Young
HAWKE

Also by David Day

Menzies and Churchill at War (1986)

The Great Betrayal: Britain, Australia and the Onset of the Pacific War, 1939–42 (1988)

Reluctant Nation: Australia and the Allied Defeat of Japan, 1942–45 (1992)

Smugglers and Sailors: The Customs History of Australia, 1788–1901 (1992)

Contraband and Controversy: The Customs History of Australia from 1901 (1996)

Claiming a Continent: A New History of Australia (1996)

Brave New World: Dr H.V. Evatt and Australian Foreign Policy, ed. (1996)

Australian Identities, ed. (1998)

John Curtin: A Life (1999)

Chifley (2001)

Celtic-Australian Identities, ed. with Jonathan Wooding (2001)

The Politics of War (2003)

Conquest: A New History of the Modern World (2005)

The Weather Watchers: 100 Years of the Bureau of Meteorology (2007)

Andrew Fisher: Prime Minister of Australia (2008)

Antarctica: A Biography (2012)

Flaws in the Ice: In Search of Douglas Mawson (2013)

Paul Keating: The Biography (2015)

Antarctica: What Everyone Needs to Know (2019)

Maurice Blackburn: Champion of the People (2019)

Young HAWKE

THE MAKING OF A LARRIKIN

DAVID DAY

HarperCollins*Publishers*

HarperCollins*Publishers*
Australia • Brazil • Canada • France • Germany • Holland • India
Italy • Japan • Mexico • New Zealand • Poland • Spain • Sweden
Switzerland • United Kingdom • United States of America

HarperCollins acknowledges the Traditional Custodians
of the lands upon which we live and work, and pays respect
to Elders past and present.

First published on Gadigal Country in Australia in 2024
by HarperCollins*Publishers* Australia Pty Limited
ABN 36 009 913 517
harpercollins.com.au

Copyright © David Day 2024

The right of David Day to be identified as the author of this work has been asserted by him in accordance with the *Copyright Amendment (Moral Rights) Act 2000*.

This work is copyright. Apart from any use as permitted under the Copyright Act 1968, no part may be reproduced, copied, scanned, stored in a retrieval system, recorded, or transmitted, in any form or by any means, without the prior written permission of the publisher. Without limiting the author's and publisher's exclusive rights, any unauthorised use of this publication to train generative artificial intelligence (AI) technologies is expressly prohibited.

A catalogue record for this book is available from the National Library of Australia

ISBN 978 1 4607 6569 2 (hardback)
ISBN 978 1 7430 9547 8 (ebook)

Cover design: Design by Committee
Front cover image: Portrait of Rhodes Scholar Mr Bob Hawke, 29 November 1952 © West Australian Newspapers Ltd
Back cover image: Bob Hawke speaking at Bi-ennial Congress of Trade Unions, 1975. NAA: A6180, 23/9/75/4.
Author photograph by Emily Day
Typeset in Minion Pro by Kirby Jones
Printed and bound in Australia by McPherson's Printing Group

In memory of John Moore
mountain climber, filmmaker, friend
1949–2019

Abbreviations

ABC	Australian Broadcasting Commission
ACSPA	Australian Council of Salaried and Professional Associations
ACT	Australian Capital Territory
ACTU	Australian Council of Trade Unions
ADB	*Australian Dictionary of Biography*
AIPS	Australian Institute of Political Science
AJA	Australian Journalists' Association
ALP	Australian Labor Party
ANU	Australian National University
ANUA	Australian National University Archives
ANZUS	Australia New Zealand United States Security Treaty
APSF	Australian Public Services Federation
ASIO	Australian Security Intelligence Organisation
ASIS	Australian Secret Intelligence Service
ATL	Alexander Turnbull Library, Wellington
BCC	Bordertown Civic Centre
BHP	Broken Hill Proprietary
BHPML	Bob Hawke Prime Ministerial Library
BL	Battye Library, Perth
BLB	Bordertown Library
BLO	Bodleian Library, Oxford
CIA	(U.S.) Central Intelligence Agency
CPI	Consumer Price Index
CPSO	Commonwealth Public Servants' Organisation
DLP	Democratic Labor Party
DSD	Defence Signals Directorate
FBI	(U.S.) Federal Bureau of Investigation

FL	Fryer Library, University of Queensland
GATT	General Agreement on Tariffs and Trade
GCA	Guild Council Archives, University of Western Australia
HSC	Higher School Certificate
ILO	International Labour Organization
JCPML	John Curtin Prime Ministerial Library
ML	Mitchell Library
NBAC	Noel Butlin Archives Centre
NCA	National Crime Authority
NFSA	National Film and Sound Archive
NLA	National Library of Australia
NSW	New South Wales
NUAUS	National Union of Australian University Students
PLC	Parliamentary Library, Canberra
PLO	Palestine Liberation Organization
PMSA	Perth Modern School Archives
RAAF	Royal Australian Air Force
RSL	Returned Services League of Australia
SLSA	State Library of South Australia
SROWA	State Records Office of Western Australia
SRSA	State Records of South Australia
THC	Trades Hall Council
TNT	Thomas Nationwide Transport
UCAA	Uniting Church of Australia Archives, Perth
UCA	University College Archives, Oxford
USAL	University of South Australia Library
UWA	University of Western Australia
UWAA	University of Western Australia Archives
WCTU	Woman's Christian Temperance Union

Contents

Author's note ... 1

Part One: Childhood

Chapter One: Origins ... 7
Chapter Two: 1929–1939 ... 30
Chapter Three: 1939–1946 ... 49

Part Two: Scholar

Chapter Four: 1946–1949 ... 69
Chapter Five: 1950–1953 ... 82
Chapter Six: 1953–1955 ... 101
Chapter Seven: 1956–1958 ... 124

Part Three: Advocate

Chapter Eight: 1958–1961 ... 149
Chapter Nine: 1962–1964 ... 168
Chapter Ten: 1965–1966 ... 187
Chapter Eleven: 1967–1969 ... 203

Part Four: President

Chapter Twelve: 1970–1971   223
Chapter Thirteen: 1971–1972   244
Chapter Fourteen: 1973–1974   267
Chapter Fifteen: 1974–1975   287
Chapter Sixteen: 1976–1977   310
Chapter Seventeen: 1978–1979   333

Endnotes   357
Bibliography   391
Acknowledgements   411
Index   414

Author's Note

When I was growing up in Melbourne, Bob Hawke was a frequent and flamboyant figure on television. Though he was president of the Australian Council of Trade Unions (ACTU) at the time, some viewers mistakenly believed that he was the prime minister. In opinion polls, Hawke's popularity was often higher than the conga line of mostly undistinguished politicians who occupied the Lodge during the late 1960s and early 1970s. As a result, it was no surprise after the dismissal of Gough Whitlam in 1975 that the Labor Party turned to Hawke in 1983 to rescue it from the post-Whitlam funk into which it had slumped.

I was studying in Cambridge when Hawke was first elected prime minister, and I remained there during much of his government. It was before the age of the internet, so my parents kept me in sporadic touch with Australian politics by sending rolled-up pages from *The Age* and *The Australian*, which I supplemented with occasional visits to the newspaper files at Australia House in London. At the time, the politics of Britain under Margaret Thatcher were competing for my attention, with the Falklands War, the long-running strikes by miners and printers, the bombing of Libya from British air bases, the cloud of radiation from Chernobyl and the outbreak of mad cow disease. The news from Australia provided a welcome distraction from this litany of disasters, as the Hawke government, after eight years of divisive leadership under Malcolm Fraser, pursued policies of reconstruction and reconciliation. I recall it as being a good time to identify as an Australian overseas, with the progressive policies of the Hawke government overshadowing the embarrassing antics of the Queensland premier, Joh Bjelke-Petersen.

I never imagined back then that I would one day write Hawke's biography. Blanche d'Alpuget had already written one in 1982, although I didn't get a copy until a British edition was published three years later. I still recall the impact of reading it during the course of several train journeys to London. With its exposure of Hawke's excessive drinking and sexual exploits, the book was unlike any other political biography I'd read. Yet he'd become prime minister despite the airing of those flaws.

It would be another twenty-six years before I decided to embark on my own biography of Hawke. I'd written biographies of three Labor prime ministers by then, starting with John Curtin and Ben Chifley before going further back in time to Andrew Fisher. They'd all been commanding leaders who'd changed the course of Australian history for the better. I was still working on the Fisher biography when I agreed to write a biography of Paul Keating, which was published in 2015. By then, I'd also decided to write a biography of Bob Hawke.

In doing so, I wanted to delve into the making of the man and his place in Australian history. There was an apparent paradox within Hawke, the Sunday School teacher and Rhodes Scholar who became an alcoholic and compulsive womaniser. To fully understand this paradox, I had to go back to Hawke's beginnings, which meant an examination of his parents, who were zealous adherents of the Congregational Church, and of their Cornish origins.

Hawke's parents first met during the First World War in a small stone-built church, set on a cliff above the Murray River in South Australia. Discovering the ruins of that church, along with the church papers in the State Library, was one of those imaginative moments that a biographer hopes to have while trying to compose a picture of their subject. Learning of how he lost his position at that church, apparently because of his affair with his future wife, and later on two occasions ran his horse and cart off the road, provided glimpses into the wildness of Hawke's father that was later seen in the son.

Along with tracking down the succession of South Australian churches in which the Hawkes had preached, I also came across numerous newspaper accounts and interviews with townspeople, which gave a surprisingly detailed account of what life was like for Hawke during his childhood. It was a story of parental pressure that likely contributed to his narcissistic personality.

I was fortunate to discover the Western Australia branch papers of the Woman's Christian Temperance Union (WCTU), of which Hawke's mother was a leading member. In the pages of those heavy, leather-bound minute books was revealed the extent of the neglect that Hawke suffered as a young teenager, while his father was away at military camp and his mother spent extended periods doing the work of the WCTU.

Despite that neglect, his parents had great ambitions for their son, ensuring that he gained entry to an academically minded school and pushing him to get a Rhodes scholarship to Oxford. A search of the papers in the University of Western Australia Archives show how Hawke failed at the first attempt, only to return with a determined campaign to amass influential referees and powerful supporters on the Rhodes committee, including the state governor. It was a sign of how he would campaign for the presidencies of both the ACTU and the Labor Party.

Just as enlightening was an exploration of Hawke's haunts in Oxford, from his primitive room in University College to the dining hall in which he gained renown for sculling a beer and then ensuring the record time was reported in the recently created *Guinness Book of Records*.

It was also in England that I tracked down the Congregational minister with whom Hawke had sometimes stayed. The Reverend Beck was ninety-nine years old and in an aged-care facility when he described a rather startling story that could have derailed Hawke's political career. He told of a furious escapade through the streets of Oxford, with the police in hot pursuit of an inebriated Hawke in his small van that was dubbed 'The Fornicatorium'. The ensuing conviction could have caused his expulsion had he not been urged by a policeman in the minister's congregation to mount an appeal rather than return to Australia in disgrace. The success of that appeal saved Hawke's future career. He went on to evade expulsion from the Australian National University in a similar fashion.

His parents asked a member of Canberra's Congregational church to meet Hawke on his arrival in the nation's capital in the hope that he might act as a chaperone for their son, but the congregant told me that Hawke's wilder side couldn't be contained. His account was borne out by female students who were there at the time. One of the students described to me the climate of fear that the frequently drunk Hawke had engendered among the small number of women residents.

Although I encountered plenty of witnesses to his predilection for excessive drinking and bawdy behaviour, Hawke managed to rise to the presidency of the ACTU. Throughout Hawke's seemingly inexorable ascent towards the prime ministership, observers had harboured misgivings about his character and his associations with dodgy businessmen, only to have his charisma and popularity trump their opposition and overcome their reservations. The decade-long research for this book has shown that they were right to have doubts and to question whether his flaws would stop him succeeding as the nation's leader.

Yet my research also revealed a different side of Hawke, a man who, in his darkest moments and in spite of all of his bravado, had his own doubts, but was determined to press on and change Australia in the process.

PART ONE

Childhood

CHAPTER ONE

Origins

There are so many questions to be explored about the tortured Labor hero Bob Hawke. But they can't be answered without first examining the lives of the couple from whom he'd sprung. Clem Hawke and Ellie Lee were both descended from migrants who'd come from Cornwall to work in the South Australian copper mines, bringing with them religious enthusiasms that would see the mining towns dominated more by churches than by pubs.

While Adelaide was known as the 'city of churches', the birthplace of Clem Hawke, Kapunda, could have been described as the 'town of churches', with the Anglican and Catholic churches more than matched by those of the Wesleyans, the Primitive Methodists, the Lutherans, the Congregationalists, the Presbyterians, the tub-thumping Salvation Army and the Bible Mission. The most imposing of all was built by the Baptists. Working alongside the churches were the temperance campaigners, who toured the countryside with their fervent messages of abstinence, and the travelling revivalists with their fearful talk of fire and brimstone and the promise of salvation for those who joined their sect.[1]

While Clem's father was an active member of the Baptist church in Kapunda, Ellie's father was a Methodist lay preacher in the tiny settlement of Greens Plains West, where he became wealthy growing wheat and barley on the dry and open plain of the northern Yorke Peninsula. Both Clem and Ellie were devout members of their respective churches, whose teachings promised eternal salvation for those who lived good Christian lives.[2] What a world it would be if everyone could be convinced to do so. Some thought they could be.

The religious fervour that conjured this vision was matched by the political optimism of the early post-Federation years, as the newly created nation of Australia moved on from the devastating depression and drought of the 1890s, and the socially progressive Labor Party loomed on the political horizon as the natural party of government. This was the religious and political background to Clem and Ellie's childhood. It would shape their own lives, and influence the upbringing of their son.

Ellie was born on 1 October 1897; she was named Edith Emily Lee but always known as Ellie. She was the second-youngest of William Lee's seven children and was raised in an area that was staunchly Cornish. To house the mineworkers and service their needs, the substantial towns of Moonta and Kadina were quickly developed, while a large copper smelter was established at the nearby port of Wallaroo. Collectively, the three towns were known as 'Little Cornwall'; they still host a regular Cornish festival today.[3]

Ellie's father had worked in the mines as a boy before he and his father began farming land on the adjacent plain. Their property was in a scrub-covered area that was first settled in the 1840s by Europeans who swiftly dispossessed the Narungga people. The pace of settlement and landclearing quickened as miners turned to farming. It was a healthier occupation and there was good money to be made from growing wheat and barley, once water had been piped in and superphosphate added to improve the soil's fertility.

Although it was a very different place to the rolling hills and hedgerows of Cornwall, the early arrivals tried their best to make it feel like home. Not only did they bring their mining and agricultural skills to Australia, they also brought a strong ethnic identity that distinguished them from other British groups. Being descended from the Celts who'd been pushed to the western edges of Britain by the Anglo-Saxons, they harboured a sense of grievance towards their conquerors and nurtured their separate identity. While there were few if any speakers of the Cornish language by the turn of the nineteenth century, Cornish words remained as names for places and things.[4] They also had their own flag and a motto, 'One and All', which helped bind them together and invest them with a sense of a common past in the face of Anglo-Saxon economic and political domination. Part of that domination was exercised by the Anglican Church, as the religious arm of the English state, as well as by the landed aristocracy and mine owners. For centuries, the Celts had resisted the church's impositions and held to ancient beliefs and practices rooted in their rural existence.

When an alternative belief system was offered in the eighteenth century by the charismatic preacher John Wesley, founder of the Methodist Church, many Cornish people became his fervent followers. Others flocked to the Congregationalists, the Baptists or one of the other Protestant sects. Rather than the cathedrals that dominated many large English towns, Cornish towns were marked by the plainer buildings of the Methodists and their ilk, which offered a religion that was more in accord with the rising democratic feelings of the people. There were no bishops or priests demanding obedience to a state-sanctioned religion, just preachers appointed by the congregations, who celebrated the sacrifice and forgiveness of Jesus.[5] Just as chapels were constructed across Cornwall, so too were they built in the settlements of South Australia, bringing Cornish customs and beliefs from the old world to the new. Their presence helped to make the Methodist Church by far the largest of the nonconformist churches in South Australia.

The Methodist church at Greens Plains West reflected the devotion of the inhabitants thereabouts, who built the church and provided lay preachers such as Ellie's father from among their number. Although the small congregation could not support a minister of their own, and the Sunday School was run by local volunteers, preachers often visited from nearby towns.[6] It was in this small church, and under the guidance of her devout and domineering father, with his 'fire and brimstone' brand of religion, that Ellie was provided with an uplifting vision of a better world in which sinfulness was banished, Sundays were kept sacred and alcohol was shunned. It was a vision that made the believers look beyond their daily toil of subduing the land and meeting the challenges of the area's climate. The vision of a better world, and the Christian faith that underpinned it, gave greater meaning to their lives and would stay with Ellie throughout her life. It was not sufficient just to attend church, sing hymns, mouth prayers and live good, Christian lives. They also had to spread the word and gather new members for the church, so that their vision of a better world could become a reality.[7]

Another institution also provided inspiration for young Ellie. The one-room, single-teacher state school offered a window into the world beyond the flat fields of stubble that surrounded the scattered settlement after each year's harvest. The female teacher, who would take Ellie away with her on holidays, showed how she might do good works and pointed to a possible pathway out of Greens Plains West at a time when women's choices were very restricted. Ellie's father expected that his daughters would become mothers and housekeepers for neighbouring farmers. By getting an education and becoming a teacher, she would have the opportunity to break free from her isolated rural circumstances, become financially independent, travel to new places and make new friendships. While her sisters stayed tied to their lives on the land, Ellie won for herself a passport to the world beyond. Had it been possible at the time, she might have become a Methodist preacher, but that career path did not then exist for women. Teaching provided her with an alternative calling, one that would still allow her to do God's work by shaping the minds of her young charges.

With the outbreak of the Great War in August 1914, and the consequent enlistment of numerous male teachers into the army, there were many vacancies to be filled in South Australia's schools. It was in the wake of the Gallipoli landing in April 1915 that seventeen-year-old Ellie enrolled at teaching college in Adelaide, where she completed the required training before being appointed in January 1916 as the sole teacher at a rural school on Kangaroo Island, where she boarded with a couple of 'cold, harsh characters', sharing a bedroom with their children. The teenage teacher was keen to bestow the benefits of education and moral improvement on her young students, particularly the girls, in the hope that they might follow her example.[8]

Ellie was not overwhelmed by the responsibility of her first appointment; the visiting inspector reported that she was 'bright, forceful, earnest, promising'. In subsequent years, she was described as 'eager', 'hard working' and 'inspiring', although that was somewhat offset by descriptions of her as 'zealous', 'dominant' and 'anxious', and exercising 'extreme control'. Nevertheless, she clearly impressed the inspectors. After a year on Kangaroo Island, she was transferred to another single-teacher school, at Wandana, ten kilometres north-east of Adelaide, where she spent two years before being transferred in January 1919 to the small settlement of Forster, on the eastern bank of the Murray River, 120 kilometres from Adelaide. The appointment would change her life. With no schoolhouse in Forster, she had to teach her class of about twenty students in the stone-built Methodist church, where the irrepressible and equally fervent Clem Hawke was the newly appointed preacher.[9]

Clem's childhood in Kapunda had some parallels with Ellie's rural upbringing. The town was as strongly Cornish and Protestant as the region around Greens Plains West, and mining had initially underpinned the town's economy. Indeed, Kapunda became Australia's first mining town when copper was discovered there in 1842 and thousands of Cornish miners were recruited to work the mine and its associated smelter. Clem's grandfather had come out with his family at the age of fourteen in 1851 and found ready work in the new colony. Large-scale mining had come to an end by the time his grandson, Arthur Clemence Hawke, was born on 5 March 1898, yet Kapunda continued to be relatively prosperous as a service centre for surrounding wheat farms and the site of major engineering works.[10]

It was an exciting time to be growing up, as Australia was transformed by the telegraph and the telephone, as well as by the advent of electricity, motorcars and the mechanisation of agriculture. Because of its greater size and quick railway connection to Adelaide, there was much less sense of isolation in Kapunda compared with Greens Plains West. Whereas Ellie had only a handful of children at her school, there were about four hundred at Clem's primary school in Kapunda, and a greater variety of jobs once he left school in April 1910. He was employed for a time delivering papers, and was also apprenticed to a blacksmith. As a teenager, Clem had followed his family's political interests by becoming secretary of the Labor Party branch in Kapunda, which saw him organise meetings for the federal election in late 1914 and the state election in early 1915. Both elections had seen Labor return to power. Perhaps because of this Labor resurgence, he dallied with the idea of one day standing for state parliament.[11]

Clem later recalled how his parents had imbued him with 'a strong sense of social justice' and 'the necessity for public service'. For that, he would need more education. So he continued his schooling, both by reading at the local library and by taking classes in shorthand, typing and Latin at the Kapunda School of Mines. He later said that the books that were most influential on his thinking were the radical theological works by W.R. Inge, the Dean of St Paul's Cathedral in London, and a history of the Tolpuddle Martyrs.[12] As this suggested, socialism and Christianity were the twin flames that would guide him through life. Although his younger brother, Albert, was drawn to the political platform, Clem and another brother, Cyril, found their calling in religion.

Like many Cornishmen, Clem had been raised a Methodist, but a teenage infatuation with the daughters of Kapunda's Baptist minister saw him baptised into that church. At some stage, Clem's father, who'd worked in the mines and on farms, also became involved with the local Baptist church. In Clem's case, he'd thought of becoming a Baptist home missionary so that he might take the teachings of the church to the far-flung settlements of the South Australian frontier. For reasons that aren't clear, he returned to the Methodist fold and became a home missionary of that church instead.[13] Having been taught by his parents 'to be contemptuous of human wickedness', Clem believed that preaching from the pulpit and ministering to the congregation was the best way to usher in a better world, one person at a time.[14]

There was more cause than ever to work for a better world. When he was just sixteen years old, Australia had become embroiled in a European war that saw killing on an industrial scale. Within a year, the fruitless British campaign on the Dardanelles Peninsula had caused thousands of Australian casualties, and the flow of recruits was starting to ebb. When the Labor government of Billy Hughes announced a plebiscite on whether men should be conscripted for the trenches, the issue tore the country and the Labor Party apart.

For Clem, the war posed a difficult dilemma. His dreams of what he might do in his life were put at risk. Although he wasn't a pacifist, Clem shared the anti-conscription and anti-war views that were held by many in the Labor Party. Indeed, his brother Albert was an anti-conscription activist in Kapunda.[15] But it wasn't easy for men of military age, who were hounded by people demanding to know why they hadn't joined up. They now faced the possibility of being forced to go. It was perhaps to escape these pressures prior to the conscription plebiscite in 1916 that eighteen-year-old Clem joined the Methodist

Home Mission, which was established to provide religious services to people living on the fringes of European settlement in Australia.[16]

Joining the mission wouldn't entirely relieve the pressure on Clem to enlist for the war. Many young members of the mission still went off to the Western Front, cheered on by the mostly pro-conscription leaders of the Protestant churches.[17] If they were over thirty years old, mission members could serve as chaplains while others worked in non-combatant roles with the Young Men's Christian Association. Most missioners, though, fought in the trenches.[18] While it would have been difficult for Clem to resist the call to arms, he could tell himself that he was making a sacrifice for a worthier cause. Out on the frontier, in Bible classes and at temperance meetings, he would be saving his fellow man by spreading the word of God, converting non-believers, rescuing backsliders and campaigning against the evils of drink and loose living.

The mission offered Clem a position that was akin to a religious apprenticeship, providing a pathway for him to be ordained eventually as a minister. The first steps along that pathway took him to Adelaide's Methodist Training Home, run by the liberal evangelist William Torr, who ensured that the young and impressionable man and his small coterie of fellow students were instilled with 'a non-fundamentalist view of Christian scripture'.[19] Then he was sent to Kalangadoo, a small town near Mount Gambier, in the south-eastern corner of South Australia. His region included the similarly sized settlement of Glencoe, which had a Methodist church to cater for the area's pastoralists and farmworkers, and the employees of the local cheese factory.

The distant conflict in Europe reached even here. In October 1916, Clem went to Mount Gambier for the Methodist District Synod, which passed a 'resolution of deep sympathy ... with all those who have been bereaved by the war'.[20] The terrible news from the battles of Fromelles and Pozières was seeping back to loved ones in Australia and filling the pages of local newspapers. Although the scale of the casualties increased the pressure for conscription as the only way to provide reinforcements, the plebiscite narrowly rejected the conscription proposal, with South Australia being one of three states to vote No.

The vote against conscription was a big setback for Prime Minister Hughes, who nevertheless pushed on with his commitment to send the maximum number of young men to war. When they didn't volunteer in sufficient numbers, he planned another plebiscite in late 1917 in the vain hope of a favourable result. It too was defeated, and more emphatically.

By now Clem had been transferred to the small and isolated settlement of Port Neill, on the distant Eyre Peninsula, where farmers were still grubbing out mulga roots on newly acquired wheat and sheep properties.[21] The trains from Adelaide didn't reach there and the roads were rudimentary and liable to be covered by sand drifts. Communication with the world was mostly by sea; locals referred to Adelaide as 'the mainland'. Such was the isolation and the primitive state of facilities that the Eyre Peninsula was regarded as 'Methodism's great frontier challenge'.[22] It was not a place for grand oratory, but for individual pastoral care and small group gatherings that brought religion to people living the toughest of lives.

Clem's base at Port Neill was notable only for its wooden jetty, its two-storey, stone-built pub and a handful of houses. He had to travel for nearly a hundred kilometres inland, taking hours on horseback or bicycle, to preach at meetings of perhaps ten people. It meant sometimes carrying the distressing news of a soldier's death to relatives largely cut off from the world. It would have been a testing time for Clem, although many of his fellow teenagers were enduring an even harsher test in the trenches of the Western Front.

*

In April 1918, as the war was coming to its climax, Clem was transferred from one side of South Australia to the other, landing at the frontier settlement of Forster, on the eastern bank of the Murray River.[23] Despite having been settled prior to Port Neill, the place had little more than a small public hall, two churches, a post office and a scattering of pastoral and wheat properties that were connected to the wider world by bullock drays and paddle-steamers. Along the meandering river, fishermen caught giant cod for the Adelaide market. Getting there would have required Clem to go by train from Adelaide to Murray Bridge, where a paddle-steamer could take him on to Forster.

One of his predecessors described his delight on seeing 'the scenic beauty of the place', with the banks of the river having been carved over time into cliffs. While a Lutheran church and a few houses were built on the riverbank, a Primitive Methodist church had been constructed of stone on the cliff above. It had been built in 1888 by a devout Christian couple, James and Elizabeth Sears, on their property, named Rossawella, which became a small, stone-built settlement of its own, complete with a store and post office. Across the river, and connected by a punt, there was a larger expanse of alluvial soil that supported scattered farms around the settlement of Walker Flat. A person standing on the steps of Clem's cliff-top church took in a fine sight that combined natural beauty and human industry.[24]

As an agent of the Methodist Home Mission, Clem had a big area to cover. He was expected to spread his message of hope by paddle-steamer or on horseback to the isolated homes along the river and to townsfolk in their tiny halls. His predecessor had spent his first Sunday preaching at one settlement in the morning, another in the evening and in Forster at night, with the congregations travelling considerable distances to attend.[25] For Clem, there was the usual round of Bible classes and temperance meetings in churches and homes, the celebration of births and marriages, and the commemoration of hard lives well lived. He also presided over the annual harvest festival and 'welcome home' occasions for returning soldiers, with their haunted eyes and sometimes damaged bodies telling of horrors that Clem could only imagine.

Clem was engaged in an important campaign of his own. He was like a general, presiding over a ceaseless battle against wickedness. He appeared to have enjoyed some success. At a meeting of fellow Methodists in July 1918, he told the large gathering that 'the Home Mission campaign had had a splendid start'.[26] In Forster, the finances of Clem's church were helped by its parallel use as a state school.

In November 1918, he helped at the school's annual picnic, where sporting events were followed by tea and a concert. It was a particularly emotional gathering that year, since the end of the war had been announced just four days before, with Clem conducting thanksgiving services throughout his circuit.[27]

The presence of the students and their teacher would have helped reduce the loneliness that he must have felt in such an isolated place. Fortunately for Clem, that loneliness would come to an abrupt end the following year, when a new teacher arrived to run the school.

*

In early 1919, having crossed in the punt, an elderly, stern-faced man and his daughter hung on to the cart seat as their horse jolted its way up the track from the riverbank to the settlement of Forster. Curious onlookers would have seen the young woman squinting through her spectacles in the bright sunlight as she looked at the scattering of houses set among the dry fields. Dressed in his clerical attire, Clem Hawke may have been there to greet her devout father and help the pleasant-faced newcomer with her luggage of clothes and schoolbooks, as she was led to her lodgings and shown the church where she soon would be teaching the local farm children.

Once her father had gone, the tall, blue-eyed missionary and the teacher were quickly smitten with each other. Clem's love affair with Ellie would have been helped by his handsome appearance, supported by a flirtatious manner and a disconcerting tendency to look people searchingly in the eye when he spoke to them. It was helped, too, by there being few unattached adults thereabouts. Ellie's relationship with Clem certainly seems to have lifted her mood, as the school inspectors were soon describing her as 'bright, earnest, sympathetic and cheerful'.[28] Love can have that effect.

The pair not only shared a religion and a Cornish background, but also a desire to build a better world from the ruins of the war and the devastation being wrought by the influenza epidemic, which was killing thousands of Australians, many of them young. While there was much rejoicing that the long war had finally ended, it had come at the cost of 60,000 Australian dead and many more men who had returned damaged in mind and body. To provide jobs for the ex-servicemen, the South Australian government encouraged hundreds of them to settle on the floodplains of the Murray, where they could continue opening the land for European farming.

Among the men and women on the returning troopships were former employees of the Methodist Home Mission who'd taken leave to go to the Western Front and now wanted to resume their vocations. Bowing to the public pressure, the mission decided that these ex-servicemen should take over as preachers along the Murray, so they could minister to the ex-servicemen who were being encouraged to settle there. It signalled the end of Clem's time in Forster.

In March 1919, little more than a year after his arrival and just a month or so after Ellie had begun teaching in his church, the 21-year-old preacher was told he was to be transferred to Kangaroo Island. It's possible that Clem's love affair with Ellie prompted calls by the landowner James Sears for his removal, since he was instructed to leave Forster without anyone being sent in his place. In fact, the post remained vacant for more than two years after his departure.

Whatever its cause, Clem's abrupt transfer meant that his relationship with Ellie was in danger of coming to an end. But neither of them was going to allow that to happen. Desperate to avoid being transferred to Kangaroo Island, Clem resigned from the Methodist Home Mission and joined the Congregational Church. Apart from anything else, it made financial sense, particularly since he now had marriage in mind. The mission's work was meant for young, single men subsisting on a meagre wage, made lower by post-war inflation. Moreover, the theological leap was not great; in fact, unification talks were being held between the Methodists, Congregationalists, Baptists and Presbyterians. Clem's new position in the Congregational Church gave him a better income and a more certain path towards ordination as a minister. Once he'd been called by a congregation to become the unordained preacher at their church, he could ask Ellie to join him. First, though, he spent some time preaching at different churches in Adelaide and became an external student at the church's Parkin College.[29] That brought Clem under the influence of the college's new principal, Dr Edward Kiek, a radical English theologian who offered courses in both arts and theology, while also teaching classes for the Workers' Educational Association.

Kiek was a Christian socialist and an anti-militarist who, prior to 1914, had said the war was against 'the interests of the working classes'. He backed away from this during the war, and also from his attachment to socialism. Rather than revolution, he now embraced the idea of creating a Heaven on Earth by 'regeneration and personal transformation'. Instead of instilling a fear of damnation into the faithful, Kiek declared that salvation would come by embracing the teaching of Jesus and living His lessons in daily life.[30]

These beliefs accorded with Clem's own political and theological predilections. More importantly, Clem recalled how Kiek had taught him that Christianity should be seen 'as a noble crusade' and not 'a passive submission to suffering and martyrdom'. As a young man who'd declined to join the forces, he was naturally attracted to this notion of Congregationalism being a muscular religion 'for red-blooded men' and 'a faith for the strong and valorous'.[31] He would later give sermons of his own entitled 'Muscular Christianity – Life's great wrestling match'.[32]

Although Clem was still unordained, he was sent in early 1920 to take over a small Congregational church at Houghton, in the Adelaide Hills, as well as to have responsibility for the church in the nearby village of Paracombe. The prosperous town of Houghton was just twenty kilometres from the centre of Adelaide and was dignified by a scattering of buildings that included a post office, a bakery, a primary school, several churches and a pro-temperance Rechabite Hall.

It was a place fit for a family, and Clem wasted little time arranging for Ellie to join him there. At the end of March 1920, she resigned from the teaching service and went to stay with her well-off parents, who were now living in the Adelaide suburb of Torrensville.[33] Two months later, on a Wednesday evening, Clem and Ellie were married in the Thebarton Methodist Church in inner Adelaide, with Albert acting as best man. Because of the flu pandemic, there was no reception afterwards.[34]

Taking up residence in the refurbished manse at Houghton, the young couple quickly became stalwarts of the district. Clem became vice-president of the local Christian Endeavour Society, chief ruler of the Rechabite Lodge and secretary of the school committee. He was also a member of Houghton's Progress Association and involved himself in sporting groups and literary societies.[35] Their lives became even busier with the birth of their first child. Prior to the birth, Ellie had gone to stay at her parents' house, which was where John Neil Hawke was born on 1 March 1921. He would be known always as Neil, because the Gaelic-derived name denoted 'champion', which was what Ellie expected him to be, according to the plan that she believed God had laid out for them both.

After passing his preliminary examinations at Parkin College, Clem gained formal admission at the time of Neil's birth. To boost the family finances, he also found work in Adelaide for the hours between classes.[36] It would have been a stressful time for the couple. While Ellie was balancing the demands of motherhood with her own church and community commitments, Clem needed to find a quiet place, away from the interruptions of parishioners and the baby, for writing essays and preparing for the classes that would allow him to be ordained as a minister.[37]

Clem joined a small class of men at the college who'd had much more education than him. Some were university graduates and some had also served in the war. It would have been a daunting atmosphere, since Kiek ran his fiefdom like a small Oxford college, with the handful of students expected to wear academic gowns and to attend one-on-one tutorials. For someone with a rudimentary education, and with a newborn baby at home, Clem would have been reassured by Kiek's focus on turning out 'good preachers' rather than 'good scholars'. Not that Clem shied away from scholarship. By the end of his first term in June 1921, he'd passed four subjects and been described by Kiek as a 'promising new student'. But the strain of it all proved too much. It was during these early months of 1921 that he drove his pony and trap off the road. Not once, but twice, on different days. With the pressures of home, of his two churches, of work and of the college, Clem suffered a breakdown, which caused him to be absent from his classes for several months and also to miss church meetings. Whether it was caused by depression or by the stress of his several roles can't be known. But when he returned to the college in late 1921, he was advised by a concerned Kiek 'to "go slow" for a time'.[38]

Clem was not a man for going slow. There was a wildness about him that would later be seen in his famous son. Rather than taking things quietly, he began to court controversy in the press. Shortly after returning to college, he sprang to the defence of the South Australian governor, who had outraged the Methodist Church by opposing the prohibition of alcohol. Clem wrote to a newspaper to defend the governor's right to express his opinions. This incited the Methodists to turn their hostility on Clem. He also attacked the government for neglecting the interests of rural school students, claiming that their education was 'nothing but a painful farce' because they were often without teachers for months and left to 'run wild'. This was forcing some farmers to move to the city 'so that their children could receive a proper education'.[39]

It was in the latter part of 1922, having just returned from a trip to Queensland, that the restless preacher decided he needed to get away. And not just to another church in South Australia. He was going to take his family to New Zealand, even though he hadn't completed his course at Parkin College. He may have been following the example of another Congregational minister, Frank de Lisle, who'd accepted a posting in Wellington and become secretary of the church's district committee. It was De Lisle who made inquiries in Australia 'for a suitable married man' to serve in Lower Hutt and who reported in August 1922 that Clem was willing to accept the post.[40]

Clem may also have been attracted to Wellington by the presence of Reed Glasson, formerly of Adelaide and now the minister at Wellington's main Congregational church. Glasson had been ordained in Cornwall before going to Adelaide in 1884, where he became a committed Christian Socialist and a frequent lecturer on politics.[41] Whatever the reason for Clem's departure, the Houghton congregation was sorry to see him go, since his ministry had been 'very successful ... especially among the young people'.[42]

Sailing to New Zealand by way of Sydney in January 1923, Clem was headed for a church just outside Wellington. In 1840, Lower Hutt had been the site of the original British settlement in New Zealand and was pretentiously named Britannia. It didn't last long as the putative capital. When a better site was found on the south-western side of the harbour, most of its population shifted there. This new settlement was named Wellington and became the country's capital, while Lower Hutt remained a satellite town.

The commercial and civic centre of Lower Hutt was established on the eastern bank of the Hutt River, while the western side was a sodden and flood-prone place that had workers' homes, a railway workshop and ancillary industries, breweries and a substantial meatworks that made the waters run red on the nearby beach. At night, Lower Hutt was a place of flickering candles and soft gaslight, of muddy streets with wandering cattle and staggering drunks. Unlike Wellington, it still lacked electricity. The poorer and less salubrious streets on the western side of the river were located in Alicetown, which was previously known as Black Swamp. It was in Alicetown that Clem's small wooden church was situated.[43]

The Hawkes went about with their customary zeal. One of Clem's earliest innovations was to introduce a half-hour of community hymn singing prior to the Sunday evening service. Ellie was just as energetic. Having borne a son, she was keen to have a daughter, and meanwhile threw herself into activities with young girls. She founded a Girls' Club at the church, which arranged a concert to raise funds for the Sunday School, which greatly increased its membership. When the Sunday School had a day-long celebration in November 1923, it was Ellie who led 'fifty little scholars' in a 'unique kindergarten demonstration', with several acting out 'the parable of the Good Samaritan', while Clem gave an evening sermon to a packed church on the topic of 'Home influence and character building'. The celebrations resumed the following Tuesday, when Ellie handed out more than a hundred prizes to her young scholars and Clem told the proud parents and friends that he planned to raise funds for a new building to house the growing Sunday School. The success of their joint ministry was evidenced by the enrolment of about seventy new children, with Clem declaring that 'there would soon be many more'.[44]

There were so many children that they couldn't fit them in the small church. Moreover, Clem worried that being 'forced to run every tiddlywinking thing in the building in which you hold divine services' was causing the church to be regarded with less reverence. That was just 'one of the things that plays on my nerves', he told the district committee. With a separate building, he predicted that he could double the school numbers to 200 or more. The church would need a loan for the whole amount, since it was by far the poorest of the eight Congregational churches in the Wellington district. The committee decided that there was no money for the Sunday School.[45]

Clem's activities didn't stop at the boundary of his church. A large part of his pastoral duty was to visit people in their homes, which he could do more easily when the church agreed to buy him a bicycle. He also served on a committee that agitated for a new high school and for the improvement of the town's facilities. In May 1924, he started the Western Hutt Advancement Association and became its first secretary, lobbying the local council to fix its ungraded dirt roads and unsealed footpaths, confine the stray cattle and install electric light and telephone lines. He also objected to the presence of 'the objectionable manure siding' at the railway station and lobbied the council to build a hall 'for social and public meetings' to encourage its people to be active citizens.[46]

As a minister, Clem also wanted to improve the moral fibre of the town's inhabitants. In a long letter to Wellington's *Evening Post* he deplored the public's predilection for 'the highly-suggestive and very questionable low-grade novel' which 'panders to the passions'. The 25-year-old preacher worried that the popularity of such novels and films meant that he could no longer assume that his congregations had even read the Bible or knew its stories. He thought people should be 'urged to read books worthy of the name'. Citing Tennyson, he observed that:

Better not be at all
Than not be noble.[47]

It was clearly going to be difficult for many members of Clem's congregation to measure up to his and Ellie's standards. For now, the optimism of his relative youth helped to keep alive the missionary zeal that had sustained him for the last seven years.[48] Yet the couple also had the impatience of youth, which was sorely tested by their experience in New Zealand.

Cycling around the rutted tracks of Alicetown, swerving to avoid cowpats as he serviced the needs of his working-class flock, Clem was forever conscious of his position as a poorly paid pastor of the most impecunious Congregational church in the district.[49] His success in filling the pews for the Sunday service and Ellie's success in doubling the Sunday School numbers were not rewarded by the district committee, which refused to provide the additional accommodation the church's numbers demanded. Just as the needs of Alicetown were neglected by the Lower Hutt council, the needs of his church were neglected by the wealthier churches.

The wealthiest of all was Reed Glasson's imposing and well-located church in central Wellington, where the long-ailing minister had preached for the last three decades. When the 66-year-old pastor announced in November 1923 that he was planning to retire, the ever-restless and ambitious Clem may have harboured thoughts of replacing him. If so, it was an overly ambitious hope. His chances of securing Glasson's support were dashed by the death of the elderly preacher just a few weeks later, which ended any faint chance that he may have had of succeeding him.

Although Clem helped to conduct the funeral service at Glasson's graveside, it soon became clear that the congregation would be looking elsewhere for a replacement.[50] Not that the recently ordained Reverend Hawke could have reasonably expected to be appointed to the leading Congregational church in New Zealand's capital. The church wanted a young replacement for Glasson, but not one as young or inexperienced as Clem. On 2 April 1924, the church's selection committee decided 'to seek a minister overseas, of outstanding ability and talents', and to offer the new minister a salary of £800, four times the stipend that Clem was being paid.[51] Clem and Ellie would be condemned to soldier on in Alicetown, dealing with a fractious congregation and crowds of unruly children, while being denied the facilities that could make their lives more bearable.

On 29 July, Clem peremptorily announced his resignation. No reason was recorded. The committee was taken aback, but unanimously accepted it, albeit 'with profound regret', and recorded their 'approval of the good work done by Mr & Mrs Hawke in the church & neighbourhood'. Feelings were so bad that no more meetings were held before the departure of the couple two months later.[52] When the district committee called on Clem to withdraw his resignation, he angrily refused, pointing to 'white livered people [who were] putting [a] report around that I have not been doing my work'. The malicious gossip may have been prompted by him going off earlier that year to tour the sights of New Zealand.[53] Clem and Ellie packed up the manse and departed with an abiding sense of bitterness and deep frustration. With their toddler Neil in tow, they boarded the train to Wellington, from where they caught a ship back to Australia. Anyone who asked was told that they were leaving for unstated 'family reasons', which is how it was explained in the press.[54] Fortunately for the young family, there was a position waiting for Clem in Australia.[55]

*

The Hawkes were a chastened couple when they arrived back in Adelaide with three-year-old Neil in September 1924. They headed back to the river where they'd first met and fallen in love. This time, they were going further up the Murray, to a Congregational church in Renmark, where they would find much work to do and more fertile soil in which to do it.[56]

Renmark had a special appeal. It had been established in 1887 as a company town by the Chaffey brothers, who brought American irrigation ideas and recruited English immigrants with the promise of making the Australian desert productive. The town was alcohol-free until the inhabitants realised that the sly-grog shops and the local distillery made that rule a bit of a nonsense. Instead of trying to enforce prohibition, a community-owned hotel was established, with the profits providing civic amenities and supporting local groups. Other cooperatives ran the distillery and a winery.[57]

In keeping with the town's progressive origins was the eccentric editor of the local paper, Harry Samuel Taylor, who'd been a leader of the New Australia settlement in Paraguay before buying the paper and renaming it the *Murray Pioneer*, with a motto of 'Each for All and All for Each'. He used the paper to espouse the cause of brotherhood and equality for white Australians, while spending Sundays as a lay preacher at the Congregational church.[58] He was Clem's kind of man, and it seemed that Renmark might be Clem's kind of town. He would later describe it fondly as 'the most progressive country town in South Australia'.[59] After taking up residence in the adobe-walled manse, one of the oldest houses in the town, Clem was inducted into the Renmark Congregational church in October 1924. The small timber church, which had been moved on rollers from its previous site, certainly needed a minister with energy who was willing to get among the people. The pews were rarely full, the Sunday School needed reinvigoration and the choir conductor had resigned. When the congregation looked askance at Clem for having arrived without his wife, he assured them that he was 'preparing the way [for her] and would write and tell her what fine people they were'.[60] Meanwhile, he set about attracting the town's attention by delivering a sermon which claimed that permanent world peace was possible if only people would commit to it. He'd given the same sermon in

New Zealand, where it had created much discussion, and he clearly hoped that headlines in Renmark would help to fill the pews of his new church.[61]

Such a sermon might suit the commemoration of the war's ending, but it was not suited to Anzac Day, particularly in a town with more than six hundred former soldiers. In April 1925, just a few months after the Hawkes' arrival, there was a whole weekend of commemoration, with businesses being closed, special entertainment for children at the showground, cyclists racing through the town, hydroplanes competing on the river and an evening reunion for ex-servicemen. For the Sunday service, Clem told the 400-strong audience how the Australian soldiers at Gallipoli had gone 'forward to face peril, pain and death [so] that liberty might cover the earth'; he wanted those in attendance to draw upon the 'the spirit of the Anzacs to ennoble and transfigure their lives'. There was no inkling of Clem's previous anti-war and anti-conscription beliefs.[62]

Once Ellie and Neil had arrived from Adelaide, the Hawkes set out to become pillars of the town, as they had been in Houghton and Lower Hutt. There were few institutions in Renmark with which they didn't become involved. Clem was on the committee of the football club and manned the gates at big football matches. He was also on the committee of the Boys' Guild, and was president of the tennis club, as well as being on the committee of the Renmark Institute and chaplain of the Masonic Club. He would later say that being a Freemason 'helped him stay the course'. He instructed and umpired the Girls' Hockey Club and judged cycling and foot races at the Renmark Show, while competing unsuccessfully in races for older cyclists. He also helped establish a branch of the Australian Nurses' Christian Movement and led Bible study classes at the local hospital.[63]

Ellie, meanwhile, taught classes at the primary school and at the church's Sunday School, and became secretary of the Renmark Sunday School Teachers' Union and president of the Church Ladies' Guild. She entered needlework in the Renmark Show and established the Renmark Girl Guides. As leader of the unit, she took the girls on weekend camps, paraded them before visiting dignitaries and went with them for a week to Adelaide during the visit of the Duke and Duchess of York. At home, she tutored young Neil, who would later excel at school.[64]

As always, alcohol and immorality were the Hawkes' targets. For his part, Clem invited visiting prohibitionists to speak from his pulpit, and vainly pressed the temperance cause onto local and state authorities. His only success came when he and his fellow ministers got the Renmark Hotel to stop selling wine with an alcohol content of 35 per cent after it was blamed for causing several men to drown in the river. As a leading member of the Woman's Christian Temperance Union (WCTU), Ellie campaigned tirelessly on the issue and represented Renmark at regional gatherings of the group. She blamed alcohol for causing problems in the home, from domestic violence to the impoverishment of families, and believed it held back the advancement of women. At Sunday School, she told children about the evils of drink and encouraged them to join the Band of Hope and sign its pledge of abstinence. She also trained them in elocution and singing and got them to act out Biblical stories, particularly the story of Esther, the Queen of Babylon who saved her Jewish compatriots from being killed by her husband.[65]

While Ellie ensured that the church was bedecked with flowers and the tea table was covered with cakes, she was also an independent woman who carved out a separate existence for herself. The strong-willed couple clearly had a relationship that was not threatened by time spent apart. Indeed, it may have been a relationship that required them to spend time apart. Whatever the case, Ellie's independence was clear in October 1926, when she accompanied Clem by train to Tailem Bend, where he caught the onward train to Adelaide for the assembly of the Congregational Church and she caught the train to Melbourne to attend a revivalist rally. It's not clear who looked after Neil on these occasions.[66]

As 'guardians of the public morals', Clem led other ministers in protesting against Sunday trading, which allowed young people to spend money from their parents that was meant for the Sunday School collection plate. Clem convinced the Renmark council to prohibit street hawkers so the 'peace of the Sabbath' would be undisturbed. He also urged the council to ask the town band not to hold any Sunday concerts prior to 8.30 p.m. But he and his fellow ministers went too far when they asked the council to ban Sunday picnics on the banks of the Murray. Clem caused even more controversy when he seized upon press reports of immorality at local dances. Although he claimed to be 'a broad-minded man', he told his congregation that he could not remain silent 'when glaring, unblushing, unashamed immorality raises its ugly head'. He blamed it on alcohol, which caused men and women to become 'worse than beasts of the field'. He warned them 'that while they are wading through a stream of vice the wrath of God was not far away'.[67]

The old notions of sin and sacrifice were being submerged by a rising wave of young Australians who'd been battered by war and the influenza pandemic and were now focused on the pursuit of pleasure. Try as he might with visiting lecturers and revivalist-style campaigns, Clem could not turn that tide. He even tried encouraging townsfolk to attend the silent film *The Ten Commandments*, which played for a week in one of Renmark's cinemas. Although he regarded the cinema as a dangerous distraction, Clem said the massive blockbuster was the best picture he'd ever seen.[68]

Try as he might, Clem was failing to increase the congregation, or to convince the hardworking and hard-drinking people of Renmark to follow the Christian path. Just as in New Zealand, the people had failed to live up to his hopes and expectations. He'd had enough. In November 1927, after just three years in Renmark and in the wake of a disastrous frost that wiped out most of that year's grape crop, Clem announced that he'd been invited to take over the Congregational church in Bordertown, almost three hundred kilometres south.[69]

The Hawkes were heading for another town on the frontier. From the oasis on the Murray, they would be heading for the edge of the Little Desert. Because of their missionary sensibility, the Hawkes would have appreciated Bordertown's relative isolation. The road to Adelaide was little more than a track – motorists were regularly lost and had to be rescued.[70] But the Bordertown church had a strong congregation, who were able to offer an annual stipend of £250, along with £26 to cover the cost of running a church-owned Chevrolet car.[71] There was also a relatively handsome manse that had originally been built for a bank manager.[72] Apart from these material inducements, Bordertown was away from the wickedness of Renmark's vine-growing region and offered a healthier moral climate in which to raise young Neil. At the time, it didn't appear likely the Hawkes would ever have another child.

Unlike in Renmark, Hawke had no trouble filling the pews. At the harvest thanksgiving service a few weeks after his arrival, so many people turned up that some were unable to get inside. The following night the church was similarly crowded for a concert, followed by supper and a sale of fruit and vegetables in the adjoining kindergarten hall. Although some might have attended simply to assess the new pastor, their coins helped fill the church coffers.[73]

This enthusiasm was more than matched by the Hawkes as they involved themselves in the doings of the town. Ellie was elected secretary of a newly formed mothers' club at the Bordertown School, which was established to raise funds for the teaching of domestic arts and crafts. She also organised an annual Children's Day, when such arts and crafts were featured. The club was just one of many activities in which she became involved, from the local croquet club to the fairs and fetes organised each year by the church and the school. Somehow, she also found time to continue tutoring Neil.[74]

Within four months of their arrival, Clem had been elected to the school committee, presided over a concert by visiting performers raising money for the blind, given an address to an Anzac Day service at the Bordertown Institute, been elected to the committee of the Bordertown Football Club, and been made president of the B-grade football club and served as its timekeeper. He also played in an intertown tennis competition and played golf and umpired hockey matches between two teams of the Bordertown Girls' Sports Club.[75]

It wouldn't have been appropriate for Clem, as a minister, to be actively involved in the Labor Party, where his political sympathies still lay. Bordertown was staunchly conservative and always strongly supported the anti-Labor candidates in state and federal elections. Instead of publicly supporting Labor, he attempted to restart the activities of the Workers' Educational Association, which provided improvement classes for men and women who'd been denied a university education.[76]

Although he'd been active in the Renmark Institute, it seems that the Bordertown Institute wasn't to Clem's taste. Instead, he helped to establish the Tatiara Literary and Dramatic Society in May 1929. The two dozen or so members met fortnightly in the institute's committee room, and interspersed talks and debates with readings from plays.[77]

Somehow, the Hawkes managed to juggle all these civic and sporting commitments with their many church obligations. Along with Ellie, Clem built up the Sunday School, convincing the congregation in a way he hadn't been able to do in New Zealand to erect a purpose-built hall to accommodate the growing number of children.[78]

Ellie hankered to have a daughter of her own, and even suggested vainly to her sister that she be given one of hers. Apart from one miscarriage, she'd had no pregnancy for eight years. Although one account suggests that it was only after having an operation in August 1928 that Ellie was able to become pregnant again, the *Bordertown Chronicle* reported that the operation in question had been for appendicitis.[79] It's possible that the couple simply required time away from the relentless commitments of church and town.

Seven months after Ellie's operation, they were able to take a relaxing holiday. A Renmark couple accompanied them on a 2000-kilometre round trip by car to Daylesford, in Victoria, and back by way of Naracoorte. Tom Beech was the irrigation officer in Renmark and a former tennis partner of Clem's. When Ellie was recuperating from her operation, she had stayed at the Beeches' Renmark home before going on to her mother's in Adelaide.[80] In March 1929, with 31-year-old Ellie now fully recovered, the four friends drove off to explore a wide swathe of south-eastern Australia. It was during this motoring odyssey that Ellie finally became pregnant again.

CHAPTER TWO

1929–1939

When Ellie became pregnant with her second child, she was certain that God would finally bless her with a daughter. She'd even chosen a name, Elizabeth. As a result, she must have felt some disappointment when she gave birth at home on 9 December 1929 and gazed down upon the swaddled infant boy. Whatever pleasure she might have felt at finally having another child, it was her first-born son who remained the centre of her attention and the repository of her hopes. Growing up, it would be a constant source of anger to her second-born son that he was never allowed by his mother to forget that she had wanted him to be a girl.

Ellie reconciled herself to his gender by concluding that it was part of God's plan. In her daily Bible reading, her eyes had often alighted on a text from the Book of Isaiah: 'For unto us a child is born, unto us a son is given: and the government shall be upon his shoulder.' The words are not a reference to worldly leaders, but to the coming of the Messiah and the divine governance of Christ. Yet it became Ellie's staunch belief, and perhaps a sign of her pathological narcissism, that she was a conduit for God, and that any child of hers would fulfil God's plan by changing the world for the better. Clem, too, was convinced that their new son was 'destined for a great future'.[1]

For the last eight years, the weight of Ellie's expectation had fallen on Neil, and he'd shown signs of realising her vision. Just ten days after her second son was born, Neil was presented with a prize for topping Grade Four at Bordertown's primary school. As for the baby, he was dubbed Robert James Lee Hawke, the first name being chosen, apparently, because it seemed distinguished and would suit the knighthood that Ellie expected he would be awarded one day. The boy would be known as Bobbie throughout his childhood. Clem would later say that they were aware that 'one prevalent meaning of the name, "Robert", was "bright in fame"'. This sense of specialness was reinforced when Clem's mentor, Dr Edward Kiek, came from Adelaide to perform the christening. But it was Neil who continued to receive the bulk of his mother's love and attention.[2]

As with many children born into a family after a long hiatus, Bobbie was indulged by his parents in ways that never happened with Neil. Whereas Neil was often physically punished by both his parents, Bobbie went through his childhood without ever feeling the sting of his mother's hand or his father's strap. While Ellie thought that God had chosen Bobbie for some special purpose, she had developed a much closer relationship with Neil than Clem had done. It was Clem who became particularly close to Bobbie, bathing and dressing the child and later reading stories to him. He was unabashed about saying that Bobbie was his favourite child, and that Neil was Ellie's favourite. Clem would later suggest that there was a mystical quality to his close connection with Bobbie, that his second child 'had an outflowing magic about him'. This unconditional love from his father would buoy Hawke throughout his life. He later told a television interviewer that 'the bond between us was just remarkable'.[3]

The birth of Bobbie had coincided with the beginning of a ruinous, decade-long depression that would see unemployment peak at more than 30 per cent. The cities were hardest hit, but the economic effects reached Bordertown when wheat prices slumped and farm incomes shrivelled. Some businesses were forced to close and the contributions in the church collection plate got progressively lighter. Within a year of Bobbie's birth, Clem was asked to take a 10 per cent reduction in his stipend and an even bigger cut in his car allowance. Henceforth, the car was only to be used on church business. Even with these economies, the church's overdraft kept increasing.[4]

As a Christian socialist, Clem had welcomed the election in October 1929 of a federal Labor government, which had come into power on a surge of public support that caused even the conservative prime minister, Stanley Bruce, to lose his seat. To the great surprise of the people of Bordertown, their own conservative MP had come close to being defeated.[5] But the incoming prime minister, James Scullin, had no panacea for the worsening economic troubles that soon swamped his government.

Rather than spending their way out of the depression, the government followed conventional economic theory by reducing government expenditure in the belief that a balanced budget was the best way to restore international confidence in the Australian economy. It was vital that the bankers of London regarded Australia as a secure place to loan their money. In the hope of boosting the nation's income, Scullin encouraged farmers to grow more wheat, which only caused prices to slump further. The government disintegrated under the pressure, forcing a new election, which saw the newly formed United Australia Party, led by former Laborite Joseph Lyons, replace Labor on the government benches.

When work became harder to find in Bordertown, Clem helped organise a community singing event, at which the churches combined to raise money for the unemployed.[6] Some of Bob Hawke's earliest memories are of people calling at the manse and receiving assistance from his father. Men humping their swags would ride the rails between Melbourne and Adelaide, jumping off the goods trains at intermediate towns. With the manse being just a short walk from the station, many of them called and waited with doffed hats as food was fetched from the kitchen or shelter was offered for the night. Hawke would later say that it was one of the formative experiences that caused him to develop a sense that 'everyone, all humans, were kin'.[7] The local railway staff were not as charitable as the Hawkes, and armed themselves with lengths of garden hose with which to beat the interlopers off the trains that stopped to take on fuel and water.[8]

Although unemployment eased somewhat in 1934, Clem disputed the view of the Adelaide *Advertiser* that the 'buoyant spirits and carefree spending' seen at a city race meeting signalled the end of the depression. The economy still had 'grave problems', wrote Clem, and people were not generally better off. During his travels around the countryside, he'd heard 'of farmer after farmer being sold up', while his investigations in Adelaide revealed 'the wretched conditions' of the unemployed. Moreover, the 'fundamental causes of depression and unemployment' were still in place and were an affront to a nation that had the resources to have 'every citizen well-fed, well-housed and well-clothed'. That was not happening, wrote the impassioned preacher, because of what he described as the man-made 'juggernaut which crushes helpless victims beneath its heartless weight'.[9] Such sentiments would have been part of the kitchen-table conversation that an impressionable young Bobbie would have imbibed, as he witnessed his loving father's anger and frustration.

While Clem wasn't in a position to mobilise the people against capitalism's injustices, he did try to ameliorate the effects of the depression on individuals and to exhort people to live better lives. One way was to abandon alcohol. The Bordertown branch of the temperance organisation the Band of Hope was re-formed in 1930 and became one of the biggest in the state, with Clem as vice-president. Nearly two hundred people signed its pledge of abstinence at the Bordertown Institute, while speakers from the group encouraged children at Sunday Schools to also sign the pledge. The group met monthly on the night nearest to the full moon, so that those walking or using horses had some light to guide them. In July 1933, perhaps with young Bobbie looking on, Ellie told the audience 'why men should not drink', a speech she also presented in nearby Wolseley and over the border in Serviceton. Back in Bordertown, she later did 'a cleverly-contrived and well-acted dialogue' explaining why alcohol should not even be part of a medicine shelf, and helped produce a play for a conference of the WCTU.[10]

As well as church and Sunday School roles, Ellie continued as secretary of the school committee and played a prominent part in its many public activities, from the pet show and May Day fair to the Arbor and Bird Day, when she helped serve up ninety litres of soup to the students who'd planted thirty pine trees around the school grounds. In March 1933, she was deputed to buy books for the library during a visit to Adelaide, and was later rewarded with a rose bowl to mark her five years as committee secretary. She also continued as an active member of the croquet club, of which she was president in 1934. Among her frenzy of activities, she was a regular visitor to patients at the hospital, was elected vice-president of the hospital's ladies' auxiliary, and organised the music for its annual fundraising afternoon at the Bordertown Institute.[11] And she continued to surround herself with young girls, filling the manse with them, which perhaps provided her with some solace at not having a daughter of her own.

Following Bobbie's birth, Ellie had several girls to live at the manse, presumably one at a time, so they wouldn't be taken out of school by hard-pressed parents who wanted them to work as domestic or farm servants. While the Hawkes' kindness might have kept those girls at school, there would have been domestic duties for them to do in the manse, since it's difficult to see how Clem and Ellie could have fulfilled their numerous obligations without drawing upon the labour of others, whether paid or unpaid. Some help may have been provided by a Miss Peggy Strachan, who was a probationer nurse and was reported to have come from Renmark to stay at the manse when Bobbie was about six months old.[12]

It was during this time that Ellie became more deeply involved with the Girl Guides. Rather than just being the local Guide leader, as she had been in Renmark, she became the district commissioner and also served as leader of the youngest girls.[13] Although he sometimes accompanied his mother to meetings of the Brownies, it was tough for young Bobbie to be noticed by a mother, whose attention was often elsewhere and whose roles often took her away from home.[14] And it was made more difficult by his mother's openly expressed preference for his older brother. His father's absences only made things worse. When Clem went on annual leave to southern Tasmania in March 1931, perhaps scouting out a new church, he left Ellie to take care of the children and fulfil her civic and church duties, during which she spoke at a function to commemorate the founding of the Bordertown School Club and made a three-level birthday cake for the attendees to devour.[15]

Recognising that a congregation needed more than just a Sunday sermon, Clem and Ellie provided a range of groups and activities to ensure that the church was a central part of their congregation's life. There were special services for men, for mothers and for young people. One of the most popular was the annual Harvest Thanksgiving Festival, which saw the church fill to overflowing and young Bobbie running about, unrestrained by either parent. Between services, there was an afternoon program of musical items, along with a brief talk by Clem on the theme of thanksgiving. There was a further concert on the Monday evening, when entertainment and religion were again combined, followed by supper in the hall.[16]

The couple were conscious that they had to compete with cinema, radio and the other distractions that were leading people away from the church. Clem became president of a committee to organise midweek meetings for young people that would combine 'devotional exercises' with 'competitions and other items'. One of the first events was a 'Garden of Surprises', which was held on a rain-affected Wednesday evening and involved a girl dressed as an angel leading four young girls around a supposed garden in the church, while a concealed choir sang hymns. To the delight of the congregation, parcels of groceries were presented to the local unemployed and sweets were given to the hospital, while Clem received a cheque for the church. A concert by several soloists and a buffet supper rounded out the evening, which had been preceded the previous Sunday by a 'Young People's service', during which Clem gave a sermon entitled 'Self-Knowledge, Self-Reverence, and Self-Control'.[17]

Just as they had in other churches, the Hawkes devoted a lot of effort to the Sunday School. Ellie taught classes in both Bordertown and the church in nearby Pooginagoric, and tutored them for the annual exam organised by the Congregational Young People's Department. Clem held a meeting of Sunday School teachers from the district's Protestant churches to hear a crusading lecturer tell them that parents had to 'impart a feeling of reverence in the child when only a few weeks old' by regularly praying over them and bringing them to Sunday School from the time they were toddlers. For the older children, any entertainment put on by the church had to have 'a high tone', and not have anything that was 'suggestive or undesirable'. It seems that Ellie and Clem didn't need to be reminded about praying over their child. Clem would later say of Bobbie that 'the child of so many prayers can never be lost'.[18]

Among his civic duties, the non-combatant Clem continued to take a leading part in the commemoration of Anzac Day, during which he eulogised the sacrifice of Australian soldiers and assured the crowd that the Gallipoli campaign had 'contributed largely to the eventual winning of the war'.[19] He also embraced the celebration of Empire Day by having a service in the church, with the pulpit and railing adorned with Union Jacks and members of the Bordertown troop of the Light

Horse attending in full uniform. Clem likened the growth of the British Empire to the growth of Christianity, and called on the audience to 'make their contribution to Imperial progress' by living righteous lives. He made a similar appeal to Bordertown's children during Empire Day celebrations at the school.[20] Among the audience was Neil, who was trying his best to live up to Clem's ideals.

In December 1932, the Bordertown School held its annual concert in the Institute hall, which was decorated with gum branches and gladioli. After displays of gymnastics, 'action songs' and nursery rhymes, it was time for the prize-giving, which is what Clem and Ellie were waiting for. They weren't disappointed. Despite having had an operation for appendicitis during the year, eleven-year-old Neil topped Grade Seven and, along with three other boys, was presented with a temperance certificate. His outstanding school marks earned him a year's free membership of the Bordertown Institute library. Not that he'd have much use of it, because he'd also been awarded a scholarship to King's College in Adelaide, a private school that had been established primarily for Congregational boys. The scholarship covered most of his tutorial fees but not the much greater cost of boarding at the school, so he was sent to live with Ellie's elderly mother.[21] This meant Bobbie would be living the life of an only child for much of the year – except that the example of his brother would always be held out to him as the ideal to which he should aspire.

During their seven years in Bordertown, the couple had become deeply involved in the community. They might have lived out their lives there. Clem hadn't experienced the rancour and frustration that had caused him to suddenly leave some of his previous churches.[22] That all changed in May 1934, when a visiting evangelist set up a huge tent in the grounds of the rival Church of Christ for a month-long program of amplified hymn singing and sermonising. The evangelist, Thomas Hagger, took his inspiration from the gospel-singing, tub-thumping evangelists of the United States. Hard-hit people who were hungry for answers flocked to his marquee like flies to a picnic. The tent throbbed with nightly entertainment, culminating in the worked-up audience being promised salvation if they agreed to be immersed in a baptismal ceremony and commit themselves to the Church of Christ. The interloper's campaign coincided with the week-long diamond jubilee celebrations of Clem's church. Part of those celebrations involved a combined Sunday School service at the Bordertown Institute, at which the Church of Christ children were notably absent. Ellie was furious.[23]

In a long letter to the *Border Chronicle*, apparently written at Ellie's instigation, Clem launched a bitter attack on Hagger, accusing him of trying to capture 'members of other churches', and arguing that his promise of salvation through immersion was contrary to the teachings of Jesus. The incendiary letter set off a month-long explosion of claim and counterclaim, with Clem suggesting that Hagger was 'Mussolini-like', had 'the fanaticism of Mohammodanism' [sic] and was set on 'white-anting other denominations'. To Clem's dismay, the Baptists and Presbyterians joined in the counterattack on him. Clem would not be silenced. Even after Hagger had dismantled his tent and left, he kept going, only to have Hagger's supporters continue to trade religious blows with him. Some of them were pillars of the town and involved with Clem in various local groups. The bitterness ran so deep that even fifty years later some townspeople were unwilling to talk about it.[24]

Clem's public outbursts revealed a level of anger and frustration with his situation that isn't apparent in the church records. The history of the church simply notes how his 'quiet humour, sterling integrity and active involvement in town affairs earned him the affectionate regard of the people'.[25] But the acrimonious dispute with Hagger harked back to his tumultuous time in Lower Hutt. Now the fiery preacher, bursting with energy, was again looking for a new start.

Within a few weeks, Clem went to the small town of Hamley Bridge, ostensibly to give sermons at the town's Congregational church. His real reason was to check out whether he wanted to shift there after the church's minister resigned. Hamley Bridge was about thirty-five kilometres west of Kapunda, where Clem had been born and where many of his family still lived. Nothing came of his visit. It's not clear whether Clem was unimpressed by the church, or the congregation was unimpressed by him. Still, he'd made clear to church officials in Adelaide that he wanted a transfer, and in September they suggested to the congregation in Maitland that it should try him out. The town of about six hundred people was on the Yorke Peninsula, not far from where Ellie had been born at Greens Plains West. Clem went there in early November to present sermons. This time, they clearly went well.

On his return to Bordertown, Clem told his congregation that he'd accepted 'a call'.[26]

Clem and Ellie were well aware that congregations and their ministers have a way of tiring of each other, and that pulpits need refreshing if the audience is to remain engaged. Some might have tired of Clem's sermons, while the messianic Ellie's tendency to be 'impatient, aggressive and dogmatic' would have caused even more members of the congregation to tire of her. The church organist later described the Hawkes as 'an interesting and different family', a polite description into which much can be read.[27]

But it was the Hawkes, rather than the congregation, who took the initiative for a change. Hagger's visit had undermined Clem's work and inadvertently created an antagonistic relationship between Clem and several prominent townspeople, with the district's Protestants dividing along sectarian lines. This had reverberated through many community organisations. The dispute had also exposed a side of Clem that he usually kept hidden from public view. It all became too much for them; they needed to move on.

*

In the late-summer heat of February 1935, there was a great gathering of Maitland worthies to welcome Reverend Hawke and his family to the town. Crowding the hall were representatives from the nearby Congregational churches of Tiparra West, Cunningham and Yorke Valley, of which Clem would also have charge, along with women and men from other Protestant churches. It was a sign of the times that there were never any representatives of the Catholic Church at these events. Presiding over the induction was the former head of the church's South Australian branch, while Maitland's mayor added to the welcome. News of their ill-disciplined younger son had preceded the family's arrival in Maitland, and Bobbie promptly proved it correct in the middle of Clem's first church service when he 'ran out of the church, climbed up a tree and tore his pants on the way down'.[28]

For Ellie, the shift to Maitland marked a return to the region of her childhood, where copper miners and farmers had brought their Cornish ways and their nonconformist religion, making the mostly flat plains of the Yorke Peninsula a place of Methodist chapels and Rechabite halls, of community hymn singing and prim godliness. For Clem, the northern Yorke Peninsula was just 145 kilometres from his relations in Kapunda. It also brought them about a hundred kilometres closer to Adelaide, where Neil remained a student at King's College.

The Maitland congregation was sufficiently well-heeled to offer Clem a stipend of £300, along with a rent-free manse, complete with a tennis court, a telephone and a supply of firewood for heating and cooking. Although there was no allowance for running a car, the stipend was more than he'd been receiving in Bordertown.[29] As in the other places where they'd served, the couple soon became prominent members of Maitland society. Ellie was elected a member of the local croquet club and threw herself into the activities of the church and the WCTU.[30]

The town had been laid out like Adelaide, with Maitland having a square grid of just five streets crossed by another five. This inner grid was bounded by a belt of shady parkland, in which sports fields, a golf course and the showground were located. Beyond the parkland was an outer square of terraces, which were designed to accommodate any future expansion of the town. It was in that outer square that the Congregational church and manse were located, which set them apart from the other churches and from most of the town's inhabitants, who lived within the central grid. Although the Maitland summers could be almost unbearable, the waters of Spencer Gulf were just twenty kilometres to the west and could be seen from some parts of the town, while Gulf St Vincent was a similar distance to the east, which meant the family could get to a beach and back in a day.

The town lay at the centre of what one newspaper called 'a veritable agricultural paradise', where tractors rather than horses had become the norm. Maitland was the service centre for these farms, with two sizeable hotels, a post office and a range of shops, banks and garages selling the essentials of life for the farmers and the town's inhabitants. There was also a handsome, stone-built Institute that boasted a library, a supper room and a hall capable of seating 450 people, which was used as a cinema on Saturday nights.[31]

Bobbie's Maitland years, when he was between five and nine, were formative ones for him. With his older brother only home during school vacations, it might have been expected that Bobbie would be showered with the love and attention that had flowed so freely to Neil. That was only partly true. Although Hawke recalled 'being enveloped by love' during his childhood, he drew a clear distinction between the 'purposeful love' of his mother and the 'mutual adoration' he had with his father.[32]

Ellie's love for Bobbie was of the conditional kind, and she made no attempt to hide the disappointment she felt at him not being the daughter she'd craved, which Ellie now knew she could never have. Bobbie was also left in no doubt that 'Neil was *her* son, her first-born, her favourite'. Although Neil was absent from the family's life for months at a time, Ellie ensured that he was nonetheless present as the exemplar for Bobbie in scholarship, sporting ability and behaviour. It was against the taller and more strikingly handsome Neil, the scholarship winner, that Bobbie would always be measured. It was a big burden of expectation for a young child. As if that weren't enough, Bobbie was also told repeatedly of his mother's narcissistic conviction that she was chosen by God, and that he, like Neil, was born of her to become 'a destined instrument of the Lord'. This was something that his father also firmly believed.[33]

The natural anxiety of a child seeking reassurance about his parents' love was complicated in the Hawke household by the presence of the girls or women whom Ellie invited to stay, or even to live with them. Ellie was again the district commissioner for the Girl Guides, and a training week in 1937 saw the manse crowded with teenage girls. Seven-year-old Bobbie found his home converted into 'an indoor camp under strict camp routine', with his mother lording it over the girls.[34] She continued her lifelong campaign to encourage the education of girls; Hawke later recalled how he often heard his mother say to a parent that a particular girl has 'talent [and] should go on'.[35]

Bobbie also had to compete for his mother's love and attention with a young woman, Gwen Geater, who moved into the manse soon after their arrival in Maitland. The Geater family were members of the Congregational church at Tiparra West, about twenty kilometres away. When Ellie discovered that the Geaters had three daughters, she insisted they give her one, which they did. One of the younger girls moved in and was taught needlework by Ellie, only to be joined soon after by the older Gwen, who helped with domestic chores.

Gwen wasn't a teenage girl but an attractive 23-year-old woman 'of feminine, dark-eyes [and] good looks', who became both a helpmate and close companion to Ellie. She would later say that she became like a 'daughter' to Ellie and 'a lifelong friend'. Gwen often found herself minding the needy Bobbie, which saw her give him the discipline that his parents were loath to do. 'I put him over my knee more times than I can count,' Geater recalled, but her annoyance was tempered by him also being 'so lovable – full of fun and affectionate'.[36]

Bobbie had to cope with the frequent absences of one or both of his parents. In August 1938, Ellie drove with Gwen to the scenic beachside settlement of Corny Point, at the tip of the Yorke Peninsula, where Ellie opened a new Guide hall and presided at the induction of Girl Guides, after which she and Gwen stayed on to holiday for a few days. It was one of many times that Ellie was absent from Maitland, with the church records showing she often missed meetings of the Women's Society. Perhaps because of these absences, she stood down as president in September 1938 and became one of two vice-presidents.[37]

The Girl Guides were the great distraction for Ellie. As the district commissioner, she often visited other groups on the peninsula to induct young girls into the movement or to attend training camps. As a leading member of the WCTU, she would also travel to meetings in other towns and cities, often accompanied by Gwen, who would later become a youth organiser for the organisation.[38] Bobbie was also left behind in early 1938 when Ellie accompanied another family on a caravan holiday to Sydney; on her return she gave 'an entertaining account' to the Women's Society. Just weeks later, both Clem and Ellie went on a caravan holiday, leaving Bobbie at the Geaters' farm, where he was 'torn between wild enthusiasm and fear' at the prospect of being away from his parents. Hawke would recall going to the farm after school and staying up late to hear broadcasts of Ashes cricket matches from England.[39]

Ellie's prolonged absences likely added to Bobbie's insecurity about her love for him, although it was his father's absences that caused him the deepest distress. Hawke's official biographer and later wife, Blanche d'Alpuget, writes of one instance when Bobbie was eight or nine years old and was so upset that he demanded a telegram be sent calling for Clem to come home, declaring dramatically: 'I can't live without him ... I'm going to die.'[40]

This type of boisterous and demanding behaviour wasn't tolerated by Gwen. Nor was it tolerated at Maitland School, where Bobbie began his education in late January 1935, although at first he resisted going at all. The brick school was located at the south-eastern extremity of the town's square grid, just over a kilometre from the manse. Bobbie would tote his satchel the length of Robert Street, the town's main thoroughfare, doubtless being distracted en route by the contrasting smells emanating from Thomas's butchery and Mullner's bakery, and the discordant noises spilling out of Gunnings' garage and the Maitland Hotel. Being relatively small in stature, he was nicknamed 'Little Bobbie' by other children and was bullied relentlessly until he allied himself with older protectors, becoming the quick-witted jester to a gang of tough-talking kids. 'Anyone who punched him had to fight me,' recalled one of these older friends. Bobbie was also troubled with respiratory problems in Maitland, perhaps brought on by the change in climate from Bordertown and hay fever at harvest time. Brains rather than brawn were his forte, and Ellie's tutoring and Clem's night-time reading of Bible stories gradually saw him begin to excel in class and grow in confidence.[41]

The school had five teachers and more than 150 students crammed into three small classrooms. It was a test of both pupil and teacher, yet he responded enthusiastically, perhaps because he related well to the headteacher, Martin Hansberry, and to the constant testing that was done. Clem acted as an exam supervisor for the external exams and spoke on occasions such as Empire Day. His presence at the school, and on the stage in the Maitland Institute Hall during the annual speech night, would have encouraged Bobbie to do well.

Each week, successful pupils were listed in the *Maitland Watch*. At the end of 1936, Bobbie joined about twenty-five other students in being presented with a prize for 'good work'. By December 1937, he was placed at the top of Grade Three. Despite earlier reports of his misbehaviour and carelessness in his work, even his conduct was now rated as 'excellent'. Unfortunately, his moment in the spotlight at the 1937 speech night was taken from him by an outbreak of polio, which caused the cancellation of the event and delayed the start of the 1938 school year until mid-March. That didn't stop him from often being listed in the local paper and topping his class again at the end of

1938. His self-confidence had grown sufficiently for him to do a solo performance at that year's Sunday School Christmas party.[42]

With Neil away during term time and usually working on farms during his school holidays, Ellie focused on getting Bobbie to emulate his older brother, whose occasional visits to Maitland provided a reminder of the sort of son that she wanted Bobbie to be.

When the school holidays in May 1935 coincided with an annual three-day Eisteddfod organised by the Congregational Church, Ellie competed alongside Neil and Gwen Geater. While Gwen and Ellie both won different parts of the elocution section, Neil won a prize by reciting a piece of prose and some scripture and doing an impromptu reading. Early the next year, his proud parents would have been at the Maitland Cycling Track, along with six-year-old Bobbie, to cheer Neil on when he competed in the club's three-mile handicap race, which he won by ten lengths from eight other starters.[43]

Newspaper reports of the Hawkes' activities in Maitland make the family's lives seem idyllic. A recently discovered home movie shows a young Bobbie riding a sheep in his garden. However, the 1930s remained a difficult time. Unemployment continued to be high, and itinerant workers were always knocking on the back door of the manse looking to do an odd job or begging for a feed. The general desperation was epitomised by the 73-year-old swaggie who succumbed to his despair and was found hanging from a tree outside Maitland. The macabre discovery was made just days before Christmas 1936, as Ellie presided over parties for the Sunday School and the Brownies and as Clem welcomed his mentor from Parkin College, Reverend Kiek, who conducted a Masonic church parade and gave a combined sermon with the Methodists entitled 'Christ and the world crisis'.[44]

Conflict had already erupted in the Pacific with the Japanese invasion of China, and there was every chance that Australia could again become embroiled in a spreading conflict and even be invaded by Japan, which could see the whole family caught up in the conflict. As a pastor, Clem tried to provide guidance for his congregation. Yet the Congregational Church was conflicted. For a time, it was affiliated to the anti-war and anti-fascist movement, and expressed its 'strong opposition' to the introduction of compulsory military training.[45] They were moves that Clem would have supported. In July 1936, he preached against the Old Testament talk of destroying people who weren't part of 'the chosen race', and pointed instead to the teachings of Jesus, which were all about 'the Fatherhood of God and the brotherhood of man'. Concluding with the words of a hymn, Clem looked forward to a world where:

> In every heart and brain shall throb
> The pulse of one fraternity.[46]

However, the growing fraternity of Italy, Germany and Japan caused the church to retreat from its anti-war stance.[47] Like many people, Clem was forced to confront the awful truth that the all-embracing love proclaimed by Jesus might not be sufficient to defeat the destructive hate of the fascist powers and their determination to dominate the world. It was perhaps a reflection of Clem's changing views when he argued in a debate that 'Britain's re-armament policy is a factor for world peace'.[48]

As war became more likely, Ellie grew increasingly fearful that Neil would enlist when he came of age.[49] For the time being, he continued to study hard at his boarding school in Adelaide. King's College had fewer than 200 students, who were taught in a large two-storey home with wrap-around verandahs, which were enclosed on the first floor to provide accommodation for boarders. It was established in 1923 by the Congregational and Baptist churches with the aim to 'win every boy for Jesus Christ'. The editors of the school magazine told their fellow students in 1932 that they were 'the spiritual heirs of the old Puritans' and they should emulate their 'intense moral fervour'. When Neil began in 1933, the school was led by a strict Baptist disciplinarian, who told one teacher having trouble with his students to 'be more of a brute'. The only restraint on the teachers was not to hit the boys about the head. One boy made money by hiring out a rabbit skin for boys to put down their trousers prior to punishment being meted out.[50] While they might not have approved of such harsh punishments, Clem and Ellie would have nodded approvingly when the head of the Congregational Church told the annual speech night in 1936 that he 'hoped that King's boys would be found foremost among those who gave their utmost in service to the State'.[51] Although she didn't want Neil joining the armed forces, this is what Ellie expected of her favourite son.

In 1937, Neil was on both the debating committee and the magazine committee, and competed successfully in the house swimming competition at the Unley Crystal Pool. He was also a member of the college's Scout troop and was awarded the highest proficiency badge. Meanwhile, he'd done so well at his studies that he was dux of the Lower Sixth Form and was awarded the prize for Scripture. Although he wasn't singled out for a distinction in the state-wide Leaving Examination, he passed his six subjects and seemed set for university. In 1938, he moved into the Upper Sixth class, only to suddenly leave school in July 1938, shortly after being appointed a house prefect.[52]

It's not clear why Neil left in the middle of the year. His parents may have been concerned for his health, as a polio epidemic had recently caused the school to be closed for five weeks. Then again, there was a story that the 'fine, manly lad', who was also described as 'moody' and 'temperamental', may have left under a cloud after unsuccessfully propositioning one of the female teachers.[53] Rather than going on to university, Neil secured a junior position in a government office and took up lodgings in a boarding house on Adelaide's South Terrace. It meant that he would spend even less time in Maitland.[54]

Worse was to come. When Clem and Ellie caught up with Neil at the funeral of Ellie's elderly mother in mid-February 1939, he'd seemed unwell. Gwen had baked a fruitcake for him, which Ellie had decorated and given to Neil, telling him not to eat it before his forthcoming birthday. Thinking little of it at the time, his parents said their farewells and returned to Bobbie and their busy lives in Maitland.[55]

It was late summer, a time when the churches held harvest festivals to mark the passing of the seasons and to give thanks for the bounty of the earth. South Australia had been suffering a prolonged heatwave, and terrible bushfires had torn across the nation's south-east, killing scores of people. A visiting preacher was invited to give the Harvest Thanksgiving service at Clem's church, while Clem had agreed to preach services in Minlacowie and Yorketown.[56] These plans were cast aside when a telephone call from Adelaide told them that eighteen-year-old Neil was gravely ill. Clem drove furiously to the capital to check his son's condition, then called Ellie to join him at Neil's bedside in a small private hospital on South Terrace. It seems that he'd contracted amoebic meningitis from the Unley pool where he used to train and compete in amateur competitions. Although a surgeon drained the fluid from his brain, there was nothing that could be done to prevent the terrible illness from taking its awful course. Despite the earnest prayers of his parents, Neil died comatose and convulsing in the early hours of 27 February 1939. Clem and Ellie were awoken that night and summoned from their accommodation but arrived too late. As they'd always done, his parents took comfort in their religion. Neil's death notice included a Biblical quote – 'The golden bowl is broken' – to reflect their conviction that their son's death had been followed by eternal life in heaven, while his mortal remains were taken back to his lodgings. The day after his death, amid unseasonal cold and wet, friends and family gathered to mourn as the undertakers carried the coffin on its journey to the Protestant cemetery in the suburb of Mitcham. Neil's tombstone simply marked his name and the date of his death.[57]

Ellie had lost her mother and her favoured son in quick succession and appeared 'totally devastated' when she returned home to Bobbie, who'd had no chance to see his sick brother or farewell him at the funeral; the family did not consider it proper 'for children to be associated with grief and death'. Although the Women's Society noted that 'a gloom had been cast over our Church life by the sudden passing', life had to continue. A few weeks after his brother's death, Bobbie decorated his bike and won a prize for it at the school's show. Clem, despite his anguish, went on with his preaching, driving to Kadina, where he counselled the congregation to live by the teachings of Jesus so that they would be 'strengthened when the testing time comes'. Presumably with Neil's death in mind, and perhaps hoping that his remaining son would take over where Neil had left off, he consoled the congregation and himself with the thought that the 'young tree may be cut down, but it will survive in some other form'.[58]

Neither Clem nor Ellie had much time for grieving or to spend with their surviving son, who seemed unaffected by the loss of his older brother. In his memoirs, Hawke would explain how Neil's term-time absences had prevented the brothers from being close. The favouritism with which his mother treated Neil was likely a bigger factor in keeping them apart, and would have caused his resentment towards his mother to transfer to Neil also. According to D'Alpuget, Hawke 'never inquired into the nature of his brother's death, never visited his grave or even discovered where he was buried'. Hawke's own memoirs devote only two paragraphs to Neil's death before turning to describe how it made him the cherished child of both his parents, rather than just of his father. Clem now encouraged Bobbie not to be so fixated on him, and to provide comfort by showing affection to his grieving mother. That was going to be difficult when his mother's love seemed to be conditional on Bobbie achieving the greatness to which she believed Neil had been destined. 'I had these two problems in childhood,' Hawke told D'Alpuget, 'my mother wanted me to be a girl, and then her son died, and I had, somehow, to replace him.'[59]

The Hawkes struggled to cope with their loss. Less than three months after Neil's death, Clem spent part of his annual leave at Kapunda, where many of his relatives still lived and where his brother Albert, now a cabinet minister in the West Australian Labor government, was visiting.[60] Ellie went on several trips of her own. After attending meetings of the Congregational Union in Adelaide in April, she travelled to Brisbane in early May for the biennial assembly of the Australasian church. Among the usual issues of church unity and the moral danger of films on children, the imminent threat of another war captured the most attention. With Germany having invaded Czechoslovakia just weeks before, and with a Pacific war looking likely, the assembly made a plea for peace and for Australia to accept more refugees from Nazi Germany.[61] After being away for about a month, Ellie was home for less than a fortnight before heading off again, this time to spend four days with the Minlaton Guide group about fifty kilometres south of Maitland.[62] With Gwen at her side, Ellie also continued as president of the Maitland WCTU, resumed her former position as president of the Women's Society, and pressed on with the organisation of a flower and cookery show. The display of flowers and cakes was held just days after German forces stormed into Poland.[63]

By this time, Ellie's attention was concentrated on the family's imminent departure from Maitland. They had been there for less than five years, but Clem was keen to be off again. The move has usually been ascribed to their anguish over Neil's death, but the Hawkes had had another falling-out with a congregation. As early as 1937, there'd been criticism of Clem's frequent absences from the Sunday services in Maitland; he was instead preaching at nearby Cunningham. This was causing attendances in Maitland, and therefore contributions, to decline. It was perhaps because of this dissension that Clem first tried to secure a church in Melbourne before deciding to join his brother in Western Australia.[64] Ellie didn't want to shift, telling Gwen, 'I won't go unless you come with me,' to which her young companion agreed, only to be prevented from doing so by her father. So it was just the bowed figure of the minister, thought by his parishioners to be on the verge of a nervous breakdown, along with his determined wife and temperamental child, who left Maitland with their bundled-up belongings in early November 1939. Their departure from South Australia meant they missed the King's College speech night, when a prize they had donated in memory of Neil was presented to a Lower Sixth Form student. Perhaps the occasion was too painful for them to bear. Now all that distress receded into the distance as the train took them slowly west towards their new lives in Perth. Not quite ten years old, Bobbie could barely supress his excitement.[65]

CHAPTER THREE

1939–1946

It was a slow journey across the Nullarbor Plain aboard the steam-driven Great Western Express. The standard-gauge line between Port Augusta and Kalgoorlie had only been completed twenty-two years earlier, and stretched for more than 1600 kilometres, much of it in a straight line. With no towns or even isolated houses for hundreds of kilometres, travellers looking out through the dust-streaked windows couldn't help but be impressed by the size and 'emptiness' of the continent.

It would have been difficult for the Hawkes to keep their unruly nine-year-old son contained over the few days of their journey. At least there was a lounge car with a piano for entertainment and tables for socialising and playing cards. There were regular stops where passengers could alight as the train took on water and coal, and longer stops in Port Augusta and Kalgoorlie, where passengers and their luggage had to be laboriously transhipped from one train to another. It must have been a relief to finally arrive in Perth on 11 November 1939, where they were greeted by Albert Hawke and heard newspaper hawkers call out headlines about the war, in which the German army was attacking along the French border.[1] Clem and Ellie might have taken some comfort from the words of the new prime minister, Robert Menzies, who counselled Australians to maintain an attitude of 'business as usual'.[2]

Clem seems to have taken this admonition to heart. The day after his arrival, he gave services at the Leederville Congregational Church.[3] It was a busy time for the family. The new church didn't come with a manse, so they had to find a house to rent that was convenient to the church and a school for Bobbie.[4] After a few weeks, they managed to secure a double-fronted brick house at 101 Tate Street, West Leederville.

Built just thirteen years before, their new home had three bedrooms, an enclosed verandah at the back and a big backyard. It allowed Clem to have a study and was large enough to accommodate visitors or to rent out a room to lodgers. Bobbie's room became little more than an alcove of the verandah, crammed with 'a single bed, a small wardrobe, a bookshelf and a side-table placed under the louvred window where he could study'.[5] West Leederville was a comfortable suburb of similar solid-brick homes on narrow, tree-lined streets with a thriving retail strip. The house was just a five-minute walk to the local primary school, where Bobbie started Grade Five in January 1940, and about twenty minutes' walk to the church in Oxford Street. It was also just a short commute by electric trolleybus into Perth.

Today, the school remains much as it was, with classrooms opening off a large central hall. It looks spacious now, and it needed to be back then because it was seriously overcrowded, with 660 pupils crammed into a school built for 550. One infant class had to be held in the hall and another in a washroom with an open archway. The numbers were so big that the school took over a nearby church hall, with the teachers' union worrying about the effect of the overcrowding on 'the children's general health'. Nevertheless, with Ellie's coaching and Clem's encouragement, Bobbie continued to do well academically, helped along by his natural ability and a home where reading the Bible, and Bible stories, was a regular activity. Hawke later claimed that he 'found little difficulty ... in being at the top, or equal top, of my classes'. In fact, from the time of his brother's death, his success was achieved by virtue of much pressure from his mother. He would later describe 'the stress of being forced to keep at his books', and recalled the pleasure when he 'escaped to play with Clem'. According to D'Alpuget, this set a pattern for life, with 'enforced labour' being followed by 'wild release with one he loved & who demanded nothing of him but joy'.[6]

Bobbie's teachers at West Leederville Primary School would have also played a part in his success, as exemplified by the enthusiasm of long-time teacher Ethel Crossley, who in 1940 led the school choir to first position in a festival at Perth Town Hall. Not that Hawke would ever pay tribute to the influence of any teacher. 'I was a loner,' he would later say. 'I wasn't interested in anyone else. I didn't depend on anyone else – I had no need for anyone else. I had my own views about life, I knew what was in my head.' This wasn't primarily a commentary on his teachers, but his parents. As biographer Stan Anson argues, the comment was Hawke's 'way of avoiding the chilling recognition that his needs were never adequately responded to by a mother who was too self-absorbed and a father who was too self-effacing'. It was also a reflection of his narcissism.[7]

Psychologists remain divided about the causes of narcissism, whether it is due to people being deprived of love at an early age and compensating with a heightened level of self-love, or whether it is due to children being assured at an impressionable age about how special they are and how they are capable of achieving anything.[8] Hawke was subject to both influences. There may also have been a genetic component too, as his mother's behaviour and beliefs displayed some of the characteristics of a narcissistic personality.

Hawke would spend his life looking for love and acceptance from the world outside. At the same time, and particularly after Neil's death, his narcissism was fed by his mother repeatedly assuring him, often in the presence of others, of how gifted he was. A contemporary recalled meeting the Hawkes in 1945 and being disconcerted by Ellie's tendency to 'talk of nothing but her marvellous son', and her displeasure when he didn't come first in all his exams. Clem added to the adulation that was heaped upon him, as did his uncle Albert. On one telling occasion, Hawke's future wife Hazel Masterson recalled how she and Bob rode up on his motorbike to the Hawke house after a game of cricket and encountered Clem and Albert in the driveway, with the two brothers 'competing in their compliments [about Bob] ... to see who could please him most'.[9]

While Bobbie enjoyed academic success, these early years in Perth also saw a continuation of the misbehaviour on which many had commented throughout his childhood. A young Hazel had first encountered him in a church play, *The Story of Esther*, which Ellie was again directing. It was soon after the Hawkes' arrival in Perth, when Bobbie and Hazel were both about ten years old. His behaviour was so bad that Hazel dismissed him as 'a brat', particularly as he was embarrassing his mother and undermining her own presentation.

Hazel was five months older than Bobbie and took performance seriously, having competed as a solo pianist at the West Australian Music Festival in 1939. As Ellie looked on, Hazel now played the role of Esther in 'a long, pink satin gown trimmed with silver braid', while Bobbie appeared on stage as a servant carrying a tray of glasses. This was his chance to get attention, so he shook the tray, causing the glasses to rattle loudly. To his mother's exasperation, the noise drowned out the voices of the other players, although Hazel later wrote that 'everyone understood that she really thought he was rather funny and that she enjoyed his pranks'.[10] It was a pattern of behaviour that was ingrained into him, as he sought the approval of his frequently distracted parents.

Once the family was settled in their new home, Ellie went back to croquet, playing regularly with the Leederville team. For reasons that aren't clear, she didn't resume her involvement with the Girl Guides.[11] Instead, as the minister's wife, she was in various church groups and taught for a time in the Sunday School. This might have been sufficient activity for most women, but not for Ellie, who devoted most of her time and energy to the WCTU. Its never-ending campaigns filled her days and many of her evenings, whether it was meeting in public halls, churches and schools, exhorting the passing parade on city streets or trying to capture the attention of beachgoers lying on the sand. Being taken to the beach by his mother could be a mortifying experience for Hawke, who recalled how she carried around 'bottles of shrivelled-up specimens of livers ... to warn about the effects of alcohol'. In Ellie's view, her temperance work was about making her Christian faith part of the daily lives of anyone who could be convinced to sign the pledge of abstinence. It was about helping to build a better world, about improving the lives of women and promoting the happiness of families. Children were particularly targeted by the WCTU, with mothers even being encouraged to sign up on behalf of their babies.[12]

The war, with its concomitant lowering of social and moral inhibitions, added to the urgency of the campaign against alcohol, gambling and 'loose living'. The WCTU wanted Perth's pubs to be closed when troopships were in port. It also argued for the federal government's national fitness campaign to include lectures on 'racial hygiene', which formed the basis of the eugenics movement that had begun in late-nineteenth-century Germany before spreading around the white world and being embraced by Adolf Hitler. The WCTU's call reflected the extent to which the campaigns for temperance and 'racial improvement' were intertwined. WCTU members were also disturbed by football matches being held on Sundays, even when the games were to raise funds for patriotic purposes. The social upheaval caused by the war, and the sense of crisis it engendered, caused one outraged resident to describe Perth as a 'modern Sodom or Gomorrah'. The president of the WCTU, meanwhile, decried the consumption of alcohol by girls, warning darkly that it 'stimulates the sex organs until the worst is bound to happen'. The organisation wanted women constables to patrol streets where females might be engaged in 'loose' behaviour, and called on the police commissioner to stop turning a blind eye to the brazen operation of the brothels that had long lined the street opposite the platforms of Perth station.[13]

Ellie's missionary zeal was inflamed as never before, with photographs from the time showing her with a serious mien, pinch-mouthed and unsmiling, as she went into battle on behalf of the Lord. She led devotions at the WCTU's annual convention in 1940, with the fifty or so women joining her in the singing of a hymn and listening to her Bible reading. She attended the WCTU Executive Committee and also the central Perth branch, which met monthly at its headquarters in Aberdeen Street. She volunteered for all manner of tasks, from organising teas to running a fete and hosting visiting officials at her home. Maggie Broadbent, a Methodist minister's wife who lodged at Tate Street with her son Peter during 1941, and who also did the household shopping and cooking, recalls how Ellie would spread pamphlets across the kitchen table as she lectured the boys on the evils of drinking and smoking. She 'drained the energy out of me', said Broadbent, who found Bobbie to be 'impossibly spoilt'. Even so, it wasn't easy for him, because Ellie was forever pressuring him to do as well as his deceased brother, which would have left him in little doubt that 'she loved Neil more than him'. There was a constant sense of loss in the house, recalled Broadbent, who noted how the still-grieving Ellie would bury her face in Neil's clothes in an attempt to recapture his presence.[14]

This behaviour would have been unsettling for Bobbie, and made even more so because Clem had become emotionally withdrawn after

Neil's death. Just over a year after arriving in Perth, Clem decided to go away altogether. Despite suffering from flat feet and varicose veins, the 42-year-old walked into Swan Barracks on 2 January 1941 to enlist as a padre in the Australian Militia. He would have the automatic rank of captain and would be counselling rather than killing. A photograph in the family's album shows a smiling Bobbie, dressed in blazer and tie, walking proudly down a city street beside his uniformed father, who looked slightly abashed in his new attire.[15]

Clem's move caused much angst among the Congregational deacons, who'd only recently called him to the church and now refused to grant him leave, forcing him to resign.[16] At least he'd be earning a higher income, and he could assuage any guilt that he harboured from not having enlisted in the previous war. Not that he would be going anywhere near a battlefield. For the next three years, Clem would be stationed at the army training camp at Northam, nearly a hundred kilometres north-east of Perth, where he provided pastoral care to newly enlisted troops before they were sent overseas or went north to repel the expected invasion. On those weekends when Clem could get leave, Bobbie 'would stand at the front gate, staring up Tate Street for the first sight of his father walking down from the trolley bus'. But for all his joy at his father's arrival home, he felt intense resentment when Clem didn't give him his undivided attention. Clem often used these weekends to preach at various churches or take Ellie out. Hawke later recalled having had 'an unbelievable tantrum' on his twelfth birthday, when his father came home on leave and refused to take him to see a pirate film, and instead took Ellie to a performance of *Pygmalion*.[17]

The isolation of the army base was mitigated for Clem by the fact that it was located in the electorate of his brother Albert, who had a house in Northam. When he was in Perth, the good-natured Albert, who had a daughter but no son of his own, had been a regular visitor at Tate Street, playing bridge and talking politics across the kitchen table. It was during this period, recalled Hawke, that he 'started to think in political terms'. Although his parents 'didn't articulate their attitude to life in party political terms', they had a great influence in 'shaping what I thought of the world', whereas Albert impressed him as a man 'who thought the world should be much more oriented towards looking after the ordinary bloke'. Among the topics they presumably discussed was the advent of the new minority Labor government under Prime Minister John Curtin, who lived nearby in the beachside suburb of Cottesloe. It may have been while listening to these discussions, and after meeting Curtin, that Bob found a lifelong political hero in the wartime prime minister. As a reformed alcoholic, a resident of Perth and a principled Labor man, Curtin would naturally be a hero to the Hawkes. A more immediate influence was Albert Hawke, who played an important mentoring role during Bobbie's adolescence and into his early adulthood, while also providing support for Clem. When Clem was stationed at Northam, the domesticity of Albert's solid, Mediterranean-style house provided him with occasional respite from his work at the army base.[18]

During school holidays, Bobbie was sent to Northam when his demanding behaviour became too difficult for his distracted mother. On top of giving Scripture lessons at Perth Girls' School, she agreed in June 1941 to become secretary of the state branch of the WCTU.[19] She would spend each day at its headquarters, where she dealt with correspondence and answered phone calls, received visitors, oversaw the work of other volunteers and represented the WCTU at meetings. Ellie's special passion was spreading the message of temperance among young girls. In October 1941, her colleagues at the WCTU applauded her 'splendid work' in doing so. Some of that effort was done under the guise of teaching first aid at Mount Hawthorn Primary School. She also held after-school classes for girls intending to enter the Temperance Essay competition, for which she was the main assessor.[20] Ellie was so busy that sometimes Bobbie wouldn't see his mother for days at a time. It's not surprising that he would later complain that the WCTU 'took up too much of mum's time, almost to my detriment'.[21]

It may have been Ellie's heavy commitments that caused her to want Bobbie to emulate Neil by attending a private school when he finished primary school in December 1941. She presumably had the Methodist Church's Wesley College in mind, but that was across the Swan River in South Perth, which would have taken him an hour or more of travel and was expensive, even with a scholarship. She may have intended him to be a boarder, as Neil had been, which would have simplified her life. Hawke later said that his mother thought a private school would make him 'a better person' and cause him to have a more cultivated accent.

Such an education would enhance his chances of achieving the great things she had in mind for him. However, Bobbie and Clem convinced her that he should try to gain admission to the coeducational and much cheaper Perth Modern School, a government school that had been established for academic high achievers from across the state, with entry by competitive exam.[22] Its four hectares of grounds with tennis courts and cricket oval, its teaching of Ancient Greek and Latin, and its teachers attired in academic gowns all combined to create the impression of a private school.[23] Moreover, it was less than two kilometres from their home, which meant Bobbie could walk there in little more than twenty minutes, or cycle in even less. But first he had to win entry.

With Clem in the army, it was up to Ellie to ensure that Bobbie did well in the exams. Taking time off from her role with the WCTU, she tutored him every afternoon with a 'fervour and dedication' that he'd never experienced before, all the while instilling in him the conviction that he was capable of achieving anything, and that gaining entry to Perth Modern would be 'a shaping point' for his career. He responded accordingly, delighting his parents by coming seventh in the statewide exam and winning a scholarship to the school.[24] Bobbie could now be forgotten as Ellie immersed herself once again in the work of the WCTU. Writing half a century later, Hawke noted with a tinge of bitterness how, 'having achieved the goal of a good educational environment for me, she could turn her boundless energies to a range of other issues'.[25] To his enduring chagrin, he was just one of her many projects.

Bobbie's first year at Perth Modern occurred against the backdrop of the Japanese capturing the British base at Singapore on 15 February 1942 and the subsequent bombing raids against Darwin and Broome. It was amid this alarming atmosphere that he traipsed down Tate Street to his new school, not knowing whether Japanese planes would appear in the skies overhead. To prepare for a possible attack on Perth, Ellie helped compile a list of WCTU volunteers for canteen work and attended a meeting in the Town Hall to discuss the possible evacuation of the city's 'very old and very young' inhabitants.[26] Some of Bobbie's fellow students stayed in the countryside until the danger of invasion had abated, while older boys dug bomb shelters in the school grounds to protect against air raids. Hawke recalled how sirens would cause the five hundred or so staff and students to 'all scamper off and get into the air raid shelters'. It always turned out to be a practice drill, but Bobbie and other boys took the opportunity to get closer to the girls than they were normally allowed in the otherwise closely segregated school.[27]

The students at Perth Modern were conscious of being the elite students of the state. The school's magazine, *The Sphinx*, told readers that 'Mod' would form their characters and mould their ideas, creating citizens who would solve 'the problems of the world'. As at English public schools, each first-year student was a 'fag' and subject to the authority of a senior student. While this could have led to bullying, Hawke claimed that his mentor was 'a nice bloke'.[28]

Nevertheless, he was bullied by his classmates. One was the future economist and financial journalist Max Newton, who described the school as a place of 'ferocious competition' in which Hawke often came off worst. Newton thought he was a 'bumptious little bastard' and recalled how they 'used to put him over the desk and bend his arms backwards and beat his chest', or 'torment him by putting his books out through the upper-level windows and on to a ledge'. Hawke later conceded that he was involved in some bullying himself, when he joined some of his classmates in directing antisemitic jibes at a Jewish student, something that would later cause him intense guilt. As for his own victimhood, the bullying receded as his physique improved, which made him better able to fight back. He ascribed this physical improvement to his diet being changed after Ellie consulted a naturopath in 1944, although it may have been simply that he was reaching the age when his hormones started to kick in.[29] Whatever the reason, his later years at school were marked by less bullying and a greater involvement in sport, although his claims of high sporting achievements are only partly borne out by the school magazine.

While Hawke claimed to have been in the school's First XI cricket team in his final two years, *The Sphinx* only listed him as a member in his final year. The previous year, he was mentioned as a player in the Second XI, along with his classmate John Stone, whose mother worked as a teacher. Although both boys were in the First XI in their final year, neither was listed among the school's top five batters or top three bowlers. Stone described Hawke as 'a slashing batsman', while *The Sphinx* agreed that Hawke's skill as a batsman was let down by his 'lack of patience'. When fielding, he was usually the wicketkeeper, which suited his short frame.

His most memorable cricket match was one that was held against the staff, when he scored ninety-three before being dismissed by the sportsmaster. Had he reached his century, tradition dictated that he would have been given a bat as a trophy. 'I knew how proud dad would be if I won it,' recalled Hawke. He was 'so annoyed' because he thought that he shouldn't have been given out, and regarded the incident as 'one of the biggest disappointments of my schooldays'. Bobbie also seems to have played for the West Perth cricket team in the Young Sports Temperance League and football for the school's third team. He recalled also having played hockey, although no record of that has been found. His other sport was tennis. He played in an inter-school tennis competition when he was thirteen and fourteen but was eliminated in the first round each time. Most of his success at tennis came in church competitions.[30]

Curiously, there is no evidence from his school days that he had any potential for leadership. His name is absent from the lists of prefects, captains of sporting teams or officials of the debating, literary, dramatic or historical societies. Neither does the school magazine have any article written by him, or any indication that he was even involved in the historical or debating societies. As for being a prefect, Hawke said that he was 'a bit of a rebel' and 'always in trouble with the headmaster and the deputy headmaster', and therefore had been barred from a position. While the headmaster might blackball a particular candidate for prefect, it was the final-year students who selected the following year's prefects from among the students in the Fourth Form. Bobbie was probably overlooked because he wasn't sufficiently popular among his peers and didn't strike them as being prefect material. He was regarded as 'a two-bob lair', said John Stone. Despite all this, he was showing interest in politics. A fellow student and future Labor senator, John Wheeldon, recalled having had 'long talks on politics' with him. And there was much to talk about, with the federal election in 1943 having brought a landslide victory for the former minority government of John Curtin, only for Curtin to die in 1945. He was given a massive funeral in Perth that Bobbie may well have attended alongside his uncle Albert.[31]

At school, high jinks remained young Bobbie's main focus. His misbehaviour had worsened in the absence of his father and with his mother's preoccupation with the WCTU. Walking home from school, he could never be sure whether Ellie would be there when he arrived, or whether he'd see her before he went to bed or even at the breakfast table. Her commitments kept her at the WCTU office for long hours and saw her attend meetings throughout Perth, often at night. In 1941, Ellie helped to collect signatures for a petition demanding a 6 p.m. closing time for licensed premises.[32] That was an easy argument to make in wartime, and early closing was quickly introduced. To guard against illicit sex, Ellie organised chaperoned dances, with one hundred carefully selected Christian girls turning out to socialise with servicemen. She also arranged good Christian homes in which men could be billeted when they were on leave. But the press still carried complaints from outraged citizens who'd seen soldiers and sailors accompanying young women to Perth's beaches for nights of drunken debauchery.[33]

Ellie devoted many of her evenings to working with young women living at the WCTU headquarters, where a collection of rooms at the rear, including bedrooms and a communal kitchen, were organised into a hostel for young women. Ellie helped to paint and furnish the place and make jam from the fruit of the fig trees in the garden. As the war clouds darkened in February 1942, with Bobbie starting at his new school and Clem absent, she spent much of her time there, sometimes staying overnight. She barely had time to type up her secretary's report for the monthly meeting of the executive, complaining that it had to be done 'during phone rings and calls in many directions'. The following month was even more strenuous: she was there most days and some nights and was left exhausted. With an attack from the Japanese seeming imminent, a trench was dug in the backyard to serve as a bomb shelter, while Ellie prayed to God to 'give us the strength to stick to our posts'.[34]

In May 1942, Ellie was so preoccupied with her mission that twelve-year-old Bobbie was left without either parent for long periods. Among her many activities that month, she spent a Saturday showing people over the hostel; she presented an evening service at the Mount Hawthorn Methodist church; she collected money on street corners for the Young Women's Christian Association; she looked for a home for 'an unwanted girl baby'; she attended a meeting of the Modern Women's Club; she filled in for the hostel housekeeper; and she attended meetings of the Cheerio Club. As if that wasn't enough, in mid-May she went off on a week's holiday with the WCTU's treasurer, Miss Lily Ayres, to a convalescent home in the Perth hills. The ailing Ayres was also overworked and soon resigned as treasurer, while maintaining a deep involvement with the organisation.[35] In August, Ellie visited the Children's Court and then the Fremantle Gaol, where she talked with girls being treated for venereal diseases, who she thought could become 'healthy useful citizens' if they were 'given a fresh start and re-education'. Although she had to take more leave in September, because she was 'very tired', her energy and enthusiasm were soon restored.[36] It's little wonder that Bobbie's behaviour, both at home and at school, provoked critical comment.

His mother didn't let up even at Christmas. Although Bobbie was home from school, Ellie remained hard at work, taking Christmas parcels to the women and girls at Fremantle Gaol on 23 December, entertaining soldiers on Christmas Eve, and on Boxing Day telling stories to children on the beach at Mosman Park. With the hostel 'full to overflowing' and a staff member sick, Ellie reported that she had to spend 'a good part of my time assisting in the hostel'. Then she took three weeks' holiday, most of which was spent at the seaside south of Perth, in the hope that she would 'feel refreshed for another year of service'.[37] In her absence, Bobbie was left in the care of the lodger, who recalled how Ellie 'wouldn't discipline Bob' and instead would tell her to 'speak to him'. Much as Gwen Geater had observed in Maitland, the wife of the Methodist minister said that Bobbie would 'always want a bit of love at bedtime – he was a devil of a kid, he'd whinge and whinge until he got his own way, but he was very affectionate. The cat would be there in bed with him, hidden under the blankets.'[38]

During Bobbie's second year at Perth Modern, his mother spent even more time at the hostel. In April 1943, she relieved the housekeeper on several occasions and then seems to have slept there for three weeks while the matron was on holiday. The following month she did likewise, this time deputising for the housekeeper for another three weeks. Yet she somehow found time to do the Mothers' Day service at the Mount Hawthorn Congregational Church and to give an address to the Mount Hawthorn branch of the WCTU. It had been 'an extremely busy month', she wrote. And it didn't stop. The following month she found a new office for the WCTU and then helped move all the files and furniture to the new premises. She went to Perth station to meet a family from Adelaide who needed assistance, gave Scripture and temperance lessons at schools and Sunday Schools, presented talks to women's groups, spoke in a debate on prohibition, and was part of a deputation to a government minister asking for improvements in Aboriginal schools. She was so busy that she bought a car and convinced the WCTU to pay for her petrol, which may have allowed her to drive to the Rechabite Hall in Northbridge, where she opened a flower show for the Good Templars, and to speak at the Methodist Kindergarten in Wembley Park.[39]

The repeated and prolonged parental absences and the onset of puberty combined to exacerbate Bobbie's misbehaviour. One of his classmates recalled how he became 'very pugnacious' and was 'often involved in punch-ups'.[40] By late 1943, his school record reveals that his misbehaviour was 'jeopardising his Scholarship'. Despite being disciplined, he continued to receive 'a number of warnings concerning his conduct'. Like many of his fellow students, he had no respect for the stern headmaster, Noel Sampson, whom he later described as 'an abominable fellow' and who now threatened him with expulsion. The final straw came when Bobbie destroyed a teacher's science experiment by blowing out the Bunsen burner when the teacher left the room.[41] It was only after Clem turned up in his padre's uniform to intercede on his son's behalf that he was saved from expulsion. 'I know my father had to come down from the army camp and plead the case of his recalcitrant son,' Hawke recounted. 'He must have been a good advocate because I stayed on.' Hawke would later say that he was 'a little boy' when his father enlisted in 1941 and 'a young man' when Clem was discharged in 1944. It was around this time, too, that he changed from being 'Bobbie' to 'Bob'. Although his father was now at home, Bob continued to play the part of the class clown. He joined the school's cadet corps, but he was often found smoking behind the quartermaster's store. Bob would be one of only three students still a private at the end of his years with the cadets. It was only in his final year that reports of misbehaviour are absent from his record. A teacher of English and maths, as well as the supervisor of the gym class and the cadets, recalled how his 'high-spirited' student 'showed little desire for leadership or for strong application to study', but was 'good in both written and oral expression' and already displaying 'his mannerisms of shrugging his shoulders and turning his eyes upwards'.[42]

He was also turning his eyes towards girls. Hawke was, as he would later tell an interviewer, 'starting to feel his oats'. As in many Australian families at that time, there was little open discussion of sex in the Hawke household. Although he was surrounded by girls and women throughout his childhood, Hawke recalled his 'terrible shock' when he learned in his late teens about menstruation. While the education of girls about sexual morality was a driving force for Ellie, she left the sex education of her son to Clem. 'In an embarrassed sort of way dad pushed a couple of books about sex at me,' said Hawke. If he had been able to have a discussion with his parents, they would doubtless have told him that sexual intercourse was for procreation rather than pleasure. That didn't stop him from frequently masturbating, but he confessed that his religious background probably caused him 'more than average guilt'.[43]

As Bob became more confident, he had two or three girlfriends during his time at school, despite the headmaster's strict segregation of the sexes until the final two years. There were not only separate gates for boys and girls to enter the grounds and separate areas during recess and lunch, but separate staircases to get students to the classrooms on the first floor, and separate classes for boys and girls during their first three years of education.[44]

Of course, there were other ways to meet girls. The Congregational Church provided one such means, with its inter-church socials and sporting events. Hazel Masterton was part of the church circle. Born on 20 July 1929, she had lived all her childhood in suburban Perth, where her father was an accountant and had built a comfortable Californian bungalow in Coogee Street, Mount Hawthorn. The family attended the local Congregational church and the children were sent to the local state school, before Hazel went on to Perth Central Girls' School, on the edge of the city. She was a bright student who was sometimes dux of her class, and did particularly well in the subjects that were designed for girls heading for work in an office – shorthand, typing, bookkeeping and commercial arithmetic – while also performing well in English and history.[45] However, music was her real love. While she had first competed on piano at the West Australian Music Festival at the age of nine, she continued to enter each year and usually came second or third in her age group, while also playing the piano and the organ each Sunday in church.[46]

Finishing school in December 1944 at the age of fifteen, Hazel collected her junior certificate and went to work as a typist for an electrical engineering firm that was housed in dingy and rat-infested premises.[47] It was still wartime and there was plenty of work to be had in Perth, where there was a large American presence. Their flying boats could be seen from the city, bobbing in the wide expanse of the Swan River or flying low overhead as they went off on patrol, while their submarines were tied up in Fremantle. And there were thousands of Australian soldiers brought home from the Middle East and readying for deployment against the Japanese. It was a head-turning time for a girl fresh out of school, as she fended off attention from servicemen on the make.

In December 1944, Hazel joined about fifty thousand other children and their parents for a Christmas party put on by the US Navy at Gloucester Park trotting track. She noted in her diary how she attended the 'Yankee party' and collected chewing gum, autographs and portraits, before later going on a river trip. On the way home, she described how she 'met [a] little soldier. Very nice but fast. Got rid of him easy when tram came.' Hazel was still of an age when she and her friends went for long bike rides, played tennis with the church team or played about on the local beach. That was where she would rather be.[48]

On Boxing Day 1944, Hazel went for a week's holiday to Keysbrook, about sixty kilometres south of Perth. In her diary, she wrote how 'Bob & Gordon came up shooting – were with us for a long time – had fun. Bob nice kid, very nice. Grown up – I didn't know him – very nice looking.' On the Saturday, she danced the hokey-pokey with him at a Mad Hatter's Ball and had a 'marvellous time'. But he was just one of a wide group of friends. In June 1946, she went to Leederville for badminton and 'laughed till we cried watching Peter, Jack, Ross & Bob playing comical game'.[49] Then, on 25 August 1946, Bob wrote in her autograph book:

> Life is mostly froth and bubble
> Two things stand like stone
> Kindness in another's trouble
> And courage in your own.[50]

These were words by the Australian poet Adam Lindsay Gordon and might have summed up Hawke's attitude to life. It was a sign, too, of the growing friendship between the pair.

With Clem discharged from the army, it might have been expected that Bob would receive some of the parental attention that he'd lacked for the last three years. However, his father was now distracted by the urgent necessity to get a job after ending his well-paid position as a padre. Although the Congregational Church was having difficulty finding preachers, no congregation was prepared to call him to their pulpit. He was left to deliver guest sermons at several churches, most of them Methodist.[51] Instead of preaching for a living, Clem became an insurance salesman, using his empathetic pastoral skills to earn about the same income as he'd been earning from the pulpit.[52] While he went knocking on doors, Ellie devoted even more time to the WCTU. A few weeks after Clem's return, she resigned as secretary and began working at the hostel, while remaining the WCTU's director of education and its superintendent of Sunday Schools. Because she was no longer writing up her activities, it's not possible to know whether her work at the hostel involved sleeping there.[53] In July 1944, just two months after taking up that job, she resigned and went to work as a teacher at the nearby Subiaco Infants' School, while continuing her voluntary positions at the WCTU.[54] On Sundays, she taught Sunday School at the Leederville church in Oxford Street, where Bob now joined her, teaching the senior boys' class.[55]

The experience of teaching alongside his mother and the return of his father probably helped Bob complete his schooling with more success than he might otherwise have achieved. Although he later claimed that he had coasted through each year 'until it got towards the exams', when he achieved 'very good results', the good results came only in his final year.[56] His school record reveals that he was 'below the average of Scholarship boys' in his first year, while his parents were warned a year later that he wouldn't get his Junior Certificate unless he 'work[ed] hard on his weak subjects'. Yet he managed to scrape through, passing nine of the ten subjects, only to slip back again the following year. In April 1945, just eighteen months out from his Leaving Certificate exams, Bob's term results were described as 'mediocre'. The message didn't get through to him. His next results remained 'borderline', and his misbehaviour was still bringing him to the attention of the headmaster. It was only in the third term that he was praised for having 'worked well'. The school remained concerned in his final year, 1946, that he would need to make 'a determined effort' to get his Leaving Certificate. He left it until the last month, being away from school for a week with a shoulder injury and then taking an additional four days off for study at home.[57]

The intensive effort worked. When the Leaving Certificate results were published in *The West Australian* on 9 January 1947, Clem and Ellie were relieved to discover that Bob had passed all his seven subjects and achieved distinctions in three. It was not as good as that of his then girlfriend, Dawn McHarrie, who scored five distinctions and was awarded a General Exhibition. Nor were his results as good as those of the studious John Stone, who used to get out of bed at 5 a.m. to study, achieved distinctions in all his seven subjects and was awarded Exhibitions in maths and physics. Bob's three distinctions were in History, Industrial History and Economics, and Art of Speech.[58] The latter subject had been done at Ellie's insistence, in the hope it might improve Bob's diction and soften the grating drawl that had characterised his speech from his time in the playgrounds of rural South Australia. While his accent remained unchanged, learning the art of speech, together with teaching restless boys at Sunday School, would have provided him with some understanding of how to hold an audience, a skill he would use to good effect in later life. For now, he could rest content that his results were sufficient to gain him entry to the University of Western Australia, where he would get his first real taste of politics.

PART TWO

Scholar

CHAPTER FOUR

1946–1949

By the time Bob Hawke finished school, the world had been at peace for twelve months. Although there were Cold War tensions in Europe, there was a sense of optimism in Australia. Soldiers were returning to peacetime pursuits and the economic depression of the 1930s was receding from popular memory. Rationing was gradually being lifted and wartime savings were being spent, sparking the beginning of a prolonged boom. Clem Hawke was back in 'civvies' and living at home, while seventeen-year-old Hawke no longer faced the possibility of being forced to don khaki himself. He would later recall the time as a period of 'unbridled optimism'.[1] The Labor government of Ben Chifley had been returned to power in Canberra with a mandate to push ahead with reconstruction, while Labor governments held sway everywhere but South Australia. Even the federal opposition leader, Robert Menzies, suggested in his New Year message that employers should share their high profits with their employees.[2] It was a sign that another tide of hope was sweeping through Australian life. Hawke would ride the wave for all he was worth, pushed along by a mother who was intent on imbuing her sole surviving child with a sense of the greatness that awaited him.

Hawke was among the youngest of about five hundred first-year students who trooped into Winthrop Hall at the University of Western Australia in March 1947 to hear the vice-chancellor encourage them to pursue the 'way of truth', hastening to add that their search should be subject to the 'limits of decency and good taste'.[3] Among the throng were hundreds of men and women who were a decade or so older than Hawke. They'd experienced the worst of mankind during the recent war and were taking advantage of the Labor government's training scheme for returned service personnel. One former serviceman had survived being aboard an Australian cruiser that was sunk in the Java Sea, only to be rescued and imprisoned by the Japanese, while another had been based in Britain and flown Atlantic patrols in a flying boat.[4] 'They were a great bunch,' recalled John Stone, and were 'so much more mature than most of us who had come straight from school'. They were also 'a pretty hard drinking crew'.[5]

With their maturity and range of life experience, they might have overwhelmed a first-year student who was less self-confident than Hawke, but he was used to dealing with worldly-wise adults such as his uncle Albert. His mother, meanwhile, never tired of telling whomever would listen that Bob was destined one day to be prime minister. The young man had even begun to predict it himself.[6] As a result, he entered university with a degree of self-assurance that belied his young age. Once he got the measure of the place, this allowed him to mix easily with fellow students and lecturers alike.

In 1947, there were little more than a thousand full-time students, which made the university about the same size as Perth Modern. Hawke would have known some of them from school already. And because he was joining the Law Faculty – one of the smallest at the university – he would quickly get to know all his fellow students. The sense of familiarity came with a liberating freedom from the restrictions that had constrained his schoolboy years. Instead of being in a school where boys and girls led largely separate lives, and where a strict headmaster was a looming presence, he was at a university where his amorous objectives could be pursued more freely. The mature cohort of former service personnel, moreover, provided him with 'wonderfully boisterous companions'. With its extensive campus on the shore of the Swan River, there was also much more room to move at the university than in the relatively cramped and closely supervised grounds of Perth Modern. Although it had only been founded in 1914, the university had been endowed by a wealthy benefactor, Sir John Winthrop Hackett, which helped it become Australia's only free university. It also ensured that the extensive campus had room for a number of ovals and other sporting grounds, with the former 'native bush and swamp lands' being landscaped in ways that befitted the site and the dignity of the institution. The landscaping included a 'cathedral of trees' that provided an outdoor auditorium for meetings and musical events. To Hawke, it was a place of 'incomparable beauty'.[7]

Being at university would have also boosted his self-confidence, since only a small percentage of children completed high school, let alone went on to university. Finishing school at fourteen and getting a job remained the norm. Fortunately, Hawke's enrolment at university didn't entail much sacrifice for his hard-pressed parents, other than the forgone pay he might otherwise have contributed to the household. Bob had won a Hackett Bursary because of his parents' relatively low income, which provided some money to cover his books and living expenses, but he nevertheless worked at various jobs during the term breaks, including labouring with the university grounds department and working as a clerk with the Fuel Board prior to the abolition of petrol rationing.[8]

In December 1947 Clem received a call from the Congregational church in Subiaco. But the appointment didn't rescue the family's finances. Unlike his previous posting in Leederville, the congregation was unable to pay for his car, telephone or postage.[9] With her position as a teacher, Ellie was now the main breadwinner, which didn't help relations in their Tate Street home, particularly as Clem had become much less straitlaced after his time with the troops and was no longer averse to the occasional tipple. Ellie found her authority being challenged both by her husband and by her teenage son.[10]

For Bob, university offered an escape from the strictures of home and reinforced the sense of there being a great crusade before him. It just wasn't clear what the nature of that crusade might be. The future poet and playwright Dorothy Hewett was editor of the university's magazine, *Black Swan*, in 1946 and was seized with a sense of mission that prompted her to join the Communist Party. She told the *Black Swan* readers that 'a feeling [was] stirring our university ... a feeling of participation in world events, of jobs to be done, and a good fight to be fought for peace and a better world'. With his family background and uncle Albert's position in the West Australian parliament, it's not surprising that Hawke counted himself among those students. The emphatic victories of the Curtin and Chifley governments in the 1943 and 1946 elections suggested that the Labor Party could be in government for years to come, and that all manner of radical changes could be in the offing. Against this exciting background, the university's

Labour Club seemed the ideal outlet for Hawke's political aspirations. After all, he had chosen to spend four years studying law because he thought it would be 'useful' in politics. So Bob was quick to join the Labour Club and become a member of its executive in his first year, assuming that it was for supporters of the Labor Party. Forty years later, Hawke would say that he'd been drawn to the club partly because of 'the vast, imaginative and compassionate immigration program [that was] then being launched by the Federal Labor Government'. His reason for joining was probably simpler. It would have seemed at first sight to accord with the views he'd imbibed from his father and his uncle. Along with the Australian Student Christian Movement (ASCM), with which he was also involved, the club had a large percentage of female members and organised a range of social activities, from film nights to dances and camping trips. Unlike the ASCM, the Labour Club camps were not chaperoned by university staff.[11]

In May 1947, the club hosted a lunchtime talk by Kim Durack, the son of a West Australian pastoralist, on the situation in the state's Kimberley region, where the overstocking of cattle was damaging the environment. Two months later, the members approved a motion calling for the Chifley government to reduce defence expenditure and redirect the funds towards education and immigration, arguing that those would be the best forms of defence. The Labour Club also campaigned on issues of immediate relevance to students, while also running 'study groups on social and economic problems' and holding 'vacation camps, dances and play readings'. Although members didn't have to be members of the Labor Party, the club advertised itself as being 'an integral part of the A.L.P.' and sent delegates to the fortnightly meetings of the party's Metropolitan Council.[12] The party may have encouraged the club as a means of attracting students to the Labor cause, but it was a broad church encompassing Laborites like Hawke, along with a sizeable number of the Catholic Right, anarchists, communists and other varieties of socialist. As the Cold War worsened and conservatives looked for evidence of communists among Labor ranks, the party's links with the Labour Club became increasingly problematic.

Despite his membership of the Labour Club, Bob's interests were also religious. His father may have drawn him towards politics, but both his parents tied him to the church. It was Ellie who'd accompanied

Bob to the Leederville church Sunday School, where they both continued to teach classes. It must have been awkward being active members of a congregation that had spurned Clem and appointed someone permanently in his place. Yet Bob had remained in charge of a class of senior boys, although the manner of his leadership raised the eyebrows of the school superintendent. Clem's successor as minister of the Leederville church noted how the teenage Bob was 'an individualist who frequently chose not to conform to the accepted pattern' and was 'a law unto himself'. It was perhaps a further indication of the narcissism that had been evident from his early childhood and was seen in his school reports at Perth Modern. It would have been difficult for the superintendent, or even the minister, to call Bob to account, given the prominent position of his parents. The reticence of the church officials to rein him in was also caused by their grudging recognition of the 'fine influence he has had over the boys', even though the minister suspected that their 'loyalty [was] to their leader rather than to the school itself'.[13] Being able to hold sway over the boys was probably early evidence of the charisma that Hawke would use to great effect as an adult.

Bob's work alongside his mother at Sunday School would have pleased Ellie, while his involvement in sport was of more moment to Clem. Try as he might, young Bob could never be the player that he aspired to be and his father hoped he'd be. He would later say that his 'first interest has been cricket [for] as long as I can remember'. Although outclassed by most of his teammates, he kept plugging away, presumably because it was Clem's favoured sport. Unlike football or some other team sports, it suited his slight frame and was a game that allowed an individual to shine. Hawke later told friends that 'God invented cricket'. His mother had convinced him that he could succeed at anything to which he set his mind, so he not only played cricket and tennis, but also baseball, hockey, squash and badminton. And not just with university teams. He also played cricket with the local Subiaco club, rising to become a member of the state junior practice club but never playing for Western Australia, perhaps because he only played with Subiaco's C-grade senior team. He also played tennis regularly with his uncle Albert, and won the church championship. Not that a church trophy amounted to much. There was a freneticism about all this sporting activity by a young athlete who was weighed down by the burden of his parents' expectations.[14] Perhaps he could satisfy them with his academic results.

When Hawke began his law degree in 1947, the department was led by Frank Beasley, born and educated in Oxford. There was only one other full-time academic, with additional teaching provided by barristers as part-time lecturers. The department had been suspended altogether for three years during the war, when Beasley was serving in the Australian Army. When teaching resumed in 1944, there were just five students. Three years later, only about a dozen students were graduating from the department annually. Fronting up for his first classes, Bob may have been surprised to find the department had just been moved to a 'wood and asbestos building on the western edge of the campus', where a chemistry laboratory had been transformed into a law library run by a female solicitor, Enid Russell, who acted as a part-time lecturer and also served as the department's secretary. Despite her presence, it was a very male-dominated department, where the initiation rites for new law students sometimes saw them forced to run naked around the university courtyard. Yet they were expected by Beasley to behave like 'scholars and gentlemen', with 'their behaviour and even attire ... to be in keeping with their high calling'. Both students and staff wore academic gowns, beneath which Bob and his fellow students were required to wear jackets and ties. Beasley also valued sport, particularly rowing, but Hawke was too tall to be a cox and too short to be a rower.[15] Neither did he impress Beasley with his first-year academic results.

It wasn't Bob's fault. With the grudging support of Clem, and after much argument with his mother, he'd got a Panther motorbike, a heavy machine with a top speed of just over a hundred kilometres an hour. It saved him a lot of time and turned heads on campus. He could cover the five-kilometre journey to the university in about ten minutes. He could save even more time by taking a scenic short cut through Kings Park, testing himself and the bike as he leaned into curves that swung gently between the trees.

It's not clear what caused Bob to crash on 11 August 1947, when he decided to pack up his books and head home during the second-term break. According to his account, he'd been off-colour with sinusitis and tonsillitis and had self-medicated with analgesics. He blamed the medications for causing him to black out and lose control as he powered the motorbike round a bend. It's more likely that he just pushed the machine further than his novice skills and small frame allowed. As the bike slid on its side into the bush, Hawke was left on the ground, screaming in agony. He might have been able to scramble back up and remount had he not been carrying the motorbike's metal stand inside his clothing. Although none of his bones were broken, he had landed on the stand and suffered such serious internal injuries that he was left in 'unspeakable' pain.[16]

With Hawke doped up to dull the agony, the doctors who gathered around his bedside decided that they needed to operate. When he was opened up, they found that his spleen had been ruptured, resulting in internal bleeding that might have killed him had the organ not been removed. Although the spleen provides a protective function for the immune system, it is not essential for life. Yet he was in danger of dying in those desperate days after the crash and the trauma of the surgery. A close friend and the president of the university's Liberal Club, John Knight, was startled to find Hawke's face 'a deep grey' when he dropped by, the same 'colour of death' that Knight had seen on his dying grandparents. Ellie and Clem feared they could lose their remaining son. Lying in his bed and coping as best he could with the post-operative pain, Hawke was confronted with his own mortality and saw the depth of his parents' distress. Any doubts that he'd harboured about their love for him were swept away. It made him realise 'what an enormous sense of tragedy dad and mum would feel, losing their only son'. Of course, he wasn't their only son but their only surviving one, and their palpable relief at his gradual recovery was impressed upon his consciousness. They took it as confirmation that he had a special destiny ahead of him – that he'd been saved for a purpose. 'It was the total turning-point of my life,' said Hawke, who now had to decide how to make use of the years he'd been given.[17] His time in hospital meant that he finished the year with poor results, scoring only two Bs and two Cs.[18] That had implications for his final degree: he wouldn't be able to achieve first-class honours no matter how well he did in subsequent years.

Once he'd recovered, Bob got back on the motorbike. Whether at university, at the cricket club or at the church in Subiaco, the bike set him apart, marking his ascension to adulthood despite being only seventeen years old. It brought him admiring looks from the boys of his Sunday School class, from his fellow students at university and from the girls who were attracted by his daredevil demeanour as he roared past. It might have been part of the attraction for young Hazel Masterson. In 1946, he'd added his name to her autograph book and the following year, after he'd got the motorbike, she'd put his telephone number in her diary.[19]

Although Hazel wrote about 'Bob' in her diaries, it wasn't always clear which Bob she meant, as she had several friends with that name and she seldom used their surnames in her diary. We do know that she was taken to the cinema a couple of times by Bob Clews, that she went swimming with a group of friends including a Bob Cornell, and that she once crammed into the back seat of a car and found herself sitting on the knees of Bob Foote. She also had Bob Barnett's phone number listed in her 1947 diary. In February 1947, she met up with a Bob at the boatsheds on North Beach, whom she described as having a 'very nice face, tall, fair, blue eyes', which isn't a description that could be applied to Hawke. It was presumably this same Bob whom she met again the following day; she was 'saved' by the arrival of her parents 'just as he was getting round to a "date". Nice though,' she added. A few days later, she wrote about how she went swimming and lay on the beach with this Bob, who 'got fresh too', with Hazel later being told that he was an 'awful flirt'. On 21 February, she saw *Gone with the Wind* with Bob Clews, and the following day won a tennis competition with 'Bob', donating the prize money to church funds. 'Bob is a bit "know-all" but we all laugh at him,' she wrote, which suggests that this last Bob may well have been Hawke.[20]

About six weeks later, at a church camp over Easter in 1947, Hazel started to take a closer interest in Hawke, who was there with his mother. In a mixed-doubles tennis match, they were on opposite sides of the net when she and her partner were beaten by Hawke and his partner. At night, they had a quiz, a 'beaut debate' and a scavenger hunt, topped off by Ellie taking Hazel and the other girls into the bush for supper. After a church service the following morning, there was more swimming and tennis. 'Gosh they are a super crowd of kids,' wrote Hazel, noting that 'Bob and Mrs Hawke spoke very well'.[21] And that was that.

Although Hazel would later say that she'd first met Bob at this Easter camp, she'd clearly met him well before that, and there is no evidence in her diary that they'd fallen in love at this camp.[22] Indeed, two days after the camp, both Bob Clews and Bob Foote were at her home. It was probably Bob Clews who was in the audience with her parents when she competed once again on the piano in the West Australian Music Festival in June 1947 and was placed second in the open age group.[23] But she wanted something more. By early 1947, she'd become tired of her job, was struggling to keep up with the work and feared that she wasn't doing it well. On one Monday morning she didn't want the weekend to end. She swam at the beach before work and complained in her diary of how she was 'longing to stay at [the] beach & be lazy. I reckon I need it & am getting crotchety.' Ten days later, she wrote that she was 'just about living on the beach'.[24] As an outdoorsy girl who enjoyed tennis, cycling to distant beaches or bushwalking in the Perth hills, she had no hesitation in April 1948 when Hawke rang and invited her to take a ride on his motorbike. This marked the real beginning of their romance.

It was a fine Sunday when Hazel was called across to her neighbour's house to take a call from Mrs Hawke, only to find that Bob was on the line. 'Pleasant surprise!' she wrote in her diary. He asked whether she wanted to take a ride to Roleystone, about thirty kilometres south-east of Perth. 'I was excited – went – had lovely time, beautiful weather.' When they returned, he took her to tea with his parents in Tate Street, before taking her the four kilometres home in time for church and supper. The brat who'd annoyed her during the church play in 1940 had grown up. And she was smitten. Her diary entry for the following day simply says: 'Thought a lot about Bob, had such a nice time.' She jumped back on his motorbike the following Sunday, holding on tight as he rode them around some of the city's beaches.[25]

Their relationship was formalised when he escorted her to the Law Ball at the end of April, where his fellow students and staff and their partners mixed with barristers and judges. Hazel described in her diary how she 'met a lot of new people [and] saw a lot of "new looks". It was [a] real flash turn out and lovely night. Bob was beaut company. Had wonderful time all round.' She didn't get home until 2.30 a.m.[26] Her attraction to Hawke was not just because he was 'beaut company'.

It was also very physical: 'I liked Bob's skin, tending to swarthy, his eyes were a good deep blue, his hair luxuriously thick, dark brown and wavy.' The attraction was mutual, with Bob judging her to have 'one of the most beautiful pairs of legs I had ever seen'.[27]

For Bob, though, it would never be exclusive. Throughout their long relationship, Hazel would have to compete with a succession of other women, although none would love Hawke as much as he loved himself.[28]

Young women were attracted by his charisma and succumbed to his charm. As one of his friends recalled, Hawke was the one who 'could always line up girls' and get them to join him and his mates on blankets at the beach. As the breakers crashed onto the sand, teenage flirting and beer-fuelled banter would turn to clumsy fumbling and eventually lovemaking among the dunes. He would later say that he'd lost his virginity at the age of nineteen. Not that there was much love expended by Hawke, whose succession of conquests was a way to reinforce his 'sense of narcissistic power'.[29] Each young woman would be discarded in turn, as he sought to sate what he would never be able to satisfy.

Also unleashed in Hawke's late teenage years was his appetite for alcohol, which proved similarly impossible to quench. As psychologists have observed, alcohol abuse is 'frequently associated' with narcissism, since it imbues narcissists with a 'sense of power and self-confidence' that is central to their identity. Although the legal drinking age was twenty-one and the university restricted alcohol consumption on campus, beer drinking was 'a distinctive aspect of campus culture', whether it was in the men's common room, the student hostel, the rooms of St George's College or the nearby Nedlands Park Hotel, run by Stephen McHenry and popularly known as Steve's pub. Hawke later described Steve's as 'a favourite haunt'. It was over beers there that an inebriated Hawke and his friends had many a political and philosophical discussion. He was forced, perhaps for the first time, to question his religious beliefs after Catholic friends challenged his 'fashionably anti-Catholic' attitudes. It was also at Steve's that Hawke was reputed to have set a local record 'for the quickest yard-glass skol', a feat that he would later reprise as a student at Oxford. Here, too, Hawke drunkenly challenged McHenry to a fight over some slight, real or imagined. Most likely, the publican had asked Hawke to leave the premises, because he was not good at holding his liquor and could be both offensive and aggressive when drunk. Although Bob confessed his drinking to his mother, Ellie couldn't convince him to stop.[30] Indeed, his dissipation was probably the most dramatic assertion he could devise of independence from his domineering mother.

Despite his mother's pressure about his studies, or perhaps because of it, Hawke hadn't applied himself during his first year. Passing his exams had seemed sufficient. But his near-death experience had invested him with a drive to do well, not just in his classes but also in his contribution to society. And his results did improve in 1948, when he achieved two As and two Bs in his four law subjects.[31] That year, he also turned his back on the Labour Club because its grab-bag of communists, socialists and anarchists was too radical for his taste. As he would later tell an interviewer, 'I was only ever a socialist briefly. I soon realised it didn't work, and really consider myself a social democrat.'[32]

In fact, the Labour Club had disaffiliated from the Labor Party in May 1948, with the aim of making it a branch of the Communist Party. The members from the Catholic Right, under law student Frank Malone, responded by establishing an ALP Club and prevailing upon the initially reluctant Hawke to be its president, while Malone became secretary and acted as its 'driving force'. Malone would later become state president of the right-wing National Civic Council after the Labor split in 1955. The formation of the ALP Club effectively ended the life of the Labour Club, which suited the Labor Party at a time when it was cleansing itself of any association with communists, and when the university was being attacked by conservative politicians for having 'a Russian Communist influence at work'. The new club also guaranteed Albert Hawke that he would have additional supporters on the party's Metropolitan Council.[33]

While Hawke supported 'the right of communists and their sympathisers to be active in the political life of the university and the country', he wasn't going to be part of a Labour Club that regularly attacked the policies of the party that his uncle would soon lead in the state parliament.[34] The student delegates to the party's Metropolitan Council would now be provided by Hawke's ALP Club, which made a point of encouraging women to be members, assuring them they were 'more than welcome. Don't be shy.'[35]

In some respects, Hawke was more conservative than his father. While he opposed Australian students being associated with the communist-dominated International Union of Students, his father was expressing sympathy for the activities of former American vice president Henry Wallace, who was trying to build peaceful connections between east and west. According to Clem, Wallace was one of the 'few statesmen big enough to have the interests of humanity at heart'.[36] There is no evidence that Bob matched his father's admiration for Wallace. His political apprenticeship was more prosaic. After being installed as president of the ALP branch, he tried to become involved in the Guild of Undergraduates, which ran the refectory that provided meals and a hostel that had a limited amount of student accommodation. It also organised the orientation week for incoming students, an annual ball for those graduating and a compulsory tuberculosis test for 'freshers'. This focus on services meant that it was less political and more conservative than student organisations at other universities, which were split into a student union that provided services and a student representative council that provided a political voice.[37] Under the umbrella of the Guild, there was a Sports Council and a Societies Council, which controlled their respective spheres of student life.

Hawke's first attempt to stand for the Guild occurred just over a year after his motorbike accident. With his opponents including the future Liberal leader Bill Snedden, and with Hawke trying to distinguish himself from the radical members of the Labour Club, his election policy declared that he had 'no intention of fermenting [sic] a revolution'. Neither was he 'wedded to a policy of atheism', having served on the committee of the ASCM. He said that he also played 'some sport, if that means anything, and I am on the Baseball Club committee'. He'd only begun playing for the baseball team that year and was reported to be a 'newcomer' to the sport. (One of the other newcomers was Rolf Harris, who was already making a name for himself as a painter and was described as a 'star turn' on the baseball team.) Hawke's failure to play for the cricket team was apparently due to the lack of any positions in the A-grade side, something he would soon put right. As for his election promises – there weren't any, other than to 'represent the interests of the student body as a whole in all matters'. It was hardly a potent message and he failed to get elected.

The successful candidates included Snedden and Bob's fellow student and lifelong bête noire from Perth Modern, John Stone.[38]

Yet Hawke was undeterred by this setback and stood again the following year, helped along by fellow law students and ALP Club members Frank Malone and John Toohey, and by the higher profile he had achieved through his activity in the ALP Club, the Baseball Club and the ASCM. Having Liberal Club president John Knight as a close friend also helped him garner votes. Hawke was part of a successful push by law students that year to take positions on the Guild, as well as on the Societies and Sports Councils. Despite the small size of the faculty, the law students and the relatively small faculty of engineers dominated the election, with Hawke, Malone and Toohey being elected to the Guild and a high-school friend Alan Barblett being elected president of the Sports Council.[39]

The end of 1949 marked the end of eight years in power for the federal Labor Party, as the government of Ben Chifley was trounced by the Liberal Party's Robert Menzies. Unlike Chifley, nineteen-year-old Hawke finished the year on a high. He had been elected to the Guild Council and been awarded the prize for being the best third-year law student. With only one more year to complete his degree, he felt sufficiently confident about his future prospects to ask Hazel to marry him. First, though, he obtained her conservative father's grudging permission. The proposal scene played out in the Masterton lounge room in December 1949, where Hawke expected her immediate and gleeful acceptance. After all, he was destined for greatness, and was already proving himself at the university, while she was working as a stenographer. Hawke wasn't seeking an intellectual equal, confiding to Hazel that he wouldn't have proposed to her if she'd been a fellow university student. He was taken aback and deeply hurt when she asked for time to consider. She only waited a day or two before accepting. Hazel's indecision was based partly on her feelings of inadequacy, but she also harboured fears about Hawke's alcohol consumption and, presumably, his reputation for philandering. She hoped that age would temper his drinking and would have expected that their engagement would satisfy his other appetite.[40] She would be disappointed on both counts.

CHAPTER FIVE

1950–1953

By 1950, the final year of his law degree, Hawke was set on going to Oxford. To do so, he would have to get a Rhodes Scholarship, only one of which was awarded in Western Australia each year. The criteria for the scholarship were not just about academic results. Candidates had to have a 'fondness of and success in manly outdoor sports', to exhibit 'qualities of manhood, truth, courage, devotion to duty, sympathy for the protection of the weak, kindliness, unselfishness and fellowship' and to show evidence of 'moral force of character and of instincts to lead'.[1]

Having been told repeatedly by his mother that he was a future leader of Australia, it was inevitable that Hawke would aspire to gaining a Rhodes Scholarship, which could open the door to whatever career he might want to pursue. However, his academic record in law couldn't put him in serious contention. He watched as John Stone and Maxwell Newton, his former classmates from Perth Modern, became the leading candidates in 1950. Perhaps because of Newton's predilection for alcoholic binges, it was Stone who secured the Rhodes and sailed off to Oxford in September 1951, while Newton won a Hackett Scholarship to Cambridge.[2]

Stone's win left Hawke particularly bitter. His rival had emerged from school with much better results and continued to do better than Hawke at university, in the exam room, on the sportsfield and in student government.[3] He'd been elected president of the Guild Council just two months before he was due to front the Rhodes committee. Stone's scholarship application ticked all the boxes and appealed to the committee because of his planned course of study in Oxford:

he intended to focus on mathematical physics, in the hope that 'his studies will eventually lead to the mathematics of nuclear physics, a relatively unexplored area'.[4] The topic would have piqued the interest of the committee, since their meeting coincided with American forces being repelled in Korea and against the background of the continuing race to build a hydrogen bomb.

Stone's thumping election victory as Guild president had been galling for Hawke. It had been a three-cornered contest between Hawke, Stone and Alan Barblett, with Stone receiving 584 votes to Hawke's 231 votes and Barblett's 127. Hawke did better in the election for positions on the Guild Council, where he received seventy-seven votes, which was the highest of any candidate. And he received some solace when he was elected unopposed as vice-president of the Guild, which could provide him with the profile among the students to be elected president once Stone stood down.[5] He might then be able to follow Stone to Oxford.

For that to happen, he would have to remain a student and be able to present a compelling case to the selection committee, which was chaired by the governor, the former conservative premier Sir James Mitchell. In April 1950, the 83-year-old Mitchell mingled with Hawke and other student politicos, who were decked out in tuxedos for the annual graduation ball in Winthrop Hall. With a twelve-piece band, the hall was decorated for the occasion with 'a tasteful arrangement of flowers, flags and palms', as eighteen debutantes came forward to be presented to the governor, with their proud parents looking down from the gallery.[6] The ball was a chance for Hawke to make an impression on the person who could determine whether or not he was awarded the Rhodes Scholarship.

His performance on the sporting field could be just as important, he knew, and Hawke spent much of his time trying to improve his cricket. He played for the Law School cricket team in the inter-faculty Goyder Cup competition, with the team being written up in student newspaper *The Pelican* as 'Hawke and Boys'. While that didn't count for much, he also played for the university cricket team. His place in the team was said to have been won after Hawke and his supporters stacked the club committee and installed selectors who would pick him despite his sometimes indifferent form. When the so-called 'Demon Bob' led the student team in a regular match against the staff, the staff easily won. Although Hawke was reported to have 'batted well', he had 'the dubious distinction of being out twice on the one ball, caught behind and stumped'.[7]

In order to stay on at the university, 21-year-old Hawke decided to follow up his law degree with an arts degree, majoring in economics. He was able to use five of his seventeen law subjects as credits towards the new degree, which meant that in 1951 he only had to do two subjects, Economics I and Economic & Social Statistics, and just four subjects in total to gain an arts degree. This part-time study gave him time to be president of the Congregational Youth Fellowship of Australasia, to which he'd been elected at a conference in Victoria in February, while Clem had been elected as president of the Western Australian branch of the church. Bob also had time in April of that year to take on a cadetship at the state office of a big American oil company, Vacuum Oil, which later became Mobil. It was here, in the personnel department, that he first developed an interest in industrial relations, albeit from the employer's side.[8]

Hawke also used that year to immerse himself in the affairs of the Guild, in preparation for the presidential election in late 1951, which would be decided by a popular vote rather than just by his fellow Guild councillors. He was helped by having the support of the student newspaper editor and fellow cricketer Terry Zanetti, who acted as his campaign manager and ensured there were plenty of stories and photographs featuring him in *The Pelican*. Hawke promised Zanetti that he would appoint him as his press secretary when he became prime minister. He also garnered support from a wide range of student groups: both the ALP and Liberal Clubs; the Student Christian Movement; the cricket and baseball clubs; and the law and arts students.

Even so, he didn't achieve the thumping victory that Stone had the previous year. When the votes were tallied in September 1951, Hawke had beaten his opponent, Bob Leschen, with 445 votes to 377. Being president would raise his profile, not only among the students and staff but in Perth society, which would be crucial if he was to secure the scholarship.[9] He went some way towards doing that a few weeks later, when he was one of several sportspeople who addressed three thousand young people at the Festival of Christian Witness, which was held in

Winthrop Hall. After music from the Salvation Army band, and with the event being broadcast on ABC Radio, Hawke told the audience that he read the Bible 'because it gave God's plan for life'.[10] And God's plan was pointing him towards Oxford.

To be sure of securing the scholarship, he also needed a swag of strong references from influential supporters. And he didn't have them. He couldn't ask the headmaster of Perth Modern, who'd almost expelled him and provided him with a lukewarm reference at the end of his schooling, merely noting that he had 'good ability and has made progress with his studies'.[11] He would have to rely mainly on his limited university contacts.

Unfortunately, two of his six referees were overseas at the time. One law lecturer submitted a reference from London, noting that Hawke's work was 'equal to that of the best students I have had'; while the young man 'might appear ... to lack personality', the referee was 'confident that he has strength of character which will eventually produce an all-round personality'. The second reference was from his lecturer in economic history, who wrote a brief note from Singapore describing him as 'always very keen, well-informed, liked by his fellows, solid as well as with a pleasant sense of humour'. As dean of the Law Faculty, Frank Beasley could have provided the strongest support, but said only that Hawke was of 'much more than average ability and possesses in a marked degree a personal and intellectual honesty'. While Beasley praised him for being 'conscientious', he also noted there was about Hawke 'a certain reserve, almost a brusqueness, of manner' and that he would 'never be spectacular; but he will always be reliable'. Other references came from the general manager of the Vacuum Oil Company and from the executive officer of the Guild, Mrs M.E. Haselhurst. She had some inkling of Hawke's abilities as a political operator, noting that during his short time as acting president of the Guild he had 'shown marked administrative ability, considerable tact, and an unswerving adherence to moral principles'.[12]

The longest reference of all came from the Congregational minister who had replaced Clem at the pulpit in West Leederville. The Reverend Ewan Watts had known Hawke for five years and suggested, presumably at the prompting of Ellie, that he had 'an intellectual ability that suggested brilliance' during his schooldays and that he'd been placed upon a pedestal by his 'hero-worshipping fellows' – which was not true of his results at Perth Modern, or of the ambivalent regard in which he was held by many of his fellow students. According to Watt, it was the influence of 'his Christian home and the Church' that prevented all this adoration from going to his head, which also wasn't true. Watt conceded that Hawke had 'very definite limitations', and there was 'still much of the impetuosity and impulsiveness of youth, that tends at times to cloud his judgment'.[13] As with the other references, the inclusion of negative comments might have been seized upon by members of the selection committee.

Hawke didn't help his cause when his application made no mention of the motorbike accident, which would have explained his poor results in first year, and while he referred to his solid sporting achievements, he put most stress on his involvement with the church. As for his plans at Oxford, he informed the committee that he would like to do the usual two-year honours course done by Rhodes scholars – Philosophy, Politics and Economics – 'with an emphasis on economics, particularly economic history leading to the evolution and significance of present-day socio-economic institutions'. On his return, he planned to continue with the work he'd been doing at Vacuum Oil in the personnel and industrial relations department.[14] It was all rather ho-hum.

The selection committee met at Government House on 28 November 1951, two days before Hawke formally took over as president of the Guild. The committee was chaired by Sir Charles Gairdner, who'd replaced the recently deceased Mitchell as governor. Gairdner had had an indifferent career in the British Army before retiring to Ireland to enjoy a life of hunting, yachting and knitting.[15] Other committee members included former Rhodes scholars, who clearly weren't impressed by Hawke's application, or perhaps by his demeanour in the interview.

In his memoirs, Hawke makes no mention of the experience, other than to note that he failed to be selected. In fact, it was another humiliation for him, because the selected candidate was another student from Perth Modern, John Hall, who'd been in the year below Hawke. He'd been a prefect and a lieutenant in the cadet corps, and in his final year at school had won seven distinctions as well as Exhibitions in Physics and Chemistry in the statewide exams. At university, Hall did an honours degree in chemistry, during which he was awarded another seven distinctions and won prizes in Chemistry and Physical Science.[16]

Although Hall's academic, sporting and leadership achievements placed him head and shoulders above Hawke, it must have seemed to Hawke that the younger man had jumped the queue. According to Hazel, he 'felt he had been robbed', not least because his 'whole focus, as well as his mother's and father's, had been set on it'.[17] He'd let them down, as well as himself. As a mark of Hawke's intense self-belief, he decided that he would try again the following year, which would be his last chance. Because Rhodes scholars had to be unmarried men, it meant that his marriage to Hazel would be pushed further into the future. It also meant that he would have to prepare a much better application.

One of the advantages of being Guild president was that it gave Hawke a non-voting seat on the University Council, which brought him into contact with a range of senior academics and other influential Perth figures who might support his next application. As head of the student body, he was also the person who welcomed dignitaries to balls and other events organised by the Guild and sat with them at the official table. One such dignitary was Gairdner, whose support would be crucial.

As president, Hawke was on the subcommittee that arranged the Graduation Ball in Winthrop Hall that year, helping to decide on the curried egg sandwiches and sausage rolls and the eight-person group that would provide the dance music. The graduates were encouraged to provide splashes of colour and dignified formality by wearing their caps and gowns, while the ball also served as a 'coming-out' occasion for those women students who, as debutantes, would be presented to the chancellor and his wife and to Hawke and a female Guild councillor. To ensure the relative sobriety of the evening, alcohol could only be consumed in the men's common room. At least, that was the rule. The reality was that copious amounts of alcohol were consumed in students' cars prior to, during and after such events.[18]

Soon after the ball, Hawke was on the stage of Winthrop Hall to farewell the university's genial vice-chancellor and former professor of agriculture, George Currie, who was leaving Perth to become vice-chancellor of the University of New Zealand. In expressing appreciation on behalf of the students, Hawke made special mention of Currie's efforts to help the fifty or so overseas students to become 'acclimatized'. This was a particular interest of Hawke's, and a matter of serious concern to the university authorities after two Asian students had suicided and another suffered a breakdown and been committed to an asylum. Others had failed to complete their courses. At the time of Currie's farewell, Hawke was pressing for the Psychology Department to set up a student counselling service and was in the process of establishing an Australia-Overseas Club. The latter was designed to reduce the barriers between local and overseas students, to prevent the open hostility that was sometimes shown towards Asian students. Hawke wanted to 'make these people feel more comfortable amongst us', and began by presiding over an afternoon tea in the refectory. He was roundly congratulated by *The Pelican* for 'making the initial move'. Hawke saw the matter in the wider context of building bridges between Australia and the emerging nations of Asia.[19] He wanted to establish an International House in Perth so that Australian and foreign students could live together, rather than having foreign students living isolated and possibly vulnerable lives in private accommodation.

Earlier in the year, Hawke and Alan Barblett had represented the University of Western Australia at a council meeting of the National Union of Australian University Students (NUAUS) at Melbourne University, where moves were being made to establish an International House along the lines of similar institutions in Europe and the United States. Apparently inspired by this, Hawke presided over a meeting of the Guild Council that agreed to investigate the possibility of establishing an International House in Perth. Once he'd received the Guild's go-ahead, he wasted no time in asking the university for a grant of land on which it could be built. This request was premature, though, since it had to come from a properly constituted body that had a reasonable chance of raising the required funds. Hawke estimated that it would need about £150,000, which would be a massive undertaking. He began by calling a meeting of interested groups on 29 May 1952, with the Guild making him its representative on the resulting committee. He also pressed ahead the following month with the first meeting of the Australia-Overseas Club.[20] And he helped to establish a committee comprising representatives from all the organisations in Perth that had an interest in creating an International House, with Hawke becoming chairman of the central appeal committee. He suggested optimistically that most of the funds would be raised from the state and federal governments and from American educational foundations, as well as from 'interested bodies and individuals in Asian countries'. It wasn't clear how that would happen.[21]

It was all part of a frenetic round of activity for Hawke, as he fulfilled the many obligations of his university and church positions and built up his credentials for the Rhodes Scholarship.[22] For the previous two years, winning the scholarship had been the object of his life. Failure was not an option. But that possibility confronted Hawke when he returned from the NUAUS council meeting in Melbourne to be told by Hazel that she was pregnant.

They'd been engaged for more than two years, and had progressed from the sand dunes and the backseat of his parents' car to the back verandah of the Tate Street house. Presumably because of their long engagement, his mother came to accept that Hazel might sleep there overnight, and she would take in a cup of tea 'and cluck about how sweet it was that Bob and Hazel were having a brotherly-and-sisterly cuddle'. Although it was a decade before the contraceptive pill became available, they did use other contraceptives. However, Hazel recalled in her memoir that her knowledge was 'meagre' and they made a 'catastrophic error'.[23] This was 1950s Australia, when unmarried mothers were still shunned and shamed, which could only be avoided if a rushed marriage was arranged to spread a veil of decency over the impending birth. However, only single men were eligible for the Rhodes Scholarship, so marriage would bring an end to Hawke's Oxford dream, which was also a dream that had excited Hazel.

They were on their own in finding a solution to their terrible predicament. Their parents couldn't be told, and when Hazel asked three different doctors she was given a 'rigid moral lecture' by each. In desperation, she tried home remedies, such as gin in a hot bath. However, she naively poured the gin into the bath rather than down her throat. The weeks were going by and her secret would soon be revealed. It was then that they finally sought an abortionist. Although illegal, abortion was widely practised and it seemed to be their only viable option if they wanted to keep their Oxford dream alive. Hazel recalled how they 'talked about it, prayed about it, made our decision, kept our secret and supported each other'. But the task was hers alone to undertake and to finance. As she later described it: 'I emptied my bank account and during my lunch hour walked two city blocks from the office to a mystery man. Goodbye innocence and modesty!' Then it was back to work, as she waited for something to happen. As she later surmised, she'd had a saline solution injected into her uterus to bring on a miscarriage. She seems to have been about three months' pregnant and it wasn't until three days later that she panicked with the pain as she began to abort the foetus. It was another two days, after hurriedly leaving work, that she finally 'aborted, alone and aghast'.[24] It became their dark secret, which wouldn't be revealed until her autobiography was published some forty years later.

Meanwhile, Hawke's chances of winning the Rhodes Scholarship were enhanced in early September 1952 with the launch of the International House Appeal. With Hawke at the helm, there were three days of events, beginning with an official opening in the refectory by Gairdner, who'd agreed to be the appeal's patron. With the hall bedecked with flags, and with overseas students serving the refreshments in their national costumes, Gairdner said that he 'strongly endorsed' the idea of an International House, which would create 'ambassadors for our country, our way of life, and our people'. He was supported by the new vice-chancellor, Professor Noel Bayliss, and a fellow member of the University Senate and headmaster of Wesley College, Dr James Rossiter. The afternoon tea was followed by a sports day and an international ball in Winthrop Hall.[25] The money raised by these events would only be a tiny fraction of the amount required to construct a building to house a hundred students. It would need much more commitment and influence than Hawke was able or willing to bring to bear. In the end, the required funds would never be raised, and the grand vision of an International House would come to nothing.[26] By the time that was apparent, Hawke would be long gone from the university and from Perth.

Apart from boosting his chances of securing the Rhodes Scholarship, the International House Appeal provided another formative political experience for Hawke.[27] However, it was his role on the Guild Council that was particularly valuable in providing experience for him as an aspiring prime minister. Seated around the council table were other students with debating skills that could sometimes outshine his, and who regularly deployed their knowledge of the meeting rules to test his chairmanship. He seems to have been outclassed during one meeting in March 1952 that went on until 3 a.m., as young tyros repeatedly put forward procedural motions to challenge his rulings or contest the motions of others. Nonetheless, Hawke's staunch supporter Terry Zanetti placed no blame on Hawke, describing him in *The Pelican* as a 'competent' and 'capable fellow ... with all the clues on chairing a meeting and presenting a matter most briefly and lucidly'. If he was 'a little dictatorial in his attitude and rulings', wrote Zanetti, it was just because of the 'annoying, time consuming, pointless and frustrating title-tattle [sic] with which he is often confronted'. Sometimes Hawke could let his anger get the better of him. At a Guild meeting in August, he was forced to apologise when a council member, John Gillett, walked out in protest at his behaviour.[28]

Despite its ultimate failure, the International House Appeal had served a useful purpose in raising Hawke's prominence before the Rhodes selection committee. He now had a much greater claim to having fulfilled one of the major criteria for the scholarship. His sporting achievements over the previous year or so were also more substantial than previously, although mainly restricted to cricket. He captained the Guild team in a match against the staff, when he abandoned his usual slashing method and scored 'a chanceless 143'. He also played for the Arts Faculty cricket team in the inter-faculty Goyder Cup, and went to Geraldton with the university cricket team for an exhibition match against the town side, where he was described by its local paper as a 'wicket-keeper and classy, free-scoring batsman'. More importantly, he toured the eastern states with the university cricket team, which also won the state A-grade pennant that year, but without Hawke being singled out for special mention. Eight players from the university team were listed among the top forty-seven A-grade batsmen for the 1951/52 season, but Hawke was not among them.[29]

Although he was elected as vice-president of the NUAUS, the Rhodes selection committee would not hear about the excessive drinking that had robbed him of the chance to become its president.

According to D'Alpuget, during the NUAUS congress meeting in Melbourne, he 'went off for a boozy weekend, returned late and still drunk on Monday morning' and thereby gave the impression of being 'too wild for the job'. This was presumably the meeting that future politician Neal Blewett also attended. It was Blewett's first NUAUS meeting and also the first time that he'd seen Hawke. It left an indelible impression on the South Australian delegate, who was four years younger than Hawke. 'We were all waiting for him to turn up at this gathering,' recalled Blewett, 'and he walked in with a blonde female delegate on his arm and in shorts and tanned and looking charismatic and spectacular. It was an overwhelming impressive entrance.' While Blewett was taken by Hawke's physique and his 'visceral gut charisma', Hawke's intense self-regard and devotion to drinking, and perhaps his womanising as well, combined to lose him the support he needed to become president.[30]

Hawke might have earned additional kudos for the Rhodes had he been successful in his plan to establish a weekly 'University Forum of the Air' on a local radio station. His idea had been to involve both undergraduate and postgraduate students in the program, which was to be moderated by a staff member, with topics that were 'reasonably controversial'. It was a format that had been used previously by the ABC, with a program called *Nation's Forum of the Air*. An episode had been recorded in Winthrop Hall in 1950, which presumably inspired Hawke's proposal.[31] However, nothing came of the project, and he made no mention of it when he reapplied for the Rhodes in late 1952.

This time, Hawke was able to present a much stronger application. He again used Beasley as one of his referees, along with five new referees who were more senior than the last lot. The most senior of all was the recently retired vice-chancellor, George Currie, who lauded Hawke as 'a manly person and ... truthful and courageous in all his work and associations' and 'sober' in his habits. That was true enough of those occasions when Currie had interacted with him, but far from true in many other social settings. As the teetotal Hazel recalled, she was 'vaguely concerned by Bob's increasing use of alcohol' at this time.[32]

Another new referee was the recently arrived professor of classics and former Rhodes scholar Mervyn Austin, who'd seen Hawke score a century in a match against the staff in early 1952 and then found

Hawke knocking on his door to consult him 'about his work' and talk about 'matters of common interest'. Although Austin wasn't one of Hawke's teachers, he formed a good impression of him after Hawke introduced him to a campus gardener who happened to be a recently arrived migrant with a background as a classical scholar. That act of kindness had impressed the professor, who found Hawke to be 'a likeable, frank, modest young man, free from any kind of affectation or obsequiousness'. But it didn't lead to a good reference. Austin thought that Hawke failed to fit 'the highest sense of the Rhodes ideal'. He was only 'an average lad, well-balanced and with some potential strength of character', but not 'likely to make any outstanding contribution to Oxford'. Nevertheless, he thought that Oxford could 'make something of his raw material' in ways that 'would not disappoint the hopes of those who felt that they discerned some faint signs of a potential Rhodes Scholar'.[33]

Austin's reference could easily have sunk Hawke's last chance to secure the Rhodes. However, much better references were provided by the professor of economics Frank Mauldon, a fellow Congregationalist, and by Selwyn Grave, who'd taught Hawke philosophy. Mauldon noted that Hawke had come second in a class of 112 students doing Economics, that he had 'a strong sense of responsibility for service to his fellows' and would be 'a very good selection as a Rhodes Scholar'. Grave thought that Hawke would 'do very much better [once he leaves university] than his academic record would indicate' and made the prescient observation that he was 'very much the sort of person that shows "promise of outstanding achievement in later life"', which fulfilled one of the scholarship's main criteria. Hawke's final and most enthusiastic reference came from James Rossiter, the headmaster of Wesley College, a member of the University Senate and chairman of the International House Appeal. He described Hawke as a 'quietly dynamic and inspiring young man' with a 'moral force of character'. Moreover, he was 'a natural leader, displaying intense enthusiasm and a facility for inspiring enthusiasm in others, and possessed of vision and drive'.[34]

For his part, Hawke crafted a much better application letter to sit alongside these references and help explain why his academic results were so much less impressive than the two previous recipients of the scholarship. He began by highlighting the motorbike accident that had cruelled his chances of getting a first-class degree. He told the committee that the near-death experience had convinced him to 'lead a full and varied life' and 'do all things to the very best of my ability'. And that was what he had done, particularly over the last twelve months. Apart from being elected president of the Guild and vice-president of the NUAUS, he was president of the Congregational Youth Fellowship and would be one of eight delegates to a forthcoming World Conference of Christian Youth to be held in India. Although he lauded his sporting achievements, they were mostly on faculty teams rather than university ones; his only sporting distinction was a half-blue in baseball. More impressive was the work he'd done in establishing the Australian-Overseas Club and chairing the International House Appeal. The weakest part of the application was Hawke's uncertainty about where his post-Oxford life might lead him. All he could say was that it would be in 'some form of public service either in the academic or other spheres of public life'. He assured the committee that, unlike at UWA, he wouldn't be distracted from his studies by becoming involved in student politics at Oxford; he was eager to study 'under the guidance of outstanding minds and personalities' so that he would be 'better equipped to be of service to my fellow men'.[35]

When it came time for the selection interview on 28 November 1952, Hawke walked through the imposing gates of Government House weighed down by the hopes and expectations of Hazel and his parents and painfully aware that this was his last chance. In his memoirs, Hawke claimed that he was the 'red-hot favourite', which he may have been. He was older than the other candidates and he'd submitted a much stronger application this time. As well, the governor, as chair of the committee, was a familiar and friendly face. Gairdner had become even better acquainted with Hawke's uncle Albert, who was now the Labor leader and who doubtless had put in a good word for his nephew. Although the committee quickly dismissed Austin's critical comments, it all threatened to come unstuck when one of the members repeatedly pressed Hawke to detail his career aspirations, only to have Hawke refuse to do so. Instead, he stood by the vague statement about pursuing 'some form of public service'. Worried that his chances were slipping away, and with his hackles raised, he turned defiantly towards Gairdner for support, assuring him that he'd 'answered the question truthfully' and wouldn't make up something just to satisfy his interrogator. According to Hawke's account, this retrieved the situation for him, with the governor later whispering his admiration for how Hawke had 'dealt with that blithering idiot'.[36] The scholarship was his.

Three days after getting the news, a triumphant Hawke waved goodbye to Hazel and his parents and boarded RMS *Strathmore*, joining the rest of the Australian delegation to the World Conference of Christian Youth in India. It was Hawke's first overseas trip and he later said that the experience changed his life. As he recounted in his memoirs, it was 'the beginning of the end of my belief in the organised Christian religion'. On board, Hawke and his fellow delegates had discussions about the themes of the coming conference. A future Anglican archbishop, Keith Rayner, was among them and recalled a shipboard conversation with Hawke that left him feeling that Hawke's 'hold on the Christian faith was rather tenuous'.[37]

The Australians were among 350 young delegates to the conference in Kottayam, a small southern Indian city in what is now the state of Kerala. The conference was radical for its time, bringing Christians of all denominations together in an ecumenical gathering in a country that had just been decolonised and was in a state of political ferment. Kottayam had a large number of Christians, with churches dating back to the sixteenth century sitting alongside ancient mosques and Hindu temples. It was also a place where extreme poverty existed alongside extreme wealth, much of it in the hands of Christians. As a result of the glaring inequality, this centre of religious devotion was also a centre of support for the Communist Party, which vied for power with the ruling Congress Party. The great disparity in wealth was to prove overwhelming for Hawke.

His religious upbringing had given Hawke a strong social conscience. He now found himself at a pre-Christmas garden party at the bishop's residence in Kottayam, with 'hundreds of poor villagers staring in through the fence' at the 'fantastically decorated cakes'. To the local Christians, wrote Hawke, 'these people seemed totally irrelevant'. Yet they were a constant feature of the conference, which was held in a temporary hall made of bamboo poles and a thatched roof. Because of the tropical heat, there were no walls, which allowed curious onlookers to crowd in their thousands around the gathering. Stricken by the sight of children sleeping in the street as he returned to his lodgings, Hawke said that he presented his windcheater to a small boy and an older sister, then 'kissed them and went back to my bed sick at heart'. He already had doubts about religion, and his time in India made him question his beliefs anew. Writing from India, Hawke complained to his father that while 'Bible study has been good', his involvement with a discussion group 'on Personal Freedom & Social Justice has been a lot of airy blithering with nothing unified or practical'.[38] It may have been his concern that caused the discussion group to observe in its final report how the world was 'plagued by the inequalities of wealth and of economic opportunity' and to recommend that Christians 'should not be afraid to be revolutionary, if the peaceful, persuasive, nonviolent techniques of Christian ethics fail to arouse the "conscience" of society'.[39]

Hawke didn't want to be 'revolutionary', but his experience was forcing him to question how religion alone could provide the best means of improving the lives of the downtrodden. At a midnight service on Christmas Eve, as his fellow delegates sang carols about 'this Saviour of all Mankind', Hawke found that his 'thoughts were in the streets of Kottayam with those children lying in the gutters'. He came away with the conviction that 'because [Jesus] died for man we as Christians are bound to serve man wherever we find him in misery and in suffering'.[40] As Clem had repeatedly impressed upon him, you couldn't believe in the fatherhood of God without also believing in the brotherhood of man. For Hawke, that would mean eschewing the church pulpit for the political platform.

When the conference ended, he accompanied another delegate on a tour of nearby states, fetching up in Mysore, where he inspected the palace of the local ruler, whose family of four was attended by sixty servants and who had seventy-six cars in the palace garage. Hawke saw the 34-year-old maharajah in one of the cars and scribbled down in his diary a derisory description of the 'great fat fellow' who lived in such luxury and yet was said to be a 'good philosopher, very religious, writes poetry'. Continuing on his homeward journey, he was taken on a tour of a hospital in Madras, where he saw 'some shocking malnutrition', and then went by way of Ceylon (now Sri Lanka), where he visited a

Buddhist friend he'd met in Perth and went to a temple where he had earnest discussions with an elderly monk.[41]

Hawke wasn't only wrestling with religion; he was also interested in the Hindu attitude towards sex. In Bangalore, he collected a leaflet about 'the latest scientific advancement to eliminate sexual disappointments, troubles and worries', which advertised a book promising to provide its readers with the 'hidden secrets' on how to become 'sexually sound' in their marriage. It was about sex for pleasure, rather than just procreation, and Hawke folded it away to take home with him. After he boarded the ship for home, he described in his diary how he was handed a parcel from someone called 'Soma', a Hindu name used for both males and females. This prompted him to write enigmatically: 'What queer things one's thoughts are!' After opening the parcel, he wrote: 'Beaut. book & once more the tormenting thoughts'. It seems that it wasn't only politics and religion that was causing the turmoil in Hawke's mind as the ship steamed towards Perth. Hawke spent his days in the usual shipboard activities of quoits, deck tennis and snoozing in the sun. At the end of one such day, after dressing for dinner, he returned to his cabin and 'changed into slacks & open shirt', which he was pleased to note 'got a few stares'. Hawke's final two days aboard were more leisurely. He spent most of his time asleep on deck, only waking to dine or play table tennis. On 12 January, he packed up his belongings and the presents bought from bazaars in India and Ceylon and prepared to meet Hazel and his parents, who would be waiting eagerly at the foot of the gangway. There was much to tell them, and some things he couldn't. For instance, he wouldn't reveal that his experiences had made him question the religion that had been such a central part of his life.[42]

That was made clear upon his return, when he flew off to Adelaide for the annual meeting of the Congregational Youth Fellowship. Clem and Ellie accompanied him, while Hazel was there as a member of the West Australian contingent. After praying for help to articulate his concerns, Hawke made an impassioned speech to the 120 young delegates, speaking vividly about the 'abject filth and squalor amid which thousands of people eked out an existence bereft of purpose or pleasure'. Painting a picture of the lavish garden party at the bishop's palace, he warned the delegates against becoming 'Garden Party

Christians', people who thought they could fulfil their faith by going to church on Sunday and ignoring 'the vast numbers of suffering people outside the Church'. For Hawke, the speech was a powerful moment. He'd spoken at student gatherings in Perth, but this rousing address was something different. It was the first time he'd stirred an audience and been swept up in its warm embrace. As he later told D'Alpuget, he had 'felt something unknown – a capacity in myself which I had never suspected – it was as if it were not I speaking but someone else'. His mother had always believed that the Lord was channelling His will through her, and Hawke now believed that God was doing likewise with him. Or so he seems to suggest, noting that the address 'had enormous impact', with 'people [being] moved in a way in which I've never been able to repeat'.[43] But to what purpose? That was something he was yet to work out.

Hazel was relieved by the reception. She had waited nervously for Hawke to give what she described as his 'stirring report'. The audience may not have realised it, but the child of the manse was tugging at the bonds of his upbringing. Looking back, Hazel realised that the report signalled 'the real beginning of his commitment to politics'. She also recalled 'a vague sense of foreboding' about what it might mean for their 'church-centred' relationship, although there is no sense of foreboding captured in a photograph taken of the couple relaxing in the summer heat, with a smiling Hawke clad just in brief shorts with his arm loosely draped around a clearly happy Hazel. Despite the smiles, there would be difficult discussions ahead with Clem and Ellie, as Hawke gradually came to terms with his changed outlook on the world.[44] As his departure for Oxford loomed closer, he also had to disentangle himself from the other organisations in his life.

One was the NUAUS, which had given Hawke some political experience on the national stage but which had nothing left to offer him. He also stepped back from the Guild. At its annual general meeting in October 1952, when its election results were announced, Hawke's name was not among the candidates, although he would remain on the council as past president. His report for the year lauded it as 'an outstanding year for the Guild', listing the achievements that had been mostly driven by his efforts and omitting the ones that hadn't quite come off. Amid an ovation from the students assembled in the

Arts lecture theatre, fellow council member John Gillett proposed a vote of thanks to the 'deeply moved' Hawke for 'the particularly fine job' he'd done. At another farewell, about sixty foreign students made a presentation to him in recognition of his role in establishing the Australia-Overseas Club; in reply, he told them of the important role they would play in coming years as their countries steered either towards democracy or dictatorship. He hoped that their experience in Australia would 'prove to them the value of democracy'.[45]

Although he was still on the council, Hawke missed some meetings. That was partly due to another accident: he had been crushed against a fence by a horse-drawn cart when working as a labourer with the university gardeners. Hawke was distracted by a cricket match on the university oval between a visiting South African Test team and the governor's team, and was left with a 'badly gashed thigh'. Members of the South African team applied a tourniquet before he was rushed off to hospital. A report in *The Pelican* described Hawke later as 'a wan, pathetic figure, who stomps about the University on a pair of crutches'.[46]

Once he was able to dispense with the crutches, a spring returned to Hawke's step as his departure for Oxford approached. He wouldn't be able to complete his Arts degree prior to boarding the ship. He'd finished four of the five required subjects, for which he had gained two distinctions and two credit passes. He'd also been employed as a temporary tutor in Economics. Although he'd proposed to do honours in Economics in 1953, he never did.[47] Hawke would have to sit his outstanding subject, Economics IIA, in Oxford or upon his return to Perth.

Although a shipping company provided a first-class cabin for Hawke as a Rhodes scholar, and despite his part-time work as a labourer and tutor and the money from his scholarship, he was so skint in his final months in Perth that he was forced to borrow £125 from a member of his father's congregation to tide him over when he reached Oxford. Not that anyone would have known this from his behaviour. The day before leaving Perth, he and his uncle Albert, who in February 1953 had become state premier, were entertained at Government House, where they played three sets of tennis against Sir Charles Gairdner and the head of the Premier's Department. Perhaps sensibly, the Hawkes were 'thrashed'; neither would have wanted to put the governor offside.[48]

Then there were the dockside goodbyes from his doting parents and a fiancée who was planning to join him the following year. Clambering up the gangplank of the *Dominion Monarch* – which was carrying butter and meat from New Zealand in its hold and five hundred well-to-do passengers in its first-class cabins and luxury lounges – a smiling Hawke was exultant. His tortuous campaign for the Rhodes was over and Oxford beckoned.

CHAPTER SIX

1953–1955

In September 1953, Hawke disembarked in England, where the effects of the last war still lingered. Unlike in Australia, some wartime rationing was still in place, and piles of rubble remained where buildings had once stood. The Australian writer Russell Braddon, who was living in London at the time, described the city as a scene of 'grey bleak desolation' where buildings had remained unpainted for a decade or more and the food was 'appalling'.[1] Not that Hawke saw much of that desolation during his first few days ashore, as he'd caught pneumonia on board ship and had to be carted off in an ambulance from the wharf in Southampton.

Having spent weeks living 'a life of luxury' aboard the plush *Dominion Monarch*, Hawke was now forced to eat the stodge that was dished up to post-war public-hospital patients.[2] Once he'd recovered, and with classes yet to begin in Oxford, he decided to linger in London. Anxious to see the sights of his imagination, he took a room in the rather grand London House, which was situated just a few blocks from the British Museum and was built to provide accommodation for students and academics from the Commonwealth.

It was while he was staying there that he encountered the 32-year-old Braddon, who had just shot to fame with *The Naked Island*, a wartime memoir about his captivity by the Japanese. They'd met on 14 September and agreed to have lunch together the following day so that Braddon could escort the young Rhodes scholar around the capital, the central parts of which had been spruced up for the coronation of Elizabeth II. In a letter to his parents in which he misspelled the name of his new acquaintance as 'Brandon', Hawke described with some excitement how the pair ate at a 'really posh' place in Piccadilly before going to Horse Guards Parade in Westminster, where fighter planes were being displayed to commemorate Battle of Britain Week and a swarm of aircraft roared low overhead. Further on, they encountered 'Old Winny and Lady Churchill' returning to Downing Street after spending the weekend with the Queen at Balmoral. Hawke described how he was 'within just a few feet of him as he stood in the doorway of No 10 and gave the characteristic V sign'. He thought that the 78-year-old Churchill 'certainly looks old and bent but still has the look of a man with plenty of life left in him'. In fact, the prime minister was recovering from a recent stroke and was being pressured by his family to retire, which he was refusing to do.[3]

After Braddon showed Hawke around Westminster Abbey, St Paul's Cathedral and the Tower of London, the pair caught the tube to Leicester Square, where the well-connected author had secured tickets to see Graham Greene's *The Living Room*, which was described by one critic as 'a terrific sermon on sin' and by a clergyman as 'sordid muck', apparently because of its portrayal of a relationship between a young woman and an older man. Hawke 'thoroughly enjoyed it' and told his parents that he enjoyed even more being taken by 'Russ' to a 'beaut café', where at 'about 10.30 at night [they] had roast lamb, vegs. mint sauce etc so you can see what a day I had – my eyes and ears were continually battered with famous places etc. which I'd heard about nearly all my life and at last was seeing'. And it was all thanks to 'Brandon', who was 'a marvellous person – knew the spots and [was] very interesting to talk to'. Braddon, whose male partner at the time described him as '100 per cent gay' with an 'energetic capacity for random dalliance', may have hoped for a dalliance with the visiting Australian student. If so, he would have been disappointed by the hyper-sexed heterosexual Hawke. The prolific Australian writer, who never publicly acknowledged his homosexuality, left no record of that night. Later, when Hawke had become prime minister, Braddon said that he'd never met him.[4]

Leaving Braddon, Hawke steamed off by train to Loders, a small Dorset village on the River Asker, where he stayed with the local policeman, Eddy Edrich, and his family. Edrich had been a British submariner who'd attended 'sing-songs' at Hazel's home during the war, and he now gave Hawke the warmest of welcomes. Indeed, Hawke felt so at home that he went there twice for brief stays during the several weeks prior to term starting in Oxford. For Hawke, staying in the Edrichs' primitive home, with its tiny scullery and a sitting room where the meals were cooked on an oven that also provided the only source of heating, was partly to save money at a time when he'd not yet received the first of his scholarship payments. The embrace of the family also helped him get over his homesickness, as he downed pints at the local pub, pulled up potatoes from their rented field or went shooting for rabbits. Eddy also made his own wine, either from elderberries or parsnips, which would have helped the two men develop a ready rapport. By the end of his second visit, Hawke could assure his parents that the 'worst of the homesickness has sort of worn off'.[5] Which was just as well, because he was about to experience another culture shock when he finally alighted at Oxford station on 8 October 1953, about a month after arriving in England.

Rather than the 'dreaming spires' of Matthew Arnold's nineteenth-century imagination, the towers of the university were begrimed by the soot of coal fires and the diesel exhausts of the constant procession of buses and lorries that clogged its main road, which provided the major artery between London and Wales and the Midlands. It was on that street in the centre of Oxford that Hawke unloaded his bags at University College, with its tall stone walls cracked by the vibration of the traffic. Tracing its history back to 1249, the male-only college was arguably the oldest in Oxford, although its buildings dated mostly to the seventeenth century.[6]

Four days after unpacking his belongings, Hawke wrote in his regular lettergram to his parents of his first impressions of 'the city of spires and long-haired intellectuals – boy oh boy are there some queer characters inhabiting this town'. He'd been busy equipping himself with 'an ancient bicycle and a very tattered gown which is a proper bum freezer only hanging a short way down the back in all its gorgeous tatters'. The gown would soon play an important role in securing an enduring reputation for Hawke as a dinkum, beer-swilling Aussie.[7] First, though, he had to come to terms with life in college.

Hawke was shown to his two-room set, a 'freezing, dilapidated study and cell-like bedroom'. There was no plumbing, just 'a washstand with a bowl', a coal fire for heating and 'some dreadful old furniture and a piece of bald carpet on the floor'. Each morning, he would be woken by his elderly 'scout', whose job it was to rouse the students, fill the bowl with warm water and light the ineffective fire. 'My servant is a good bloke,' Hawke told his parents, '[and] does nearly everything for me including cleaning my shoes – what a life eh!' To take a bath, Hawke had to scamper in his dressing-gown, sometimes through snow, across the quadrangle to one of the few bathrooms.[8]

Hawke was clearly shocked and perhaps even a little intimidated by the mix of squalor and privation in Oxford, overlaid as it was by the weight of history and tradition. And he was experiencing it without the supportive company of his close friends, his fiancée and his ever-encouraging parents and uncle.

The photograph of that year's college intake shows an unsmiling Hawke to be of slightly less than average height compared to his contemporaries as he stood on the highest of five temporary tiers that were set against a creeper-clad stone wall, with his hair perfectly coiffured and his face displaying a rather distant but confident look that belied the unease he was feeling. Yet with the apparent assistance of the college classicist, he signed into the college register in the customary manner with a Latin flourish as *'Robertus Jacobus Lee Hawke ex universitate Australiae occidentalis'*. He was one of ninety new students at the college, which included nine other Rhodes scholars, including Hedley Bull from Sydney, who was two and a half years younger than Hawke and intent on doing a BPhil in Politics. Bull would go on to enjoy a distinguished career in Britain and Australia as a political scientist. The new students were welcomed after dinner by the college's master, American law professor Arthur Goodhart, who told the assembled young men of the college's 'essential character as a gentlemen's club, of the privileges of members, and the need for discipline'. The novelist V.S. Naipaul, who also attended University College in the 1950s, described to his father how the 'atmosphere of the college is more of a club than anything else', with students retiring after dinner to the Junior Common Room, where they 'drink and smoke and talk'. There was also drinking to be had in the college's cellar, which was open each evening for students to imbibe a quick pint or two before going up to dine in the hall.[9]

To that extent, Hawke was in his element. He also played to the larrikin Australian image that he was fond of projecting, acting the colonial clown rather than attempting to mimic the plummy accents of the mostly English students and college fellows. After a drinking session one evening, Hedley Bull was with Hawke on a balcony overlooking the High Street when Hawke tipped a bucket of water onto the head of one of the university's two disciplinary officers, known as proctors, who was bustling along on the pavement below.[10]

For the incoming Rhodes scholars, there was also a welcome from the warden of Rhodes House, Brigadier Bill Williams, a historian with a first-class honours degree from Oxford who'd married and later divorced a New Zealand woman. During World War II, he'd served in military intelligence under General Montgomery. After the war he returned to academia, becoming editor of the *Dictionary of National Biography*, where it was said 'his acute estimate of character, ability to judge real rather than assumed merit, and dislike of humbug and pomposity stood him in good stead'. After also being appointed in 1952 as warden, he brought those qualities to bear when he met Rhodes scholars for the first time and later assessed their progress at the beginning of each term. In some ways, Williams was much like Hawke, being a keen lover of cricket but without the skills, the physique or sufficiently good eyesight to become a first-class cricketer. Like Hawke, he was also the son of a Congregational minister, only to become, like Hawke, an agnostic. Slouched in the chair of his study at Rhodes House, probably with a glass of dry sherry at hand, the warden's slight, bespectacled figure would have seen through the veneer of the overconfident Australian, while still recognising the potential within.[11]

With its dining hall and library, Rhodes House offered a more modern and congenial place for Hawke to study, alongside students from across the world and with a library collection that included large holdings of Australian material from the nineteenth century onwards. Not that study was much on his mind during that first year in Oxford. Hawke had planned on a two-year honours degree in Philosophy, Politics and Economics, known as PPE, which was designed for students who'd already completed a first degree. It would allow him to learn from some of the world's greatest thinkers, and to specialise in whatever subjects within those three branches of learning sparked his interest.

Initially, he was excited by the prospect, telling his parents that 'the facilities for study are really good, the standard of lecturing promises to be very high, and what a great variety of things there are to do'. The first week of classes fulfilled his expectations, as he attended lectures 'from guys right up in the front rank of their subjects', including Hungarian economist Thomas Balogh. But he was taken aback by the amount of work expected from PPE students, who were required to write weekly essays which they had to read out for comment and criticism by their tutors. Hawke's tutor was a young, Ulster-born economist, Tom Wilson, whose book *Modern Capitalism and Economic Progress* had argued against the British Labour Party's post-war program of nationalisation and proposed instead for Britain to become a more egalitarian, property-owning democracy.[12]

The Oxford academic system was more demanding than that of the University of Western Australia, and having his work subject to critical examination each week affronted Hawke's narcissistic nature. Moreover, it would interfere with his other pursuits, whether it was playing on the local golf course, going to the theatre with his fellow Rhodes scholar from Perth, John Hall, enjoying Sir Thomas Beecham conducting the Royal Philharmonic Orchestra at the Sheldonian Theatre or downing pints at the pub. During those first weeks, he also went to hear the Labour leader Clement Attlee address the Student Union; he afterwards asked for Attlee's autograph, because, as he rather pompously told his parents, 'it may prove of interest to others than myself'. In late November, Hawke went to Cambridge with Hall and a scratch team of other Australian students, including Stone, to play the annual Australian Rules football match against their Cambridge counterparts. Hawke wasn't good at football but excused his poor performance by telling his parents that he was matched against a Cambridge student who'd once played for South Australia. Cricket remained his game of choice, and he was already training in the nets with the Oxford team. He wanted to return with a coveted Oxford Blue, which he could only obtain by playing in the traditional match against Cambridge at Lord's cricket ground in London. That would please his father above all. After being 'advised that politically it was a good thing to do', Hawke also joined the Oxford University Air Squadron, which would teach him to fly in a two-person Chipmunk with a top speed of

240 kilometres per hour. He was almost prevented from doing so when an eye test revealed that he was colourblind. It was only after he proved that he could distinguish between red, green and white that he was allowed to proceed. Becoming a member of the squadron would pay him a handy £60 a year and allow him to add a service record of sorts to his political résumé. Although it would take up at least six hours a week, it would also give him access to the squadron's headquarters, which had 'the best club facilities in Oxford'.[13]

As the grey days of winter closed in and the end of Michaelmas term loomed, Hawke became homesick and disconsolate. He told his parents that he was looking forward to 'the break from the steady routine of having to prepare two essays every week'. Not only was he weighed down by the demands of his tutors, he was surrounded by students who, usually, were younger than him, despite most of them also having done two years' national service, and who were sometimes smarter than him and not overly friendly. Like Hawke, Hedley Bull was taken aback by the frostiness of the English students, complaining that he'd twice 'said hallo to an English student living here, but on each occasion he stared frigidly back. The lousy bastard. All the Australians complain of this.' Rather than trying to ingratiate himself with his English counterparts, Bull noted, Hawke 'seems much concerned to assert his colonial nationalism'. This struck Tom Wilson as brashness: he noted on Hawke's student card that he was 'bright, efficient, a bit superficial' and said his self-confidence could prevent him from 'realising that he still has a good deal to learn'. Hawke was now being matched against some of the best students the world could produce. He would also be competing with his bête noire, John Stone, who'd switched from maths to PPE and would graduate in 1954 with a first-class honours degree and a prize in Economics. Hawke was also being forced to cope without the constant affirmation that had been provided by his parents. To remedy this, he tried to find a way for his father to swap churches for a year with a Congregational minister from Colchester, only to discover that the minister was only interested in going to Sydney.[14]

Just weeks after arriving in England, and in a sign of his desperate loneliness, Hawke pressured Hazel to give up her job, as well as her work with the church and Sunday School choir, and get to Oxford before Hawke was seduced by 'all the delights which are available to the uninhibited Oxford undergraduate'. He warned that he'd been 'thrust into an environment which is full of opportunities for the satisfaction of my varied tastes, to which if I succumbed in their entireties, would only succeed in taking me away from you'. He assured Hazel that he didn't want that to happen. Nor did he want her to come earlier than they'd planned just so she could protect him from his 'weaknesses', but because he'd 'made a choice about the person with whom I want to spend the rest of my life'. That must have struck 24-year-old Hazel as somewhat strange, since she presumably thought Bob had made that decision when they'd become engaged four years earlier. Yet here he was emphatically instructing her to 'GET ON THAT SHIP DARLING FOR YOUR SAKE AND MINE'. Anxious not to have him slip away, and excited by the prospect of travel and the life that might await her, Hazel immediately booked her passage. In the interim, Hawke sent an avalanche of letters professing his love and offering practical advice about the voyage, including how to avoid men who might have seduction in mind. When the ship docked at Southampton in December 1953, Bob was the first up the gangplank, having used the good offices of the West Australian agent-general to sidestep the usual formalities. Bundling her into the two-seat baker's van that he had bought with money sent to him by Hazel after she'd sold the car they'd owned in Perth, Hawke tootled off to spend Christmas with the Edrich family in Loders, where they feasted on two geese. Hawke reported to his parents that he now weighed well over seventy kilograms, while Hazel was 'getting quite a backside on her'.[15]

Although the betrothed couple had been able to sleep together in the cramped conditions of the Edrich house, they would have more trouble doing so in Oxford, where Bob would not be able to have her in his bed, at least not when the servant came to light the fire in the morning. After staying as long as they could in Loders, they drove back to Oxford, arriving in the pitch dark with nowhere to stay. Hawke described to his parents how they turned up on the doorstep of the Reverend Geoffrey Beck, the Congregational minister in Summertown, on the northern outskirts of Oxford. Apparently throwing themselves on the mercy of Beck and his wife, Joy, Hawke reported that 'they have asked me to stay with them till I go back into College next Thursday'. Beck provided a rather different account, saying that Hawke had knocked on his door the previous November, when Hazel was on her way to England, and made 'a silly request' for him and Hazel to 'come and live with us', which Beck politely declined. Apart from the question of propriety, the two-storey manse at 42 Lonsdale Road had limited accommodation, with the Becks' three daughters in one bedroom and their young son in the other, which was also used for occasional visitors. Hawke had placed the hospitable minister in a quandary. In the middle of winter and late at night, Beck could hardly demand that they sleep in the van.[16]

The visitors' book at the Beck manse reveals that Bob and Hazel stayed there for nine days, during which time the couples became good friends. Hawke wrote cheekily in the book that he had 'developed a "washed up" feeling' there, because he'd had the apparently unusual experience of helping wash the dishes. Beck was about ten years older than Hawke; he was a strong supporter of the ecumenical movement and played cricket for the university team. He regarded Hawke with a degree of indulgence, later describing him as 'a good example of an Australian away from home going to his church but behaving in all sorts of student ways and late nights'. Perhaps to help out the minister, an elderly member of the congregation agreed to put Hazel up in her house on nearby Woodstock Road, while another rented out their garage for Hawke's van. Hazel also found a temporary job doing secretarial work for the local office of the Anglican church, cycling off each day to the centre of Oxford. Even when Hawke was back in college and Hazel was living in her rented room, the couple were frequent visitors to the manse. 'Their place is just like a home to us now,' wrote Hawke on 25 January, 'and there's rarely a day goes by that we haven't been in there for some thing or other.' They also became regular members of Beck's congregation at the church on Banbury Road, and sometimes acted as childminders so Joy could attend the evening service and the Becks could enjoy some private time together. For their part, Hawke and Hazel had to snatch whatever time they could, whether it was in the manse, in Hawke's college rooms, at Hazel's boarding house or in the back of the van, which became known by his friends as 'The Fornicatorium'. In March 1954 Hawke lent the van to Hedley Bull so his friend could have a honeymoon in the Cotswolds after his fiancée arrived from Sydney.[17]

When Hawke returned to college, he abandoned PPE in favour of a Bachelor of Letters degree. According to a future Rhodes scholar and Labor leader, Kim Beazley, the BLitt degree was for students who wanted to have fun during their time at Oxford. Rather than having to write essays each week, attend lectures and tutorials and sit written examinations, they just had to write a minor thesis. Hawke told his parents that the idea had originated with Tom Wilson, who supposedly suggested that he do a BLitt thesis on 'the development of the Australian economy since the war'. Hawke assured them that this appealed to him since 'I could bring in the political factors involved' and perhaps expand the thesis to make it eligible for a PhD. It would be a coup if he could return to Perth as Dr Hawke; he would then be well placed to secure a plum academic position, either at UWA or some other Australian university. Wilson's recollection is somewhat different, suggesting that it was Hawke who decided on the switch to a BLitt and that Wilson had been 'disappointed' to lose him as a student, since Hawke was 'obviously such an interesting person'. The young economics tutor partly blamed himself for there not being sufficient 'intellectual rapport' between them.[18]

As Hawke's supervisor for the BLitt, the university selected 48-year-old Colin Clark, a father of nine children and the director of the university's Agricultural Economics Institute. He was the author of a well-regarded treatise, *The Conditions of Economic Progress*, a book that placed facts and statistics above theories and speculations. The Oxford-educated Clark had worked as a lecturer in Cambridge, stood unsuccessfully for the British Labour Party and had been close to the leading economist John Maynard Keynes, who once described Clark as 'a bit of a genius'. During a visit to Australia, Clark had been a visiting professor at UWA in 1938, where he'd got to know Albert Hawke, before being employed in several economic advisory positions by the Queensland Labor government, during which time he'd joined the ALP. Clark's brilliance, his embrace of Keynesian economics, his fond attachment to Australia and his apparent sympathy for the Labor Party seemed to make him a good fit for Hawke.[19]

However, unknown to Hawke, his Catholic supervisor was attached to the notion of Australia becoming a primary-producing nation of small farmers, based on high immigration, rather than encouraging greater industrialisation and the concentration of the population in cities. This was an idea Clark had been propounding in concert with the right-wing Catholic ideologue B.A. Santamaria, whose supporters had been infiltrating the Labor Party since the war and would soon break away to form the Democratic Labor Party (DLP). As Wilson later noted, 'Clark's views must have surprised and dismayed' Hawke. They'd also raised eyebrows among Clark's fellow economists, and sparked 'a whispering campaign reflecting on his sanity'. Although Clark still considered himself as 'a [British] Labour Party man, [he] had reached the conclusion that the welfare state should be largely scrapped', believing that people should pay for their own health and education. Unknown to Hawke, he also opposed the system of quarterly adjustments to Australia's basic wage, arguing that it was exacerbating the inflation induced by the Korean War. Hawke was a passionate supporter of automatic adjustments, believing they were necessary to compensate workers for the effects of inflation. Two weeks before arriving in Oxford, he had mentioned in a letter to his parents that the 'abolition of quarterly basic wage adjustments' was a 'dangerous' decision by the Commonwealth Court of Conciliation and Arbitration during 'a period of continually rising prices'.[20]

Fortunately for Hawke, there was sufficient Australian historical material in the Rhodes House library to support his proposed thesis, which he later described as being 'virgin territory for a scholar' that he was 'uniquely equipped to research'.[21] That may have been true in Britain but it was hardly true back home, where there was no lack of knowledge or understanding about the topic, and where there was much more historical and current material. As always, Hawke had to portray everything as a personal success, informing his parents on 10 February that his BLitt course had been approved on the 'general subject of wage determination in Australia and [I] have been most fortunate in securing Colin Clark as a supervisor', describing him as 'one of the most competent and certainly one of the most controversial economists in the world today'. Moreover, Clark had told him that 'this field of research is practically untouched and that good work in it will open up unlimited possibilities so I am getting stuck into it with a will and sincerely hope that it will lead to a Doctorate'. He made similar comments in a letter sent to the church member in Perth who'd lent him £150, with Hawke lauding Clark as 'one of the foremost economists in the world today'. Although he noted that Clark was 'an ardent R[oman]

C[atholic]', which can sometimes 'tend to colour his work' and would likely cause them to have 'differences of opinion', Hawke felt that 'at all times I should be sure of stimulating supervision'.[22]

The two men started on a positive note. No longer burdened by weekly essays and tutorials, Hawke told his parents that 'the work is going well now'. He described how he was 'really interested in it' and excited by the idea 'that at the end of the course there are not just more examinations but the publication of a substantial bit of work that you've achieved yourself'. While he pushed ahead with his reading, with Hazel taking shorthand notes as he leafed through his library books, he also threw himself into extracurricular activities. He asked his financial supporter in Perth for a further loan – this time £200 – so they could see more of the country and also travel to Europe.

A fortnight after starting on his thesis, Hawke went to London with members of the Oxford cricket side to practise in the nets, before spending Easter touring Devon and Cornwall with Hazel, camping along the way in their van.[23] Graduating with a BLitt, or perhaps a PhD, would be good, but returning with a cricket Blue would be just as satisfying. For that to happen, he'd have to work hard at his game. During the English summer of 1954, he strapped on the batting pads practically every day and headed to a cricket pitch for a match or to practise in the nets. The *University College Record* reported that 'some very good totals were amassed [by the college cricket team], due often to good batting by R.J.L. Hawke'. His batting was sufficiently good for him to graduate to the Oxford Authentics, the university cricket team then led by the future Test cricketer Colin Cowdrey, who was three years younger than Hawke. According to Geoffrey Beck, the brash Australian became friendly with Cowdrey, which helped to win him a place as twelfth man. Hawke was 'a good cricketer but not of first-class standard', said Beck, who suggested that he got 'one or two games [only] because he could offer a lift to two or three of the team' in his van. Nevertheless, along with Beck but without Cowdrey, Hawke toured with an Oxford team to northern England and Scotland during the summer of 1954, playing against a variety of school, university and town teams.[24] The team wasn't Oxford's First XI, which would play against Cambridge at Lord's that July. For that match Hawke was named twelfth man; he was briefly called onto the field, only to earn the guffaws of the crowd when he fumbled the ball, which went through to the boundary for four. There was still a chance he could do better the following summer and earn the coveted 'full blue'. If he failed, it wouldn't be for want of trying, although Brigadier Williams worried that Hawke's 'intellectual over-certainty on the one hand and eagerness for a Blue on the other, may prove a difficult combination'.[25]

Hazel often traipsed along to matches in the surrounding villages during those long English weekends, seizing the opportunity to explore the picturesque surrounds and wander among the headstones of the churchyards while Bob played.[26] Although Hawke had been desperate for Hazel to join him in Oxford, she was excluded from much of his day-to-day life. He would continue to live alone in his all-male college; Hazel could visit but would have to leave the grounds by 10 p.m. She couldn't be at his lectures or tutorials, nor would she be among his mates at the pubs he frequented, or at the Air Squadron club or the exclusive, all-male Vincent's Club, which limited its membership to 150 and was for sports-minded students, most of whom had earned a Blue. Perhaps because of his friendship with Cowdrey, Hawke had wangled his way into that hallowed space, with its bar and dining room and views from the third floor across High Street. It was 'a warm comfortable place', wrote Cowdrey, 'with its deep leather armchairs, polished wood, tankards of ale, and laughter'.[27] Hawke's ribald stories would have marked many a night in that venerable institution.

Hazel had her own life, working during the day, firstly at the Anglican Diocesan Office and then as a typist at the Institute of Statistics, where she also whiled away the summer evenings by playing tennis on nearby courts. At the institute, she did a lot of work for Tom Balogh and also, with Bob, took care of his house when he was away. To earn extra money, she typed up theses for students when she wasn't taking down shorthand from Bob or typing up his research notes.[28]

Spending so much time on cricket, while also taking a five-week summer camping trip across western Europe with Hazel, meant that Hawke fell further and further behind in his research. Moreover, the little reading he had done was causing him to reconsider his topic, which would put him even further behind. Rather than an economics-driven examination of wage determination in Australia, Hawke now wanted to examine the 'Arbitration Court and the function it performed in the Australian community', only to have Clark argue against it. According to Hawke, his supervisor declared that the topic was 'of no interest to me, and what is more important, it would be of no interest to the University of Oxford'. That wasn't how Clark recalled their conversation. He told D'Alpuget that he thought it was 'a very good subject for a thesis' but was concerned that 'Hawke did not seem to have any real interest in the economic implications of wage arbitration'. When Clark asked another economist to interview Hawke, the same conclusion was reached. Clark later explained how Hawke had 'turned up in Oxford with an I-know-it-all-already attitude', believing that 'if we just showed him one or two more tricks of the trade he could be a complete authority on wage fixing'. According to Clark, his new student 'did not know any economics at all [and] was far too stubborn to learn any'. Hawke regarded Clark's attitude as a personal slight and became even angrier after discovering, on his return to Australia, that Clark had been an opponent of automatic adjustments to the basic wage. He never forgave him, declaring in his memoirs that Clark's rejection of the change to the thesis was driven by a desire to prevent 'a bright and committed young fellow probing the ground he had contaminated', and that he was trying to 'divert attention from his own dishonesty by denigrating my work as a scholar'.[29]

That was not wholly true. For the past year, Hawke had frittered away his time, seduced by the delights of Oxford and England and desperate to secure a place in the cricket team. According to Hedley Bull, Hawke had earned a reputation as a playboy and was 'well-known for sport, for drinking, and, of course, for women'.[30] Now he was in the first term of his final year, and Clark feared that Hawke's topic was 'too ambitious' and that, because of cricket, he'd done 'very little work' over the eight months since starting the BLitt. With time running out, Clark suggested to the college's senior tutor on 11 October 1954 that Hawke should either switch to doing a one-year diploma, perhaps in economics and politics, or ask for an additional year from the Rhodes Trust so that he could return to PPE with some chance of completing that degree. There is nothing in the correspondence to suggest that Clark had anything but Hawke's best interests in mind. Indeed, he assured the senior tutor that he was 'sorry to have to say all this' because he liked Hawke 'and his father even better'. The comment about Hawke's father is curious, since there is no indication that Clark had ever met Clem. It was presumably an inadvertent reference to Bob's uncle Albert, whom Clark had met while in Perth and who was still premier of Western Australia. A similar mistake was made by the college dean, who wrote on Hawke's student card that he was the 'spoilt son of an Australian politician'. That may have been because Hawke had misled both men about the identity of his father (in the same way that he would mislead people about his true height). When Hawke was confronted by the senior tutor that same morning with Clark's advice, he said that he was 'greatly surprised and disappointed', claiming that he'd 'done quite a lot of work and that he had a great deal of material with which to begin his thesis'. Although he angrily dismissed the idea of dropping his unwritten thesis, he was now on notice that 'his situation is a bit dicky'.[31]

More time was lost as the college sought to resolve the dispute by finding an academic who was prepared to take on the testy, overconfident student and supervise the topic he was adamant about doing. Peace was restored by swapping Hawke from economics to political history and finding a supervisor in the Politics department. This was the Gladstone Professor of Government, Kenneth Wheare, a 47-year-old Australian who specialised in the study of the constitutions of the British Commonwealth. The phlegmatic professor was a much better fit for Hawke's narcissistic personality and his changed topic. Unlike Clark, who was apt to pontificate, Wheare knew little about the wage system in Australia and was happy for Hawke to teach him, rather than the reverse, which was how Hawke liked it. Although he would later say that the appointment of Wheare was due to the intervention of Brigadier Williams and (presumably) the dean or senior tutor of University College, Clark claimed also to have had a role in negotiating the transfer, caustically observing that 'we got him to ... write a thesis in the sub-faculty of politics, which we thought would be easier'. He didn't regard Hawke as a serious student, noting that his 'principal interest was cricket'. As Hawke's new supervisor, Wheare would have just a year to focus his student's attention on the task at hand and prove Clark wrong. That would take some doing. As Williams noted at the end of Hawke's first year, his 'self-confidence has muffled from him the fact that in his work he has still far to go and much to learn'.[32]

It was going to be a busy year. Hawke not only had to research and write up his BLitt thesis but also study for the final subject of his UWA arts degree, on which he had arranged to be examined in Oxford in February 1955.[33] He also moved out of his college rooms and spent 'some months' living with the Becks. He hoped that Beck would allow Hazel to move in as well, but the minister refused. Allowing the unmarried couple to live together in the manse would raise the eyebrows of his parishioners in the 'prim and proper' middle-class neighbourhood, where Hawke and Hazel were among the few people in the congregation who were under fifty. Somewhat to Beck's surprise, the age of the female parishioners didn't stop Hawke from commenting on their comeliness or otherwise. While he was living at the manse, Hawke would usually be gone after breakfast and wouldn't be seen again much before bedtime. To Beck, it seemed that he regarded their home 'almost as a hotel'. The understanding was that he would vacate the small back room any time that it was required for a visiting churchman, with Hawke going to stay with Hazel in a flat she shared with an Australian couple.[34]

Although Beck says that Hawke didn't drink alcohol while he was staying at the manse, there were surely nights when the binge-drinking student returned to his room the worse for wear. According to Hedley Bull, Hawke 'would drink most nights'.[35] One of those nights was when he downed two and a half pints of lager in record time. There was a tradition at University College that allowed students to be challenged by the president of the Junior Common Room if they came to dinner wearing a loud tie, failed to wear their gown, spoke ill of a woman or swore while at the table. It was failing to wear a gown that saw Hawke challenged. Students would grab any available gown hanging outside the hall and walk into dinner as if it were their own. When Hawke found his had been purloined, he went in without one and was promptly challenged. The butler was duly summoned with his stopwatch and Hawke was forced to drink two and a half pints from a pewter cup that was kept specially for that purpose. If he managed to do it within twenty-five seconds without his lips leaving the cup, and also managed to beat his challenger, he would escape the humiliation of having to pay for both their beers. The college record had been set by a South African student, who'd done it in thirteen seconds. Hawke rose to the challenge, setting a new record of eleven seconds. As he later observed with some satisfaction, the 'feat was to endear me to some of my fellow Australians more than anything else I ever achieved'. That may have been because Hawke ensured it would come to their notice by having it listed as a world record in the second edition of the bestselling *Guinness Book of Records*, which was first published in 1955 by twin brothers Norris and Ross McWhirter, who'd been Oxford graduates and members of Vincent's, where they'd presumably shared an ale or three with Hawke, and who needed entries for their book.[36]

While that brought him fame, another of his many drinking episodes almost brought his time in Oxford to an end. After learning to fly the Air Squadron's rudimentary Chipmunks – Hawke later boasted of having 'engaged in acts of lunacy over the Cotswolds' – he joined his fellow airmen at the squadron's annual dinner on a rain-sodden night in November 1954. Amid much heavy drinking, one of them became so drunk that the inebriated Hawke offered to drive him back to his college, with the Scottish cricketer Jimmy Allan accompanying them. It was well after midnight, after leaving the college, that two constables patrolling in their car saw Hawke's little van shoot out of a side street onto St Aldgate's, the city's main thoroughfare, and speed off, driving erratically and dangerously fast. Suspecting the van was stolen, they took off after it. The pursuit went on for more than two kilometres before the police finally drew abreast of Hawke and signalled him to stop. With the driver honking his horn and the other constable shining a torch at him and waving his arm out of the window, Hawke responded by honking his own horn, making a rude gesture and speeding away until he reached the squadron's car park, perhaps hoping that, dressed in their dinner suits, they might be able to blend in with the many similarly attired students. No such luck. The police car pulled in behind them, only to have the drunken Hawke reverse into them, possibly because he'd failed to apply the handbrake.[37]

If Hawke hadn't damaged the police car, he might have escaped with a caution. It didn't help that he was also 'very aggressive [and] sarcastic and seemed to think he was being persecuted', warning the police that it would be their word against his and Allan's in court. Unimpressed, the police summonsed him on four charges, the most serious of which was dangerous driving. When the case came before the magistrates the following January, Hawke pleaded guilty to the three minor charges and not guilty to dangerous driving. With his mates looking on from the gallery, and despite Beck appearing as a character witness and Allan supporting his story, he was convicted on all counts and fined a hefty £21/10/- and had his licence suspended for two months. Hawke was distraught at the possible implications of the conviction, which he feared could see him sent home in disgrace. That possibility seems to have caused him to suffer a bout of depression, with Brigadier Williams describing how the result of the case 'put him off his over-certain stroke for a while'. Hawke feared the reaction of his parents and his supporters back home, since his letters had painted a very different picture of his activities in Oxford. In fact, he was convicted at around the same time for trying to make off with a street lamp and fined £5. He would later say that he'd been fined £40 for the driving offence, rather than £20, and been disqualified for six months, rather than two, which had left him feeling both 'terribly ashamed' and 'very angry' because he regarded it as a stitch-up. He said that he 'decided to appeal, and if I lost the appeal to throw it in and go home'.[38]

The distraction of the court case would not have helped with Hawke's performance in the examination for his final Arts subject, which he nevertheless passed, albeit without distinction. He could now add a second degree to his résumé. But he was unlikely to get an Oxford degree to go with them unless the Rhodes Trust gave him additional time to complete his thesis, still barely begun. An additional term would suffice, giving him until the end of 1955. The senior tutor at University College supported his appeal for extra time, noting that Hawke had 'a rather rocky beginning which was due to difficulty with his subject and to some extent with a hope that he was going to get a Blue'. Now, with Wheare attesting that Hawke was 'doing very good work', and with the senior tutor agreeing that he was 'now behaving very sensibly and working very hard', the Rhodes Trust complied with Hawke's request. It would have been embarrassing for the Trust to have one of their scholars return home a failure.[39] Now he just had to clear his court record.

It was apparently a policeman in Beck's congregation who had suggested that Hawke should appeal, predicting that the police witnesses wouldn't be so confident in giving their evidence before a judge of a higher court, and that was how it turned out. Hawke's barrister got the hapless constables to describe how Hawke had put his arm out the rolled-down window in the rain to make a rude gesture, only for the barrister to point out that this was physically impossible, given that the window had to be opened by sliding it across rather than rolling it down. That stumble discredited the police evidence and, after Jimmy Allan told the judge he was a student at the same college that the judge's father had attended, Allan's evidence was given a degree of credibility that it had not received from the magistrates. With his appeal won, a triumphant Hawke and his supporters thronged into Vincent's, where Hawke was hero for a day, although a relieved Brigadier Williams thought he was lucky to get away with it.[40]

The court cases provided ample material with which to amuse his mates in the pub, but the newspaper reports also had the potential to ruin his reputation, both in Oxford and back in Perth. Yet, despite his worries, Hawke came through with his reputation relatively unscathed. As so often during his life, most people overlooked his misbehaviour, whether because of his status, their fear of his possibly aggressive response or a feeling that his infractions were peccadilloes compared to his attractive qualities and the contribution he might make as prime minister, which he never tired of telling people he would become. As Williams observed in the wake of the court case, one 'can't help liking' him because 'he gets cracking (he is a bundle of energy)'.[41]

So it was that Hawke's wild behaviour at Oxford didn't prevent him from securing a scholarship to a six-week summer school in 1955. Hazel drove him to London, where he caught a train to Salzburg, in the American-occupied part of Austria. The seminar series in American studies had been established at the beginning of the Cold War in 1947 by students and staff from Harvard University, led by Austrian historian Clemens Heller, and was financed largely by private foundations and the US State Department as part of the American effort to stem the spread of communism in post-war Europe. After that first seminar, the US Army prevented Heller and one of the other participants from returning to Salzburg for fear they were too left-wing. The seminar was held in the lakeside Schloss Leopoldskron, a beautiful eighteenth-century palace, which had been built by an archbishop who was responsible for expelling Protestants from the city. During the interwar years, the building had been restored by the theatre director Max Reinhardt, who founded the Salzburg Festival.[42]

The students for the seminar were drawn from Europe and the United States and recognised as future leaders of their countries, while the distinguished academics came from several American universities to lecture on American culture, history and politics. Hawke was attracted to that particular summer session because it was on the American industrial system, which offered him the opportunity to contribute the results of his own research on the Australian system. There was also a rich program of extracurricular activities, from sport to dances and concerts, organised by the students, who lived and dined onsite in communal conditions. Part of the purpose of the seminar was to establish linkages among the students and with the American faculty members.

Twenty-five-year-old Hawke seems to have become closest to the Jewish-American labour economist Ben Seligman, who was seventeen years his senior and, according to Hawke, 'took me under his wing' and tolerated his wild behaviour. Seligman would soon become an economist with the Union of Automobile Workers, before becoming a professor at the Massachusetts Institute of Technology and director of its research centre for labour relations. Among many other topics, he would write about the effects of automation and the economic causes of poverty in the United States. He was the economist Hawke might have been if his life had taken a different course. It's impossible to know what Hawke gleaned from the Salzburg Seminar and his conversations with Seligman. At the least, they provided him with some American comparisons for inclusion in his thesis, while on a lighter note his friendship with Seligman saw the pair catch a spectacular performance of Mozart's *The Magic Flute*, as part of the Salzburg Festival, with scenery by Austrian expressionist painter Oskar Kokoschka. Described by one critic as a 'miracle-work', it wasn't sufficiently impressive to keep the hard-living Hawke awake.[43]

Salzburg was a brief hiatus in Hawke's frantic final year, as he kept up his campaign to secure a cricket Blue and raced to complete his BLitt thesis, still hoping to take it further to a PhD. Hawke's chances of a Blue were reduced when Colin Cowdrey graduated and departed the cricket team, yet Hawke played on. One academic recalled how Hawke 'drank excessively, wenched excessively, played cricket excessively' in summer, and in the winter stopped drinking and wenching and studied as if his life depended upon it, only to begin again when the following summer dawned. His final summer in Oxford was the best one yet. Blessed with good weather, he and Hazel filled their days with tennis, swimming or punting on the river. Hawke also played cricket practically every day that summer, including a game with other players from the British Commonwealth in a benefit match against an English county side. The practice and the playing were to no avail. That year, he couldn't even secure a place as twelfth man in the Oxford team. Brigadier Williams noted sagely that 'his cricket is a little like the rest of him – he starts hitting a bit too early in an innings'.[44]

With the end of his time in Oxford fast approaching, Hawke had to get serious about his thesis and his future. On Wheare's recommendation, and with his supportive reference, he applied in August 1955 for a scholarship to the Australian National University, proposing to continue his partially completed study of the arbitration system with a view to graduating with a PhD.[45] If successful, it would be his fourth degree. Meanwhile, as the days shortened, he squirrelled himself away in a corner of the Rhodes House library, spreading out his notes from parliamentary debates, arbitration reports and newspaper records as he wrote successive drafts of the 70,000-word thesis. Hazel would type these up in her digs after work before Hawke discussed them with Wheare.

Because Wheare had been content for Hawke to go his own way, there was no friction between the pair, despite Wheare's conservative views. Hawke recalled 'many hours of lively discussion ... over numerous glasses of his dry sherry', which helped to shape the work that Hawke finally submitted in November 1955. He might have struggled had he not also had the help of Hazel and several friends, whether it was commenting on his drafts or helping with the typing. It was 'some tribute to him', noted the bemused Brigadier Williams, 'that everyone does rally round. He has a host of friends: it's all slightly inexplicable until one remembers that one is one of them oneself.'[46] That had been so for most of Hawke's life, and would continue.

His thesis – 'An Appraisal of the Role of the Australian Commonwealth Court of Conciliation and Arbitration with Special

Reference to the Development of the Concept of a Basic Wage' – was based on his reading of the Federal Convention Debates of the 1890s and Commonwealth parliamentary debates from 1903 to 1904, as well as Commonwealth arbitration reports, law reports and labour reports, and buttressed by reference to just twenty-four books. Of these, Hawke singled out conservative historian Keith Hancock's history, *Australia* (1930), as being 'particularly stimulating', while disparaging the radical historian Brian Fitzpatrick's *The British Empire in Australia* (1941) and his *Short History of the Australian Labor Movement* (1940) as giving 'a quite misleading interpretation of the circumstances of the creation of the [Arbitration] Court'. Hawke was not immune from his own misleading interpretations, with the first sentence claiming that 'the first colonists landed at Port Phillip [rather than Port Jackson] in 1788'. Beyond that opening blooper, his thesis traced the development of the arbitration system, with Hawke showing how the court had assumed increasing authority to set the basic wage however it saw fit. Rather than following the historic Harvester judgment of 1907, when the court had awarded a wage increase based upon the need for workers to maintain a reasonable standard of living for themselves and their families, the court increasingly based its decisions on the capacity of employers to pay any increase. The 1953 basic wage judgment went further, partly at the urging of Colin Clark. It agreed to abandon the automatic quarterly increases altogether, arguing that their abolition would bring the runaway inflation under control.[47]

According to Hawke, the judges of the Arbitration Court were lawyers rather than economists and shouldn't have based their 1953 judgment on 'inadequate' economic arguments about the cause of post-war inflation. The fact that the court then denied it was doing so provoked Hawke to even greater heights of rage: he declaimed angrily in his thesis that the court had 'carried this senseless denial of the relevance of theory and policy to an almost unbelievably ridiculous extreme'. He would have been angrier had he realised that the court had been influenced by the arguments and lobbying of his former supervisor. Concluding his thesis, Hawke called for the power of the court to set the basic wage, the various margins for skill and the hours of work to be removed altogether. Instead, the court should be simply a court of appeal for industrial disputes, while a new bureau composed of employer and employee representatives should be established to set the basic wage, skill margins and hours of work. This bureau should set the basic wage according to the needs of workers, with automatic adjustments for inflation and increases in productivity. For Hawke, it was all about 'maintaining harmonious and equitable industrial relations'. Although the examiners duly passed his thesis in January 1956, noting that he knew much more about the topic than they did, it was as much a job application as an academic thesis. As D'Alpuget observed in her biography of Hawke, the thesis was 'at heart, a politician's speech'.[48]

With his Oxford degree confirmed, Bob and Hazel set about preparing for their return to Perth by ship. Although Hawke now had three degrees, he would have felt little sense of triumph. Whereas John Stone had returned with a first-class honours degree in Economics, Hawke had done the equivalent of an Australian honours thesis, and had failed to win the coveted Blue. The final observation on Hawke's college student card noted that he was 'not very clever or industrious, but he improved a great deal as a person while he was here'. Ensconced in his study at Rhodes House, Williams also thought Hawke was 'much improved' and confessed that he would 'miss him and his brash ways'.[49]

Hawke had wanted to return home as Dr Hawke, but his passion for sport and his propensity for carousing had got in the way. Reverend Beck recalled how, as Hawke and Hazel were taking their leave in the hallway of the Summertown manse, his wife 'was almost ticking Bob off for the way he treated Hazel', telling him that 'if he was going to marry her, he'd got to behave better, not really thinking of his other girlfriends'.[50]

However remorseful Hawke was, and however much his behaviour upset Hazel and disturbed his close friends, he was not about to change. After all, his narcissism and his upbringing had convinced him that he was no mere mortal and subject to normal strictures. That conviction had helped both to empower and hobble him. It was a burden that he'd taken with him to Oxford, and it would return with him to Australia.

CHAPTER SEVEN

1956–1958

The first thing Bob and Hazel did after arriving back in Perth in February 1956 was get married. It marked the end of a six-year engagement that had seen their relationship tested by an unplanned pregnancy and subsequent abortion, and then by Hawke's philandering and binge-drinking, in both Perth and Oxford. Hazel had learned to look the other way. After all, they'd also had plenty of good times, travelling England and exploring Europe in their van, and she'd pursued pastimes of her own. Now, with Ellie looking on from the front pew of the historic Trinity Church on Perth's St George's Terrace and with Clem helping to officiate, the couple exchanged vows, while Hawke's mates from his university days, now married and embarked on respectable careers, provided support.

On his mother's instruction, no alcohol was laid out in the adjoining church hall where the reception was held, which meant their thirsty friends were left to drink warm fruit juice and soft drink on the stinking-hot day. Hawke compensated for that when the newlyweds spent the night in a city hotel before driving off in his parents' car to stay four nights at Caves House, a licensed two-storey guesthouse set above the spectacular rocky beach at Yallingup. The place was popular with honeymooners, although theirs was no normal honeymoon. They spent part of their time working on four talks that Hawke was doing for ABC Radio, with Hazel pounding away at a portable typewriter as he dictated to her in the shade of the extensive garden.[1]

It was a brief break before they turned their backs on Western Australia, not knowing whether they would ever return to live there. As for many graduates of the time, Perth seemed to offer no future.

Some of Hawke's contemporaries sought careers in Britain or the United States, while others drifted across the Nullarbor to find challenging careers in Sydney or Melbourne. A few headed to the fast-growing national capital to work in the public service. That was where the Hawkes were headed after he was successful in securing a well-paid scholarship to do a PhD in the Law Faculty of the recently established Australian National University, where he'd have little if any teaching to do and plenty of opportunities to travel for his research.[2]

Before leaving Perth, 26-year-old Hawke underwent a medical examination, a requirement for the scholarship. The doctor found him to be healthy, which was true enough. Then, presumably taking Hawke's word for it, he certified that Hawke was 179 centimetres tall. In fact, Hawke was 173 centimetres tall, about the average height for Australian males at the time. Photographs from the 1950s suggest that the weight on the medical certificate was about right at sixty-eight kilograms, although the certificate's claim about him being 'temperate' in his drinking was well wide of the mark.[3]

Despite having the scholarship, Hawke dallied with the idea of using his uncle's influence as West Australian premier to secure preselection for a federal seat in Canberra. The thought of more years at university before getting a proper job weighed on his mind. A seat in parliament would allow him to catch up and perhaps surpass the career trajectories of his friends, while also satisfying his mother's ambition and his own desire to be employed in the service of the public. However, the 1950s and 60s were not a fruitful time for people aspiring to be Labor MPs. Whether such an offer was in his uncle's power at the time can't be known, but it was never made, and a penniless Hawke decided to explore the prospects of an academic career. He would also lay more groundwork for a possible future in politics, far from his mother's censorious gaze.[4]

As the train slowly took him away from his former life in Perth, Hawke had plenty of time to think about what might lie ahead in a life that had so far failed to live up to his parents' exalted hopes, or his own. Despite the distance, he would be weighed down by the burden of those expectations in Canberra.

His mother had already expressed her disappointment on his return from Oxford. She'd expected that he would come down the gangway in Fremantle hailing her in a voice that was more like that of Prime Minister Bob Menzies than of the porter handling their luggage. No such luck. As she greeted Bob and Hazel, she couldn't help expostulating in dismay: 'You don't sound any different from when you went away.' She had always feared that his distinctive Australian drawl would be a barrier to success in public life and had hoped the experience of living in England would achieve what his schoolboy elocution lessons had failed to do.[5] Little did she realise that her son's defiant attachment to his Australian accent, as well as his penchant for beer drinking, would provide a more certain pathway to political success.

Like Hawke, the Australian National University had unfulfilled promise. It had been established by the Chifley government along the lines of Princeton's Institute of Advanced Study and was meant to bring together leading academics and postgraduate students across a core range of disciplines, from medicine and physics to political science, history and law. The teaching of undergraduates would be left to the long-established Canberra University College, which largely operated out of army huts in the nearby city centre and taught part-time courses to public servants.

Kenneth Wheare had advised on the shape of the ANU's Research School of Social Sciences and even been mooted as one of its possible professors, only to decline the offer. Instead, it would be his student who would step from the train in Canberra, intending to write a PhD thesis. It would mean three years of study under the supervision of Professor Geoffrey Sawer, a 46-year-old lawyer who'd graduated from Melbourne University and then worked as a solicitor and barrister before becoming a senior lecturer in law and later taking charge of Australia's wartime propaganda broadcasts to Japan. When Hawke arrived in March 1956, Sawer had just returned from a sabbatical in London, and was both the founding Professor of Law and the Dean of the Research School of Social Sciences. He was well connected politically. Apart from being a member of the CIA-backed Congress for Cultural Freedom, he was a friend of Labor leader and former High Court judge H.V. 'Doc' Evatt, and was well known to Prime Minister Menzies. Sawer met Hawke and Hazel the day after the couple's arrival and, with Hazel unwell, took Hawke off to lunch and 'showed him around', pointing out the office adjacent to his own that Hawke would be able to use. He would be his first graduate student and the only student in the law school, which had just one other staff member, Sam Stoljar, who entertained them all at his flat at University House that night with 'sherry and [a recording of soprano Elisabeth] Schwarzkopf'.[6] In Oxford, Hawke had been supervised by a professor of agricultural economics and then by a professor of government; now he would be supervised by a lawyer for a thesis 'on the assessment of the basic wage by industrial tribunals in Australia'.[7] Once again, Hawke would know more about the subject than his supervisor.

In 1956, Canberra was enjoying a post-war boom but still had little more than thirty thousand people. Although the federal parliament had been established there in 1927, the city remained a national capital in the making. Most of its monumental buildings were yet to be built, and the Molonglo River hadn't yet been dammed to create Lake Burley Griffin. Canberra's monuments at this time were the mountains that surrounded its spreading suburbs. The city itself was a reflection of the post-war migration that was transforming the ethnic make-up of Australia. Together with the nearby Snowy Mountains Scheme, the construction of houses and office buildings in Canberra attracted an army of workers from a range of backgrounds, who were forced to find accommodation in barracks-like conditions, often located across the New South Wales border in Queanbeyan. Many were Italians. Indeed, there were so many Italians that by 1957 Canberra had its own Italian-language newspaper, while a union newsletter had pages in Italian, German and Polish. As for the university, it was in an early state of construction when the Hawkes arrived, with a mishmash of old timber buildings that had served as a hospital and other facilities, all of them scattered across the expansive bushland campus. The two staff members of the Department of Law were housed in the former hospital's labour ward.[8]

In those early years of the university, the grandest of its buildings was University House, designed to be an Australian version of an Oxford college. It followed the Oxbridge tradition by having high table in its hall and a Latin mass before dinner. Money was splashed about to ensure that it was aesthetically attractive from a distance, with sculptures in the landscaped grounds and bespoke furniture and fittings in its spacious rooms. It was one of the smartest places in

Canberra, and had been opened in 1954 by the Duke of Edinburgh during the new Queen's tour of Australia. There was accommodation for unmarried and some married staff without children, graduate students and visiting academics, as well as a library, a Great Hall, a Ladies' Drawing Room, a music room, a bar and meeting rooms adorned with modern art and set along an elongated, ornamental pond. It was hailed as 'the best hotel in the city'. As well as providing accommodation, its various amenities made it a focal point for the university's academic and social life. It was here that Bob and Hazel fetched up with their luggage to begin their married life proper on 20 March 1956.[9]

Bob was in his element. Canberra was a relatively youthful place, filling up with young men and women and married couples, where hormones and alcohol combined to make a sex-charged cocktail. Hawke later described it as 'incestuous but exciting'.[10] It was 'a place without grandmothers', as British historian David Fieldhouse observed after spending several years there in the 1950s, where the normal restraints didn't necessarily apply.[11] Public servants, politicians, diplomats and academics came from elsewhere and lived in the bush capital, mostly without their extended family. Moreover, as Hazel would later observe, 'most Canberrans were just sailing through to somewhere else', whether it was an overseas posting for diplomats, a big-city appointment for public servants or a position at a major university for academics.[12]

Hawke's parents clearly feared that their son might succumb to the pressures that had sent him off the rails in Perth and Oxford. In an attempt to provide a restraining influence, and to encourage him to remain within the church, they contacted the minister of Canberra's Congregational church, the Reverend Alan Farr, requesting that he look after the young couple. At church on 25 March, Farr asked one of his congregation who was living at University House to meet up with the new arrivals. Niel Gunson was well chosen. He'd begun a PhD in the Department of Pacific History and came from a family with a long involvement with the Congregational Church. He was aware of Bob's existence already, having heard stories from a female cousin in Melbourne with whose family Hawke had stayed a few years previously while attending a church youth camp. Gunson's cousin had developed a crush on Hawke, 'and vice versa'. Now Gunson was being asked to make himself known to the Hawkes, with the church secretary telling him that Hawke was 'a remarkable young man and one day will be prime minister of Australia'. Gunson met the Hawkes in the foyer of University House and invited them to his room for coffee, with Hawke remarking that Gunson's cousin was a 'beaut looker'. As a sign of Hawke's growing political passion, no sooner had he downed two cups of coffee than he headed off to the old hospital for a Monday-night meeting of Canberra's ALP branch, which was under the chairmanship of political scientist and biographer Professor Finlay 'Fin' Crisp, while Hazel was taken by Gunson to a lecture by an American Buddhist monk on 'design for living', part of a popular quest for meaning in a world that had been battered senseless by war and was now threatened with an even worse one.[13]

There was hope for an end to the Cold War after the death of Joseph Stalin and a speech by his successor, Nikita Khrushchev, in February 1956, which conceded some of the mistakes and crimes of the previous regime, only for that hope to evaporate when Soviet tanks crushed the Hungarian uprising in October that year. Instead of easing, the Cold War intensified.

Hawke was one of many Australians who was trying to make sense of it all. He went with fellow student and future New South Wales Liberal leader Peter Coleman to sit in the public gallery at Parliament House to watch Evatt and Menzies debate the dramatic events that were unfolding in Europe. Hawke also accompanied Coleman to a public lecture by the American writer James T. Farrell, who was there as chairman of the American Committee for Cultural Freedom, part of the Congress for Cultural Freedom. Although the lecture was held in the hall of Canberra University College, with a reception at University House, most academics stayed away and Hawke seems to have been unmoved by Farrell's anti-Soviet rhetoric. It's not clear if he also went with Coleman to hear B.A. Santamaria give a lecture which, according to Coleman, 'stunned the packed hall'. It was the culmination of a conference of Santamaria's National Catholic Rural Movement, during which the fervent anti-communist painted a picture for the five hundred delegates of an idyllic Australia based on 'independent family farms' rather than a concentration of population into industrialised cities.[14] Such views were anathema to Hawke, not least because they were underpinned by the economic thinking and Catholic beliefs of Colin Clark, with whom he'd fallen out so badly.

Those Cold War years were a tumultuous time for Labor. After the defection of the Soviet spy Vladimir Petrov in 1954, Evatt had defended some of his staff who'd been accused of being communists, and had attacked the largely Catholic, right-wing branch of the party in Victoria, accusing it of being run by the far-right and secretive 'Movement' led by Santamaria. The subsequent furore caused the Victorian branch to split and the Catholic dissidents to form the Australian Labor Party (Anti-Communist), later to be renamed the Democratic Labor Party. No such split occurred in the New South Wales branch, which also included the Australian Capital Territory. That meant that the staunchly anti-communist members of the party – known as the 'Groupers' because of their membership of industrial groups that were trying to wrest control of trade unions – remained uneasily within Labor's ranks in New South Wales and represented a majority of the Canberra branch.[15]

The divisions that Santamaria caused in the Labor Party were a political gift to Menzies, who was returned with a landslide victory at the federal election in December 1955, courtesy of preferences from the DLP. When the new parliament opened, just a few weeks before the Hawkes arrived in Canberra, the government benches had a familiar face from Hawke's time at UWA, Bill Snedden, who sat alongside another newcomer, Malcolm Fraser. A young economics lecturer from Melbourne – Jim Cairns – was among the new Labor MPs lining up behind Evatt.

Snedden wasn't the only one of Hawke's former rivals to be in Canberra. John Stone had returned from London to a senior position in the Treasury, while Max Newton had been appointed political correspondent for *The Sydney Morning Herald* and the *Australian Financial Review*. The economist Ron Hieser recalls that Hawke and Newton were 'very different and intensely competitive with each other'. The then hard-drinking historian Manning Clark described Hawke, Hieser and Newton as 'an inseparable trio, who went everywhere together, drank together'. One day, they arrived at his house to play table tennis, 'rushing in together – it was like a snowball – then rushed out together, a sort of ballet'.[16]

The 35-year-old Hieser had been a member of the Communist Party but was now attached to the Labor Party and part of Evatt's circle of advisers. Married with two children, Hieser had won a scholarship to ANU before becoming an economics lecturer at Canberra University College. Hawke became a part-time lecturer there in June 1956, giving two lectures a week on Introduction to Legal Method.[17] Hieser was 'a notorious character in the history of the university', observed historian Robin Gollan, 'but was a very able economist until the grog got the better of him'. Like Hawke, he was a keen cricketer and aggressive when drunk. Indeed, Sawer said he was 'very aggressive, drunk or sober'.[18] Hawke and Hieser could often be found drinking together in one Canberra bar or another. On one occasion, the inebriated pair had exhausted their money and were so desperate for additional alcohol that they rang Hawke's old friend from UWA's Liberal Club, John Knight, at his office in the Treasury to cadge a loan. When Knight tried to fob them off, Hawke and Hieser stormed into his office, demanding that he lend them £5, and then rolled out toilet paper to the door of the departmental head. They were only prevailed upon to leave when Knight was lent the money by his immediate superior.[19] Another of Hawke's drinking companions was Manning Clark. On one occasion, Hawke had to pick up the heavily drunk Clark from the gutter and drive him home, where Clark's wife upbraided Hawke for leading her husband astray.[20]

As the Cold War continued to cast its chill on Australian politics, and despite hydrogen bombs being tested off the West Australian coast, spreading radioactive debris across the continent, it was difficult for a left-wing party led by an increasingly inept and erratic leader like Evatt to gain traction. Shortly after Hawke joined the local Labor branch, a fellow member, professor of economics Heinz Arndt, launched a blistering attack on Evatt and called for a return to Chifley's more avuncular and moderate style of Labor leadership. Many in the Labor Party and the trade union movement were yet to accept that Australians were living in a new boomtime world, where the pre-war problems of unemployment and stagnant growth had been replaced by their opposites. The German-born and Oxford-educated Arndt wanted them to face the new reality. He'd already caused an outcry in Labor ranks when he joined with other economists to support a rise in taxation to end the inflationary spiral that the economic boom had caused. That outcry became louder when the Menzies government went ahead and levied a raft of taxes, some of which affected working people.[21]

Hawke may well have been in the audience when Arndt presented the Chifley Memorial Lecture, which roundly criticised Labor's lack of policies for countering inflation, arguing that it was thereby failing to protect the interests of working people. Although the lecture led to calls for Arndt's expulsion from the party, Hawke thought the economist was proposing 'constructive criticism in an objective fashion'.[22]

Amid this political turmoil, Hawke was intent on establishing a public profile for himself. Within a month of his arrival, he'd penned a long letter to *The Canberra Times* setting out the legal rights of workers who'd become unemployed because of cutbacks to government spending, and who were being harassed because they'd fallen behind on payments for goods they'd bought on hire purchase. He also engaged in correspondence with the editor of *The Sydney Morning Herald* about his familiar hobby horse, calling for the reinstatement of quarterly cost-of-living increases for workers' wages and contesting the paper's claim that this would only worsen inflation. At the same time, Hawke was becoming involved in Labor politics. After joining the party's ACT branch, he was soon elected as its junior vice-president and one of its delegates to the state electoral council. Hawke told his parents that the branch was controlled by the right-wing Groupers and was riven between pro- and anti-Evatt factions. Crisp led the latter faction, colourfully describing Evatt as a 'power-hungry desperado'. The faction supporting Evatt was allowed in 1956 to form its own branch, a move that was opposed by Crisp and initially by Hawke, who thought it would threaten the ability of the branch in the centre of Canberra to have good discussions and attract interesting speakers. He changed his mind after being persuaded that a suburban branch would attract new members to the party. Meanwhile, Hawke was elected as one of two student representatives on the University Council.[23] He had much bigger dreams.

As his mother had told him for years, Hawke believed his God-given destiny was to be prime minister. It was not in a branch meeting in a stuffy meeting room of the old Canberra hospital where he belonged, but in the prime minister's office in Parliament House, which he could see in the distance from University House. Hawke would catch the bus across the Molonglo River to attend sittings of the parliament, where visitors could watch debates and mingle with politicians and journalists in King's Hall. Meanwhile, on Sundays, he would cross the paddocks with Hazel to attend Canberra's Congregational church in Civic, not only for the morning service but also for the Men's Fellowship Teas in the evening. At one such tea, recalled Niel Gunson, Bob 'berated members for organising lawn-mowing for the aged instead of lobbying to save the world'. Hazel told Gunson that another church meeting had turned into a 'fiasco' after one member walked out, apparently taking offence at Hawke's argumentative stance.[24] Hawke was impatient to make the world better and didn't believe that could be done by pushing a lawnmower or preaching from a pulpit, as he'd watched his father do for decades. It was still unclear to him how his time in Canberra would serve his own mission in life.

There was a pervading sense of transience about Canberra. It was also a very male-dominated place, from the federal parliament and the public service to the military college and the university. Of the nineteen PhD students who enrolled with Hawke in 1956, only one was a woman, while the total student population of seventy-four included just eight women. When the Hawkes arrived at University House, there were thirty-six male students and four female students in residence, although there were other women residents who were academics or the wives of students or staff.[25] While most postgraduate students took their studies seriously and availed themselves of the cultural events and cross-disciplinary discussions, there was also a 'blokey', alcohol-fuelled culture among some of its residents. During Hawke's time in Canberra, that culture took on a new intensity, with him as one of the ringleaders. Perhaps it was the pressure of being singled out as a West Australian, with his distinctive accent a regular matter of comment, and of having to prove himself intellectually in ways that he'd avoided in Oxford. Manning Clark suggested that having to measure up in the meritocracy that was Canberra prompted Hawke to resort to an unpleasant aggressiveness, often fuelled by alcohol, in some of his dealings. 'Canberra was not kind to him,' said Clark, 'he was not considered top flight as an academic, he felt he had to prove his worth, as a West Australian, to the Eastern States.' Within a year of Hawke's arrival, professor of political science Leicester Webb described with horror the 'almost open sexual adventures among some men and women residents, while rowdy behaviour and drunkenness are far too prevalent'.[26]

Initially, under Hazel's watchful eye, Hawke seems to have behaved well, reading for his thesis, going to church each Sunday, playing tennis on the church court, potting billiard balls with fellow students at University House, attending Labor branch meetings, playing cricket and watching debates from the public gallery in parliament. And their marriage seemed to be a happy one. A close friend recalled how Bob and Hazel 'had a good, very warm, very happy relationship' and were 'very flirtatious with each other ... they were physically demonstrative, and there was a lot of giggling that went on'.[27] Gunson recalled how Hazel was 'very much the dutiful wife', although he thought 'she would have liked to have asserted her own independence more'. While they were living at University House, meals and cleaning were provided. They didn't have a kitchen, just a bedroom, a bathroom and a combined lounge and study. It was as if they were on holiday. But their stay didn't last long. In about May 1956, Hazel discovered she was pregnant, which Sawer thought was 'silly of them'.[28] Because children were prohibited at University House, the couple were compelled to move out. Fortunately, there were flats for married students and staff about two kilometres away in Masson Street, Turner. For Hazel, the shift was a blessing, because it brought her closer to her job as a receptionist and secretary at the Indian High Commission. It would be the first time they'd fended for themselves as a married couple. Bob cultivated fruit and vegetables in the garden of the flats and competed with neighbours to see who could grow the best tomatoes. They bought an old Austin car, which allowed them to access the limited range of shops in Civic and occasionally to venture further afield.[29]

While the couple might have presented a picture of domestic bliss at the flats, Hawke remained a member of University House and was a regular drinker at its bar, as well as at a couple of Canberra pubs. It was in the married student flats that Hawke became friends with Coleman, who later recalled how Hawke's 'indiscretions, passions, strange intensities, blindnesses and charm ... had helped make my

Canberra days tolerable'.[30] His charisma and manic energy made him a force of nature that Coleman clearly found attractive. Others found him exhausting, or worse.

It could be exhausting for Hawke as well. Gunson attended one party at the Colemans' flat 'where Bob was sleeping on the floor and was still there when everybody left'. It was perhaps just as well that the drink on this occasion caused him to adopt a supine state. Often, it was quite the opposite. Gunson described how 'Bob was very unpleasant when he was drunk, very unpleasant'. Margaret Steven was a resident in University House at the time and recalled several gatherings where she'd encountered Hawke with 'glass in hand', and how he'd struck her as being 'a colossal show-off, repellent'. Whereas other residents involved themselves in intellectual discussions, she felt that Hawke was 'an empty man, basically'. She concluded that he was 'a guy in a hurry, he knew more than anybody else and he wouldn't restrain himself in any discussion'.[31]

A fellow resident at University House was the Singapore-born Emily Sadka, whose Jewish parents were originally from Baghdad and Bombay. She had graduated from Oxford in 1941 with a history degree and eventually fetched up in Perth, joining her parents, who'd fled from Singapore prior to its fall to the Japanese. During Hawke's time at UWA, she'd worked as a tutor in the Department of History and doubtless would have encountered Hawke when he was seeking support for the International House Appeal. Now she was in ANU's Department of Pacific History. Photographs of Sadka reveal a serious, exotic-looking woman who was described by one of her fellow academics as 'a beautiful person'. Soon after his arrival in Canberra, Hawke spent a lot of time in the room of the now 35-year-old Sadka, whom D'Alpuget described as 'a woman of rare strength of character'; she claimed that Sadka and Hawke were intellectual soulmates rather than bedmates. While Sadka may have played the part of a muse to the inebriated Hawke, his behaviour provoked rumours of there being something more. Hawke's drinking mate Sam Stoljar, who'd been tossed out of University House in June 1956 after 'openly sleeping' with a married research student, described how the 'flighty playboy would make fifty thousand circles around Emily's door before he would knock'. Manning Clark described it as 'a very touching relationship'.

Similarly, a woman on Sadka's staircase described how she 'would hear Bob whispering "Let me in, Emily" late at night after he had spent the day boozing with his low-down friends', suggesting that the remorseful Hawke 'was a soul in torment, looking for purification'. He would also have been looking for alcohol after the bar had closed. Sadka, said Gunson, 'wasn't afraid of him' and, 'being the gentle person she was, she let him in ... because he wasn't physically attracted to her she wasn't in danger'.[32]

Hawke's descent back into heavy drinking seems to have begun in late 1956. He'd joined the Northbourne Cricket Club in September, but there were so many players that he had trouble getting picked for an A-grade game. Nor did he play more than a few matches with the university club, which was captained by Hieser, who didn't think much of Hawke's abilities. His desire to see a big score next to his name, together with his experience in Oxford, had made him averse to risk-taking. 'He had no spark to his batting,' said Hieser, 'he was prod and poke.' Manning Clark also watched him play and noted how Hawke wasn't a very good cricketer and was terrified of failing. Even when he wasn't playing, Hawke would go along to watch and drink with the players. Hieser recalls seeing Hawke watching one match in his shorts, all the while 'admiring and stroking his bare legs during the game'.[33]

Hawke later moved to the Turner Cricket Club, where the opening game saw him bat at number three and score 'a breezy 62 before being well caught'. He was sufficiently handy with the bat that he played for the ACT team in a match against the Goulburn team, only to have heavy rain bring play to an early close when he and his fellow batsman 'appeared set for a long stay at the wickets'. In an interview with D'Alpuget, Hawke described another occasion when the ACT team was playing in Newcastle and he played as if possessed, as the bowlers 'went through contortions to try to get me out but I just hit them and hit them – fours and sixes – until I was 78 not out'. Hawke claimed that a New South Wales selector was so impressed by his performance that he suggested he try out for the state team. It makes a great story, but no evidence has been found to support it. He certainly played with the ACT team in Newcastle on a blisteringly hot weekend in January 1958 but was run out for twenty-two.[34]

By December 1956, Hawke's drinking was such that Gunson mentioned it in his diary. Some thought that the drinking, and the 'loutish' behaviour that accompanied it, may have been prompted by Hazel's pregnancy, with Hawke subconsciously rebelling against the approaching burden of parenthood.[35] But it wasn't the first time he'd gone through bouts of heavy drinking and unbridled womanising. And the imminent birth of his first child, which he was convinced was going to be a boy, was just one of the factors contributing to the turmoil he was going through. He was also struggling with his thesis, as he was unable to develop an economic theory to explain the system of wage fixation.[36] Hawke may have made more progress had he been supervised by an economist rather than a lawyer. There was a lot riding on it. For one thing, he found any failure hard to take, and in Canberra there was no Colin Clark he could blame. If he was unable to secure a PhD, he mightn't get a good academic job. That said, he wasn't sure that he wanted an academic career, since he'd been asked by the Australian Council of Trade Unions (ACTU) to help with its basic wage case.

Back in June, for the purposes of his thesis, Hawke had sought permission from the ACTU to attend a special trade union congress that had been convened to discuss the unions' campaign for the restoration of automatic adjustments to the basic wage and the federal government's inclusion of penal clauses in its new Conciliation and Arbitration Act. Whereas the removal of cost-of-living increases undermined the living standards of working people, the imposition of penal clauses threatened trade union officials with jail for defending the interests of their members. The trade unions' campaign had obvious appeal for Hawke, while he had obvious appeal for the ACTU's English-born president, Albert Monk, and its new secretary, Harold Souter, who'd formerly served as its research officer. Not only was Hawke a qualified lawyer with some training as an economist, he had links to the Labor Party and his uncle was a Labor premier. Moreover, his Oxford thesis had been on the arbitration system and automatic cost-of-living adjustments, which was the issue of the moment. He came with a recommendation from the Canberra economist and statistician Horace 'Horrie' Brown, who'd been a friend of Ben Chifley, an economic adviser to the Labor Party and an expert witness for the unions in the 1952–53 basic wage case, only to have his painstaking and innovative evidence about productivity disregarded by the judges. Although Brown couldn't attest to Hawke's academic achievements, he could vouch for Hawke's palpable passion for the cause of working people.[37]

Following his experience at the trade union congress, Hawke approached Souter in September 1956 requesting details of the process involved in the ACTU's upcoming application for an increase to the basic wage, telling Souter that he 'would very much like to come down and get an idea of the procedure – and of course, if I can help in any way you know I would be glad to do so'.[38] On 6 November, Hawke received a call from Souter, asking him to fly to Melbourne to advise the ACTU's high-powered barrister, Richard 'Dick' Eggleston. Eggleston was an old friend of Sawer's, who had recommended Hawke's services to him. After going to Melbourne for the day on 8 November, Hawke was then joined by Souter for a week-long wage conference in Canberra, before they both flew back to Melbourne for the resumption of the wage case. Returning to the heavily pregnant Hazel in Canberra at the end of the week, he again left on the Monday to attend the court sittings in Sydney. It was a heady experience for a postgraduate student to be a participant in the process that he was writing his thesis about. It was made even better by the ACTU paying for all his expenses and insisting that they pay him an honorarium, which came on top of his scholarship money. As Hawke put it to his parents, '[H]ow lucky can you be?' By helping Souter prepare the union case, wrote Hawke, he was 'right in the middle of the show getting the best possible idea of how the whole thing works'. Moreover, he was 'enjoying it all immensely', not only because he was applying his 'academic and research experience to some practical use' but also 'because the union blokes are beaut fellows with whom it is a pleasure to be working'.[39] After nearly a year in Canberra, it seemed that he'd found his mission in life. He just didn't know it yet.

Hazel gave birth to their first child, a daughter, on 19 January 1957. In the same way that his mother had been convinced that he would be a girl, Hawke had been certain they would have a boy. In a letter to his parents in October 1956, he told them that Hazel would soon stop working, even though she was experiencing 'no troubles at all with young Junior'. The following month, he described how 'the young bloke gets livelier with each passing week'.[40] Hazel didn't have any preferences about their baby's gender. She just had a sense of 'indescribable' relief to be pregnant, after fearing that her abortion might have made her infertile. Hawke was also stressed by it all, telling Souter on 15 January that his 'fingernails remain their thoroughly well-bitten selves despite the fact that my wife continues to hold out for what seems an unnecessarily long time'.[41]

When she finally gave birth, it was a Saturday and Hawke was playing cricket. According to his probably apocryphal account, he was at the crease when he was told the news, which supposedly caused him to be bowled out for a duck. They named her Susan Edith, with the second name a nod to Hawke's mother.[42] In the wake of Susan's birth, Hawke's behaviour became more outrageous than ever. One episode, just five weeks later, became a legendary chapter in the history of University House.

Different versions of the event abound. Although she wasn't with him that night, Hazel tried to make light of it in her memoirs, saying simply that he 'jumped into the ornamental lily pond at University House late one night and upset a visiting bishop and, of course, the warden, with his loud, bawdy remarks'.[43] It was rather more than that. For one thing, the warden wasn't there on the night in question, 24 February 1957. Sawer, who also wasn't there, had to deal with the aftermath and later gave two versions of what happened.

In the first interview, done for the National Library in 1971, Sawer conceded that he had 'some difficulties with [Hawke], mainly arising from the fact that at this particular time he was going through some difficult personal circumstances with his wife and he was drinking far too much', noting that he was 'thrown out of University House through getting involved in drunken orgies and scenes of one sort or another'. In a diary entry at the time, Sawer described the 'row over drunken party at U[niversity] H[ouse] last night – Hawke and [history student Ted] Docker ringleaders. Hawke very bad – aggressive, bad language, abused women. Not very apologetic either. He's been humming around UH thus for 4 weeks.' Nearly twenty years later, Sawer gave more details in an interview for the ANU Archives, describing how Hawke had embarked on a drunken spree with several of his inebriated mates, including Docker, and was caught trying to climb up to a small window above the door of a terrified female student, 'who was in bed on the other side of the door. He was drunk, of course, and he was quite frequently drunk.'[44]

The assault on the female student's room was just part of the pandemonium, which went on into the early hours of the morning, upsetting a bevy of visiting Anglican bishops who were trying in vain to sleep. The details of the incident remain contested among the participants, the complainants, the shocked witnesses and those who heard about it at one remove or more. But it was the culmination of riotous behaviour that had been going on for weeks and in which Hawke had played a prominent role. According to Margaret Steven, there were 'about four or five of them and they hunted in a pack … They were violent. You wouldn't go near them without a hockey stick at least, really ugly, and that's the memory that remains with me.' They would 'get roaring drunk and go around the place banging on the doors and demanding more drink'. On the night in question, with every word being magnified in the quadrangle, 'the racket wakened me and I remember standing at the window in the dark looking out and watching these guys and hearing them and laughing to myself because I thought everybody else who had a room looking onto the quadrangle must have been watching too'. There was much 'splashing, roaring', recalled Steven, and 'I think someone fell in the water'.[45]

Some accounts have Bob stripping naked and swimming the length of the shallow ornamental pool before upsetting the outraged clergy with his bawdy shouting. The account given by Hazel in her memoir doesn't make any mention of him being naked. It also omitted his badgering of the female student. Other accounts claim it was one of his drunken mates who swam naked, egged on loudly by a similarly drunk Hawke. After interviewing Hawke for her biography, D'Alpuget says that he threatened to throw a professor into the pool before later that night 'swimming in it'. The professor concerned was 51-year-old anthropologist and former lieutenant colonel W.E.H. Stanner, who was also the bursar of University House. Some students thought it was all a bit of a lark. One woman recalled being 'most amused' on hearing 'obscenities floating through the still Canberra air'. She'd 'heard about rags in Melbourne. Now we had one of our own.'[46] At best, it was boorish behaviour by the apparently manic Hawke. These days, it would be seen as something worse and would probably lead to expulsion, and perhaps criminal charges. Even back then, there were serious, career-threatening consequences.

The university couldn't afford the scandal. It had already been the butt of regular criticism in the federal and state parliaments for supposedly harbouring a nest of communists who were living off taxpayers.[47] It didn't want Hawke's drunken escapades to be splashed across the front pages of the tabloids. The professors who'd been threatened and insulted were determined that the reputation of the institution would be best protected, and their own outrage assuaged, by disciplining the students concerned. Then, if the behaviour ever became public, the university could point to the punishment.

Stanner wanted to send Hawke and the others out of Canberra on the next train, but the deputy master of University House, distinguished physicist Mark Oliphant, decided to have them formally disciplined by a hastily assembled committee of the vice-chancellor and the deans. Hawke was deemed 'the ringleader in this as in many other unpleasant incidents' and agreed by the residents to be 'the major culprit'. According to the official account, it was 'only Hawke and Docker [who] used filthy language and [were] excessively exhibitionist'. Hawke had 'incited the others to the worst excesses of the evening. It reduced one of the woman residents to tears by an insulting remark made in the presence of Dr Stanner.' When appearing before the committee chaired by the vice-chancellor, Hawke denied being the ringleader and claimed not to remember using bad language, but he admitted urging others into the pool, although not going in himself, and also to being 'solely responsible for reducing [a] girl to tears'.[48]

Although he apologised, there was damning evidence from the other accused students about Hawke's behaviour. He was only saved from being expelled by the intercession of Sawer, who reminded his colleagues that Hawke was a Rhodes scholar and that his thesis was promising. He also said that his 27-year-old student 'suffered of adolescence perpetuated by [the] Oxford system'. That was unfair to Oxford. In this, as in other similar episodes during his life, Hawke's behaviour was likely to have been an expression of his particular form of narcissism, which had been evident since his childhood. Sawer's intervention and Hawke's contrition ensured that he escaped relatively lightly. One student was cautioned and the others fined, while Hawke,

Docker and another of the rowdies were banned from University House. 'Horrible day,' wrote Sawer in his diary. In a letter to the master, Hawke promised 'that the stupidity of the events has impressed itself on me' and would not be repeated. There was little chance of that, now that he'd been banned from the premises. And he was unsuccessful when he tried six months later, with Sawer's support, to have the ban lifted. Hawke was also forced to resign as the student representative on the University Council.[49]

Canberra was a small community and Hawke could ill afford to earn the enmity of its senior academics, upon whom his future employment might depend. He was several years older than most graduate students and would be lucky to get his PhD before he was thirty. Moreover, with the birth of Susan, Hazel was no longer able to work, which meant they would be spending the next two years living on Hawke's scholarship money and his earnings from his part-time lectureship at the university college.

Adding to the pressures was the apparent impasse he'd reached with his thesis. As Sawer recalled, Hawke had 'wanted to try to produce an economic explanation, an explanation in terms of economic theory of the basic wage'. However, it wasn't a topic for which an economic theory could be developed, not even by Sawer's overly confident student, who fancied himself as an economist despite his relatively limited study of the subject. Hawke's efforts to develop a theory were in vain. He and his supervisor consulted 'every blooming economist in the country and none of them would come to this party', said Sawer. They all said it was 'complete nonsense'. Nevertheless, Sawer still believed that Hawke could produce an acceptable thesis. It just wouldn't be of 'very high standing'.[50] Hawke was on firmer ground when he limited himself to talking about the history of arbitration, which he knew inside out and which he made the topic of a talk to the Law Society that Sawer thought was 'excellent'.[51]

It was while beset by these worries that Hawke gave vent to his anger after being confronted by a policeman while he was double-parked at the shops in Civic. It was just two days before their infant Sue's first birthday, and Hazel had insisted that he stop the car so she could go into a store. When the policeman demanded he park properly, Hawke refused to do so, claiming it was unsafe while he was holding the baby.

Unless, of course, the policeman would like to hold their daughter until he could park and return to get her. With neither man budging, and the car remaining stubbornly double-parked, Hawke was issued with a parking infringement. Rather than paying it, he appeared in court to cross-examine the policeman and argue the injustice of the charge, noting that he wasn't causing any obstruction on the wide street. As Hawke well knew from his experience in Oxford, magistrates don't like going against the evidence of police officers. Yet he pressed ahead and suffered the inevitable result when the magistrate told Hawke that he could easily have placed Sue safely on the floor in the back of the car so he could comply with the police direction. Rather than appealing the decision, as he'd done in Oxford, Hawke let the trifling matter lie.[52] He was leaving Canberra and would put the embarrassment of another court case behind him. More importantly, he'd be sidestepping the intractable problem of his thesis. Fortunately for Hawke, a new opportunity had presented itself.

The Oxford thesis, together with his legal training and his PhD studies, had allowed him to present himself as an expert on the basic wage. Indeed, he boasted that he 'knew more about the basic wage than anyone else in the country'. Now he'd helped to prepare the union arguments when the basic wage case was being decided over the summer of 1956–57. Hawke hadn't put the arguments himself; that was left to Eggleston. But Hawke had been in attendance, fidgeting with frustration when Eggleston's junior barrister was left in charge of the case after Eggleston hived off to London to represent employers in a case before the Privy Council. According to Hawke, his carefully prepared facts and arguments were 'butchered by the junior! I suffered the tortures of the damned.' He later prepared a report on the decision for the ACTU, spending several weeks during the winter of 1957 at his parents' house in Perth, where he was able to show off baby Susan. While there, he corresponded with Harold Souter, suggesting how the ACTU should approach the next wage case and offering to do 'anything else you would like me to do'.[53] His sights were clearly shifting from a life in academia to a career with the unions.

Hawke attended the next basic wage case, bringing folders of research material to inform the union arguments. The chief judge and president of the commission, Sir Richard Kirby, watched with amusement from the bench, noting that Hawke 'was unable to sit still and we could see he was nearly going mad with frustration, wanting to jump up and have a say'. Much to Kirby's consternation, Hawke later barged into his chambers, 'introduced himself as a research scholar and started asking questions as if he were entitled to, ignoring the fact that I was of judicial rank and deciding a matter that he was involved in'. Hawke pressed Kirby on the ability of the court to decide 'very important questions of national economics' when none of the judges had any formal economic qualifications. Despite a sneaking admiration for the uppity young man, Kirby showed him the door.[54]

Hawke's brashness, together with his legal and economic training, made him attractive to Albert Monk, who approached him after a union dinner in a Sydney pub and proposed that Hawke go to Melbourne and work as the ACTU's research officer. While the appointment of a university-educated person was a novel idea at a time when unions were traditionally run by officials elected from among their members, Monk recognised Hawke's passion for public service and perhaps sensed his need to perform on a bigger stage. Hawke also needed the money. Not that Monk and Souter were offering him a permanent job. According to their account, they wanted him to provide the facts and figures and legal arguments that their barrister could deploy in arbitration cases. In other words, he would be doing full-time what he had been doing on a casual basis for an honorarium. And the position was only meant to be occupied by Hawke for perhaps two years, after which he would be expected to allow another young academic to take his place. In Souter's view, the union movement would thereby gradually amass a number of academics who would be 'interested in and sympathetic to us, and that they would spread knowledge of wages arbitration throughout the university system'.[55]

The limited nature of the position caused Hawke to procrastinate, as he weighed his options and consulted with Hazel and Sawer. If he accepted the ACTU position, there was a danger that he might close the door on the academic life to which he was still somewhat attracted. Although Arndt had wanted him to teach a course on industrial relations for the Commerce Faculty at Canberra University College, with the lectureship also involving a course on industrial law for the Law Faculty, there was no guarantee he would be selected for this, given his reputation and the quality of the applicants who were likely to apply when the position was advertised internationally in September 1957. Moreover, the students were mostly public servants pursuing courses part-time, which meant the classes were held at night in the huts of an old workers' hostel.[56]

In the event, Sawer convinced him not to accept an academic position until he had completed his PhD, which Sawer was confident he could do by May 1958, along with a 'publishable book'. Neither of those things happened. His supervisor was less averse to Hawke accepting the offer from the ACTU. He was conscious that his student's attributes were more suited to the calling of an advocate than a professor. After supervising him for more than two years, Sawer felt that Hawke 'did not have the makings of a first-rate academic' because he 'lacked a kind of analytical acuity, which a really first-rate research lawyer needs'. Anyway, said Sawer, he 'genuinely associated himself with the Labour movement' and 'had its interests at heart and on the whole was more attracted with the prospect of being an industrial advocate'. Sawer hoped that the job in Melbourne 'would straighten him up and result in his going on drunken benders less frequently'. Sam Stoljar agreed with Sawer's assessment, noting that being a scholar 'requires the kind of devotion which Bob does not have – all his interests led him away from the sleepier, less energetic, lazier if you like, academic's devotion'.[57]

There was another possible career move. Albert Hawke was still premier of Western Australia and had encouraged his nephew to try for a seat in the federal parliament. But when Hawke made inquiries in October 1957, he was advised by Albert and the party's powerful state secretary, Joe Chamberlain, that the chances of him securing preselection for a federal seat were not good. Anyway, he was told that there was little point in putting his name forward, since there was no chance of Labor winning any additional seats at the next election. Albert and Clem talked it over too, and urged Bob instead 'to strengthen your position & wait until next time'.[58] The position in Melbourne was much more attractive and didn't preclude the possibility of Hawke later completing his thesis and going on to pursue an academic career. Hazel, meanwhile, was mindful of their precarious finances and hopeful that the ACTU position might provide a pathway to the political career Hawke craved.[59] No doubt she was hopeful, too, that it would lead to a moderation of the heavy drinking and wild behaviour that had characterised their last year in Canberra.

Hawke couldn't help leaving Canberra without having a spat with Sawer over his removal expenses, with the library also pursuing him for overdue books. Sawer, too, suspected that he 'probably has a lot of my books'. At least Sawer's books were returned prior to Hawke's departure in late May 1958, which meant that the Hawkes' farewell party – where Sawer, ironically, presented him with books – had a 'pleasanter atmosphere' and Hawke was in 'very good spirits'. Sawer was ambivalent about his departing student, describing him in his diary as 'arrogant, selfish, drunk, but also [a] good sport, generous, good brain'. All in all, a 'weird mixture', wrote Sawer, who was disappointed that 'my first student has been little help to the University or the Department but we've done him a little good & enabled a trained man to enter a necessary job – legal expert with ACTU'.[60]

Hawke himself later wrote of having had a sense that his move to Melbourne represented 'a point of destiny'.[61] So it would prove to be.

PART THREE
Advocate

CHAPTER EIGHT

1958–1961

There was little sense of triumph when Bob and Hazel packed Susan and their belongings into their Ford Zephyr in mid-1958. They were heading south to Melbourne in a car that had been bought with a loan from Hazel's father. Hawke had failed to achieve the hoped-for PhD in Oxford. Now he'd failed to achieve it in Canberra, or to write the book that he'd promised his supervisor, Geoffrey Sawer. And he was leaving the city in debt.

All this perhaps explains why he devoted little more than a paragraph of his memoirs to the two largely wasted years that he'd spent at the ANU. His former Oxford supervisor Colin Clark may well have had Hawke in mind when he wrote in his 1958 book, *Australian Hopes and Fears*, that Rhodes scholars 'include a number who never seem to feel quite sure of themselves once they come back to Australia'.[1] If Hawke ever read Clark's comments, it would have provided him with further cause for anger. Yet there was some truth in the observation.

After spending nearly twelve years at university, Hawke was just six months shy of his twenty-ninth birthday. It was a time when most people were long settled into their careers and raising families. He'd boasted for years of one day becoming prime minister. As part of this journey, he'd established a place for himself in Labor's ACT branch and secured a seat on the New South Wales Electoral Council. In the process, he'd become acquainted with some of the party's most powerful identities, benefiting from his relationship with his uncle Albert. If his own political ambition was to be realised, he would have to start anew in Melbourne. At least the ACTU provided a better launching pad for that ambition, with Hawke later noting that it would take him 'into the heart of the labour movement' and fulfil his oft-repeated desire to be of 'public service'.[2]

For years, the ACTU's two full-time officials and their few support staff had been crammed into three small rooms in the historic Trades Hall building in Lygon Street, Carlton. Back then, almost every occupation had its own trade union, from felt hatters to rubber workers, and most Victorian unions had their offices in that wide wedding cake of a building. Most of the union officials drank at one of the two pubs across the street, the Dover or the Lygon (later renamed the John Curtin), depending partly upon their political allegiances. As a mark of its growing power and influence under the presidency of Albert Monk, the ACTU had moved out of Trades Hall, having bought land on the opposite side of Lygon Street and built a two-storey office building. Surplus space upstairs was rented out to the legal firm Maurice Blackburn, which specialised in working on behalf of trade unions and the ACTU, mainly on workers' compensation cases. To remind its officials of their national reach and responsibilities, the wood that was donated to panel the walls had come from every state.

The building was only four years old when Hawke was welcomed by Monk and Souter to take up Souter's old position as research officer. Apart from the two officials, there were only three other staff when Hawke arrived. They were the secretaries for Monk and Souter and a female junior assistant.[3] The appointment of a university graduate in law and economics was a sign that the organisation was embarking on a process of expansion and modernisation to make it better able to serve its constituent unions, which were struggling to remain relevant in a nation that was being transformed by unprecedented levels of immigration and industrialisation.

Many of the immigrants were stepping ashore at Melbourne's Station Pier and working in the shops and factories that had sprung up to service the burgeoning population. In the late nineteenth century, the city had been the biggest in Australia and one of the leading commercial and cultural cities of the British Empire, only to stagnate during the interwar years, when immigration subsided and the White Australia policy stunted the nation's imagination. That was all changing by the time of the Hawkes' arrival in Melbourne, as European immigrants asserted their presence in the city and the country's racially restrictive immigration policy increasingly became an embarrassment to its people and an impediment to the country's future security and prosperity.

The lessons of World War II, the hosting of the Olympic Games, the advent of television and the arrival of Asian students under the Colombo Plan combined to lift the racial blinkers from the eyes of a growing number of Anglo-Celtic Australians. Apart from anything else, the war had taught them that their nation's security relied on it having a larger population, which could only come from beyond the British Isles.[4] That was something that Hawke had long known and welcomed, even if Melbourne's growing population made it difficult for him to find a home within easy reach of his work. It would be the biggest city in which the couple had ever lived, but it wasn't unfamiliar to Bob.

Hawke had visited Melbourne numerous times, in his roles as a student leader, church youth group leader and adviser to the ACTU. He knew that the north and west of the city were largely crowded with working-class families crammed onto relatively small blocks of land, while the south and south-east boasted more salubrious homes set among large gardens and with easier access to the beaches of Port Phillip Bay. Within days of starting their search, the couple had decided on the beachside suburb of Sandringham, which was a few kilometres beyond the wealthy beachside suburb of Brighton and located at the end of a trainline that took about half an hour to disgorge commuters into the city.

The suburb was reminiscent of Perth during their easygoing childhoods. According to Hazel, who was already pregnant with their second child, they decided they 'wanted to be near the sea'.[5] Of course, the beaches of Port Phillip were very different from those of Perth, where dunes overlooked the breakers rolling in from the Indian Ocean. In contrast, the narrow, sandy beach and sheltered waters of Sandringham were set below a red cliff, from where bathers could look down upon the jetty and yacht club at Half Moon Bay, together with the rusting hulk of the colonial warship HMVS *Cerberus*, which had been sunk off the beach to provide a breakwater and diving platform for bathers.

Bereft of savings when they arrived in Melbourne, Hawke had to secure an advance on his salary before he could pay the deposit on the house at 13 Keats Street. For the auction price of £4400, they got a four-roomed, low-slung timber bungalow, about thirty years old and largely devoid of adornment. Tacked onto the rear, a lean-to provided a narrow sunroom looking out onto the deep, north-facing backyard, mostly grassed, which made it ideal for children and outdoor entertaining. The front of the house looked onto a wide street with a mix of brick and timber houses of similar vintage, all displaying Art Deco features and built on large blocks shaded by trees of middling height. A great attraction of Keats Street was the ten-minute walk to the beach and similarly short walk to the station and shops of Sandringham. There was also a hospital, a private girls' school and several golf courses close by.[6]

Although Bob could reach Sandringham station in a brisk twelve-minute walk on the days that Hazel needed the car, he mostly drove at a frenetic pace the twenty kilometres to his office in Carlton. There was much for him to do. As the research officer, he was expected to prepare the material that the ACTU would present to the recently formed and non-judicial Commonwealth Conciliation and Arbitration Commission as part of its argument to lift the basic wage and restore the automatic adjustments that had been stopped in 1953. Back then, productivity figures had been presented to the court after being compiled for the ACTU by Canberra economist Horrie Brown. The country was grappling with inflation caused by the Korean War and the court had interrogated Brown for a week, putting his newly developed measurement of productivity under such sustained scrutiny that he had a heart attack.[7] At the end of it all, the ACTU argument for a wage rise based upon productivity improvements was rejected. Moreover, in an attempt to reduce inflation, the court stopped the automatic adjustments to the basic wage.

Undeterred, the ACTU had continued to compile figures to reinforce its arguments about post-war productivity increases. Souter had shouldered that task when he was research officer and now it devolved to Hawke, who acted like a solicitor, amassing evidence that the ACTU's barrister could deploy to fight the upcoming wage case, which was due in 1959. It required him to read through industry and government reports to extract relevant figures, and also to meet with union officials, either at Trades Hall or at the bar of the Lygon Hotel, to hear about their first-hand experience of productivity improvements in the nation's factories and workplaces.[8]

Hazel might have hoped that the teetotal Souter, with his upbringing as a Seventh-day Adventist, would exercise a good influence on Hawke.[9] No such luck. Pubs in Victoria closed at six o'clock, which saw a lot of heavy drinking in the hour between the end of work and the publican calling 'Last drinks, please'. The custom of shouting a beer for all one's companions increased the consumption that would otherwise have occurred, although Hawke was notorious for not shouting a round when it came to his turn. There was so much work for Hawke to do as he met union officials and discussed industrial issues, and he often did it with a beer in hand. As Hazel later conceded, his ability to more than match his companions glass for glass helped him overcome the prevailing prejudice among union officials against university graduates. It led to 'heavy sessions' at the bar. Peter Coleman recalled meeting Hawke after work in 'a pub in Lygon Street that displayed faded pictures of sundry political hacks or heroes on its walls and then [going off] to a party across the road ... where drunk officials sang snatches about the bush, the wild west and the deep south'. At the end of it all, Hawke drove home, dropping Coleman off along the way, with Coleman describing how Hawke 'shot along St Kilda Road hunched over the wheel peering moodily through rimless glasses. At the junction he swung into orbit and spun around the circus a dozen times looking for the right exit, the right way home. Each time as we sped past I would call out: "There it is! There!" – each time too late.' On one of the nights that Hawke took the train, he fell asleep, either through inebriation or overwork or both, and was taken all the way back to the city, where the otherwise empty train was put away in the yard for the night. When Hawke awoke, he was forced to 'stumble back along the track in the dark and hail an expensive taxi ride home'.[10]

The blokey culture of trade unions in the 1950s was a reflection of the prevailing sexism in Australian society, where women were still expected, and sometimes required, to resign from their employment when they married. It was generally accepted that there was a world of work peopled mainly by men, and a domestic world of women and children where fathers were often a remote presence. That was particularly true in middle-class and working-class families of Anglo-Celtic background.[11] It was also true of the Hawkes, with Hazel leaving paid employment just before she had her first child and not returning to work until her children were adults.

After leading a much more interesting life in Oxford and Canberra, Hazel wasn't wholly satisfied with her position as a mother and homemaker. For some time, she had few friends of her own in Melbourne and was largely excluded from Bob's life. He had the ACTU office staff to do any secretarial tasks and no longer required her assistance. It was only on weekends that she would get some insight into his new world, when he might spread his wage case papers across the lounge-room floor or when some of his union mates called around for a barbecue or to help with concreting the driveway, painting a room or building a carport. But handing around bottles of beer or sharing sausages among the backyard throng was very different from the exciting life she'd formerly led.

Perhaps trying to recapture earlier times and connect her world to Bob's, Hazel would occasionally take Susan in her pusher to visit him in his office, or seek him out in the back bar of the Lygon Hotel. She might even sit with Susan in the public seats of the Arbitration Commission as he advocated on behalf of the unions. She was perhaps trying to see for herself whether his new responsibilities, at both home and work, had caused him to abandon his old roistering ways. In that, she would have been disappointed, since the behaviour that had been frowned upon by professors at both Oxford and the ANU, and which had almost led to his expulsion from both those places, was tolerated and even admired by some of the union and Labor Party officials with whom he now socialised. Souter wasn't one of them. He ordered modesty boards for the front of the desks of the three female staff members, so the lascivious newcomer couldn't eye off their legs. Souter also instructed that none of the young women were to be alone with Hawke when he moved to an upstairs office or worked there on weekends.[12] It was a wise precaution, but Souter couldn't prevent him from pursuing a string of women in his ceaseless search for the unconditional love that always eluded him.

He thought he'd found it when he began an affair during his early days at the ACTU with a petite, red-haired ballet dancer, Beverley Richards. Born in New South Wales, she moved with her family to Adelaide in the late 1930s, where she began ballet lessons and was soon winning competitions. In 1950, she was chosen to dance with the Australian National Theatre Ballet in Melbourne, and toured with that company throughout Australia and New Zealand. She went to London in 1952 to continue her studies, returning home in December 1954 to tour with the recently formed Walter Gore Ballet. But success eluded her. It wasn't long before Gore had returned to London and Richards was struggling to find regular work as a dancer, and was appearing instead in an American musical comedy, *Bells Are Ringing*, which proved a flop in Melbourne when it was staged in April 1958. It was around this time, through her friendship with a female employee of the ACTU, that she met Hawke. Although he was having an affair with an air hostess at the same time, his relationship with Richards would be one of his longest and most intense.[13]

While Hawke grappled with his new position and was seldom home for dinner, the pregnant Hazel concentrated on being a mother to young Susan and making gradual improvements to the facilities and decoration of their two-bedroom home, with its sitting room and dining room off the central hallway and a small kitchen and a laundry at the rear. To cover some of its bare boards, Souter gave them a carpet, while a friend from Canberra who'd earlier moved to Melbourne helped Hazel with 'sewing and painting' and provided 'an old briquette heater', since there was no heating in the house apart from the fireplace in the sitting room. Laundry was done manually in a copper trough, with the washing then put through a wringer. The house was unsewered, which meant the toilet was located towards the back of the garden. Rather than going outside during wintry nights, the family used chamber-pots. They'd bought a new mattress, but they slept with it on the floor because they couldn't afford a bed. Hazel slowly amassed other essential items of furniture, buying them cheaply at auction or knocking them together from whatever materials she could gather or buy. For entertainment, they had a record player and, courtesy of Ellie Hawke, a piano. Buying one of the newly introduced black-and-white television sets was a luxury they couldn't yet afford.[14]

Occasionally, they would go to a friend's house to watch Graham Kennedy's popular variety show *In Melbourne Tonight*, but they both thought such suburban pastimes were 'tame ... after our carefree past', Hazel later wrote. Sitting silently in front of a television set would have also tested the patience of the garrulous Hawke. Although the couple enjoyed some idyllic evenings listening to records, Hawke began spending less and less time at home as he was drawn to his work, along with the heavy drinking and womanising that had come to characterise his adult life. 'Before long I was seeing very little of him,' recalled Hazel, who usually had dinner alone with her infant daughter. Weighed down by her growing loneliness, she flirted with 'the idea of fleeing Melbourne', but never did, accepting that she had 'a job to do, and there I stayed'. In truth, Hazel's options were limited. As a pregnant woman with a young child, she could go back to Perth and stay with her parents or leave Bob and live a life of poverty in Melbourne. To what purpose, though? It would be difficult to openly acknowledge the problems in their marriage, particularly to her father, who'd been critical of Bob and with whom she did not get on. Instead, she dispelled her loneliness and sadness by immersing herself in caring for Susan, soaking up the sun on the beach and enjoying a sense of achievement from her homemaking. She also took solace from Hawke's work at the ACTU. She believed in his life's mission and accepted that the piles of paperwork that he brought home would take all his attention at weekends.[15]

A big test came in early 1959, when the ACTU Executive asked Hawke to act as their advocate during the basic wage case. In the view of the commission, any increase to the basic wage had to be based on the economy's 'capacity to pay' rather than responding to the changing rate of inflation. It thereby scrapped the historic and rather problematic Harvester decision of 1907, which had required employers to pay a wage that was sufficient for a male worker to support a wife and three children in 'frugal comfort'.[16] The Harvester decision had certainly made no allowance for women workers with family responsibilities, who continued to be paid much less than men. Now the 1953 decision had made it much worse for both men and women, as inflation was allowed to erode their 'real' wages.

Invoking 'the capacity of the economy to pay' as the basis for any increase had opened the door for employers and the Menzies government to argue that the economic circumstances of the mid-1950s did not justify anything more than the most minimal increase to wages. Fortunately for workers, the state of full employment and the availability of overtime allowed many of them to work additional hours and their unions to demand over-award payments.[17] But those unskilled workers who relied solely on the basic wage were adversely affected by the ruling in 1953, which was still in place when Hawke began work in Melbourne.

When he'd assisted the ACTU barrister, Dick Eggleston, Hawke had watched in palpable frustration as the judges, who were lawyers with no training in economics, blithely dismissed the unions' economic arguments. In his Oxford thesis, Hawke had complained of untrained judges being expected to follow arguments and economic theories based upon competing statistical evidence from unions, employers and the federal government. Invariably, they came down on the side of the employers and the government. The ACTU had tried to circumvent the arguments about the economy's 'capacity to pay' by arguing that increasing productivity justified workers being given a wage increase. However, the notion of being able to measure economy-wide increases in productivity was still a novel one and beyond the ken of the judges, much to Hawke's annoyance.[18]

With each case, the ACTU's arguments about productivity were becoming more sophisticated, as additional material was compiled from company and government reports. However, the economists on the witness stand were questioned by an ACTU barrister who had no more formal economic training than the judges he was trying to convince. Eggleston's repeated failure to win over the judges, and his decision in 1958 to take on a case in London and leave the basic wage case to his junior, helped to convince the ACTU Executive that their legally trained research officer should be given a chance to prove his mettle by representing the unions. It would also save the ACTU a great deal of money if it could avoid having to pay a barrister and an instructing solicitor for the several months that a basic wage case took.[19]

For Hawke, after less than six months in the job, this was a great compliment, but it also presented him with a challenge. For all his grandiose talk about being an economist, he had limited training in the subject and would require intensive tutoring if he was to convince the judges to abandon the notion of 'capacity to pay' as the basis for deciding on any increase.

The hapless Horrie Brown, who'd recommended Hawke to the ACTU, was the obvious economist to approach for help. Hawke was also assisted by two up-and-coming economists. The first was Brown's

ANU colleague Wilfred Salter, who'd been a friend of Hawke's at UWA before going off to England to do a PhD at Cambridge. The second was Eric Russell, an economist from the University of Adelaide. Like Hawke, they were also jovial and sports-loving, fond of a drink and keen to leave the world better than they'd found it. All were political economists who agreed with Hawke that the commission was not only depriving workers of their rightful increases, but also holding back productivity growth in the broader economy. By relying on the dubious notion of 'capacity to pay', the commission was keeping wages low in declining industries, and thereby keeping unproductive industries alive that should have been encouraged to transform or allowed to contract or even expire. At the same time, growth industries with a greater 'capacity to pay' were being burdened with higher wages and had their growth prospects thereby hampered. The highly protected Australian economy was thus less competitive than it might otherwise have been, and consumers were forced to pay higher prices.[20]

While Hawke was hunkered down, Hazel's pregnancy was coming to term. The imminent birth was unfortunate timing for Hawke. The wage case was due to begin on 24 February and the baby was due not long after. With so much riding on the outcome of the case, not just for the workers of Australia but for Hawke's career at the ACTU, he suggested to Hazel that she and Susan should fly to Perth so that she could have the baby there and her parents could provide her with the company and assistance she would need.

In the event, that option became redundant after Hazel sought relief from the heat one day on the beach at Sandringham, and later panted her way up the cliffside path with two-year-old Susan in a pusher. Late the following night, after spending part of the day on her feet making an apricot chutney from a neighbour's fruit, she felt the first signs of an early labour. In a panic, and with Bob not home, she called her doctor, who confirmed her fears and then had the doctor call Bob, who came home to arrange for Susan's care before driving Hazel to a nearby hospital and then going home to sleep. When he called by the hospital the next morning, Hazel was able to show him his longed-for son, who was six weeks premature and weighed just 2.3 kilograms. According to Hazel, Hawke was overcome with a mixture of 'emotion at the birth of his son, and exhaustion'. A bout of jaundice saw young Stephen detained for several days in hospital, while Hazel returned home to take care of Susan, expressing milk for her new baby which Hawke would take into hospital each morning on his way to work.[21]

Stephen's birth and the consequent turmoil at home added to Hawke's exhaustion. He couldn't let it distract him from the task at hand. He would hide himself away in his upstairs office for days, with the publican's wife, Rosie Harding, bringing him meals as he scribbled out notes and got his mind around the arguments he planned to present to the three judges. One of the judges, 72-year-old Justice Alfred Foster, lived in Sandringham, just around the corner from Hawke, and may have witnessed or heard of Hawke's more intemperate suburban moments. He had been a member of the Victorian Socialist Society alongside future prime minister John Curtin before joining the Labor Party and becoming, like Curtin, a staunch anti-conscriptionist in World War I. Appointed as a County Court judge and later as a judge of the Arbitration Court, he had reduced the working week from forty-four hours to forty, and in 1950 increased the basic wage by a massive £1 a week at a time when it was just £7 a week. Foster had long wanted to restore the quarterly cost-of-living adjustments and so was sympathetic to the ACTU case, but he feared that having Hawke as its lead advocate would jeopardise the chances of convincing his two fellow judges. Privately, Foster urged Monk to engage a senior barrister in place of Hawke. Although his intervention was arguably improper, Foster's fear was a reasonable one. However, the ACTU Executive decided to press ahead with Hawke.[22]

All Hawke's strengths were on display when the case opened in Melbourne on 24 February 1959. Journalists, union officials and judges were left agape as the 29-year-old Hawke angrily tore into the decision of 1953 and demanded that the judges admit the error of their ways.[23] Kirby was the only one of the three who'd been involved in the 1953 decision and, unknown to Hawke, had been among the minority who'd opposed abolishing cost-of-living adjustments. But because the judges had decided to present the 1953 decision as a unanimous one, Kirby became the focus of Hawke's attack. The usually amiable judge thought Hawke was behaving like a religious zealot, demanding 'confession and repentance' for the supposed transgression of 1953 rather than convincing the court to change its view by persuasively arguing the case. Regardless of his sympathy for Hawke's arguments, Kirby resented being told by Hawke that he'd been 'a bloody fool and a crook' for being part of the court that made the decision in 1953.[24] It was as if Hawke were channelling his mother on the beaches of Perth, when she used to breathe fire and brimstone and brandish a cirrhotic liver in the faces of bemused bathers.

Mustering all the passion of which he was capable, Hawke beseeched the judges to accept the ACTU case on behalf of all the workers who'd been left short-changed for the last six years. The previous year, the judges had given them a miserly increase of just five shillings and no cost-of-living increase at all. The result of the various decisions had caused the workers' share of national income to slump from 60 per cent in 1953 to just 50 per cent in 1959. Hawke now demanded they be given a ten-shilling increase in the basic wage, along with an extra twelve shillings to make up for the cost-of-living payments they should have been paid.[25]

Over the three months of sittings, Hawke set out the evidence to support the ACTU's demands. He put Salter on the stand to present statistics showing that workers who relied on the basic wage had been receiving a declining portion of the national cake, while Russell explained how workers were also being denied their rightful reward for the post-war productivity improvements they had helped to achieve. Foster quickly set aside his reservations about Hawke and became a supportive voice on the bench. The others were more circumspect. Kirby later confided that he didn't understand the economic theory and consulted privately with other leading economists 'to help me understand in some depth what Hawke was talking about'. Just as telling as the evidence from the economists were Hawke's probing questions of the witnesses testifying on behalf of the employers, who cited the supposed inability of employers to pay and of the economy to bear any increase in the basic wage. Along with the barrister for the Menzies government, they argued instead for it to be reduced even further. Hawke skewered their arguments when he showed that the evidence presented by one of their witnesses, which had previously been accepted by the court, was false. It might have been game, set and match had Hawke taken a less confrontational approach. While his full-throated advocacy buoyed the union officials sitting behind him, it failed to impress the judges in front of him. While Kirby and Justice Francis Gallagher were willing to agree with Foster that the court had been wrong to base its decisions on the economy's supposed 'capacity to pay', they refused to concede that the court had also been wrong to stop the cost-of-living increases.[26]

When announcing their decision in June 1959, they broke with tradition and gave their separate views on the case. As expected, Foster was the most sympathetic. He wanted to restore the cost-of-living increases and increase the basic wage by £1. This would have been a triumph for Hawke, but he failed to win over Kirby and Gallagher. Despite the passion of Hawke's advocacy and the strength of his evidence, Kirby suggested that the increase should be only fifteen shillings, while Gallagher wanted it to be ten shillings. Eventually, they settled on an increase to the basic wage of fifteen shillings for male workers and eleven shillings and threepence for female workers. As for the automatic cost-of-living increases, Kirby argued that an annual review of the basic wage was preferable to quarterly increases based upon a rudimentary price index provided by the Commonwealth statistician. The latter, argued Kirby and Gallagher, carried the risk of increasing inflation. Their stand was a bitter blow for Hawke's campaign to have the automatic increases restored. At least he could take some satisfaction from the size of the increase he'd won, which was 50 per cent more than he'd demanded and more than double the previous year's increase. It would go within days into the pay packets of about two million workers. The judges had also conceded that, in future, the annual wage case would take account of both productivity improvements and inflation.[27]

Although the ACTU Executive denounced the increase of fifteen shillings as 'inadequate' and expressed 'complete disappointment' at the court's refusal to reinstate the quarterly adjustments, that was partly bluster.[28] The employers had more reason to be upset, not least because their highly paid barristers and witnesses had been bested by a loud, feisty union advocate who was economically and legally literate. And they became more upset when Hawke went on to win a 28 per cent increase for skilled tradesmen in a 'margins' case, which determined the amount above the basic wage that tradesmen were to be paid. The commission had not increased margins for five years, so there was a lot of catching up to do, even though the state of full employment had seen many tradesmen receive over-award payments in lieu of increases to their margins.[29]

Nevertheless, the two cases were embraced by unionists as marking the end of a long drought, and Hawke was embraced as the advocate who had persuaded the heavens to open. In his memoirs, he wrote of being hailed as 'the new young hero who had turned the system around', allowing workers once again to have a chance of using the 'arbitration system to get a share of the increasing real output they were helping to create'.[30]

The ACTU rewarded him by appointing a young research assistant, Ralph Willis, to help him prepare for the next case. Willis was a commerce graduate from Melbourne University and was working as a researcher in the Department of Labour and National Service. As a staunch Labor supporter and with his father a union organiser, the softly spoken Willis was going to be much more comfortable working for Hawke. Hopes were high that the coming years would see quarterly adjustments restored to compensate for inflation, and productivity accepted as the measure for increasing the real value of the basic wage. Together, Hawke and Willis wanted to drive a stake into the heart of the 1953 decision.[31]

After little more than a year in Melbourne, Hawke knew he had made the right decision to suspend his PhD and leave Canberra. Once the painstaking research and forensic advocacy was done, he would reappear in the pub, where his 'extraordinary stamina' would give way to 'idiocy'. It could take the intervention of Rosie Harding and her two sons to subdue him, sometimes locking him in a cupboard until someone was prepared to drive him home. As Hawke basked in the adulation, he knew there was no going back. He'd found his calling. Whether seated behind the desk in his upstairs office at the ACTU, performing in the hearing room of the Arbitration Commission or speaking to workers outside countless factory gates, he would campaign to improve the lives of ordinary Australians by righting the economic injustices to which so many were subject. This was the brotherhood of man, about which his father – who was now chairman of Western Australia's Congregational Union and chaplain of the freemasons – had talked so often.[32]

It would require a zealous devotion to the cause, which would mean even less time spent at home. To provide company and presumably protection for Hazel, they got a German shepherd pup, which they named Tessie. Not that Hazel had time to walk a frisky dog, now that she also had two young children. Fortunately, a friend of Hawke's – a research chemist named Bill Mansfield, the unmarried brother-in-law of the Canberra economist Ron Hieser – came by to exercise the dog. Apart from taking responsibility for Tessie, Mansfield also played tennis with Hawke on those Sundays when he was free from work.[33]

Convinced that the Arbitration Commission had left the door ajar for the reintroduction of quarterly adjustments, Hawke looked forward with great anticipation to the basic wage case in 1960. This time there would be no holding back. However, he didn't get a chance to assail the judges or closely question the witnesses for the employers. The economy had taken a turn for the worse, caused partly by the federal government lifting import restrictions, which had the effect of unleashing pent-up demand and raising prices. The inflationary impact was exacerbated by the 1959 basic wage decision, although that was yet to work its way fully through the economy. But the judges were anxious not to accelerate the inflationary effect of their previous decision and agreed with warnings from the federal government, which now employed Dick Eggleston as its advocate to argue against the ACTU submission.

In previous years, the government hadn't taken sides but had simply set forth the facts about the economy. Its new stance meant that Hawke was snookered before he began. As he pointed out, when times had been tough, the commission had rejected wage increases for fear of causing increased unemployment, and when times had been buoyant, it had rejected the union claims for fear of increasing inflation. And that was what it did this time. His hard work in presenting the ACTU case for an increase of £1/2/- and the reintroduction of quarterly payments was for nought. Instead of listening to several months of evidence based on his extensive research, the judges brought the case to an early close, accepting the government's submission that it wasn't the time to increase the existing inflationary pressures. The decision was blasted by the ACTU Executive as 'cowardly, evasive and spurious'. Hawke was similarly snookered when he asked the commission to increase annual leave for workers from two weeks to three. Although the commission acknowledged that additional leisure time was justified, it decided that 'the present was not an opportune time to grant the increase'. On this reasoning, wrote Hawke, 'the Unions can never win'.[34]

Hawke was distraught. He'd been convinced that his success in 1959 would see the Arbitration Commission take a more even-handed approach in which fairness would be their guide. His optimism had been misplaced and he came to see that his left-wing drinking companions were right: the Arbitration Commission was rigged against working people. He later reflected how the 1960 decision had made him 'crooked on the system' and was 'a factor in drawing me to the Left'. But his faith in the system was partially restored in early 1961, when the judges expressed greater sympathy with the union case. This time, Hawke's case was helped by having the venerable economist Sir Douglas Copland argue on behalf of the unions. At the time, Copland was perhaps the most distinguished economist in Australia, having been Professor of Economics at Melbourne University, the wartime prices commissioner for the Curtin government and the inaugural chair of the Australian Productivity Council. By the time he appeared at the commission, Copland was chair of the Committee for Economic Development of Australia and a director of several companies. His conservative pedigree would have helped to convince the judges of the sense of his arguments.[35]

But it was the frenetic Hawke, sporting his Oxford tie, who oversaw the campaign, with three days of opening arguments and twelve days of closing arguments that attacked previous judgments with a degree of vitriol that delighted the audience of unionists. His anger was partly driven by having learned, one Sunday morning at Foster's Sandringham home, about the role played in the 1953 decision by Colin Clark and B.A. Santamaria. Such was Hawke's anger that Kirby later recalled how the union advocate 'would stand there shouting, saying in effect I was a bloody idiot'. It was during this case that Hawke so intimidated an economist called by the employers that he declined to take the stand, for fear that his reputation would be ruined by Hawke's forensic questions. It was Hawke at his fiercest, with no quarter given to witnesses or judges. His closing statements saw him easing off his shoes and standing in his socks, with his voice giving out as he leaned on the lectern for support. The judges were affronted at first, then impressed, and finally sufficiently convinced to decree that annual increases would take account of inflation and every three years would compensate for increases in productivity, unless the employers could convince the commission otherwise. For the current year, they awarded an increase of twelve shillings.[36] The door that Hawke had prised open in 1959, only to see it slam shut in 1960, had been forced ajar.

The decision brought more adulation for the young advocate, which didn't help his relationship with Hazel, who'd given birth to their third child, Rosslyn, in November 1960. Even with Willis as his research assistant, Hawke was busier than ever. Apart from the burden of work at the ACTU, and the after-hours socialising at the pub and with his lovers, the interstate sittings of the Arbitration Commission opened up new opportunities, taking him away from the gaze of those who might easily recognise him. Willis often accompanied him on these trips and recalls how Hawke would book them into a pub in a side street in sleazy Kings Cross, where, after their work was done, Hawke would set off alone into the night. There is an account of him scaling a building in Kings Cross to access Beverley Richards' bedroom, and of him urinating in one of her clothes drawers when he woke one morning, apparently too inebriated to find the bathroom. Being the father of three children had done nothing to improve his behaviour. Hazel had endured this for years, hoping that he would one day put it behind him. But as Hawke revelled in his growing fame, she realised that he hadn't changed his ways and might never do so, particularly now that his public profile was enhancing his charisma and attracting women intent on a casual dalliance, or, like Richards, wanting more. Hazel blamed the drinking, which may have facilitated his drive for ceaseless sexual conquest, but it was hardly the cause of it. What was she to do? They were living largely separate lives and she feared that questioning his fidelity would only confirm what she suspected and spark arguments that could end their marriage. She would later say that she 'chose to remain silent', which was not quite true, since his attempts to keep his affairs secret only allowed her doubts to fester and provoked screaming arguments when a jilted Beverley Richards phoned their home.[37]

In his memoirs, which were published two years after revelations by Hazel in her own memoirs, Hawke claimed that he'd been unaware of the pain he was causing her. He blamed it on his sudden elevation to 'national hero status [which] is not the easiest thing to handle and certainly my behaviour at times was excessive and unintelligent'.[38] Indeed, the adulation was more than many would have been able to bear. His public persona as an advocate at the ACTU was overshadowing that of its two senior officials, Albert Monk and Harold Souter. It was Hawke who was hailed by officials at the annual ACTU Congress, who was increasingly quoted in the press and appeared on television, and who found himself the centre of back-slapping attention at the Lygon Hotel.

Although Souter had intended Hawke's position at the ACTU to be a short-term interlude in an academic career focused on law and industrial relations, there would be no going back. Hawke made that very clear when he went to Canberra on the Australia Day weekend in January 1962 to attend the annual summer school of the Australian Institute of Political Science (AIPS), where he spoke on the social and political effects of Australia's economic growth. He was speaking in the context of the rising unemployment caused by Menzies' ill-judged credit squeeze, which had almost cost him the prime ministership at the election held just weeks before. Had he remained at ANU, Hawke would likely have been among the audience rather than standing on the podium and speaking on behalf of millions of workers.

Some months previously, the AIPS had asked him to write an article on unemployment but he'd been prevented from doing so by Souter and Monk, who were always reminding Hawke that he was an employee and not an elected official. Perhaps they thought it was safe to send him to a gathering of academics, where the irate advocate was unlikely to cause more than a little tut-tutting over the teacups. Hawke was determined to do more than that. Letting fly from the outset, he used his typed-out talk to describe his audience as 'polite and comfortably situated people applauding platitudes, uncritical when confronted with nonsense and sublimely unaware of the economic and political realities which face this country'. In fact, the audience of more than seven hundred was drawn from 'nearly every walk of life and major interest in the community'. Hawke's anger was provoked by the presence of Colin Clark, who was warmly applauded for an opening address that decried the Australian preference for factories over farms and railed against the recent decisions of the Arbitration Commission. Clark called for a reduction in tariff protection, a repudiation of a state-planned economy and an embrace of competition, an increase in immigration and a shift of workers from factories to farms to encourage greater exports of primary products. Hawke was having none of this, declaring that his former supervisor was speaking on behalf of the DLP and 'its perverted programme for Australia'. Instead of Clark's prescription, Hawke harked back to the planned wartime economy of the Curtin and Chifley governments, which stood in contrast to the haphazard development of the Menzies years, with its alternating periods of 'minimum growth and ... stagnation'. Only a 'planned society', thundered Hawke, would allow 'the community's resources [to be] allocated and utilised for the benefit of the society as a whole'.[39]

Returning to Melbourne, he would have realised that his outburst would have no effect on the direction of the country. Even his work at the ACTU, where he could make only gradual improvements to the lives of Australians and was hamstrung by his subordinate position, could do little to effect fundamental change. He knew he would have to lift his sights higher.

He'd been talking for decades about becoming prime minister and remained confident that he would achieve his destiny. It was in 1961 that a young industrial lawyer, John Button, who'd begun working in the ACTU building for Maurice Blackburn, first encountered Hawke 'surrounded by cronies' in the adjacent smoke-filled bar. By the late afternoon, recalled Button, Hawke 'was mostly somewhere between less than sober and out of his brain'. Button was taken aback at their first meeting when an apparently sozzled Hawke offered him the position of attorney-general in a Hawke government. 'I hear you're not a bad lawyer,' Hawke said, 'you can have it if you want.' Button was 'flabbergasted'. It was not the reaction expected by Hawke, who responded with 'a frosty stare' and they 'never spoke of it again'. Although Button would become a senior minister in both the Hawke and Keating governments, he would never be the attorney-general.[40]

The incident provided confirmation, if such were needed, of Hawke's continuing conviction that he was on an ascendant political trajectory. He was the coming man, and would soon have his first chance to prove it on the hustings.

CHAPTER NINE

1962–1964

Ever since 1949, Labor had been kept out of power by the divisive and fear-driven politics of the Cold War. When the Labor Party split in the 1950s, the DLP had used its preferences to keep the Menzies government in power. So long as Labor was unlikely to gain government, it was difficult for Hawke to imagine how he might chart a course to the prime ministership. That had suddenly changed in November 1960, when Menzies moved to curb the boom that had been caused partly by the wage increases that Hawke had won in 1959, combined with the government's ill-advised lifting of import restrictions several months later. The resulting credit squeeze had caused a recession that saw unemployment spike at a post-war high of more than 2 per cent. Australians had become so used to full employment that they looked darkly on a government that threatened their prosperity.[1] They were given an opportunity to vent that anger when Menzies called an election for December 1961.

Instead of facing off against the brilliant but erratic 'Doc' Evatt, Menzies found himself campaigning against Labor's new leader, Arthur Calwell, and its energetic deputy leader, Gough Whitlam, who'd worked as a barrister in Sydney before being elected to parliament in 1952. With his home in the southern Sydney suburb of Cronulla, and then in Cabramatta in western Sydney, Whitlam was living among the aspirational middle class, who were often forced to reside in unsewered homes on unmade roads. With Whitlam's influence, the party broadened its appeal beyond its traditional base among the industrial working class to encompass the professional middle class of the burgeoning suburbs.

Labor came close to regaining power in 1961, almost unseating the Menzies government. The party was on such a roll that it seemed, on the night of the count, that Calwell had won the election. Even as the counting continued over the next several days, Calwell remained hopeful that the surprise swing of 4.6 per cent would be sufficient to make him prime minister. However, despite Labor winning 50.5 per cent of the two-party-preferred vote, Menzies managed to hold on by the narrowest of margins. The Labor Party had performed best in Queensland, where a policeman named Bill Hayden defeated a government minister, and where Labor won eleven seats to the government's seven. In the Labor stronghold of New South Wales, the election saw twenty-seven Labor MPs returned to the government's seventeen. It was a different story in Victoria, the stronghold of the DLP, where Labor won only ten of the thirty-three seats. That poor showing, together with an electoral system that was tilted against Labor, saw Menzies returned with a majority of one seat.[2]

Hawke would have been as disappointed as Calwell. The Liberals' stranglehold on Victoria might explain why he hadn't made any attempt to stand at that election. In fact, there were no safe Labor seats open to him in 1961, so he would have had to stand in a Liberal-held seat if he'd wanted to enter parliament that year.

Interestingly, there was one electorate, Maribyrnong, where the Labor candidate came within several hundred votes of winning and where Hawke's youth, charisma and growing public profile might have been able to tip the balance for the ALP, and perhaps therefore have enabled Calwell to claim the prime ministership. Had it worked out that way, it would have ended the Menzies era, produced much-needed economic and social reform and probably avoided Australia's participation in the Vietnam War, thereby saving Australians – and perhaps the Vietnamese and Americans as well – from that needless horror.

For Hawke, though, it was probably best that he hadn't been a candidate. He'd only been working at the ACTU for two and a half years and there was much for him to contribute to the labour movement. He still hadn't fully redressed the injustice of the 1953 basic wage decision. Because the recession of 1961–62 had suppressed the inflationary surge of the 1950s, the ACTU couldn't make an argument in 1962 for a cost-of-living increase to the basic wage or to margins. It decided instead to demand an extra week's annual leave for workers, which would make it three weeks in total and four weeks for seven-day shift workers. The commission agreed in principle with Hawke's arguments but decided, in its usual cautious way, to delay implementing the additional leave until it was clear that the economy had absorbed the effects of the wage increases the ACTU had won the previous year.

That set the stage for 1963, when Hawke laid out evidence showing that the now-growing economy could afford to pay the increase in annual leave. The judges agreed, which represented a great victory for Australian workers. However, it didn't put additional money in their pockets to reward them for the productivity increases they had helped to achieve. Nor did it compensate them for the cost-of-living increases that had occurred since the commission's decision in 1959. Rather than seeking an increase in the basic wage, Hawke now called on the commission to increase the margin paid to fitters and for any increase to flow on to the skill margins paid to other workers. Willis sat alongside him, taking charge of a mountain of material at the union table and handing documents across to Hawke whenever a judge raised a query or the employers' advocate, Jim Robinson, raised an objection. Robinson had difficulty arguing the employers' case, given that full employment had returned and the country was experiencing rising prosperity.

While the judges didn't give Hawke everything he wanted, they did award a 6 per cent increase to compensate for the cost-of-living increase since 1959 and a further 4 per cent to compensate for the increase in productivity. It meant that the fitters' margin increased by ten shillings, which was a far cry from the fifty-three shillings Hawke had demanded. Any further increase would have to await the basic wage case that was set for 1964.[3]

Once the presentation of their cases was finished, Hawke and Robinson usually traipsed off to the nearby Beaufort Hotel on the corner of Queen and Little Bourke streets, where they would hold a court of their own, along with Willis and George Polites, executive director of the Australian Council of Employer Federations. The hotel's public bar was reached by way of the Queen Street entrance, while the entrance on Little Bourke Street gave access to the saloon bar and the lounge, which was described by a newspaper as being 'furnished like a club'. The arguments of the commission would be left behind as the men joined other after-work drinkers in the smoke-filled surrounds, lining up their seven-ounce glasses of beer before the barmaid shouted 'Last drinks' at six o'clock. Since the hotel served meals to guests staying in the bedrooms above, there was always the option of retiring to the lounge on the pretext of having a meal and thereby sidestepping the strictures of the licensing law. With his performance done for the day, the gregarious Hawke would relax and enjoy the badinage with Robinson, who'd been born the son of missionaries in China and whom Willis described as 'a very suave, articulate, friendly, intelligent guy'.[4]

Life was going well for Hawke. He'd cemented his place at the ACTU and now had a secretary and a research assistant with him upstairs, while Monk and Souter and their assistants remained below. In between court cases, it remained his habit to spend time in the adjoining pub, sometimes at lunchtime and often after work, swapping stories with unionists who'd risen through the ranks to become shop stewards or paid officials. Hawke relished socialising with these representatives of the workers, and with workers themselves, whether they were from the left or right of the labour movement; according to Willis, he 'could spend hours listening to their stories'.[5] It was akin to the life he'd led in the student pubs of Perth and Oxford, as well as in Canberra, where the stories were mostly about sport and women. Now they included tales of bosses and politicians and working lives, whether in the factories or on the wharves. As he listened, one eyebrow cocked, Hawke was imbibing the ethos and history of the labour movement, and learning its songs. They would be hymns that he learned by heart and would sing enthusiastically at labour gatherings for the rest of his life. By now he'd stopped going to church and had turned his back on the lessons that his father and mother had preached from the pulpit, and which he had impressed in turn upon the boys in his Sunday School classes in West Leederville. He was left with his father's powerful and inspiring notion about the 'brotherhood of man'. This was his new religion, and the pub his church.

Hawke and his drinking companions would often kick on at the nearby Police Club. He had become friendly with the Police

Association's secretary, Bill Crowley, after helping him win a big pay rise for new recruits in the early 1960s. At the end of the night, and with a bit of concentration, he usually managed to drive himself home to Hazel without mishap, although he was once sent the bill for a telephone pole that he'd apparently toppled.[6]

But getting home safely wasn't the end of it. If he was too drunk or too late, or smelled too much of perfume rather than cigarettes and beer, he would have to run the gauntlet of a stern-faced Hazel in her dressing-gown. She knew there were other women, as there always had been, and this ate away at their relationship. She later wrote of how their marriage was in a mess. But she was in a bind. She couldn't stop his dalliances. Nor would she leave him. She still loved him and remained committed to his mission in life. Moreover, it wasn't all bad times. They still found time to spend together, whether it was touring the Snowy Mountains Scheme or blackberrying with friends in Gippsland. And she was pregnant with their fourth child.[7] However, rather than bringing them together, this pregnancy would test their relationship anew.

That was partly because Hawke's long relationship with Beverley Richards had come to a stormy end. It might have worked out differently had Richards been able to find ample work as a dancer and developed a life of her own. But she found that dancing engagements were hard to come by, and she'd become as obsessed with Hawke as he had seemed to be with her. When he decided to get off this destructive merry-go-round, Richards resisted in ways that brought the soured relationship to the notice of his colleagues – and of Hazel. One account describes how Richards threw stones at the window of his office and tried to waylay him when he was coming and going on Lygon Street. She would also frequently ring his home in Keats Street, hoping to catch him there. When Hazel had been away with the children, Richards had stayed there with Hawke, which would have been brought to Hazel's notice by well-meaning neighbours, or perhaps made plain by the signs left behind of their tryst. When Hawke finally sought to bring this long-running relationship to an end in 1963, it was said to have prompted Richards to threaten him with blackmail and for the pregnant Hazel to become involved with warning his lover off. She would later say that 'nobody would ever know how hard it was'.[8] It wasn't a good atmosphere in which to give birth, but that wasn't the only problem.

Hazel was used to giving birth prematurely, but this time it was different. Unknown to her doctor, the placenta was sitting above the opening of the uterus. In early August 1963, when she was barely seven months pregnant, she began to haemorrhage and had to be rushed by ambulance to the nearby Mordialloc Hospital, where she underwent an emergency caesarean and was treated for severe blood loss. She was lucky to survive.

Their baby boy was not so fortunate. Having been partially starved of oxygen, he was born with a blue tinge to his skin and was whisked off to a humidicrib in a city hospital before Hazel had been able to see him. With their three other children cared for by friends and neighbours, a distraught Bob shuttled between the two hospitals, sitting by Hazel's bed as he assured her 'how well formed he was and what a strong little body he had', and then sitting beside their baby's crib. 'I sat and watched him die – for 24 hours I watched him die,' Hawke later recalled. The fact that the baby was otherwise perfectly formed only made his death harder for both of them. A relative lack of oxygen in utero and the premature birth had caused his lungs to collapse from atelectasis, leaving him unable to get sufficient oxygen into his bloodstream. Unaware that their son's life was draining away, Hazel suggested that he should be named Robert James, in the hope that this 'might lift Bob's spirits', and presumably to attach Hawke more strongly to her. It could be his last chance to have a namesake, since she feared that 'it might be their last child', which would mean that he would miss out on having the Biblical seven children he had wanted.[9]

Just four days after being born, Robbie had drawn his last breath. The loss of their child, with Hazel blaming the premature birth on the stress she was under, made it a terrible time for both of them. It was made worse for Hazel by never having seen her son and by having to remain in hospital for an extended period. When it was time to go home, she moved into a friend's house for several more weeks of recuperation. Apart from being livid with Hawke, she was also angry at herself, wrongly believing that her failure to consult a specialist had sealed her son's fate.

As for her anger at Hawke, she later recalled how she'd 'abused him terribly about the mess our marriage was in' when he'd visited her in hospital. The stress from his infidelities and drinking was made worse by the manner of their son's death. There had been so much left unresolved in the previous few years that their grief over the tragedy was buried rather than being worked through. While Hazel sought solace in her friend's home, a tearful Hawke drank with his mates at the pub, where he railed against the burial procedure for stillborn babies and those dying soon after birth. 'Robbie should have a funeral,' he shouted. But there wouldn't be one. With Hazel still in hospital, Ralph Willis was the only person who accompanied Hawke to see the tiny white coffin laid out alongside others at Melbourne's general cemetery in Carlton. There was 'a big pit in the ground', recalled Willis, 'with all these white coffins in it'. Although there was 'sort of a service', only the undertakers were listed on the death certificate as witnesses to the burial. 'It was a pretty traumatic moment for Bob,' Willis said. The life he'd imagined for himself seemed to be slipping away.[10]

Weighed down by the death and by guilt due to his behaviour, the grieving Hawke was drinking so much by the time that Hazel finally returned home that it almost killed him. One morning, when he was already drunk and insisted on taking a reluctant Hazel to a football match, he collapsed in the taxi from alcohol poisoning. Delirious and fearful of dying, he was eventually sent home from hospital to dry out. With his life in disarray, Hawke's inability to control his alcoholism and moderate his behaviour might have led him to lose his position at the ACTU and be divorced by Hazel. But the quietly alcoholic Albert Monk could hardly take issue with Hawke's drinking, particularly as it seldom seems to have affected his work, while Hazel forgave him his trespasses, as she always had. 'What you lose on the swings, you pick up on the roundabout,' she would tell their children. It was a personal philosophy that helped her through the hard times. His criticisms of her during their shouting matches had caused Hazel to doubt her own worth, but she still felt attached to him and believed that he remained at heart a good man doing valuable work on behalf of ordinary Australians. Their early passion for each other would never be recaptured, but she reconciled herself to their changed situation by thinking of their relationship less as a marriage and more as a transactional partnership, where the children and Bob's career were paramount.[11]

That career was about to take a dramatic new turn when Bob was persuaded, with Hazel's support, to stand for the federal seat of

Corio when Menzies called an early election for November 1963. After Calwell's close-run result in the 1961 election, there was a real chance of Labor getting over the line and of the 33-year-old Hawke being able to make the switch into federal parliament. It might provide the hoped-for path to the prime ministership.

The Corio electorate, which centred on the industrial city of Geelong, was a good seat for Hawke. His victories at the Arbitration Commission had seen him hailed as the hero of the workers, and there were plenty of workers employed in Geelong's car factories and wool-processing plants, the aluminium refinery and associated workshops, as well as on the docks and railyard. As the South Australian Labor MP Clyde Cameron assured him, 'Your standing with the workers is almost legendary,' with Cameron predicting that Hawke would 'win by thousands'.[12]

In fact, it wasn't such a sure thing. There was a large rural hinterland and the seat had alternated between Labor and the conservatives ever since it had been created in 1900. It had most recently been held by Labor from 1940 to 1949. The electorate was far from Sandringham, which meant Hawke would be regarded as an outsider. That wasn't an insurmountable obstacle. The bigger obstacles were the grief from which the Hawkes were both still suffering, the shadow of his mistress and the health effects of his heavy drinking. Perhaps because of that, he hadn't sought Labor endorsement until it was privately offered to him by the party's state secretary in an aside during an ALP dinner. Having an outsider foisted upon them wouldn't please the local party members and voters, but Hawke promised to live in the electorate if they elected him. What's more, he loudly proclaimed his newfound love for Geelong's VFL football team. As a sign of his earnest intention, and to help with the campaigning, the party rented a beachside house on The Esplanade at Portarlington, where the family lived for two months. It was that local address that he rather misleadingly wrote on his nomination form.[13]

If Hawke was a young hero to some of the voters, his Liberal opponent was a legend. Fifty-nine-year-old Hubert Opperman had been an international cycling champion in the 1920s and '30s, as well as being a marathon runner, before later turning to politics, securing the seat of Corio for the Liberals in the 1949 election. The genial sportsman, known affectionately as 'Oppy', was now the minister for shipping and transport in the Menzies government. Turfing him out of parliament would be like shooting Phar Lap.

Or so Opperman hoped. Although the economy had improved since the last election, and full employment had returned, he still feared that his young challenger might snatch the seat back from the Liberals. And it seemed that Hawke could well be successful. He had a growing national profile, as was evident when he flew to Sydney on the day of his nomination to appear on a television panel discussing the economy. He also had the support on the ground of union officials, including Willis and the office manager of the ACTU, who travelled to Geelong to campaign and door-knock on his behalf, operating out of four offices in the city and its suburbs. The local party members fell in behind him, despite some resentment.

Hawke's campaign secretary was a railwayman and a Geelong Trades Hall official, Gordon Scholes, but the real campaign director was the ALP's state organiser, George Poyser, who came from Melbourne for that purpose. According to Scholes, 'the money came down the highway' as well. It was a sign of the seriousness that the ALP attached to taking Corio back from the Liberals. Apart from massive meetings in public halls and at factory gates, Hawke's profile in the electorate was established with a raft of radio ads, orchestrated by the state Labor MP and media personality Doug Elliot, and by full-page spreads in the conservative *Geelong Advertiser*. The lavish spending was made possible by the surreptitious support of a shipping magnate, Rod Miller, who was engaged in a bitter dispute with Opperman over Miller's plan to use foreign-built but Australian-crewed oil tankers on the Australian coast. According to the ageing and now overweight Opperman, Labor's spending was far greater than his, and he'd also lost his long-time campaign manager. Feeling beset on all sides, he described how he 'began to panic' as he cycled around the electorate shouting out greetings to puzzled pedestrians.[14]

Hawke had his own problems. The workers at factory gates may have hailed him for the wage increases and the three weeks' annual leave he'd secured for them, and others might have been impressed by pamphlets extolling his academic record and his service with the Oxford University Air Squadron. But voters were also showered with allegations about the supposed communist associations of the Labor candidate and his party. It was a sign of his desperation that Opperman made wild allegations about there being six communists among the ALP leadership. The DLP and the Catholic Church chimed in with a shrill chorus accusing Hawke of being 'a disguised Communist'. Hawke was particularly shocked to hear children from a Catholic school taunt him as a communist when he attended the opening of a new parish hall. The heat of the campaign, with several meetings each day, took its toll on Hawke's fragile health, and was likely exacerbated by more drinking, which may have been prompted by the presence in Geelong of his former mistress, who was determined to unsettle him. Hawke was forced to recuperate in bed for three days, where the still-grieving Hazel took care of him, as well as of the campaign workers who slept over in their temporary home. The pressure on Hazel was 'a bit of a nightmare', said Willis. Others noted how she was 'easily upset'. While Hazel managed the ever-changing crowd at breakfast and cared for her three children, she was not up to sitting alongside Bob on the stage in Geelong's public halls, where his jilted lover would sit determinedly in the front row trying to catch his attention. Ignoring her presence as best he could, Hawke concentrated in his speeches on economics, explaining at length how Labor planned to pay for its promises. 'He was used to speaking for days in the Commission,' said Willis, but that 'wasn't good training for concise speeches'. He didn't have 'the sensitivity towards an audience that a good actor has', observed the future South Australian premier Don Dunstan, and he came across as 'too strident'.[15]

Yet Hawke had good support from Gough Whitlam, who was on stage with him as 750 people watched televisions set up around the hall to play Menzies's pre-recorded campaign launch, before Whitlam and Hawke responded with replies on behalf of Labor. It was a novel idea that turned the Liberal launch into a quasi-debate in which Menzies had no right of reply. The fact that Labor organised this with Whitlam was another indication of the party's hopes that Hawke could dislodge Opperman from Corio. Arthur Calwell was there for the opening of Hawke's campaign in the Plaza Theatre, with the pair arguing in the street outside as to who should speak first. Hawke insisted it should be him but Calwell pulled rank, explaining that he needed to speak first to ensure it was reported in time for the morning's newspapers. The presence of Calwell and Whitlam reinforced the widespread expectations that Menzies might lose the election if sufficient voters objected to being forced to another early poll. Even the 68-year-old prime minister thought it could go either way. That was certainly how it seemed in Corio, where Hawke 'drew crowds everywhere he went'.[16]

Although Hawke enjoyed an early surge of support on the hustings, Opperman was an experienced long-distance athlete and gradually gained on his young challenger. With Miller's connivance, Hawke had tried to entice Opperman into greeting the first arrival in Geelong of Miller's oil tanker. After initially accepting the invitation, a suspicious Opperman wasn't there when it steamed into harbour. It was just as well, because the tanker's side was draped with a massive banner exhorting the people to vote for Hawke, who was left lonely and frustrated on the wharf at his thwarted attempt at political theatre. Hawke strode away to vent his anger in the studio of the local radio station, where he contemptuously derided his opponent's failure to attend. Rather than helping his campaign, Hawke's intemperate behaviour eroded the favourable impression he had created among voters during its first weeks. According to the embattled Opperman, whose tottering campaign had been buttressed by the arrival of several experienced media advisers, Hawke's early lead was 'nullified by his increasing bitter vehemence'. While Hawke's stridency may have unsettled Corio voters and created a minor headwind, his relative youth and energy might still have won against the aged Opperman, who was so rattled by Labor's campaign that he refused to accept Hawke's challenge of a public debate.[17]

In the event, Opperman's desperate campaign was saved when the last days of the election were caught up in a cyclone of international events that diverted the attention of voters and gave Menzies an unassailable advantage over Labor's hapless leader.

The Cuban missile crisis of October 1962 had been dangerous enough, but it was far from Australian shores. Not so the 'confrontation' between Australia's populous neighbour, Indonesia, and the newly formed federation of Malaysia. It began when Indonesia's president, Sukarno, sent irregular troops in raids across the Malaysian border on the island of Borneo in early 1963, and steadily escalated until a riotous mob attacked and burnt down the British embassy in Jakarta that September. The long-held Australian fears of an Asian invasion were exacerbated by Indonesia also having a popular Communist Party and the Soviet Union providing support for Sukarno. A little further north, the United States was sending forces to prop up the authoritarian regime of South Vietnam's Ngo Dinh Diem, as Washington continued its ill-fated attempt to prevent that country's reincorporation with North Vietnam.

The Australian government had encouraged the American involvement in South-East Asia and agreed to send training forces to South Vietnam, a move that would see it tagging along into that increasingly bloody quagmire. It had also agreed to have an American naval communications base built in Western Australia, which would allow the Americans to communicate with their nuclear-armed submarines. At the same time, the threat of nuclear war was heightened when the United States resumed nuclear testing in response to Soviet tests. It was in this fearful atmosphere that Hawke derided Australia's defence preparedness, claiming that even if all the country's defence forces were gathered around Geelong, they'd be unable to stop the city being overwhelmed.[18]

These worrying developments were a blessing to Menzies' electoral chances, which were further enhanced when he announced a massive order for an expensive, and still untested, American fighter bomber, the swing-wing F-111, which promised to ward off any attack from Australia's north. The election also saw further upheaval in Vietnam, with riots by Buddhist protestors being brutally suppressed by Diem, only to have his generals, at the prompting of the Americans, topple and assassinate him on 2 November. Calwell's response to the regional mayhem and Cold War rivalry was to call for a nuclear-free South Pacific, only to quickly abandon the proposal when it was mocked by Menzies. When Calwell attempted to turn the attention of voters towards domestic issues, they were distracted by Menzies promising for the first time to assist non-government schools and to provide science blocks to all schools, regardless of their affiliation.

Although some commentators thought a Labor victory might still be possible, the assassination of President John F. Kennedy in Dallas, Texas, on 22 November 1963, just a week before Australian voters went to the polls, extinguished any hopes Calwell might have had of becoming prime minister. It also sounded the death knell for Hawke's hopes in Corio. When he was told of Kennedy's death, Hawke's immediate reaction was to think it had been the television entertainer Graham Kennedy who'd been killed. But the assassination of the US president would dominate the news during the campaign's final week, with fears that the Soviets had been involved.

Hawke tried his best to steady his campaign and reassure voters by prevailing upon Hazel to agree to a Kennedy-like family portrait, which was displayed as part of a large advertisement in *The Geelong Advertiser* two days before the election. The photograph could also have been designed to reassure voters about the state of his marriage and allay any rumours that might have been circulating. Unfortunately, the small photograph was overshadowed by the verbose advertisement, probably composed by Hawke, which focused on rebutting Opperman's allegations about communists in the ALP. With Labor putting so much effort into Corio, Menzies was driven there on the eve of the election for two lunchtime meetings at the Ford factory. Having only held onto power in 1961 by a single seat, he was determined that Corio wouldn't cost him this election. With media reports of an assassination threat having been made against him, Menzies was surrounded by masses of uniformed police, while detectives on a rooftop kept watch on the crowd of factory workers below, as catcalls rang out and heads turned when one joker let off a firecracker.[19] The meeting was a great piece of political theatre by the worn-out Menzies just as the campaign curtain came down.

When the election results were tallied the following night, it was clear that Menzies had won a historic victory, gaining an additional ten seats. It gave him a 22-seat majority over Labor, the biggest Menzies had ever achieved. Although the early votes looked good in Corio, Hawke realised that DLP preferences would doom his chances. Returning to Portarlington late on election night, he woke six-year-old Sue to tell her that he'd done well but hadn't won because of 'the bloody DLP'. It took a week to finalise, as Hawke's lead on first-preference votes was steadily whittled away by the distribution of DLP preferences and the counting of postal votes. By the end, he had been easily defeated on the final two-party count, receiving 22,456 votes to Opperman's 25,666 votes. Nevertheless, he'd scored a swing to Labor on first preferences of more than 3 per cent when there'd been a national swing against Labor of 2.4 per cent. It was some small solace, even if it was helped by him being in top spot on the voting paper and thereby enjoying the so-called donkey vote. For Hawke, who couldn't abide losing any contest, the result was a bitter disappointment. He told friends and supporters that another week would have seen him defeat Opperman, but that was baloney. He'd been soundly defeated by an ageing pedal-pusher who'd outsmarted him and who would continue to hold the seat until retiring in 1967. Although the *Geelong Advertiser* noted Hawke's 'truly energetic and relentless campaign', the paper had helped Opperman by giving the minor DLP candidate more headlines and column inches than Hawke.[20]

Instead of entering federal parliament and beginning his political ascension, Jesus-like, at the age of thirty-three, Hawke would have to return to his role at the ACTU and wait for a more propitious moment. Although Clyde Cameron consoled him with the assurance that 'there is not the shadow of doubt that at the next election you will be a Member of the Federal Parliament', Hawke was not so sure. In his memoirs, he devoted little more than a paragraph to his defeat and declared, with hindsight, that the result 'was the best possible outcome' since it saved him from spending nine years of 'sterility' on the opposition benches.[21]

There was much for him to think about as he and Hazel packed up the Portarlington house and headed back to Melbourne. In attempting to fulfil his supposed destiny, he'd fallen at the first hurdle.

There was no telling when Hawke would get another chance. It would depend upon a winnable seat becoming available in Victoria and on Hawke being able to convince the state executive or the local branches of his suitability. There was no point looking to his own local branch, located at the southern end of the wealthy Balaclava electorate, which had been held since Federation by conservative representatives. At least the election campaign for Corio had allowed his political aspirations and abilities to be flagged to the party, and his platform skills to be honed. That would have been the lesson with which Hawke consoled himself as he marked his thirty-fourth birthday and prepared himself for the great challenges that awaited him as the advocate for the ACTU.

The first came in the basic wage case beginning in February 1964, when the employers proposed a radically new approach to wage-fixing. Their counsel, Jim Robinson, argued that the long-accepted system of the basic wage, on top of which were margins for skill, should be replaced by a single-tier system of a total wage, which could be increased annually, but only in line with productivity improvements. It would mean that workers would be forced to accept changes to their work practices, such as increasing mechanisation or speeding up production, if they wanted to gain any movement in their wages. Under the employers' plan, there would be no compensation for inflation. If accepted by the Arbitration Commission, it would destroy the victory Hawke had won in 1961 and return workers to the dark days of the 1950s, when their wages had been eroded by cost-of-living increases.

With Kirby presiding, and thousands of workers protesting in the street about the attempt to kill off the basic wage, the commission was in a bind. There was no supportive testimony from economists appearing for the employers: Hawke had dealt with them so aggressively in past cases that they were not prepared to risk their reputations by sparring with him from the witness box. It meant that Kirby was swayed instead by his reluctance to retract the recently agreed principles that underpinned the 1961 decision and return to the disastrous decision (for workers) of 1953. Although the four judges unanimously refused to accept the employers' argument about a total wage, they were split on the size of the wage increase, which was finally decided on Kirby's casting vote. The increase of twenty shillings a week was much less than the fifty-two shillings Hawke had argued for, which had included twenty shillings for inflation, but he'd seen off the employers' attempt to introduce the concept of a total wage. When the hearings concluded in Sydney, he and Robinson joined Sir Richard Kirby for a function at a golf club, where the three drank for much of the day. An inebriated Hawke berated Robinson for calling the bemused Kirby 'Sir Richard' or 'Your Honour', rather than doing as Hawke did and calling the racehorse-owning judge 'Dick'.[22]

Although Hawke had defeated the employers' proposal and gained an increase in workers' wages, two of the judges had made known their dissatisfaction with the underlying principles of the 1961 decision. Their attitude put Hawke on notice that there would be an increasingly fierce

Look at me! Bob Hawke, age twenty, with the world at his feet.
(*John Curtin Prime Ministerial Library, Hazel Hawke Collection*)

The ruins of the church above the Murray River where Hawke's parents, Clem and Ellie, first met and fell in love. The remains of the post office can be seen in the foreground. *(David Day)*

Clem and Ellie, with their bridal party, on their wedding day in Adelaide in 1920. They were about to embark on a lifelong mission to save the world. *(University of South Australia Library, Bob Hawke Collection, Item RH25/F1/12)*

The infant Bobbie in the garden at Bordertown, 1930. *(JCPML, Hazel Hawke Collection)*

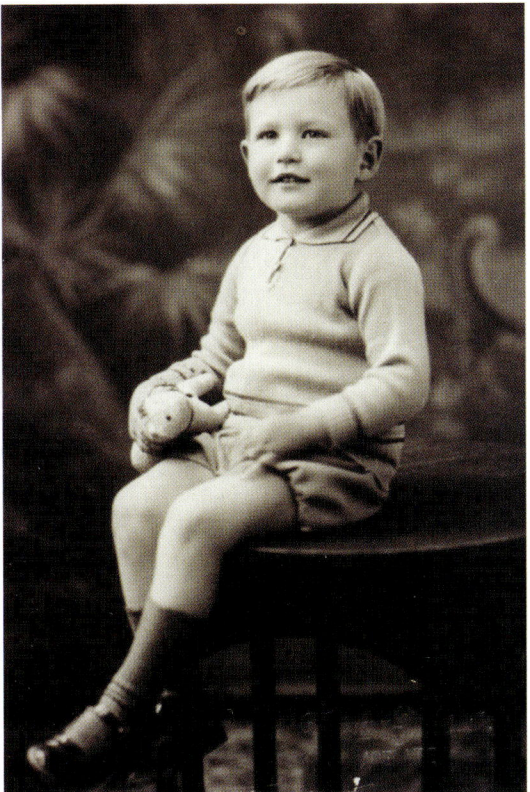

Already gaining a reputation for being uncontrollable, an angelic-looking Bobbie poses with his teddy. *(JCPML, Hazel Hawke Collection)*

Teased about his diminutive stature, Bobbie uses a chair to get level with his brother, Neil, in this family photo taken in Maitland, c. 1935. *(USAL, Bob Hawke Collection, Item RH25/F20/1)*

With the Congregational manse at one end and his school at the other, Bobbie had to walk the length of Maitland's main street each morning. *(State Library of South Australia)*

The thick stone walls of the Maitland church couldn't contain Hawke's father for long, with the congregation complaining that he was spending too much time at subsidiary churches. *(SLSA)*

With his mother's help, young Bobbie gained admission to selective state school Perth Modern, setting himself up for future success. *(JCPML, Hazel Hawke Collection)*

In 1941, Clem enlisted as a padre in the Australian Militia. The frequent absence of both parents worsened their son's behaviour and nearly caused his expulsion from Perth Modern.
(JCPML, Hazel Hawke Collection)

Hawke described a cricket match between staff and students at Perth Modern, in which he just missed out on scoring a century, as 'one of the biggest disappointments of my schooldays'.
(State Library of Western Australia, BA3010/120)

Hawke and Hazel make a happy couple at an Easter camp in 1949. *(JCPML, Hazel Hawke Collection)*

The University of Western Australia cricket team, 1952. Hawke stands in the back row, third from the right. *(JCPML, Hazel Hawke Collection)*

Hawke sits astride his Panther motorbike, 1951. Despite being thrown from this bike and suffering serious injuries in 1947, Hawke continued riding for several years. *(JCPML, Hazel Hawke Collection)*

Bob and Hazel present an uncharacteristically dour image for their engagement photo in 1952, Bob perhaps miffed at Hazel's hesitation to commit herself to him. *(JCPML, Hazel Hawke Collection)*

With his arms folded and head cocked to the side, Hawke is standing in the front row of students, second from the right, as they listen to a talk, possibly during Orientation Week, outside UWA's Winthrop Hall. *(UWA Archives, 5864P, courtesy of The West Australian)*

For the benefit of a press photographer, Ellie helps Hawke pack for his voyage to India for the World Conference of Christian Youth in 1952. *(JCPML, Hazel Hawke Collection)*

Although it would never be built, the International House Appeal strengthened Hawke's second application for the Rhodes Scholarship. Here, four overseas students bid him farewell as he heads for Oxford. *(JCPML, Hazel Hawke Collection)*

Hawke (front row, middle) ran a successful campaign for the presidency of the Student Guild Council in 1952, further strengthening his application for the Rhodes Scholarship. *(UWA Student Guild)*

Aged nearly 25, Hawke (back row, fourth from right) would have been one of the oldest students in University College's induction photo for 1954. *(University College, Oxford)*

Hawke and Hazel reunited after her arrival in Oxford in 1954. *(JCPML, Hazel Hawke Collection)*

The baker's van that Hawke drove in a furious police chase through Oxford and which became known by fellow students as 'The Fornicatorium'. *(JCPML, Hazel Hawke Collection)*

Hawke, a member of the Oxford University Air Squadron, poses beside the two-man Chipmunk trainer aircraft that allowed him to claim a service record of sorts when he later made his first bid for parliamentary office. *(JCPML, Hazel Hawke Collection)*

On a stinking hot day in 1956, the bridal party poses on the steps of Trinity Church in Perth, with their respective parents standing behind them. *(JCPML, Hazel Hawke Collection)*

In 1956, Hawke is photographed with the family's car outside the married students' flats in Canberra. *(JCPML, Hazel Hawke Collection)*

In January 1957, around the time of the drunken incident involving the ornamental pool at University House, Hawke and Hazel pose with their new baby, Susan. *(JCPML, Hazel Hawke Collection)*

This plain timber house in Keats Street, in the Melbourne suburb of Sandringham, was the Hawkes' first home. They lived here from 1958 to 1964. *(JCPML, Hazel Hawke Collection)*

With his jilted lover regularly embarrassing Hawke at public meetings, a last-minute advertisement for the Corio by-election in 1963 was designed to portray Hawke as a happily married family man. *(JCPML, Hazel Hawke Collection, courtesy of ALP Victoria)*

A full desk on his first day as president of the ACTU. His 'office wife', Jean Sinclair, would bring order to his office. *(News Ltd/Newspix)*

Businessman Sir Peter Abeles visited Hawke after he became president of the ACTU. Showering him with gifts, it began a friendship that never waned. *(Anton Cermak/The Sydney Morning Herald)*

The Gippsland bush provided the Hawke family with an occasional escape from Bob's increasingly helter-skelter life. Here they are at Agnes Falls in the mid-1960s. *(USAL, Bob Hawke Collection, Item RH33/F27/19)*

When Hawke was depressed by Israel's plight during the Yom Kippur war of 1973, Abeles (not pictured) paid for him to visit Cairns for a spot of sport fishing, where Hawke caught this 343-pound (155-kilogram) black marlin. *(USAL, Bob Hawke Collection, Item RH27/4/F33/1)*

Hawke and political staffer Glenda Bowden at the ALP's Terrigal conference in February 1975. His louche behaviour added to the image of a government out of touch with voters, who were being impacted by rising inflation and unemployment. *(The Sydney Morning Herald)*

Hawke and Prime Minister Gough Whitlam enjoy a beer at the ALP conference in Terrigal, February 1975. Rather than setting Labor up for nearly three more years in power, the conference helped propel Labor towards the Dismissal and electoral defeat. *(Russell McPhedran/Fairfax)*

Hawke addresses a lunchtime rally at Parliament House to protest against the sacking of the Whitlam government, 1975. *(National Archives of Australia)*

Based in Geneva as the administrative head of the International Federation of Commercial, Clerical and Technical Employees, Helga Cammell was the woman Hawke dubbed 'Paradiso' and almost married. *(The Age)*

Hawke's biographer, long-time lover and later wife, Blanche d'Alpuget. *(Graeme Thomson/Newspix)*

Posing for the camera while facing the possibility of divorce, the Hawkes visit China's Great Wall in 1978. *(JCPML, Hazel Hawke Collection)*

Following the death of his mother, an angry Bob Hawke berates delegates during the debate on uranium mining at his final ACTU congress in September 1979. *(Michael Rayner/The Age)*

Despite repeatedly failing to give up the grog, Hawke realised he had to overcome his alcohol addiction if he was to ever become prime minister. *(Andrew Chapman)*

The cartoonists loved him. Geoff Pryor of *The Canberra Times* marks Hawke's decision to enter parliament in October 1979. *(Geoff Pryor/National Library of Australia)*

battle to defend his great victory of that year. There was also a battle going on at the ACTU, where Hawke had become the organisation's de facto spokesman, much to the chagrin of Harold Souter, who was keen to keep him in his place as an employee rather than see him strutting around Australia as if he were an elected official. Hawke had even been on a three-month study trip to Canada and Britain in mid-1962, taking Ellie along to show her his old haunts in Oxford and call on Reverend Beck.[23]

Unlike Souter, Albert Monk was happy for Hawke to take on speaking engagements that would otherwise have fallen to him. Short and stout with thick glasses, Monk was a nervous speaker who was uncomfortable on television; he was now in his early sixties and looking towards retirement. As ACTU secretary, Souter might have taken on some of these engagements himself and lifted his own public profile, but he didn't have the charisma or the fiery presence that Hawke could bring to the platform. Moreover, the role of secretary was largely an administrative one, running the office and ensuring that unions were paying their dues, rather than being a public voice. For Hawke, the public appearances provided an opportunity to make valuable political contacts across Australia and to further raise his profile, not only within the trade union movement and the Labor Party but among the general populace. He was regularly quoted by the newspapers' industrial roundsmen, who would hobnob with him in the bar, scribbling down stories in their beer-stained notebooks.[24]

If they wanted a story from Souter, journalists would have to catch him at his desk in the ground-floor office, perhaps sipping on a sarsaparilla. Professionally, his teetotalism was a problem for him, keeping him from socialising over a beer with many of his fellow union officials at the Lygon or the Dover. Those informal connections were helping to establish Hawke's bona fides in the labour movement and could prove crucial when union officials decided on Monk's successor as ACTU president.

It would have seemed inconceivable to some that the position of president could go to a young university graduate who'd not risen through the ranks and won the presidency as the culmination of a long trade union career. After all, the English-born Monk had been approaching fifty when he'd become president in 1949 and had been employed by unions all his working life.[25] But times were changing, and Hawke had already shown his ability by taking on the temporary position of research officer and within months assuming the position of advocate. Souter was aware that the presidency could be in Hawke's sights.

Despite suffering from hypertension and having had a possible heart attack when visiting Prague in 1959, Monk hadn't yet signalled when he might retire, but it couldn't be more than a few years away.[26] Souter was determined that he, rather than Hawke, would take over, so it was important that Hawke not be allowed to portray himself as Monk's natural successor by speaking on behalf of the ACTU.

When the ALP's federal secretary, Cyril Wyndham, invited Hawke to join both the party's Economic Planning Committee and its Industrial Committee in March 1964, Hawke readily agreed, only to be taken aback to hear that the planning committee had met six months later without him receiving notice of it. Hawke suspected Souter of destroying the letter. He told Wyndham that future letters should be sent to his home rather than to his office. While the seventeen-member ACTU Executive wasn't about to silence their young advocate, it did offer a sop to Souter by instructing that Hawke only speak with the approval of Monk, and not accept speaking engagements off his own bat. That was hardly going to rein him in.[27]

At home, Hazel may have wanted to rein him in too, so that he could spend more time with the family and less time working his extraordinarily long days at the office while he was fighting a case at the commission. Too often, he topped off those days by drinking and wenching. As he became better known, recalled Willis, there was 'a fair bit of that, women throwing themselves at him, almost', adding that 'Bob wasn't so much going looking for it as it came looking for him', although 'he was interested if they were good enough'. It was part of the package that Hazel had accepted, however reluctantly, when she'd decided enthusiastically to live her life with him. The excitement they'd enjoyed in Oxford had been tempered by his dalliances with other women, and had subsided even more with the shift to Canberra and then the birth of their children. His absences and infidelities became harder to take after the death of their second son, when she was left to grapple largely alone with her bereavement. Once Rosslyn was old enough to go to kindergarten, Hazel had considered doing further education by correspondence, only to have the idea dismissed by Hawke, who told her that she 'had plenty to do already'. It was perhaps to distract Hazel from her ongoing grief and the continuing problems in their marriage that Hawke suggested they move to a bigger house, telling her that it would 'lift our spirits'.[28]

For him, it would also be a mark of his success as an advocate and his rising status as a public figure. Their house in Keats Street, with its small kitchen and lounge and scattering of children's toys underfoot, was a humble abode in which to host the social gatherings, of friends or of colleagues, that Hawke held on many a weekend. As a result, when trade union and party officials trooped up the driveway, bottles of beer in their arms, they usually congregated around the barbecue or spread across the backyard. It also made it difficult to host overnight visitors in any comfort. The Hawkes had been in the house for six years and both aspired to something better, preferably in Sandringham, where Hazel now had friends and the children were going to school.

Their chance came in July 1964, when they noticed a house for sale just a short walk away at 25 Royal Avenue. It came complete with an adjoining block but was a 'soulless place, painted battleship grey', recalled Hazel, and had been on the market for more than a year. In desperation, the owner offered the house for £12,500 and the adjoining block for £5000. Although it was a bit further from the Sandringham shops, the house was marginally closer to the beach, while Sandringham East Primary School was just two kilometres away. Importantly, it was bigger and brasher than their Keats Street home, and the neighbouring block sported a run-down tennis court.[29] It was not unlike Hawke's childhood in Maitland, where the manse had a tennis court on which he first developed his love of that game, and where he also practised with the cricket bat, as Neil or Clem or Gwen Geater lobbed balls his way. This new home would allow him to socialise on a more expansive scale and help set him apart from his associates. From having one of the humblest houses in Keats Street, they would be moving to one of the better houses on perhaps the biggest block in a grander street in upper-middle-class Sandringham.

The new home was beyond their means, but they had a supportive bank manager who extended an overdraft for the expensive property, even though Hawke was only earning about £2000 a year at the time. They were also helped by the vendor, who agreed that they wouldn't have to commit to buying the adjoining block immediately. Instead, he would give them a one-year option, after which they could choose to purchase it or not, as their financial circumstances dictated at the time. The struggles that Hazel had endured when they'd moved into their first home and she had to knock together cupboards and make do without modern appliances and facilities could now be left behind them.

Indeed, the home itself would be left far behind them when Hawke took advantage of a wage case in Perth to bundle Hazel and the kids and the dog into their station wagon and drive across the Nullarbor to stay with Clem and Ellie for a few weeks. While Hazel caught up with her family and friends, and Susan and Stephen were sent to Hawke's old primary school in West Leederville, Hawke fought for a £3/1/- increase in the state basic wage. He was opposed by his familiar adversary Jim Robinson, and was roundly defeated, only managing to secure an increase of three shillings. On a more positive note, Hawke made contact with old university mates and strengthened his relationships with local union and party officials.[30] Much had changed since he'd left Perth eight years before. He was now a person of some importance, and on a trajectory that was likely to take him much further.

By the time the family arrived back in Melbourne, the house contract had settled and he was able to ease the fully loaded car along the driveway of their new home. Hazel might worry about the size of their mortgage, but the purchase confirmed that Hawke was making his mark. Whether the house would give the couple more than a transient lift to their spirits was another matter.

CHAPTER TEN

1965–1966

The size of their new home in Royal Avenue was a sign of the success that Hawke had achieved during those six years in Melbourne, while the size of the overdraft was a sign of the inveterate optimism with which he faced his future. It was also a reflection of the general optimism that pervaded Australia in the mid-1960s, as the new generation who'd come to adulthood in the relatively prosperous post-war years became accustomed to full employment and ever-rising living standards. Women were starting to sense that a larger life could be possible outside of their homes, as the first stirrings of a new wave of feminism began to be felt. As well, millions of immigrants from Britain and Europe were transforming Australia's ethnic make-up and adding their energy and confidence to the country. Many were also strengthening the labour movement, bringing their political ideologies and experiences from the old world to the new. Some had fled communism in Eastern Europe and huddled in the comforting political arms of the DLP or Liberal Party, while others had fled right-wing dictatorships and looked to the Labor Party, or perhaps the Communist Party, to create a fairer future for them in Australia. But a Labor government wasn't going to happen anytime soon.

In such prosperous times, most Australians were loath to oust the Menzies government, which shored up its support by appealing to a mix of Cold War fears about communist China and older fears about an Asian invasion, whether from China, Japan, India or Indonesia. Although Australian forces were still involved in fending off Indonesian attempts to undermine the newly created nation of Malaysia, these fears coalesced into a focus on Vietnam after the United States decided, with Australia's encouragement, to commit ground forces to prevent the spread of communism across South-East Asia. Instead of allowing the creation of a single Vietnamese nation, as had been agreed with the departing French colonial power in 1954, Washington would back a succession of regimes in South Vietnam, which had to be supported with increasing amounts of American munitions and manpower.

When there was a brief exchange of fire between an American destroyer and several North Vietnamese torpedo boats in August 1964, the incident was used as a pretext to begin a proper war, which led to Australian forces joining in. Otherwise, it was argued, the Chinese, who'd exploded their first nuclear bomb in October 1964, would thrust southward all the way to Australia. The Australian commitment proved popular with the public and divided the Labor Party, with Arthur Calwell, who'd been an anti-conscription campaigner in both world wars, being much more forthright than his deputy, Gough Whitlam. It didn't bode well for the party's chances at the federal election that was due in 1966.[1] Nor did it bode well for Hawke's political aspirations.

Over in Western Australia, his uncle's experience offered proof, if such were needed, that the political tide wasn't running Labor's way. He'd been tossed out as premier in 1959 and lost the next two elections, culminating in the most ignominious defeat of all in 1965.[2] For now, his nephew would focus his long-term attention on getting the numbers for the ACTU presidency, whenever that might happen. The position offered him an opportunity to improve the lives of Australian workers and their families, while also promising him the public plaudits and power that he craved, and which an opposition backbencher couldn't deliver. It also provided a possible launching pad into federal politics.

Even as the ACTU advocate, Hawke was receiving a lot of public attention, and not just at the time of basic wage decisions. He was becoming a recognisable and sought-after figure on public platforms. His distinctive, drawling voice was heard frequently on the radio and his carefully coiffured hair and often scowling face were seen on the increasing number of television sets in Australian homes, with Hawke pulling at his earlobe as he tried to intimidate his interviewer.

When Menzies had called a half-Senate election for December 1964, hoping to hold on to his narrow majority, the Labor Party had asked Hawke to record two television spots. Although the campaign centred on defence, after Menzies announced young men were going to be conscripted for overseas service, Hawke's focus was elsewhere. While Calwell concentrated his campaign on the conscription announcement, Hawke focused on the economy, reprising some of the arguments he'd made at the Arbitration Commission about inflation and the wage regulation system, accusing Menzies of 'criminal negligence' because of his failure to produce 'continuous and rapid growth'. This had cost Australians dearly, argued Hawke, not only financially but in the nation's ability to defend itself. In the telecasts, Hawke presented more like an academic at a seminar rather than a rabble-rousing trade union official, in stark contrast to Calwell with his passionate speeches and the furious anti-conscriptionists who shouted down Menzies in public meetings.[3]

It was all for nothing. The Labor campaign had failed to resonate with voters, who were transfixed by the vision of foreign threats from the north. Although Menzies lost a seat, it was picked up by the Country Party. And while Labor's vote held steady, it also lost a seat, which was picked up by the DLP. It meant that seventy-year-old Menzies was safe and that Australia would continue its slide into the Vietnam quagmire.

Hawke had a more important election in view. He just didn't know when it would occur. With Albert Monk continuing to be cagey about the timing of his retirement, Hawke had to concentrate his energies as ACTU advocate on improving the wages and conditions of working people. That meant defeating the employers' campaign for the concept of a total wage. So far, Hawke had been successful. But the employers kept proposing the concept to the commission, hoping that the ever-changing composition of judges on the bench would shift the balance their way. The basic wage case in 1965 gave them another chance.

Hawke prepared for the case with his customary zeal. For all his drinking and carousing, he was able to work extremely long hours when the occasion demanded. As Willis recalled, 'He was very responsible and if he had work to do he made sure he did it and he wouldn't let drink get in the way of that.'[4] It was the mark of a high-functioning alcoholic. This was just such an occasion, since the employers' proposal threatened to undo all the gains he'd achieved and send the trade union movement back to the detested decision of 1953, which he'd attacked so vociferously in his Oxford thesis and had the satisfaction of unravelling during successive cases before the commission.

There was a shock in store for Hawke. Rather than responding to the ACTU's wage claim, the employers in January 1965 presented their claim first, putting Hawke on the back foot. The employers' claim resubmitted the total wage concept, which they wanted based solely on productivity gains, and also argued for the ACTU's basic wage and margin cases to be heard together. Either outcome could spell disaster for the gains made by Hawke. And there was no telling how it would go, since he would be facing a new combination of judges sitting alongside the usually sympathetic president of the commission, Sir Richard Kirby, and his offsider, deputy president John Moore. It meant long hours of preparation in the summer heat, when the upper floor of the ACTU building, with its flat roof and lack of air conditioning, could be almost unbearable. 'I remember working there stripped to the waist it was just so hot,' said Willis. Their effort was in vain. Robinson had got Hawke's measure during the state case in Perth, and used that experience to expose Hawke's weaknesses when the case opened in March 1965. Robinson began by bombarding the judges with militant union material that called for strikes and other union activity to pressure the commission. Along with the advocate for the Commonwealth government, John Kerr – who would later earn notoriety as governor-general – Robinson urged the judges to frame their decision in a way that would promote price stability rather than spark an inflationary spiral.[5]

As if to buttress Robinson's arguments about militant unionists, the public seats in the commission chamber were crowded with angry workers, who shouted encouragement as Hawke laid out the union case in his usual passionate way. When the hearings shifted to Sydney, police had to be employed to keep hundreds of wharfies at bay when they besieged the street outside. While Kirby and Moore were accustomed to Hawke's invective, the other three judges were not willing to tolerate Hawke's political theatre and personal attacks against the judges who'd made the 1953 decision. Hawke compounded the offence by angrily attacking the two judges from the 1964 case who'd questioned the principles he'd succeeded in having the commission accept in 1961. He might have got away with it, had the two judges in question not been on the bench in front of him. Hawke's anger increased when Justice Gallagher denied that workers had any right to strike, while Justice Charles Sweeney took great umbrage when Hawke referred to the 'stupidity' of a previous decision. Undeterred, Hawke went on regardless until he lost his voice, which forced the hearing to adjourn for a week.

Despite the fireworks, Kirby had been confident that Gallagher and Moore would join him in a majority decision to cement the 1961 decision. He was astounded to discover that he was in a minority. Gallagher and the two other judges had secretly agreed to set aside the principles from 1959. To Hawke's horror, a stunned and humiliated Kirby led his fellow judges into the chamber and promptly handed over to Gallagher. The president of the commission could only sit in silence as Gallagher enumerated the reasons for the shock decision.[6]

The three judges rejected any increase at all to the basic wage and awarded only a six-shilling increase to margins. Although their decision also rejected the employers' argument for a total wage, it decreed that the basic wage and margin cases be heard simultaneously, which was tantamount to having a total wage. They also railed against strikes, which were on the increase, declaring them to be 'relics of past thinking' and 'a calamity to all concerned', and decreed that wage increases had to be set in a way that promoted price stability. As such, they had to be based upon the discredited concept of the economy's 'capacity to pay', whatever that meant and however it was meant to be measured, rather than upon increases in productivity and prices. All this meant that the wages and salaries of workers would fail to maintain their value in real terms. The decision outraged blue-collar and white-collar workers alike, and helped cement the growing links between the ACTU and the two main umbrella groups representing white-collar workers: the Australian Council of Salaried and Professional Associations and the Commonwealth Public Service Organisations. If the decision was humiliating for Kirby, it was also humiliating for Hawke. All his victories at the commission had been swept away by three judges who'd been angered by his intemperate performance.[7]

Rather than acknowledging it as a personal defeat and taking some responsibility for it, Hawke focused his attention on the humiliation suffered by Kirby, with whom he'd grown close. In his memoirs, he devoted just a paragraph to the 1965 case, all of which he used to attack Kirby's colleagues for what he angrily called their 'sheer intellectual incompetence' and 'shoddy reasoning'. Hawke could never abide losing at anything, whether it was on the cricket field or in the Arbitration Commission. Just as he would stride to the crease determined to improve upon a previous poor performance at the wicket, so he took the 1965 commission decision as a challenge that demanded a response. Apart from anything else, his career depended upon him restoring his own credibility and reputation. 'I steeped myself in that judgment as I had in no other,' wrote Hawke. He was 'determined to destroy it', not least because he 'found it utterly offensive that a decent man like Kirby had been publicly humiliated by such a low-grade piece of work'. While the employers were just as appalled by the treatment of Kirby and would have preferred a more balanced, and therefore lasting judgment from the commission, the union movement was furious. At workplaces, there was general disillusionment with the industrial relations system; some unionists downed tools in protest and called for a national strike. The ACTU decided instead to adopt Hawke's recommendation to take the unprecedented step of appealing, only to have the commission refuse to review its decision. Any redress would have to wait until the next basic wage case.[8]

It wouldn't have helped Hawke's mood when he returned to Sandringham, where Hazel was struggling to make a comfortable home from their awkwardly designed and basically furnished new home. It was certainly a bigger house, which allowed the three children to have their own bedrooms as well as a playroom, but the kitchen was small, there were no curtains, they had to borrow a dining table and there was only one gas fire in the lounge room to heat the whole house. 'Most people said that it looked as if we couldn't afford to live in it,' recalled Hazel, because 'all the furniture was second-hand'. She was in charge of the domestic finances, and the size of their mortgage ensured there was no splurging on new furnishings, and it was several years before they could afford to have central heating installed. Their financial problems added to the tensions in their relationship. Hawke's grandiosity and Hazel's careful budgeting didn't sit well together. Their finances were so tight that she felt impelled to take in a lodger, Jill McKissack, who also watched over the three children if Hazel needed to go out in the evening. Fortunately, they'd managed to acquire the adjoining block with the tennis court just before the one-year option expired, after a newspaper in Sydney mistakenly described Hawke as the communist leader of the Waterside Workers' Federation and Hawke sued for libel. It was just one of many libel actions Hawke would launch against media proprietors, with several of them ending in lucrative settlements. D'Alpuget calculated that six of the actions brought Hawke more than $60,000 in total. In the most celebrated case, in 1974, Kerry Packer coughed up $25,000, which paid for a swimming pool in their backyard. Hawke took great delight in pointing it out to guests as the 'Packer pool'.[9]

In Keats Street, their weekend social life had revolved around the backyard barbecue. Now their guests could spread across their expansive and informal garden and spill onto the tennis court, where Hawke would play like a demon against those who dared to challenge him. Willis, who was still unmarried and would sometimes mind the house when the Hawkes were away, occasionally gave it a go. He was no match for Hawke at tennis. Nor could he beat him at golf. 'Bob wasn't a great golfer,' he recalled, but he was 'much better' than Willis. One person who did beat Hawke on the local golf course was young Don McIntosh, who lived nearby and played a few times with Hawke soon after the family arrived in Sandringham. McIntosh played off a handicap of just four and soundly beat Hawke each time. Although others remember Hawke being passionate about winning, McIntosh doesn't recall Hawke as getting upset, perhaps because of his partner's youth or because he wasn't part of Hawke's circle of friends and associates. With Willis, it was different. 'You played anything with him,' recalled Willis, 'he was absolutely trying 100 per cent to win.' And he always did win, and was triumphant, when the pair were playing tennis or golf. However, Willis was good at squash, which had become popular during the 1960s, and 'beat him easily'. That was enough for Hawke. After that single defeat, 'we never played again', said Willis.[10]

When he'd won handsome increases in the basic wage or margins, Hawke was always feted by the hundreds of union officials attending the subsequent congress of the ACTU. Not so in the wake of the commission decision in 1965, when left-wing unionists at the ACTU Congress in September 1965 decried what they described as the ACTU's 'scholarly approach' to wages policy and called for the ACTU to argue for the basic wage to be £22, based upon the needs of workers, rather than continuing to push for increases based upon prices and productivity. This had been a constant refrain of left-wing unions since the 1950s and had popular appeal, since it harked back to the Harvester judgment of 1907. It didn't have to be supported by the reams of complicated statistical evidence and economic theories that Hawke brought to bear. It just had to be justified by a sense of what was widely considered fair.

Now the attack on Hawke's 'scholarly approach' struck a chord with many of the delegates, who'd been fending off the anger of their members ever since the judges' decision had been handed down. One union official even called for the commission to be burnt down, noting that Hawke was 'no doubt a very able man but the workers are in revolt'. Although Hawke hadn't been mentioned by name in the opening attack, it was clear that the criticism was directed at the ACTU's advocate rather than just its wages strategy. Hawke responded by pointing to the increases he'd managed to achieve for workers in the four years prior to the present year's setback, noting that there'd been a 6 per cent increase in real wages and that he was planning to demand an increase of at least thirty-four shillings at the next basic wage case. That allowed him to narrowly win the debate. But the closeness of the vote revealed the extent of the anger within the union movement.[11] Now it was even more important for Hawke to achieve a sizeable increase in 1966.

There was another reason why Hawke had to retrieve his reputation at the upcoming wage case. His media profile, particularly on television, had elevated his public stature to such an extent that he was now being talked about as a possible successor to Monk. Another failure at the commission could cruel his chances by confirming the criticism and prejudice he'd encountered because of his academic background. To overcome that prejudice, he had to build up his support among the union officials who'd be attending the congress at which the next president was going to be decided.

Although Monk hadn't given any indication when that would be, Hawke wasn't going to wait for the starter's gun. By late 1965, he was enlisting supporters and seeking out those who might campaign on his behalf. When he went to Adelaide to give a talk to trade unionists, he was met at the airport by a young political apparatchik, David Combe, and immediately asked to be taken to the nearest pub, exclaiming, 'I gotta have a beer.' They had another beer at Combe's home and more beers at two other pubs before finally fetching up at Hawke's hotel, after which they joined others and 'ended drinking all night'. It didn't prevent Hawke giving a 'brilliant' speech the next day, or from using the opportunity to enlist Combe effectively as a campaign manager within the South Australian labour movement. 'He was very open to me,' said Combe, 'about his ambition to be President of the ACTU, and asked me to sound people out, to try to find support.' Which Combe gladly did, after being captivated by Hawke's charisma and seeing him perform on the union platform.[12]

Hawke approached many union officials directly, often over a beer at the Lygon or during his many interstate trips. Some were more crucial than others, such as the secretary of the Miscellaneous Workers' Union in New South Wales, Ray Gietzelt, who wielded considerable influence among left-wing unionists. If Hawke could get him on board, others would surely follow. Hawke's efforts to establish his credentials were not helped when, exasperated, he ended one of his early approaches to Gietzelt by threatening: 'If blokes like you won't support me, I might as well go back to the ANU!'[13] That was exactly where his critics alleged Hawke had his natural home, rather than representing workers at the ACTU.

He kept at it regardless, after work in the pub, at meetings of the ACTU Congress and when he was away at speaking engagements or interstate hearings of the commission. Acting as the ACTU advocate, with its necessity for frequent interstate travel, gave Hawke opportunities to meet with trade union and Labor leaders whom he might otherwise seldom see. That was good for his future advancement in the trade union movement and in the party as well. Willis usually flew with him. Travelling with Bob was 'adventurous', he recalled, because he was 'certainly keen to sort of let his hair down a bit' and 'sometimes there might have been a woman involved' – which didn't help the atmosphere at home with Hazel.[14]

It was a mark of Hawke's narcissistic personality that, rather than working quietly behind the scenes and swearing fellow conspirators to secrecy, he was upfront about his ambition. He had only one realistic competitor, the man working away assiduously in the office below, for whom the presidency seemed the natural progression from his position as ACTU secretary. It also seemed natural to the many union officials who had a high regard for Souter, who was now on notice, if he hadn't been before, that Hawke was pursuing the position that Souter considered rightfully his after a lifetime's dedication to the union movement. For the moment, Souter could be content that his right-wing supporters had a majority among the sixteen men who comprised the ACTU Executive.

The open competition for the presidency made for a very tense atmosphere in the office, which became 'bloody awful' once the gloves were off, recalled Willis, who was now in an awkward position, not least because he 'thought it was the wrong thing for [Hawke] to be doing'. He couldn't comprehend why Hawke would want to become president, which Willis regarded as 'a sort of nothing job compared to what [Hawke] is doing in the commission'.[15]

Hawke had his reasons. He had a vision, which he never tired of telling possible supporters, of 'a much more unified and much better resourced union movement', one that would be able to achieve, in tandem with the Labor Party, 'a much better quality of life for working people'.[16] By becoming president, he would also free himself from the limits imposed by Monk on his public appearances and statements, allowing his public stature to be even more enhanced. Even if the presidency didn't provide an eventual pathway into parliament, it had intrinsic satisfactions of its own and allowed him greater opportunities to effect positive changes for Australia. First, though, he had to win the basic wage case that started its hearings in March 1966, with his proud parents taking the opportunity of a holiday in Melbourne to attend some of the sittings.

The case was complicated by the recent report of a committee that had been initiated by the Menzies government and chaired by businessman Sir James Vernon. The committee had conducted an in-depth inquiry into the state of the Australian economy, canvassing everything from 'the availability of credit, the distribution of the workforce, the balance of payments and trends in costs, prices, wages, productivity and the standard of living'.[17] The inquiry had been instigated in the wake of the

1961–62 recession and was meant to answer Labor's criticisms about Menzies' mismanagement of the economy. Because the committee was dominated by businessmen, who naturally regarded wage increases and strikes as a danger to growth and productivity, the thousand-page report said as much when Menzies tabled it in parliament in September 1965. That was unfortunate for Hawke, because it gave powerful ammunition to the employers and the government, while also exerting considerable influence on the thinking of the judges as they prepared to sit on the basic wage case. In a hastily written memo for Monk, Hawke decried the report as 'essentially a private enterprise "be-kind-to-business (especially manufacturers)" report', which urged the Arbitration Commission to regard the maintenance of price stability as being central to its task.[18]

When Hawke commenced his arguments before the commission, Kirby wasn't there to hear them. He'd appointed former employers' advocate and now senior judge Syd Wright to chair the case along with Moore and Gallagher. Wright had been on long-service leave in 1965, so wasn't involved in that year's case, while only Gallagher had been part of the three-judge majority that had brought down the decision that had so infuriated Hawke.

The case began on 8 March 1966 and Hawke let fly. On and on he went for three weeks, leaning on the lectern as he launched into a sustained attack on past judgments, but particularly the 1965 decision, which he berated as 'outrageous' and 'absolute humbug', much to the chagrin of Wright, who asked him to abbreviate the history lessons and avoid making personal attacks on the judges. Hawke couldn't stop himself. When an irate Gallagher likened him to a soapbox Demosthenes, the Greek orator who'd roused the citizens of Athens with inflammatory rhetoric to oppose Philip of Macedon, Hawke not only refused to resile from the comments that had provoked the judge's ire but suggested the judge was not giving him 'the respect I am entitled to receive'. Willis suspected that Hawke 'really enjoyed being attacked because he could attack back and he was confident that he had the answers. He was in his element, in a sense.' Moreover, as Hawke defiantly told the judges, they shouldn't get upset by his comments because he was speaking not as Bob Hawke but as 'the representative of ... 80% of the Australian population', which was a gross overstatement. The charged atmosphere and clear hostility from two of the three judges did not bode well for Hawke's chances of winning the case, which weren't high anyway after the 1965 decision and the Vernon report. 'It was really a backs-to-the-wall job,' he recalled.[19]

As expected, Robinson made much of the Vernon report when he rose to present his opening arguments on behalf of employers. If the report's conclusions were accepted by the commission, it would undercut the entire ACTU case. Fortunately for Hawke, a chance meeting at Essendon airport in Melbourne with the economist Keith Hancock provided him with some powerful ammunition. Although Hancock had written the report's chapter on wages, which Robinson had cited, he had since written a paper arguing that Australian workers hadn't been properly compensated for increases in prices and improvements in productivity. Hawke had cited that paper during his three-week-long opening address, but this hadn't stopped Robinson from using the Vernon report as the main support for the employers' case. Hawke had to knock that support out from under them. And he decided to do it in the most dramatic way possible. It would run the risk of damaging his reputation, imperilling his chance of winning a deserved wage increase for working people and perhaps fatally injuring his campaign for the ACTU presidency. Rather than riffling through the report, as Robinson had done, he would put Sir James Vernon on the witness stand and subject him to sustained questioning about the report's conclusions. First, though, he had to clear it with Monk, who feared that Hawke's high-wire approach was 'too radical'. Curiously, it was Souter who convinced Monk to let the ambitious advocate have his way. According to Hawke, his rival 'had recognised what was in the best interests of the people we represented and, ignoring his own interests, acted accordingly'.[20] Or perhaps Souter was hoping the strategy would blow up in Hawke's face.

When Hawke asked for members of the Vernon committee to be subpoenaed to give evidence, it set off a barrage of objections from Robinson and the barrister for the federal government, the silver-haired John Kerr, whom Hawke loudly derided as the 'Liberace of the Law' whenever he walked into the commission. Hawke's opponents could see where he was headed and, to the amusement of the judges, were desperate to prevent the prominent businessman and his committee members from being put on the spot.

When a majority of the judges agreed that Vernon and his colleagues could be put on the stand, the committee members were represented by a bevy of barristers, who raised objections to them having to answer questions from Hawke about the report's conclusions on wages. Eventually, it was Vernon himself who insisted on answering the questions, only to find himself agreeing with Hawke that the statistics used by the committee about wage stability were wrong and that workers had indeed seen their wages eroded. According to former ACTU Executive member Terry Winter, who was now an arbitration commissioner, Hawke handled Vernon brilliantly, putting aside his usual aggressive stance to be suitably 'deferential and courtly'. Indeed, observed Winter, 'Bob could have been in velvet knee-breeches'. The judges were left little choice but to decide in favour of the ACTU. Hawke's great risk had paid off, and his pleasure was made all the sweeter by having his parents in the public gallery, with 63-year-old Ellie clacking away on her knitting needles.[21] Reversing its decision of the previous year, the Arbitration Commission decreed that wage increases had to be based both on price increases and productivity, thereby restoring the principle that Hawke had achieved earlier.

But there was never a complete victory for Hawke at the commission. Although he didn't mention it in his memoirs, the case wasn't just about re-establishing the principle that inflation had to be considered when determining wages. The ACTU had also wanted an increase of $4.30 to the basic wage and of $5.90 to the margin paid to electrical fitters, which would have led to pro-rata payments for other skilled tradesmen, along with the return of quarterly cost-of-living adjustments. Not only were the quarterly adjustments refused by the commission when it brought down its decision on 8 July 1966, it also refused to increase margins. As for the basic wage, it awarded an increase of just $2. As always, the fight would have to go on, particularly as the commission accepted in principle the employers' argument that a total wage should replace the present combination of the basic wage plus margins for different skills.[22] Before that was implemented, however, it would have to be argued anew at the commission in 1967.

Meanwhile, Hawke had another important role to play. On 20 August 1966, he clambered aboard an aircraft that would take him to Port Moresby. He had been enlisted by the territory's Public Service

Association to conduct a wage case on behalf of Indigenous public servants, who were paid a pittance compared to their expatriate colleagues. The case had important symbolism for the inhabitants of an Australian colony that was slowly moving towards its inevitable independence, with some of the leaders of the independence movement, such as future prime minister Michael Somare, being subject to the discriminatory wage ruling by the public service arbitrator, who was controlled by Canberra rather than by the locally elected House of Assembly.

The case was just as important for Hawke, who later described it as 'one of the most stimulating experiences of my whole career'.[23] The palpable injustice offended his sense of what was right and fair. He'd seen for himself the poverty and injustice of life in newly independent India. Now he would confront the poverty and injustice Australia imposed on its own colonial peoples.

It would be very different from arguing a case at the commission, however, and Hawke had a lot of work to do, gathering background information about the economy and society and amassing the statistics and witness statements that he needed to buttress his case. He'd spent a week in Port Moresby in June 1965, consulting with local officials of the Public Service Association and advising them what information he would need to argue the case. He had planned to visit other centres but had been laid low by illness. Now, with the 1966 wage case behind him, he was back.

Rather than sitting in an air-conditioned office in Port Moresby, Hawke would talk to the Indigenous officers working in different parts of the country. Accompanied by the 26-year-old lawyer for the Public Service Association, Paul Munro, Hawke spent a couple of weeks flying in small planes around cloud-shrouded mountains to some of the most distant parts of the territory, even crossing the Bismarck Sea to Manus Island, where they also went fishing.

The day before the case was due to resume with a conference in Port Moresby, they were nearly 800 kilometres away at Wewak, in the far north-west of the territory. Having to catch a flight to Port Moresby early the next morning, Munro described how they went off for a 'few drinks', which turned into the sort of session that Hawke was used to having in Melbourne. His young companion was appalled at

Hawke's behaviour and worried that he would be in no condition to catch the flight, let alone put the arguments at the 9 a.m. conference with the government representatives. As was often the way with Hawke, though, he somehow managed to rise to the challenge, perhaps because what was a large quantity of alcohol for Munro was not so unusual for Hawke. It was something that Munro discovered early the next morning. Hawke not only boarded the aircraft 'as bright as a button' but performed brilliantly at the conference by calling the bluff of the government barrister, who was proposing that an increase in allowances for the expatriate officers be dealt with first. No way, retorted Hawke, conscious that it would be regarded as a betrayal of the Indigenous officers. He threatened to 'bloody-well withdraw the local officers' claim', which caused the administration to cave in and agree to offer an interim increase. Munro was blown away by 'Hawke's negotiation style and brilliance [that] was so effective, so dramatic, so different from anything I had witnessed before'. Then again, Munro was a young lawyer and this was his first real experience with an industrial case.[24] And it was just the first round in a match that would take several months to decide.

Hawke took Hazel and their three young children along with him when the case recommenced in January 1967, setting them up in a house in Port Moresby that came complete with a servant, who did their shopping, cooking and cleaning. While the children went to primary school for three months, Hazel was left at a loose end and took up reading the novels she'd never had the time for before. When the case began, she could often be found in the public gallery, sitting alongside the local trade union officials and their members as they watched Hawke wave his hands in the air in rhetorical flourish. Much to the amusement of those sitting behind him, Munro recalled, Hawke also had a habit of 'allowing his left hand to work its way under his trouser belt into the vicinity of his buttock crack, while standing on one leg, the other propped on a chair'. Beyond the case itself, Hawke acted as an agent of change in the stultifying, white-dominated society, giving talks to multiracial audiences on trade unionism. Gregarious as ever, Hawke would take Hazel and the children to social occasions with a mix of journalists, academics, public servants and local activists, often ending up at the home of journalist Don Hogg, a New Zealander of Māori heritage who ran an SP betting operation from the shed next door. The Hawkes' eldest daughter, Sue, recalled how their visits to the Hogg home 'would be punctuated by discussions of form, placing of bets, and races run in Australia played on the radio'. It was during this time that Hawke placed a few bets of his own and 'became hooked for life', obsessed by the challenge of picking winners. Back home in Australia, he would develop contacts in the racing world that could give him an edge on the 'mug' punters.[25]

Unfortunately for the Indigenous public servants, Hawke had more luck with his bets than with their case. Despite his vigorous prosecution, his three months in Port Moresby did not produce the desired result. As Hawke conceded in his memoirs, the interim increase only produced a 'marginal improvement' in their wages. Nevertheless, he believed that his conduct of the case produced a larger benefit by giving heart to independence activists, whose number included some of the same public servants. On the family's final night in Port Moresby, Hawke invited some of those Indigenous officers to a party at the house, where they mixed with his new-found coterie of journalists, unionists and public servants. During the raucous and beer-fuelled tropical evening, full of back-slapping and reminiscences, he tried to set an uplifting tone by encouraging the crowd to join in a rousing rendition of 'We Shall Overcome'. Hawke likely learned the song at union events in Melbourne, but it had its origins in gospel hymns and nineteenth-century slave songs, before being adapted in the twentieth century as an anthem for striking workers, only to be adapted again and be popularised by the American civil rights movement in the 1960s.[26] Its spiritual form and origins would have resonated with Hawke, reminding him of his hymn-singing Sundays in the church, while its recent iteration as an international anthem for labour and civil rights activists would have resonated with his identity as an emerging labour leader guiding Australian workers out of the wilderness of wage slavery.

There was much further to go on that journey. First, he had to get back to Melbourne, which was where he now headed with Hazel and their sun-bronzed children.

CHAPTER ELEVEN

1967–1969

There was much that needed to be changed in Australia after sixteen years of increasingly sclerotic government under the leadership of Robert Menzies, who'd won seven elections in a row before finally retiring at the age of seventy-one in January 1966. Menzies had just been appointed by the Queen to succeed the recently deceased Winston Churchill as Lord Warden of the Cinque Ports and proudly flew that fourteenth-century ensign at the Lodge and on his official Bentley.

Hoping to give the government a more modern face, Liberal MPs elected the younger and more progressive Harold Holt as their leader. No matter how much Menzies had wanted to stem the tide of change – whether it was the White Australia policy, the decolonisation movement sweeping the world or the 'Swinging Sixties' that were transforming Australian society – the changes were coming regardless. With Holt's predilection for skin-diving and having his photo taken alongside his bikini-clad daughters-in-law, there was a sense that he was comfortable with some of these changes. But there was one he didn't want to make, which was the Australian determination to see US troops deployed in Vietnam. Menzies had committed a thousand Australian soldiers there in April 1965, and Holt doubled their number the following February. Among them were the first echelon of conscripts.[1]

Conscription and the war dominated the federal election that Holt called for November 1966, after hosting a popular visit by US President Lyndon Johnson. With foreign policy at centre stage, and fear of China rampant, Holt earned a resounding endorsement from voters, winning a two-party-preferred swing of more than 4 per cent. It gave him eighty-two MPs in the House of Representatives, compared to just forty-one for the Labor Party.

It was a disastrous result for the ageing Arthur Calwell. Many had seen the disaster coming, but Calwell had refused to avert it by resigning beforehand. He now shared the dubious distinction with his predecessor, H.V. Evatt, of having been defeated at three elections in a row. When the leadership was thrown open in April 1967, Gough Whitlam took the role he regarded as rightfully his, easily defeating the former Special Branch policeman turned economist Dr Jim Cairns, and promptly proceeding to modernise the party and prepare it for government. Of his four-man leadership team, three were barristers, which was the sort of modern Labor Party Whitlam wanted. He also wanted Hawke as part of his team. As deputy leader, he had suggested to Hawke that he again stand against Opperman in Corio. Hawke declined.[2] He could see Labor heading for another loss under Calwell and had his eyes firmly fixed on succeeding Monk as ACTU president.

When Opperman was dropped from Holt's ministry after the election and then retired altogether, Whitlam urged Hawke to stand in the resulting by-election. Although Opperman's departure made the seat more winnable for Labor, Hawke again refused, fearing that he would repeat his earlier defeat, particularly since Holt had won the federal election so handsomely. Moreover, the position of an opposition MP could not compare in power and prestige with the prospect of becoming president of the ACTU. On a practical level, it might have been difficult for him to be preselected for Corio in any case, since the Labor candidate at the 1966 general election, Gordon Scholes, wanted to stand again. The former train driver and heavyweight boxer had served as Hawke's campaign secretary in 1963. He was two years younger than Hawke and well known in the area, being president of the Geelong Trades and Labour Council.

In the event, Whitlam embarked on a determined effort to support Scholes by moving into a Geelong motel for ten days of intense campaigning. It was part of the new Labor leader's drive to lift the party's dismal vote in Victoria, which was vital if he was ever to become prime minister. The campaign worked. When the votes were counted, he'd helped Scholes achieve an incredible 11 per cent swing to Labor, turning Corio into a safe Labor seat. The party has held it ever since.[3]

It wasn't the only time that Hawke had resisted pressure to stand for federal parliament. In August 1965, he had been invited to nominate for the Liberal-held seat of Robertson, centred on Gosford, New South Wales, where a branch secretary assured him he would have the numbers to secure the nomination and predicted he would win the seat.[4] Hawke was uninterested. Apart from not wanting to shift his family, a provincial electorate, whether in New South Wales or Victoria, couldn't offer him the satisfactions, acclaim and national profile that were on offer at the ACTU. As he told Whitlam: 'If I become president of the ACTU I shall always be involved in decisions', whereas if he won a seat in parliament, 'I'll be involved in decisions only when we get in'. The problem for Hawke was that Monk was still refusing to say when he was going to retire, and there was no way Hawke could hasten that event. However, he continued to let everyone know that he saw himself as Monk's successor, regardless of the bitter atmosphere and awkwardness this caused in the ACTU office.[5]

It wasn't Hawke's colleagues who had to be won over, but the hundreds of union officials who would eventually assemble for the biennial ACTU Congress that would decide the issue, as well as the ACTU Executive members, who would appoint an acting president in the event of Monk retiring between congresses. Either way, the decision on the presidency would determine the future direction of the union movement.

A possible direction was set out in a newspaper article in January 1967. Indeed, it may have been inspired by Hawke himself during one of his many discussions with industrial relations reporters in the back bar of the adjacent Lygon pub, with its red linoleum floor and cream walls. The article compared Australia's union movement with those in the United States and Europe, lamenting the lack of Australian officials who could 'examine the unions critically, suggest new ideas [and] present sophisticated schemes for tomorrow's world'. It decried the officials who'd risen through the ranks from the workshop floor for making unions 'obstructionist in their approach, resistant to technological change [and] frightened of advance'. By holding on to nineteenth-century forms and practices, such officials were doing a disservice to their members and the economy, limiting the prosperity that might otherwise be possible if the workforce was more mobile and flexible and was represented by fewer and larger unions. It called for the appointment of 'economists, lawyers, sociologists [and] psychologists'. If such forward-thinking people were appointed, the argument went, the union movement would have a much more 'integral and fully productive role in Australian society and a vested interest in its prosperity and future', which is what it should have, since 'organised labor today is big business if it is run properly'.[6] These were views that Hawke had come to embrace after nearly a decade at the ACTU, although he had to avoid articulating them in public for fear of alienating the very officials whose support was vital for his success, and who remained suspicious of people drawn from academia.

When the right-wing Australian Workers' Union (AWU) finally affiliated with the ACTU in January 1967, Hawke's chances of becoming president didn't improve. The fiercely anti-communist union was one of the oldest in Australia and remained one of its biggest, with 180,000 members. Decades before, it had aspired to cover all Australian workers, and was now a largely rural-based union of shearers, miners and agricultural workers, as well as covering the thousands of workers on the Snowy Mountains Scheme. The union's general secretary was a former canecutter, Tom Dougherty, who had only agreed to affiliate after an extra position was added for him on the sixteen-member ACTU Executive. The union would now send a sizeable block of delegates to future congresses. Its affiliation had been negotiated between the tough-talking Dougherty and Souter, who hoped to benefit from the change in numbers on both the executive and at the congress. That spelt trouble for Hawke, since the AWU had derided him as an 'egghead' when he was first appointed as ACTU advocate. The union's affiliation was expected to cement the right-wing control of the executive and to reinforce the right-wing majority that usually dominated the congress.[7]

The next congress was due in August 1967, when Monk would be two years past the usual retirement age of sixty-five. Power and position can be difficult to relinquish voluntarily. That's particularly true when it necessitates a substantial drop in income, which is what Monk would face when he retired. Despite his deteriorating health, he was determined to hold on for as long as he could.

In the meantime, Hawke huddled with the various faction leaders over a beer as he sought their support. His calculations were based on the contest occurring at the forthcoming congress or, failing that, at the succeeding one in 1969. The big danger for Hawke would be for Monk to resign in between the two congresses, which would see the appointment of an acting president. Given the factional numbers on the executive, that would almost certainly be Souter, which would give him a likely unassailable advantage when congress decided on a permanent appointee. Hawke had to hope that Monk would hold on until the 1969 congress, which would allow him and Souter to fight on a more even footing. There was little he could hope to gain from the upcoming national wage case. With the hearings beginning in March 1967, the commission was likely to implement the employers' proposal for a total wage, which it had accepted in principle the previous year.

The ACTU continued to oppose the total wage, believing that workers would be better off with the basic wage, provided it was adjusted for prices and productivity and supplemented by margins for skills. With Kirby back as chair of the bench, Hawke reprised his arguments from the previous year, arguing for an increase of $7.40 in the basic wage, an increase of $5.90 in the margin paid to electrical fitters, which would flow on proportionally to other skilled workers, and the restoration of automatic quarterly adjustments. Kirby and his colleagues were having none of it. Rather than allowing the case to drag on interminably, they declared on 5 June that the commission would implement the employers' concept of the total wage by awarding 'a flat increase of $1.00 to all award wages of male and female workers and the same amount to the minimum wage, which was to be retained permanently'. In money terms, it was another disappointment for Hawke, as well as for the unions and the many workers who didn't have the industrial strength to compel their employers to top up the basic wage and margins with over-award payments. He convinced the ACTU Executive to launch a High Court case to appeal against the decision, only to see it tossed out. Trying to put a good spin on his defeat, Hawke told the executive that the decision by the Arbitration Commission had benefited low-income and women workers, because it made the introduction of equal pay for women more feasible. As for workers generally, Hawke immediately began to search for ways to turn the concept of the total wage to their advantage – perhaps they might even be better off. But that would mean embracing the concept, which union officials remained loath to do, having spent their lives operating under a system that had begun with the venerated Harvester decision.[8] It would be akin to the Pope giving up on God.

For more than sixty years, the basic wage had been all about setting a wage that would be sufficient for a male wage-earner to support a wife and three children in frugal comfort. The possibility of a woman having to support a family, either as a single mother or as the wife of a disabled husband, was not considered, and nor were any of the other family permutations in which a woman was the primary breadwinner. On a broader level, the injustice of gender-based wages was increasingly being questioned, as women became a larger part of the workforce and the women's movement raised demands for equality across Australian society.

The ACTU had been slow to heed those demands. Its constituent unions had been largely composed of male workers employed in factories, on farms or down mines, while unions with large numbers of female workers, such as nurses, teachers, bank tellers and many office workers, were not affiliated with the ACTU. That was changing, as white-collar organisations developed closer links with the peak body. Although the overwhelming majority of union officials at the ACTU Congress were men, and the executive would be all-male throughout Hawke's time, there had been a call at the 1965 congress for the ACTU to make a claim the following year for equal pay, and to do so every year until it was won. Although Hawke had some sympathy for the cause, Monk rejected the move, arguing that equal pay should be achieved through parliamentary means rather than through the commission. This had been the union view ever since World War II, when the ACTU accepted equal pay for women doing war work, on the proviso that women would be displaced from those jobs once men returned from the war.[9] Although there was little inclination in parliament to legislate equal pay, the campaign was gathering pace as part of an international, largely youth-driven rebellion that was challenging the status quo.

Hawke was facing a rebellion of his own, as his three children grew older and Hazel resumed the search for more fulfilment in her life. Their home was often a battlefield. Hawke was consumed more than ever with his work, his travel and his extramarital interests. It was difficult for Hazel to assert herself in a house where Hawke's needs overshadowed practically everything else. In a small act of defiance, as well as trying to be 'vogueish', she'd taken up smoking. Although he smoked cigars himself, Hawke objected to this. Hazel persisted, partly as an act of rebellion, but also because it provided an antidote to the anxiety from which she suffered. Although the family had 'many good times', recalled Hazel, 'the unhappiness the children saw and heard when Bob and I argued was hard to bear'. They had to put up with him arriving late for family events, or not arriving at all, and they had to endure 'the yelling late at night or in the mornings', when he might stumble in with a drinking companion. Hawke's humour was not improved by frequent bouts of ill-health. Most resulted from his drinking, lack of sleep and periods of excessive work. He sometimes complained of back pain, but more frequently of suffering from debilitating infections, whether it was the flu or sinus trouble. These may have been a result of him losing the protective function provided by his spleen. Then again, he also claimed to have an infection when he needed to recover from one of his many benders. Each day, the children learned to take the temperature of their parents' relationship and act accordingly. Susan recalled how 'the approach of another patch of irritability, marital tension, storms, distress, then sometimes collapse ... were the unwelcome part of the family landscape'.[10]

There were arguments when Hazel made clear that she was determined to create a life for herself beyond Royal Avenue. She'd long yearned for a larger life but had been stymied by Hawke's opposition, perhaps because he recalled the many times when Ellie had deserted him as a child or because he couldn't face the prospect of Hazel having achievements of her own. He'd opposed Hazel doing a night course when the children were infants, but they were now at school. She'd tried to obtain part-time work, but the difficulties were so daunting that she gave up. She still wanted to do night classes, but she couldn't count on Hawke returning home with the car in time for her to go.

Not to be thwarted, she finally bought a cheap car from a friend, which allowed her to begin matriculation classes, starting with English, one night a week at the local high school. While she was at class, a female lodger helped with child-minding. Ralph Willis was also available for child-minding, which gave him the opportunity to explore Hazel's classical music collection. At first, she didn't have a clear aim in mind with the night classes, other than to make something more of her life. If Hawke objected, she could always point to the example of his mother, who'd recently begun a university degree, which she would never complete. For Hazel, it became another small act of defiance at a time when Hawke's attention was increasingly consumed by his campaign for the presidency. Hawke would later concede that they were years when 'the family suffered dreadfully'.[11]

His campaign became more intense with the approach of the 1967 congress, which would elect the ACTU Executive for the next two years. Hawke had feared the influence of the Souter supporters who controlled the executive, but in the event it was the Souter camp that was disappointed by the outcome. Hawke's supporters emerged with an additional seat on the executive after Joe Riordan of the right-wing Clerks' Union lost his position to Ray Gietzelt of the Miscellaneous Workers' Union. Riordan's defeat also ended his chance of becoming a possible third candidate for the presidency. That meant Hawke and Souter were likely to be the only contenders, and Hawke was now in the stronger position. If an acting president had to be appointed before the 1969 congress, it was likely that Hawke would get the nod. Hawke would have also been encouraged by the congress's decision to approve an increase in affiliation fees paid to the ACTU by its members, with the funds adding three additional officers – an industrial officer, an education officer and a publicity officer – to the existing five officers. The expansion would boost the ability of the ACTU to service its affiliated unions and lift its public profile. The increased budget would be crucial for Hawke if he was to achieve his grand vision for the ACTU and for himself as its future president.[12]

His ultimate ambition of becoming prime minister, meanwhile, required him to become more deeply involved with the Labor Party. After losing out in Corio, Hawke concentrated on boosting his influence within the party, which could help to lay the groundwork for an eventual switch to federal parliament. As noted earlier, he'd become a member in 1964 of an Economic Planning Committee established by the federal Labor Party, which reported its conclusions to the Labor Conference in July 1967. With Whitlam also a member, the committee carried substantial clout. Its recommendations combined the traditional Labor demand for a fairer share of the nation's wealth with proposals for how that wealth could be increased. It also supported policies to channel the flow of overseas investment towards the creation of new industries, and to prevent it being used to buy up existing industries.

All this was part of Whitlam's reshaping of the Labor Party and its policies. He'd won clear endorsement for his leadership and the party with the Corio by-election in July 1967, and again with the Capricornia by-election in October 1967, where Doug Everingham defied predictions of a Liberal win by scoring a swing that saw Labor easily hold the North Queensland seat. The results in those two seats at opposite ends of the country boded well for the half-Senate election in November that year. The war in Vietnam was again a major issue after Holt announced an increase in the Australian commitment to three battalions. It was no longer proving to be a vote-winner. When the Senate results were tallied, Whitlam found that there'd been a swing of 5.7 per cent against the government.[13] A month later, with his worried mistress looking on, Holt dived into rough seas off Portsea's back beach, never to be seen again.

The disappearance of the prime minister, and his eventual replacement by the former fighter pilot John Gorton, was just one of many unsettling events during the late 1960s, as the post-war generation took issue with the world they'd inherited. They marched in the streets against conscription and the war in Vietnam, against the patriarchal power structure that denied women equal rights, against the racism that oppressed Indigenous Australians and against the American bases that dotted the outback. They took hallucinogenic substances and birth control pills, the men grew their hair long and, much to Hawke's delight, the women wore their skirts short. Angry songs of protest became hits. Authority was under attack.

Although Hawke's three children were too young to be part of this rebellion, their time would come. Aside from their parents' stormy relationship, they had an otherwise privileged life. Unlike many Australian children of the time, they lived in a big house and had safe beaches nearby. Neighbouring children would often join them to play on their tennis court; Hawke would bowl a cricket ball to young Stephen there, much as Clem had done with him in Maitland.

At first, the children were sent to the nearby Sandringham East Primary School, but the Hawkes decided that they'd go to private schools for their secondary education. Susan led the way in 1969 after winning a scholarship to Firbank Grammar School, an Anglican girls' school about seven kilometres away in well-to-do Brighton. Fortunately, it was accessible by train from Sandringham, with the school being close to North Brighton station. Meanwhile, Hazel continued with her own education as she pursued her ambition to pass the Higher School Certificate, with a view to going on to university. This time, she studied politics at a night school in the city.[14]

The social turmoil of the late 1960s was matched by industrial turmoil, as workers used the conditions of full employment to demand a fairer share of the national cake and railed against attempts by governments and employers to rein them in with the threat of massive fines and even jail for striking or holding unauthorised meetings. Hawke's performances in the theatre of the Arbitration Commission had redressed some of the inequities of the 1950s basic wage decisions, but many unskilled workers, particularly women and the lower-paid, still struggled to keep their incomes rising in real terms.

Rather than depending upon the Arbitration Commission, skilled workers were able to use their industrial muscle to achieve over-award payments from employers whose profits were protected by tariffs and who were able to recoup the additional wage payments by increasing their prices. But the value of money put into pay packets courtesy of over-award payments would be reduced by rising prices at petrol stations, shops and the new supermarkets that were appearing in Australian cities. This was something that impressed itself upon Hawke during his brief reflective moments between cases.

He was also conscious of the cost to the economy – and to workers – of the ceaseless demarcation disputes between unions, as officials fought to cover some or all of the workers in a particular business or industry. Of course, that was beyond his remit as advocate. His role was about defending the achievements won at the Arbitration Commission, pushing back against attempts to change the historic relativities between the wages of different workers, protecting margins and over-award payments, and always, like an angry Oliver Twist, asking for more.

There was a new militancy afoot in the late 1960s, with 1968 being a particular year of rebellion around the world, whether it was students facing off against police from behind barricades on the streets of

Paris, occupying buildings at the University of Tokyo or being beaten by batons in the streets around the Democratic Party convention in Chicago. Demonstrations against conscription and the Vietnam War were also convulsing the campuses of Australian universities and regularly spilling out onto city streets, where students would be beset by police on horseback.

The actions of the students might have been widely deplored, but they gave heart to workers and their elected officials to resist encroachments on their own hard-won rights. The year began with a bitter dispute involving workers in the metal trades after the Arbitration Commission, under Justice Gallagher, decided to award them an increase, only to allow employers to absorb the increase into their existing over-award payments. Widespread fury resulted, as workers went on a series of strikes for more than a month and held a national strike on 6 February. Employers responded by asking the Industrial Court to invoke the penal clauses of the industrial legislation and fine union officials for contempt when they defied orders to call off the strikes. It was a costly exercise for both sides, although the workers were judged the winners after Justice Kirby held a new hearing that did away with Gallagher's decision.[15]

The militant mood in the factories and the union offices suited Hawke more than Souter. And he was further advantaged when the balance on the ACTU Executive tipped in his direction in February 1969, after a right-wing member died and was replaced by a left-wing supporter of Hawke, making it nine to seven in his favour. Monk hadn't given any indication as to which contender he favoured. Had it been Hawke, Monk might have been expected to retire in early 1969, which would have allowed Hawke the advantage at the subsequent congress of being able to appear as the acting president. But Monk wasn't about to give an advantage to either man. Instead, he simply signalled in March 1969 that he was going to retire at the forthcoming congress and fired a parting shot at 'the so-called left wing', which was out to capture control of the ACTU Executive. It meant that the identity of his successor would depend on the numbers each contender could amass by the time the five-day congress kicked off at Paddington Town Hall in Sydney during September. Numbers were everything, and the intervening few months saw unions pay the affiliation fees that they usually left owing during the years that a congress wasn't held. Not only were their fees paid up, but some unions suddenly found they had more members than they'd previously declared, and therefore a right to send more delegates. Some small unions also decided to affiliate so they could add their delegates to the growing throng.[16] While that went on, Hawke and Souter campaigned hard for their support.

The unseemly fight splashed into the public domain when Souter released a statement that took up Monk's allegation about a left-wing push to take control of the ACTU, with Souter claiming that a 'pro-communist alliance front of the so-called New Left' was set on using 'dictatorial pressure tactics' to take control. This pre-emptive shot across the bows of Hawke's campaign was formulated by one of Souter's Victorian supporters who had links to Santamaria's clandestine Movement, and was meant to rally the right-wing unions by transforming the power struggle into a fight for the soul of the union movement. Which it was, in a way, since the modernising Hawke certainly had a much wider vision for the future role of the union movement than the narrow industrial focus favoured by Souter. With his opponent painting him as a tool of the communists, Hawke hit back with a statement claiming that he had 'the support of many unions not normally classified as being on the Left' and suggesting that Souter was a creature of the Santamaria-inspired 'extreme Right-wing', which had caused the devastating split in the Labor Party in 1955. Each side threw punches in public, briefed journalists in private, quietly took union officials aside to seek their support and carefully tallied up their respective numbers.[17] However, there was no guarantee that assurances given over a beer would transform into numbers on the floor of the congress.

The political division within the union movement came into sharp focus on 15 May 1969, and Hawke was the beneficiary. Laws had been passed to impose fines and even jail terms when unions ordered their members to stop work in defiance of orders from the Industrial Court. Over the previous thirteen years, fines totalling more than a quarter of a million dollars had been levied against unions, most of which went unpaid, while a trifling amount had been levied against employers for breaching various awards. When the secretary of the Melbourne Tramways Union, Clarrie O'Shea, refused to pay an $8000 fine after his members went on strike over the introduction of buses without conductors, he was brought before the Industrial Court, where Justice John Kerr sentenced him to jail for contempt. While the right-wing unions affiliated with the Victorian Trades Hall Council (THC) declared that O'Shea was a committee member of the Communist Party and that the issue was a communist plot to radicalise the union movement, the many left-wing unions that had been suspended from the THC called a twenty-four-hour stoppage. It sparked a popular campaign that saw a million workers down tools and many of them throng Melbourne's streets to protest against the injustice of jailing a union official for defending the interests of his members. The matter pitched the left-wing unions that supported Hawke against the unions that supported Souter, with Hawke's majority on the ACTU Executive ensuring that it backed the Australia-wide campaign. The impasse between the defiant O'Shea in his cell and the autocratic Kerr in his courtroom only ended when one of Monk's rich friends stumped up the money to pay the fine. The campaign had worked. Governments and employers and the Industrial Court were on notice that they could expect a massive reaction if they made another union official into a martyr. The Hawke forces were exultant. And it was Hawke who seemed to represent the future of the union movement.[18]

When the delegates walked up the Oxford Street hill to Paddington Town Hall on Monday, 8 September, the talk was all about the contest for the presidency. A beaming Hawke and his numbers men circulated among the delegates, trying to get definite assurances of support from unions in the political centre while making sure that none of the left-wing unions had second thoughts about supporting him. As he always did, Hawke portrayed himself as the certain winner, telling journalists that he was sure of securing a majority of a hundred; his hope was that this would unsettle Souter and encourage support from those delegates wanting to have supported the winner.

Hawke had brought Hazel along in a dress she'd bought for the occasion. Her conspicuous presence by his side, he hoped, might cause some of the socially conservative delegates to wonder about the veracity of the widely circulating stories about his womanising. Although the vote wouldn't be held until Wednesday morning, there was much to do before then. In an early blow to his rival, Hawke had used his majority on the executive to ensure that the committee charged with checking the credentials of the hundreds of officials thronging the cavernous hall would be controlled by his supporters, rather than by the returning officer and a scrutineer from each side. Every vote would make a difference, so any likely supporters of Souter who could be disallowed on one pretext or another would be a plus for the Hawke camp. Eventually, 754 delegates were approved and the congress got down to business.[19]

It began with Monk presenting his last presidential address, which concluded with the formal announcement of his retirement. A swift tactical move by Souter's supporters proposed that Monk's term should conclude at the end of the year rather than at the end of the congress; they hoped to take Hawke by surprise and goad him into opposing the motion, which might drive some of the moderate delegates into the Souter camp. And if Hawke was elected president, this move would give Souter an extra three months to prepare for his takeover. Hawke wasn't going to be outwitted. His numbers man, Charlie Fitzgibbon of the Waterside Workers' Federation, quickly declared the Hawke camp's support for the delay and called for it to be made a unanimous vote of the congress and for the delegates to give Monk a standing ovation.

The Souter camp tried again to give their man an advantage by seeking to bring on a debate about equal pay during the time that was allotted for Hawke's address. A debate on equal pay, after Hawke had just lost the ACTU's application, would have allowed his critics to attack him and might peel away some of his wavering supporters. It would also postpone his set-piece address until after the vote for the presidency on Wednesday morning. Again the Souter camp failed, losing by 120 votes, which buoyed the confidence of the Hawke forces. This meant that Hawke would have half an hour to impress the delegates with his report and to stir the emotions of the audience as he attacked the perfidious actions of the Gorton government, the rapacious steel pricing by BHP and the harsh wages policy of the employers – which he dismissed as 'the same old tart dressed up in fine new clothing' – before ending with a heartfelt appeal for unity. It was Hawke at his best. As he sat down, well satisfied with his performance, Souter rose at the rostrum to propose the adoption of the economic report, which had, ironically, been written by Hawke. The delegates looked down at the printed copies of the report in their hands and couldn't believe it when Souter mumbled his way through a reading of it rather than seizing the chance to respond to Hawke's policy speech. It 'went over like a lead balloon', recalled one of Souter's shocked supporters. The contrasting performances confirmed one of the major differences between the candidates. As Willis noted, Hawke 'was obviously good on TV' and delegates 'knew he could hold his end up publicly', whereas Souter 'had no great public speaking attributes, or capacity to present a case or anything. He was just a bloke who'd worked hard for the union movement and was respected.'[20]

Their starkly different presentations capped the first two days of a congress during which nearly everything had gone Hawke's way. There was still no telling how delegates would vote on Wednesday morning, despite the factional control that union chiefs tried to exert. In the event, when the result was announced that afternoon, the numbers were closer than Hawke had predicted. Instead of a majority of a hundred delegates, he only secured 399 votes to 350 for Souter. Delegates who were claimed by Hawke to be in the bag were found not to be there. Monk might have swung more votes Hawke's way, but he remained above the fray. Nevertheless, it was a good win for Hawke and a satisfying culmination to his two-year campaign. 'Great, another win, here we go, next phase,' thought Hazel as she joined in the jubilation of his supporters. When Hawke leapt up to acknowledge the cheers reverberating around the hall, his hand was shaken by Souter, whose camp still had a surprise or two to pull. When the votes were tallied for the executive, two of the candidates Hawke had supported were defeated, which meant the new executive would be split evenly between left and right, with the president providing the casting vote. From 1 January 1970, that would be him. The delegates would find, if they didn't know already, that their decision on the presidency had also decided the future direction of the trade union movement. As Hawke made clear in his acceptance speech, he would be taking the ACTU into new areas, fighting non-industrial issues and broadening the movement to incorporate the growing army of white-collar workers.[21] But that was for the following year. In the meantime, there was another election campaign to fight.

A federal election had been announced by Prime Minister Gorton, to be held on 25 October 1969. Delegates wondered how far the imperious figure of Gough Whitlam would cut into the massive Liberal majority won by Harold Holt, who'd been in political trouble well before he disappeared beneath the waves. As for the hard-drinking Gorton, his fondness for young women had caused political scandal and he could not hide the disunity that existed within his senior ranks, particularly between him and his treasurer, the diminutive, squeaky-voiced Billy McMahon. This election would be the first big electoral test for Gorton. He was defending his large majority by concentrating on familiar, fear-driven issues around the Vietnam War and the expansion of China and the Soviet Union, while also promising improvements in social welfare and increased spending on education. He claimed that the Labor Party was dominated by trade unions, and could point to the recently elected, left-wing ACTU president to prove his point. However, Whitlam – like Gorton a former airman – knew a thing or two about shooting down an opponent and navigating his way out of trouble.[22]

When he launched Labor's campaign on 1 October, Whitlam gave an inspirational speech that invited voters to join his 'crusade to give all our people the opportunities to which they are entitled in a rich and growing nation'. It was a political pitch that was suited to the times. After twenty-five years of economic expansion, Whitlam called for the nation's fruits to be used for equal educational opportunities, to provide access to housing and affordable health care and to ensure a dignified retirement in well-planned cities. Whitlam wanted to 'restore and widen freedoms and civil liberties', end conscription, bring the troops home and have a foreign policy that would make Australia a partner with the nations of the region. The classically educated Labor leader also wanted to 'liberate the creativity and ingenuity of our people' so as to 'build a truly great and good civilisation here in these southern oceans'. Turning Australians away from the Cold War politics of the last two decades, he assured voters: 'The future is with Australia; the future is with Labor.' A subsequent opinion poll suggested he might be right. It showed Labor on 45 per cent and the government on 42 per cent, which implied that Labor could claw back a lot of Holt's landslide. For the first time, Labor was helped by the DLP, which refused to commit its preferences to the Liberal Party after being upset by a government statement suggesting that Australia 'need not panic' about Soviet naval expansion into the Indian Ocean. With the opinion polls suggesting that the government was set for a drubbing, some Labor supporters dared to dream of victory.[23]

Gorton made things worse for his government by running an abysmal campaign that had his colleagues sharpening their knives for the post-election autopsy, only for Gorton to be saved by the skewed electoral system. Although Labor won a majority of the votes, Gorton held onto a slim majority of the seats. When the counting concluded, Whitlam had fallen four seats short of becoming prime minister, while an unchastened Gorton managed to win the post-election leadership ballot against McMahon.[24] Still, few had any illusions that he would survive until the following federal election, due by the end of 1972.

The eighteen new Labor MPs included a swag of university-educated professionals, which diluted the strength in the Labor caucus that had previously been enjoyed by former trade union officials. Among the newcomers was a 25-year-old party apparatchik from the New South Wales right wing, Paul Keating, who had a gleam in his eye, walked with a confident stride and disported himself in stylish clothes that suggested a level of political ambition belying his youth and lack of higher education.[25]

For Hawke, it was all rather academic. Approaching his fortieth birthday, he would soon take the leadership of the Australian trade union movement, which would involve challenges aplenty and provide opportunities to build his public profile in ways that had not been possible when he'd been an employee. While the prime ministership had beckoned him for decades, the prospect of a parliamentary career per se held no attraction. He wanted to be called to the prime ministership by the acclamation of the people and was prepared to bide his time.

PART FOUR

President

CHAPTER TWELVE

1970–1971

The turbulent 1960s had come to an end. The youthful uprisings across the world that had seen students and young people demand an end to the Vietnam War, to racial and economic injustice and to imperialism had produced profound cultural changes but not many fundamental political or economic changes. That was certainly true in Australia, where the Gorton government remained, at least in public, an enthusiastic participant in a war that had cost the lives of several hundred Australian soldiers, including conscripts, and hundreds of thousands of Vietnamese soldiers and civilians and that was spreading to Laos and Cambodia. Although it had been a popular electoral policy under Menzies and Holt, the war was being increasingly questioned by Australians who saw the fighting and the bombing on the nightly news, and by the young men who were liable to be conscripted to fight there. Even in black and white, the terrified faces of the Vietnamese civilians, the haunted looks of the soldiers and the photographs of atrocities were forcing Australians to reappraise the conflict.

It wasn't the only thing they were reappraising. The political verities of the 1950s and '60s were being challenged by a new generation who took peace and prosperity for granted and wanted a better world. Aboriginal people demanded land rights, women demanded gender equality, people questioned the environmental cost wrought by the post-war development binge and workers demanded a bigger share of the resulting prosperity. The turbulence would take various new forms, and Bob Hawke would play a leading part in several of its manifestations.

A vision of a better and more egalitarian world had long been the driving force for Hawke, who had just turned 40 when he handed over his position to Ralph Willis and moved downstairs into Albert Monk's old office. As leader of Australia's unionised workforce of nearly two million people, Hawke was finally able to live out his father's notion about the brotherhood of man in ways that hadn't been possible when he'd been subject to the command of Monk and Souter. Not that his power as president was completely untrammelled. His two-year campaign for the presidency and the slim majority that he'd won at the ACTU Congress exacerbated the bitter divisions on the seventeen-man ACTU Executive, which meant that his initial authority was limited. Souter may have publicly shaken Hawke's hand after the vote was declared, but the secretary and his many supporters couldn't hide their suspicion that the presidency had been somehow stolen from Souter's grasp by secret deals and manoeuvrings. In Victoria, there'd been a split in the Trades Hall Council that had seen left-wing unions suspended two years earlier after they refused to pay their affiliation fees unless they were given greater representation on the THC Executive. The right-wingers who now controlled the THC regarded Hawke and his supporters as 'dangerous extremists'.[1] Hawke would have to build his authority over time.

Hawke could have used his bare majority of supporters on the executive to push his proposals through, but that could have brought his presidency to an early end. Instead, he would emulate Monk's adroit leadership, his own experience as student president of the UWA Guild and the lessons he drew from Albert Hawke (and presumably also from Clem), whose example had taught him 'the importance of having decent human relations with people within your own party' and a 'readiness to meet with people you didn't necessarily agree with'. Rather than ramming things through, he would have to keep his ever-present anger contained and seek compromises that would allow the executive to reach unanimous decisions on as many issues as possible. With Labor likely to win the next federal election, it was important that strikes didn't impede its path to power and that the Labor leadership took union concerns on board. To that end, Hawke called a meeting of the Commonwealth Labor Advisory Committee in January 1970. With Hawke in the chair, three fellow members of the executive met with Whitlam and six of his senior Labor team in the ACTU boardroom, where they discussed current campaigns for higher wages and shorter hours, equal pay and four weeks' annual leave. The wish list was long and Hawke made sure that the unions could bring more pressure to bear on the Labor leaders by including representatives of the two peak white-collar organisations in future meetings of the committee. As for himself, he was kept busy during that first year, rushing from one protracted dispute to the next, as the level of industrial strife rose to new heights. He also tried flexing his muscles by imposing a ban on the live export of merino rams, only to be thwarted by Prime Minister Gorton, who offered an RAAF base and its refuelling facilities for the flights.[2]

Hawke's style of leadership and the expansive vision he had for the ACTU were evident at the first executive meeting in late February 1970. Instead of the usual concentration on industrial issues, Hawke invited Dr H.C. 'Nugget' Coombs, who was chair of the Australian Council for the Arts and also of the Council for Aboriginal Affairs, to speak to the rough-hewn union officials about the arts as well as about Aboriginal disadvantage. Coombs had been a student at Perth Modern, one of the founding members of the Labour Club at the University of Western Australia and, like Hawke, had served as president of its Guild. As well as Coombs, he had Tom Roper from the NUAUS speak about educational inequalities, while two independence activists from Papua and New Guinea, Albert Maori Kiki and Gavera Rea, reported on the situation of trade unions and the independence movement in that territory. The executive was generally happy to go along, agreeing to establish committees on the arts and on Aboriginal affairs. In regard to the latter, Hawke envisaged that the ACTU could take the lead in 'fighting against discriminatory practices in jobs and wages', while also telling journalists that he and Souter would visit Papua and New Guinea with a view to reinforcing its nascent trade union movement, perhaps by establishing an office in Port Moresby, where he claimed that employers were 'getting away with murder'.[3]

While Hawke's first executive meeting led to a flurry of initiatives, some of which would never be implemented, another issue proved more problematic. Hawke wanted the executive to express support in principle for the upcoming Vietnam Moratorium on 8 May 1970, which took its inspiration from the American Moratorium to Stop the War in Vietnam, held in October 1969, and the massive marches that had occurred across America in November following the disclosure of the My Lai massacre. In Australia, the Moratorium would not just be a march but a symbolic sit-down against business as usual. This deliberate act of civil disobedience alarmed authorities, provoking the Minister for Labour and National Service, Bill Snedden, to liken the organisers to 'political bikies who pack-rape democracy'.[4]

Despite Hawke's motion being in accord with existing ACTU policy, which demanded Australian troops be withdrawn from Vietnam, and although more than seventy federal Labor MPs had declared their support for the Moratorium, the issue split the executive down the middle. While the seamen and the wharfies opposed the war and had already black-banned ships carrying munitions, some right-wing unions were just as staunch in support of the war. Hawke tried to reach unanimity by phrasing the motion in the most moderate terms. It simply called on unions 'to support activities which are in line with declared ACTU policies', provided they were 'conducted in a disciplined and orderly fashion that will bring credit to the Trade Union Movement'. Rather than calling on all trade unions to down tools for the Moratorium, which some unions planned to do, the motion merely provided sanction for those unions taking part. It still failed to achieve unanimity. Instead, Hawke had to use his casting vote to ensure its approval, only to have a powerful right-wing representative from New South Wales, John Ducker, call for it to be referred for approval to the Trades Hall Council in each state, where Ducker was confident it would fail to secure majority approval. Which is what happened. Not that it mattered, since many unions would go ahead anyway. Hawke also would not resile from his own opposition to the war.[5] Ultimately, however, it wasn't Hawke but the softly spoken Jim Cairns who led the Moratorium movement, risking his political reputation by becoming the titular leader of a protest that many feared would turn violent.

It was Cairns who ensured that there was only a brief sit-down in the Melbourne streets, rather than the two hours that some of the more radical activists wanted. Hawke played no role in these organisational debates. Neither did he join the march. In April 1970, he had flown to Geneva to attend the annual meeting of the International Labour Organization (ILO) for the first time. As ACTU president, he was on its governing body, which met four times a year in Switzerland. Hawke went by way of Jakarta, and it was here that he encountered Blanche d'Alpuget for the first time.

D'Alpuget was a single child who'd been raised by journalist parents who'd wanted a boy, much as Hawke's mother had wanted a girl. Her father had encouraged D'Alpuget to pursue masculine activities, such that she thought of herself as a boy until she hit puberty.[6] She would later recount how she'd had 'many lovers' and had enjoyed an open marriage with her Australian diplomat husband, Tony Pratt, during the decade they'd been together. The pair had been in Indonesia in 1966, where Pratt worked as an intelligence officer, and had just arrived back in Jakarta and were staying in the room next to Hawke's at the five-star Hotel Indonesia. Hawke first set eyes on her at a party where she wore a white dress made by her mother. She recalled how 'we just clicked'. And they met again early the following day when Hawke banged on their hotel door, shouting, 'Wake up, you bastards!' as he was meant to be taken by Pratt to visit a factory. Then, when D'Alpuget later went for a swim in the hotel's pool, Hawke was there in his bathers, disporting his body and displaying the scar on his stomach from his teenage motorbike accident. The fact that he rode a motorbike, spoke with a 'flat Australian voice' and was a trade unionist all marked him down in her eyes. After all, she wrote, 'I was a very pretentious young diplomat's wife'. There were no 'sexual sparks', at least not from D'Alpuget, but 'he was definitely interested', she thought. Indeed he was. Hawke said he 'was immediately very much attracted to Blanche not simply because of her considerable beauty but her character and her probing mind and a charm that ... I found very compelling'. Nothing came of it. 'I didn't know who the hell he was,' wrote D'Alpuget, who had misheard his name and thought he was called 'Robin'. They just had a long talk, and that was that. The following year they met in Jakarta again. This time, Hawke and daughter Susan attended a party of embassy folk at Pratt's house, where the partygoers drank and danced and argued into the early morning about the war in Vietnam. At one point, presumably drunk, Hawke exclaimed loudly to D'Alpuget, who was sitting next to her husband, 'I want to fuck you.' It would be another five years before he'd get the chance to do so.[7]

His April 1970 visit to Geneva by way of Jakarta brought Hawke into contact with many of his trade union counterparts, allowing them to compare notes on the common challenges they faced. These ranged from the technological advances that were displacing workers, to the growing tendency of transnational corporations to shift their operations to low-wage countries and the use by governments of oppressive powers to limit workers' wages and conditions.

The ILO was more than just a meeting place for trade unionists. It had been established in 1919 by the League of Nations, the predecessor of the United Nations, to bring together representatives of governments, employers and trade unionists. They met in the hall of a grand building on the shores of Lake Geneva. The Australian delegation included diplomats and government ministers, along with employer and trade union representatives, of whom Hawke would be just one. Yet he quickly made a name for himself when he defended the organisation against criticism from the US delegation after a Soviet representative was appointed as an assistant director-general. In the words of one official, they had been 'struck by his energy, frankness, dynamic approach, his quick understanding and spontaneous friendliness', and now they 'saw that he had courage'. But the demons that so often beset Hawke in Melbourne also travelled with him to Geneva, springing out when he was drunk. At a succession of cocktail parties, delegates were taken aback by his 'swearing, boozing and womanising', with the attending Australian diplomats having to usher 'a roaring drunk Hawke' into a car and off to his hotel. He'd been to Geneva before on behalf of the ACTU but was there now as its president. He revelled in the relative anonymity of the beautiful city, with its permanent population of little more than 300,000 people.[8] It provided a welcome break from the pressure of being Bob Hawke in Australia, where he had become immediately recognisable and increasingly acknowledged as one of the country's most powerful political figures.

As ACTU president, Hawke began lifting his public profile even higher. Unlike Monk, he opened his door to journalists and made himself available for countless interviews on radio and television. By July 1970, he was being called 'the ACTU dynamo' by the Melbourne *Sun News-Pictorial's* industrial roundsman, Barry Donovan, who described how Hawke 'welcomes tough questions and thrusts back hard at them. He is a union leader unlike any this country has ever seen before. His image, like his sideburns, is shaped for 1970.' Indeed,

Hawke quickly became such a ubiquitous presence on television that a viewer in Perth complained about seeing him 'being interviewed and giving his opinions' on three consecutive nights. He had become a celebrity whose colourblindness and lack of dress sense caused him to choose clothing that was a bit too loud and sharp. Combined with his strident manner, it made him noticed during televised interviews and debates with government ministers. It would have been a particular pleasure when he was judged by journalists to have won a television debate with his former Guild rival Snedden. Such was Hawke's profile after just seven months as president that he was widely considered to be 'a strong contender' for leadership of the Labor Party once he'd 'built up a solid reputation as the ACTU's leader'. As if to signal his political aspirations, Hawke was elected in June 1970 to the state executive of the Victorian party, although he told Donovan that he had 'absolutely no thoughts at present about going into Parliamentary politics'.[9]

Neither would Hawke become deeply embroiled in the backroom business of the Labor Party, or even in his local branch in Sandringham. Yet the party couldn't hope to win office without making some fundamental changes to the organisation of the Victorian branch, which was effectively under the control of an outside body, the Trade Union Defence Committee, which represented the left-wing unions that had been expelled from the Trades Hall Council. The president of the branch was George Crawford, from the Plumbers and Gasfitters Employees' Union, while the secretary was a graduate of UWA and a former member of the university's Liberal Club, Bill Hartley, who would become a passionate supporter of the Arab cause and a source of much mischief in the party. An informal grouping of mainly middle-class party members, known as the Participants, was doing what it could to wrest control of the state branch from the Hartley faction, but had to operate secretly for fear of being expelled for acting as 'a party within the party'.

One of the prime movers behind the Participants was the lawyer John Button, while its newsletter was edited by Bob Murray, from the Sandringham branch. Button would sometimes encounter Hawke in an Italian barber shop on Lygon Street, where the latter would be having his handsome head of hair carefully 'sculpted'. Button would listen as Hawke made 'wry observations about the deplorable state of the Labor

Party in Victoria'. Despite being a member of the state executive, which gave him an inside view of the branch's deplorable state, Hawke was never an active member of the pro-Whitlam reform group, perhaps because he didn't want to offend the left-wing unionists who'd helped to make him ACTU president.[10] Matters were nonetheless brought to a head following the 1970 state election, and Hawke found himself in the middle of it.

The Labor Party had had hopes of doing well at the state election under the fresh-faced leadership of the urbane Clyde Holding. The rough-hewn Liberal premier Henry Bolte had been in power for fifteen years, and there was a widespread sense of it being time for a change. However, Holding's chances of victory were stymied when Crawford and Hartley issued a statement in the final week of the campaign declaring that the party couldn't support Holding's commitment to continue state aid for non-government schools. This was a policy that had divided the party throughout the 1960s and finally been decided by the federal conference in 1969, which had agreed, at Whitlam's urging, to support state aid. As a result, Crawford and Hartley had not only destroyed Holding's chance of becoming premier but had contravened the party's federal policy. Their action made it clear that the branch would have to be brought to heel if Labor was to have any hope of winning government in Canberra.

It wasn't Hawke who led this move, but the South Australian MP and former AWU official Clyde Cameron, who'd been promised the position of Minister for Labour in a future Whitlam government. At Cameron's urging in August 1971, the federal executive agreed to investigate a list of charges against the Victorian branch, and two weeks later dismissed the state executive. Hawke had been concerned that the federal intervention could split the party, but agreed after the event to join the advisory council that had replaced the state executive until the branch could be reinstated. He was also appointed as one of two Victorian representatives to the party's federal executive.[11] With the Victorian branch effectively subdued, Whitlam could look forward with greater confidence to the next federal election.

At the ACTU, Hawke lost no time in expanding the scope of his new position and broadening the ambit of the organisation. He began by adding to the existing seven staff. As education officer he appointed Peter Matthews, a former lecturer who'd been on the staff of the UK Trades Union Congress. Matthews would soon be complaining to Paul Munro that Hawke had given him no guidance as to what he should be doing. Munro explained that he would 'have to work it out for yourself', noting that Hawke 'will give you a free hand unless you stuff it up'. As information officer Hawke appointed Geoff Gleghorn, a former industrial relations journalist with the *Australian Financial Review*. With Willis taking over Hawke's previous role, his former assistant now needed an assistant of his own. Hawke took the then radical step of appointing Jan White, a 22-year-old economics graduate who, when she went to the pub after work, drank a lemon squash rather than a beer.[12] Which was probably just as well.

It was White, known as Jan Marsh after her marriage, who was meant to be assisting Willis at the 1970 wage case, only for Willis to find that Hawke insisted on presenting the opening arguments, as if he were still the advocate, and then leaving Willis to present the detail. That was not something that Hawke would have accepted when he began as advocate, and Willis was not happy at being upstaged on his first appearance as if he were incapable of holding his own after ten years as Hawke's assistant. 'It didn't look good for me,' recalled Willis, and he was unsettled even more because he 'didn't know exactly what [Hawke] was going to say'. It was the usual angry, tub-thumping presentation, the tenor of which can be seen in the heavily inscribed, handwritten notes that have been preserved in the ACTU papers in the Noel Butlin Archives Centre. Against several points, Hawke wrote 'HAMMER THIS' or 'BASH' or 'KNOCK THIS IN DETAIL'. He hit out at the 'ABSOLUTE BLOODY SMARMINESS' of his opponents and lashed the 'ABSOLUTE HOPELESSNESS' of their arguments, which he described as 'BASICALLY OFFENSIVE TO LOGIC', 'BLOODY NONSENSE' or simply 'CRAP'. After completing his opening address based upon such notes, Hawke slumped down beside Willis, allowing his young advocate to get some small revenge when he was asked a question by one of the judges and told the judge that he'd have his assistant, Hawke, look it up. 'The whole bench laughed at this,' recalled Willis, 'and I thought, "Oh shit, what have I said," and Bob's mumbling under his breath, "Cheeky young bastard."'[13]

When the ACTU called a three-hour strike in August 1970 in protest at Gorton's niggardly budget, the prime minister attacked Hawke as 'a would-be dictator'. Liberal MPs were convinced that linking Hawke to Whitlam's rising political star would cause it somehow to explode. So Gorton made frequent references to Hawke and the ACTU during the subsequent half-Senate election campaign in November 1970, warning that the union campaign for a thirty-five-hour week would destroy the economy. Gorton was egged on by the Liberal Party's president, Bob Southey, who'd seen Hawke up close at a dinner and told Gorton that the union leader 'really is an intimidating and unattractive creature' who 'actually does think in terms of class warfare'. But the world was changing in ways that didn't suit the government's election hopes, particularly as the generation of post-war 'baby boomers' began to add their names to the electoral roll. Although Whitlam lost ground during the half-Senate election, Gorton lost even more, with dissatisfied voters opting for the newly formed Australia Party and the DLP, along with a slew of independent candidates. The balance of power in the Senate was now held by the independents and the DLP, which marked a watershed in the make-up and role of the increasingly assertive upper house.[14]

The government's attacks on Hawke only lifted his profile and approval ratings and led to even more media appearances, which allowed audiences to judge him for themselves. Most were persuaded that the larrikin unionist was both entertaining and standing up for their interests. Whereas few Australians would have known Albert Monk's name, there were few who didn't know Hawke's. And many knew him by sight from his increasingly frequent appearances on television. As for the Liberal government, it just couldn't resist attacking him in the hope that doing so would tarnish Labor's growing electoral appeal. Hawke usually sidestepped the attacks or responded with effective rejoinders that were relayed by way of his many media contacts. He was a shameless self-promoter who gave his private telephone number to any journalist who wanted it and many others besides, much to the annoyance of ACTU staff, who had to field the calls in the office, and of Hazel, who had to deal with the many calls that came at all hours to their home.[15]

Financially, Hawke was better off once he became president of the ACTU, earning about $9000 a year, or about $110,000 in today's terms.

He could have earned much more in the private sector, either as a lawyer or an economist, but Hawke told journalist Barry Donovan: 'I personally don't think about money. I don't feel financial frustration in any way.' The size of his Sandringham property suggested otherwise, as did the assiduous way he pursued actions for defamation. One of the lawyers he used in his defamation actions was Peter Redlich, who later noted how Hawke would frequently ring him asking whether one media report or another could justify him making a demand for damages.[16] Then again, the family needed the money, as they would be incurring additional expenses now that he and Hazel had decided to send their children to expensive private schools. Susan had already begun at Firbank, albeit with the assistance of a scholarship, and Stephen and Rosslyn would soon follow to private schools. It was always a balancing act for Hazel to ensure there was sufficient to pay their hefty mortgage.

For her part, Hazel was forced to abandon her education plans when Bob became president. After achieving excellent school results as a teenager, and then working with academics in Oxford and for the Indian High Commissioner in Canberra, she'd been keen to carve out a career for herself as the children came to the end of their primary schooling. Hazel's Higher School Certificate night classes in the city just weren't tenable when Bob sometimes spent about half the year travelling interstate or overseas, on top of the long hours he spent at work, in the pub or pursuing the love interests that came his way. Studying had been important for Hazel's faltering self-esteem.[17] She might also have been making provision for the possibility that he might leave her altogether. Now she was back to being a full-time mother and a part-time wife. The 1970s would be a dark decade for her.

On the surface, her life might have seemed idyllic. The family was living in a relatively luxurious home, complete with a tennis court and swimming pool. Hazel was a good tennis player and played in a weekday women's competition, as well as playing with Bob and another couple on Sunday mornings. She also allowed a tennis coach, Mick Sweetnam, to coach children on the court on weekday afternoons, in return for which he helped her improve her game. The court and the pool attracted local children, which Hazel encouraged, since it was reminiscent of her own childhood in Perth, where neighbourhood children were in and out of each other's houses and took over the street for games. Once, when she saw children playing with a tennis ball on the street, Hazel had no hesitation in inviting them to use the court. Bob was not amused. One of the children later recalled how he returned that night and 'poured himself out of the car'; it was clear he was 'completely pickled'. When he saw them on his court, he 'went apoplectic' and sent them scampering home as he yelled out, 'Next time fucking well ask!' A month or so later, Hazel again offered them the use of the court, only to have a furious Hawke repeat his drunken tirade. The children had already run from the court after seeing him arrive home, looking as though 'he was going to have a heart attack' as he screamed at their disappearing figures: 'Next time fucking well ask!' Other children, who went along with their parents, had a different experience when Hawke was sober and was happy to bowl a cricket ball to them. One of them was the future cricketer Shane Warne, whose mother worked as a cleaner for Hazel and helped out when they were entertaining. In 2018, Warne recalled how the kids 'used to have a hit on Bob's tennis court' and were sometimes joined on the court by Hawke, who would introduce them to 'visiting heavies – politicians and celebrities – who played too. We loved Bob.'[18]

There were happy times for Hazel as well. Some of these occasions occurred when Hawke took the family to Adelaide for the state's annual Labor Day celebrations, so he could parade through the city's streets as ACTU president, enjoying the cheers of the onlookers. The march was a celebration of unionism and served as the prelude to a day of activities that culminated with a dinner dance. The first time, Hawke had rung Clyde Cameron, the chair of Labor's industrial relations committee, and asked to be put up for the weekend. Thinking it was only Hawke and Hazel, Cameron offered to let the pair sleep on his couch, only for the Hawkes to turn up with their small children and dog. For the next several years, the family stayed instead at the home of Mick Young, a former shearer who'd become the powerful federal secretary of the Labor Party in 1969 and the federal member for Adelaide in 1974. 'Bob and Mick got a bit wild sometimes,' recalled Hazel, 'and Mick had a tendency to sing the very rousing hymns of his Irish heritage in the VERY early hours'. Hawke could match him song for song with the Congregational hymns of his childhood, which he would mix with the stirring songs of the labour movement. The stays in South Australia served a political purpose, lifting Hawke's profile there and reminding people that the state was the place of his birth and might one day provide an electorate to launch his career in federal politics. And there were the times they spent at the Gippsland hobby farm of their local doctor. These moments stood out for the family because they were high points in years marked more by Hawke's long absences.[19]

He made a brief reference in his memoirs to the pressures on Hazel during the 1960s and '70s, claiming that he'd been largely oblivious to the strain he'd put on the family. If he really was unaware, it wasn't due to Hazel not voicing her objections plainly and loudly at times. At other times, she stayed silent for the sake of the children and herself. The Hawkes' mutual friend from their Canberra days, Peter Coleman, recalled his shock when he discovered in 1972 how the formerly 'bright and vivacious' Hazel had changed into 'a cold, tough woman', with Coleman concluding that 'she must have had a rough spin'.[20]

For Hazel, there was the burden of 'running a household and garden and coping with the media and everything that came to the door, or the letterbox, telephone or answering machine', which could include anonymous threats, packages of excrement and torrents of abuse. She was also 'coping with three teenage children and all their friends who came and went constantly'. She also had to cope with the knowledge of her husband's constant philandering. Drinking seemed to help Hazel, as did some of her friendships with women. Although she read the works of Simone de Beauvoir, Germaine Greer and Betty Friedan, she struggled to free herself from traditional ideas about the role of women, which she had absorbed during her upbringing in Perth. She and Sue urged Hawke to read these books, but Hazel came away feeling that he hadn't understood them. When Greer toured Australia to publicise *The Female Eunuch*, she appeared with Hawke on the ABC's *This Day Tonight*. Looking on was the show's researcher, Vera Wasowski, who later recalled how:

> Bob believes passionately that he's the most brilliant man on the planet. Germaine believes that she's the most brilliant human who ever lived. They're fascinated with each other, and also insanely competitive. Bob shows he's on the side of women, up to a point. He says complimentary things about Germaine, and also a few

condescending things ... after the show I'm interested to see her come on to Bob, not waiting for him to show he adores her. Bob's going to be prime minister one day: he knows it; she knows it. Their mutual fascination is an acceptance of equality. They're twins in their vanity, also in their immaturity. Both are adolescents, forever.

Certainly, there was little change in his subsequent behaviour towards the women in his life. Hazel continued to rail against the way she and their children were treated by a husband who was too distracted by the pursuit of his ambition and his pleasures to pay them sufficient notice. They had to seize whatever family moments that he deigned to give them.[21]

During his decade as ACTU advocate, Hawke had spent long days arguing before the often-hostile judges of the Arbitration Commission for workers to be given their fair due, only to find wages often falling behind once inflation was taken into account. Increases to the total wage were not enough, particularly for women and the poorly paid. Hawke recognised that there was another side to the equation. If there was a limit to what he could achieve with wages, perhaps he could do better by limiting price rises, or even reducing them.

The opportunity to tackle prices came when he was approached by Lionel Revelman, the part owner of Bourke's, a discount department store on the corner of La Trobe and Elizabeth streets in Melbourne. After being an articled clerk for the firm of Maurice Blackburn and then a barrister, Revelman had given up law to run a tow truck operation before joining his brother at Bourke's, where the pair became engaged in a long-running price war with Myer's, the dominant department store in Melbourne, which had been helped by manufacturers refusing to supply goods to discount retailers. Shops such as Bourke's had to source their supplies from manufacturers or importers who had no such requirement, which meant that they were unable to sell many popular brands and were struggling to survive. This system of resale price maintenance caused consumers to pay higher prices for a wide range of goods, from socks to washing machines, which thereby lowered the living standards of all Australians. The federal government had promised to ban it but nothing had been done.[22]

When Revelman came knocking on Hawke's door in October 1970, the two quickly struck up a friendship and sketched out an agreement, under which the ACTU agreed to pay $1.75 million for a 50 per cent stake in Bourke's. The money would only be payable after five years, during which time any profits earned by Bourke's would be divided equally between the two stakeholders. The partnership seemed relatively risk-free for the ACTU, since it could withdraw from the deal without penalty at any time during those five years, while Bourke's would reap the benefit from the additional customers that the association was meant to produce when unions encouraged their members to patronise the store. More importantly for Bourke's, the ACTU promised to use its industrial muscle to destroy the system of resale price maintenance. With Hawke at the helm, the union movement would do what the government had failed to do. For Hawke, it promised to provide the first building block for a much larger and more influential union organisation, along the lines of those he'd seen during his travels in West Germany, where unions owned one of the country's largest banks and insurance companies, along with a housing finance and construction company. Being the champion of the Australian consumer would also boost his profile and popularity, particularly after he began appearing in the store's television advertisements.[23]

Although manufacturers and rival retailers tried to defend the system of resale price maintenance, Hawke and Revelman had their measure. Soon after the ACTU took up its stake on 1 January 1971, the offending manufacturers were given an ultimatum to supply Bourke's or face the full fury of the union movement, which threatened to impose a black ban on any company that didn't comply. In the event, the imposition of the black bans was delayed after Hawke fell ill with one of his frequent infections. The campaign couldn't be prosecuted without him.

When he recovered, Hawke came back in full fighting mode, focusing his attention on Dunlop, a massive industrial conglomerate that made everything from tyres and sports gear to underwear. With the wharfies banning the handling of Dunlop goods at Australian ports, transport workers refusing to deliver to their factories and Dunlop workers going on strike, Hawke had the company's chairman, Eric Dunshea, by the throat. Hawke also had the public and much of the media willing him on. Despite being warned that attacking Hawke would only cause him to 'become a large national figure commanding an immense amount of personal sympathy', the new prime minister, Billy McMahon, went ahead anyway, declaring in parliament that Hawke was using the 'great trade union movement' for the 'aggrandisement of the company [Bourke's] he has taken over'. Hawke shot back, explaining that the union campaign would 'reduce prices and halt the extortionate profits many companies were making at the expense of the consumer'. That should lead to lower inflation, said Hawke, for which he expected the government's support.[24] Not that he needed any help from McMahon, since Dunlop raised the white flag after holding out for little more than a day.

On 17 March, Dunshea's chauffeur dropped his boss at the door of the ACTU, where the media were waiting. After some discussion in Hawke's office, the two men fronted a press conference, at which Dunshea agreed that Dunlop would henceforth supply its goods to Bourke's, which would be free to sell them at a discount. The journalists were disappointed to see that there was no humiliation for Dunshea, who later recounted to D'Alpuget how Hawke 'answered most of the questions for me, before the Press could get stuck into me; and avoided the use of the term "surrender"'. The relieved businessman said that Hawke 'made it as gentle, easy and honourable as any person could'. For Hawke, this was about more than just resale price maintenance. He told journalists it was 'part of a fundamental extension of the aims of trade unionism in Australia', and could see the ACTU move into 'credit unions, hire purchase, insurance, health and medical benefits schemes, housing co-operatives – perhaps even newspapers'. Indeed, said Hawke, there was 'no end' to what the union movement might do. When it was all over, Revelman gathered up Hawke and the staff to celebrate with champagne at the Lygon pub, now renamed the John Curtin, and then took Hawke to his locked-up store to fit him out with tennis gear so they could play a game at his Balwyn mansion. The pair would play many games of tennis over the succeeding year, until one day Revelman was stricken with a heart attack, dropping his racquet and dying in Hawke's arms. It was one of the most traumatic experiences of Hawke's life.[25]

The whirlwind campaign against Dunlop reaped a rich reward for Bourke's, for the ACTU and for Hawke, who was hailed as the people's champion. The South Australian Farmers' Union talked of setting up a joint company with the ACTU to process Australian farm produce, with the farmers even talking of affiliating with the ACTU, but nothing came of it. Nevertheless, other manufacturers quickly followed Dunlop's example and began supplying Bourke's with their goods, while the federal government finally introduced its long-promised ban on resale price maintenance. Journalists searched in vain for any other example 'in the world in which trade-union power had been used so devastatingly on an issue that involved the commercial operations of the economy'.[26] And it was all due to Hawke's leadership. He'd tasted fame before, but this was of a different magnitude.

Because of the Bourke's campaign, women's magazines also sent writers along to the ACTU office, and they liked what they saw. When 54-year-old journalist Ailsa Craig strolled along Lygon Street to meet with Hawke, his aggressive demeanour on television had led her to expect a big bully, only to discover that he was 'lean, spare and nothing like ten-foot tall'. She described for the readers of *Woman's Day* how he had 'a fashionably thick head of hair and nice side-levers', and said that 'energy streams out of him like an electric current' such that it 'almost strikes you a physical blow'. Moreover, he has 'some of the sheer male magnetism of Richard Burton' and is 'what Liz [Taylor] herself would call a sexy man'. The interview must have been conducted in the John Curtin, because the manager, Dawn Bemrose, confirmed to her that 'he's got charm all right' and the staff 'like him a lot', while Hawke's secretary, Corinne Millane, agreed that Hawke was 'a beaut boss' who was 'so easy to work for'. The only person prepared to reveal his darker side was Marjorie Cropper, an English barmaid, who complained that 'he's always trying to take a rise out of me. I don't feel at ease with him. I think he's, well ... arrogant.'[27]

Being described as 'a sexy man' would have pleased Hawke, as would his first appearance in an opinion poll, which found that 42 per cent of Australians approved of his performance while just 30 per cent disapproved and the remainder were undecided. Many would have approved of him advocating for the workers during the 1960s and now standing up for consumers. Many would also have related to the tough-talking, larrikin persona that he presented in media interviews. Most saw through the hysterical attempts of his political opponents to paint him as a dangerous radical. Sure enough, he was a radical, but in the tradition of those who'd fought for the abolition of slavery and for universal suffrage, rather than a Robespierre who wanted to put capitalists and their flunkeys in tumbrels. His experience at three universities hadn't seen him become attached to any particular political philosophy. His narcissism made him resistant to the idea of being a follower of any great thinker. He would say that he wasn't beholden to teachers at school and nor was he beholden to any academic theorist. 'Some people may have their guiding-star philosophers,' he boasted, 'but not me.' He proclaimed himself a socialist and agreed 'that while the means of production are in private hands, they will be dominated by the call of private profits'. Not that he wanted to tear down capitalism. He accepted the existing economic system and acknowledged that present-day Australians had become inherently conservative and resistant to radical change. Those who wanted 'complete socialism' in Australia were 'up shit creek', since not even the wartime emergency had been able to bring that about. As he told a writer for the American magazine *Time*, he was 'realistic enough to see that most Australians don't want socialism; therefore we must make the system we have work better'.[28]

No sooner had he disposed of resale price maintenance than Hawke was confronted with an issue that would divide the union movement and threaten to destroy his popularity. It arose from a planned tour of Australia during the winter of 1971 by the all-white South African rugby union team, which was to be followed in the summer by a visit from the similarly segregated South African cricket team. The apartheid regime had become an international pariah ever since the world saw photographs of its police fatally shooting sixty-nine protestors, including many women and children, in the town of Sharpeville in 1960 and the subsequent jailing of many anti-apartheid activists, including Nelson Mandela. The civil rights movement in the United States and decolonisation in Africa and Asia added to South Africa's isolation, while protests in Britain had seen the proposed tour of its cricket team cancelled in 1970, only for it to be invited to Australia.

When the rugby and cricket tours were announced, the great majority of Australians believed that politics should not intrude into sport. Hawke was not one of them. His deep-felt beliefs and life experiences had made apartheid anathema to him, as it was to many in the union movement and Labor Party. But he trod warily. Not only was he confronting Australians' love for sport, but racism remained fairly rampant in Australia, as much in the union movement as elsewhere. Initially, Hawke said he would 'boycott the tour as a personal gesture against apartheid', only to have some union leaders demand that the ACTU impose a 'complete boycott'. At the same time, Whitlam was fearful of the electoral effect and urged him to refrain from imposing a boycott and demand instead that the government order the tour's cancellation. Few Labor MPs took a prominent stand against the tour, although Bill Hayden did so in Brisbane, where he addressed a crowd from the back of a truck.[29]

While a broad-based protest movement, led by students and the churches, proposed to block any matches from going ahead, Hawke was more circumspect. He wrote to the South African government suggesting that the issue could be solved if its teams were chosen according to a non-discriminatory selection policy. Even a token non-white player in the rugby and cricket teams would suffice. Billy McMahon immediately accused him of 'attempting to intimidate' the South Africans. With McMahon refusing to stop the tour, Hawke announced after an ACTU Executive meeting on 13 May that the organisation would ask its affiliated unions to impose boycotts on the team 'as an act of conscience'. Later, he spoke to a meeting of some fifty union officials crammed into the ACTU boardroom, where a young Bill Kelty listened in admiration as Hawke laid out the case against apartheid. Kelty was an economics graduate from La Trobe University who'd gone on to become a research officer with the Storemen and Packers' Union. He described how Hawke's 'call for action was quietly and emotionally delivered but at the time it sounded like an army of trumpeters. There was plainly a tear for all to see.' After speaking for forty minutes, Hawke had convinced them of the cause. 'It still is the best speech I have ever heard,' recalled Kelty.[30]

Hawke was hoping that the executive's decision would cause the tour to be cancelled, while he pressured the commercial sponsors of the subsequent cricket tour to withdraw their support. However, the rugby tour wasn't going to be cancelled so long as it had the support of the federal government.

While expressing his personal abhorrence of apartheid, McMahon continued to declare that the tours were a matter for the sporting organisations and that apartheid was a matter for South Africa. An election was due within eighteen months and McMahon was beginning to sense a political opportunity. With the prospect of trade union bans and riots in the streets, McMahon offered the South Africans the use of air force planes so they could circumvent any union bans on their transport. That prompted Hawke to suggest that the RAAF would then have to be renamed 'the Royal Apartheid Air Force', claiming that it 'demonstrated the absurd lengths the Australian government was prepared to go to identify itself with the racist government of South Africa'. McMahon saw the South Africans as providing a possible opportunity for an early law-and-order election and for cutting Hawke down to size. Journalist Don Whitington claimed that Hawke's 'public and private life is already under close surveillance by his political enemies', and that the Australian Security Intelligence Organisation (ASIO) has been used to obtain evidence about people the Government regard as hostile'. They wanted to destroy Hawke politically before he made his anticipated move into parliament.[31]

For a time it seemed the government might have won. Even *The Age*, which had long been an opponent of such tours, thought Hawke had 'overplayed his hand on this issue'. His stand saw him subjected to death threats; he also received hate mail at home, while black paint was tipped over Hazel's car and their children were taunted and bullied at school. Things became so bad that the Hawkes' home was placed under police guard. While some unions imposed a boycott, the tour organisers were able to circumvent them.

Just as the South Africans were about to arrive in Perth, Hawke was due to fly to Geneva for the annual meeting of the ILO and to present an inaugural lecture in Israel, financed by the Jewish communities of Melbourne and Sydney in memory of the recently deceased Labor senator Sam Cohen. He took fourteen-year-old Susan along with him, planning to leave her at an Israeli kibbutz to gather information for a school essay on the conflict between Palestinians and Jews, only to face a conflict of his own as they were forced to walk a gauntlet of jeering rugby supporters at Perth airport, where the South African team was about to arrive. Staying overnight at his parents' Tate Street home while a security guard kept watch outside, Hawke had to negotiate the lifting of a ban imposed on his plane by aircraft refuellers, who'd objected to being ordered by their federal union not to provide services to the South African team, with the president of the local union branch describing Hawke as 'a dictator who was using apartheid to impose his will on the trade union movement'. Hawke declared that he 'merely enunciate[d] the views of the union movement' and that the government had 'compounded our position in the eyes of the world as a racist country'. When their plane finally took off, it was forced to return because of a bomb threat, only to take off again a couple of hours later.[32]

For Hawke, it would be a life-changing trip.

CHAPTER THIRTEEN

1971–1972

As anti-apartheid protesters stormed onto rugby fields and workers downed tools in support, Hawke left the growing mayhem behind. When he landed in Tel Aviv, he was already an unabashed supporter of the Jewish state at a time when the Labor Party had an even-handed policy towards Israel and the Arab states.

Hawke's attachment to the Israeli cause can perhaps be traced back to his childhood, when he'd acted for his mother in several performances of the story of Esther, the Old Testament story about the Jewish wife of the Persian king who had persuaded him to abandon his plan to kill his Jewish subjects. Possibly Hawke was also atoning for the jibes he'd directed at the Jewish students of Perth Modern. As a boy of small stature, he'd also been attracted to the story of Samson and Delilah, as well as that of David and Goliath; he later imagined himself as David when going in to fight against the phalanx of barristers at the Arbitration Commission. To many people, it seemed that the story of David and Goliath was being played out in modern Israel, as the newly formed state battled for survival against its much larger Arab neighbours. Hawke's sympathy for Israel was strengthened by his friendship with a group of Jewish businessmen who pledged him their support and played to his narcissism by embracing his future claims to political leadership. There was also his admiration for the Israeli trade union and kibbutz movements, which were a central part of the Israeli economy. If he'd been able to remake Australia from scratch, Hawke would have drawn on the example of the two-decades-old Israeli model, with the ACTU playing a role akin to that of its Israeli counterpart, the Histadrut.[1]

It was an official from the Histadrut who met Hawke and Susan and took them on a two-week tour of Israel. Hawke would later recall how looking out from the car on the 'dry, dusty landscape dotted with ancient olive trees evoked all the memories of those biblical stories which had enthralled me as a child'. It made real the images he had conjured up in his young imagination, while a visit to the Holocaust museum and his late-night discussions with Israelis made him painfully conscious of the history that had driven so many of them to leave the refugee camps of war-shattered Europe, turning their backs on the countries of their birth so they could sink their energies into the soil of a land where so many ancient stories had been created. As for the Palestinians, many of whom had been killed or driven out during the process of Israel's creation to live in the refugee camps of surrounding countries or exist under Israeli military rule in Gaza and the West Bank, Hawke believed it was incumbent on the Arab countries to form a separate Palestinian state, in which they could live in peace alongside the Jewish state. Such arguments were reinforced for him during an emotional meeting with the Israeli prime minister, Golda Meir, who'd been the first Israeli representative in Moscow and was passionate about attracting people from the Jewish diaspora to live in Israel. The result of Hawke's visit was to make the Israeli cause even more strongly his own; he told a press conference in Tel Aviv that Australia should do all it could to achieve agreements with the Arab nations that would ensure the security of Israel as a Jewish state. He also accepted a mission to convince the Soviet Union to pressure its Middle East allies to recognise Israel and for Moscow to allow the emigration of those Soviet Jews who wanted to leave.[2]

After the nineteen-day tour of Israel, Hawke left Susan behind to experience life on a kibbutz while he flew to Geneva. After his meetings there, he returned to fetch her for the flight to Moscow. This was a delicate diplomatic enterprise for which Hawke had little experience. Although his role as ACTU president had put him in charge of the organisation's international relations, he was no diplomat. He was used to presenting his case to the Arbitration Commission, doing deals on behalf of trade unions with governments and employers, and convincing workers who were exhausted by prolonged strike action to accept a settlement that was less than what they'd been fighting for.

He had no experience in convincing a communist government in the midst of a Cold War to change its strategy in the Middle East or to give up one of its pawns in that complicated game: the denial of exit visas to the so-called Jewish refuseniks.

Nonetheless, Hawke thought that success was his to grasp. This was because he knew the leader of the Soviet trade union movement, Alexander Shelepin, from his work at the ILO and had even engaged in a vodka-drinking contest with the Russian, which Shelepin had won. However, his Soviet counterpart wasn't just a genial, hard-drinking trade union leader. He was a graduate of the Moscow Institute of History, Philosophy and Literature who'd gone on to be head of the Soviet secret police, the KGB. He'd been a staunch Stalinist before attaching himself to Stalin's successor, Nikita Khrushchev, whom he had then helped overthrow, with the apparent aim of taking the top job himself. Rather than favouring détente with the West, Shelepin wanted to continue the hardline approach that had led to the 1962 missile crisis with the United States. Unfortunately for Shelepin, the notion of détente was in the ascendant among Soviet powerbrokers, and by 1971 he had become a relatively lonely figure on the ruling Politburo. Hawke seems to have been unaware of this, and went equipped with little more than his charm and the force of his moral suasion when he and Susan flew from Moscow to the Baltic resort where Shelepin was holidaying.[3]

In their discussions, which stretched over some sixteen hours, Hawke tried to draw a parallel for the historically minded Shelepin between the nascent state of Israel and the Soviet Union, which had been similarly surrounded by hostile armies in the immediate aftermath of its founding in 1917. He argued that the Soviet Union should stop arming its Arab allies for war and instead get them to guarantee the borders of Israel, since Israel's continued existence would help to keep those Arab nations as client states of the Soviet Union. He also argued for more Soviet Jews to be allowed to emigrate to Israel. Although Shelepin gave a hearing to Hawke, it's difficult to point to any outcome arising from his intercession, since it would have been one of many such discussions that others were also having with different levels of the Soviet government. Nevertheless, Hawke left the resort convinced that his history lesson had made the desired impression on Shelepin.[4] But nothing came of it. What the trip had done was reinforce

Hawke's emotional and intellectual attachment to Israel, creating in him a prolonged fascination with the country and its people, while also deepening his links with Australia's Jewish community.

Hawke's emotional attachment was on display in October 1971 when he delivered the inaugural Sam Cohen Memorial Lecture in Melbourne. Hawke had been one of the last people to see Cohen alive, when they'd crossed paths in Adelaide during the 1969 election campaign. While Hawke went on to catch his plane to Melbourne, fifty-year-old Cohen had gone off to a meeting in Adelaide, where he suffered a fatal heart attack. It had been Cohen who'd played a large part in crafting Labor's vexed policy on state aid to schools, thereby helping to end the bitter divisions within the party on that issue. In his lecture, Hawke paid homage to Cohen for his contribution to the party, to the campaign against antisemitism in Australia and to the state of Israel. Although he kept his Soviet discussions secret from his Australian audience, Hawke repeated the points he'd made to Shelepin about the right of Israel to exist as a Jewish state within secure borders, about the 'fanatical determination of the Israelis to defend their territory or perish' and about the parallels that could be drawn with the Soviet Union's early post-revolution history. Lastly, he referred to Cohen's concern with education and the difficulties caused by the messy division of responsibility and funding for education between the state and federal governments. This was a symptom of a wider problem, argued Hawke, brought about by the division of powers under the constitution, which had arisen from nothing more meaningful than 'the meanderings of explorers in the British colonies of more than a century ago'.[5] It was an argument that Hawke had made before and to which he would return.

While he'd been in Europe, the Springboks' rugby tour had proceeded in the face of fierce protests. The matches had been disrupted by thousands of protestors, who'd invaded the grounds and let off smoke bombs in vain attempts to have the tour called off. Conservative state governments were determined to facilitate the games, sometimes surrounding rugby grounds with barbed wire, while Queensland premier Joh Bjelke-Petersen took the extreme step of declaring a state of emergency. Although the rugby tour went on, the cricket tour was abandoned, since cricket could hardly be played in the midst of smoke bombs and whistles. The protests also ensured that no other South African team would tour Australia until apartheid was ended.[6]

Hawke had given his imprimatur to the union bans on the rugby team and had pressured the cricket authorities into abandoning the summer tour, but he wasn't central to the mass movement that had turned rugby grounds into battlefields between young protesters and baton-wielding police. Although he'd been out of the country when most of the action had taken place, he was nonetheless held accountable by many Australians for the staunch stand he'd taken. The popularity he'd reaped by fighting Dunlop on behalf of consumers had dissipated by the time of the rugby tour, as Australians took exception to unionists interfering with their enjoyment of sport. That loss of popularity caused some Labor MPs to worry that Hawke could endanger their chances at the federal election due by the end of 1972. The issue encouraged some of his right-wing opponents at the upcoming ACTU Congress to move for the organisation to limit its activities to industrial issues.[7]

When delegates gathered for the congress in Melbourne on 30 August 1971, Hawke had been president for just over eighteen months and was already widely regarded as a likely future prime minister, partly because he never tired of saying so. As he rushed from one industrial dispute to another, resolving strikes that had run their course and were ripe for settlement, his political stature grew apace. The political strikes were more problematic. They were seen as being beyond the business of the union movement and intruding on issues that were properly the business of government. It all came to a head at the congress.

In his fiery opening address, Hawke confronted the matter head-on, paying particular attention to the campaign against apartheid and portraying the right-wing attacks as part of a broader campaign by government and employers in reaction to the recent successes of the ACTU. A majority of the delegates agreed with him. Hawke was also pleased to see delegates choose moderation over militancy, rejecting calls for widespread strike action to achieve their wage claims. However, they weren't prepared to embrace Hawke's vision of an ACTU that mimicked the size and capacity of some of its overseas counterparts, denying him the recommended doubling of affiliation fees that was required to pursue such a course. The congress settled instead on an increase of just 50 per cent, despite Hawke vacating the chair to argue the case from the floor of the congress. This meant that his plans for expanding the role of the ACTU were effectively hobbled. He would press on nonetheless, in the hope that the partnership with Bourke's and other commercial activities might provide the funds. At least he could be happy about the outcome of the executive elections, which saw his supporters take ten of the seventeen positions. This would allow him to steer the ACTU in a more pragmatic direction. He'd become somewhat of a sabre-rattling socialist in order to secure the presidency two years before. Now he could stow the papier-mâché sabre away.[8]

Although Hawke acted as the great conciliator during disputes, many people still regarded him as a radical socialist who wanted to tear down the system. That was partly because of his aggressive manner with journalists, which Australians often witnessed on their televisions or heard on their radios. 'His method of being interviewed is to intimidate the interviewers,' wrote one journalist, 'put them off-balance, and once he has the initiative, to rephrase questions, refuse to answer them ... or give answers which are not actually answers to the questions asked.' People were misled into equating this rudeness with radicalism. It was just his style that was 'militant and abrasive', said Nugget Coombs, who told D'Alpuget that he 'can be as charming as he can be offensive; with fine even-handedness he is as disagreeable to his friends as he is to his enemies'.[9]

It was during the ACTU Congress that this supposedly dangerous radical was named Victorian Father of the Year. As he freely admitted, there were few men in Victoria less deserving of that honour: it was Hazel, he told journalists, who performed the roles of both father and mother to their three children. Worried about how she would receive news of the award, he hived off to the pub for a solid session of drinking before prevailing upon Ralph Willis and his fiancée, Carol, to accompany him home, telling Willis 'I need a bit of protection'. It was 'one of the great ironies of Bob's life', wrote Willis, that 'for all that he loved and was proud of his family he had hardly been a model father, a fact that Hazel forcibly related to him' when he walked in the door. Willis recalled how Hazel 'had an absolute piece of him', telling him 'what a jerk he was to be Father of the Year' when he was 'always coming home late and never here for the kids and when you are here, you're drunk'. It had been getting much worse since he'd become ACTU president, when there'd been so many more demands on his time and so much more travelling, both interstate and overseas.[10]

Apart from the requirements of work, he'd also chosen to be away, whether it was to stay late in the pub, spend nights with different women or take off to the races on Saturdays. Horses had become another of his obsessions: Hawke would check form guides in his office on Fridays and ring his growing network of racing contacts for tips. The hours he spent comparing the weights and form of racehorses, combined with the telephoned tips, helped him win many of the small bets he laid with bookmakers.

That wasn't the only pleasure he enjoyed at the racetrack. There was also the adulation from the crowds, which was showered on the readily recognised figure, who lapped it up and wanted to stay until the bar had closed and the last people were leaving. It was at the Caulfield races in 1972 that Hawke first became acquainted with Col Cunningham, a keen golfer, lifelong Labor supporter and the owner of a small bus company. Cunningham had friends across the sporting world, including champion jockey Roy Higgins and international golfer Jack Newton. Cunningham and Hawke became firm friends after Hawke asked him to play a round of golf. The street-smart Cunningham was a few years younger than Hawke and was able to immerse him in a world outside of politics and the trade unions. He very quickly became Hawke's boon companion, driver and bag-carrier, idolising Hawke and being a frequent visitor to Sandringham.[11]

Hawke had been introduced to Cunningham by Eddie Kornhauser, who'd fled Germany with his brother in the late 1930s and fetched up in Australia, where they set up fur shops in Melbourne and Sydney. While operating the Sydney shop in the early 1950s, Kornhauser entered a partnership with a Kings Cross nightclub owner, Abe Saffron, who controlled various criminal enterprises, from sly grog and sex shops to prostitution and gambling, as well as being involved in Frank Sinatra's tour of Australia. According to Louis Nowra, Saffron was said to be 'inordinately proud of his penis and as a party trick would whip it out and compare it favourably to those of his cronies'. While Saffron's involvement in the entertainment business afforded him some legitimacy, his illicit businesses were protected by paid-off politicians and police. Some of his ill-gotten gains were channelled into property development and investments, including blocks of flats and hotels, which were useful for holding sex parties at which powerful men could be filmed in compromising positions and thereafter be caught in Saffron's grip. When six o'clock closing was still in force, Kornhauser had been enlisted by Saffron to be a 'front man', acting as the licensee of one of several pubs so that beer could be ostensibly purchased for sale at the pub and then trucked across town to his unlicensed nightclub and sly-grog operation for sale at huge mark-ups. That experience seems to have shown Kornhauser the great profits that could be made from pubs and property development, which is presumably what led him to become the owner of the John Curtin pub, which is where it seems likely Hawke first met him. Experience had presumably also taught Kornhauser the value of having influential politicians and senior police onside. He would later become one of the so-called white-shoe brigade on the Gold Coast: he would be charged and acquitted in 1991 of bribing the crooked Queensland politician Russ Hinze.[12]

There were many members of the Labor Party, from Whitlam down, who wondered about the nature of Hawke's relationships with influential members of the Jewish community. Some were concerned that these friendships were responsible for Hawke adopting a pro-Israel stance that was at odds with official party policy. There was also concern that the naive union leader was exposing himself to the possibility of being corrupted by those who might ask him to use his influence to benefit their business interests. Hawke's relationship with Revelman had sparked rumours to this effect, with some union officials claiming that the deal with Bourke's was done to rescue the struggling department store rather than to benefit the ACTU and its members. There was some truth in this, although the ACTU also benefited when it moved its office from Lygon Street to the top floor of Bourke's, which Revelman allowed them to occupy for a peppercorn rent. Although there is no evidence of Hawke accepting bribes, Kornhauser certainly attempted to make him even more beholden by offering to sell him a plot of land on the Gold Coast at a ridiculously cheap price. Its sale would have allowed Hawke to reap a quick and easy profit. Rather than rejecting it out of hand, Hawke consulted Labor lawyer and close confidant Peter Redlich, who'd represented the ACTU in legal cases and Hawke in libel suits, and had been involved with Hawke in the intervention in the Victorian ALP. Wisely, Redlich urged him not to accept the compromising offer.[13]

There were other offers that Hawke did accept, many of them from wealthy businessman Peter Abeles. Fifteen years older than Hawke and a man of similarly large appetites, the softly spoken and urbane Hungarian Jew from a wealthy family had been born in Austria and survived both World War II and the subsequent communist takeover. Fleeing to Australia in 1949 with his wife, Claire Dan, who'd worked as an entertainer in post-war Europe (and who claimed that Abeles had raped her prior to their marriage), he embarked on a number of small business enterprises and property speculations in Sydney before establishing a trucking company with another Hungarian, George Rockey. They were so successful in undercutting their competitors that Abeles and his wife were soon living with two adopted daughters in a 1920s English-style manor house in Bellevue Hill, with extensive views of Sydney Harbour. When the couple divorced in about 1970, Abeles bought a grander hillside mansion in Vaucluse. Originally built for the Grace retail family in the 1920s, the six-bedroom 'Villa Igiea' was reminiscent of a Mediterranean estate and was named after a mansion in Palermo, Sicily. Abeles lived in a city where the corruption of politicians and police was rife, the detection and prosecution of corruption was hardly pursued, and the dividing line between organised crime and legitimate business was often difficult to discern. Indeed, Abe Saffron's ill-gotten gains were said by his son to have made him a go-to lender of last resort for both Peter Abeles and media tycoon Kerry Packer.[14]

In 1967, Abeles' private trucking company, Alltrans, had merged with a larger public company, Thomas Nationwide Transport (TNT), with Abeles soon becoming the sole managing director. Abeles quickly accelerated the company's growth overseas, while also moving into shipping and expanding its rail operations, all the while forging links with politicians who might facilitate the expansion. One of his closest links was to the notoriously corrupt New South Wales premier Sir Robert Askin, with whom he regularly played bridge and poker. Some of Askin's fortune may have come from the payment by Abeles of at least $20,000, which reportedly changed hands when the premier recommended Abeles for a knighthood in 1972. According to one account, Abeles also took care of Askin's gambling debts and, when Askin retired in 1975, hosted a farewell dinner and appointed Askin as a director of TNT, giving him a large swag of shares in the company and an office in TNT's multistorey building in Redfern. Abeles was one of several closely connected Hungarian businessmen, mainly property developers, who were dubbed the 'Hungarian mafia' by a Labor MP speaking under parliamentary privilege. Liberal leader John Dowd would later claim that 'it doesn't make much difference which political party forms the government in New South Wales, because the real power lies in the hands of an extra-parliamentary group' that included 'Sir Peter Abeles, Sir Arthur George, Sir Paul Strasser, John Charody, Abe Saffron and a few others'. The close-knit cabal were distinguished by the knighthoods that Askin had sold several of them, along with the valuable political favours he had done them. The knighthoods helped to give these relatively new arrivals a degree of status and credibility when doing deals or pressuring politicians and public servants. According to crime writer Tony Reeves, these wealthy Hungarians were part of a group he dubbed The Brotherhood, which encompassed businessmen, politicians, senior police and crime figures.[15]

The harbourside city had reeked of corruption among its political and business elite and police force long before Askin became premier, and the stench would continue after his passing. With no anti-corruption commission, police and some politicians in other states were similarly compromised. Whether through naivety or venality, Hawke would become caught in this corrupt web.[16]

It was shortly after becoming ACTU president that Hawke received a call from Abeles requesting a meeting. Just as Abeles had courted Askin and influential Liberal ministers in Canberra, appointed former Labor premier and governor-general Sir William McKell as chairman of Alltrans, and was alleged to have paid off some officials of the Transport Workers' Union (TWU), Abeles now intended to draw Hawke into his circle of pliant politicians. Laid up with a bad cold, and perhaps wanting privacy for their discussion, Hawke asked him to come to his Sandringham home. Abeles had embarked on a big expansion plan for TNT and couldn't allow his business to be crippled by industrial action. That was where Hawke came in. Along with several other conglomerates, Abeles had presided over a consolidation of the road transport industry and the widespread use of owner-drivers rather than direct employees. It meant that many of the company trucks could be sold, while the mainly non-union owner-drivers, who were paying off their trucks on hire purchase, could be played off against each other to keep company profits extraordinarily high. Because of the industry consolidation, there were just four main transport companies, which allowed them to raise their freight rates faster than their labour and other costs. TNT was the biggest. Having Hawke on board would help to preserve this highly profitable arrangement while the company was experiencing rapid growth and facing increased militancy by owner-drivers, who were joining the TWU en masse. Although Abeles instructed his executives to pursue 'a policy of complete co-operation with the unions', he sought to moderate his drivers' militancy by paying off union officials with shares in the company. According to Abeles, he and Hawke became the 'closest friends' within twelve months of that first meeting, with Abeles lavishing his new friend with expensive gifts.[17]

One of Abeles' closest associates was a fellow Hungarian named Bela Csidei, whom he treated as a son and who'd sold sly grog on behalf of Abe Saffron before going on to become a drug dealer and Abeles' conduit to the American mafia. He was instructed by Abeles to 'take care' of Hawke when he was in Sydney because 'he's going to be the next Prime Minister'. Csidei said that he 'became a keen student of the clever way [Abeles] could manipulate the powerbrokers at the very top of the political tree' and arranged to meet Hawke at the Boulevard Hotel. 'By midday', recalled Csidei, 'we had polished off a bottle of Johnny Walker Black Label', during which Hawke 'politely declined' his offer to get some girls and instead asked for information about Abeles. Csidei told him that 'Sir Peter was indeed powerful, and a man of his word'. Which seems to have reassured Hawke, who was 'more than comfortable strutting the plush carpets of mahogany row'. According to Csidei, he was 'a bit of a champagne Charlie, old Hawkey, one of the original Limousine Lefties. He loved the good life.'[18]

The recently opened Boulevard was Sydney's second international hotel and was ten storeys higher than its major competitor, the Qantas-owned Wentworth Hotel. With an interior designed by Hungarian refugee George Surtees, it became Hawke's regular haunt during his frequent visits to Sydney. The twenty-five-storey hotel was built by the shopping centre developers Frank Lowy and John Saunders as part of a planned three-building Westfield Centre, which was meant to be the centrepiece of a redeveloped William Street, the wide avenue connecting the city to the bright lights and seedy haunts of Kings Cross. Urban planners had had dreams of the street becoming Sydney's Champs-Élysées, but they were swept away by the property crash of the mid-1970s. Buildings bought up by developers were left vacant or dilapidated, while the vision for the interconnected Westfield Centre was also scaled back. Only the office tower accommodating the Westfield company headquarters, together with the adjoining hotel, which opened in May 1973, were ever built. The building industry downturn didn't auger well for the Boulevard. While its upper floors enjoyed views of the harbour, its lobby looked out on the district's rundown surrounds, where sex workers loitered and alcoholics shuffled past to a nearby homeless shelter. It meant that the well-heeled customers coming to patronise the hotel's Champs-Élysées Cosmetic Salon or eat food from the kosher kitchen sometimes had to avert their eyes from the sight of the passing pedestrians. Far above the local hoi polloi was the cocktail bar on the twenty-fifth floor, where female staff were dressed in Carla Zampatti clothes, while the adjoining swimming pool had panoramic views and boasted underwater music. One floor below was a Japanese-style bathhouse, which offered saunas and massages.[19]

Hawke would arrive at the Boulevard in a chauffeur-driven limousine, courtesy of Abeles, before ascending to the spacious comfort of his high-rise Lady Nelson suite, where businessmen were entertained, union disputes resolved and political deals done. The suite was reportedly paid for by Abeles but may have been provided gratis by the hotel owners. The suite had the advantage of having doors opening onto different corridors, which allowed his visitors to come and go in a more surreptitious manner. Not that there were many guests in the hotel's early years, when international tourism to Australia had barely begun. Despite the advent of jumbo jets, an increase in the Australian dollar and expensive airfares between Tokyo and Sydney meant that the expected rush of tourists failed to eventuate, leaving the occupancy rate at a loss-making 30 per cent. So instead of the bathhouse being enjoyed by throngs of Japanese tourists, it was frequented by leading figures of Sydney's underworld, who were profiting from the thousands of American service personnel visiting Sydney on leave from Vietnam, who were patronising the illegal casinos, nightclubs and brothels of Kings Cross and consuming the drugs that were widely on offer. A regular patron was George Freeman, a 'racing identity' and operator of illegal casinos who became involved in the drug trade and had powerful police in his employ. Indeed, the bathhouse was so 'well-known as a meeting-place for men who dabbled in illegal matters' that the police often had it under surveillance. The facility was on the floor above Hawke's suite, and he was wont to have a sauna and massage to relieve himself of the physical effects of his alcoholism. While there, he may have become acquainted with Freeman and even laid bets on horse races with him. If his losses became too great, Abeles would bail him out.[20] Hawke also used Abeles to underwrite his business initiatives at the ACTU.

In August 1972, Hawke brought Abeles to a meeting of the ACTU Executive to convince his colleagues to support a travel company to be known as ACTU-New World Travel. Despite some reservations, the proposal was approved, with the company to be owned equally by the ACTU and Abeles. It was intended to provide discount travel for unionists and produce profits that could be ploughed into other ACTU initiatives. If all these business plans were implemented, Hawke boasted, they would 'bring about a radical change in the structure of Australian society as a whole'. His ambitious plans fell flat when the ACTU-affiliated unions failed to give their enthusiastic support. The right-wing officials thought that the ACTU should stick to its traditional role, while the left-wingers were suspicious of links with people like Abeles. More to the point, Abeles was a trucking magnate, not a travel agent, and he didn't make the required commitment to ensure the venture's success. Which was why Abeles and TNT were soon replaced as the ACTU's partner by Isi Leibler's successful travel agency, Jetset Travel. Even that would never live up to Hawke's hopes. Neither would his plan for the ACTU to provide insurance and banking services for unionists, cheap housing for workers or a holiday village on the New South Wales coast, despite union officials from Israel and West Germany visiting Australia in 1972 at Hawke's invitation to advise on the implementation of his grand plans. He hoped they would lend money to the enterprises, but none was ever forthcoming.

The insurance plan almost came to fruition but was scrapped on the day that Hawke intended to announce it, after journalist Neil Mitchell advised him that the insurance company he was about to partner with was dodgy. While he had more success with a plan to disrupt petrol retailing by establishing a small network of discount petrol stations, to be known as ACTU-Solo, it never posed a major threat to the big oil companies. His vision of emulating the commercial activities of the West German or Israeli union movements was never realised. Nor was his plan to shift the ACTU to Canberra and build its headquarters on a 'prestige site'.[21]

Finances were simply not Hawke's forte. That was also true on a personal level. All the money he spent on betting and alcohol, as well as on other entertainments of one sort or another, put pressure on the family budget. Although Hawke's frequent threats to launch defamation actions brought in occasional dollops of money, which were mostly spent on house renovations, he was so hard up one Christmas that he borrowed $300 from the publican of the John Curtin. His reckless spending and gambling losses opened the door wider for Abeles, who covered some of his gambling debts, paid his children's school fees and the mortgage on the house, provided chauffeur-driven cars in Melbourne and Sydney, gave jobs to his former lovers and covered the cost of his accommodation in swanky hotels. Both Abeles and Hawke denied that there was any quid pro quo provided by Hawke for this largesse.[22]

It was the lack of time Hawke spent at home that most rankled with Hazel, who was concerned about the effect it was having on their teenage children. If his absences were work-related, the family might have been able to accept it. However, they knew from the heated, late night arguments, as well as the early-morning, alcohol-fuelled blow-ups and the sight of him sloping off to the races on Saturdays, that 'much of the time that he spent elsewhere ... was optional and actively sought out by him'. When he was at home and occupied with family matters, recalled Susan, he was 'hungover and irritable at what he perceived as its banality'.[23] In a way, Hawke couldn't help himself. He'd been neglected as a child by parents who'd often been absent from home as they pursued their own obsessive missions to save the world. Anyway, he wasn't the only father who thought it was sufficient for him to provide the material comforts of life and leave the parenting to the mother.

Hawke could have rejected the Father of the Year award, but he needed to improve his image among women after being voted 'Male Chauvinist of the Month' by the feminist *MeJane* magazine. It had followed a television interview earlier that year with an equal pay campaigner and postal worker, Zelda D'Aprano, during which Hawke had reached across to feel whether she was wearing a bra. As D'Alpuget later observed, 'his language, his excessively virile swagger, the way he stood – legs straight, calves pushed back, hips forward – his every public gesture revealed dominance, including sexual dominance'.[24] While some women found that attractive, and he was frequently having women proposition him, many more were put off by the language he used and the demeanour he displayed on television. He tried to appeal to women by promising that Bourke's would provide them with cheaper cosmetics and pharmaceuticals, but their political support would have been more assured if he'd won them equal pay. At the time of Hawke's Father of the Year award, a poll revealed that he had an approval rating of only 26 per cent among women, compared to an overall approval rating of 32 per cent. That probably wasn't helped when, after being asked by *Woman's Day* for a message to the women of Australia, he blurted out: 'Tell them I'm glad they're as pretty as they are and I hope they stay that way.'[25] It was as if he were the local Lothario rather than the leader of a trade union movement that had a growing number of women as members.

Under Albert Monk's leadership, the ACTU had left it to government to legislate equal pay, which a succession of Liberal governments had declined to do. It was only in 1969, after Hawke had made equal pay part of his platform for the presidency, that he took an equal pay case to the Arbitration Commission. Although Hawke was heavily involved at the time in his campaign for the presidency, Willis believed that he 'gave the case everything that he could muster'. D'Aprano was one of the women who demonstrated with placards outside the commission and later sat watching Hawke make the 'irrefutable' case against discrimination on the basis of gender, with the all-male advocates arguing their respective cases before the all-male judges. 'The women sat there day after day as if we were mute,' fumed D'Aprano, 'while the men presented evidence for and against our worth.' Although the commission agreed with Hawke's arguments, it only granted equal pay for women doing work of equal value to men in the meat industry, which had been used as a test case. According to D'Aprano, 9 per cent of women in that industry were receiving equal pay anyway, and the decision would only extend equal pay to 3 per cent more women, which meant most women still missed out. Moreover, for other industries, 'every union would have to establish an individual case of proof in every classification of work performed'. It turned out that Monk had been right: women would do better if they waited for a Labor government. They would also have done better if Hawke and the ACTU had mobilised women into a mass campaign, which might have been able to pressure governments, employers and male-dominated unions to accept the principle of equal pay and put it into practice. Instead, it was left to D'Aprano and a small band of like-minded women to take action on their own: they chained themselves across the entrances to the Commonwealth Government offices and the Arbitration Commission to publicise their cause.[26]

With the election due by the end of 1972, the McMahon government was desperate to create a political bogeyman to scare voters from embracing Whitlam's new-style Labor Party. The politics of the Cold War had lost much of their purchase on the Australian psyche and the country's commitment to Vietnam was in tatters. The world was changing in ways that had not been anticipated even five years before. The government had to find a new bogeyman, and Hawke again seemed to fit the bill.

After the tumult of the Springbok rugby tour and a series of disruptive strikes during the last two years, it had been easy for governments to heap the blame onto Hawke and, because of his position on the ALP Federal Executive, to spread it onto the Labor Party as well. The Liberals also wanted to tarnish Hawke's reputation in order to hamper his widely anticipated move into politics. That became more difficult after the 1971 ACTU Congress, when Hawke's position was reinforced by the election of the moderate Cliff Dolan as the ACTU's senior vice-president. From being perceived by the public as a fomenter of strikes, Hawke became seen instead as the union peacemaker after he stepped in to bring a series of long-running strikes to an end or averted threatened strikes before they happened. As he told delegates at the congress, unions must have 'a preparedness to compromise', so long as they don't contravene their 'basic principles'.[27]

When a strike erupted in the oil industry in June 1972, causing aircraft refuellers to join in and the petrol supply to run short, it seemed that the government might have the law-and-order election campaign it craved. McMahon urged the employers not to negotiate, even suggesting that troops might operate the refineries. This just caused the strikers to be as recalcitrant as the employers, and to stick fast to their demands for higher pay and a thirty-five-hour week. The dispute was tailor-made for Hawke. He just had to wait for each side to become exhausted. Meanwhile, he had the workers retain sufficient refining capacity to keep essential services running. McMahon came under mounting pressure to bring the dispute to an end but wasn't sure how to do it. He threatened to hold an emergency session of parliament to deregister the striking unions, only to be lampooned in the press. Hawke was having his own troubles getting both sides to agree and used another breakdown in his health to his advantage. He took to his bed in Sandringham, while Gleghorn called in the reporters, who were handed beers by Hazel as Hawke, attired in his dressing-gown and stroking the family's cat, promised sufficient oil to keep the bowsers going. At the same time, he threatened to expose the price gouging by the foreign oil companies. With Hawke appearing to have the advantage, the labour minister, Phillip Lynch, requested a meeting, only to be told that it had to be held at the ACTU offices. Hawke then set the scene by forcing Lynch and two other ministers to pass through a phalanx of photographers as they paid homage to his power. The dispute was brought to an end in mid-August, when the oil companies conceded most of the union demands, including higher wages and a 17.5 per cent annual leave loading.[28]

Instead of providing a political victory for McMahon, the successful conclusion to the strike became another triumph for Hawke. He followed it up by announcing that the ACTU would be claiming an 18 per cent increase in the national wage and a further claim for equal pay for the many women doing work of equal value to men. McMahon's attempt to depict Hawke as a dangerous radical pulling the strings of the Labor Party had failed. Not that such claims ever had much credibility when the party was led by the forceful figure of

Gough Whitlam and when Australians were well acquainted with and mostly accepting of Hawke's straight-talking persona. Of course, most of them didn't witness Hawke when the grog had taken hold and he was letting fly at enemies, real and imagined.

Such an occasion occurred just prior to the 1972 election, when Hawke had been in Canberra for talks with the whisky-drinking Treasury secretary Sir Frederick Wheeler. With a few drinks under his belt, Hawke later accompanied Wheeler to a gathering of industry representatives at the then swanky Canberra Rex hotel, where he encountered his old bête noire John Stone, who was now Wheeler's deputy. The pair hadn't met since they'd both been in Canberra in the 1950s. Stone was taken aback when Hawke immediately became 'most aggressive, very nasty', telling Stone that Labor was going to win the coming election and 'you're gonna be the first person out the bloody door'. Stone remembered being called 'all sorts of names'. One person within earshot was Labor's shadow treasurer, Frank Crean, who warned Whitlam of Hawke's threat. A furious Whitlam assured Stone the next day that 'you've got nothing to fear from me', noting that 'Hawke can say what he likes but he's not going to be running the country'. Such behaviour was commonplace for Hawke and was often dismissed as being part of his endearing larrikinism. He'd also developed a reputation as a 'playboy', which seems to have done him no harm. Indeed, by February 1972, an opinion poll found that he had an approval rating of 39 per cent, compared with 34 per cent for Whitlam and 28 per cent for McMahon. Five months later, Hawke's approval had increased to 48 per cent.[29] The change did not bode well for McMahon's chances in the election.

When the British television personality David Frost flew into Sydney for a series of political interviews later that month, Hawke had been lined up as one of the four interviewees. First was the hard-of-hearing McMahon, who assured Frost that Hawke's popularity had slumped a 'tremendous amount' because of the oil dispute. Alluding to the widespread speculation about Hawke becoming Labor leader one day, McMahon predicted that Hawke would depose Whitlam as prime minister if Labor won the upcoming election. If McMahon's prediction was meant to frighten the viewers, it didn't work. An opinion poll released just after the interview revealed that Hawke's approval rating had risen to 60 per cent. Yet the Liberals still tried to portray Hawke as the power behind Whitlam. McMahon had confided to Frost and the millions of television viewers that he would be praying for his government's election victory. He would need to do so, because the opinion polls suggested that only divine intervention could ensure him a win. Whitlam was also interviewed by Frost and said he would fight to stay on in the unlikely event of him losing the election, which would be his second as leader.[30]

When it was Hawke's turn to be interviewed, he seized the opportunity to denigrate Whitlam and spruik his own credentials as Labor leader. Just weeks before the election, he told millions of television viewers that Whitlam 'lacks the personal warmth of a Curtin or a Chifley', and that he would struggle to provide the cohesive leadership the party required. It was an extraordinary claim for Hawke to make on the eve of the election campaign. On 4 October, he took another swipe at Whitlam during a Rotary luncheon in Canberra, noting that the Labor leader was 'not as outgoing, warm and genial as some people', and that his own career trajectory could see him moving into parliament 'within a year or so'. He followed up those headline-making remarks the following day by saying that 'if I went into politics I would aspire to leadership'. And so he should, suggested the retiring Arthur Calwell, who had no regard for Whitlam and called for the preselected Labor candidate for his former seat of Melbourne, Ted Innes, to stand aside in favour of Hawke. Even if Innes were prepared to do so, which he was not, there was no time for that after McMahon announced the election would be held on 2 December. Despite encouraging opinion polls, which gave Labor a lead of about 3 per cent over the Coalition, Whitlam knew it was going to be a tight race and he would need Hawke's help to get Labor over the line.[31]

For much of the twentieth century, it seemed that the Labor Party was only elected to government to clear up the mess left by conservative governments. Menzies and his successors had reaped the benefits of the nation-building projects of the Curtin and Chifley governments and promoted additional developments of their own. With the international economy enjoying a long boom, driven by the rebuilding of war-racked Europe and Asia and the wars in Korea and Vietnam, Menzies had presided over one of the longest booms of all. Behind a high tariff wall and with a high rate of immigration boosting demand, manufacturing industries had prospered and been able to pay relatively high wages to their workers. They needed high wages, because the prices of household durables and vehicles were made inordinately high, and their quality kept inordinately low, by the lack of competition from imports, while the system of resale price maintenance had hampered competition among retailers until Hawke had brought it crashing down. Hawke knew there was much more to do if Australian manufacturers were ever going to become internationally competitive, but there was a limit to what he could do as ACTU president when most unions were strong supporters of tariff protection and their members saw the apparent benefits in their pay packets. However, there were some troubling economic signs on the horizon, as both inflation and unemployment showed slight increases in 1972. Although unemployment was still only 1.8 per cent of the workforce by June of that year, Hawke told journalists that the rising trend confirmed that Australia was in the midst of an unemployment crisis.[32]

Despite the sluggish economy, the shadows over Australia's prosperity didn't seem to trouble the Labor speechwriter Graham Freudenberg when he composed Whitlam's campaign speech for the coming election. After twenty-three years of Coalition governments, there was a sense of inevitability about a Labor victory when Whitlam's tall figure stood on the stage of the Blacktown Civic Centre on 13 November 1972, intoning to the excited audience and the millions watching on television that 'It's Time' for Labor to take charge. The Murdoch papers thought so too and pushed Labor's cause. A group of intellectuals led by historian Manning Clark also urged Australians to vote Labor in order to 'benefit both the major parties, on which the vitality of our political system depends'. It's doubtful whether that appeal to the national good would have carried much weight with the self-interested voters, who were used to drawing up a balance sheet of the competing election promises to determine which one offered the most. On that score, Whitlam had much to offer, from ending conscription to higher pensions, a universal health scheme, land rights for Aboriginal people and free universities, all to occur in the context of a grand commitment to 'give new life and meaning … to liberty, equality, fraternity'. There were almost two hundred election promises, many of them directed at distributing the bounty of the post-war prosperity 'to secure a fairer share for all', although McMahon warned that the promises would unleash 'a flood of inflation such as we have never known'.[33]

In contrast to Labor's previous election launches, this was all about the leader. Despite being recently elected as the party's vice-president, Hawke was conspicuously absent from the stage, excluded because of fears that the Liberals would use his prominent presence behind Whitlam to suggest that the union leader was pulling the party leader's strings. Hawke and other leading Labor figures had to find a seat as best they could. The eight-hundred-strong audience, many wearing 'It's Time' T-shirts, gave ovations and stamped their feet as the senior MPs and party members, along with celebrities from the entertainment world, entered the hall. The loudest cheers erupted when Hawke appeared, wearing an 'It's Time' badge on his lapel. The left-wing MP Tom Uren watched with amusement as a beaming Hawke then jostled with the shadow labour minister, Clyde Cameron, for a seat in the front row.

Being relegated to sit among the masses was a come-down in more ways than one for Hawke. If Whitlam won, Hawke would be dislodged from his position as the most popular and arguably the most powerful political figure in the country. That downgrading was illustrated when the statuesque figures of Gough and Margaret Whitlam entered the hall, unleashing a crescendo of cheers and applause and foot-stamping, with some audience members climbing onto their chairs to get a clear view of the soon-to-be prime minister. The enthusiasm was so vocal during his speech that Whitlam was forced to omit several pages to ensure it fitted into his allotted time on television. Once the speeches were done and the television broadcast had ended, the stage was crowded with the singers and actors who had come out in support of the Labor campaign. Australia had never seen such political theatre before, and Hawke joined in with gusto, providing more amusement to Cameron, who told a colleague that he was 'unable to dictate to my typist the thoughts that went through my mind as Bob Hawke shook hands with Little Pattie but you know Bob as well as I do and I think my thoughts would pretty well correspond with your own'.[34]

Whatever reservations Hawke may have had about being overshadowed by Whitlam, he threw himself into the campaign and attracted thousands of people to meetings in cities and towns, whether it was haranguing workers at factory gates, addressing farmers from the back of a truck or making passionate orations to city workers in their lunchtimes. He would later claim, not without justification, that along with Whitlam and the Labor Party secretary Mick Young, 'no-one worked harder for the long-awaited victory than I'. Sometimes he spoke alongside Whitlam. At the last Melbourne rally, he stood on the stage with Whitlam at St Kilda Town Hall and watched as the Labor leader reminded the four thousand euphoric supporters about Ben Chifley's 'light on the hill' and called on them to 'set it aflame again'. On other occasions, it was more low-key as he visited electorates to support the local Labor candidate. Hazel recounts one such trip when she accompanied Hawke and his media adviser, Geoff Gleghorn, to a town in northern New South Wales. They'd missed the scheduled flight and were forced to fly in a four-seat aircraft low along the coast. It was late at night before the meeting had concluded in a local hall and the trio were able to repair to their motel. Hazel recalled how her tired husband emerged from his shower and 'flopped on his back, naked, spread-eagled across the bed' in front of her and Gleghorn. As they moved about the country, there was immense enthusiasm for Whitlam and it seemed to Hazel that a Labor victory was assured.[35]

When the votes started to be counted on 2 December, however, the winner wasn't immediately clear. McMahon had been defending a narrow majority of just nine seats, and opinion polls had suggested that Labor would secure a swing of about 3 per cent. That would be enough to wipe out McMahon's majority, but the Liberals and Country Party also had the advantage of a gerrymander that allowed a variation of up to 20 per cent in the number of voters in each seat. In practice, this meant that Labor electorates in the cities had many more voters than conservative electorates in the country. That factor had helped Gorton defeat Whitlam in 1969, despite Labor winning more than 50 per cent of the two-party-preferred vote. Everyone knew it could happen again.

While Whitlam watched the vote count from a motel near his home in Sydney's Cabramatta, Hawke and Hazel were among the Labor supporters crammed into the party's Melbourne headquarters. This time, there was no doubt about the result on election night. Although there had been a late swing back to the government, the increase of

2.6 per cent in Labor's primary vote was sufficient. Whitlam was able to walk back to his home and stand before the television lights in his crowded backyard to claim victory before the day was out. No sooner had he done so than journalists in Melbourne were asking Hawke about his own leadership ambitions. He fobbed them off, saying that 'the future can look after itself'.[36] In fact, Whitlam's victory had made Hawke's political future look more distant and uncertain. After all, Whitlam might emulate Menzies and stay in the Lodge for more than sixteen years.

CHAPTER FOURTEEN

1973–1974

When Labor lost the 1949 election, Bob Hawke had just celebrated his twentieth birthday. Now he was forty-three and there was another Labor government in Canberra. His entire adult life had been lived with Australia being ruled by a succession of Liberal governments.

It's not surprising that Whitlam and his ministers were driven by pent-up political pressure amid a widespread public expectation for them to change Australia in ways that had been resisted for nearly a quarter of a century. There was such a sense of urgency that Whitlam and his deputy, Lance Barnard, formed a short-lived two-man cabinet to implement changes that could not wait for a full cabinet to be formed. Conscription was ended, draft resisters were released from jail, the remaining troops were withdrawn from Vietnam, diplomatic relations were established with China, racially selected sports teams were banned from Australia and sales tax was lifted from the contraceptive pill. When the United States used B-52 heavy bombers against the North Vietnamese capital of Hanoi at Christmas 1972, killing thousands of civilians, two of Whitlam's ministers condemned the action and supported a ban on American shipping, which Hawke did his best to have called off.[1]

In retrospect, Whitlam's flurry of activity unsettled many voters and set an unfortunate tone for a government that lacked control of the Senate. For Hawke, there was another unfortunate effect: Whitlam was dominating the stage. The big man's victory inevitably diminished Hawke's political stature. As Hawke later conceded, he had difficulty 'coming to terms with the fact that the unions, and the ACTU in particular, were no longer the only effective voice of working men and women in Australia'.² Workers could now look to the Whitlam government and its new labour minister, former AWU official Clyde Cameron, to fulfil their demands for better pay and conditions and for an industrial relations system that wasn't geared towards protecting the economic interests of employers.

There was an immediate dividend for female workers when Cameron applied to reopen the equal pay case that the ACTU had been running in tandem with the national wage case from October 1972. Although the hearings had concluded, the commission agreed to hear evidence from the new government. Mary Gaudron, one of New South Wales' few female barristers, was appointed by Whitlam to represent the government. Hawke was not amused. Although it could prove crucial in convincing the commission to broaden the application of equal pay to many more women, any credit would accrue to Whitlam and Cameron rather than to Hawke and the ACTU.

When Cameron flew to Melbourne on 7 December to meet with the ACTU Executive, he was surprised to find that Hawke and Souter were nowhere to be found. Although it had been Hawke who'd invited him, the pair had walked out, leaving the remaining union officials to listen to Cameron's explanation of the incoming government's plans for industrial relations. As well as the equal pay case, these included legislating to give four weeks' annual leave to Commonwealth public servants in the expectation that this would flow through to the private sector. Hawke's snubbing of Cameron was due to his annoyance at the government's intervention in the equal pay case. Moreover, participating in a meeting with Cameron, where the minister was the centre of media attention, would only confirm Hawke's diminished political stature for television audiences. Hawke had been advocating for equal pay since 1969, with limited success. Now the commission agreed with Gaudron's submission that equal pay should be extended to women doing work of equal value to men. The decision brought many more women within its compass, while giving employers nearly three years to implement the decision in full. At the same time, the commission rejected the ACTU's call for the minimum wage to be made equal for men and women. Once again, it was the Whitlam government that saved the day by implementing the decision immediately for public servants, which pressured private employers to follow suit.³

Hawke's memoirs make no mention of the equal pay decision. Indeed, he only devotes eight pages to the three years of the Whitlam government, and ignores its long list of achievements. But he does make space for criticism of Cameron. While conceding that Cameron was 'a man of immense abilities', Hawke noted that his 'capacity for hatred ... was boundless' and embellished by 'venomous sarcasm, a deadly sense of humour, a thin smile which played around his mouth and a fascinating capacity to look a person in the eye and ... tell the most outrageous porky'.[4]

The equal pay case was just the first of several issues that saw the two men at loggerheads. It was followed by Cameron's determination to appoint an outsider to succeed Sir Richard Kirby as president of the Arbitration Commission. Hawke was not the only person who was aghast at Cameron's announcement, but it was Hawke who got Whitlam to overrule Cameron and appoint Kirby's long-serving deputy, John Moore. The antipathy between Hawke and Cameron was exacerbated when Cameron forced union elections to be more democratic and introduced a raft of measures into the public service in the hope it would become a pacesetter for the private sector. As well as the increase in annual leave, these included the introduction of maternity leave and so-called flexi-time to allow public servants to align their working hours with their personal circumstances. Most importantly, Cameron threw the government's support behind the union arguments for higher wages, which saw the Arbitration Commission give unprecedented and long overdue increases that decisively shifted the balance between wages and profits.[5] Cameron was doing with the stroke of a pen what Hawke had been unable to do in more than a decade at the ACTU.

Some union officials were also becoming more forthright in their demands and less inclined to defer to Hawke's leadership. They worried about the disarray in his office and pressured him to appoint a personal assistant, the English-born Jean Sinclair, an economics graduate who'd worked for an American management consultancy, McKinsey & Company, and who would become Hawke's 'office wife'.[6]

New issues were also coming to the fore. In Sydney, Jack Mundey of the Builders Labourers Federation initiated a series of actions that went beyond the traditional union concern with wages and conditions. After being contacted by a local residents' action group anxious to protect an area of parkland, Mundey declared a ban on it being cleared for luxury housing. It was the first of many 'green bans' that saw the union intervene to protect heritage buildings and areas from being cleared, the most famous being the historic Rocks area overlooking Sydney Harbour. They were the first in the world to do so, with the term 'green bans' later adopted elsewhere. The union also used its industrial muscle to demand that women be employed on formerly male-only building sites, and deployed creative means to buttress their industrial demands, such as walking off a building site midway through a concrete pour. Workers in other industries were also taking matters into their own hands, sometimes in defiance of their union officials. The dissatisfied workers at the Ford Motor Company rebelled when their officials negotiated a derisory pay offer. Alienated by the nature of their work on the production line, they defied the officials by going on strike and vandalising the factory in June 1973, smashing windows, destroying structures and flooding the interior with a fire hose. Whether or not he understood the workers' anger, Hawke didn't condone their tactics. Nor did he support Mundey's radical notion that building workers should be able to refuse their labour for socially deleterious construction.[7] Such New Left ideas, which also influenced the Whitlam government, were anathema to Hawke, despite his earlier support for taking industrial action on the issue of South African sporting teams.

Workers were not only reaping the rewards of a Labor government in their wages and conditions, but they were also looking forward to promises of universal healthcare, cheaper pharmaceuticals, increased pensions, greater government spending on education, and action on issues ranging from multiculturalism to the environment.[8] And it was Whitlam and his ministers whose images were splashed across front pages and the television news. Not that Hawke had disappeared altogether. There were still plenty of industrial disputes to resolve. Nevertheless, he must have wondered during these early months of the Whitlam government whether he could have been standing there in Whitlam's place if only the voters of Corio had embraced him more wholeheartedly or if he'd stood in one of the subsequent elections. From the time of Whitlam becoming prime minister, Hawke seems to have eschewed the chance of entering into a more productive partnership with the new government. For their part, Whitlam and his ministers felt no pressing need to defer to Hawke or to feed his ego.

Feeling partially shut out from decision-making and the national conversation, Hawke decided to break his way back in. In a reprise of his stand against racially selected sporting teams, he now made a stand against French government plans to conduct nuclear tests in the Pacific. Although Britain had conducted several such tests in Australia in the 1950s, there was now a widespread movement to have nations sign the Partial Nuclear Test Ban Treaty of 1963, which banned the testing of nuclear weapons in the atmosphere, under water or in outer space. Atmospheric tests like the French were planning on Mururoa atoll in the South Pacific in July and August 1973 were particularly opposed because they dispersed radioactive material around the Southern Hemisphere, with doctors warning about the fallout affecting unborn babies in Australia through the water supply and fresh milk. Although Whitlam had spoken out against the French tests, there was a limit to what he was prepared to do. He'd made an election commitment to take the French government to the International Court of Justice on the issue and, on coming to power, quickly signed the Nuclear Non-Proliferation Treaty.[9] Neither act was going to stop the French government from continuing with its testing program. Although the attorney-general, Lionel Murphy, convinced the International Court to issue an interim injunction against the tests, the French refused to attend or to recognise any adverse ruling.

With some unions imposing their own bans on French businesses, Hawke saw a chance to make his mark on an issue about which he felt deeply, which was popular with the public and the media, and on which Whitlam had limited options. To ramp up the pressure, he flew to Mexico to address the International Confederation of Free Trade Unions, which represented nearly 100 million trade unionists. Although he'd been briefed by scientists about the threat to human life posed by atmospheric tests, the actual threat was limited and was unlikely to have any effect at all on people living in the Northern Hemisphere. As a result, Hawke received a respectful hearing but no firm commitment of industrial action from European or North American union officials. Undaunted, he headed to Geneva, where he perhaps expected more help from his colleagues at the ILO. Again, the action in Geneva was symbolic, with Hawke challenging the leader of the French delegation, Alexandre Parodi, in the grand surrounds of the conference hall before leading a walkout of two hundred worker representatives as Parodi rose to speak.[10] Of course, it didn't prevent the tests from going ahead as planned.

Nevertheless, the issue had brought Hawke back to centre stage, and he was determined to stay there. His first three years as ACTU president had lifted his profile and popularity, but he was now struggling to stay in the spotlight. Neither did he have the power he'd enjoyed when there was a Liberal government. Although he was also on Labor's federal executive, he had to be re-elected at each state conference. Rather than just being the ACTU president, he decided to also seek the presidency of the Labor Party, which was due to be decided by the federal executive on 6 July 1973, prior to the party's triumphant federal conference in Surfers Paradise. 'I'd earned it,' he would later say, adding that he was 'ambitious for it' and 'cherished it'. Hawke conceded in his memoirs that he'd sought the position because he 'had a keen sense of the distinction of being ... at the age of forty-three, the leader of both the industrial and political wings of the labour movement'. He said that he wanted to act as a bridge between the political and industrial wings of the labour movement and was doing the party a favour by letting it exploit his popularity. That popularity was evident when the two other candidates withdrew, allowing him to emerge in triumph before the cheering conference delegates. He was cock-a-hoop when he returned from Surfers Paradise with Hazel, cracking open a bottle of champagne in his office and ringing his mother in Perth, who exulted: 'The prophecy of Isaiah has been fulfilled!'[11]

Questions were quickly raised as to how he could serve the trade union movement and the Labor Party at the same time. After all, he'd just been at odds with Whitlam on the issue of black-banning French trade and communications. And how was the public supposed to know whether he was speaking on behalf of the party or the ACTU? Moreover, there was a political danger for the party by having Hawke as its president, since it had been a constant refrain of conservative politicians that the Labor Party was the submissive creature of left-wing trade unions. Hawke's elevation threatened to bear that out.

Hawke refused to acknowledge the inevitable conflicts of interest that would arise between the two positions, telling journalists: 'If you can't ride two horses at once, you shouldn't be in the bloody circus!' Which was a ridiculous rejoinder and failed to answer the point. Anyway, he assured the many doubters, he only intended to keep both roles until the next biennial party conference. It was another promise that wouldn't be kept. Being party president meant that he couldn't be taken for granted by Whitlam and his ministers, or by those union leaders who were inclined to challenge his authority as ACTU president.[12] It also meant that he devoted even less time to his paid position with the ACTU, although he still made time for gambling, drinking and women.

Ever since the English model Jean Shrimpton had set Melbourne racegoers agog in 1965 with a white dress that ended a daring thirteen centimetres above her bare knees, the miniskirt had been de rigueur for most young women. Which was just fine for a 'leg man' like Hawke. And there were more women than ever who wanted to make the acquaintance of this charismatic celebrity with his distinctive head of hair. Hawke was often happy to oblige, particularly when he was drunk. With several beers under his belt, he would also go looking for women to seduce; D'Alpuget noted his 'outrageously public propositioning of women when he was drunk'.[13] There were no mobile phones on which to record his gross behaviour and no internet on which to post videos of him staggering about, foul-mouthed, in public. Neither was there a #MeToo movement, or even much of a feminist movement in the early 1970s. Some union officials looked askance at his behaviour, and a few were horrified and wrote him off as a result, but his position as ACTU president was never threatened. The media didn't report it and most of his friends and associates seem to have brushed it off as 'Bob being Bob', just as most people had done when he was a university student. After all, he was often exciting to be around, which meant that his sins were frequently forgiven when he sobered up and expressed remorse.

One of his lovers in 1973 described the times they had together. She accepted his many casual liaisons because, she later said, he 'would always return to me', which led her to believe that she 'was his favourite'. Moreover, when they were together she found him to be 'such good fun'. They'd both gone to Congregational Sunday Schools and she recalled one afternoon they spent in a suite at Sydney's Park Regis hotel 'sitting up in bed and drinking champagne and singing Congregationalist hymns at the top of our voices'. The suite was provided by a margarine company for the use of Labor Party officials. There were other times that weren't fun at all. Late one night at the Canberra Rex, Hawke was so drunk that David Combe appealed for the same woman to take him upstairs to his room, only for Hawke to stagger down the corridor banging on doors, screaming, 'Wake up, wake up.' His lover hoped he would collapse on his bed, 'but he turned nasty and physically attacked me – he didn't punch me, but he manhandled me. He was very rough. It was awful.' When she managed to get away, she left a note beside the bed, only for Hawke to borrow a car from the hotel manager and turn up at her place early the next morning, peering through his sunglasses as he abjectly apologised. There was no pretence that it could ever be a permanent relationship. It was 'just sex', she said, and that was sufficient, although Hawke could become 'very jealous' if he thought she had other lovers, and would often pester her to profess an exclusive love for him, which she declined to do. 'It used to drive him mad,' she said. For his part, he would suggest they holiday together, even go to Geneva, only to forget about it almost immediately. Eventually, she ended the affair by shifting to Sydney and not giving him her new phone number. He found it nonetheless and made a drunken call to her in the middle of the night.[14]

Despite Hawke's pursuit of different women, he made it clear that he wouldn't leave Hazel, noting the 'tremendous debt' he owed to her for having 'brought up our kids single-handed'. Yet when he spoke to Hazel on the phone, he could be 'so contemptuous and bitter', said his lover. On one occasion, she recalled him shouting into the phone: 'I fucking told you I couldn't get home on Thursday – can't you understand anything?' With Hawke usually absent from home, Hazel would sometimes have the help of her 76-year-old widowed mother, who came from Perth in 1973 and stayed in Sandringham for six months. It was a shock for her mother to see the state of the family and to find her daughter smoking and drinking. Her mother's presence allowed Hazel to accompany Hawke on one of his frequent overseas jaunts, during which he called on trade union officials in Singapore and Tehran before landing once again in Tel Aviv, where he left Hazel for nearly a week to be escorted around the country by a Histadrut official. He then continued on to meetings of the ILO in Geneva.[15] His frequent visits to Geneva were marked by the same bouts of drunken womanising that had long been the norm for him in Australia. His behaviour became the bane of the Australian diplomats who were delegated to chaperone him.

Among his casual affairs in Geneva, one woman stood out. The German-born Helga Cammell was a stunningly beautiful woman with long blonde hair who worked in Geneva as the administrative head of the six-million-strong International Federation of Commercial, Clerical and Technical Employees. At the invitation of the right-wing Federated Clerks' Union, the 37-year-old feminist visited Australia in March 1975 as part of the first International Women's Year, which was supported by the Whitlam government. During her three-week visit, the local clerks' union provided her with a well-connected publicist, Noel Tennison, who'd worked for Santamaria's National Civic Council and the DLP, as well as for the Liberal Party. Tennison ensured that she was interviewed on current-affairs programs and her speeches were splashed prominently across the pages of newspapers. He described in his memoir how the 'feminine feminist was media-modified from International Woman of the Year into Australia's 1975 Calendar Girl as she crossed her long legs and dangled her high IQ in front of hard-nosed industrial reporters and feature writers'. She told journalists that women often need to be reminded that they are the equal of men, confessing that even she was forced to suppress an occasional 'unconscious doubt'. Her relationship with Hawke wouldn't have helped in that regard. But she was smitten with his charm and energy, his larger-than-life personality and his role in the fight for equal pay. Cammell would later tell D'Alpuget that Hawke gave her 'strength and hope', and that she was impressed by his 'love of mankind'. She also accepted that he 'cannot belong to anyone'.[16] That was just as well, because Hawke's gaze remained fixed on the prime ministership, with the presidencies of the ACTU and the ALP providing the stepping stones.

George Polites, the head of the Australian Council of Employer Federations, would later say that Hawke's acceptance of the party presidency was his 'great mistake as a union leader', because it caused the ACTU's influence and power to diminish. Although the party position meant Hawke was in greater demand by the media, he exercised less authority as ACTU president and the organisation began a steady decline in importance.[17]

That was seen within days of his elevation to the presidency, when Whitlam announced a 25 per cent reduction in the tariffs that protected local industries. It was done at the urging of the former Reserve Bank governor, Nugget Coombs, who'd become an adviser to Whitlam and wanted to stem the inflationary pressures produced by the government's expansionary program at a time when the economy was already running at full tilt. Something had to give. Coombs suggested that the dollar should be floated in the hope that it would cause the price of imports to drop. Failing that, import duties should be cut to produce the same effect. Whitlam opted for the latter and, with the assistance of Jim Cairns, managed to convince caucus to support the move. The announcement was made late on the afternoon of 18 July 1973, after businesses and the stock exchange had closed for the day. Companies were able to appeal against cuts that harmed their business and retrenched workers were promised income support and retraining.

Although the tariff reduction had big implications for jobs in certain industries and marked a dramatic shift from Australia's traditional attachment to protectionism, Hawke was not consulted. That was probably just as well. When he heard the news the following morning, he yelled for his secretary to 'Get me fucking Whitlam!' and then had a 'blazing row' with the prime minister. His anger wasn't just about the tariff cuts, but about the lack of consultation by a government that had largely sidelined him and the union movement. By day's end, despite some of the directly affected unions and businesses howling their outrage, Hawke was telling the media that he supported the decision. Lindsay North of the Textile Workers' Union had to remind him that his 'main job is to look after the trade union movement'; Hawke had 'a choice of which hat he wears and today he is wearing the wrong hat'. In the event, the cheaper imports were slow to arrive and the workers who lost their jobs were easily absorbed elsewhere.[18]

While Whitlam had suggested during the 1972 campaign that his government would not be increasing taxes, Hawke had argued for him to keep the tax door ajar, warning that the government might need that option as a means of controlling the economy, to provide the money for Labor's ambitious programs and to redress twenty-three years of regressive Liberal tax changes. Hawke had been concerned that Whitlam had little understanding of economic policy and offered to introduce him to some eminent economists, in the same way he had been tutored after becoming the ACTU advocate. Whitlam declined. He was the captain of the ship and didn't see any need to understand how the engine worked. He had economists in the Treasury and the Reserve Bank, along with Coombs and the treasurer, Frank Crean. With the long economic boom showing little sign of stopping, and full employment continuing, Whitlam saw his role as allocating the resulting bounty to pay for his many election promises.

The prime minister wasn't the only one who was slow to see the economic storm that was about to engulf Australia and eventually destroy his government and damage his reputation. According to Whitlam, Hawke was also blind to the clouds on the horizon. 'Bob was just as hopeless as everyone else,' recalled Whitlam, and 'cannot turn round now and say he knew better'. Hawke had been appointed by Whitlam to the board of the Reserve Bank, and began attending its meetings in September 1973, which would have given him a good overview of the deteriorating economic situation. Despite that, he 'was no help', said Whitlam.[19]

Although it seemed manageable at the time, the many new demands on the economy were causing both wages and prices to rise strongly. By the end of 1973, average weekly earnings had risen by nearly 15 per cent and inflation to more than 13 per cent.[20] What was worse, inflationary expectations had taken hold as workers raced to keep their wages ahead of the strongly rising prices and employers raised prices even higher in response. The government had few levers to pull once these inflationary expectations took hold.

For more than half a century, the Labor Party had been trying to convince Australians to change the constitution so that the federal government would have power to control both prices and incomes. Despite the failure of successive referendums, the caucus forced Whitlam to try once again to get power over prices. In the face of objections from the business community and the opposition parties,

Whitlam also agreed to seek power over incomes, with a referendum being set for 8 December 1973.

That put Hawke in a bind. The party's federal executive had called for an affirmative vote on both questions, while the ACTU Executive only supported a vote in favour of the prices question while opposing the incomes question. Hawke had long supported the idea of the government having power to control prices, and he'd even suggested in July that he might support the notion of it having power over incomes as well. However, the ACTU Congress had met since then and come out strongly against the government having power over incomes, for fear of a future Liberal government using it to deny workers their rightful wage increases.[21]

Hawke's second congress as president had been a difficult one. He had appeared nervous and had uncharacteristically read his hour-long presidential speech to the nearly seven hundred bored delegates, of whom only twenty-three were women. Hawke never knew what alliances would be forged between normally antagonistic forces to stymie his proposals or change the composition of the executive in ways that might threaten his control. While he was successful in having the ACTU's commercial activities approved, and in securing an increase in the affiliation fee, he was unable to get approval for the appointment of a full-time vice-president. Hawke had wanted his close ally, the moderate secretary of the Waterside Workers' Federation, Charlie Fitzgibbon, to take the position, in the hope that he would one day succeed him as president. That would make Hawke's eventual transition to politics easier, while also removing some of the day-to-day pressure that was on him as president. It would have meant that Fitzgibbon became the third elected official in the office alongside Souter, with Fitzgibbon taking effective charge during the many months each year when Hawke was absent from Melbourne.

It was Souter who convinced the congress not to support the proposal, despite Hawke angrily berating those officials who said they felt stampeded on the issue. Hawke also lost some of his control of the executive when right-wing and left-wing unions combined to elect the fractious Norm Gallagher from the Builders Labourers Federation, a member of the Maoist-aligned Communist Party of Australia (Marxist-Leninist), in place of a more amenable Hawke supporter from the opposing Communist Party of Australia. The right was also strengthened by the election to the executive of the powerful, Yorkshire-born John Ducker of the New South Wales Labour Council. Hawke could live with all that, but he would have been less pleased to watch Whitlam stride into the hall to a rapturous standing ovation and become the first prime minister to address an ACTU Congress.[22]

That rapture soon ebbed as Whitlam sought the support of the labour movement for his referendum on prices and incomes. After first accusing union officials of sabotaging the government by calling for people to vote No on the incomes question, Whitlam tried to assuage their concerns about the incomes power being used to reduce real wages. Hawke wasn't troubled, because he was convinced that Australians would defeat both referendums anyway. He would have been fortified in that view when Labor failed to win a by-election for the seat of Parramatta after the sitting Liberal member retired. There was a 6 per cent swing against Labor, partly prompted by a government announcement in the middle of the by-election campaign about a plan for a western Sydney airport, with flight paths over the electorate. The poorly timed announcement was an 'act of imbecility', declared Hawke, which showed that the government was not 'keeping in touch with what is happening at the grass roots'. Donning his ACTU hat, Hawke then announced that he'd be opposing the referendum on incomes, telling an interviewer that the government should raise income taxes to control inflation. Although Whitlam hit back, it was all for nothing. The squabbling helped to ensure that the two questions were soundly defeated.[23]

The inflationary pressures weren't all home-grown. They were also driven by international factors, as the Vietnam War boosted raw material prices and increased inflation around the world. The inflation accelerated when oil-producing nations in the Middle East suddenly imposed an embargo on selling oil to nations that supported Israel during the Yom Kippur War. That war had begun when Syria and Egypt launched a sudden attack on 6 October 1973 to retrieve the territories they'd lost to Israel in 1967. It saw the Arab armies enjoy spectacular success in its first days. From the south-west, the Egyptian army crossed the Suez Canal and pushed deep into the Sinai Peninsula, while from the north-east the Syrians stormed across the 1967 ceasefire line to recapture the Golan Heights and push into northern Israel. These were places that Hawke had toured in 1971, and he was distraught at the possibility that Israel might be defeated. However, the invaders were quickly repelled, with the Israeli forces pushing back into Syria and routing the Egyptians in the Sinai. Despite this, Hawke was said by Peter Abeles to have been in 'in a VERY bad way for six months'. Taking the opportunity of an ILO meeting in Geneva, Hawke flew to Israel in the wake of the war to see the situation for himself. When the usual Histadrut representative wasn't there to greet him – he'd been called up into the army – Hawke insisted on scouring the northern battlefield in a fruitless search that took him past blown-up tanks and into Syria itself, before he finally turned back towards Jerusalem.[24] The sights and smells of the recent battles left a deep impression on him.

The effect was compounded when he met again with Israel's prime minister, Golda Meir, who was still traumatised by the human cost of the war and how close the nation had come to annihilation. Hawke would later say that it was 'the most emotional meeting I've ever had in my life with anyone'. When she showed him photographs that she said were of Israeli soldiers who'd been tied up and executed by the Syrians, Hawke asked for copies to take home to show Australians. Then he was asked to make another mission to Moscow to impress upon the Soviet Politburo member Alexander Shelepin the determination of Israelis to defend their country, even to the point of using nuclear weapons. During his subsequent meeting with Shelepin, Hawke again called on the Russian to pressure the Arab nations to recognise Israeli sovereignty and for the Soviet Union to allow the emigration of more of its Jewish citizens. This time, as well as being an unofficial emissary of Israel, Hawke was in Moscow as the president of both the ACTU and Australia's ruling party, which should have given him more heft. But there were bigger international influences at play in Moscow, as the American president, Richard Nixon, sought a rapprochement with China, which raised the fear in Russian minds of an anti-Soviet alliance one day forming between those countries. It was considerations such as this, rather than Hawke's fevered intercessions, that caused Moscow to keep its Arab allies on a tighter leash and make moves towards détente with Washington. A more liberal attitude towards Jewish emigration was part of that changing Soviet stance.[25]

The passion that Hawke brought to the issue was reminiscent of his mother's temperance campaign on the beaches of Perth, when she beseeched beachgoers to sign the teetotal pledge. Flying back over those same beaches on 24 November, Hawke held an emotional press conference at Perth airport, during which he flourished the gruesome photographs of the Israeli soldiers, much as Ellie had flourished a wizened liver in a glass jar. Then he railed against Labor's 'even-handed' policy in the Middle East, claiming that it was driven by the politics of oil. 'That's all right for the politicians,' said Hawke angrily, 'but I understand what truth and democracy are all about and I don't put my knees on the same altar as the politicians.' On this occasion, Hawke was purporting to be speaking as a private citizen. That was a bit too clever and wasn't going to be accepted by Labor MPs or the party's executive. Whitlam was still the minister for foreign affairs as well as prime minister, and he was not amused by the party president decrying his government's foreign policy. He haughtily pointed out to Hawke that the policy was a bipartisan one that had predated Labor's coming to power. Hawke's outburst also upset those Australians who were just as passionate about the Arab cause and the plight of the Palestinian refugees. It was presumably a supporter of the Arab cause, claiming to be a member of the Black September terrorist organisation, who rang Hawke at the ACTU just as an executive meeting was about to begin and threatened to kill his children. Hawke was distraught. All the political pressures had suddenly become personal. After being given a sedative, he was driven home to bed, while his children were collected from school and his house was put under police guard. Hawke also got himself a rifle. Fortunately for the people of Sandringham, he never had cause to fire at shadows in the street.[26]

These were testing months for Hawke and there was little solace to be had at home, where he and Hazel were in a state of intermittent domestic warfare and his teenage children were becoming rebellious. Hazel's diary bears this out. On 25 November 1973, she scribbled down a stream of telephoned abuse from Hawke, apparently verbatim: 'You are a shit, a lying bitch. You are nothing, nothing, & if I could be rid of you I would. I despise you.'[27]

Close friend Col Cunningham recalled how the couple 'were going to bust up 8 million times – I don't know how many times they were going to bust up but they didn't. How could you have a normal marriage? He'd make it abnormal – he'd come home one day, then you wouldn't see him for a week.' Putting a good gloss on it, his long-time secretary and lover Jean Sinclair thought the pair had 'a very strong marriage, despite constant fighting'. They both 'loved fighting, they thrived on it', recalled Sinclair. It was to people like Cunningham and Abeles, rather than his political or union associates, that Hawke turned in moments of stress. 'Bob was in a very high emotional way at that time,' Abeles told D'Alpuget, describing how he listened patiently as they 'spent practically the whole night together talking and talking, just to give him an opportunity to let of[f] problems and steam'. Amid it all, Hawke and Abeles flew off to Cairns for several days of marlin fishing. 'We didn't talk politics or anything,' said Abeles, 'we just had a good time.' After failing to land a marlin one day, despite a three-hour struggle, Hawke caught a smaller one the following day, which Abeles later described as weighing 390 kilograms but which a photograph of a tousle-haired Hawke on the Cairns wharf shows to have been just 155 kilograms. It was far from being one of the 500-kilogram monsters that were occasionally caught off Cairns, but it still took him four hours of strenuous effort on the sixty-kilogram line. It left him so exhausted that he slept on the boat for several hours.[28]

The struggle over the Arab–Israeli issue was more exhausting. He'd begun the year with an emotional speech to the Australian and New Zealand Zionist Federation, during which he explained his staunch support for Israel and why that nation's survival was important for everyone. Wearing a yarmulke on his head and escorted by bodyguards, Hawke received a standing ovation from the packed audience. Their response left him in tears.[29]

Although he'd declared that he was speaking as an individual rather than on behalf of the Labor Party or the ACTU, he was determined to change the party's even-handed approach to the conflict. In the wake of his speech, Hawke raised the issue at a meeting of the party's federal executive in February 1974, demanding that it reconsider its stance and accusing the government of 'abasing themselves at the barrel of oil'. Both Hawke and his pro-Arab opponent on the executive, Bill Hartley, were spoiling for a fight. While Hartley wanted the government to explicitly support the Arab states, Hawke wanted it to express support for Israel's right to exist as a Jewish state. In the event, the status quo was maintained after the ALP executive split eight-all on the issue. Any other outcome would have been embarrassing for Whitlam, since the government's policy had the support of both the caucus and the party conference.[30] Hawke's failure to win over the executive left him stressed and disconsolate, while the threats to his life and those of his family fed his paranoia and saw him take even greater solace in alcohol.

One of his lovers recalled an occasion in early 1974 when he was so drunk during an intimate dinner at the Boulevard Hotel that he behaved in a 'horrifying' manner. The death threats had made him so paranoid under the influence of alcohol that he thought an approaching waiter was a terrorist intent on attacking him. Unleashing a torrent of abuse, Hawke tried to punch the waiter before being restrained and asked to leave. When his lover finally got him back to his room, he was so strung out that he was convinced the adjoining suite was 'full of Arabs who were going to murder him'. When he awoke the next morning and had sobered up, he discovered a note from his lover describing his disgusting behaviour and declaring that she wanted nothing more to do with him. As so often happened, a contrite Hawke insisted on taking her to lunch, when she 'told him exactly what he had done'. Hawke promptly 'burst into tears'. He'd been so paralytic that he had no memory of it. 'I don't know why I do these things,' was all he could say.[31]

Without sufficient insight into the reasons for his actions, Hawke was destined to continue the self-destructive cycle of sexual transgressions, emotional breakdowns, outbursts of drunken anger and outrageous behaviour, often acted out in public, which was sometimes followed by fleeting but intense feelings of remorse. Indeed, the cycle would intensify as his private life fell apart, his drinking worsened and he failed to chart a sure path to his ordained position as prime minister.

To get there, Hawke believed that he would first have to drive out the Socialist Left faction so that the Labor Party's policies could better reflect what he regarded as the inherent conservatism of Australian voters. Reducing the power of the left in the Labor caucus would also reduce his problems as prime minister, whenever that day came. He'd been telling people about it for decades. He had to tread more carefully now that he had a national profile as president of both the ACTU and the ALP. It was made even trickier because he wanted to be held aloft by his supporters, handed a safe electorate and presented by caucus with the keys to the Lodge. Once, when driving past the Lodge, he'd talked offhand to one of his lovers about 'when I live there'.[32]

With his political ambition widely acknowledged among the public and the media, Hawke did nothing to discourage journalists from asking him when he was going to stand for parliament. It suited him politically to be portrayed as the future prime minister, and it boosted his ego for journalists to keep pestering him about it. The television presenter Mike Willesee – the son of Labor's foreign minister, Don Willesee – had a knack for prising answers out of Hawke, whose appearances on his show enhanced its ratings. Once, when Hawke was reluctant to appear, Willesee sent a Rolls-Royce, complete with a beautiful woman and a bottle of champagne, to wait for him to emerge from his office. It was a winning combination. The woman convinced him to get in the car, while the alcohol made him more unguarded in answering Willesee's seductive questions under the glare of the studio lights.[33]

When Hawke appeared on the show on 31 March 1974, the Labor preselection contests for the House of Representatives election, due in 1975, were only about six months away. Willesee was keen to create a headline by getting Hawke to say whether he had any intention of standing at that election. In his usual teasing fashion, Hawke didn't dismiss the idea out of hand. 'I certainly have not planned for it,' he said, while readily conceding that 'a circumstance could arise' that could see him standing. And would you like to be prime minister, asked Willesee, to which Hawke replied: 'In certain circumstances, yes.' Then he was off to the green room for another go at the bar. Apart from Hawke, Willesee noted in his memoirs how the former prime minister Billy McMahon and his wife, along with other 'Liberal bigwigs', were also in the studio and stayed for drinks. When a very drunk Hawke joined the gathering, accompanied by 'a woman of some standing', he promptly put his arm around her and declared loudly: 'I fucked this sheila fourteen times last night.' There was shocked silence. Oblivious to the reaction, Hawke continued in a similar vein as Willesee surreptitiously got the barman to set up in an adjoining room and have the other guests move there. Eventually, it was just Willesee, the garrulous Hawke and his companion. Finally realising that the room was empty, the sozzled Hawke was told that the others had all gone home, which allowed Willesee to usher him out of the building.[34]

Hawke's comment about possibly standing for parliament had been made on the assumption that the next election wouldn't be happening for eighteen months. That changed within days, when Whitlam was forced to an early poll by an opposition that had never accepted the legitimacy of his government. With a half-Senate election due in mid-1974, the Liberal leader, Billy Snedden, used his Senate majority to prevent Whitlam from implementing some of his core campaign promises, particularly the universal health insurance plan, the establishment of a petroleum and minerals authority, industrial relations reforms and the introduction of a bill to reduce the gross disparities in the size of electorates. Matters were brought to a head when Whitlam attempted a political manoeuvre that backfired.

In an attempt to gain an advantage in the half-Senate election, Whitlam tried to add an extra Senate vacancy in Queensland by appointing a DLP senator, Vince Gair, as ambassador to Ireland, only to be outsmarted by Queensland's premier, Joh Bjelke-Petersen, who immediately issued the writs for the election before Gair could formally resign. It meant that only five positions would be contested, rather than six. The remaining Senate vacancy would be filled by the Queensland government after the election. The tit-for-tat political games then saw Snedden announce that the opposition would take the extreme step of blocking a government money bill in order to force Whitlam to dissolve both houses of parliament. It was a challenge Whitlam was happy to accept.[35]

Rather than having an election for the House of Representatives and just half of the Senate, Whitlam made it an election for the full Senate. He also put forward four referendum questions to be decided at the same time. The first was to have simultaneous elections for both houses of parliament; the second allowed people in the ACT and the Northern Territory to vote in referendums; the third allowed the Commonwealth government to grant assistance to local governments and borrow money on their behalf; and the fourth proposed that the House of Representatives and state parliaments should be chosen directly and democratically by the people on the basis of 'one vote, one value', thereby ending the gerrymander in some states, where greater weight was given to the votes of rural electors. While the opinion polls suggested Whitlam would retain control of the lower house, the full Senate election gave him a chance of winning the upper house as well.

This election could have been Hawke's chance to enter parliament and eventually succeed Whitlam as prime minister. There were suggestions that he should stand against Snedden in the Melbourne seat of Bruce, which wouldn't have taken a big swing for Hawke to win. Although Whitlam encouraged the idea, Hawke demurred, citing 'family pressures and the demands of his post as Federal ALP leader and President of the ACTU'. He told a press conference that he would enter parliament at a time of his choosing and 'when his candidature would not be seen as a gimmick'. The truth was that if he was going to enter parliament, he wanted a safe Labor seat that wouldn't require much work to hold.[36]

Setting aside his criticisms of the Whitlam government, Hawke went off on the campaign trail to fight for its re-election. Dressed in his characteristically loud shirt and tie, Hawke appeared with Hazel at the University of New South Wales, where he was greeted with a rapturous response by thousands of students. 'The mere physical presence of the charismatic Bob Hawke was electrifying,' reported the student newspaper, which described how the students applauded his 'penetrating incisive spontaneous remarks'. He presented a different picture at Whitlam's launch of Labor's election policies, where he sat stony-faced on the stage of Blacktown Town Hall as the prime minister railed against the injustice of being forced to an election just halfway through his term and asked voters to renew his mandate.[37]

Whereas it would have been galling for Hawke to see the attention directed at Whitlam, the reception at the university was a balm to his ego and a foretaste of what he might expect if he ever became prime minister. Whatever the voters decided now, Hawke would remain ensconced at the ACTU for the foreseeable future, enjoying the power, privileges and freedoms of that position, and the popularity that often went with it.

CHAPTER FIFTEEN

1974–1975

The result of the 1974 election was a stark warning for the Whitlam government. The Labor landslide that seemed likely as the first votes came in on election night had subsided by midnight, leaving a shocked Whitlam unable to declare victory before tired television viewers went to bed. It took a week before the outcome was certain. Labor's majority in the House of Representatives had been reduced from nine seats to five, and Whitlam had failed to secure his hoped-for majority in the Senate. As for the four referendum proposals, they were soundly defeated. His political honeymoon was over.

The close-run election increased the criticism of Whitlam within the Labor caucus, which voted to replace his dependable deputy, Lance Barnard, with the softly spoken but more mercurial and ambitious Jim Cairns. On the other side, Snedden had been dominated in debates by Whitlam's commanding presence, and the election campaign had confirmed that Snedden wasn't able to perform any better on the hustings. He made himself a laughing stock with a post-election assertion that the Liberals hadn't lost, they just didn't 'win enough seats to form a government'. Yet Snedden held on as leader. He'd had the position for less than eighteen months and there was no widely acceptable successor. While the shadow minister for industrial relations, Malcolm Fraser, hungered for the leadership, he didn't have the numbers for a successful challenge. Meanwhile, the economic peril engulfing the world economy was beginning to affect Australia in ways that would threaten Labor's election program and the jobs and wages of the millions of workers led by Hawke and the ACTU.[1]

The steep increase in petrol prices sparked by the Arab oil embargo of October 1973 took time to work its way around the world. As it did so, it pushed up inflation, both at home and abroad. This occurred at the same time as the Whitlam government was boosting wages and improving working conditions to redress the historical injustice in income distribution caused by twenty-three years of Liberal governments. Many employers simply increased their prices to pay for the wage increases, which thereby eroded their benefit and prompted workers to demand even more. The inflation rate was the highest since the Korean War. When some employers began to lay off workers in response to the government reining in consumer demand, the economy started to stagnate. In fact, the rate of economic growth had been slowing for several years and had dropped to a historical low of less than 4 per cent. This put economists in a quandary. The conventional Keynesian response to a downturn in demand was to encourage spending by companies and consumers. But that would only accelerate inflation. On the other hand, if the government focused on reducing inflation by raising taxes and reducing government spending, that would exacerbate the recession and increase unemployment, which was already at a post-war high of more than 2 per cent.[2] What was to be done?

Had the referendums on prices and incomes been accepted, the government would have had more power to rein in inflation. Without that constitutional power, and with conditions of stagnation also affecting other advanced economies, the Whitlam government began to founder. When Treasury officials urged Whitlam to hit the economy with 'a short sharp shock', his ministers took fright at the effect that would have on unemployment, as well as on the spending plans of their departments. They believed that Treasury officials were intent on blocking the government's initiatives and were leaking information to the opposition. Over the protests of Whitlam and his treasurer, Frank Crean, the government pressed ahead with its promised election program, boosting government spending by 10 per cent. As ministers in cabinet approved each other's spending plans willy-nilly, it became 'like a lunatic asylum', Crean later said. In the wake of the 1974 double dissolution, Whitlam held a joint sitting of parliament to push through the legislation that had been twice rejected by the Liberal-controlled

Senate. Most important was universal health insurance, which had been bitterly opposed by the Liberals, the medical insurance companies and many doctors. The trade unions took their cue from the government and from the improved wages and conditions that it had granted to public servants, demanding the same benefits from private employers, including an additional week's annual leave, a thirty-five-hour week and annual leave loading. Female public servants had also been granted twelve weeks' paid maternity leave, and up to twelve months' unpaid leave. With Whitlam also abolishing university fees, there seemed to be no limit to the largesse that the struggling economy was capable of bestowing upon its people.[3]

With hindsight, Hawke pointed to the 'fiscal irresponsibility' of the Whitlam government from the time of the 1974 election as marking the beginning of its electoral doom. It wasn't helped by the ceaseless industrial disputation that beset a wide range of industries that year. There were workers in the clothing and textile industries upset by the tariff cuts, while metal workers, coalminers, postal workers and builders' labourers all walked off the job, seeking further improvements in their wages and conditions. Others went on strike because their wages or conditions had declined relative to other workers in the same company or industry. Electricians at General Motors Holden walked out in March when they were aggrieved at losing relativity with other skilled tradesmen at the company. When one factory shut down, the dispute spread to plants in other states, and it dragged on for more than two months before the 'fireman' Hawke intervened. These disputes over relativities, or demarcation disputes between different unions, were the bane of his life. In this case, the bitterness between the workers had threatened to descend into bloodshed. It was more evidence, argued Hawke, for the smaller craft unions to amalgamate into industry-wide unions so workers could focus on their real enemy – the employers. In doing so, they 'should not be sucked in by talk of a common purpose', since the means of production in Australia were controlled by just a small number of people, often overseas corporations.[4]

It wasn't just political and industrial disputes that occupied Hawke. When Frank Sinatra organised an international comeback tour in 1974, Hawke found himself drawn into a dispute between the blue-eyed crooner and Australian unionists. Fifty-eight-year-old Sinatra had once likened female American journalists to '$2 hookers', which prompted a female journalist in Sydney to ask cheekily whether the recent bout of inflation had caused him to elevate his value of them. In the absence of any press conferences, journalists riffled through old newspaper cuttings to write stories about his links to the mafia and produced picture spreads of his former wives and partners, describing them as 'Sinatra's molls', while photographers besieged his hotel and pursued his Rolls-Royce. It put him in a sour mood by the time he arrived in his private jet for a concert at Melbourne's refurbished Festival Hall on 9 July, which wasn't helped when his bodyguards punched their way past the photographers and TV cameramen who were angling for a shot of the ageing, hard-drinking singer. When Sinatra got on stage in front of thousands of adoring fans, he vented his anger about the press: 'They keep chasing after us. We have to run all day long. They're parasites who take everything and give nothing. And as for the broads who work for the press, they're the hookers of the press. I might offer them a buck and a half.' It was the assaults on photographers as much as the insults that provoked the Australian Journalists' Association (AJA) to call for a black ban on his tour until the singer apologised for his comments and his bodyguards' behaviour. Rather than apologising, Sinatra declared that he was cancelling the tour and returning to the United States. Barry Donovan was involved with the AJA and urged Hawke to stop Sinatra from leaving Melbourne. Putting a call through to the control tower at Tullamarine, Hawke demanded that Sinatra's private jet not be allowed to take off, only to be told that it was already on the runway with its engines running. Despite his escaping Melbourne, Hawke warned that Sinatra would 'never get out of Australia' unless he apologised or was able to walk on water.[5]

The stalemate continued as Sinatra resumed his residence in the presidential suite on the twenty-third floor of Sydney's Boulevard Hotel, while his representatives sought a solution. When Whitlam was approached, he suggested they get Hawke to intercede with the unions. Although one account has Hawke remaining in Melbourne, waiting for the two sides to become willing to accept a negotiated settlement, he actually landed in Sydney less than twenty-four hours after Sinatra and made his way with several local union officials to the familiar surrounds of the Boulevard, where they found a bottle of Courvoisier and a box of cigars laid out on the table in Sinatra's suite, while the singer remained in another room. After several hours of negotiations with Sinatra's manager, a compromise was eventually reached and a 'half pissed, almost legless' Hawke descended to confront the waiting media. In a written statement read out by Hawke, each side made an apology of sorts for their behaviour. The AJA regretted 'any physical inconvenience' caused to Sinatra and his party by the enthusiasm of their members, while the singer regretted 'any physical injury suffered by persons as a result of attempts to ensure his personal safety'. He also acknowledged that the journalists and photographers were only doing 'their professional duties', and his comments in Melbourne were not intended to besmirch the 'moral character of the working members of the Australian media'. The two concerts in Sydney were allowed to go ahead, with Gough and Margaret Whitlam meeting Sinatra in his dressing room prior to one of them. Meanwhile, Clyde Cameron amended Sinatra's work permit, allowing one of the concerts to be televised to satisfy the Melbourne fans.[6]

Although the spat reaffirmed Hawke's reputation as the great conciliator, it didn't help the reputation of the unions. And it didn't bring Hawke more than a brief moment in the spotlight. Whereas he'd had an approval rating of 60 per cent prior to the 1972 election, an opinion poll two years later ranked him only third as preferred Labor prime minister. Then again, it wasn't a great result for Whitlam either. The prime minister received support from a mere 39 per cent of respondents, with 17 per cent preferring the flamboyant South Australian premier, Don Dunstan, who'd done much to shatter that state's conservative reputation, not least by wearing pink shorts on the steps of Adelaide's Parliament House. Only 14 per cent opted for Hawke. It put Hawke on notice that he wasn't the only possible successor for Whitlam. Another poll in mid-September showed that his approval as ACTU leader had slumped to just 43 per cent, probably driven down by a series of strikes in essential services that had caused widespread disruption. Perhaps the message to be taken from the two polls was that he should remain at the ACTU rather than head for Canberra.[7] There was much for him to do. From his office at Bourke's, he had to defend the workers from the boffins in the Treasury, supported by several ministers in the Whitlam government, who wanted workers to bear the burden of reducing inflation. Which would mean thousands of them being thrown out of work.

The government was repeatedly advised by Treasury officials that inflation could only be reduced by cutting demand for goods and services with the aim of increasing unemployment. It was believed that forcing a reduction in demand and accepting the consequent rise in unemployment would cause a moderation in wage increases, which would help inflation to stabilise. The hardship caused by such a policy would be suffered by the thousands of workers who would become unemployed and by those whose wages would decline in real terms. The Treasury approach was opposed by a majority of the Labor caucus and by the ACTU, with Hawke arguing that it wasn't inflation per se that was the problem but inflationary expectations, which caused workers to demand higher wages in expectation of future price increases. To cut this self-defeating spiral, he proposed that workers be offered tax cuts to moderate their wage demands. Casting around for other solutions, Jim Cairns wondered whether the government should delay metric conversion and the introduction of colour television for fear they would prove to be inflationary, only to have both go ahead. At the same time, ministers pressed on with their spending plans.[8]

Constrained by the demands of the caucus, Crean brought down a late budget in September 1974 that increased government spending by a whopping 32.4 per cent, which ensured that the inflationary pressures continued unabated. When businesses struggled under these pressures or from the reduction in tariffs, the government kept some of them afloat with grants to help them restructure. It also announced a plan to retrain redundant employees, and introduced import controls to provide some shelter for the clothing and footwear industries that had been hit hard by tariff cuts. Some companies couldn't be saved. The British-owned Leyland Motors had been assembling cars in Australia since the 1950s until it made the ill-fated P76 model and faced increasing competition from superior Japanese imports. Five thousand workers lost their jobs when Leyland closed its Sydney factory. Trade unionists on the wharves tried to save other car workers by banning the unloading of car imports, while the government raised the import duty on vehicles. Hawke rushed from one dispute to another, attempting to bring the warring sides together.[9] He had less success bridging the gulf between trade unions and the Labor government.

His relations with labour minister Clyde Cameron remained strained, with Cameron directing his communications with the ACTU through Souter rather than have to deal with Hawke, whom he dismissed as a 'show pony'. Back in 1973, Hawke had excluded Cameron from addressing that year's ACTU Congress. The two men were a generation apart in age and were competing to be the hero of the workers, with Cameron often gaining the kudos for securing improvements in wages and conditions. That began to change when Cameron started to worry that the inflationary effect would destroy the government. When Qantas offered its pilots and engineers a 27 per cent salary increase, Cameron and the transport minister referred it to a tribunal, prompting Hawke to demand that the government stay out of such disputes. When Hawke went on to call for greater consultation from the government, Whitlam rounded on him, demanding that trade unions should consult with the government before they called strikes, which were threatening the government's standing with voters. Hawke quickly backed down, telling journalists that the lack of consultation by ministers was not because of any antipathy towards the unions but because they were preoccupied with 'clearing up 23 years' mess'.[10]

Although there had been repeated bursts of antipathy between Whitlam and Hawke, whether it was in interviews with journalists or shouting down the phone line or across the table at meetings of Labor's federal executive, when Hawke was the chairman and able to call the prime minister to order, it didn't serve the interests of either side for the Labor government to lose office. Moreover, Hawke knew that extricating Whitlam from his political troubles would help to bring the union leader back to centre stage.

At times Hawke was pelted with abuse by hostile audiences and gave just as good in response. One such occasion was an episode of the popular ABC television program *Monday Conference* on 30 September 1974, when he faced down about two hundred people drawn from a range of largely hostile organisations and let fly with loud invective at audience members who dared to challenge him. A reviewer in *The Canberra Times* noted how 'almost his first words [to an interjector] were "Shut-up ya mug"'. It went on like that for sixty minutes, during which he mostly 'treated his audience like a group of very dull children' but was also occasionally 'patiently humble, sentimental and ever-so-honest'.[11] With his angry nature on full display for the million-strong television audience, this was Hawke in full performance mode, rolling his eyes in disgust and bristling at the temerity of those who contradicted him. At the same time, the palpable anger of the audience was a reflection of the antipathy that the Whitlam government and the strike-prone union movement had evoked in some parts of society, particularly among farmers and the small business community. That antipathy was set to worsen as the government struggled for solutions to its economic problems.

The British Labour government of Harold Wilson was grappling with similar problems of stagflation and tried to solve them by offering a raft of social welfare measures in return for unions moderating their wage demands. Dubbed a 'social contract', it was quick to attract interest in Australia, where Hawke and Cairns brought together a meeting of 256 union delegates in late September 1974 to see whether such a social contract might work in Australia. The meeting was held in the wake of the government's big-spending budget, which had been brought down in the vain hope that workers might respond by reining in their wage claims. However, Hawke couldn't stop unions from making big wage claims, and the government couldn't stop the Arbitration Commission from agreeing to them. As an alternative, Hawke suggested that the ACTU might support a new referendum on prices and incomes. He'd opposed the previous one, which had then been rejected by voters, so that suggestion was never going to fly. The best that could be hoped for was closer consultation between the ACTU and the government on economic matters. That would require a meeting of minds between the grandstanding prime minister and the wannabe prime minister. While Hawke would welcome the attention such consultation would bring, it was unlikely to result in positive outcomes for an economy that was careering beyond the government's control.[12] It was also a government in increasing disarray. Whitlam's authority was being steadily diminished as he struggled to balance the demands of his caucus, the calls by Hawke and the trade unions, and the advice coming from the Treasury and university economists.

Hawke's private life, too, was in continuing disarray as he tried to balance its competing elements, deal with his unachieved ambition and live with the threats on his life. According to the policemen who were protecting him at the time, the pressures on Hawke were so great that at times he was left 'a gibbering idiot'. He enjoyed some periods of respite when he took Hazel and the kids to spend several days out of the limelight on his doctor's farm in Gippsland. These were brief breaks in their turbulent life. Back home in Sandringham, the situation was getting worse. The children were bereft of the steadying influence that their father might have provided, had he been present and able to empathise with them. Hazel struggled to cope on her own and found herself smoking and drinking more than was healthy for her. Once she got so drunk at a friend's barbecue that she had to be helped home by the children and put to bed. Rather than sympathy from Hawke, there was only anger. When friends suggested she develop outside interests, the couple sought help from David Scott, the director of the Brotherhood of St Laurence, a charitable arm of the Church of England that was employed by the ACTU to supply research material on poverty. Their dinner with Scott did not go well. Both of them got drunk and Hazel had to be sent home in a taxi, while Hawke failed to return home at all. Hazel was eventually convinced by Susan to see a therapist to work through her many issues. It was during this therapy that she was encouraged to make another approach to Scott, who suggested she volunteer for half a day per week with the Family Centre for Low Income People. The experience would change her life.[13]

For Hawke, there was no life-changing experience in the offing. He had his succession of lovers and his coterie of wealthy friends, who in combination provided time away from the pressures of his work and the demands of his family. Wherever he went, he couldn't escape from himself, other than to the oblivion produced by drink, momentary distractions in different bedrooms or fleeting bursts of public adulation. According to Col Cunningham, there was little enjoyment to be had at home. Cunningham described how Hawke would return home after restoring industrial peace to the nation and expect to be hailed for his achievement, only to have Hazel demand that he dry the dishes. 'He likes someone to fuss over him,' said Cunningham, 'and not treat him like a dog.' Not receiving adoration at home, he would go elsewhere. 'There were plenty of times when he could have gone home,' recalled Cunningham, 'but didn't want to.' Hawke would frequently hive off for lunch to the Chevron Hotel in South Yarra, an extensive four-storey edifice extending over several wings and topped with a tower. It had been built in 1934 with a sense of luxury and style, and boasted such novelties as ensuite bathrooms, a swimming pool and a tennis court. The Chevron was famous for having hosted actor Ava Gardner during the filming of *On the Beach* in 1959, with its nightclub having become a swanky feature of Melbourne's limited nightlife. The hotel was owned by Eddie Kornhauser, who wanted to transform the site into a multistorey office, hotel and casino complex. According to Kornhauser, Hawke came to lunch with him at the Chevron three or four times a week. On one occasion, when he was avoiding Hazel's wrath, she called Kornhauser and angrily demanded to speak to her husband. 'I know Bob is with you! I'll cut your throat,' she was said to have screamed.[14]

On other occasions, Hawke would escape with Cunningham to the Gold Coast. Once the pair went to the Sands Hotel at Surfers Paradise for two nights, before planning to head south to Ocean Shores in northern New South Wales, where Cunningham had a condominium adjoining an eighteen-hole golf course. The American-owned development on former dairy farms had attracted Hollywood celebrities after singer Pat Boone became involved in the development company, with movie stars Clint Eastwood, William Holden and Fred MacMurray jetting in to play in the Pat Boone Celebrity Golf Classic. It was a way of shifting the seven thousand house lots, some of which were sold to CIA operatives in South-East Asia and gullible US soldiers visiting Kings Cross. Many were still undeveloped at the time of Hawke's visit. One of the salesmen for the development was Michael Hand, who would become a co-founder of the notorious Nugan Hand bank, which was used by the CIA and drug dealers alike for money laundering, while one of the directors was the private secretary of his partner Frank Nugan, whose family was associated with the Griffith mafia.[15]

En route to Ocean Shores, Hawke attracted a mass of admirers on the beach at Surfers Paradise before borrowing a newfangled jet ski and powering off through the surf. Cunningham was supposed to be acting as his minder and was appalled to see him 'risking his bloody life, 300 yards out to sea. But he'd do anything.' It was characteristic of Hawke's manic behaviour, which became much worse when alcohol was involved. 'He was the worst drunk, and pest,' recalled

Cunningham. 'I used to be embarrassed for him. It was just awful to see the guy ... belittling himself in front of people, and people saying, "look at that drunk".' This time it happened in the Gold Coast's leading restaurant, the Hibiscus Room, where Hawke berated the well-heeled diners. 'He gave them a helluva night,' said Cunningham, putting on a performance that was 'v[ery] anti-establishment ... swearing, uncouth'. Fortunately, it didn't escalate into a physical confrontation before Cunningham contained him and got them back to the Sands Hotel. Early the next morning, Cunningham bundled him into a car for the drive to Ocean Shores.[16]

In his hungover state, looking out on the subtropical forest and glimpses of surf beach, the drive to the Lodge must have seemed further off than ever. No matter how much he wanted to become prime minister, there were too many barriers and Hawke couldn't be certain he could surmount them. There was the problem of finding a safe Victorian seat, of which there were just a handful, and he could only have a hope of nabbing one if a sitting member retired. There were powerful politicians in caucus who were determined to prevent him from securing a safe seat because they didn't want to see him succeeding Whitlam as Labor leader. As journalist Alan Ramsey observed, 'for all his leadership credentials and strong public support', Hawke lacked the most 'basic qualification of all – a seat in parliament and [he had] no early prospect of getting one'.[17] Even if a seat became available, he would have to win preselection in the face of opposition from the Socialist Left, which remained powerful in the Victorian branch.

One such seat was Melbourne Ports, which Crean had held since 1951. Towards the end of 1974, after having many of his deflationary policy proposals frustrated by the caucus, Crean told Whitlam that he wanted to resign from parliament and become chairman of the Commonwealth Bank. His electorate had a sizeable Jewish component, which might have been expected to support Hawke. However, the state Labor leader, Clyde Holding, wanted to make the transition to federal politics and had his own eyes on the seat. In the event, Whitlam consulted Hawke, who advised him not to give Crean the bank job and instead to encourage him to remain in parliament. According to Whitlam, Hawke feared that the resulting by-election could produce an anti-government swing that might imperil Labor's hold on the seat and destabilise the government. Hawke was probably also thinking about his long-term ambitions, and not wanting one possible avenue to Canberra being closed off. In the event, Crean's possible resignation was leaked to the media, creating a furore that prevented it from going ahead. Whitlam suspected that Hawke had been responsible.[18]

Other political disasters for the government were more difficult to avoid. Just seven months into the Whitlam government's second term, a tropical cyclone swerved from its expected course and destroyed Darwin on Christmas Eve 1974, levelling much of the city and killing at least seventy-one people. Whitlam was on a five-week tour of Europe, so it was left to the acting prime minister, Jim Cairns, to deal with the disaster, organising the evacuation of most of the inhabitants and putting in place the plans for Darwin's reconstruction. He did such a good job that there was talk that Whitlam might be displaced as leader by his popular deputy. Whitlam didn't return until four days later and was hardly home before he flew back to Europe to resume his talks with European leaders and complete his grand tour of the continent's archaeological ruins, only to have a disaster occur at the other end of Australia, when a cargo ship brought down the Tasman Bridge over the Derwent River, killing twelve people and dividing Hobart in two. Whitlam could only fulminate in frustration at this further intrusion on his carefully planned trip, while Hawke was left to wonder about a prime minister who could be so distant and so oblivious to the concerns of his constituents.[19]

After all, it wasn't as if the government was secure and was guaranteed to serve out its full three years. The economy was in a mess and the government had only a slim majority in the House of Representatives and was beset in the Senate by opposition MPs, who were determined to bring down Whitlam at the earliest opportunity. Yet that prospect seemed far away when Labor delegates humped their suitcases into the Florida Hotel, overlooking the beach at Terrigal on the New South Wales Central Coast, for the biennial ALP conference in February 1975.

The tone of the Terrigal conference was set by Whitlam, resplendent in a Hawaiian shirt, while 45-year-old Hawke sprawled by the hotel pool, beer in hand, wearing a too-tight pair of speedos and displaying a torso that was turning to flab. Presuming that everyone would admire his body as much as he did, he was snapped by photographers taking off to the beach with 23-year-old Glenda Bowden, a bikini-clad political staffer from Jim Cairns' office, with whom he had a brief affair. She would later say that although Hawke was an 'average lover', he had a 'voracious sexual appetite'. Many women could have attested to that. Not to be outdone, a misty-eyed Cairns caused headlines when he was caught up in the holiday atmosphere and told a tabloid journalist that he had a 'kind of love' for his recently appointed office manager, Junie Morosi. It was a love that wouldn't end well for either of them, or for the government. It was that sort of conference, held in a holiday resort by casually dressed delegates whose leaders seemed oblivious to the peril that was steadily engulfing them. Hawke was happy to absorb the sun and compete for media attention, drinking greedily from a succession of schooners and trying to bed a string of women.[20]

The political correspondent for *The Canberra Times*, Gay Davidson, was one of them. She went to Hawke's hotel room for an interview, only to watch him strip to his underwear and lie back across the bed. When she showed a reluctance to join him, he wheedled her into at least removing her shoes and sitting on the edge of the bed. When it became clear that she would go no further, Hawke turned on her. He didn't take rejection well and usually showered such women with insults, presumably so he could feel that it was he who was spurning them. In this case, he told Davidson: 'God you've got ugly feet.'[21] It was no way for her to treat the president of the party, he must have thought, after he'd been hailed by the conference for his opening oration.

While Hawke's hastily written speech had canvassed some of the government's shortcomings, it had concluded with an upbeat assessment that assured delegates they had no reason to fear the government's defeat, so long as they 'get behind the Prime Minister and the Government'. That was in spite of Labor being trounced at the Queensland state election just two months before. Whitlam spoke in a similarly positive vein, rousing his listeners with a vision of future success 'through 1975 and beyond', provided they exhibited 'the crusading spirit of '72 and the deep determination of '74'. However, unemployment was already at a post-war high of around 5 per cent, while inflation was more than 15 per cent and rising sharply. As for the industrial peace that was promised by an incoming Labor government working in concert with the trade unions, the number of working days lost to strikes had more than doubled in 1974. Yet the conference had little to offer as solutions. It was 'a schemozzle', said Hawke in retrospect, with Whitlam and his ministers paying little more than lip-service to the idea of consulting the forty-nine assembled delegates. That was hindsight talk. As chair of the conference, Hawke had been as responsible as anyone for the schemozzle, and for the derisory way the conference was reported by journalists and colourfully portrayed by photographers. Indeed, it was Hawke who'd agreed to a publicity stunt at the newly opened Old Sydney Town theme park, inland from Terrigal, where he posed for photographers as if he was having his bare back whipped in the manner of a convict.[22] It wouldn't be long before Australians would be doing likewise to the Whitlam government.

During the conference, Whitlam had decided that he would promote his reformist attorney-general, Lionel Murphy, to the High Court, which would give it a progressive majority for the foreseeable future. It was a laudable objective for a Labor leader who was anxious not to have his political initiatives ruled unconstitutional by the eminent judges. But he would also have wanted Murphy gone from his ministry so that he would not be able to transfer his undoubted talent and ambition from the Senate to the House of Representatives, from where he might challenge Whitlam for the leadership.

Perhaps more importantly, Whitlam wanted to remove his gregarious, champagne-swilling attorney-general from the government for fear of the political embarrassment Murphy might cause if his associations with Sydney's criminal underworld came to light. He was alleged to have done favours for the ruthless crime boss Abe Saffron, who'd become rich selling sly grog with Eddie Kornhauser before going on to control the vice trade and illegal casinos. Saffron was alleged to have supplied young Filipino sex workers to Murphy, who was also said to have been close to Junie Morosi, which prompted members of the Liberal Party to employ a private detective, Tim Bristow, to break into Morosi's Sydney townhouse to hide listening devices and gather any documents involving Murphy's business activities. Unfortunately for Bristow and his two associates, including a Liberal Party official, Murphy learned of the imminent break-in and had Commonwealth

Police officers lying in wait to arrest the intruders. Although Bristow escaped, his two associates were nabbed, only to be dealt with lightly when Bristow rushed around to the home of Murphy's long-time friend, the well-connected bookmaker Bill Waterhouse. According to Bristow's account, Waterhouse phoned Morgan Ryan, who was Abe Saffron's solicitor of choice and a mate of Murphy, to have him intervene with the New South Wales police. This mad escapade involving Murphy didn't cause any headlines at the time, but it confirmed Whitlam in his determination to be done with his corrupt attorney-general.[23]

With Murphy out of the way, Whitlam's success at the next election, due in 1977, would rest on him being able to reduce unemployment without causing a further rise in inflation. In an effort to put a brake on prices, the government had created the Prices Justification Tribunal, which had compelled companies to justify their price increases, while trade unions were asked to moderate their wage demands in return for the government supporting a system of quarterly wage indexation. Although it kept inflation a percentage point or two lower than it might otherwise have been, the Prices Justification Tribunal could only apply moral pressure on companies that raised their prices, while quarterly wage indexation meant that workers were chasing sharply rising prices as they watched their wages fall in real terms.[24]

That put Hawke in a bind. While he might want to support the aims of the government, his trade union constituents demanded that he support the interests of their members. He might have escaped from the bind by giving up the Labor presidency after one term, as he'd promised to do, but he was determined to stay put. There was too much satisfaction to be had from occupying both positions, which put him on a political pedestal that almost equalled that of the prime minister, and that saw Hawke, rather than Whitlam, open the Labor conference and chair meetings of the federal executive. And it was Hawke who had greater sway with the trade union movement. But the ALP presidency had imposed an additional load on him, with executive meetings, media appearances, correspondence and telephone calls, and requests from party branches. No support staff came with the position, so he spent even less time at home.

Perhaps feeling remorse for his neglect, Hawke combined his attendance at a conference in Belgrade in late May with a two-week family holiday, during which they drove through Greece to visit the ruins at Delphi before continuing on to the tourist sights of Athens. From there, they set sail on a yacht on a five-day voyage around the Greek islands. According to Hazel's account, it was an idyllic time that ended all too soon. Moreover, it had been interrupted by political turmoil at home, after Whitlam accepted the resignation of his former deputy, Lance Barnard, who was promptly appointed as ambassador to Sweden. It was a fit of madness by Whitlam, and also by Barnard, since it would necessitate a by-election in his Tasmanian electorate of Bass, which had been hit hard by the reduction in textile tariffs, and where farmers were smarting at the removal of subsidies from superphosphate. Hawke was incredulous, later describing the move as 'one of the stupidest political decisions in living memory'. He could see the political trouble that Whitlam was creating for the government, particularly as the Liberals had dumped Snedden and put Malcolm Fraser in his place. Giving the new opposition leader a by-election in a knife-edge seat was putting the future of the Labor government in peril, and Hawke didn't hold back from expressing his anger in a series of heated telephone calls from his Athens hotel. His outrage was all in vain. Whitlam had felt an obligation to repay his former deputy for his years of loyalty, and wished to redress the action of the caucus in displacing Barnard as deputy prime minister in favour of Cairns.[25]

As Hazel and the children flew home to Melbourne, Hawke went to Geneva for meetings of the ILO and presumably trysts with Helga Cammell. It was clear that his holiday with Hazel had changed nothing. As Susan later noted, the family was set to resume their 'all-but separate lives', much as before. Hazel was left to handle the domestic arrangements and arrange schooling for two of their teenage children, after both Stephen and Rosslyn became unhappy at their schools. Stephen was rebelling against the conservative milieu of Melbourne Grammar, where Hawke would sometimes sit with the reforming Liberal premier Dick Hamer on Saturday mornings as they watched their sons play cricket, much as Clem had done with Bob. Stephen would later describe the school's 'arrogant, self-satisfied, self-seeking congregation of teenagers' and his attempts to make a stand against its rules. Disciplined for speaking out against instances of racism, he took to smoking 'grass' in the nearby Botanic Gardens. Although he was in his final year, it was clear that he would be risking his final results if he stayed at a school that he loathed. It was up to Hazel to make the arrangements. Insisting that Hawke accompany them, she took Stephen and Rosslyn to inspect an alternative school at Langwarrin South, about thirty-seven kilometres away. It was at Woodleigh School that the pair would complete their secondary education, while Susan began a degree at Monash University.[26]

Hawke had been in Europe when the Bass by-election was held on 28 June 1975, which saw Labor take a 14 per cent drubbing. It was a great boost for Fraser in his first electoral test as opposition leader, and made the Liberals more determined than ever to force Whitlam to another early election.

They had much material to work with. For the last six months, the government had been trying to tap into the sea of 'petrodollars' that were flooding the oil-rich nations of the Middle East and needed somewhere to be invested. Cameron and Cairns were involved in the talks, while Whitlam and his resources and energy minister, Rex Connor, had nation-building projects on which to spend $4 billion of such loan money, including a transcontinental pipeline and a uranium enrichment plant. During the Terrigal conference, Connor had been busily trying to contact a Pakistani-born businessman and undischarged bankrupt named Tirath Khemlani, who claimed to have contacts with several Middle Eastern leaders who had cheap funds to invest. Even though the $4 billion was reduced to $2 billion, it was too good to be true. Secret talks went on for several months before the backdoor dealings were finally exposed, bringing discredit on Connor and Cairns and forcing Whitlam to instruct that his government's negotiations with Khemlani be brought to an end, and that only Cairns was permitted to negotiate the borrowing of funds from overseas. The issue continued to dog Whitlam for the remainder of his time as prime minister, and he was forced to sack Connor for continuing to negotiate with Khemlani after his authority had been withdrawn. Cairns, too, was sacked when it was discovered that he'd started negotiations for a loan from American sources, wrongly assuring Whitlam that he hadn't agreed to pay any brokerage to the Melbourne businessman who was supposedly setting up the loan. Cameron was also sacked after falling out with Whitlam over the government's economic policy. An increasingly confident Fraser watched as the government imploded.[27]

The loans affair had been news to Hawke, who, as president of the party, might have been expected to have been told, at least in general terms, of the proposed arrangement. On returning from Geneva in mid-July, he criticised Whitlam for not consulting him. Had he been consulted, Hawke would have railed against the idea of raising funds from Middle Eastern potentates in case it came with conditions concerning Australia's relations with Israel. Even though no funds were forthcoming, Hawke's anger and dismay at the government's political naivety was reinforced when he later had occasion to have a conversation with Khemlani on an international flight, after which he could only wonder anew about how the Whitlam government 'had allowed itself to be conned by this unimpressive little shyster'.[28] Not that Hawke hadn't been conned by a few shysters in his time.

Although Whitlam had barely served a year of his second term, the political chaos in Canberra pointed towards another early election if the opposition could find an issue that would justify the Liberal-controlled Senate blocking the budget, thereby forcing Whitlam back to the people. Try as he might, there was little that Hawke could do to shore up a government that was falling apart. Nor could he prevent Fraser's machinations in parliament from coming to their eventual conclusion.

Amid the chaos, Hawke played the part of political commentator standing above the fray, untouched by the mud that was being thrown about so freely in Canberra. By late July, a writer in *The Age* thought he was 'easily the most popular Labor politician in the country'.[29] He was pestered by journalists about when he would gallop to the rescue of the embattled Labor Party by standing for a seat in parliament with a view to succeeding Whitlam. That would not be easy. The party's rules prevented him from challenging a sitting member, and there was still considerable opposition to him within both the Victorian branch and the caucus in Canberra. What's more, others were positioning themselves to be Whitlam's successor. Foremost among them was Bill Hayden, who'd brought the Medibank legislation to fruition as social security minister before replacing Cairns as treasurer in June.

Yet such was Hawke's self-belief that he kept the stories of his transfer to Canberra bubbling away, saying that he would talk to people about a possible seat and the support he might receive in the caucus. But there was no vacancy. Neither were any sitting MPs prepared to resign to make their seats available for Hawke. Not that he would have wanted to stand for parliament at a time when the party seemed destined for an extended period in opposition.

Instead, Hawke threw himself back into his role as ACTU president, settling a difficult postal dispute and launching the business venture that partnered the ACTU with an independent petrol retailer, Solo. Even though Souter had done most of the work to get the business established, it was Hawke who gained the kudos when the chain of petrol stations, mainly in Melbourne and emblazoned with 'ACTU-Solo' signage, offered fuel at a significant discount. It was like Bourke's all over again, with Hawke this time taking on the multinational oil companies in a campaign that was sure to be popular. Jetting in from Geneva, he posed at an ACTU-Solo bowser, petrol pump in hand, for the benefit of photographers and film crews. Consumers might have lauded his initiative, but the new company soon became caught up in the political turmoil that was besetting the government. The opposition alleged that the government had provided ACTU-Solo with access to locally produced crude oil to which it was not entitled. A royal commission into the petroleum industry found that Souter, as a director of ACTU-Solo, had misled the government about the price it was paying for a quantity of overseas crude oil. Hawke had been overseas during the negotiations and was absolved of blame, but Souter was compelled to resign from the various board positions he'd garnered from the government. Hawke expressed his 'terrible sorrow that this should happen' to 64-year-old Souter 'in the twilight of his career'. With the government beset on all sides, Whitlam announced that no further allocations of local crude oil would be given to the company. That didn't end the matter. The Liberals accused Hawke of being involved and demanded that the royal commission be reopened so Hawke could be put on the stand and even have the police consider charging him under the Crimes Act. Denying everything, Hawke went on television with Liberal senator Ivor Greenwood, challenging him to repeat his accusation outside the safety of parliament. Silence ensued.[30]

Further trouble came in October 1975, when the treasurer, Bill Hayden, confided to Hawke the details of the budget he was about to announce in the hope it would be greeted favourably by the trade unions, only to have Hawke say that, if asked by journalists, he would have to tell them truthfully of his foreknowledge. If he was intending to undermine Hayden as Whitlam's likely successor, he was outwitted when Hayden released the story himself. Much to Hawke's chagrin, that put Hawke under pressure, since the budget included a $2 levy on crude oil, which the opposition claimed was meant to advantage ACTU-Solo. These issues soon became moot when the Coalition used its Senate majority to block the budget, which sparked their long-hoped-for political crisis. Hawke urged Whitlam to call a half-Senate election in the hope of securing a Labor majority in the Senate, while some trade unions threatened strike action if the Senate did not relent. It might have been possible to call the opposition's bluff, since some Liberal senators were uneasy about blocking the budget of a popularly elected government, but Whitlam was outmanoeuvred by a secret understanding between Fraser and Governor-General Sir John Kerr.[31]

The finish to the political drama came quickly. Rather than allowing Whitlam to break the deadlock by calling a half-Senate election and letting the people decide, Kerr concluded that he would decide the government's fate. With Fraser secretly waiting in another room of Government House, Kerr pounced upon the unsuspecting Whitlam and presented him with a letter of dismissal. It was an extraordinary act that ignored the majority that Whitlam still enjoyed in the House of Representatives. Paul Keating would later say that if he'd been prime minister, he would have defied the governor-general. Not so Whitlam, who went quietly, wrongly believing that his majority in the House of Representatives would compel Kerr to reinstate him. It was only when he discovered that Fraser had been appointed as caretaker prime minister and parliament had been prorogued that Whitlam's outrage was released on the steps of Parliament House. Speaking to the angry crowd that had gathered below, he urged them to 'maintain your rage and enthusiasm'. As the news percolated through Australia, workers downed tools and huge crowds marched in protest along city streets. Amid calls for a national strike to force the fall of Fraser's caretaker government, Australians looked to Hawke for leadership. If there was going to be any resistance, he would have to direct it.[32]

Hawke was already on his way to Canberra to consult with Whitlam that evening, telling the now opposition leader: 'I told you so. Fancy appointing that bastard [Kerr].' But what were they to do? Hawke's positions as ACTU and ALP president placed him in a predicament. Wearing his ACTU hat, he could support the growing calls for a strike, but he couldn't see how that would reverse the course upon which Kerr had set the country. Wearing his ALP hat, he was conscious that a national strike could cruel Labor's chances at the inevitable election, since it would be portrayed as the unions trying to prevent the Australian people from expressing their views on the government's dismissal. Hawke also feared that a national strike could cause the country to descend into chaos and violence. 'We are on the edge of something quite terrible,' he warned. '[I]t is important,' he added, 'that the Australian people should respond to leadership.' Some of his critics thought that it was leadership that Hawke was singularly failing to provide by refusing to rally the union movement in defence of the government. But Whitlam and Hawke had both trained as lawyers and had an ingrained respect for legal forms and procedures. It wasn't in the nature of either man to take to the streets for a political cause. They would place their trust in the fair-mindedness of the Australian people, who had, after all, responded well when Whitlam had been forced to an early election in 1974. Of course, that time had been different: he'd gone to the election as prime minister. This time he'd be going as a sacked politician, burdened by the baggage of the 'loans affair' and other scandals, and weighed down by an economy marked by rising inflation and growing unemployment.[33]

For three years, the conservatives had denied the legitimacy of the Labor government, despite two elections confirming it in power. By meekly accepting its dismissal, the Labor government had implicitly accepted the arguments of its opponents. Whitlam might have imagined that the coming election could be fought on the misuse of constitutional proprieties by Kerr and Fraser, but such arguments only had purchase with staunch Labor supporters. By making Fraser the caretaker prime minister, Kerr had given him the mantle of legitimacy and allowed the Liberals to make Whitlam's dysfunctional government the issue.

Hawke had no illusions about how the poll would pan out. The day after the dismissal, as angry marchers coursed their way through the centre of Melbourne, Hawke sat in his office with Bill Kelty, from the Storemen and Packers' Union, and Jean Sinclair to consider the options confronting the union movement. He recognised that the marches could not resurrect the Labor government. And he wasn't going to exacerbate the political divisions created by Kerr and Fraser by calling a national strike. Instead, he would accept Kerr's action and go forward to an election that he knew would see Whitlam's demise. Rather than striking, he called on workers to donate a day's pay to replenish Labor's much-depleted electoral coffers, while confiding to Kelty that he believed Labor would lose not only the upcoming election, but the one after that as well. No matter; Fraser had ruined his own reputation by the way he'd come to power, and wouldn't be able to 'wage war with us', said Hawke. Once the Whitlam years were well in the past, voters would turn back to Labor when they saw that 'we are the people of consensus and we demonstrate that we have learnt our lessons'. According to Hawke, it would be a platform of consensus that 'will deliver us Government' and there was nobody 'better placed [than him] to be PM'.[34]

Although he was convinced that Whitlam had no chance of winning, Hawke threw himself into the campaign as if he really believed victory were possible. *The Age* called him 'a tower of strength', with Hawke predicting that inflation, unemployment and industrial disputes would all be lower under Labor. But voters had lost confidence in Labor as an economic manager; Hawke hadn't helped matters by earlier describing Whitlam as 'economically illiterate'. While the passion and size of the Labor crowds gave a misleading glimmer of hope, the opinion polls told a different story. They had favoured Labor in the lead-up to the dismissal, when the Liberals were blamed for immersing the country in political chaos; now they'd swung against the sacked prime minister, who was trying in vain to keep the focus of voters on the manner of his sacking rather than on his dysfunctional government and the deteriorating economy.

On the day of the election – 13 December – Hawke took his family to Canberra for the count, with the numbers going up on a board in a school hall that served as the national tally room. Commentating for Packer's Channel Nine alongside Bill Snedden, Hawke watched in dismay as supposedly safe Labor seats fell to the Liberals. It was worse than he'd feared. With tears in his eyes, he quickly conceded that Labor had lost. 'We've had the guts ripped out of us,' he said. He was forced to stay under the lights of the television cameras as Labor's humiliation became clear. He would later describe it as 'one of the longest and loneliest nights of my life'.[35]

The Whitlam experiment had ended. Despite his distress on the night, Hawke realised that the scale of the government's defeat would demand that a new leader be found to rebuild the shattered party and chart a course back to government.

CHAPTER SIXTEEN

1976–1977

Sitting in the national tally room on election night, Bob Hawke watched as Gough Whitlam arrived to the half-hearted cheers of his disappointed supporters before turning to the television cameras to acknowledge his government's defeat. Within minutes of arriving, a devastated Whitlam turned heel and shrank back into his car. Thirty Labor MPs were swept from the House of Representatives, providing Malcolm Fraser with an overwhelming majority.

As the scale of his defeat became clear, Whitlam began planning for a successor. His first choice was the former treasurer, Bill Hayden, the only Labor MP who looked likely to survive in Queensland. However, Hayden had enrolled to do a law degree and wasn't sure on election night that he'd be able to hold his seat. It was only then that Whitlam turned to Hawke, calling him to the Lodge on the Sunday morning, where the two men sat by the pool. With the grim headlines of the Sunday papers spread out before him, Whitlam got straight to the point, confiding that Hayden had declined the leadership mantle and urging Hawke to stand for parliament as soon as possible. Whitlam had told David Frost in August 1973 that he wanted to remain prime minister for about eight years, and he'd repeated that ambition during the 1975 campaign.[1] Now he was gone a few weeks shy of three years. This was Hawke's chance.

It was what he'd been dreaming about for decades. Whitlam's speechwriter, Graham Freudenberg, was also at the Lodge and confirmed to Hawke an earlier commitment to be his speechwriter in the event of Hawke becoming the Labor leader. Freudenberg then helped to write a joint statement for Whitlam and Hawke, in which they placed themselves 'at the disposal of the will of the party'. The implications of the statement seemed clear: Whitlam was going out and Hawke was coming in.

Flying home to Melbourne, Hawke was accompanied by his close ally Bill Landeryou, the federal president of the Storemen and Packers' Union. Landeryou later recalled how the pair had first met at the bar of the Lygon in the early 1960s, when Hawke was 'being loud and destroying his brain cells at a rapid rate'. They'd remained close ever since. The son of a timber worker, Landeryou had become president of Young Labor when he was twenty-two, state secretary of the Storemen and Packers when he was twenty-eight and federal president when he was thirty-eight. He'd transformed the union, bringing Simon Crean and Bill Kelty on board and adopting a more militant industrial stance that secured much higher wages for the union's formerly underpaid workforce. Now he was Labor's leader in the Victorian Legislative Council, and the leader of the powerful Centre Unity faction. He was the quintessential back-room operator who preferred to call the shots from the shadows. He was not only Hawke's numbers man, but also claimed to be his 'personal confidant and close friend'. Landeryou realised that Hawke's success required him to stay quiet until a seat could be lined up and the numbers in caucus guaranteed. To keep the lid on Hawke's irrepressible enthusiasm, Landeryou stayed with him for a day and a half while the necessary phone calls were made. It was all for nothing. The Canberra press gallery had been briefed that Hawke was aiming to be the new Labor leader. Whitlam later denied that he'd let the news out, pointing the finger instead at the party's federal secretary, David Combe.[2]

Whatever the source, Hawke could contain himself no longer. His impatience would be his undoing. Less than twenty-four hours after the meeting at the Lodge, Hawke was being anointed in the newspapers as Whitlam's heir apparent. A report in *The Age* claimed that Whitlam had agreed to support Hawke and that 'a safe Victorian seat will be available to Mr Hawke when he decided to make his move'. When questioned about the report, Hawke said that 'it would have to be in the next three years'. He wasn't the only possible contender. For several years, Don Dunstan had been mentioned as a likely Labor leader, and again he was being cited as the politician most able to rescue Labor's political fortunes. The influential political editor of *The Age*, Allan Barnes, argued that Dunstan was the 'one man in the movement who has shown by performance that he has the qualities of leadership which Federal Labor desperately needs'. It was only if Dunstan refused that 'a lot of Labor people might have to swallow their reservations and quickly find a seat for that most difficult but talented man, Robert James Hawke', who already knew that Dunstan wouldn't be leaving Adelaide. The previous year, he'd offered to support Dunstan as Labor leader if the South Australian wanted to go first. Dunstan assured him that he had no federal aspirations. Dunstan's lack of interest buoyed Hawke's confidence about his own chances, but he was snookering himself with arrogant statements about becoming leader. The former treasurer Frank Crean, who also had leadership aspirations, was one of those who made clear that Hawke couldn't count on the support of caucus.[3] Hawke pushed on regardless.

Interviewed on television, Hawke confirmed that he had Whitlam's support and, in his usual boasting manner, declared that he could get Labor back into government at the next election if caucus elected him as leader. It was a presumptuous statement that was made worse when he said he was only prepared to represent a safe Victorian seat, which meant that one of five Labor MPs – Jim Cairns, Frank Crean, Gordon Bryant, Ted Innes or Harry Jenkins – would have to make way for him. As Whitlam later observed, one of them might have been prepared to retire if they'd been approached quietly, but Hawke had 'put their noses out of joint' by publicly pressuring them to go. Moreover, he'd now stirred up his enemies in the resurgent Socialist Left, who were on notice to organise against his preselection, while the Victorian branch called on Whitlam to renounce the deal with Hawke and take the party to the next election. This effectively killed Hawke's immediate political ambitions. Even if he could get preselection for a safe Labor seat, he would face opposition in caucus. By promising to be much more consultative and less imperious than Whitlam, he only upset Whitlam, who decided to remain as leader, while Crean, Bryant and New South Wales MP Lionel Bowen announced that they would stand for the leadership rather than have Hawke lead the party. Hawke's chances were further diminished by word getting around that he'd had drinks at the Boulevard Hotel with Rupert Murdoch, who was persona non grata with caucus after his papers had campaigned against the Whitlam government. That ill-advised tête-à-tête allowed Hawke's opponents to depict him as Murdoch's creature, which some of the caucus already believed.[4] His fleeting opportunity to succeed Whitlam had passed as suddenly as a summer storm.

Hawke had recognised that the dismissal had opened the way for him to develop an alternative ALP vision that might attract disillusioned voters back to Labor. While he appreciated how long that might take, he knew also that Fraser was hobbled by the manner of his coming to power and was confronted by the same intractable economic problems that had bedevilled his predecessor. Hawke was confident that the solution to the twin challenges of inflation and unemployment could only be found in consultation with the union movement. Which is where he came in. After three years of the public's attention being focused primarily on Whitlam, it would now be back on him. As for becoming Labor leader – that could wait.

For the time being, Whitlam declared, he would remain as leader, which was duly confirmed by a somewhat reluctant caucus in acknowledgement of Whitlam's exalted status among party members. At the same time, the caucus decreed that another leadership ballot had to be held in May 1977, in the hope that a viable successor would have emerged by then. That gave Hawke more than a year to find a safe seat in which to stand. Not that he was set on doing so. His indecision was such that he repeatedly asked people for their opinion. Members of the public thought he should stand, sometimes hailing him as a political messiah. The Israeli ambassador also pressed him to do so, while many in the labour movement wanted him to remain as ACTU leader, protecting workers from the union-bashing inclinations of the Fraser government.[5]

Returning to centre stage in defence of workers had obvious appeal for Hawke. His inclination to remain at the ACTU was strengthened when he discovered in February 1976 that Whitlam and Labor's federal secretary, David Combe, had sought a donation of US$500,000 from Iraqi leader Saddam Hussein to help the cash-strapped party fight the 1975 election. Despite being party president, Hawke had been unaware of the madcap deal when it was discussed in November 1975 at the instigation of a fellow member of the national executive, Bill Hartley.

During a meeting with Iraqi representatives, Whitlam was alleged to have assured them that the pro-Israeli Hawke would never become prime minister. When the funds failed to materialise, Combe had to convince the Commonwealth Bank to increase the party's overdraft, which was when Hawke was told. He was justifiably aghast at the news that Hartley had manoeuvred the party into seeking funds from a despotic enemy of Israel. It showed an extraordinary lack of judgement by Whitlam and Combe – it was like the loans affair all over again. Hawke called Combe and other senior officials to his home on 15 February, a Sunday, to discuss the political implications, which threatened to do lasting harm to Labor's reputation if it ever became known. In fact, the intermediary who had first suggested the plan to Hartley, the Sydney businessman Henry Fischer, had flown to New York, offering a tell-all story to Rupert Murdoch and claiming that he would try to get Whitlam to accept the money in person and have the handover secretly filmed. Meanwhile, Combe had accepted responsibility and offered to resign. Not wanting Combe to be the fall guy, but hoping that Whitlam might be forced to resign, Hawke convinced the meeting to delay any action until there'd been an investigation by the federal executive.[6]

The news of the Iraqi money had come at an embarrassing time for Hawke, whose commitment to Israel was about to be recognised by the Jewish community. At the urging of Eddie Kornhauser, thirty Jewish businessmen from Melbourne and Sydney had each contributed $1000 to pay for the dedication in Hawke's name of a newly planted forest on an Israeli kibbutz. It was while he was grappling with the secret Iraqi issue that Hawke addressed a gathering of the donors on 19 February. With Kornhauser looking on, Hawke spoke with his head bowed in mortification at the knowledge of the attempted Iraqi loan. 'I was too ashamed to look at them,' he later told Kornhauser. Rather than staying to oversee the party's investigation, Hawke flew to Europe for meetings of the ILO. It was during a stopover in Jerusalem that he received a call from Murdoch indicating that the news of the Iraqi money would soon be published. 'Well, we're done for,' thought Hawke, who cancelled his attendance in Geneva and flew to Athens, which was where he was staying when the sensational news broke.[7]

Murdoch himself had taken charge of the story, which ran on the front pages of his newspapers for more than a week, as the details were drip-fed to outraged readers. Hawke rushed back to Melbourne to convene a two-day meeting of the federal executive. It was an awkward time for the party, because the Victorian Labor leader, Clyde Holding, was in the throes of a state election campaign that he was now doomed to lose. Over drinks at his home, a furious Hawke told journalists that Whitlam couldn't survive, which prompted Murdoch's *Daily Telegraph* to announce: 'Hawke to axe Whitlam'. It wasn't within Hawke's power to axe anyone, and the headline only caused further resentment within caucus at the apparent alliance between Hawke and Murdoch. While he would have liked to see Hartley driven from the party, Hawke was more forgiving of Combe, who was an important ally as the party's national secretary. In the event, no one was put to the sword. The remorseful Whitlam retained a lot of support, including from Hayden, who wasn't ready to make his move yet, although he did return to the shadow ministry after standing down in the wake of the 1975 election defeat. Whitlam couldn't be sacked without threatening the party as a whole. Neither could Hartley's power base be ignored, particularly after he blamed the imbroglio on a nefarious combination of Israeli intelligence and the American CIA, abetted by Fischer, Murdoch and anti-Whitlam forces in the Labor Party. When the Fraser government ordered an investigation by the federal police and the intelligence services, there was a closing of ranks behind Whitlam at a caucus meeting on 17 March; the opposition leader also sued the Murdoch press for defamation.[8]

Although the Iraqi affair had wounded Whitlam, some of Hawke's public comments had rebounded to hurt him as well. Caucus was already resentful about Hawke making damaging statements during the term of the Whitlam government, despite being president of the party. Loyalty is everything in the Labor Party, and Hawke was seen as putting his political interests above those of the party. He couldn't stop himself. After the election loss, he'd upset some in the caucus when he'd publicly called on Labor MPs not to boycott Governor-General Kerr's opening speech to the new parliament. It had prompted Hayden to tell journalists at the National Press Club that Hawke had not been 'terribly helpful to the Labor Government with some of his impulsive, intemperate comments and his occasional emotional outburst', and that he should 'save politics for when he becomes a politician'. After being let off by the federal executive and the caucus, Whitlam was soon back in form, loosing off a shot of his own against Hawke, declaring that he wasn't 'as intellectually well equipped for leadership as I know Bill Hayden to be'.[9] The political tryst between Whitlam and Hawke on the night of the election loss had been a one-night stand. With Hayden showing renewed signs of wanting the leadership, Whitlam was going to throw whatever support he could muster behind Hayden rather than Hawke. But it was Hawke's political star that burned brighter among the public.

A report in *The Economist* in late March 1976 described Hawke as 'the most important man in the country' after Fraser and 'the strongest candidate' to replace Whitlam. In the meantime, he could only get stronger as he played the role of trade union negotiator with Fraser. This was how Hawke had predicted things would play out once the Fraser government took power. Although Fraser had won a handsome election victory, he noted that he was 'keenly aware of the need for healing' and wanted to be seen 'to govern for all Australians'. That wouldn't be easy. Many in the labour movement were averse to cooperating with the man who'd shamelessly bent political conventions to make himself prime minister. Hawke had no such compunction about seeking a basis for cooperation with Fraser. He wanted to protect the union movement from the worst instincts of the Fraser government, which wanted workers to accept a reduction in their real wages and planned to reduce spending on health and social welfare measures. Such moves would undo some of the most important initiatives of the Whitlam government, as well as undermine nearly two decades of Hawke's achievements at the ACTU. In particular, Hawke had fought for workers to receive wage rises in return for increases in productivity, and for their wages to be maintained in real terms. This had worked well in the 1960s and early '70s, only to fall apart in the wake of the oil price shock of 1973, when wage demands set off a spiral in prices that often left workers worse off. Hawke remained keen to emulate the British Labour governments of Harold Wilson and James Callaghan and institute a 'social contract', offering government benefits and tax cuts in return for unions moderating their wage demands.[10]

During the first half of 1976, and despite the reservations of the ACTU Executive, Hawke reached out to an apparently receptive Fraser to see whether they could find the basis for a productive relationship that would suit both their purposes. After all, Fraser had promised voters that he would maintain wage indexation and Medibank, and introduce tax indexation. Although he'd committed to abolish the Prices Justification Tribunal, Fraser announced after the election that he would defer doing so. For his part, Hawke could offer to help end the remorseless wage-price spiral, if Fraser agreed not to attack trade unions and committed to compensating workers for reducing their wage demands. It was naive of Hawke to believe that the Liberals might set aside their ingrained antipathy towards the trade union movement and their hostility to Hawke as a likely future Labor leader. Yet it seemed to hold promise as Hawke and Fraser, both former Rhodes scholars, took each other's measure during a series of early meetings in Canberra and informal discussions at the Lodge, often leavened with lashings of liquor.

Although Fraser was six months younger than Hawke, he was fitter and twenty centimetres taller, which added to his formidable presence. As they sat together, Hawke was taken aback by the size of Fraser's thighs, but unsurprisingly believed that he had the better brain. The chances of them reaching agreement on how best to tackle inflation and unemployment were slim. Fraser was grappling with a massive budget deficit and believed that inflation could only be controlled by greatly reducing government spending. That meant cuts to government services and higher unemployment. Only when inflation was tamed would he turn his attention to stemming unemployment. Hawke's call for programs to deal with unemployment would cost money that Fraser was loath to spend. He also reneged on his commitment to support wage indexation.[11]

By the time of the budget in May 1976, it was clear that trade unions would have a fight on their hands to retain employment in industries like ship-building, after the government allowed the Australian National Line to have four bulk carriers built in Japan rather than use a local shipyard. Retrenchments also continued in the textile industry, following the Whitlam tariff cuts, and in the car industry, which was under pressure from Japanese imports. However, the raft of harsh changes to the industrial relations laws failed to materialise. Even though Fraser gave employers the power to sue unions that used so-called secondary boycotts to pressure businesses involved in industrial disputes, no employer wanted to fire the first shot. The atmosphere of compromise, which Hawke had predicted, had largely come to pass.

Although some unionists were so angry at Hawke for compromising with Fraser that they occupied the ACTU offices, he argued that the movement's responsibility to the unemployed compelled unions to moderate their wage demands in return for tax concessions. In the wake of the attempted deal-making, a leaflet in Victoria described Hawke as 'a most despicable person' who was selling out workers. Anyway, the possibility of a meaningful deal was limited because Hawke couldn't control the wage demands of individual unions, or the decisions of the Arbitration Commission or the state industrial tribunals.[12]

With Fraser's massive majority setting him up for at least six years as prime minister, he was determined to dismantle some of Whitlam's legacy and reduce the influence of the trade unions. Whitlam was powerless to stop him. The fight had gone out of him and he could sometimes be found sleeping on the couch in his office. Only the trade unions had a chance of doing so by calling stoppages in protest. And there was no issue more calculated to stir the anger of trade unionists than that of Medibank, the forerunner of Medicare. It was only a few months before the 1975 election that people had received their Medibank cards in the mail. The scheme provided basic hospital cover and reimbursed 85 per cent of a doctor's consultation fee. It was to be paid for by a 1.3 per cent levy on taxable incomes, which still left the government picking up a considerable part of the cost. Fraser had an ideological objection to a universal medical scheme and was keen to reduce the burden on his budget. Because of the scheme's popularity, he had to tread carefully. In May 1976, he announced that people could opt out of the scheme by buying private insurance and set up a government-owned company, Medibank Private, for that purpose. Alternatively, people could pay a 2.5 per cent levy on their taxable income. It was widely seen as the first step in a plan to dismantle Medibank entirely, which provoked calls for a national strike.[13]

The millions of Australians who'd been angered by the dismissal of the Whitlam government looked to Hawke to save Medibank. They were destined to be disappointed. He'd resisted calls for a national strike in protest at Whitlam's dismissal and he wasn't about to call one to defend Medibank. Hawke was convinced that he could talk Fraser around on the issue. However, Fraser had come to realise that his one-on-one meetings with Hawke had only served to increase the stature of the ACTU president while diminishing his own. Anyway, he wasn't willing to make concessions on Medibank. Instead of agreeing to a meeting with Hawke, he delegated the responsibility to his health minister, Ralph Hunt. When Hawke took Ralph Willis and Jan Marsh to Canberra to meet with Hunt in late June, they flew into a brick wall. Not only was Hawke unable to gain any concessions that could allay the anger of his union constituents, but his behaviour in the capital raised serious questions about his fitness for political office.[14]

After having an inconclusive meeting with Hunt at Parliament House, Hawke went off to a boozy dinner with his colleagues at Bacchus Restaurant before adjourning to the Canberra Rex for more drinks. He had a major speech to deliver to hundreds of people at the National Press Club the following lunchtime and had not decided on a topic. It was only that evening, half-tanked, that he scribbled down a few points that could be strung together into a speech. When he stepped up to the podium, a glass of white wine in hand, he gave the 400-strong audience his take on the defeat of the Whitlam government and presented suggestions as to how government could be improved in the future, presumably under his leadership. The crowd included a mix of journalists, public servants, Labor MPs and staffers, along with a sprinkling of diplomats. They were eager to check out the credentials of the possible future prime minister. Hawke certainly caught their attention. After describing some of Whitlam's ministers as 'dills', he proposed that future prime ministers should be able to draw on people from outside parliament to make up at least half of their ministry. This was done in the United States but didn't fit with Australia's system and wouldn't be welcomed by caucus members who aspired to be ministers. Hawke's off-the-cuff speech was widely derided in the press and raised questions about his suitability to be a politician, let alone a prime minister.[15]

That concern was borne out by Hawke's behaviour at the luncheon and his subsequent failure to achieve anything when his talks resumed with Hunt. He 'drank liberally' as he waited for journalists to finish asking their questions and then, amid nervous laughter from the audience, he attacked one of them for asking a question he had misunderstood, only to apologise later. Never one to leave while the bar was still open and while he was the centre of attention, Hawke retired with the Press Club committee to the boardroom to drink some more before heading off late to Parliament House to resume his discussions with Hunt, who'd been waiting around for an hour and soon had to leave for another engagement. When journalists asked him about the failure of their brief discussion, Hawke angrily told them to 'piss off' before heading back to Melbourne. In the eyes of many observers, the trip had been an unmitigated disaster. Journalist Mungo MacCallum questioned the wisdom of Hawke describing some Labor ministers as 'dills' when he might soon be wanting one of them to step aside for him, while fellow journalist Paul Kelly thought his 'impetuous outbursts must call into question whether he possesses the stability needed to lead a major party'. The *Nation Review* was more forthright, arguing that 'Labor's man of destiny stands exposed as a loud, foulmouthed bully'.[16]

It was an ugly side of Hawke that was seen too often, whether he was drunk at the racetrack or picking a fight at the pub. He was 'an animal with women', said Kornhauser in 1981, recalling a 'very unpleasant scene' in a crowd at the races: a drunken Hawke had abused the wife of a policeman, who he believed, rightly or wrongly, wanted to bed him because of his celebrity status. 'Piss off,' he screamed. 'You only want to be fucked.' In March 1976, Abeles and his business partner, George Rockey, were said to have paid for a penthouse at the Sydney Hilton, where Hawke was set up with an escort. The next day, Hawke returned the favour for Abeles.[17]

His casual dalliances continued. When Blanche d'Alpuget came calling to interview him for a biography she was writing of Sir Richard Kirby, they had a brief fling that neither thought would lead to anything more serious. Hawke thought of leaving Hazel but couldn't: she had borne four of his children and raised the three surviving ones, not to mention having had an abortion so that he (and she) could go to Oxford. Yet their relationship continued to sour, with Hazel confessing to a confidante that she had a 'love-hate' relationship with him. She couldn't give him the adulation that his narcissism demanded and that was showered on him in public. Their Sandringham home should have provided a welcome haven from the pressures of his work. Expensive renovations had modernised and expanded the interior, installed a swimming pool and provided the tennis court with lighting and a new artificial surface. However, he and Hazel were caught in a destructive vortex of recriminations and remorse over his behaviour. They remained married because neither was prepared to accept a divorce that would force them to sell their mortgaged home, divide the limited proceeds and live poorer, separate lives.[18]

Hawke's behaviour also caused problems in his relationships with the children, who had mostly left home. Susan was doing a law degree at Monash University, while Stephen had finished school and moved to Tasmania, resisting his father's pressure to attend university and choosing instead to pursue his own path in life. Initially he lived in a shepherd's hut in the bush and immersed himself in environmental issues. Rosslyn moved interstate and lived in a succession of share houses, causing Hazel to be 'worried about the world [Rosslyn and her friends] inhabited'. It was a very different world to her own childhood, and she was concerned that dabbling in marijuana could lead to the taking of harder drugs. Hazel was right to be concerned, but she could hardly preach about the dangers of drug-taking, given the amount of alcohol and tobacco in which she and Bob indulged. According to a frequent visitor to the Sandringham home, 'there was a kitchen noticeboard with a marijuana leaf pinned to it', apparently placed there as a joke by one of the children. Hawke's life was so busy that Hazel would complain that he was barely home one day a month. According to one observer, the children were forced to make an appointment if they wanted to see him, only to have him occasionally fail to keep them.[19] There was so much for him to do – so many horses to back, so many women to bed, so many interviews to have, so many disputes to settle, so many drunken stories to tell. There was also Israel to be saved from its enemies, Australian workers to be protected from the depredations of the conservative government, and his elusive political ambition to be pursued in the face of hostility from many in the Labor Party.

Despite Hawke's attempts to prevent the national strike over the Medibank changes, it went ahead on 12 July, with a limited turnout of workers and no impact on the government's plans. Ironically, it helped

Hawke, since it convinced the ACTU Executive that there was little to be gained by striking over political issues, and that a policy of consensus was likely to be more fruitful in the face of a hostile government. Such a policy spoke to Hawke's strengths as a negotiator and conciliator, which were on public display during the several industrial disputes that convulsed the country that year, from transport workers to air traffic controllers. Watching Hawke performing this role on the television news reinstated his power and prestige in the minds of the public. They hadn't witnessed his drunken performance at the National Press Club, while his novel suggestions for outside appointments to the ministry would have confirmed for them that Hawke was a person who could shake up Canberra.

As always, his popularity kept his political hopes afloat. Six months after the 1975 election, his approval rating had soared by ten percentage points to 62 per cent, which made him the most popular political leader in the country. By comparison, Fraser had an approval rating of 53 per cent and Whitlam just 41 per cent. It's not surprising that Hawke was widely depicted as the Labor leader in waiting, with *The Bulletin* publishing a painting of Hawke on its front cover. Yet he gave no indication as to when he might make the shift into politics. Hawke had suggested to Whitlam that he would like to spend about six years as president of the ACTU before entering politics. Although he'd now had six years in that job, he still held back from making any announcement.[20] Yet the time could have been ripe for him to do so.

In the wake of his election defeat and his embarrassment over the Iraqi funding deal, Whitlam was a husk of his former self. Under the new caucus rules, he would have to stand for the leadership in May 1977, when Hayden was widely tipped to replace him. If Hawke could convince an ageing Victorian MP to retire early, he had a chance of being elected at a by-election, joining caucus and mounting a bid of his own. But none of the MPs in safe Victorian seats were willing to stand down in his favour. Frank Crean was said to hate Hawke and to be saving his seat of Melbourne Ports for his son, Simon, who was then an official in the Storemen and Packers' Union. As for Jim Cairns, he thought Labor had done Hawke 'a great disfavour by convincing him too soon that he is a great man', and that it would be a 'regression' for Labor if Hawke became leader. The other three MPs also showed no signs of shifting. In the face of their recalcitrance, Hawke's allies had the rules changed to allow sitting MPs to be challenged for preselection. This change was designed to facilitate a tilt against Cairns, only for Hawke to decline to do so. According to the frustrated Victorian ALP president, Peter Redlich, who'd helped to orchestrate the change, 'Hawke was too frightened to make his run.' It was making Hawke appear more indecisive than Hayden, wrote Mungo MacCallum, while some in the party were questioning whether he was serious about wanting to become prime minister.[21] Others were adamant that he never should be allowed to do so.

The trappings of high office were given to him nonetheless. Because of the perceived threat from terrorism, and the threat to Hawke's life from driving his ACTU-provided Holden Premier station wagon while drunk, George Rockey arranged for him to have the services of a former Northern Territory policeman, Chris Crellin, as a chauffeur and bodyguard and the use of an Australian-built Ford LTD limousine, with both being paid for by ACTU-Solo. No longer would he have to fly first-class with politicians from Canberra and watch them being picked up by LTDs at Melbourne airport while he went off in his more humble Holden, sometimes driven by Col Cunningham. The new Ford was the same model that the prime minister had when he was in Melbourne, although Fraser, with his tall frame, found its back seat cramped. Hawke, with his much smaller stature, had no such problems in the back, which was fitted out so he could work on the go. He also enjoyed privileges when travelling overseas, where senior Australian diplomats were on hand to smooth his passage and protect him from himself. Meetings with foreign dignitaries were commonplace, whether it was with the Pope in Rome, the prime minister of Israel or a leading member of the Politburo in Moscow.[22]

When he went to Israel in late December 1976 for the dedication of the forest in his name, the then defence minister, Shimon Peres, had planned to be in attendance, only to be prevented by a political crisis in Tel Aviv. Instead, there were a hundred or so guests, including the secretary-general of the Histadrut and a number of Jewish Australians on a study tour. The latter were seated near their buses as Hawke, accompanied by Hazel and his parents, clambered up a rocky path to inspect the trees and stand by the cloth-covered plaque commemorating the occasion. With Ellie on one side, Clem on the other and Hazel in her red leather coat, a tearful Hawke in his brown suede jacket pulled aside the cloth before telling the small crowd about his love of social-democratic Israel and its people, and lauding the way they had 'turned the swamps and stony ground into fertile land'. It was a familiar trope that Israel had used to justify its dispossession of the Palestinian people. At the time, Hawke embraced it without question, perhaps recalling how his mother had turned the hard ground around their Maitland manse green with new growth. He didn't seem to realise that his forest – which lay in the Israeli settlement of Kerem Maharal, twenty kilometres from Haifa – was on the site of the pre-existing and prosperous Palestinian village of Ijzim, whose three thousand inhabitants had resisted the Israeli takeover in April 1948 until finally being forced to flee, never to return. In their place, Jewish refugees from Czechoslovakia were settled in the substantial, stone-built houses of the Palestinians and deployed to till the irrigated plantations and fields of the Palestinian farmers.[23]

Back home, Hawke's behaviour at public events continued to be deplorable once he had a few beers under his belt. When Queen Elizabeth visited Canberra on 8 March 1977 as part of her silver jubilee tour of Australia, dining with the governor-general at Government House, Hawke was on hand with Hazel and hundreds of other notables at a dinner in the Rose Garden of Parliament House. While Hayden used the occasion to mingle with his colleagues, confirming that he would stand for leader in the forthcoming vote, Hawke and Hazel spent the evening sitting at a table with the elderly newspaper magnate Sir Warwick Fairfax, to whom Hawke complained that *The Sydney Morning Herald* wasn't sufficiently supportive of the ACTU, the Labor Party and himself. Writer Thomas Keneally was also on Hawke's table, and describes how Hawke was 'very pissed' as he called Fairfax a 'geriatric, Presbyterian fuckwit'. Despite the booze, says Keneally, Hawke's palpable vigour was such that he gave the impression of being 'the coming man'. Journalist Paul Kelly was also there, describing how Hawke 'drank up and spoke out' in his usual style before putting 'his arms around Lady Fairfax who was wearing an attractive, off-the-shoulder summer gown'. Later, the inebriated Lothario had a beer poured onto his coiffured head by a Labor staff member. Hawke had behaved just as terribly during another television interview with David Frost, when his boorish performance, apparently fuelled by alcohol, provoked a torrent of critical letters and phone calls from viewers. Although he partially redeemed himself by doing two toned-down interviews on the ABC's *This Day Tonight*, the drunken incidents added to his reputation as a larrikin and a playboy, diminishing him in the eyes of some of the Labor MPs who might have to decide one day whether to elect him as their leader.[24]

His path to the prime ministership became more complicated when the Labor caucus met in May 1977 to vote on Whitlam's leadership. It could have provided an opportunity for Hawke to stand, had he been able to secure a seat. The vote was expected to see a transition from Whitlam to Hayden, until Whitlam announced that he intended to stand for re-election as leader. He still had strong support in party branches and among those MPs who believed that he'd been wrongly dismissed. The MPs even forgave him for the Iraqi affair. There were barely enough of them. When the votes were tallied, Whitlam only won because of his own vote and that of his son Tony, who'd secured preselection for a safe Labor seat at the 1975 election, together with the vote of the seriously ill Rex Connor, who'd left his sickbed to vote against Hayden. With caucus splitting thirty-two votes to thirty, Labor was left with a discredited and demoralised leader and no chance to move on from the lingering memories of his dysfunctional government.[25]

Liberal MPs broke out the champagne. The result suited Fraser, since he would have a much better chance against Whitlam than against Hayden. The result also suited Hawke, since it left the leadership question unresolved and gave him the chance to prepare for a run in Victoria against the strong opposition he would be sure to encounter. In the meantime, he relished his position as de facto leader of the forces opposing Fraser's increasingly discredited economic policies.

After nearly eighteen months in power, the Coalition government had failed to reduce the rate of inflation or unemployment. The retained Prices Justification Tribunal had been unable to moderate price rises. Meanwhile, wages continued to chase after increases in the Consumer Price Index, albeit with a slight lag and less than full indexation, which ensured that wages were gradually being reduced in real terms. There had been talk of implementing a short-term freezing of wages and prices in the hope it might break the damaging cycle, but it was easier to freeze the wages of workers than it was to freeze the prices of their household consumables, particularly when they were imported, let alone such items as rent and mortgage interest. And there was no talk of freezing the incomes of the wealthy who lived off capital. Nevertheless, Fraser embraced the idea of freezing wages when it was proposed at the premiers' conference. In concert with the three Liberal premiers, the federal government presented a case to the Arbitration Commission arguing for a wage freeze for three months, while promising that prices would also be frozen. Hawke was having none of it. He'd presided over the fiftieth-anniversary dinner of the ACTU, a grand affair in the Great Hall of the National Gallery of Victoria, where distinguished guests had been met with platters of prunes and bacon, pineapple and bacon, and chicken livers and bacon, along with red and black caviar and smoked oysters, before sitting down to a four-course meal that finished with larded fillet of beef and bombe Alaska. The well-fed diners were entertained by two opera singers before listening to a toast by Sir Richard Kirby, to which an inebriated Hawke responded with a heartfelt speech on behalf of the ACTU's nearly two million members and 'those millions who have gone before', in which he lambasted Fraser's attacks on the trade union movement and promised 'WE WILL FIGHT' if the government didn't back down.[26]

Hawke was in no mood to have workers take a pay cut to solve Fraser's economic problems. Instead, he wanted workers to be given a tax trade-off in return for forgoing wage increases. That was the argument he'd been making for the past year, and he repeated it when he took centre stage at the Arbitration Commission to lead the union attack against the proposed wage freeze, pointing out how it wouldn't be matched by a comprehensive price freeze. He also berated the Fraser government for its attacks on unions and called for a national conference of all parties to reach agreement on how to tackle inflation. Fraser was furious. He refused the idea of a national conference and rejected out of hand the idea of a tax trade-off, for fear of it blowing out the government's deficit.[27]

The defeat of the proposed wage freeze was a victory for Hawke to savour, reminiscent of his time as an advocate. However, there were some in the Labor Party who were concerned about Hawke continuing to be president of both the ACTU and the Labor Party, because of the conflict of interest it created and the lightning rod Hawke became for government attacks. The leader of the Labor Left, Tom Uren, had no time for Hawke and saw an opportunity to end his time as president when his second two-year term concluded on the eve of the party's biennial national conference in Perth in July 1977. Having been a prisoner of war near Nagasaki in 1945, Uren was a staunch opponent of Australia's participation in uranium mining. The issue was going to be discussed at the upcoming conference and it could prove crucial for the anti-uranium cause to have a sympathiser presiding over the conference. Uren claimed to have twelve supporters on the eighteen-person national executive and proposed that the genial Mick Young should take Hawke's place as president.

Hawke went prepared. On the flight to Perth, he'd asked journalist Neil Mitchell to sit with him and gave him an exclusive story that he was going to run again for president. It was front-page news in *The Age* and put his opponents on notice that they would have to roll him publicly if they wanted the presidency. Once in Perth, Hawke quickly gathered Combe and other supporters in a bedroom of the Sheraton Hotel, where, over many a drink, they hit the phones to those they thought could be won over, including an appeal to Mick Young not to stand. Still unsure of his numbers, Hawke gave a pre-recorded radio interview designed to be broadcast just prior to the executive meeting, in which he implied that he had the numbers to win. It had the desired effect. His opponents crumbled and he was re-elected unopposed. No one wanted to be responsible for inflicting a humiliating defeat on the leader of the trade union movement and the most popular political figure in the country. Of course, Hawke could have avoided the whole thing by declaring beforehand that he had never intended to stand for a third term. However, he couldn't abide the thought of being rolled and of not presiding over the Perth conference, where he'd invited his parents to see him in action. Despite the criticism of him filling both roles, he wanted the prestige that the ALP presidency brought him, and the extra publicity it provided.[28]

Buoyed by the win, Hawke went off to a Press Club luncheon, where he told journalists that he would only be interested in giving up his ACTU presidency if he could be assured of becoming the Labor leader and not be forced to 'put my bum on a backbench seat'. This wasn't news to anyone who'd been following Hawke's utterances on the subject, but it was an obvious insult to those caucus members who'd had their bums on those seats for years. Hawke was declaring that the normal rules didn't apply to him, that he was indeed the messiah and should be ushered to a safe electorate and drafted to the leadership by acclamation of the caucus. The reaction from the press and from Labor MPs was predictable. Some took umbrage at his arrogance while others wondered whether he was deliberately provoking a negative reaction in order to close off the political option and not be derided for lacking the gumption to take the leap into parliament. While most of the media thought he'd destroyed his political prospects for all time, Hawke felt otherwise. His popularity among the public was secure and his self-belief was boundless. While his comments had been lubricated by alcohol, they were made by a man who was willing to await the party's call, which he confidently believed would come when Labor was ready to grab the reins of power again. Had he played his cards differently, he might have been able to finagle his way into a safe electorate, since Jim Cairns decided a few weeks after Hawke's embarrassment to announce his retirement. When journalists asked whether he was making way for Hawke, Cairns archly replied: 'Yes, and for Bing Crosby and a few other people like that.'[29]

Cairns was not alone in resenting Hawke for expecting to be made leader without first having proved himself in parliament and without having done the hard work developing policy or organising numbers within the party. Hawke had left it to others to do much of this on his behalf, allowing him to swan in later to make a headline speech at a Labor conference. Indeed, it had been largely due to appeals on the phone by John Ducker and David Combe that Hawke was able to gather the numbers to retain the presidency at the 1977 conference. There was also a fear that Hawke's behaviour with alcohol and women could destroy him and bring the party into disrepute. In Perth, when two young women asked him for an autograph, he told them he would only do it in his bedroom. When they took the elevator to his room, along with their boyfriends and several journalists, a night of drinking saw one of the young women stay with Hawke. It was after this night of minimal sleep that Hawke was woken by an ABC Radio presenter and gave a disgraceful interview, still drunk, saying 'you blokes poop your pants' and then had his customary brandy for breakfast. In the hotel foyer during the same conference, Hawke had approached Susan Ryan, then a Labor senator for the ACT, suggesting she come up to his room, only to have Ryan brush him off. She was one of only three women, all of them senators, in the Labor caucus of sixty-three. Not one to take rejection well, Hawke dismissed her, saying that she had 'a scraggy body'. Ryan wasn't the only woman he approached in Perth. As D'Alpuget wrote, several delegates and journalists reported that the inebriated Hawke 'had propositioned them with his usual frankness and on rebuff had become sarcastic'.[30]

Although Uren failed to topple Hawke as president, he was successful in having the conference take a tougher stance on uranium mining. Delegates rejected the pro-uranium policy proposed by Paul Keating as shadow minister for minerals and energy and supported by Hawke, embracing instead a moratorium on new mines. It was agreed to keep the moratorium in place until at least the next party conference. On this issue, Hawke was in the minority. A ban on uranium mining was popular with the party membership and had broad cross-factional support, with the successful conference motion being proposed by the moderate Labor leaders of Victoria and South Australia, Clyde Holding and Don Dunstan. Not that it mattered much. While Labor's opposition might deter some mining companies, there was little prospect of a Labor government coming to power before 1980 at the earliest. Anyway, the motion had included an escape clause, which acknowledged that the caucus or the Labor government had authority to change the policy at will. Hawke was quick to point this out, much to the ire of the Victorian branch officials who supported the tougher stance. Hawke hadn't spoken on the uranium issue during the conference, but he did speak on the equally vexed issue of building an American radio navigation base in Australia as part of a worldwide network being established at the instigation of the US Navy to communicate with its nuclear-armed submarines. The base was going to be built in New Zealand but was switched to Victoria after protests from New Zealanders who feared it could be a target in a nuclear war. At the conference, the issue again pitched left against right, and Hawke's speech was credited with ensuring the narrowest of victories for the motion in favour of the base.[31]

Uranium mining was also an issue at the ACTU Congress in September 1977, when Hawke and his allies managed to head off another attempt by left-wing unions to ban it. Instead, the congress decided to survey the membership of the relevant unions and then leave it to the ACTU Executive to make the decision. Whatever the survey might reveal, Hawke's control of the executive ensured that mining would continue. His control was made more certain when John Ducker, a powerful figure of the New South Wales right, was elected as the ACTU's junior vice-president instead of the left-wing Jim Roulston.

Not everything went Hawke's way. The delegates decided that the organisation's three senior paid officials, including its president, should no longer be employed for life, which effectively had been the case for Monk, Souter and Hawke. At the time, 47-year-old Hawke was coming to the end of his eighth year as president. Under the old arrangements, Monk had remained as president beyond the normal retirement age of sixty-five, while Souter had retired as secretary at the September congress, just prior to his sixty-sixth birthday. Hawke might have been able to hold on regardless of the new limit, but he would have to shore up his numbers at each congress and keep watching his back to ward off possible challengers. And he would have to boost his flagging enthusiasm for his role in the union movement.[32] What else could he do? He'd never wanted to practise law or work in business, and there was still no clear path to Canberra, where caucus members were anxious to anoint a successor who might lead them back into government.

Despite Hayden's denials, it seemed inevitable that he would mount another challenge for the leadership before the next federal election, which was due by late 1978. Indeed, the Labor caucus soon began turning against the poorly performing Whitlam and by August 1977 was discussing how he could be pressured to resign in favour of Hayden. In such circumstances, the diffident Hayden could expect to enjoy a honeymoon period with voters that might help him win the 1978 election, or the one after. Alternatively, Hawke might find his way into parliament and mount a challenge of his own. Either outcome would be a political nightmare for Fraser, who much preferred a second contest against Whitlam. It was for this reason, and to pre-empt the worsening economic conditions, that he called an early election for

10 December 1977. It would be the fourth in five years, and industrial relations would be at the core of his campaign.[33]

Although the number of industrial disputes had markedly declined in the face of rising unemployment, the lead-up to the election announcement saw Australia convulsed by several strikes that caused massive stand-downs across the country. The most bitter dispute occurred in Victoria's Latrobe Valley, where more than two thousand maintenance workers at the coal-fired power stations agreed to impose work bans and later went on strike. The Victorian government's refusal to have their margins indexed for inflation had seen their income fall behind that of their counterparts in other states and in private industry.

As the weeks went by, the lack of maintenance began to affect the state's power supply and caused other industries to stop. Householders were banned from using electric heating or lighting in more than two rooms at a time. Although the strikers returned to work to await a decision by the Arbitration Commission, they went out indefinitely when the commission refused their application for a wage increase. When they were threatened with dismissal, the furious workers set up picket lines to prevent scabs taking their place, while other unions refused to do their work. With the state and federal governments threatening to jail the union officials, and with the strikers and those laid off suffering great hardship, Hawke had the tricky task of convincing the angry maintenance workers to return to work while an inquiry was held into the value of their work. Being at the end of their financial tether, they had little option, although the inquiry would take six months and ultimately award them much less than they wanted.[34]

While Hawke's mediation hadn't earned him much respect among the maintenance workers, it did reinforce his reputation as an industrial peacemaker. It also undermined Fraser's strategy for the forthcoming election campaign, when the unions in general, and Hawke in particular, were intended to be the targets of Liberal attacks. The early election was designed to catch the Labor Party unprepared. It was also designed by Fraser to avoid having to face the voters in 1978, when unemployment was expected to worsen.

The Labor Party was certainly unprepared. Its finances were still feeling the effects of the 1975 election, while the organisation hadn't developed new policies for its tired leader and shattered caucus to take to the people. Whereas Fraser offered cuts to income tax, the best that Whitlam could promise was to cut payroll tax in the hope that it would create jobs and redeem his reputation for economic management. Hawke had been recuperating from a chest infection (or another bender) and was unable to convince Whitlam that he needed something more attractive for voters. When the campaign began, Hawke crisscrossed the country, launching fierce attacks on the economic mismanagement of the Liberal Party while being unable to extinguish in voters' minds the memories of Whitlam's mismanagement. He tried to make the arrival of several boatloads of Vietnamese refugees a potent election issue, but his arguments were dismissed by the government and largely ignored by voters.[35]

At the end of the campaign, Hawke was once again found sitting on a television panel in the Canberra tally room, enjoying the nibbles and drinks during breaks, as the dismal results were revealed. It was worse than he'd feared. Labor's vote was even lower than in 1975. It seemed to some observers that the party was destined to spend a further decade or more in the political wilderness.

CHAPTER SEVENTEEN

1978–1979

Standing naked in front of the mirror in his hotel suite, Hawke had much to ponder as he lovingly combed his luxuriant mane of hair. Described as 'a real peacock' by one of his lovers, he would comb his hair 'for five minutes at a time'. He had also taken to dyeing it, and wouldn't wash his hair in the presence of women for fear they would notice the bare patch that appeared when it was wet. On this occasion, Hawke was at the Canberra Rex with Hazel, the pair having gone there from the Canberra tally room with a distraught David Combe and journalist Kate Baillieu after the devastating election defeat. Hawke's exhausting month of campaigning had been for nothing. Malcolm Fraser remained firmly in charge, holding a massive majority of forty-eight seats, while Labor's shambolic campaign had rendered Whitlam twice repudiated. He had no option but to resign as leader and pass the baton to Bill Hayden. As he contemplated the implications, Hawke wouldn't have been downcast, since he couldn't envisage Hayden achieving the massive swing required for Labor to win government at the next election. Nor could he envisage the caucus keeping Hayden as leader once the more popular Hawke had secured a seat in parliament. Meanwhile, he and Hayden were appointed by the party to chair a committee of inquiry into the electoral loss, looking particularly at ways to invigorate its demoralised and divided base and better communicate its 'policies and ideals'.[1]

By calling an early election, Fraser had stopped Hawke from mounting a bid for the Labor leadership. It meant more years for Hawke at the ACTU, where his presidency had provided him with unparalleled power, acclaim and celebrity. However, it hadn't been as triumphant as he might have liked. After eight years at the top, many of his bold initiatives had failed to bear the fruit that he'd promised. Despite that, his leadership had allowed the ACTU to enjoy a prominence and importance that far exceeded anything that it had had before. This was despite its inherent weaknesses in staffing and finances, and its inability to compel adherence from its affiliated unions. Much of the achievement was due to the persistence, ability and self-belief of Hawke, who pressed on when others might have wilted and who was able to marshal and direct the political forces that emerged from within the labour movement in the 1970s. By 1977, a Melbourne University politics course titled 'Who rules Australia?' concluded that trade unions had the most power in the country. And such was Hawke's prominence in the media that some people believed that he, rather than Malcolm Fraser, was the prime minister. Opinion polls tended to bear out that belief. They usually showed Hawke as Australia's most popular political figure, while focus groups regarded Hawke 'as the only national leader who is consistently respected and thought likely to handle the job of Prime Minister'.[2] Such polls helped to keep his political hopes alive and supported the widespread assumption among the public that one day he would be prime minister.

It added to the heavy burden of expectation that his mother had placed on his shoulders, which was made all the heavier by Hawke repeatedly declaring that his ultimate ambition was the prime ministership, only for him to baulk at repeated opportunities since the Corio by-election in 1963 to take the leap into politics.[3] Ellie had never stopped asking him about it over the years, as she listened to the news of his activities whenever he visited Perth or his parents made their occasional trips to Melbourne. Those visits came to an abrupt end in early 1978, when Ellie's high blood pressure caused her to suffer a stroke, from which she only partially recovered. That didn't lighten the weight of her expectations. Moreover, after nearly a decade at the ACTU, Hawke had come to realise the limits to what he could achieve there, even as its president, and what more might be possible if he became prime minister. If he was to change Australia for the better, he would have more opportunity to do so in the prime minister's office at Parliament House than in the ACTU office atop Bourke's. But there remained considerable barriers to its achievement. Some were political and some were personal.

Not least of his problems was his abuse of alcohol. It had almost caused his expulsion from both Oxford and ANU; it had resulted in his admission to hospital for alcohol poisoning; it had produced behaviour that might have been considered criminal; and it had brought regular humiliation upon himself, his family and friends. For years, he'd mostly got away with it in the hard-drinking culture of the trade unions and the Labor Party, and while hobnobbing with some equally hard-drinking journalists. He was open about his drinking problem and promised to give up alcohol if he ever became prime minister. The admission might have been expected to harm his popularity but had the opposite effect. Many voters admired him more for his drinking than for his education or his achievements. 'Let's face it, Hawke is a pisspot like us,' was a response of focus groups, with his drinking being 'symptomatic of an essential ordinariness ... which has strong appeal'. But the bouts of excessive drinking, and the bad behaviour that accompanied it, raised questions about his fitness for high office, not only in the minds of some supporters and journalists but also in his own. Blanche d'Alpuget was in a good position to see that Hawke was 'out of control' by the late 1970s, which she blamed on the booze. His marriage with Hazel seemed irretrievably broken. D'Alpuget claimed that since November 1978, the Hawkes 'were under the intolerable emotional pressure of having decided to divorce while continuing to live together in the same house, both of them unable to make the final break of physically separating, both of them wracked [sic] by guilt and depression'. Fearing that Hawke was going to divorce her, Hazel consulted a lawyer to ascertain her rights. But she wouldn't initiate the divorce. When Hawke suggested in the late 1970s that she move out of the house, she called his bluff and refused. He didn't have it in him to force the issue. It was a stand-off.[4]

The marital impasse was just one part of a dark time in Hawke's life. Uncertainty about the trajectory of his relationships was matched by uncertainty about his political future. It was one of several periods in his life when he sank into a deep depressive state, which was made worse by the deteriorating health of his mother, who suffered a second and more severe stroke in May 1978, which put her into a coma. Not expecting her to survive, Hawke made several flying visits to Perth, where Ellie was now confined to a nursing home. The pressure he felt to enter politics became more intense, although it was now unlikely that Ellie would live to see him become prime minister.

Back in Melbourne, he reduced his drinking for several months, only to relapse once again. Col Cunningham recalled the struggles he had trying to convince Hawke to stop his heavy drinking. 'He would never call it a day,' said Cunningham, who added that Hawke treated each day as if it was 'his *last* day'. After watching the cricket at the MCG, Cunningham found himself taking Hawke off for yet more drinking before finally getting him home late at night. He was 'looking old, and in a drunken stupor', recalled Cunningham, who warned Hawke that his drinking would kill him. Hawke was unmoved: 'I'm a mere nothing – just a spot. What difference if I die?' His depression was so deep that he welcomed the prospect of death and was relieved when he experienced the symptoms of what he believed to be a brain tumour, which he thought would end his worries, only to have it diagnosed as the effects of flying with a bad cold.[5]

Although he'd finally retired as ALP president in August 1978, Hawke's heavy round of commitments included a visit to Vancouver in early November, where he attended the congress of the Socialist International. Accompanying him was ALP secretary and long-time drinking companion David Combe. The congress brought together the leaders of social-democratic parties from both the developed and developing world, with former chancellor of West Germany Willy Brandt presiding, while delegates included the soon-to-be French president, François Mitterrand, and the future Israeli prime minister and later president Shimon Peres, with whom Hawke was already friendly. It was the stopover in San Francisco that would later bring media attention to Hawke's trip. Until 1983, though, the details of the stopover would remain secret.

The stop in San Francisco was done at the request of Abeles, apparently because his American business interests had been endangered by the recent conviction and gaoling of high-ranking mafia hitman Jimmy 'the Weasel' Fratianno, for involvement in the murder of another mafia leader. Fratianno was a powerful figure on the American West Coast who'd been bought off by Abeles and helped ease the way for TNT's shipping lines with the mafia-controlled waterfront unions on both the West and East coast. By making secret payments to mafia members who controlled the unions, the industrial troubles that had hampered Abeles' American businesses had been solved. That cosy arrangement was now threatened, with Fratianno agreeing to provide the FBI with information against other senior mafia figures. The code of silence was broken. Abeles needed to be assured that he wouldn't be caught in the spotlight and that his freight business in America wouldn't be affected by Fratianno's cooperation with authorities. The man with the answers was Rudy Tham, who ran the San Francisco branch of the mafia-controlled Teamsters Union and who'd been shown over TNT's Sydney operations by Abeles in 1974. It was to Tham that Hawke was directed by Abeles. But Tham was nowhere to be found. He was apparently laying low after evidence from Fratianno had caused him to be indicted several weeks previously for defrauding union funds.[6]

Instead, after landing in San Francisco and being put up in hotel rooms funded by Abeles, Hawke and Combe were taken by Abeles' representative to a local espresso bar that was owned by a leader of the West Coast mafia, Sal Amarena. Because it was such a regular hangout of the mafia, the bar was under surveillance by the FBI, whose agents had filmed various meetings with organised crime figures from Australia, including Abeles' close associate Bela Csidei, when they'd been organising drug shipments. It was Halloween on the day of Hawke's visit, and there are differing accounts of what transpired. According to Hawke, he had been amused when Amarena joined them at the table and spoke with a gangster-like accent reminiscent of the *Godfather* movies. It was a brief 'meeting of total innocence and one-offedness', Hawke would claim. Combe's account was very different. Rather than it being a brief meeting, he would later say they 'spent a very pleasant few hours with [Amarena and] met a few of his associates'. What occurred during those 'pleasant few hours' was never publicly detailed by Combe. But Abeles asking Hawke to meet with the mafia had the potential to damage, or even destroy, Hawke's political ambitions if it ever became known.[7]

While Hawke's relationship with the beneficent Abeles never wavered, his relationship with Hazel was on the brink of collapse. In January 1979, when he was made a Companion in the Order of Australia, she refused to attend the ceremony in Canberra. He took

Clem instead. It was the highest honour under the system established by the Whitlam government, and Hawke was deluged with letters of congratulation from well-wishers, including from Whitlam himself, who welcomed Hawke as 'a good companion and a great mate'. Amid the congratulations, some were aghast that Hawke had accepted an honour that two other prominent Australians – author Patrick White and former Reserve Bank governor Nugget Coombs – had returned in the wake of Whitlam's dismissal. Novelist Xavier Herbert had been a great admirer of Hawke, describing him as 'the One Just Man in Sodom', but now wrote to him in sorrow at the news of his inclusion 'amongst the usual bunch of Colonial suck-holes'. Rather than renouncing the honour, Hawke added it to his growing collection. He was doubtless buoyed by the avalanche of congratulations, among which was a letter from historian and fellow cricketer Manning Clark, who was then in the United States. Clark had been similarly honoured four years earlier and was 'proud that our country ... has [had] the wisdom and the grace to recognise your great achievement', which meant there were now two Companions 'who know how to play a straight bat'.[8]

The honour had been a bright spot during a terrible time for Hawke, as he faced a stand-off with the Socialist Left, which had regained a powerful place in Labor's Victorian branch and was now led by the more pragmatic Trades Hall Council president, Jim Roulston. Under Bill Hartley and George Crawford, the faction had been the bête noire of Whitlam when he'd been striving to have the Labor Party present a moderate, electable face to Australian voters. Hawke wanted to drive Hartley from the party altogether and had tried in January 1979 to have the federal executive expel him, only to be thwarted by state Labor leader Frank Wilkes, who feared that it would divide the party and cruel his chances of winning the upcoming Victorian election. Instead, a public showdown between Hawke and Hartley was set for the state Labor conference in April, when Hawke was due to present the report of his industrial committee, which union officials in the Socialist Left were hoping the conference would reject. With the state election due in 1980, it was crucial for the party that Hartley and his supporters were sidelined.

Journalist Peter Blazey provided a colourful account of the ensuing confrontation, describing how 'Hawke's entrance at the back of the

Fitzroy Town Hall ... electrified the gathering. He was by far the best dressed delegate wearing a yachting jacket with silver accessories and a face as tanned as a peacock.' He was there to present the committee report and defeat the motion against its adoption from the Socialist Left. Hawke took them head-on. According to Blazey's account, his extempore speech was 'one of the most excoriating attacks heard within the Labor movement since the 1955 split', with the arguments of his opponents being dismissed by Hawke as 'the ravings of infant minds'. The Socialist Left motion was lost. Wisely, Hartley didn't speak. And for all of Hawke's histrionics, or perhaps because of them, Roulston won top billing in the votes for the two state delegates to the federal executive, with Hawke coming second.[9]

When the conference broke up, Hawke went across the road to the Napier Hotel to celebrate among his admirers in the crowded bar, while a morose Hartley and Blazey headed to the less hostile surrounds of another pub, where Hartley declared over a beer that he and his supporters would oppose Hawke's preselection, no matter which seat he tried to get. Although the mood of the conference favoured Hawke, his preselection for a federal seat would be decided by the local branches, where the Socialist Left held more sway. Not that Hawke had definitely decided to jump into politics, as Blazey discovered when he joined Hawke at the Napier and found him 'doing his superstar number'. Watching on, Blazey discerned 'almost a sexual glamour to him ... Some women were offended by it, others attracted. It was not just the aphrodisia of power; it contained an element of repressed bloodlust. He had just "done over" his worst enemy in the most humiliating way possible.' Amid the shouting and the backslapping, Blazey also heard Hawke asking yet another journalist whether or not he should go into parliament, only to be told again that he should. Blazey thought Hawke had 'probably left his run too late', and anyway he 'prefers the acclamation, the exquisite indecision'. Hawke had been stoking the stories about his parliamentary ambitions for nearly two decades. 'As a true ham,' wrote Blazey, 'he fully savours tantalising his audience.' Holding back from taking the leap suggested that he lacked the courage required of a great politician, suggested Blazey. There was also a psychological need that was being satisfied. After all, Hawke was already 'the most popular politician in the country without really being one. He loves the applause too much to give it up now.'[10]

While that was true, the matter was more complicated than that. Hawke loved the power and the applause that came with being president of the ACTU, but he also loved the bonhomie it brought, whether in the back bar at the John Curtin or addressing workers on a picket line. He much preferred that to living among politicians, whom he considered 'a much more bitchy, jealous lot'. He liked the financial security that came with being president, on top of which he had stipends from other positions, whether it was as a member of the Reserve Bank board or the board of the ILO, as well as the backhanders from wealthy friends like Abeles. There was also the freedom he enjoyed as president, with little check on his movements, as well as the schmoozing with political and business powerbrokers, which would not occur to the same extent if he was an opposition MP.

Then there was his complicated private life: his lover and muse in Switzerland, Helga Cammell, whom he nicknamed 'Paradiso' and whose relationship with Hawke was sustained by his frequent visits to the ILO; the women in several Australian cities who counted themselves as his lovers, and the many one-nighters during his months away from home each year. His marriage to Hazel might be over, but there was also Blanche d'Alpuget, to whom he had recently suggested marriage. In November 1978, he had told D'Alpuget during a drunken binge of his intention to divorce Hazel and marry her. He'd been tossing up between D'Alpuget and Cammell, when he had a dream during which the women were on a roulette wheel that stopped at D'Alpuget. On several levels, the distant Cammell would have been an impractical choice for Hawke, even if he was besotted with her and she'd been willing to marry him. Anyway, he interpreted the dream as a sign that he was meant to marry D'Alpuget. She wasn't sure, though, that she wanted to marry him. As she later reflected, he was so self-obsessed that he knew little about her and couldn't even pronounce her surname. Moreover, he was subject to drunken rages that terrified her. This part of his life, which had long fulfilled a deep, narcissistic need to enjoy a succession of conquests and be smothered in love, however fleeting, might change irrevocably if he went to Canberra and became subject to the close media scrutiny that a parliamentary career entailed. Divorce might also cruel his chances of becoming prime minister. For much of 1979, he would wrestle with the decision about standing for parliament and the likely ramifications it could have for his life.[11]

Apart from the implications of divorcing Hazel, his heavy drinking could also destroy his political ambitions, since there would be less tolerance for his wild behaviour in public as a politician in Canberra. He had the measure of the industrial journalists in Melbourne, but the parliamentary press gallery could prove to be a more critical audience. Hawke was still drinking heavily in May 1979, when he made another visit to Moscow to advocate on behalf of the 'refuseniks'. He'd made their cause his own and was passionate in his advocacy.

Just as passionate was Isi Leibler, the wealthy owner of Jetset Travel, who'd enlisted the ACTU as a business partner and who'd become Hawke's close friend. It was Leibler who encouraged Hawke to make this further visit, and who provided him with extensive briefing notes, in the belief that the times were propitious for a breakthrough on the issue. Leibler also encouraged Hazel to go, hoping that her presence might provide Hawke with the emotional support that was likely to be required during the difficult negotiations, while Hawke hoped her presence would be politically useful in Moscow.

After a week of consultations in Israel, the Hawkes flew to Moscow, where Hawke met with Soviet officials and attended private gatherings of several refuseniks. A jubilant and inebriated Hawke was convinced that the authorities had agreed to open the way for them to emigrate in an orderly fashion. When he flew on to Rome, where Leibler was waiting, Hawke was so drunk and emotionally overwrought that he couldn't sit up in the embassy car that collected him and Hazel from the airport. Believing it to be the greatest achievement of his career, he broadcast the news to the world, only to have the Soviet government issue a denial. The refuseniks were a pawn in the game of nuclear chess being played between Moscow and Washington, and the Soviets weren't going to sacrifice their pawn to an Australian union official who had little to offer in return. Hawke was inconsolable, fearing that the refuseniks would suffer for his failure, as might his political prospects in Australia. When he and Hazel arrived in Geneva, they were both 'so abrasive with drink' at an Australian reception that the attending diplomats had to bundle the couple into a car and send them back to their hotel. Hawke was so depressed that he considered suicide.[12]

His year only got worse. The anger and frustration Hawke had expressed at the state Labor conference was repeated a few weeks later, when the Victorian election failed to produce the anticipated Labor victory. Once again, the Socialist Left seemed to have been the cause. As the results became clear, Hawke finally committed to making his long-awaited announcement, declaring in May 1979 that he would decide before the end of the year whether or not he would be entering parliament. He was teetering on a precipice. It was 'a very dangerous period in his political and personal life', observed Leibler at the time, predicting that a misstep could cause Hawke to 'degenerate into an alcoholic, broken down wreck'. But he couldn't keep humming and hawing about entering politics and railing against the Socialist Left at party conferences, only to see the party lose a succession of state and federal elections because of voters' fears about Socialist Left influence. As for Hayden, he had to ensure that none of the Victorian MPs retired before the election and thereby provided an opening for Hawke. He had to keep him out of parliament until the 1980 election, by which time Hayden hoped he would be prime minister himself.[13] For that to happen, Hayden had to ensure that he could go to the people with policies that were suited to the straitened economic times.

The ALP conference in July 1979 was the place where those policies would be thrashed out. Amid the political horse-trading at Adelaide's Festival Centre, all eyes would be on the sparks between Bill Hayden and the man who wanted his position. While Hayden had to prove his credentials as party leader and prospective prime minister, Hawke had to show that he had the makings of a successful politician. The conference would turn into a cockfight between the two. The only problem was that Hawke wasn't there on the opening day of the conference, and was planning to miss the second day as well because of his involvement in the negotiation of a dispute with Telecom that threatened the shutdown of the telephone system. He was also spending long, sleepless nights in the arms of Blanche d'Alpuget, whom he expected soon to marry.

Hawke's successor as ALP president, Tasmanian politician Neil Batt, wanted him to present the report of the economic committee that he'd chaired, which proposed holding a referendum to give the federal government power over both incomes and prices, despite this having been rejected at repeated referendums over the decades. If the delegates agreed to it, Hawke planned to take the proposal to the ACTU Congress in September. Yet he had asked his fellow committee member Ralph Willis to present the report to the Labor conference. Batt had argued that Hawke's presence was necessary to ensure that Hayden scored an emphatic win on the policy. This would have been regarded by Hawke as a good reason not to be there. It was only when Hayden called to tell him that his presence was required that a reluctant Hawke bowed to the pressure.[14] His speech could allow him to launch another devastating attack on the Socialist Left and portray himself as the person who'd saved Hayden.

When Hawke arrived late on the morning of the debate, taking a seat on the rostrum as Willis made his opening speech, he had no idea that he was walking into a trap set by Hayden. At first, Hayden had appeared to go along with the committee's proposal and had met with right-wing powerbrokers, including Wran and Ducker, to get them to agree. Confident of the numbers, Hawke believed that he could mount a reprise of his performance at the state Labor conference. Paul Kelly describes how 'Hawke, tanned and fit, was ... furiously making speech notes and preparing himself for a major attack on the left'. Then it all fell apart when Hawke went off to lunch at the state parliament. The pragmatic Socialist Left figure Bob Hogg convinced his factional associates (and long-time Hawke opponents) Tom Uren and Jim Roulston to formulate a compromise resolution so that Hayden could have the big win he needed. The amended resolution would bridge the gap between the factions by removing any mention of a referendum. Hayden immediately agreed to move the resolution, which would allow him to present himself as the undisputed leader of a united party. As the delegates drifted back into the conference after lunch, Hawke learned to his horror that the compromise had been reached without Hayden consulting him. Angry beyond measure, he refused to present his speech and had to be restrained by Ducker from openly challenging Hayden's authority on the conference floor.

Hawke had been outwitted by an exultant Hayden, and it was against his party leader that he turned his full fury. At the bar of the Gateway

Inn later that day, the exhaustion and the alcohol and his innate anger combined to get the better of Hawke. Surrounded by journalists who kept plying him with drink, Hawke declared that Hayden was 'a lying cunt with a limited future' and their relationship was 'finished'. Hawke was notably absent the following morning when Hayden presented a triumphant leader's speech that was met with a prolonged standing ovation. Then, when an exhausted Hawke was trying to make an interstate phone call in the conference press office, he was suddenly surrounded by television cameras and radio microphones, which recorded him rounding on the journalists, shouting at them, 'Fuck off!' His outburst was played on the evening news. Hawke's behaviour was regarded by most commentators as having extinguished his chances of a parliamentary career. The headline across the front page of *The National Times* summed up the general view: 'Hawke: The end of the road?' And it might have been the end, had Hawke not been buoyed by his strong self-belief and the messages from concerned well-wishers, including a late-night call from daughter Ros, who told a strung-out Hawke that she loved him, causing him to burst into tears.[15]

Despite the doom-laden headlines, Hayden's deal with the Left, after seeming to make a commitment to the Right faction, caused the right-wing powerbrokers from New South Wales, Graham Richardson and John Ducker, to question Hayden's trustworthiness and credentials. As for the irrepressible Hawke, he usually dismissed critical prognostications by journalists about his political future. And he did so again. When he gave a speech in Sydney a few days after the Adelaide debacle, he told those who'd been reading his political obituary that they could now witness his 'coming back, Lazarus-like, from the grave to which I have been confined'. He was convinced that he was the smartest, best-qualified and ablest person to be prime minister. Repeated polls over the years also told him that he was the most popular. Anyway, he was now committed to a political future and wouldn't be diverted by the media reaction to his drunken behaviour. That said, Hawke's commitment would only be irrevocable once he'd gained preselection for a winnable seat and had gone on to win it. In July 1979, he hadn't formally nominated for the seat of Wills, which covered several inner-northern, industrial suburbs of Melbourne. Its member, Gordon Bryant, had announced his retirement. With the vote being set for September, Hawke and his supporters would have to ensure his numbers in the branches and on the electorate council, who would choose the candidate. The Socialist Left was already organising against him and had chosen a strong candidate in a young party official, Gerry Hand. That was a serious annoyance. Rather than being waved into the seat unopposed, Hawke would have to have the numbers when the preselection vote was held. He was so peeved by Hand's candidature that he briefly decided against nominating, before changing his mind once again. Amid all the politicking and backroom number-crunching, Hawke also had to prepare for the week-long ACTU Congress, which was due to begin on 10 September. As usual, it would open with his presidential address, when he was widely expected to announce his retirement. However, in the weeks beforehand, he was still procrastinating.[16] Leaving the ACTU for a shot at the prime ministership would risk his position of power and influence for the possibility of suffering a life-defining failure, which he continued to shrink from doing.

With the preselection vote just a few weeks away, and Hawke visiting Sydney for a meeting of the Reserve Bank board, he met with Abeles and Rockey in his suite at the Boulevard Hotel. D'Alpuget was also there. Her account of that night reveals his continuing indecision. With the press predicting that his forthcoming presence at the opening of an electoral office in Wills confirmed that he was standing for the seat, his two friends wanted to know whether he'd made the decision. When Hawke said he was still unsure, Abeles took him into the bedroom for a private talk, during which he pressured Hawke not to stand, arguing that he 'would be doing so on the Left's terms'. Over dinner with D'Alpuget, Hawke said he'd already realised that possibility but he remained undecided. After carousing with D'Alpuget until 4.30 the next morning, he woke two hours later to declare that he wouldn't be standing. In his groggy state, he then tried unsuccessfully to contact Hazel before ringing Jean Sinclair, who'd been urging him to enter parliament, to explain the reasons for his decision. Among the factors he cited was the indignity of having to justify his candidature to the preselection committee and the prospect of having to appear on platforms with Hartley, whom he 'hated ... more than he hated Fraser'. Indeed, he said that he was 'closer, ideologically, to the left-wing of the Liberal Party than he was to the Socialist Left'. With the weight of indecision having finally lifted, Hawke was exultant, promptly cancelling his attendance at a board meeting of the Reserve Bank and flying back to Melbourne. A huge burden had lifted from his shoulders, but he decided to wait until after the upcoming ACTU Congress to make his decision public.[17] It was at this crucial moment in his life, on the Saturday before the congress, that he received news from Perth that his 81-year-old mother had died.

The person who had imbued him with the conviction that he was destined to be prime minister had been mostly unconscious for months in a Subiaco hospice, and now would never know whether her religiously driven prediction had been borne out. He'd seen her just weeks before, and would describe in the opening paragraph of his 1994 memoirs how he'd held her hand and thanked her for 'all she had done to encourage and equip me for life's journey'. Although she was in a coma, she supposedly replied: 'It was a pleasure, son.' Hawke would later say: 'No one had a greater influence on my life and my destiny than my mother Ellie.' Yet his relationship with his mother was more conflicted than is normal. When describing her to D'Alpuget, the only word he repeatedly used was 'strong'. It must have seemed tragically ironic to Hawke that the mother who'd been more absent than present in his life, and who'd placed this heavy burden on his shoulders, should die now.[18]

When the hundreds of union delegates gathered the next morning at Melbourne's Dallas Brooks Hall to receive the expected announcement of Hawke's retirement, they were disconcerted to hear him, distraught, apologising for not having come to a decision. Perhaps if Ellie had been proudly sitting in the audience, he might have done so, but only Hazel and a friend from the Brotherhood of St Laurence, Connie Benn, were there. With his mother's funeral to be held the following day, he still hadn't decided any of the several big questions, personal and political, that confronted him. So he stuck to the usual presidential script of attacking the government for the growing unemployment and calling for a conference of government, union and employer representatives to agree on solutions to the economic problems. He also had a dig at Hayden's wages policy, arguing that it was useless without a referendum giving the government power to rein in prices as well.[19]

Despite their unresolved talk of divorce, Hawke and Hazel flew together to his mother's funeral in Perth. 'After he had kissed his mother goodbye in her coffin,' wrote Hazel later, 'Bob repeatedly said how very cold she was.' Stephen, who'd left Tasmania to work with a First Nations community in the Kimberley, came south to join about ninety people for the ceremony at the Karrakatta Cemetery prior to the cremation. Hawke returned to Melbourne for the rest of the ACTU Congress, Hazel remained in Perth for several days to help Clem sort out the physical remains of his married life.[20]

Hawke had earlier suggested to Clem that he should come and live in their Sandringham home. Hazel hadn't been consulted and could barely conceal her fury. She'd developed a relatively independent and satisfying life for herself and didn't fancy being forced to be Clem's carer. Fortunately, it wasn't something Clem wanted either. He was set on joining his retired brother Albert in Adelaide, where he'd also be close to his childhood roots and the rest of his extended family.[21]

In the midst of his grief, Clem was troubled by the news from Hawke that he might be getting a divorce so that he could marry D'Alpuget. As Clem and Hazel organised things in the Tate Street home and Hazel prepared their lunch, he asked her about the planned divorce. 'This whatsername,' said Clem. 'What is she about?' Hazel was taken aback, later describing in her memoir the emotional moment as she considered how to respond, before telling him straight: 'She wants to marry him. And perhaps he wants to marry her.' Clem, at his pastoral best, 'embraced and held me tight', wrote Hazel, who recalled that 'it was the only time I had ever known him to make a spontaneous gesture of close physical affection, and it moved me greatly'.[22] At the time, Hazel wasn't certain that Bob would follow through with his plans. Indeed, he wasn't sure himself.

If the previous ACTU Congress had been a triumph of Hawke's presidency, the 1979 gathering was almost as much of a disaster as the recent ALP conference in Adelaide had been. His fall from grace was there for all to see when delegates from the left and right combined to defeat Hawke's moderate candidates for the executive. Instead of Charlie Fitzgibbon and other supporters getting up, the congress voted for a more militant set of representatives, including the militant Norm Gallagher of the Builders Labourers Federation. It was a time when unionists were being threatened with imprisonment by governments, and when both government and employers were determined to curb the wage demands of the workers. Instead of the tactics of negotiation and mediation that Hawke had used to such effect over the previous nine years, the congress wanted to push back with national strikes and bans in the event of any unionists being jailed. If he stayed on, Hawke was set for a difficult time.

Rather than trying to mollify the angry militancy of his audience, he used the emotional issue of uranium mining to hit back at his opponents. The issue had already been thrashed out at the Labor Party conference, where Hawke had been in the pro-uranium minority and Hayden had overseen a decision that called for a ban on its mining and export. With the support of the outgoing executive, Hawke wanted the mines that were presently operating to be exempt from any ban. He was heading for another loss, but he didn't seem to care, declining an offer from Bill Kelty 'to lead the debate so I should not suffer a personal defeat'.[23]

It was a fight that Hawke was determined to have. He'd had arguments about uranium with his family, and his daughter Susan was demonstrating outside with the anti-uranium activists who were being held back by police. He didn't deny the dangers of nuclear power, the problems of waste disposal and the perils of nuclear proliferation, but he believed that Australia was better placed to influence those issues in international forums if it continued to be a uranium producer. There was also the pragmatic reality that workers in the uranium mines wouldn't obey an ACTU ban that required them to walk away from their well-paid jobs.

With these arguments in mind, Hawke ignored the muffled shouts from outside and the occasional interjections from inside the smoke-filled hall and proceeded to berate his opponents as 'wankers' and purveyors of 'sloppy morality', taking particular aim at Tom Uren. Because the ban on uranium mining couldn't be enforced, it would thereby destroy the credibility of the labour movement, warned Hawke. In fact, Ray Gietzelt declared that members of his Miscellaneous Workers' Union would continue to mine uranium in defiance of the decision. Hawke thought it was an issue that could be argued on purely rational grounds and made no attempt to seek a compromise. But there were rational reasons that could be deployed by both sides. When the debate concluded and the vote was taken, Hawke had only 318 votes in support of the executive motion and was overwhelmed by the 512 votes against. His fiery attacks had rebounded to his discredit. His position was further undermined when delegates rejected his call for a period of wage restraint and supported instead a militant wages policy, and then piled on further humiliation by voting against an indexed increase of 150 per cent in the affiliation fees, which were necessary if the ACTU were to be rescued from the financial problems in which it had become mired during Hawke's presidency. Instead of the $750,000 in additional funding requested, the congress only approved an extra $200,000. The ACTU secretary, Peter Nolan, suggested that their desperate finances could require retrenchments among their twenty-one staff and fewer trips overseas.[24]

If Hawke had been hoping to leave the ACTU on a high note, he had failed to achieve it. Quite the opposite. *The National Times* described it as his 'week of agony', while the *Australian Financial Review* thought it 'must raise questions as to his political judgment, his influence in the trade-union movement and perhaps more importantly his desire to remain as ACTU president'. While Hawke still refused to say whether he was going to stand for Wills, the outcome of the congress made staying on at the ACTU much less appealing. He would be hamstrung, both financially and politically, and likely to lose popularity if the ACTU Executive backed a more militant approach to industrial relations. Moreover, Fraser was daring him to make the leap, telling journalists that Hawke was 'quite plainly one of the most discontented people with whatever position he has held', and that 'the whole of his life has been the run-up to Wills'. The Liberals were languishing in the opinion polls, and the haughty grazier was worried about losing the 1980 election. He hoped that Hawke's preselection for Wills would lift his own chances of victory at the coming poll, since he expected it would destabilise Hayden's leadership and raise questions in voters' minds about Hawke launching a post-election bid to topple him.[25]

Still Hawke dithered. He feared being blocked by the Socialist Left from taking a safe seat, and even dallied with the idea of standing for the Liberal seat of Isaacs, in which he lived and which only required a 6 per cent swing to win for Labor. Even if he could secure Wills, he was torn by the implications of his decision. He couldn't be sure that the Labor caucus would welcome his election to parliament, which could leave him with insufficient support to secure the leadership. He certainly wasn't interested in being anything less than leader.

Peter Abeles had suggested that Hawke create a political party of his own, much as Don Chipp had done with the Australian Democrats. Abeles even offered to fund it. Such a party would be a moderate centre party with the aim of attracting disaffected voters and MPs from the two major parties. And Abeles would be pulling its strings. At the same time, Abeles was also promoting the prime ministerial aspirations of the New South Wales Labor premier, Neville Wran, and maintaining a close relationship with the federal government's Liberal foreign minister, Andrew Peacock. One of his executives recalled an occasion when he needed Abeles to sign a document on a Saturday morning and rang him at home, only to be told that he was hosting a barbecue attended by Hawke, Wran and Peacock.[26]

It's not clear how seriously Hawke considered the proposal from Abeles to lead a third party. The idea would have appealed to his narcissism, and Hawke would have avoided the uncertainties of securing a majority in caucus to topple Hayden. However, he wanted more than just the leadership of a political party. He wanted to be prime minister. Creating his own party was a risky way of achieving that, since most Labor MPs would be loath to leave the party to line up with Hawke. The history of the DLP would have been a cautionary tale in that respect. It wasn't a model that Hawke would want to emulate. Hard as it was, he would have to trust his chances to the caucus in the hope that his ability, charisma and popularity would win him its support.

According to Hazel, he was so worried about it all that he collapsed at a friend's house on Friday, 21 September, 'under the combined pressures of alcohol and anxiety'. It was just nine days before he had to submit his nomination for preselection, and it also happened to be his dead mother's birthday. Taking matters into her own hands, Hazel slipped him two sleeping tablets rather than have him go to a scheduled speaking engagement that night. Somewhat restored by the following morning, he asked Eddie Kornhauser to come to Sandringham to go over his options. Kornhauser urged him to nominate, as did Hazel, who told him that he would regret it forever if he didn't. At Kornhauser's insistence, Hawke rang Hayden to tell him that he would probably run in Wills, waiting until the Sunday morning before telling Hayden that he was definitely running.[27]

That afternoon, Hawke finally took the fateful step, holding a packed press conference in the ACTU boardroom, where, with a composed Hazel providing symbolic support by his side, he announced that he was going to nominate for Labor preselection in Wills. With journalists scribbling away and newspaper photographers and television cameramen jostling in the crammed room for the best angle to capture the moment, a grim-faced Hawke, his forehead bathed in sweat, said that he was entering the fray to oppose those who wanted the party to be 'a vehicle for advancing the fantasies of any extremist group'. It was a jab at Gerry Hand and the Socialist Left. Rather than pursuing 'fantasies', Hawke wanted the party to represent 'the thoughts and aspirations of the great majority of Australian men and women', so that it could 'help to weld Australians together'. As for challenging Hayden, he simply said that he would be a candidate if the leadership ever became vacant. So much in his life would change because of this momentous decision, although he hadn't yet resigned from the ACTU and wouldn't leave it for almost another year.[28]

There were many messages of congratulation and promises of support from the many Australians who'd long hoped he'd make the switch to parliament. As a close friend, Isi Leibler wished him well, while warning that 'your only obstacle to otherwise inevitably becoming PM of this country will be the need to overcome your effervescence and frequent inability to tolerate fools'.[29]

A message that he would have treasured came from D'Alpuget, who wrote from Canberra to his office at the ACTU telling him of her delight at the news. She said that she'd 'been frightfully anxious about you in these past months: it was like watching a beautiful big motorcar being revved at maximum, in neutral, and being shaken – not to pieces – but to a damaging extent'. His drawn-out distress over the decision had left her feeling that, for the sake of his health, 'any decision would be better than none'. Of course, as she readily admitted, her interests as a biographer lay in him making the switch to politics, to which his whole life had been directed, rather than having to end her book 'on a note of regret, of hope abandoned'. Now that 'you've made the proper choice, in terms of your own history', wrote D'Alpuget, 'existence will transform again to living – for months, you were merely existing, I felt'. She assured him that he was 'on the side of the angels' in the coming contest for Wills. Despite supporting his decision, D'Alpuget was distraught, and even considered suicide, when Hawke told her that it meant he could no longer marry her, since divorcing Hazel could prevent him from becoming prime minister.[30]

Of course, standing for preselection didn't mean he would win. His numbers man was powerful backroom operator Bill Landeryou, who led a team that had been busily securing assurances of support from the seventy-member preselection committee. Only thirty of the committee members were chosen by the local branches, while the remainder were selected randomly from a hundred-strong panel chosen by the state conference.

Gerry Hand was just as busy with his supporters from the Socialist Left. Thirty-seven-year-old Hand was a former textile worker from Warrnambool and had been secretary of the South-West Victoria Trades and Labour Council and a Labor Party organiser. He had nominated four weeks before the poll and was sufficiently confident of his numbers to have bought a home in the electorate and shifted his family there. The Hand camp issued a four-page broadsheet called *Wills Labor Call* that was sent to branch secretaries throughout Victoria. There was no explicit attack on Hawke in its pages, but plenty of implicit ones. Apart from a glowing profile of Hand by journalist Stan Anson, there was a reminder about the importance of keeping uranium in the ground, another about the role of the Labor 'rat' Billy Hughes in World War I, implying that Hawke might emulate Hughes, and another by Jim Roulston suggesting that, unlike Hand in Warrnambool, Hawke had settled industrial disputes without necessarily ensuring that the best interests of the workers were protected. This was the polite side of the contest. There were also desperate measures by each side to shore up their numbers.[31]

For Hawke, having to compete for preselection was another humiliation. As he bemoaned to Jean Sinclair, 'I must justify myself as an ALP candidate to the preselection committee in preference to the likes of that unknown Jerry [sic] Hand.' An editorial in *The Sydney*

Morning Herald agreed. While acknowledging Hawke's 'untamed streak of narcissistic wilfulness and arrogance, and his distasteful resort to personal abuse in place of logic in debate', the paper argued nonetheless that making 'one of Australia's most incandescent, most dynamic, most able figures' go through the preselection process was 'an extraordinary belittlement'.[32]

Along with Hand, Hawke was interviewed in the normal way by the preselection committee prior to the vote. Bob Hogg thought it was all over once Hawke submitted his nomination, since Labor 'could not afford to defeat him'. If the preselection panel voted against Hawke, Hogg feared, it could cause a schism in the Victorian party, as Hawke and his supporters would be certain to take up their cudgels against the Socialist Left with even greater vigour. Moreover, an adverse decision was sure to be overturned by the federal executive, since the party was unlikely to spurn the country's most popular political figure, particularly when it was predicted that Hawke's presence on the ballot at the next election could add 2 per cent to Labor's primary vote.[33]

In the event, there was no need for the federal executive to intervene. The vote, held on 14 October 1979, went Hawke's way thirty-eight to twenty-nine. It wasn't the overwhelming result he wanted and believed he deserved. Although it was a clear win, his supporters regarded the twenty-nine votes cast against him as 'a massive insult'.[34] It set the stage for another bitter campaign by Hawke against his enemies in the Socialist Left. That would be a sideshow, though. The main event would be in Canberra, once he became the Labor MP for the safe working-class seat. It was then that his political battle would begin in earnest.

In fact, some shadow-boxing had already begun. Just a few days before Hawke's preselection, an article in Kerry Packer's influential weekly magazine, *The Bulletin*, was headlined 'Profile of a future PM' and written by journalist and future Labor premier Bob Carr. But it wasn't Hayden or Hawke who was being profiled. According to Carr, it was the snappily dressed Paul Keating, who'd been recently elected as ALP president in New South Wales, who was well placed to succeed Hayden. It was a warning to Hawke, wrote Carr, that 'the caucus he seeks to enter already includes men of vaulting ambition'.[35]

Hawke already knew that Keating was the hungriest and best situated of his potential rivals, with a powerful base in the New

South Wales Right and admirers in caucus. Although the numbers in caucus mattered, Keating lacked the national profile of Hawke, with polls continuing to rate Hawke as the most popular political figure in Australia, whereas Keating didn't rate at all. That fact alone would focus the minds of Labor MPs whenever it came time to choose Hayden's successor. Keating was also fourteen years younger than Hawke, which encouraged Hawke to think that his rival could be convinced to wait his turn.

He'd tried to stitch up such an arrangement before submitting his nomination for Wills, suggesting to Keating that, as leaders of the Centre Unity factions in their respective states, they form an alliance to act against Hayden whenever the time was right. Hawke wanted an acknowledgement that he should go first as the older man, and then be succeeded by Keating. Such an alliance could have given Hawke a clear run at the leadership after the 1980 election. However, Keating was too ambitious and too smart to provide such an open-ended commitment. He equivocated, telling Hawke that his attitude at the time of any future leadership contest would depend on how well Hawke performed in parliament, since there were many MPs who thought Hawke would prove himself unsuited to the parliamentary arena. If that proved true, warned Keating, 'then there's one body you'll have to step over – and that's mine'.[36]

Meanwhile, Hawke would have six months or more before the federal election to make a dignified exit from the ACTU after a decade as president and more than twenty years working for the trade union movement. His farewell dinner was less dignified. He talked for so long that several of the guests fell asleep; Norm Gallagher was snoring loudly. Jean Sinclair thought it was 'a dreadful evening'.[37]

Hawke had been a polarising figure when he'd been appointed. While his decade at the helm had forced some union leaders to acknowledge that he'd been a positive influence on the organisation, others pointed to the sometimes yawning gap between his declared aspirations and his eventual achievements. Much to Hawke's chagrin, *The National Times* provided its readers with a balance sheet of his successes and failures, listing all the projects he had announced and been unable to bring to fruition – including a hire-purchase company, an insurance company and a housing finance company – and the many initiatives that had been achieved: the ban on the Springboks, the ending of resale price maintenance, the campaign against penal sanctions, the creation of ACTU-Solo and ACTU-Jetset Travel, the introduction of maternity leave (albeit mostly unpaid), the creation of the federally funded Trade Union Training Authority and the ACTU's amalgamation with white-collar unions. Some of Hawke's campaigns had been only partially achieved, such as the thirty-five-hour week and equal pay, while some commercial initiatives, such as the partnership with Bourke's, had failed to live up to his optimistic projections. His vision of having the ACTU emulate its counterparts in Israel and Germany could never be fully realised so long as it remained an underfunded, loose amalgamation of powerful, independently minded unions.[38]

Still, the force of Hawke's personality and charisma, together with his boundless energy and pragmatic approach, had lifted the profile and influence of the ACTU beyond the wild imaginings of the congress delegates who'd voted in favour of his appointment back in 1969. In the process, his own profile had been lifted to such an extent that, by the end of his term, he was regarded as the most influential and most popular political figure in the country.

Now, at fifty years of age, Hawke was about to parlay his position at the ACTU for the leadership of the Labor Party and then, in quick order, the prime ministership. That had been his ultimate goal for decades, but he'd either been thwarted by circumstance or suffered a temporary loss of confidence.

This would be the biggest gamble of his life and success was far from guaranteed, as he pursued the destiny that his recently departed mother had laid out for him. It was like reaching the Everest base camp and looking towards the summit. Many observers doubted that he had the temper or ability to make the climb to be a successful parliamentarian, let alone prime minister. Ellie wouldn't be there to see his triumph or to lament his failure, she and Clem had shaped him in ways that might serve him well. His narcissism had given him an over-weaning self-confidence that he could deploy to overpower political opponents and silence querulous journalists. He'd already left a considerable mark on Australian public life. Greater opportunities lay ahead.

Endnotes

PART ONE: CHILDHOOD
Chapter One: Origins
1. D'Alpuget, *Robert J. Hawke*, pp. 3–5; G.D. Crabb, *Baptists at Kapunda, 1865–1949*, self-published, Sydney, 2015, p. 222.
2. D'Alpuget, *Robert J. Hawke*, pp. 3–5; Stan Anson, *Hawke: An Emotional Life*, McPhee Gribble, Melbourne, 1991, pp. 18–19.
3. *Kadina and Wallaroo Times*, 27 September 1924.
4. Martyn Wakelin, *Language and History in Cornwall*, Leicester University Press, Leicester, 1975, Chapters 3–4.
5. Ian Soulsby, *A History of Cornwall*, Phillimore, Chichester, 1986, p. 106.
6. For a report on the church and Sunday School, see *Yorke's Peninsula Advertiser*, 13 September 1918.
7. *Australian Christian Commonwealth*, 27 February 1925.
8. *Daily Herald*, 26 August 1914; *Observer*, 8 March 1919; D'Alpuget, *Robert J. Hawke*, pp. 1–6.
9. Personnel record of Edith Emily Lee, GRS 9084/1/19, SRSA; *Education Gazette*, 31 January 1920, GRG 18/170, 1915–20, SRSA.
10. There is some confusion about the birth date, and even the name, of Clem Hawke. While his school record lists his birthdate as 5 March 1897, his birth certificate shows him to have been born on 5 March 1898. Both of these records agree that his name is Arthur Clemence, although an internet search turns up a number of other incorrect dates and different variations of his name. By the time of his marriage in June 1920, he lists his name as Clement Arthur Hawke and his age as twenty-three, and Ellie's as twenty-two. If he was twenty-three in June 1920, it would suggest that he was born in 1897 rather than 1898. He may have said he was twenty-three so that the marriage certificate would show him to be older than Ellie. For details, see birth certificates of Arthur Clemence Hawke, 5 March 1898, and Edith Emily Lee, 1 October 1897, and marriage certificate of Clement Arthur Hawke and Edith Emily Hawke, 2 June 1920, Genealogy South Australia; (Boys) Kapunda Primary Schools Admission Registers, GRS 9180/1/P, 1878–96, SRSA.
11. (Boys) Kapunda Primary Schools Admission Registers, GRS 9180/1/P, 1878–96, SRSA; D'Alpuget, *Robert J. Hawke*, pp. 3–4; *Daily Herald*, 22 December 1914.
12. *Canberra Times*, 20 March 1983.
13. *Kapunda Herald*, 19 September 1930; D'Alpuget, *Robert J. Hawke*, p. 5.
14. *Canberra Times*, 20 March 1983.
15. Phillip Pendal, 'Albert Redvers (Bert) George Hawke', *Australian Dictionary of Biography*, Vol. 17; *Canberra Times*, 20 March 1983.
16. *Argus*, 3 March 1925.
17. Jim Moss, *Sound of Trumpets: History of the Labour Movement in South Australia*, Wakefield Press, Adelaide, 1985, pp. 239–40.
18. *Australian Christian Commonwealth*, 2 March 1917; *Chronicle*, 16 March 1918, p. 37; Michael Gladwin, *Captains of the Soul: A History of Australian Army Chaplains*, Big Sky Publishing, Sydney, 2013, p. 35.
19. Arnold Hunt, 'William George Torr', *Australian Dictionary of Biography*, Vol. 1221

20 *Narracoorte Herald*, 13 December 1916.
21 *Naracoorte Herald*, 17 April 1917.
22 Arnold Hunt, *This Side of Heaven: A History of Methodism in South Australia*, Lutheran Publishing House, Adelaide, 1985, pp. 241–44.
23 *Register*, 20 April 1918.
24 By the time the author visited, Rossawella had been reduced to ruins.
25 *Australian Christian Commonwealth*, 20 September 1918.
26 *Australian Christian Commonwealth*, 19 July 1918.
27 *Mount Barker Courier*, 29 November 1918.
28 D'Alpuget, *Robert J. Hawke*, p. 3; *Australian Christian Commonwealth*, 19 December 1919; Personnel record of Edith Emily Lee, GRS 9084/1/19, SRSA; see Notes by D'Alpuget, MS 7348/3/14, D'Alpuget Papers, NLA.
29 *Register*, 23 December 1922.
30 Walter Phillips, 'Edward Sidney Kiek and Winifred Kiek', *Australian Dictionary of Biography*, Vol. 9; Walter Phillips, *Edward Sidney Kiek: His Life and Thought*, Uniting Church Historical Society, Adelaide, 1981; Margaret Knauerhase, *Straight on Till Morning: A Brief Biography of Edward Sidney Kiek*, E.S. Wigg, Adelaide, 1963.
31 *Canberra Times*, 20 March 1983.
32 Ro Ross, 'Ellie Hawke, 1897–1979: The True Kingmaker', in Adair Dunsford (ed.), *Remarkable Women of the South East*, South East Book Promotions Group, Mount Gambier, n.d., p. 20.
33 Personnel record of Edith Emily Lee, GRS 9084/1/19, SRSA.
34 *Register*, 28 February 1920; *Chronicle*, 22 May 1920.
35 For details of Clem Hawke's salary of £15 per month and the renovations to the manse, see Houghton Congregational Church Treasurer's Book, SRG 95/32/4, SLSA; *Register*, 23 December 1922.
36 *Kapunda Herald*, 8 June 1950.
37 *Chronicle*, 26 March 1921; *Register*, 26 March 1921.
38 Hawke was not the only student to collapse. Kiek reported to the board of governors in July 1920 that the external students were so zealous that he worried they would 'suffer from undue application to their studies', with one of them having 'temporarily collapsed'. That may have been Clem, because the Houghton church minutes in October 1920 reveal there was a rumour he was about to resign due to ill health. College Journal, May 1920–March 1923, and Letter, Edward Kiek to Board of Governors, 22 July 1920, SRG 95/76/1, SLSA; Houghton Church Minutes, SRG 95/32/1/2, SLSA.
39 *Australian Christian Commonwealth*, 6 January 1922; *Advertiser*, 11 March 1922.
40 *Chronicle*, 14 January 1922; Minutes, 2 July, 7 August and 4 December 1922, Wellington District Committee Minute Book, ACC MSY-3049, Congregational Union of New Zealand Papers, ATL.
41 Race Mathews, *Australia's First Fabians: Middle-class Radicals, Labour Activists and the Early Labour Movement*, Cambridge University Press, Melbourne, 1993, pp. 58–59; *The Cyclopedia of New Zealand*, Cyclopedia Company, Wellington, 1897; *Nelson Evening Mail*, 2 May 1894; *Evening Star*, 26 December 1888; *Star*, 23 February 1895.
42 *Register*, 23 December 1922; Letter, Clem Hawke to Lewis, 4 November 1922, ACC 91-295-3/16, Congregational Union of New Zealand Papers, ATL.
43 For details about Lower Hutt and Alicetown, see David McGill, *Lower Hutt: The First Garden City*, Lower Hutt City Council, Lower Hutt, 1991, p. 145; George Kaye, *Bygone Days in Lower Hutt*, Lower Hutt City Council, Lower Hutt, 1987, pp. 98–99; Barbara Scott (ed.), *Sun, Sand and Sweat: Recollections of a Seaside Village*, Petone Historical Society, Petone, 2015.
44 *Evening Post*, 31 January, 30 August and 23 November 1923; Minutes, 5 August 1923, Wellington District Committee Minute Book, ACC MSY-3049, and Minutes, 25 April 1923, Lower Hutt Church Meeting Minute Book, MS-Papers-5363, Congregational Union of New Zealand Papers, ATL.
45 Letter, Clem Hawke to Lewis, 24 October [1923], and other documents in ACC 91-295-3/16; Minutes, 3 December 1923 and 5 May 1924, Wellington District Committee Minute Book, ACC MSY-3049, and Church Meeting Minute Book, Terrace Congregational Church, 28 November 1923, ACC MSY-0162, Congregational Union of New Zealand Papers, ATL.

46 *Evening Post*, 2, 7 and 13 May 1924; *Press*, Canterbury, 15 August 1924; Minutes, August 1923, Lower Hutt Church Meeting Minute Book, MS-Papers-5363, Congregational Union of New Zealand Papers, ATL.
47 *Evening Post*, 7 April 1923.
48 *Evening Post*, 24 May 1923, 13 March, 21 April 1924; Minutes, 5 January and 5 February 1923, 5 May 1924, Wellington District Committee Minute Book, ACC MSY-3049, Congregational Union of New Zealand Papers, ATL.
49 Minute Book, Wellington District of the Congregational Union, ACC 91-295-3/02, Congregational Union of New Zealand Papers, ATL.
50 *Evening Post*, 10 November, 19 and 21 December 1923.
51 Church Meeting Minute Book, Terrace Congregational Church, 2 April 1924, ACC MSY-0162, Congregational Union of New Zealand Papers, ATL.
52 Minutes, 28 May, 25 June and 29 July 1924, Lower Hutt Church Meeting Minute Book, MS-Papers-5363, and Minute Book, Wellington District of the Congregational Union, ACC 91-295-3/02, Congregational Union of New Zealand Papers, ATL.
53 Minute Book, Wellington District of the Congregational Union, ACC 91-295-3/02, and Minutes, 4 August and 1 September 1924, Wellington District Committee Minute Book, ACC MSY-3049, Congregational Union of New Zealand Papers, ATL.
54 Although Ellie's father died fairly suddenly in Adelaide on 22 August 1924, Clem had resigned several weeks prior to when he would have received that news. *Chronicle*, 4 October 1924; *Australian Christian Commonwealth*, 27 February 1925.
55 Church Meeting Minute Book, Terrace Congregational Church, 3 September 1924, ACC MSY-0162, Congregational Union of New Zealand Papers, ATL; *Press*, 15 August 1924; *Murray Pioneer*, 10 October 1924.
56 In October 1927, Clem gave a talk in Adelaide on 'The Wider Work of the Church and the Romance of the Outback', which suggested that he was still being driven by the missionary zeal that had taken him from Port Neill to Forster and across the Tasman to Lower Hutt. *Glenelg Guardian*, 13 October 1927.
57 I am grateful to Renmark historian Heather Everingham for her hospitality and helpful insights into the town's history. For Renmark's history, see Sydney Wells, *Paddle Steamers to Cornucopia: The Renmark-Mildura Experiment of 1887*, Murray Pioneer, Renmark, 1986; Elizabeth Storry et al. (eds), *Pictorial History of Renmark: Celebrating 100 Years, 1887–1987*, Murray Pioneer, Renmark, 1987; G. Arch Grosvenor, *Red Mud to Green Oasis*, Raphael Arts, Renmark, 1979; F.M. Cutlack, *Renmark: The Early Years*, Nancy Basey, Melbourne, 1987; Dudley Coleman, *Golden Heritage: A Story of Renmark*, Renmark Irrigation Trust, Renmark, 1954; Y.M. Johnson, *The Renmark Hotel, 1897–1997: The First Community Hotel in the British Empire*, Y.M. Gurr, Renmark, 1997.
58 Melissa Bellanta, 'Transcending Class? Australia's Single Taxers in the Early 1890s', *Labour History*, May 2007; Malcolm Saunders, 'Harry Samuel Taylor', *Australian Dictionary of Biography*, Vol. 12, Melbourne University Press, Melbourne, 1990; Malcolm Saunders, 'Harry Samuel Taylor, the "William Lane" of the South Australian Riverland', *Labour History*, May 1997; *Murray Pioneer*, 30 November 1917.
59 Church History Committee, *Renmark Wilkinson Memorial Church, 60th Anniversary*, Renmark, 1949, p. 9.
60 *Murray Pioneer*, 17 October 1924, 15 July 1927.
61 *Murray Pioneer*, 7 November 1924.
62 *Murray Pioneer*, 1 May 1925, 12 November 1926, 22 and 29 April 1927.
63 *Murray Pioneer*, 30 January and 3 April 1925, 6 August, 24 September and 17 December 1926, 11 March, 30 September and 23 December 1927, 9 March and 6 April 1928; *Chronicle*, 4 July 1925; *Observer*, 11 July, 5 and 12 September 1925; *Register*, 2 September 1925.
64 *Murray Pioneer*, Renmark, 9 April, 14 May, 4 June, 6 August, 3 and 17 September 1926, 27 May, 14 October, 16 and 30 December 1927, 3 February 1928 and 15 March 1929.
65 *Murray Pioneer*, 20 November 1925, 26 November, 3 and 24 December 1926, 8 April and 11 November 1927.
66 *Murray Pioneer*, 8 October 1926.
67 *Murray Pioneer*, 23 May 1925, 12 March and 19 November 1926.
68 *Murray Pioneer*, 13 November and 11 December 1925.

69 *Murray Pioneer*, 11 November 1927.
70 Alan Jones, *Tatiara: The First 140 Years, 1845–1985*, District Council of Tatiara, Bordertown, 1986, pp. 350–52, 755–57.
71 Bordertown Cash Book 1922–45, SRG 95/58/2/4/3, SLSA.
72 The house is so substantial that it was being used until recently as a Centrelink office, whose staff kindly allowed the author to inspect it.
73 *Border Chronicle*, 25 November 1927, 16 December 1927, 20 January and 2 March 1928; *Observer*, 4 February 1928.
74 *Register*, 6 and 11 April 1928; *Border Chronicle*, 10 May and 28 June 1929.
75 *Border Chronicle*, 6, 13, 20 and 27 April, 18 May, 8 and 29 June and 19 October 1928, 12 April 1929; *Register*, 20 April 1928; *Naracoorte Herald*, 8 June 1928.
76 *Border Chronicle*, 15 June 1928.
77 *Register*, 11 May 1929; *Border Chronicle*, 10 May 1929, 14 and 21 June 1929, 5 February 1932.
78 See undated handwritten notes in Congregational (Bordertown Pastorate) Papers, BLB; Jones, *Tatiara*, p. 774.
79 D'Alpuget, *Robert J. Hawke*, pp. 5–6; *Murray Pioneer*, 31 August 1928.
80 *Murray Pioneer*, 18 February 1927, 16 November 1928.

Chapter Two: 1929–1939
1 D'Alpuget, *Robert J. Hawke*, pp. 1–2, 6.
2 D'Alpuget, *Robert J. Hawke*, pp. 1–2, 6; *Border Chronicle*, 20 December 1929, 28 February and 20 December 1930; Letter, Clem Hawke to D'Alpuget, 12 January 1981, MS 7348/3/17, D'Alpuget Papers, NLA.
3 Transcript of 'Bob Hawke', *Elders with Andrew Denton*, ABC TV, 14 July 2008; D'Alpuget, *Robert J. Hawke*, p. 8.
4 Minutes of Church Meeting, 3 July 1930, 13 January 1931, 17 January 1934, SRG 95/143/1/2; Bordertown Cash Book 1922–45, SRG 95/58/2/4/3, SLSA.
5 *Border Chronicle*, 18 October 1929.
6 *Tatiara: The Good Country*, Tatiara Pastoral, Agricultural and Industrial Society, Bordertown, 1976; Minutes of Church Meeting, 3 July 1930, SRG 95/143/1/2, SLSA.
7 Hawke, *The Hawke Memoirs*, p. 4.
8 Dunsford (ed.), *Remarkable Women of the South East*, p. 17; *Border Chronicle*, 19 January 1934.
9 *Advertiser*, 7 April 1934.
10 *Border Chronicle*, 21 and 27 March, 26 September and 12 December 1930, 20 August, 2 and 30 September 1932, 5 and 12 May, 21 July, 11 and 25 August, 15 September and 10 November 1933; *Chronicle*, 27 March 1930.
11 Ross, 'Ellie Hawke', in Dunsford (ed.), *Remarkable Women of the South East*, p. 18; *Border Chronicle*, 28 March 1930, 11 September 1931, 18 March, 8 April, 27 May, 24 June, 1 September, 2 and 23 December 1932, 10 February, 17 March, 18 August and 3 November 1933, 5 January, 2 and 23 March 1934.
12 *Tatiara Schools Commemoration*, Tatiara Schools Commemoration Committee, Bordertown, 1988, p. 109; Interview with Elva Cleggott, in *My Memories: Recollections and Images by Residents of the Tatiara*, Bordertown High School, 1985, p. 3, BLB; D'Alpuget, *Robert J. Hawke*, pp. 6, 12; *Murray Pioneer*, 30 May and 26 September 1930; Ross, 'Ellie Hawke', in Dunsford (ed.), *Remarkable Women of the South East*, p. 19.
13 *Border Chronicle*, 29 July and 7 October 1932, 27 October 1933; *Advertiser*, 11 September 1934.
14 *Border Chronicle*, 7 November 2002.
15 *Huon Times*, 16 April 1931; *Border Chronicle*, 27 March 1931, 10 April, 7 August and 10 September 1931; *Advertiser*, 10 April 1931; *News*, 9 and 10 April 1931.
16 *Border Chronicle*, 27 February 1931, 6 May 1932, 17 and 24 February 1933.
17 *Border Chronicle*, 8 April 1932, 21 July 1933.
18 *Advertiser*, 20 March 1931; *Border Chronicle*, 20 March 1931, 7 and 21 July 1933.
19 *Advertiser*, 27 April 1932; *Border Chronicle*, 29 April 1932, 27 October 1933.
20 *Border Chronicle*, 20 May, 10 June 1932, 2 June 1933.
21 *Advertiser*, 30 December 1932, 18 January 1933; *Border Chronicle*, 23 December 1932; Notes by D'Alpuget on Neil Hawke, MS 7348/3/13, NLA.

Endnotes   361

22 *Border Chronicle*, 26 August and 7 September 1932.
23 Dennis Nutt, 'Thomas Hagger: A Burning Flame', Churches of Christ booklet, 2015; *Border Chronicle*, 30 March, 6, 13, 20 and 27 April, 4 and 11 May 1934; Notes on Bordertown by D'Alpuget, undated, p. 5, MS 7348/3/13, D'Alpuget Papers, NLA.
24 *Border Chronicle*, 4, 11, 18, 25 May and 1 June 1934; Notes on Bordertown by D'Alpuget, undated, p. 5, MS 7348/3/13, D'Alpuget Papers, NLA.
25 *Bordertown Congregational Church: A Centenary Report, 1874–1974*, p. 4, BLB.
26 *Chronicle*, Adelaide, 7 June and 15 November 1934; *Advertiser*, 14 July 1934; Minutes of Combined Deaconate, 21 September 1934, Associated Congregational Churches Minute Book, SRG 95/143/18, Vol. 1, SLSA.
27 D'Alpuget, *Robert J. Hawke*, p. 2; Vida Maney (compiler), *Great Women of the Good Country*, Bordertown, n.d., p. 172.
28 *Advertiser*, 13 February 1935; *Kadina and Wallaroo Times*, 13 February 1935; Yorke Peninsula Congregational Churches, Preachers' Plan of Services, SRG 95/143/6, SLSA; Philip Payton, *The Cornish Farmer in Australia*, Dyllansow Truran, Trewirgie, 1987, pp. 76–89; Note of an interview with Gwen Geater by D'Alpuget, MS 7348/3/13, D'Alpuget Papers, NLA.
29 Combined Deaconate Minutes, 18 November 1934, Associated Congregational Churches Minute Book, SRG 95/143/13, SLSA.
30 *Advertiser*, 28 February and 8 August 1935; *Chronicle*, 23 May 1935; D'Alpuget, *Robert J. Hawke*, p. 17.
31 *Register*, 11 August 1916, 6 July 1926; 'Maitland: Gem of the Peninsula Wheatbelt', *Chronicle*, 8 September 1932.
32 Hawke, *The Hawke Memoirs*, p. 4.
33 D'Alpuget, *Robert J. Hawke*, pp. 1–2; Graham Little, 'The Two Narcissisms: Comparing Hawke and Keating', in Judith Brett (ed.), *Political Lives*, Allen & Unwin, Sydney, 1997, pp. 16–27; Anson, *Hawke*, pp. 14–31; Notes by D'Alpuget on Neil Hawke, and Note of an interview with Maggie Broadbent by D'Alpuget, MS 7348/3/13, NLA.
34 *Advertiser*, 21 July 1937.
35 Ross, 'Ellie Hawke', in Dunsford (ed.), *Remarkable Women of the South East*, p. 19.
36 D'Alpuget, *Robert J. Hawke*, p. 16; Note of an interview with Gwen Geater by D'Alpuget, and Letter, D'Alpuget to Hawke, 20 March 1980, MS 7348/3/13, D'Alpuget Papers, NLA.
37 *Pioneer*, 2 September 1938; Minutes of the Congregational Church Women's Society, Maitland, SRG 95/143/1, Vol. 2, SLSA.
38 *Advertiser*, 4 September 1935, 25 January and 3 June 1936; *News*, 27 August 1936; *Pioneer*, 27 September 1935, 28 August 1936; *Kadina and Wallaroo Times*, 29 January 1938; Minutes of the Congregational Church Women's Society, 6 April and 4 May 1938, SRG 95/143/1, Vol. 2, and Maitland Congregational Church Minutes, 1935–39, SRG 95/143/8/6 Vols 1–6, SLSA.
39 Minutes of the Congregational Church Women's Society, Maitland, 6 April 1938, SRG 95/143/1, Vol. 2, SLSA; Hawke, *The Hawke Memoirs*, p. 10.
40 D'Alpuget, *Robert J. Hawke*, pp. 16–17.
41 D'Alpuget, *Robert J. Hawke*, pp. 14, 16; Bob Hawke's school report for 1937, BCC; John Hurst, *Hawke: The Definitive Biography*, Angus & Robertson, Sydney, 1979, p. 5.
42 *Education Gazette*, 16 January 1939, SRSA; *Maitland Watch*, 17 and 18 December 1936, 17 December 1937, 3 June and 16 and 23 December 1938; Bob Hawke's School Report for 1937, BCC.
43 *Chronicle*, 23 May 1935; the programs for the Maitland Competitions can be found in SRG 95/143/6, SLSA; *Advertiser*, 5 February 1936.
44 *Advertiser*, 24 December 1936.
45 Minutes of the Council of the Congregational Union, 31 March–5 April 1935, and Minutes of the Executive Committee of the Congregational Union, 14 April 1935, SRG 95/3/1, Vol. 5, SLSA.
46 *Laura Standard and Crystal Brook Courier*, 10 July 1936.
47 For the church's changing view about war, see Congregational Union Executive Committee Minutes, 11 December 1934, 9 July 1935 and 14 April 1936, and Minutes of the Congregational Union Council, 31 March–5 April 1935 and 2–11 March 1937, SRG 95/3/1, Vol. 5, SLSA.

48 *Advertiser*, 29 March 1938.
49 D'Alpuget, *Robert J. Hawke*, p. 17.
50 For a history of King's College, see J.R. Davis, *Principles and Pragmatism: A History of Girton, King's College and Pembroke School*, Pembroke School Council, Adelaide, 1991.
51 *Advertiser*, 16 December 1936.
52 *Advertiser*, 20 and 27 February, 5, 15 and 29 May, 10 December 1937, 8 January and 19 March 1938.
53 Notes by D'Alpuget on Neil Hawke, MS 7348/3/13, NLA.
54 Clem continued to support the college, speaking at a dinner in Maitland of the Old Collegians in October 1938, which resolved to raise money for a scholarship, and then holding a service the next day in his church. *Advertiser*, 7 October 1938.
55 D'Alpuget, *Robert J. Hawke*, pp. 17–18; Notes on Maitland by D'Alpuget, undated, p. 13, and Note of an interview with Gwen Geater by D'Alpuget, MS 7348/3/13, D'Alpuget Papers, NLA.
56 *Pioneer*, 24 February 1939.
57 *News*, 27 February 1939; *Chronicle*, 2 March 1939; *Advertiser*, 27 and 28 February 1939; D'Alpuget, *Robert J. Hawke*, pp. 17–18; Notes of interviews about the Lee family by D'Alpuget, undated, MS 4378/3/13, and Letter, Clem Hawke to D'Alpuget, 12 January 1981, MS 7348/3/17, D'Alpuget Papers, NLA.
58 Notes of interviews about the Lee family by D'Alpuget, undated, MS 4378/3/13, NLA; Minutes of the Congregational Church Women's Society, Maitland, March 1939, SRG 95/143/1, Vol. 2, SLSA; *Maitland Watch*, 31 March 1939; *Kadina and Wallaroo Times*, 19 April 1939.
59 Hawke, *The Hawke Memoirs*, p. 5; Anson, *Hawke*, p. 28; D'Alpuget, *Robert J. Hawke*, pp. 19–20.
60 *Kapunda Herald*, 1 June 1939.
61 Minutes of the Congregational Church Women's Society, Maitland, 3 May 1939, SRG 95/143/1, Vol. 2, and Maitland Congregational Church Minutes, 20 June 1939, SRG 95/143/8, Vols 1–6, SLSA; *Queensland Times*, 16 May 1939; *Chronicle*, 29 June 1939; *Courier Mail*, 25 May 1939; *Daily Mercury*, 25 May 1939; *Telegraph*, 24 May 1939.
62 *Mail*, 1 July 1939; *Pioneer*, 7 July 1939.
63 *Advertiser*, 16 August and 12 September 1939; *Maitland Watch*, 20 October 1939.
64 Maitland Congregational Church Minutes, 26 July 1937, SRG 95/143/8/6, Vols 1–6, and Letter, Clem Hawke and Bayly to Congregational Church Women's Society, 2 August 1937, SRG 95/143/3, Yorke Peninsula Congregational Churches, Preachers' Plan of Services, 1935, SRG 95/143/6, and Minutes of the Congregational Church Women's Society, Maitland, SRG 95/143/1, Vol. 2, 2 August 1939, SLSA; D'Alpuget, *Robert J. Hawke*, p. 17.
65 Hawke, *The Hawke Memoirs*, p. 6; Note of an interview with Gwen Geater by D'Alpuget, MS 7348/3/13, D'Alpuget Papers, NLA.

Chapter Three: 1939–1946
1 *West Australian*, 27 October and 11 November 1939.
2 David Day, *The Politics of War*, HarperCollins, Sydney, 2003, pp. 16–34; David Day, *Menzies and Churchill at War*, Angus & Robertson, Sydney, 1986, p. 8.
3 *West Australian*, 11 November 1939.
4 The salary for his new position was £300 per annum, but with no rent-free manse or any allowance for a car, telephone or firewood. Minutes of Church Deacons Meeting, 31 May and 19 July 1939, West Perth-Leederville Congregational Church, ACC 3572A/9, BL.
5 Hawke, *My Own Life*, Text, Melbourne, 1992, p. 34. A view of the home and its present interior was viewed by the author on www.realestate.com.au. It looks much as it would have done in 1939.
6 The author visited West Leederville Primary School in August 2017 and is grateful to its principal, Fiona Kelly, for her assistance; West Leederville School Journal, 1939–41, S3626/A1412, SROWA; Note by D'Alpuget on the pages of the *Bulletin* article about Hawke, 15 January 1980, MS 7348/2/11, D'Alpuget Papers, NLA.
7 Ethel Crossley finally retired in 1947 after forty-two years' teaching at West Leederville. *West Australian*, 16 March and 22 June 1940; *Sunday Times*, 7 December 1947; Hawke, *The Hawke Memoirs*, p. 7; D'Alpuget, *Robert J. Hawke*, p. 17; Anson, *Hawke*, pp. 28–29.

8   'Oddly, there seem to be two developmental pathways to narcissistic personality disorder: one is overly indulgent parents; the other is neglectful or authoritarian parents.' Theodore Millon, Roger Davis et al., *Personality Disorders in Modern Life*, John Wiley & Sons, New York, p. 308; Anson, *Hawke*, pp. 18–27; Little, 'The Two Narcissisms'.
9   D'Alpuget, *Robert J. Hawke*, p. 27; Hawke, *My Own Life*, p. 37.
10 *West Australian*, 29 June 1939; *Woman's Day*, undated cutting from Newspaper cutting book, Hazel Hawke Papers, JCPML; Hawke, *My Own Life*, pp. 31–32.
11 *West Australian*, 24 December 1940, 8 and 22 March, 1 and 29 April, 3 May 1941.
12 See Gail Reekie, 'War, Sexuality and Feminism: Perth Women's Organisations, 1938–1945', *Australian Historical Studies*, Vol. 21, No. 85, 2008, pp. 576–91; *Sunday Times*, London, 13 July 2003.
13 *Mirror*, April 1940; the author is grateful to Christine White, president of the West Australian branch of the WCTU, for allowing me to research the voluminous records of the organisation. Minutes of the State Executive, 12 November 1940 and Secretary's Report for the December [1940] Executive Meeting, Minute Book of Executive Meetings and Conventions, 1939–44, WCTU, Perth; for the links between temperance and eugenics, see Grant Rodwell, '"There Are Other Evils to Be Put Down": Temperance, Eugenics and Education in Australia, 1900–1930', *Paedagogica Historica*, May 2015.
14 Minutes of the Annual Convention, 17–22 August 1940, p. 165, and Minutes of the State Executive, 10 September 1940, p. 186, Minute Book of Executive Meetings and Conventions, 1939–44, and Minute Book of the Perth Branch, 1940–51, WCTU, Perth; D'Alpuget, *Robert J. Hawke*, pp. 16–17, 20–21; Note of an interview with Maggie Broadbent by D'Alpuget, MS 7348/3/13, D'Alpuget Papers, NLA.
15 Service record of Arthur Clarence Hawke, www.dva.gov.au; *West Australian*, 18 April 1941; *Border Chronicle*, 30 May 1941. The photo can be seen in D'Alpuget, *Robert J. Hawke*.
16 Minutes of Church Deacons Meeting, 1 July, 5 and 16 December 1940, 28 January 1941, West Perth-Leederville Congregational Church, ACC 3572A/9, BL.
17 D'Alpuget, *Robert J. Hawke*, p. 21; *West Australian*, 4 October and 15 November 1941.
18 Hawke, *The Hawke Memoirs*, p. 16; D'Alpuget, *Robert J. Hawke*, p. 25; Greenward Consulting, Heritage Planning and Policy, 'Heritage Assessment of 17–87 and 16–78 Gordon Street, Northam', Shire of Northam, April 2015; *Daily News*, 18 February 1947; Interview with Bob Hawke on behalf of Phillip Pendal, BL.
19 *Daily News*, 20 September 1945; Minutes of the State Executive, 10 June 1941, and Minutes of the Convention, 21 August 1941, Minute Book of Executive Meetings and Conventions, 1939–44, WCTU, Perth.
20 Minutes of the State Executive, 8 July, 12 August, 9 September, 14 October and 9 December 1941, Minute Book of Executive Meetings and Conventions, 1939–44, WCTU, Perth.
21 D'Alpuget, *Robert J. Hawke*, p. 21.
22 D'Alpuget, *Robert J. Hawke*, p. 22; Hawke, *The Hawke Memoirs*, pp. 7–8; Interview with Bob Hawke by Paula Hamilton, 13 March 2001, PMSA.
23 For a history of the school, see Sphinx Foundation, *Perth Modern School: The History and the Heritage*, B+G Resources Enterprises, Perth, 2005; see also Perth Modern School Class of 1942–46, *Then, Now and In Between: A Reunion Memento*, Perth, 1996.
24 D'Alpuget, *Robert J. Hawke*, p. 22; Hawke, *The Hawke Memoirs*, pp. 7–8; *A Celebration of Contribution: Tales of the Courage, Commitment and Creativity of Modernians 1911–1963*, Department of Education, Perth, 2016, p. 220; Interview with Bob Hawke by Paula Hamilton, 13 March 2001, PMSA.
25 Hawke, *The Hawke Memoirs*, p. 8.
26 Minutes of the State Executive, 10 February 1942, Minute Book of Executive Meetings and Conventions, 1939–44, WCTU, Perth.
27 Sphinx Foundation, *Perth Modern School*, p. 94; Author interview with John Stone.
28 *The Sphinx*, June 1944, Robert Hawke Student Record, 1942–46, and Interview with Bob Hawke by Paula Hamilton, 13 March 2001, PMSA.
29 D'Alpuget, *Robert J. Hawke*, pp. 21–22; Clyde Packer, *No Return Ticket*, Angus & Robertson, Sydney, 1984; pp. 100–102; *Sydney Morning Herald*, 30 August 1986; Interview with Bob Hawke by Paula Hamilton, 13 March 2001, PMSA.

30 *Daily News*, 28 March 1942, 3 April 1943; *The Sphinx*, June 1945, July and November 1946, PMSA; D'Alpuget, *Robert J. Hawke*, p. 23; Interview with Bob Hawke by Paula Hamilton, 13 March 2001, PMSA; Author interview with John Stone; *Call and Bailey's Weekly*, 15 March 1945; Reference for Robert Hawke by headmaster Noel Sampson, 26 November 1946, Student Record of Robert Hawke, UWAA.
31 *The Sphinx*, July 1946, PMSA; *Sydney Morning Herald*, 30 August 1986; Interview with Bob Hawke by Paula Hamilton, 13 March 2001, PMSA; Author interview with John Stone.
32 *West Australian*, 21 and 25 August 1941.
33 *West Australian*, 1 April and 24 September 1942; *Daily News*, 8 October 1941; *Western Mail*, 1 October 1942; Minutes of the State Executive, 11 November 1941, Minute Book of Executive Meetings and Conventions, 1939–44, WCTU, Perth.
34 *Cobbers*, 1 January 1942; *West Australian*, 20 February 1942; Minutes of the State Executive, 14 October 1941, 10 February and 10 March 1942, Minute Book of Executive Meetings and Conventions, 1939–44, WCTU, Perth.
35 Minutes of the State Executive, 12 May, 14 June and 11 August 1942, and undated typescript page, Minute Book of Executive Meetings and Conventions, 1939–44, WCTU, Perth.
36 Minutes of the 1942 Convention and Minutes of the State Executive, 5 September and 13 October 1942, Minute Book of Executive Meetings and Conventions, 1939–44, WCTU, Perth.
37 Minutes of the State Executive, 9 February 1943, Minute Book of Executive Meetings and Conventions, 1939–44, WCTU, Perth.
38 D'Alpuget, *Robert J. Hawke*, pp. 20–21.
39 Minutes of the State Executive, 13 April–November 1943, Minute Book of Executive Meetings and Conventions, 1939–44, WCTU, Perth; *West Australian*, 21 September and 20 November 1943.
40 D'Alpuget, *Robert J. Hawke*, pp. 21–22.
41 Interview with Bob Hawke by Paula Hamilton, 13 March 2001, PMSA.
42 Robert Hawke Student Record, 1942–46, and Interview with Bob Hawke by Paula Hamilton, 13 March 2001, PMSA; Service record of Arthur Clarence Hawke, www.dva.gov.au; D'Alpuget, *Robert J. Hawke*, pp. 22, 24; *Sydney Morning Herald*, 30 August 1986; Author interview with John Stone; Letter, Frank Constantine to D'Alpuget, 7 September 1979, MS 7348/3/17, D'Alpuget Papers, NLA.
43 D'Alpuget, *Robert J. Hawke*, p. 22.
44 Sphinx Foundation, *Perth Modern School*, pp. 286–90; *West Australian*, 19 February 2011.
45 Hazel Masterson's Class Reports from Perth Central Girls' School, JCPML; Hawke, *My Own Life*, pp. 27–29.
46 *West Australian*, 29 June 1939, 14 July 1941.
47 Hawke, *My Own Life*, pp. 29–30.
48 Hazel Hawke Diary, December 1944, Hazel Hawke Papers, JCPML 01271/1, JCPML; *Sunday Times*, 24 December 1944; *Daily News*, 26 December 1944.
49 Hazel Hawke Diary, 26 December 1944, Hazel Hawke Papers, JCPML 01271/1, JCPML.
50 Hazel Masterson Autograph Book, 1939–46, JCPML 01269, JCPML.
51 Minutes of the Executive Committee of the Congregational Union of Western Australia, 10 December 1945, ACC 1616A/F2, Congregational Union Papers, BL; Report of the Executive and the Home Mission for the Six Months ending 30 September 1944, ACC 1616A/F2, Congregational Union Papers, BL; *West Australian*, 10 June, 16 September and 4 November 1944.
52 For details of Clem's income during the years 1947–50, see Student file of Robert Hawke, UWAA. It wasn't until December 1947 that Clem was offered a position at the Subiaco Congregational Church. Minutes of Quarterly Church Members Meeting, 31 October 1947, and Special Meetings, 7 December 1947, 11 January 1948, W.A. Congregational Church Subiaco, Members' Minute Book, 1920–1953, ACC 3530A/5, BL.
53 Undated typescript page, Minute Book of Executive Meetings and Conventions, 1939–44, and Minutes, 4 May, 1 June and 9 July 1944, Minute Book of the Perth Branch, 1940–51, WCTU, Perth.
54 Record of Service Card for Edith Emily Hawke, Education Department, SROWA.

55 Typescript History of the Leederville Congregational Sunday School, c. 1945, ACC 3076A/7, BL; West Perth-Leederville Congregational Church Sunday School Minute Book, 4 December 1939, 7 October 1942, 13 October 1943, and undated appeal by Leederville Congregational Sunday School, ACC 3572A/19/257/18-19, and Leederville Congregational Church Sunday School file, ACC 3076A/5, BL; *West Australian*, 26 October 1940.
56 *Cambridge Post*, 7 December 2013; Interview with Bob Hawke by Paula Hamilton, 13 March 2001, PMSA.
57 *West Australian*, 16 January 1945; Hawke's Student Record, PMSA; Letter, Frank Constantine to D'Alpuget, 7 September 1979, MS 7348/3/17, D'Alpuget Papers, NLA.
58 Author interview with John Stone; *West Australian*, 9 and 16 January 1947.

PART TWO: SCHOLAR
Chapter Four: 1946–1949
1 Bob Hawke, 'Towards a Better Australia', in Perth Modern School Class of 1942–46, *Then, Now and In Between*, p. 26.
2 *West Australian*, 1 January 1947.
3 *West Australian*, 4 and 11 March 1947; *Mirror*, 15 March 1947.
4 *Daily News*, 19 December 1947.
5 John Stone, 'The Early 1950s', in Julie Quinlivan (ed.), *Student Days: The University of Western Australia Student Guild, a Collection of Memoirs*, Guild of Undergraduates, Perth, 1988, p. 67; Christine Shervington, *University Voices: Traces from the Past*, University of Western Australia, Perth, 1987, pp. 48–49.
6 D'Alpuget, *Robert J. Hawke*, pp. 26–27; Interview with Bob Hawke on behalf of Phillip Pendal, BL.
7 Fred Alexander, *Campus at Crawley*, University of Western Australia Press, Perth, 1963, pp. 218, 238; Hawke, *The Hawke Memoirs*, pp. 11–12; R.J. Ferguson, *Crawley Campus: The Planning and Architecture of the University of Western Australia*, University of Western Australia Press, Perth, 1993, p. 52; George Seddon and Gillian Lilleyman, *A Landscape for Learning: A History of the Grounds of the University of Western Australia*, University of Western Australia Press, Perth, 2006, pp. 81–82.
8 Student File of Robert Hawke, UWAA; *Daily News*, 9 February 1950.
9 Minutes of Quarterly Church Members Meeting, 31 October 1947, and Special Meetings, 7 December 1947, 11 January 1948, W.A. Congregational Church Subiaco, Members' Minute Book, 1920–1953, ACC 3530A/5, BL; *West Australian*, 19 March 1983.
10 D'Alpuget, *Robert J. Hawke*, pp. 26–27.
11 Hawke, 'Towards a Better Australia', p. 26; *Pelican*, 4 July 1947; Interview with Bob Hawke on behalf of Phillip Pendal, BL; Robert Pullan, *Bob Hawke: A Portrait*, Methuen, Sydney, 1980, p. 40; Drew Cottle, 'The University of Western Australia Labour Club, 1925–1949: A Nursery of Political Radicals?', *Critical Studies in Education*, Vol. 40, No. 1, 2010.
12 *Pelican*, 2 May and 4 July 1947, 25 February 1948; G.C. Bolton, 'Kimberley Michael Durack', *Australian Dictionary of Biography*, Vol. 14.
13 Letter, Ewan Watts to Rhodes Selection Committee, 8 September 1951, Hawke's Rhodes Scholarship File, 1A/14/D/5 Cons 345, UWAA; Report of the Subiaco Sunday School, 21 February 1947, ACC 3572/19, UCAA. Clem preached for a time at Cottesloe's Congregational Church in early 1947 before securing a more permanent position later that year in Subiaco. *West Australian*, 1 and 22 February, 29 March and 20 September 1947.
14 Application for the Rhodes Scholarship, 30 August 1951, Hawke's Rhodes Scholarship File, 1A/14/D/5 Cons 345, UWAA; *West Australian*, 4 January, 9 February and 1 March 1947; *Sunday Times*, 14 November 1948; Interview with Hawke on behalf of Phillip Pendal, BL; Blanche d'Alpuget, *Bob Hawke: The Complete Biography*, Simon & Schuster, Sydney, 2019, p. 34.
15 Fred Alexander, 'Frank Reginald Beasley', *Australian Dictionary of Biography*, Vol. 13; Marion Dixon, *Looking Back: A Short History of the UWA Law School, 1927–1992*, UWA Law School, Perth, 1992, pp. 12–17, 28, 30; Alexander, *Campus at Crawley*, pp. 232, 477.
16 D'Alpuget, *Robert J. Hawke*, pp. 30–31; Hawke, *The Hawke Memoirs*, p. 13; *West Australian*, 12 and 16 August 1947.

17 D'Alpuget, *Robert J. Hawke*, pp. 31–32; Hawke, *The Hawke Memoirs*, pp. 13–14.
18 Statement of Passes, Robert Hawke, 23 September 1952, Hawke's Rhodes Scholarship File, 1A/14/D/5 Cons 345, UWAA.
19 Hazel Masterson Autograph Book, 1939–46, JCPML 01269, Hazel Masterson Diaries, 1947 and 1948, JCPML 01271/3 and 4, JCPML.
20 Hazel Masterson Diaries, 9 February 1946, 21 and 22 January, 13, 14, 18, 21, 22 February and 5 May 1947, JCPML 01271/2 and 3, JCPML.
21 Hazel Masterson Diary, 5–8 April 1947, JCPML 01271/3, JCPML.
22 *West Australian*, 30 November 1994.
23 Hazel Masterson Diary, 25 and 26 June 1947, JCPML 01271/3, JCPML.
24 Hazel Masterson Diary, 2 and 12 February 1947, JCPML 01271/3, JCPML.
25 Hazel Masterson Diary, 4, 5, 11 and 30 April 1948, JCPML 01271/4, JCPML27
26 Ibid.
27 *West Australian*, 30 November 1994; Hawke, *The Hawke Memoirs*, p. 17.
28 For discussion of Hawke's narcissism, see Graham Little, 'Leadership Styles: Fraser and Hawke', in Brian Head and Allan Patience (eds), *From Fraser to Hawke*, Longman Cheshire, Melbourne, 1989, pp. 21–36; Little, 'The Two Narcissisms'; and Anson, *Hawke*.
29 D'Alpuget, *Robert J. Hawke*, p. 41; Note by D'Alpuget on the pages of the *Bulletin* article about Hawke, 15 January 1980, MS 7348/2/11, D'Alpuget Papers, NLA; Millon, Davis et. al., *Personality Disorders in Modern Life*, p. 279.
30 Millon, Davis et. al., *Personality Disorders in Modern Life*, pp. 303–304; Jenny Gregory (ed.), *Seeking Wisdom: A Centenary History of the University of Western Australia*, University of Western Australia, Perth, 2013, p. 181; D'Alpuget, *Robert J. Hawke*, pp. 38–40; Bob Hawke, 'A Different World', in Quinlivan, *Student Days*, p. 71; Letters (copy), Bob Rogers to D'Alpuget, 25 June and 9 November 1980, and Interview with Justice John Toohey by D'Alpuget, MS 7348/3/15, D'Alpuget Papers, NLA; Maxwell Newton also became addicted to alcohol during his time at the university. In one of his final exams, he recalls being 'so drunk I could hardly write', but he still emerged with a first-class honours degree that won him a scholarship to Cambridge. Packer, *No Return Ticket*, pp. 102–103.
31 Statement of Passes, Robert Hawke, 23 September 1952, Hawke's Rhodes Scholarship File, 1A/14/D/5 Cons 345, UWAA.
32 *Sunday Times*, 13 July 2003.
33 Hawke, *The Hawke Memoirs*, p. 16; *West Australian*, 12 November 1947; Bobbie Oliver, *Unity Is Strength: A History of the Australian Labor Party and the Trades and Labor Council in Western Australia, 1899–1999*, API Network, Perth, 2003, p. 184; *Pelican*, 24 September and 12 October 1948; Drew Cottle, 'The University of Western Australia Labour Club, 1925–1949: A Nursery of Political Radicals?', *Critical Studies in Education*, Vol. 40, No. 1, 2010, pp. 51–52; Pullan, *Bob Hawke*, pp. 38–39.
34 Hawke, 'Towards a Better Australia', p. 26; Hawke, *The Hawke Memoirs*, p. 16; *West Australian*, 12 November 1947; Oliver, *Unity Is Strength*, p. 184; *Pelican*, 24 September and 12 October 1948.
35 *Pelican*, 24 February 1949.
36 *Daily News*, 24 February 1948.
37 Gregory, *Seeking Wisdom*, pp. 179–80; Quinlivan, *Student Days*, p. 58.
38 *Pelican*, 24 September and 12 October 1948.
39 *Pelican*, 5 and 12 October 1949; see also *Pelican*, 25 February 1948, which reports the performance of the cricket club during the 1947/48 season, noting the outstanding players and making no mention of Hawke; Alexander, *Campus at Crawley*, p. 471; Cottle, 'The University of Western Australia Labour Club, 1925–1949'.
40 D'Alpuget, *Robert J. Hawke*, p. 42; Hawke, *My Own Life*, p. 40; Sue Pieters-Hawke, *Hazel: My Mother's Story*, Pan Macmillan, Sydney, 2011, p. 55; Hawke, *The Hawke Memoirs*, p. 18. Although both Bob and Hazel note in their separate memoirs that they became engaged in early 1950, it was announced in *The West Australian* on 31 December 1949.

Chapter Five: 1950–1953
1 Sphinx Foundation, *Perth Modern School*, p. 350.
2 Newton, *Maxwell Newton*, pp. 45, 64–65; Author interview with John Stone.

3   Hawke also lost to Stone during a meeting of the Guild Council, when Hawke and Barblett tried to have the Guild change a memo that suggested Australian students and those of the Communist bloc were similarly committed to the democratic ideal. The wording of the memo had caused a fuss in *The West Australian*, but Stone saw off Hawke's attempt to have it changed. Guild Council Minutes, 18 July 1950, GCA; *West Australian*, 5, 13 and 15 July 1950.
4   *West Australian*, 2 December 1950.
5   Election Results 1950, Guild Council Minutes, and Guild Council Minutes, 30 November 1950, GCA.
6   *Pelican*, 31 March and 21 April 1950.
7   *Pelican*, 31 March 1950; D'Alpuget, *Robert J. Hawke*, p. 41.
8   Hawke, *The Hawke Memoirs*, p. 17; Student File of Robert Hawke, UWAA; *Kapunda Herald*, 8 June 1950; *West Australian*, 16 February 1951.
9   D'Alpuget, *Robert J. Hawke*, pp. 35–36; Pullan, *Bob Hawke*, p. 40; Election results, 1951, Guild Council Minutes, GCA; *Pelican*, 5 October 1951.
10 *West Australian*, 4, 7 and 8 October 1951.
11 Reference by Noel Sampson, 26 November 1946, Student File of Robert Hawke, UWAA.
12 Letters, Parsons to Rhodes Selection Committee, 16 September 1951, Gamba to Rhodes Selection Committee, 11 September 1951, Frank Beasley to Rhodes Selection Committee, 18 September 1951, and Tuohy to Rhodes Selection Committee, 10 September 1951, Hawke's Rhodes Scholarship File, 1A/14/D/5 Cons 345, UWAA.
13 Letter, Ewan Watts to Rhodes Selection Committee, 8 September 1951, Hawke's Rhodes Scholarship File, 1A/14/D/5 Cons 345, UWAA.
14 Application Form for the Rhodes Scholarship, 30 August 1951, Hawke's Rhodes Scholarship File, 1A/14/D/5 Cons 345, UWAA.
15 Peter Boyce, 'Sir Charles Henry Gairdner', *Australian Dictionary of Biography*, Vol. 17.
16 *West Australian*, 29 November 1951; Sphinx Foundation, *Perth Modern School*, p. 353; *A Celebration of Contribution*, p. 219.
17 Hawke, *My Own Life*, p. 44; Interview with Hazel Hawke by D'Alpuget, undated, MS 7348/3/16, D'Alpuget Papers, NLA.
18 Graduation Ball Sub-Committee Minutes, 4 March 1952, and Guild Council Minutes, 27 March and 17 April 1951, 15 April 1952, GCA; *Pelican*, 24 April 1952.
19 Gregory, *Seeking Wisdom*, pp. 216–19; *Pelican*, 4 April and 9 May 1952; Hawke, 'Towards a Better Australia', p. 26; Guild Council Minutes, 23 November 1951, GCA.
20 Guild Council Minutes, 11 March, 20 May, 17 June and 7 July 1952, GCA, UWA; *Pelican*, 23 May 1952.
21 *Pelican*, 18 July and 1 August 1952; International House Committee Minutes, 15 July 1952, GCA; *West Australian*, 6 August 1952.
22 Student Record of Robert Hawke, UWAA.
23 Hawke, *My Own Life*, pp. 42–43; D'Alpuget, *Robert J. Hawke*, p. 42.
24 *West Australian*, 30 November 1994; Hawke, *My Own Life*, pp. 44–46.
25 *West Australian*, 6 August 1952; Guild Council Minutes, 29 July and 13 August 1952, and Guild Council Annual Report, 2 October 1952, GCA.
26 Gregory, *Seeking Wisdom*, pp. 216–19; D'Alpuget, *Robert J. Hawke*, pp. 37–38.
27 Hawke, *The Hawke Memoirs*, p. 19.
28 *Pelican*, 4 April 1952; Guild Council Minutes, 13 August 1952, and Finance Committee Minutes, 1 September 1952, GCA.
29 Guild Council Minutes, 11 March 1952, GCA; *Pelican*, 4 and 24 April and 9 May 1952; see also *Pelican*, 2 February 1951, which reports a big improvement in the performance of the university cricket team. Of the several matches mentioned during the 1950/51 season, Hawke is only singled out once, after he'd contributed 56 runs to the team's total of 151; *Geraldton Guardian*, 14 December 1950; *West Australian*, 9 April 1952.
30 D'Alpuget, *Robert J. Hawke*, p. 32; *Pelican*, 4 April 1952; Author interview with Neal Blewett.
31 *Pelican*, 4 April 1952; *West Australian*, 11 January 1950; *Northam Advertiser*, 15 August 1952.
32 Letter, George Currie to Reynolds, 6 November 1952, Hawke's Rhodes Scholarship File, 1A/14/D/5 Cons 345, UWAA; Interview with George Currie by D'Alpuget, 29 July 1979, MS 7348/3/15, D'Alpuget Papers, NLA; Hawke, *My Own Life*, p. 47.

33 John Melville-Jones, 'Mervyn Neville Austin', *Australian Dictionary of Biography*, Vol. 19; Letter, Mervyn Austin to Secretary, Rhodes Committee, 11 November 1952, Hawke's Rhodes Scholarship File, 1A/14/D/5 Cons 345, UWAA.
34 Letters, Selwyn Grave to Secretary, Rhodes Committee, 6 November 1952, James Rossiter to Secretary, Rhodes Committee, 14 November 1952, and Reference by Frank Mauldon, 10 November 1952, Hawke's Rhodes Scholarship File, 1A/14/D/5 Cons 345, UWAA.
35 Personal Statement by Hawke, n.d., Hawke's Rhodes Scholarship File, 1A/14/D/5 Cons 345, UWAA.
36 Hawke, *The Hawke Memoirs*, pp. 19–20; *Western Mail*, 11 December 1952; Report by Gairdner on the Committee's Interview of Hawke, Student File of Robert Hawke, UCA.
37 Hawke, *The Hawke Memoirs*, p. 21; Email to the author from Archbishop (ret.) Keith Rayner, 19 December 2019.
38 Letter, Hawke to his father, 22 December 1952, Hazel Hawke Papers, JCPML 00429/1-28, JCPML; Email to the author from Archbishop (ret.) Keith Rayner, 19 December 2019.
39 Although Hawke claims to have attended a Communist Party meeting in the town square, the report of the conference says that the few curious delegates who set off for the square were prevented by police from doing so. Hawke, *The Hawke Memoirs*, pp. 21–23; D'Alpuget, *Robert J. Hawke*, pp. 45–47; *West Australian*, 14 January 1953; *Footprints in Travancore: A Report of the Third World Conference of Christian Youth in Travancore, India, December 11–25, 1952*, American Committee for the Third World Conference of Christian Youth, Coonoor, Tamil Nadu, c. 1953.
40 Speech by Bob Hawke, *Congregational Youth Fellowship of Australia and New Zealand Conference Magazine*, 17 January 1953, Uniting Church History Centre, Adelaide. I am grateful to David Hilliard for sending me a copy of this magazine.
41 Hawke diary, 26 December–1 January 1952, RH 6/2/5-11, BHPML; Hawke, *The Hawke Memoirs*, p. 22; D'Alpuget, *Robert J. Hawke*, pp. 47–49.
42 Hawke diary, 6–12 January 1952, and 'Sex' leaflet, RH 6/2/5-11, BHPML; Letter, D'Alpuget to Rogers, 14 October 1980, MS 7348/3/18, D'Alpuget Papers, NLA.
43 *Congregational Youth Fellowship of Australia and New Zealand Conference Magazine*, 17 January 1953; D'Alpuget, *Robert J. Hawke*, p. 49; see also diary note by Hawke, in which he muses: 'The greatest charge that can be made against the Church is one of irrelevancy.' RH 6/2/5-11, BHPML.
44 Hawke, *My Own Life*, pp. 46–47; *News*, 20 January 1953; *Mail*, 7 February 1953; D'Alpuget, *Robert J. Hawke*, pp. 48–50.
45 Guild Annual General Meeting, 2 October 1952, Guild Council Annual Report, 2 October 1952, and Hostel Committee of Management Minutes, 21 July 1953, GCA; *Pelican*, 10 September 1952; *West Australian*, 6 August 1953.
46 *Pelican*, 23 April 1953.
47 Robert J. Hawke, staff file, and Student File of Robert Hawke, UWAA.
48 Letter (copy), Hawke to Geoff Brown, 19 February 1954, MS 7348/3/15, D'Alpuget Papers, NLA; *West Australian*, 15 August 1953.

Chapter Six: 1953–1955
1 Interview with Russell Braddon by Vivienne Rae-Ellis, NLA; Stephen Alomes, *When London Calls: The Expatriation of Australian Creative Artists to Britain*, Cambridge University Press, Melbourne, 1999, pp. 95–96; Nigel Starck, *Proud Australian Boy: A Biography of Russell Braddon*, Australian Scholarly Publishing, Melbourne, 2011.
2 D'Alpuget, *Robert J. Hawke*, pp. 54–55; Letters, Hawke to his parents, 26 August and 10 September 1953, Hazel Hawke Papers, JCPML 00429/1-28, JCPML.
3 Letter, Hawke to his parents, 16 September 1953, Hazel Hawke Papers, JCPML 00429/1-28, JCPML; Martin Gilbert, *Never Despair: Winston S. Churchill, 1945–1965*, Heinemann, London, 1988, pp. 884–86.
4 Letter, Hawke to his parents, 16 September 1953, Hazel Hawke Papers, JCPML 00429/1-28, JCPML; *Guardian*, 12 November 2003; Nigel Starck, 'Russell Reading Braddon', *Australian Dictionary of Biography*, Vol. 19, 2019; Starck, *Proud Australian Boy*, pp. 113, 121.

5   Letter, Hawke to his parents, 6 October 1953, Hazel Hawke Papers, JCPML 00429/1-28, JCPML; Hawke, *My Own Life*, pp. 56–58.
6   Brian Bamford, *The Substance: The Story of a Rhodes Scholar at Oxford*, R. Beerman Publishers, Cape Town, c. 1960, pp. 20–21; *University College Record, 1954–55*, UCA; Robin Darwall-Smith, *A History of University College, Oxford*, Oxford University Press, Oxford, 2008, provides an excellent history of the college. I am grateful to Dr Darwall-Smith for guiding me through the Hawke-related material in the college archives.
7   Letter, Hawke to his parents, 12 October 1953, Hazel Hawke Papers, JCPML 00429/1-28, JCPML.
8   Darwall-Smith, *A History of University College, Oxford*, p. 475; Hawke, *The Hawke Memoirs*, p. 23; D'Alpuget, *Robert J. Hawke*, p. 55; Bamford, *The Substance*, p. 37; Letter, Hawke to his parents, 12 October 1953, Hazel Hawke Papers, JCPML 00429/1-28, JCPML.
9   Robert Ayson, *Hedley Bull and the Accommodation of Power*, Palgrave Macmillan, Basingstoke, 2012, p. 20; J.D.B. Miller, 'Hedley Norman Bull', *Australian Dictionary of Biography*, Vol. 17; Bamford, *The Substance*, pp. 24–25, 42; Photograph of the 1953 student intake, UCA; I am grateful to Dr Darwall-Smith for explaining the custom in regard to newcomers signing the college register; Gillon Aitken (ed.), *Between Father and Son: Family Letters: V.S. Naipaul*, Alfred A. Knopf, New York, 2000, pp. 27–28; *University College Record, 1953–54*, UCA.
10 *Age*, 24 July 1979.
11 Bamford, *The Substance*, pp. 28–29; 'Sir Edgar Trevor Williams', *Oxford Dictionary of National Biography*; *New York Times*, 30 June 1995.
12 Letters, Hawke to his parents, 12 and 19 October 1953, Hazel Hawke Papers, JCPML 00429/1-28, JCPML; Hawke, *The Hawke Memoirs*, p. 24; *Independent*, 7 August 2001; *Guardian*, 20 September 2001; Thomas Wilson, *Modern Capitalism and Economic Progress*, Macmillan, London, 1950, pp. 256–58.
13 According to the Reverend Geoffrey Beck, Hawke had joined the squadron after being 'advised that politically it was a good thing to do'. Author interview with Rev. Geoffrey Beck; Letters, Hawke to his parents, 2, 15 and 23 November 1953, Hazel Hawke Papers, JCPML 00429/1-28, JCPML; Greg Hassall, 'Bob Hawke's family photo album', November 2014, www.abc.net.au; Hawke, *The Hawke Memoirs*, p. 24.
14 Darwall-Smith, *A History of University College, Oxford*, p. 493; Ayson, *Hedley Bull and the Accommodation of Power*; D'Alpuget, *Robert J. Hawke*, pp. 55–56; Letter, Hawke to his parents, 26 October and 23 December 1953, Hazel Hawke Papers, JCPML 00429/1-28, JCPML; Hawke, *The Hawke Memoirs*, pp. 23–24; Dean's Cards for Robert Hawke, UCA. Kindly copied for the author by Dr Darwall-Smith following his student records becoming available after his death.
15 Hawke, *My Own Life*, pp. 49–51; Pieters-Hawke, *Hazel*, pp. 53–56; Hawke, *Memoirs*, pp. 23–24; Letter, Hawke to his parents, 30 December 1953, Hazel Hawke Papers, JCPML 00429/1-28, JCPML.
16 Letter, Hawke to his parents, 7 January 1954, Hazel Hawke Papers, JCPML 00429/1-28, JCPML; Author interview with Rev. Geoffrey Beck; Hawke, *My Own Life*, pp. 54–55.
17 I am grateful to the present owner of the Lonsdale Road home, Julia Sleeper, for allowing me to view the house. For Beck's involvement with ecumenicism in Oxford, see Geoffrey Beck, 'The Blackbird Leys Saga: Part of the Story', Oxford, 2005; Michael Hopkins, 'Congregationalism in Oxford: The Growth and Development of Congregational Churches in and around the City of Oxford since 1653', MA Thesis, University of Birmingham, 2010, pp. 70–72; Letters, Hawke to his parents, 7 and 25 January 1954, Hazel Hawke Papers, JCPML 00429/1-28, JCPML; Author interview with Rev. Geoffrey Beck; Visitors' book of the Beck family, kindly provided to the author by 99-year-old Rev. Geoffrey Beck on 3 April 2018; D'Alpuget, *Robert J. Hawke*, p. 59; Hawke, *My Own Life*, pp. 55–58; Ayson, *The Education of Hedley Bull*, p. 19; Coral Bell and Meredith Thatcher (eds), *Remembering Hedley*, ANU Press, Canberra, 2008, p. 3.
18 Letter, Hawke to his parents, 9 December 1953, Hazel Hawke Papers, JCPML 00429/1-28, JCPML; Letter, Tom Wilson to D'Alpuget, 3 December 1981, MS 7348, Box 3, Folder 19, D'Alpuget Papers, NLA; Student File of Robert Hawke, UCA; Letter (copy), Hawke to Geoff Brown, 19 February 1954, MS 7348/3/15, D'Alpuget Papers, NLA; Author interview with Kim Beazley.

19 'Colin Grant Clark', *Australian Dictionary of Biography*, Vol. 17; *Australasian Post*, 12 January 1950; Letters, Hawke to his parents, 1953–55, Hazel Hawke Papers, JCPML; Australian Labor Party Membership Ticket, 1 January 1948, Box 1a, Colin Clark Papers, FL; Letter, Clark to D'Alpuget, 6 August 1980, MS 7348, Box 3, Folder 19, D'Alpuget Papers, NLA; Colin Clark, *The Conditions of Economic Progress*, Macmillan, London, 1951; Donald Markwell, 'Keynes and Australia', *Research Discussion Paper*, Reserve Bank of Australia, September 1985; Alex Millmow, 'Colin Clark and Australia', *History of Economics Review*, Summer 2012.

20 Hawke, *The Hawke Memoirs*, pp. 25–26; D'Alpuget, *Robert J. Hawke*, pp. 56–58; Letter, Tom Wilson to D'Alpuget, 3 December 1981, MS 7348, Box 3, Folder 19, D'Alpuget Papers, NLA; Letter, Hawke to his parents, 25 September 1953, Hazel Hawke Papers, JCPML 00429/1-28, JCPML; Millmow, 'Colin Clark and Australia', p. 61.

21 Hawke, *The Hawke Memoirs*, pp. 25–26; D'Alpuget, *Robert J. Hawke*, pp. 56–58.

22 Letter, Hawke to his parents, 10 February 1954, Hazel Hawke Papers, JCPML 00429/1-28, JCPML; Letter, D'Alpuget to Clark, 23 August 1980, MS 7348, Box 3, Folder 19, D'Alpuget Papers, NLA; Letter (copy), Hawke to Geoff Brown, 19 February 1954, MS 7348/3/15, D'Alpuget Papers, NLA.

23 Letters, Hawke to his parents, 15 and 29 February 1954, Hazel Hawke Papers, JCPML 00429/1-28, JCPML; Letter (copy), Hawke to Geoff Brown, 19 February 1954, MS 7348/3/15, D'Alpuget Papers, NLA.

24 *University College Record, 1952–53* and *1953–54*, UCA; *Manchester Guardian*, 15 July 1954.

25 Author interview with Rev. Geoffrey Beck; D'Alpuget, *Robert J. Hawke*, p. 61; Hawke, *My Own Life*, pp. 61–62; Hawke, *The Hawke Memoirs*, p. 27; *Birmingham Daily Post*, 7 July 1954; Comments on Hawke for 1953/54 by Bill Williams, MS 7348/3/15, D'Alpuget Papers, NLA.

26 Hawke, *My Own Life*, pp. 55–62; Pieters-Hawke, *Hazel*, pp. 58–59.

27 Colin Cowdrey, *M.C.C.: The Autobiography of a Cricketer*, Hodder & Stoughton, London, 1976, p. 49; For a history of Vincent's, see Simon Lee, *Vincent's: 1863–2013*, Third Millennium Publishing, London, 2014.

28 Pieters-Hawke, *Hazel*, pp. 62–63; Hawke, *My Own Life*, pp. 55–62.

29 Hawke, *The Hawke Memoirs*, pp. 25–26; D'Alpuget, *Robert J. Hawke*, pp. 56–58; Letters, Colin Clark to D'Alpuget, 6 and 28 August 1980, and D'Alpuget to Colin Clark, 23 August 1980, MS 7348, Box 3, Folder 19, D'Alpuget Papers, NLA; Letter, Colin Clark to Gregory Clark, 25 November 1957, in Brenda Niall and John Thompson (eds), *The Oxford Book of Australian Letters*, Oxford University Press, Melbourne, 1998, pp. 254–55.

30 *Age*, 24 July 1979.

31 Student File of Robert Hawke, and Dean's Cards for Robert Hawke, UCA.

32 Ibid.; Ayson, *Hedley Bull and the Accommodation of Power*, p. 22; Letter (copy), Hawke to Geoff Brown, 31 October 1955, and Comments on Hawke for 1953/54 by Bill Williams, MS 7348/3/15, D'Alpuget Papers, NLA.

33 Student File of Robert Hawke, UWAA.

34 Author interview with Rev. Geoffrey Beck; Perilla Kinchin, *Seven Roads in Summertown: Voices from an Oxford Suburb*, White Cockade Publishing, Oxford, 2006, pp. 16–18, 45.

35 *Age*, 24 July 1979.

36 Ayson, *The Education of Hedley Bull*, p. 19; Bamford, *The Substance*, pp. 45–47; Hawke, *The Hawke Memoirs*, p. 28; Lee, *Vincent's*, p. 111; Malcolm Knox, 'The "Guinness World Records"', *The Monthly*, December 2009–January 2010. Contrary to many popular accounts, Hawke didn't establish his record by drinking a yard-glass in an Oxford pub but in the hall of University College.

37 Author interview with Rev. Geoffrey Beck; Cutting from the *Oxford Mail*, January 1955, in Hazel Hawke Papers, JCPML; Newspaper cuttings, c. March 1955, MS 7348/3/15, D'Alpuget Papers, NLA.

38 The street lamp incident may have been on Guy Fawkes Night, when students traditionally 'scour the streets, tipping over cars, exploding stink-bombs, and removing traffic signs'. Bamford, *The Substance*, p. 50; Cutting from the *Oxford Mail*, January 1955, in Hazel Hawke Papers, JCPML; D'Alpuget, *Robert J. Hawke*, pp. 59–60; Comments on Hawke for 1953/54 by Bill Williams, MS 7348/3/15, D'Alpuget Papers, NLA.

39 Student File of Robert Hawke, UWAA; Student File of Robert Hawke, UCA.

40 Author interview with Rev. Geoffrey Beck; D'Alpuget, *Robert J. Hawke*, pp. 59–60; Newspaper cuttings, c. March 1955 and Comments on Hawke for 1953/54 by Bill Williams, MS 7348/3/15, D'Alpuget Papers, NLA.
41 Comments on Hawke for 1954/55 by Bill Williams, MS 7348/3/15, D'Alpuget Papers, NLA.
42 John Gillard Watson, 'The Salzburg Seminar', *Higher Education Quarterly*, Vol. 11, No. 4, August 1957; Details of the building and the history of the seminar series can be found on the Salzburg Global Seminar website, www.salzburgglobal.org; *New York Times*, 6 September 2002; Günter Bischof, 'Two Sides of the Coin: The Americanization of Austria and Austrian Anti-Americanism', in Alexander Stephan (ed.), *The Americanization of Europe: Culture, Diplomacy, and Anti-Americanism after 1945*, Berghahn Books, New York, 2008, pp. 159–62.
43 Joseph Warren Beach, 'The Salzburg Seminar', *CEA Critic*, Vol. 12, No. 7, October 1950; Henry Nash Smith, 'The Salzburg Seminar', *American Quarterly*, Vol. 1, No. 1, Spring 1949; Robert Mead, 'The Salzburg Seminar in American Studies', *World Affairs*, Spring 1954; Ben Seligman, *Most Notorious Victory*, Free Press, New York, 1967; Ben Seligman, *Economics of Dissent*, Quadrangle Books, Chicago, 1968; Oskar Kokoschka, *Designs of the Stage-Settings for W.A. Mozart's Magic Flute, Salzburg Festival, 1955/56*, Verlag Galerie, Salzburg, 1955; D'Alpuget, *Robert J. Hawke*, pp. 61–62.
44 Letter (copy), Hawke to Geoff Brown, 31 October 1955, MS 7348/3/15, D'Alpuget Papers, NLA; D'Alpuget, *Robert J. Hawke*, p. 61; *Coventry Evening Telegraph*, 11 June 1955; Hawke. *The Hawke Memoirs*, p. 27; Comments on Hawke for 1954/55 by Bill Williams, MS 7348/3/15, D'Alpuget Papers, NLA.
45 See documents in Hawke student file, ANUA 78/12, ANUA.
46 Hawke, *The Hawke Memoirs*, pp. 25–27; Letters, Hawke to his parents, 1953–55, Hazel Hawke Papers, JCPML; J.R. Poynter, 'Sir Kenneth Clinton Wheare', *Australian Dictionary of Biography*, Vol. 16; Interview with Kenneth Wheare by Catherine Santamaria, February 1975, NLA; *Pelican*, 29 July 1949; D'Alpuget, *Robert J. Hawke*, p. 61; Comments on Hawke for 1955/56 by Bill Williams, MS 7348/3/15, D'Alpuget Papers, NLA.
47 R.J.L. Hawke, 'An Appraisal of the Role of the Australian Commonwealth Court of Conciliation and Arbitration with Special Reference to the Development of the Concept of a Basic Wage,' BLitt thesis, 1956, Oxford University.
48 Hawke, 'An Appraisal of the Role of the Australian Commonwealth Court of Conciliation and Arbitration', pp. 279–82; Hurst, *Hawke*, pp. 24–25; Hawke, *The Hawke Memoirs*, p. 28; D'Alpuget, *Robert J. Hawke*, p. 62.
49 Dean's Cards for Robert Hawke, UCA; Comments on Hawke for 1955/56 by Bill Williams, MS 7348/3/15, D'Alpuget Papers, NLA.
50 Author interview with Rev. Geoffrey Beck.

Chapter Seven: 1956–1958
1 Hawke, *My Own Life*, pp. 60–65; Pieters-Hawke, *Hazel*, pp. 64–65; D'Alpuget, *Robert J. Hawke*, pp. 63–64; Hawke, *The Hawke Memoirs*, p. 28; The author stayed at Caves House in 2016; Hawke devotes less than a sentence of his memoirs to his marriage and honeymoon.
2 Letter (copy), Hawke to Geoff Brown, 31 October 1955, MS 7348/3/15, D'Alpuget Papers, NLA.
3 See medical certificate in Hawke student file, ANUA 78/12, ANUA. A decade later, when he went to Papua and New Guinea, Hawke again listed his height on the entry permit as being 5'10½", or about 179 centimetres. Temporary Entry Permit, 20 August 1966, RH 6/19/211, BHPML; Seth Rosenthal et al., 'The Narcissistic Grandiosity Scale: A Measure to Distinguish Narcissistic Grandiosity from High Self-Esteem', *Assessment*, Vol. 27, No. 3, 2020, pp. 13–14.
4 D'Alpuget, *Robert J. Hawke*, pp. 62–63; Letter, Hawke to his parents, 24 October 1956, Hazel Hawke Papers, JCPML 00429/1-28, JCPML; Hawke student file, ANUA 78/12, ANUA.
5 Interview with Bob Hawke by Paula Hamilton, 13 March 2001, PMSA.
6 For a history of the ANU, see S.G. Foster and Margaret Varghese, *The Making of the Australian National University: 1946–1996*, Allen & Unwin, Sydney, 1996; Interview with Geoffrey Sawer by Mel Pratt, 1971, MS 2688, Box 11, Geoffrey Sawer Papers, NLA;

Interview with Geoffrey Sawyer by Daniel Connell, 1990, ANUA; Hawke, *The Hawke Memoirs*, p. 28; Schwarzkopf had toured Australia in 1949. Geoffrey Sawer diary, 21 March 1956, MS 2688/1/3, Geoffrey Sawer Papers, NLA.
7. *The Australian National University Report for 1956*, p. 33, ANUA.
8. E.V. Davies, J.E. Hoffman and B.J. Price, *Canberra: A History of Australia's Capital*, ACT Ministry for Health, Education and the Arts, Canberra, 1990, pp. 88–93; Nicholas Brown, *A History of Canberra*, Cambridge University Press, Melbourne, 2014, Chapter 5.
9. Foster and Varghese, *The Making of the Australian National University*, pp. 71–73; For an excellent history of University House, see Jill Waterhouse, *University House: As They Experienced It: A History 1954–2004*, University House, Canberra, 2004; Jim Gibbney, *Canberra, 1913–1953*, Australian Government Publishing Service, Canberra, 1988, pp. 261–62; *Canberra Times*, 21 March 1956, 16 April 1989; Brij Lal and Allison Ley (eds), *The Coombs: A House of Memories* (second edition), Australian National University Press, Canberra, 2014, p. 10; Jim Davidson, *A Three-Cornered Life: The Historian W.K. Hancock*, UNSW Press, Sydney, 2010, pp. 236–37.
10. Mark McKenna, *An Eye for Eternity: The Life of Manning Clark*, Melbourne University Press, Melbourne, 2011, p. 300.
11. Brown, *A History of Canberra*, p. 147; Comment made to the author by David Fieldhouse, Cambridge, c. 1984.
12. Hawke, *My Own Life*, p. 66.
13. Niel Gunson, *Daniel Gunson: Gippsland's Pioneer Congregational Minister, 1847–1915*, N. Gunson, Canberra, 1983; Niel Gunson, *Reminiscences of the Gunson Family in New Zealand and Victoria*, N. Gunson, Canberra, 1994; Author interview with Niel Gunson; Extracts from Niel Gunson's diary, 25–27 March 1956, provided by Gunson to the author. Although they'd all joked about the idea of Hawke becoming prime minister at the manse in Oxford, Beck didn't 'think he quite thought it a joke'. Author interview with Rev. Geoffrey Beck.
14. Peter Coleman, *Memoirs of a Slow Learner*, Connor Court Publishing, Ballarat, 2015, pp. 79, 81–83; *Canberra Times*, 25 and 26 April 1956.
15. Letter, Hawke to his parents, 24 October 1956, Hazel Hawke Papers, JCPML 00429/1-28, JCPML.
16. Notes of an interview with Ron Hieser by D'Alpuget, MS 7348/2/11, D'Alpuget Papers, NLA; Interview with Manning Clark by D'Alpuget, 21 April 1980, MS 7348/3/15, D'Alpuget Papers, NLA.
17. For details of Hawke's appointment at Canberra University College, see documents in RH 6/14/141, Hawke Papers, RHPML.
18. *Canberra Times*, 16 April 1953, 18 January 1955; Interview with Robin Gollan by Stephen Foster, 1993, ANUA; Waterhouse, *University House*, p. 45; Russel Ward, *A Radical Life: The Autobiography of Russel Ward*, Macmillan, Melbourne, 1988, pp. 219–20; Stephen Holt, 'Bob Hawke's Boon Companion', *Quadrant Online*, 17 May 2019; Interview with Geoffrey Sawer by D'Alpuget, undated, MS 7348/3/15, D'Alpuget Papers, NLA.
19. Geoffrey Sawer diary, 26 October 1956, MS 2688/1/3, Geoffrey Sawer Papers, NLA; D'Alpuget, *Robert J. Hawke*, pp. 67–70.
20. McKenna, *An Eye for Eternity*, p. 302.
21. *Argus*, 1 February 1956; *Canberra Times*, 16 March and 24 April 1956; H.W. Arndt, *A Course through Life: Memoirs of an Australian Economist*, Australian National University, Canberra, 1985, p. 29.
22. Peter Coleman, Selwyn Cornish and Peter Drake, *Arndt's Story: The Life of an Australian Economist*, Asia Pacific Press, Canberra, 2007, pp. 150–57; Arndt, *A Course through Life*, p. 36; *Canberra Times*, 28 July, 2 and 15 August 1956; *Argus*, 28 July 1956; T.W. Swan, 'Perceptions in Kaleidoscope', *Australian Economic Review*, 4th Quarter, 1986, p. 45; Letter, Hawke to Editor, *Sydney Morning Herald*, 3 August 1956, RH 6/14/141, Hawke Papers, RHPML.
23. Letter, Hawke to Editor, *Sydney Morning Herald*, 4 April 1957, RH 6/3/13, Hawke Papers, BHPML; Letter, F.E. Chamberlain to Secretary, Canberra ALP Branch, 10 April 1956, MS 5243/15/14, Crisp Papers, NLA; *Canberra Times*, 11 December 1956, 29 January, 12 February and 29 April 1957; Stephen Holt, 'Professor Crisp and the Attempted anti-Evatt Putsch', in Brian Costar, Peter Love and Paul Strangio (eds), *The*

Great Labor Schism: A Retrospective, Scribe, Melbourne, 2005, pp. 128–37; Letter, Hawke to his parents, 24 October 1956, Hazel Hawke Papers, JCPML 00429/1-28, JCPML.
24 Email to the author from Niel Gunson; Extracts from Niel Gunson's diary, April–May 1956, provided by Gunson to the author.
25 *Australian National University Report*, 1956, ANUA.
26 Interview with Manning Clark by D'Alpuget, 21 April 1980, MS 7348/3/15, D'Alpuget Papers, NLA; Waterhouse, *University House*, p. 181.
27 Pieters-Hawke, *Hazel*, p. 70.
28 Waterhouse, *University House*, p. 97; Author interview with Niel Gunson; Geoffrey Sawer diary, 30 May 1956, MS 2688/1/3, Geoffrey Sawer Papers, NLA.
29 Hawke, *My Own Life*, pp. 65–70; Letter, Hawke to his parents, 24 October 1956, Hazel Hawke Papers, JCPML 00429/1-28, JCPML.
30 Coleman, *Memoirs of a Slow Learner*, p. 85.
31 Author interview with Niel Gunson; Author interview with Margaret Steven.
32 Emily Sadka, staff file 1947, Agency 74, Series 63, Consignment 507, UWAA; *West Australian*, 17 July 1947; *Western Mail*, 25 February 1954; *Canberra Times*, 25 March 1954; Geoffrey Sawer diary, 12 June 1956, MS 2688/1/3, Geoffrey Sawer Papers, NLA; Niel Gunson, 'Hexagonal Reflections on Pacific History', in Brij Lal and Allison Ley (eds), *The Coombs: A House of Memories* (second edition), Australian National University Press, Canberra, 2014, p. 71; D'Alpuget, *Robert J. Hawke*, pp. 70–71; Author interview with Niel Gunson; Author interview with Margaret Steven; Author interview with Ruth Butterworth; Notes of an interview with Sam Stoljar by D'Alpuget, MS 7348/2/11, D'Alpuget Papers, NLA; Interview with Manning Clark by D'Alpuget, 21 April 1980, MS 7348/3/15, D'Alpuget Papers, NLA.
33 *Canberra Times*, 20 September 1956; Notes of an interview with Ron Hieser by D'Alpuget, MS 7348/2/11, D'Alpuget Papers, NLA; Interview with Manning Clark by D'Alpuget, 21 April 1980, MS 7348/3/15, D'Alpuget Papers, NLA.
34 D'Alpuget, *Robert J. Hawke*, p. 66; *Canberra Times*, 14 October and 10 December 1957, 3 January 1958.
35 Author interview with Niel Gunson; Extract from the diary of Niel Gunson, 4 December 1956, provided to the author by Gunson; Author interview with Margaret Steven.
36 Interview with Geoffrey Sawer by Daniel Connell, 1990, ANUA; Interview with Geoffrey Sawer by Mel Pratt, 1971, NLA.
37 Margot Kerley, 'Horace Plessay Brown', *Australian Dictionary of Biography*, Vol. 13; Robert Murray, 'Reginald Roslyn Broadby', *Australian Dictionary of Biography*, Vol. 13; Peter Yule, 'History of the ANU College of Business and Economics', unpublished MS, 2012. I am grateful to Peter Yule for making this manuscript available to me.
38 Letter, Hawke to Harold Souter, 26 September 1956, RH 6/14/141, Hawke Papers, RHPML.
39 Letter, Hawke to his parents, 18 November 1956, Hazel Hawke Papers, JCPML 00429/1-28, JCPML; D'Alpuget, *Robert J. Hawke*, pp. 75–76; see also Letter, Harold Souter to Hawke, 9 January 1957, RH 6/8/67, Hawke Papers, BHPML.
40 Letters, Hawke to his parents, 24 October and 18 November 1956, Hazel Hawke Papers, JCPML 00429/1-28, JCPML.
41 Letter, Hawke to Harold Souter, 15 January 1957, RH 6/14/141, Hawke Papers, RHPML.
42 Pieters-Hawke, *Hazel*, p. 73; Hawke, *My Own Life*, pp. 69–70.
43 Hawke, *The Hawke Memoirs*, pp. 28–29; Hawke, *My Own Life*, p. 70.
44 Interview with Geoffrey Sawer by Mel Pratt, 1971, MS 2688, Box 11, Geoffrey Sawer Papers, NLA; Interview with Geoffrey Sawer by Daniel Connell, 1990, ANUA; Waterhouse, *University House*, pp. 180–83; Geoffrey Sawer diary, 25 February 1957, MS 2688/1/3, Geoffrey Sawer Papers, NLA; Author interview with Niel Gunson; Author interview with Margaret Steven; Author interview with Ruth Butterworth.
45 Author interview with Margaret Steven.
46 Interview with Geoffrey Sawer by Daniel Connell, 1990, ANU Archives; Hawke, *My Own Life*, pp. 69–70; D.J. Mulvaney, 'William Edward Stanner', *Australian Dictionary of Biography*, Vol. 18; Waterhouse, *University House*, pp. 180–83; Foster and Varghese (eds), *The Making of the Australian National University*, p. 204; D'Alpuget, *Robert J. Hawke*, p. 66; Email to the author from Niel Gunson, 26 October 2019.

47 Interview with Robin Gollan by Stephen Foster, 1993, ANUA.
48 Waterhouse, *University House*, pp. 180–83; Letters, Mark Oliphant to Arthur Trendall, 28 February 1957 and Mark Oliphant to Vice-Chancellor, 27 February 1957, ANUA 10/82, Mark Oliphant Papers, ANUA; See documents in Hawke student file, ANUA 78/12, and Minutes of Disciplinary Committee, 25 February 1957, Minute Book 1, ANUA 34/1, ANUA.
49 Waterhouse, *University House*, pp. 180–83; Letters, Mark Oliphant to Arthur Trendall, 28 February 1957 and Oliphant to Vice-Chancellor, 27 February 1957, ANUA 10/82, Mark Oliphant Papers, ANUA; Geoffrey Sawer diary, 25 February 1957, MS 2688/1/3, Geoffrey Sawer Papers, NLA; See documents in Hawke student file, ANUA 78/12.
50 Interview with Geoffrey Sawer by Mel Pratt, 1971, Oral History Collection, NLA; Interview with Geoffrey Sawyer by Daniel Connell, 1990, ANUA.
51 Geoffrey Sawer diary, 26 November 1957, MS 2688/1/3, Geoffrey Sawer Papers, NLA.
52 *Canberra Times*, 15 May 1958.
53 Letters, Hawke to Harold Souter, 18 March 1957, 16 June 1957 [from his parents' home in Tate Street], N21/854, ACTU Papers, NBAC.
54 D'Alpuget, *Robert J. Hawke*, pp. 72–77.
55 D'Alpuget, *Robert J. Hawke*, pp. 78–80.
56 *The Australian National University Report for 1956*, p. 33, ANUA; Arndt, *A Course through Life*, p. 22. The advertisement for the position, with its closing date of 28 September 1957, can be found in RH 6/14/141, Hawke Papers, RHPML.
57 Interview with Geoffrey Sawer by Daniel Connell, 1990, ANUA; Interview with Geoffrey Sawer by Mel Pratt, NLA; Peter Yule, 'Hieser, Hawke and Harsanyi: Three "Might-have-beens" in the History of CBE', *Margin*, ANU College of Business and Economics, Autumn 2011, pp. 22–23; Yule, *History of the ANU College of Business and Economics*; Hawke student file, ANUA 78/12, ANUA; Sawer gave a different view when he spoke to D'Alpuget in about 1980, suggesting that Hawke could have become a first-rate academic. Interview with Geoffrey Sawer by D'Alpuget, c. 1980, MS 7348/3/15, D'Alpuget Papers, NLA; Notes of an interview with Sam Stoljar by D'Alpuget, MS 7348/2/11, D'Alpuget Papers, NLA.
58 Letter, Bill Titterington to Hawke, 17 October 1957, RH 6/15/147, Hawke Papers, RHPM.
59 Hawke, *My Own Life*, pp. 70–71.
60 Geoffrey Sawer diary, 23, 25 and 29 May 1958, MS 2688/1/3, Geoffrey Sawer Papers, NLA.
61 Hawke, *The Hawke Memoirs*, pp. 29–30. This didn't stop Hawke in 1959 from asking Sawer for a two-year extension to his time at ANU so that he could keep alive the possibility of completing his PhD. Sawer claimed that he 'firmly refused' to support it, which caused Hawke to be 'very cross'. In fact, Sawer had been sympathetic and suggested Hawke be asked to submit a progress draft of his thesis by March 1960, which he was unable to do. He was then dropped from the ANU in June 1960 after being deemed unable to complete his PhD in the permitted time. Draft memoir by Sawer, pt. 49, p.3, MS 2688/18/4, Geoffrey Sawer Papers, NLA and Hawke student file, ANUA 78/12, ANUA.

PART THREE: ADVOCATE
Chapter Eight: 1958–1961

1 Colin Clark suggested that Rhodes scholars should be given the scholarship when they are eighteen years old, rather than in their twenties, when their focus is more on marriage and career. Colin Clark, *Australian Hopes and Fears*, Hollis & Carter, London, 1958, p. 298.
2 Hawke, *The Hawke Memoirs*, p. 30.
3 *Herald*, 26 June 1953; *Barrier Miner*, 12 June 1954; D'Alpuget, *Robert J. Hawke*, pp. 93–94.
4 Gwenda Tavan, *The Long, Slow Death of White Australia*, Scribe, Melbourne, 2005, Chapter 5.
5 Hawke, *My Own Life*, p. 73.
6 The house is unrecognisable today. The timber exterior of the front four rooms was bricked over by subsequent owners in the 1970s and the lean-to at the back demolished

to make way for a greatly expanded home. I am grateful to the present owner, Heather Copley, for explaining its past configuration. Pieters-Hawke, *Hazel*, pp. 79–80; Hawke, *My Own Life*, pp. 73–74; Author interview with Heather Copley.
7   Blanche d'Alpuget, *Mediator: A Biography of Sir Richard Kirby*, Melbourne University Press, Melbourne, 1977, p. 159.
8   Jim Hagan, *The History of the A.C.T.U.*, Longman Cheshire, Melbourne, 1981, pp. 261–62; Hawke, *The Hawke Memoirs*, pp. 34–38.
9   D'Alpuget, *Robert J. Hawke*, p. 92.
10 Coleman, *Memoirs of a Slow Learner*, p. 85; Hazel Hawke, *My Own Life*, pp. 74–77.
11 John Murphy, *Imagining the Fifties*, UNSW Press, Sydney, 2000, pp. 34–36, 48, 88–89.
12 Hawke, *My Own Life*, pp. 77–79; D'Alpuget, *Robert J. Hawke*, pp. 90–91, 93–94; Pieters-Hawke, *Hazel*, pp. 83–87.
13 Interview with Patsy Zeffel by D'Alpuget, c. 1980, MS 7348/2/12, and Letters, D'Alpuget to Beverley Richards, 2 February 1981 and Beverley Richards to D'Alpuget, 15 February 1981, MS 7348/3/19, D'Alpuget Papers, NLA; Troy Bramston, *Bob Hawke: Demons and Destiny*, Viking, Sydney, 2022, p. 107; *Sport*, 27 October 1939; *Advertiser*, 10 May 1943, 23 July 1945, 29 April and 8 May 1947, 5 July 1951, 13 December 1952, 10 December 1954; *News*, 18 April 1950, 7 November 1952; *Advocate*, 22 March 1951; *Barrier Miner*, 30 July 1951; *Herald*, 8 December 1954; *Australian Jewish News*, 18 April 1958.
14 Murphy, *Imagining the Fifties*, p. 187; Pieters-Hawke, *Hazel*, pp. 79–80, 87; Hawke, *My Own Life*, pp. 74–78; Hawke, *The Hawke Memoirs*, p. 33.
15 Hawke, *My Own Life*, pp. 78–79.
16 T.W. Swan, 'Perceptions in Kaleidoscope', *Australian Economic Review*, 4th Quarter, 1986, p. 46; Glenn Stevens, 'Inflation and Disinflation in Australia: 1950–91', Reserve Bank of Australia Conference Paper, 1992; Hagan, *The History of the A.C.T.U.*, pp. 11, 135.
17 Murphy, *Imagining the Fifties*, p. 185.
18 Hagan, *The History of the A.C.T.U.*, Chapter 9; D'Alpuget, *Mediator*, pp. 155–57; D'Alpuget, *Robert J. Hawke*, pp. 75–76.
19 D'Alpuget, *Mediator*, pp. 157–58; Hagan, *The History of the A.C.T.U.*, pp. 220, 294–95.
20 John Pitchford, 'Wilfred Edward Graham Salter', *Australian Dictionary of Biography*, Vol. 16; G.C. Harcourt, 'Eric Alfred Russell', *Australian Dictionary of Biography*, Vol. 16; G.C. Harcourt, 'The Systemic Downside of Flexible Labour Market Regimes: Salter Revisited', *Economic and Labour Relations Review*, Vol. 23, No. 2, 2012, pp. 117–18; For an essay on the life and work of Eric Russell, see G.C. Harcourt, *Selected Essays on Economic Policy*, Palgrave, Basingstoke, 2001, Chapter 3. Geoffrey Harcourt provides an obituary of Wilfred Salter in G.C. Harcourt, *The Making of a Post-Keynesian Economist: Cambridge Harvest*, Palgrave, Basingstoke, 2012, Chapter 17.
21 Hawke, *My Own Life*, pp. 65–6; Pieters-Hawke, *Hazel*, pp. 82–83.
22 Bryan Harding, *Always in Need of Reform: Reflections of a Policeman*, self-published, Kilmore, 2022, p. 104; Constance Larmour, 'Alfred William Foster', *Australian Dictionary of Biography*, Vol. 8; Constance Larmour, *Labor Judge: The Life and Times of Judge Alfred William Foster*, Hale & Iremonger, Sydney, 1985; D'Alpuget, *Robert J. Hawke*, pp. 76–77, 80; D'Alpuget, *Mediator*, pp. 28, 30–31.
23 Hawke's scrawled notes for one such case can be found in the Noel Butlin Archives Centre in Canberra, with his anger at the employers and the judges being palpable. See note by Hawke in N68/1321, ACTU Papers, NBAC.
24 D'Alpuget, *Mediator*, pp. 123–38; Interview with Kirby, cited in D'Alpuget, *Robert J. Hawke*, p. 81.
25 *Canberra Times*, 25, 26 and 27 February 1959; Larmour, *Labor Judge*, pp. 226–27; Hurst, *Hawke*, pp. 28–31.
26 Hawke, *The Hawke Memoirs*, p. 38; Hagan, *The History of the A.C.T.U.*, p. 294; D'Alpuget, *Mediator*, p. 158; *Tribune*, 15 April and 3 June 1959; G.C. Harcourt, *Post-Keynesian Essays in Biography: Portraits of Twentieth-Century Political Economists*, Macmillan, Basingstoke, 1993, p. 127; Harcourt, *Selected Essays on Economic Policy*, p. 56.
27 *Canberra Times*, 6 June 1959.
28 *Tribune*, 10 June 1959.
29 Hagan, *The History of the A.C.T.U.*, pp. 294–95; D'Alpuget, *Robert J. Hawke*, pp. 84–86; D'Alpuget, *Mediator*, p. 161.

30 Hawke, *The Hawke Memoirs*, pp. 39–40.
31 Author interview with Ralph Willis.
32 Harding, *Always in Need of Reform*, p. 104; *West Australian*, 12 March 1959.
33 Hawke, *My Own Life*, p. 80.
34 Hawke, *The Hawke Memoirs*, p. 39; Hagan, *The History of the A.C.T.U.*, pp. 295–96; D'Alpuget, *Robert J. Hawke*, p. 86; Letter, Harold Souter to ACTU officers and secretaries of affiliated unions, 13 April 1960, and 'Annual Leave Judgment', Memo by Hawke, 21 December 1960, along with other documents in N21/1429, ACTU Papers, NBAC.
35 D'Alpuget, *Robert J. Hawke*, pp. 96–97; Marjorie Harper, 'Sir Douglas Berry Copland', *Australian Dictionary of Biography*, Vol. 13; Hagan, *The History of the A.C.T.U.*, pp. 296–98.
36 D'Alpuget, *Robert J. Hawke*, pp. 96–99; Marjorie Harper, 'Sir Douglas Berry Copland', *Australian Dictionary of Biography*, Vol. 13; Hagan, *The History of the A.C.T.U.*, pp. 296–98; D'Alpuget, *Mediator*, pp. 162–67.
37 Author interview with Ralph Willis; Interview with Patsy Zeffel by D'Alpuget, c. 1980, MS 7348/2/12, D'Alpuget Papers, NLA; Hawke, *My Own Life*, pp. 82–83; D'Alpuget, *Robert J. Hawke*, p. 88; Bramston, *Bob Hawke*, p. 107.
38 Hawke, *The Hawke Memoirs*, p. 40.
39 'Social and Political Aspects of Australia's Economic Growth', paper presented by Hawke at the Summer School of the Australian Institute of Political Science, January 1962, and other documents in N21/968, ACTU Papers, NBAC; for the main papers presented at the summer school, together with Hawke's response, see John Wilkes (ed.), *Economic Growth in Australia*, Angus & Robertson, Sydney, 1962.
40 D'Alpuget, *Robert J. Hawke*, p. 99; John Button, *As It Happened*, Text Publishing, Melbourne, 1998, p. 117.

Chapter Nine: 1962–1964
1 A.W. Martin, *Robert Menzies: A Life*, Vol. 2, Melbourne University Press, Melbourne, 1999, pp. 432–43; Gavin Souter, *Acts of Parliament*, Melbourne University Press, Melbourne, 1988, pp. 448–49.
2 A.A. Calwell, *Be Just and Fear Not*, Lloyd O'Neil, Melbourne, 1972, pp. 204–11; Martin, *Robert Menzies*, Vol. 2, pp. 430–36; Scott Prasser et al. (eds), *The Menzies Era*, Hale & Iremonger, Sydney, 1995, pp. 60–68; Ross McMullin, *The Light on the Hill*, Oxford University Press, Melbourne, 1991, pp. 290–92; Souter, *Acts of Parliament*, pp. 448–50.
3 Hagan, *The History of the A.C.T.U.*, pp. 300–302; Hurst, *Hawke*, pp. 36–37; Stevens, 'Inflation and Disinflation in Australia: 1950–91', pp. 5–10; D'Alpuget, *Robert J. Hawke*, p. 99.
4 Author interview with Ralph Willis; Hurst, *Hawke*, pp. 37–38; *Herald*, 14 August 1935; D'Alpuget, *Robert J. Hawke*, p. 114; for a profile of Polites, see *Age*, 23 August 1971.
5 Author interview with Ralph Willis.
6 Ibid.; Interview with Bill Crowley by D'Alpuget, n.d., MS 7348/3/15, D'Alpuget Papers, NLA.
7 Hawke, *My Own Life*, pp. 93, 97.
8 As the author discovered during the research for this biography, the presence of other women in the house when Hazel was away was common knowledge in the street; Interview with Patsy Zeffel by D'Alpuget, c. 1980, MS 7348/2/12, D'Alpuget Papers, NLA. As for Beverley Richards, it seems that the end of her relationship with Hawke coincided with the end of her career on the stage. Although she worked as a choreographer and ballet teacher, a search of the Australian Live Performance Database found no mention of her being involved in a live performance between May 1962, when she appeared in an ABC Television production of *Lola Montez*, and August 1992, when she was in her early sixties and was listed as a dancer with the Australian Ballet production of the *Nutcracker*. For details, see www.ausstage.edu.au.
9 Hawke, *My Own Life*, pp. 88–89; Pieters-Hawke, *Hazel*, pp. 91–94; Interview with Hazel Hawke by D'Alpuget, undated, MS 7348/3/16, D'Alpuget Papers, NLA.
10 Author interview with Ralph Willis; Death Certificate of Robert James Hawke, 2 August 1963; Hawke, *My Own Life*, pp. 89–93; Pieters-Hawke, *Hazel*, pp. 93–96.
11 Hawke, *My Own Life*, pp. 93–94; Pieters-Hawke, *Hazel*, p. 89.
12 Daniel Oakman, *Oppy: The Life of Sir Hubert Opperman*, Melbourne Books, Melbourne, 2018, p. 258.

13 D'Alpuget, *Robert J. Hawke*, pp. 100–104; Pieters-Hawke, *Hazel*, pp. 97–98; Hawke, *My Own Life*, pp. 94–95; Hawke, *The Hawke Memoirs*, p. 41; Author interview with Ralph Willis; *Geelong Advertiser*, 9 November 1963.
14 H.H. Opperman, *Pedals, Politics and People*, Haldane Publishing, Sydney, 1977, pp. 376–78; Hawke, *The Hawke Memoirs*, p. 41; D'Alpuget, *Robert J. Hawke*, pp. 102–109; Author interview with Ralph Willis; 'Sir Roderick William Miller', *Australian Dictionary of Biography*, Vol. 15; Interview with Gordon Scholes by Gary Sturgess, August 2010, Oral History Collection, NLA; *Geelong Advertiser*, 9 November 1963; D'Alpuget interview with George Poyser, 11 October 1980, MS 7348/3/14, NLA.
15 In September 1964, Beverley Richards was reported to have choreographed a ballet for the Rex Reid Dance Players at the Emerald Hill Theatre. *Australian Jewish News*, 8 June 1962, 25 September 1964. D'Alpuget, *Robert J. Hawke*, pp. 104–107; Pieters-Hawke, *Hazel*, pp. 98–99; Hawke, *My Own Life*, pp. 94–96; Author interview with Ralph Willis; Interview with Patsy Zeffel by D'Alpuget, c. 1980, MS 7348/2/12, and Interview with Don Dunstan by D'Alpuget, March 1980, MS 7348/3/15, D'Alpuget Papers, NLA; McMullin, *The Light on the Hill*, p. 295; Oakman, *Oppy*, pp. 262–67; *Geelong Advertiser*, 12, 14, 15, 16 and 19 November 1963.
16 Martin, *Robert Menzies*, Vol. 2, pp. 474–76; Interview with Gordon Scholes by Gary Sturgess, August 2010, Oral History Collection, NLA.
17 Opperman, *Pedals, Politics and People*, p. 378; D'Alpuget, *Robert J. Hawke*, pp. 105–108; *Geelong Advertiser*, 21 and 22 November 1963.
18 *New York Times*, 19 September 1963; Gregory Pemberton, *All the Way: Australia's Road to Vietnam*, Allen & Unwin, Sydney, 1987, Chapters 5–6; David Goldsworthy (ed.), *Facing North: A Century of Australian Engagement with Asia*, Vol. 1, Melbourne University Press, Melbourne, 2001, Chapter 7; Souter, *Acts of Parliament*, pp. 454–55; *Geelong Advertiser*, 14 November 1963.
19 Colm Kiernan, *Calwell*, Nelson, Melbourne, 1978, pp. 240–43; McMullin, *The Light on the Hill*, pp. 293–95; D'Alpuget, *Robert J. Hawke*, pp. 107–108; Pieters-Hawke, *Hazel*, p. 98; *Geelong Advertiser*, 22, 25, 27, 28 and 30 November 1963; Interview with Gordon Scholes by Gary Sturgess, August 2010, NLA.
20 Oakman, *Oppy*, pp. 267–68; Hawke, *The Hawke Memoirs*, p. 41; D'Alpuget, *Robert J. Hawke*, p. 103; Pieters-Hawke, *Hazel*, p. 99; Martin, *Robert Menzies*, Vol. 2, pp. 471–79; *Geelong Advertiser*, 2 and 12 December 196322
21 Ibid.
22 Hurst, *Hawke*, pp. 37–41; Hagan, *The History of the A.C.T.U.*, pp. 302–304; D'Alpuget, *Mediator*, pp. 187–98; D'Alpuget, *Robert J. Hawke*, pp. 109–16.
23 Author interview with Rev. Geoffrey Beck, who kindly showed me the family guest book, which Hawke and his mother signed on 1 August 1962; D'Alpuget, *Robert J. Hawke*, p. 99; Hawke, *My Own Life*, p. 107.
24 D'Alpuget, *Robert J. Hawke*, pp. 99–100; Hurst, *Hawke*, pp. 33–34; Interview with Harold Souter by D'Alpuget, 27 June 1980, MS 7348/3/16, D'Alpuget Papers, NLA; Author interview with Ralph Willis.
25 Peter Love, 'Albert Ernest Monk', *Australian Dictionary of Biography*, Vol. 15; D'Alpuget, *Robert J. Hawke*, pp. 92–93; Author interview with Ralph Willis.
26 A note from the Prague hospital where Albert Monk had been treated for several days in April 1959 can be found in Hawke's papers. It's not clear when it came into Hawke's possession, but he may have found it in Monk's files after taking over from him as president. Note by Dr Jindrich Karpisek, 22 April 1959, RH 6/2/5, BHPML.
27 D'Alpuget, *Robert J. Hawke*, p. 100; Hurst, *Hawke*, p. 34. In 1961, Souter had prevented Hawke from writing an article for the Australian Institute of Political Science on the unemployment problem. For this correspondence and that with Wyndham, see documents in N21/968 and 975, ACTU Papers, NBAC.
28 Hawke, *My Own Life*, p. 97.
29 Notes of an interview with Hazel Hawke by D'Alpuget, undated, MS 7348/3/16, D'Alpuget Papers, NLA.
30 Pieters-Hawke, *Hazel*, p. 104; Hawke, *My Own Life*, p. 98; D'Alpuget, *Robert J. Hawke*, p. 117.

Chapter Ten: 1965–1966

1. Martin, *Robert Menzies*, Vol. 2, pp. 495–97; Pemberton, *All the Way*, pp. 209–12; Goldsworthy (ed.), *Facing North*, pp. 286–93.
2. McMullin, *The Light on the Hill*, pp. 300–301.
3. Martin, *Robert Menzies*, Vol. 2, pp. 499–501; 'A.L.P. Telecast – Senate Election 1964', and 'Senate Election 1964 – G.T.V. 9', undated election telecasts by Hawke, RH 6/8/56-68, BHPML.
4. Author interview with Ralph Willis; D'Alpuget, *Robert J. Hawke*, pp. 94–95.
5. Hagan, *The History of the A.C.T.U.*, pp. 304–306; D'Alpuget, *Robert J. Hawke*, pp. 94–95, 119–23; D'Alpuget, *Mediator*, pp. 199–213; Author interview with Ralph Willis.
6. Author interview with Ralph Willis; Hurst, *Hawke*, pp. 44–45.
7. D'Alpuget, *Mediator*, pp. 208–10; Hagan, *The History of the A.C.T.U.*, pp. 304–306; Hurst, *Hawke*, pp. 42–45; Press statement by the ACTU, ACSPA and CPSO, 12 July 1965, RH 6/10/84, BHPML.
8. Hawke, *The Hawke Memoirs*, pp. 41–42; D'Alpuget, *Robert J. Hawke*, pp. 119–23; Hagan, *The History of the A.C.T.U.*, pp. 304–306.
9. Pieters-Hawke, pp. 103–104; Hawke, *My Own Life*, pp. 98–99; D'Alpuget, *Robert J. Hawke*, p. 118; for some details of Hawke's libel actions, see notes by D'Alpuget in MS 7348/1/5, D'Alpuget Papers, NLA.
10. Author interview with Ralph Willis; Author interview with Don McIntosh; See also interview with Col Cunningham by D'Alpuget, 4 April 1981. MS 7348/2/12, D'Alpuget Papers, NLA; Roy Higgins (with Terry Vine), *The Professor*, Caribou Publications, Melbourne, 1984, p. 124.
11. *Industrial Newsletter*, 21 September 1965, RH 6/16/154, Hawke Papers, BHPML; D'Alpuget, *Robert J. Hawke*, pp. 127–29; Hagan, *The History of the A.C.T.U.*, pp. 261–62.
12. D'Alpuget, *Robert J. Hawke*, p. 126.
13. D'Alpuget, *Robert J. Hawke*, pp. 125–27.
14. Author interview with Ralph Willis.
15. Ibid.
16. Reminiscence of Paul Munro, in Sue Pieters-Hawke (ed.), *Remembering Bob*, Allen & Unwin, Sydney, 2019, p. 17.
17. Martin, *Robert Menzies*, Vol. 2, pp. 463, 476, 530–31.
18. Handwritten memo, Hawke to Albert Monk, undated, c. 1965, RH 6/14/139, Hawke Papers, BHPML.
19. D'Alpuget, *Robert J. Hawke*, pp. 129–31; Hawke, *The Hawke Memoirs*, p. 42; Hagan, *The History of the A.C.T.U.*, p. 307; Hurst, *Hawke*, pp. 47–49; D'Alpuget, *Mediator*, pp. 216–17; Author interview with Ralph Willis.
20. Hawke, *The Hawke Memoirs*, pp. 42–44, 47; D'Alpuget, *Robert J. Hawke*, pp. 129–31; Hurst, *Hawke*, p. 49.
21. Hawke, *The Hawke Memoirs*, pp. 43–44; D'Alpuget, *Robert J. Hawke*, pp. 120, 129–35; Interview with Terry Winter by D'Alpuget, 29 March 1976, MS 7348, Box 4, Folder 22, D'Alpuget Papers, NLA.
22. Hagan, *The History of the A.C.T.U.*, pp. 307–308; D'Alpuget, *Robert J. Hawke*, p. 136.
23. Hawke, *The Hawke Memoirs*, pp. 44–5.
24. *South Pacific Post*, 16 June 1965; Press statement by J.G. Smith, Public Service Association, 15 June 1965, and Letter, Smith to Albert Monk, 15 June 1965, RH 6/10/85, BHPML; Hawke, *The Hawke Memoirs*, p. 44; Pieters-Hawke (ed.), *Remembering Bob*, pp. 10–18; D'Alpuget, *Robert J. Hawke*, pp. 136–50; Michael Somare, *Sana: An Autobiography of Michael Somare*, Niugini Press, Port Moresby, 1975, p. 48; Albert Maori Kiki, *Kiki: Ten Thousand Years in a Lifetime*, Cheshire, Melbourne, 1968, pp. 144–50, 181–82; Author interview with Ralph Willis.
25. Hawke, *My Own Life*, pp. 100–105; Pieters-Hawke (ed.), *Remembering Bob*, pp. 14–15; Pieters-Hawke, *Hazel*, pp. 108–10; D'Alpuget, *Robert J. Hawke*, pp. 136–50.
26. Hawke, *The Hawke Memoirs*, p. 45; D'Alpuget, *Robert J. Hawke*, pp. 137–39; *Guardian*, 12 September 2017.

Endnotes 379

Chapter Eleven: 1967–1969

1. Martin, *Robert Menzies*, Vol. 2, pp. 541–46; Souter, *Acts of Parliament*, pp. 458–60; Tavan, *The Long, Slow Death of White Australia*, pp. 156–57; Robin Gerster and Jan Bassett, *Seizures of Youth: The Sixties and Australia*, Hyland House, Melbourne, 1991, pp. 110–11.
2. McMullin, *The Light on the Hill*, pp. 313–17; Hurst, *Hawke*, pp. 46–47.
3. Interview with Gough Whitlam by D'Alpuget, 26 June 1981, MS 7348/2/12, D'Alpuget Papers, NLA; Hurst, *Hawke*, pp. 53–54; McMullin, *The Light on the Hill*, pp. 317–18; Jenny Hocking, *Gough Whitlam*, Vol. I, Miegunyah Press, Melbourne, 2008, pp. 292–93; Interview with Gordon Scholes by Gary Sturgess, August 2010, NLA.
4. Letter, F.E. Carr to Hawke, 15 August 1965, RH 6/10/84, BHPML.
5. Author interview with Ralph Willis; Hurst, *Hawke*, p. 54.
6. *Australian*, 27 January 1967.
7. D'Alpuget, *Robert J. Hawke*, pp. 80, 155–56; Mark Hearn and Harry Knowles, *One Big Union*, Cambridge University Press, Melbourne, 1996, p. 284; Greg Patmore, 'Tom Nicholson Pearce Dougherty', *Australian Dictionary of Biography*, Vol. 14.
8. Hagan, *The History of the A.C.T.U.*, pp. 309–11; D'Alpuget, *Mediator*, pp. 227–28; Hurst, *Hawke*, pp. 51–52.
9. *Industrial Newsletter*, 21 September 1965, RH 6/16/154, Hawke Papers, BHPML; Hagan, *The History of the A.C.T.U.*, pp. 112–13.
10. Hawke, *My Own Life*, pp. 99–100, 118–19; Pieters-Hawke, *Hazel*, pp. 112–13; Interview by the author with an anonymous informant; D'Alpuget interview with George Poyser, 11 October 1980, MS 7348/3/14, NLA.
11. Pieters-Hawke, *Hazel*, pp. 111–12; Hawke, *My Own Life*, p. 126; D'Alpuget, *Robert J. Hawke*, p. 159; Author interview with Ralph Willis.
12. Mark Hearn and Harry Knowles, *One Big Union*, Cambridge University Press, Melbourne, 1996, p. 284; R.M. Martin, 'The ACTU Congress of 1967', *Journal of Industrial Relations*, September 1967; Hagan, *The History of the A.C.T.U.*, p. 270; Hurst, *Hawke*, pp. 55–59; D'Alpuget, *Robert J. Hawke*, pp. 154–57.
13. Official Report of the ALP Conference, Adelaide, 31 July 1967, PLC; Hocking, *Gough Whitlam*, Vol. 1, pp. 299–302.
14. Hawke, *My Own Life*, pp. 108–109, 113; Pieters-Hawke, *Hazel*, pp. 110–12, 145; Pieters-Hawke (ed.), *Remembering Bob*, pp. xx–xxii.
15. D'Alpuget, *Mediator*, pp. 218–25; Hurst, *Hawke*, pp. 50–51.
16. Hawke, *The Hawke Memoirs*, pp. 45–48; D'Alpuget, *Robert J. Hawke*, pp. 159–60; Hurst, *Hawke*, pp. 64–66; Hawke, *My Own Life*, pp. 105–106.
17. Hurst, *Hawke*, pp. 64–74; D'Alpuget, *Robert J. Hawke*, pp. 163–69; Hawke, *The Hawke Memoirs*, pp. 47–50.
18. K.W. Hince, 'Australian Trade Unionism 1968–9', *Journal of Industrial Relations*, September 1969; D'Alpuget, *Robert J. Hawke*, pp. 160–62; Hurst, *Hawke*, pp. 72–74; Hagan, *The History of the A.C.T.U.*, pp. 269–70; John Merritt, 'The Trade Union Leader Who Went to Gaol', *Canberra Historical Journal*, September 2007.
19. Hawke, *My Own Life*, p. 106; D'Alpuget, *Robert J. Hawke*, pp. 166–69; Hurst, *Hawke*, pp. 75–77; R.M. Martin, 'The A.C.T.U. Congress of 1969', *Journal of Industrial Relations*, Vol. 11, No. 3, 1969, pp. 261–62.
20. D'Alpuget, *Robert J. Hawke*, pp. 168–71; Hurst, *Hawke*, pp. 76–79; R.M. Martin, 'The A.C.T.U. Congress of 1969', pp. 262–64; Author interview with Ralph Willis.
21. Hawke, *My Own Life*, p. 106; Hurst, *Hawke*, pp. 78–79; D'Alpuget, *Robert J. Hawke*, pp. 170–71; R.M. Martin, 'The A.C.T.U. Congress of 1969', pp. 263–64.
22. Ian Hancock, *John Gorton*, Hodder, Sydney, 2002, pp. 33–34, 236–39; Souter, *Acts of Parliament*, pp. 485–86; Patrick Mullins, *Tiberius with a Telephone*, Scribe, Melbourne, 2018, pp. 286–88.
23. Hocking, *Gough Whitlam*, Vol. 1, pp. 333–35; Hancock, *John Gorton*, pp. 234–40; Mullins, *Tiberius with a Telephone*, pp. 284–88.
24. Peter Howson, *The Life of Politics: The Howson Diaries*, Viking Press, Melbourne, 1984, p. 562; Mullins, *Tiberius with a Telephone*, pp. 293–300.
25. John Faulkner and Stuart Macintyre (eds), *True Believers*, Allen & Unwin, Sydney, 2001, p. 106; David Day, *Paul Keating: The Biography*, HarperCollins, Sydney, 2015, Chapter 7.

PART FOUR: PRESIDENT
Chapter Twelve: 1970–1971

1. *Age*, 2 April 1970.
2. Interview with Bob Hawke on behalf of Phillip Pendal, BL; Minutes of the Commonwealth Labor Advisory Committee, 15 and 16 January 1970, N21/1179, NBAC; *Australian Financial Review*, 29 September 1971; *Bulletin*, 18 April 1970; Hancock, *John Gorton*, p. 310.
3. Hurst, *Hawke*, p. 84; *Tribune*, 11 March 1970; Drew Cottle, 'The University of Western Australia Labour Club, 1925–1949: A Nursery of Political Radicals?', *Critical Studies in Education*, Vol. 40, No. 1, 2010, pp. 44–45. The Blacksmiths and Boilermakers' Union had paid for Kiki to attend the ACTU Congress in 1969. *Papua New Guinea Post-Courier*, 14 October 1969 and 27 February 1970. Margo Beasley, *Wharfies: A History of the Waterside Workers' Federation of Australia*, Halstead Press, Sydney, 1996, p. 235.
4. Paul Strangio, *Keeper of the Faith: A Biography of Jim Cairns*, Melbourne University Press, Melbourne, 2002, pp. 208–209.
5. D'Alpuget, *Robert J. Hawke*, pp. 172–73; Hurst, *Hawke*, pp. 84–85; *Tribune*, 11 March 1970; Saunders, 'The Trade Unions in Australia and Opposition to Vietnam and Conscription: 1965–73', *Labour History*, No. 43, November 1982.
6. *Age*, 24 August 2013.
7. Interview with D'Alpuget by Mia Freeman, www.mamamia.com.au/podcast/blanche-dalpuget-interview, 2018; Blanche d'Alpuget, *On Longing*, Melbourne University Press, Melbourne, 2008, pp. 15, 21; Bramston, *Bob Hawke*, pp. 209–10; Graham Little, *Speaking for Myself*, McPhee Gribble, Melbourne, 1989, pp. 167–68; Transcript of 'Just Call Me Bob', *Australian Story*, ABC TV, 10 November 2014; *Age*, 20 March 1982.
8. D'Alpuget, *Robert J. Hawke*, pp. 220–21.
9. Author interview with Ralph Willis; *Sun*, 24 July 1970; undated newspaper cutting c. 1970, Newspaper Cutting Book, Hazel Hawke Papers, JCPML.
10. Button, *As It Happened*, pp. 138–42.
11. McMullin, *The Light on the Hill*, pp. 327–32; Daniel Connell, *The Confessions of Clyde Cameron, 1913–1990*, ABC Books, Sydney, 1990, p. 194; Judith Walker, 'Restructuring the A.L.P. – N.S.W. and Victoria', *Australian Quarterly*, Vol. 43, No. 4, December 1971. For a detailed history of the intervention, see John Daniel Fitzgerald, 'Federal Intervention in the Victorian Branch of the Australian Labor Party, 1970', MA Thesis, La Trobe University, 1975.
12. Hurst, *Hawke*, p. 83; Pieters-Hawke, *Remembering Bob*, p. 15; *Sunday Australian*, 21 March 1971.
13. Handwritten notes by Hawke, undated, c. 1970, N68/1321, ACTU Papers, NBAC; Author interview with Ralph Willis.
14. Hancock, *John Gorton*, pp. 295, 299–300; Hocking, *Gough Whitlam*, Vol. 1, p. 365; Frank Crowley, *Tough Times: Australia in the Seventies*, Heinemann, Melbourne, 1986, p. 60.
15. D'Alpuget, *Robert J. Hawke*, p. 223–24.
16. *Sun*, 24 July 1970; Interview with Peter Redlich by D'Alpuget, 30 March 1981, MS 7348/2/12, D'Alpuget Papers, NLA; Peter Redlich's political and legal relationship with Hawke is briefly explored in Philip Chubb and Barry Donovan, *Chance Is Worth a Thousand Plans: Peter Redlich and the Creation of a National Law Firm*, Holding, Redlich & Co., Melbourne, 2013.
17. Hawke, *My Own Life*, pp. 108–109; Pieters-Hawke, *Hazel*, pp. 119–20.
18. Pieters-Hawke (ed.), *Remembering Bob*, pp. 60–61, 100–102; Hawke, *My Own Life*, pp. 10, 113; Shane Warne, *No Spin*, Ebury Press, Sydney, 2018, p. 22.
19. Hawke, *My Own Life*, pp. 107–10; Bill Guy, *A Life on the Left: A Biography of Clyde Cameron*, Wakefield Press, Adelaide, 1999, p. 235.
20. Hawke, *The Hawke Memoirs*, p. 40; D'Alpuget, *Robert J. Hawke*, p. 194.
21. *Canberra Times*, 13 November 1994; Hawke, *My Own Life*, pp. 100, 105, 118, 121–22; Pieters-Hawke, *Hazel*, pp. 102, 146, 149–50. According to Hazel, Hawke's reading of these feminist books did not result in any 'metamorphosis' in his attitudes, just 'a continuation of small behavioural changes'. Note by Hazel on the draft of D'Alpuget's biography, 24 February 1982, MS 7348/3/19, D'Alpuget Papers, NLA; Vera Wasowski, *Vera: My Story*, Black Inc., Melbourne, 2015, p. 194.

22 D'Alpuget, *Robert J. Hawke*, pp. 179–80; Hurst, *Hawke*, pp. 95–96; Hawke, *The Hawke Memoirs*, p. 57.
23 *Bulletin*, 6 March 1971; *Sunday Australian*, 21 March 1971; *Nation*, 3 April 1971.
24 *Age*, 16 and 18 March 1971; *Australian Financial Review*, 19 March 1971.
25 *Sunday Australian*, 21 March 1971; *Herald*, 19 March 1971; Hawke, *The Hawke Memoirs*, pp. 56–58; D'Alpuget, *Robert J. Hawke*, pp. 179–86; Hurst, *Hawke*, pp. 95–98, 110.
26 *Age*, 19 March 1971; undated newspaper cutting c. 19 March 1971, Newspaper Cutting Book, Hazel Hawke Papers, JCPML.
27 *Woman's Day*, 19 April 1971; *Age*, 3 August 2010.
28 *Sun*, 24 July 1970, 4 May 1971; *Farrago*, 7 August 1970; *Time*, 24 May 1971.
29 *Papua New Guinea Post-Courier*, 7 and 27 April 1971; *Canberra Times*, 9 and 27 April, 7, 14 May, 6 July 1971; *Tribune*, 14 April 1971; For a good overview of the anti-Springbok movement, see Stuart Harris, *Political Football: The Springbok Tour of Australia, 1971*, Gold Star Publications, Melbourne, 1972, pp. 216–24.
30 *Canberra Times*, 27 April, 14 May 1971; D'Alpuget, *Robert J. Hawke*, pp. 190–92; Pieters-Hawke, *Remembering Bob*, pp. 44–46.
31 Hawke, *The Hawke Memoirs*, pp. 58–59; Mullins, *Tiberius with a Telephone*, pp. 416–21; *Age*, 28 June 1971; *Sun*, 1 June 1971; *Sunday Australian*, 6 June 1971; D'Alpuget, *Robert J. Hawke*, pp. 190–92; Pieters-Hawke, *Remembering Bob*, pp. 44–46; Harris, *Political Football*, pp. 62–63.
32 *Canberra Times*, 23, 24, 25 and 26 June 1971; *Age*, 25 and 28 June 1971; *Herald*, 28 June 1971; *Australian*, 28 June 1971; undated newspaper cutting c. June 1971, Newspaper Cutting Book, Hazel Hawke Papers, JCPML; Pieters-Hawke, *Hazel*, pp. 127–31; D'Alpuget, *Robert J. Hawke*, pp. 189–94; Hawke, *My Own Life*, pp. 110–12.

Chapter Thirteen: 1971–1972
1 D'Alpuget, *Robert J. Hawke*, pp. 14–15; Hurst, *Hawke*, pp. 99, 102–104; For Hawke's itinerary in Israel, see MS 7348/3/14, D'Alpuget Papers, NLA.
2 Hawke, *The Hawke Memoirs*, pp. 72–75; Pieters-Hawke, *Hazel*, 130–31; Hurst, *Hawke*, pp. 102–103; D'Alpuget, *Robert J. Hawke*, pp. 192, 246–54; Yacov Livne and Yossi Goldstein, '"Let My People Go": The Beginnings of Israel's Operation to Open Soviet Immigration Gates', *Soviet and Post-Soviet Review*, No. 47, 2020.
3 T.H. Rigby, 'The Soviet Politburo: A Comparative Profile 1951–71', *Soviet Studies*, July 1972, p. 11; Hawke, *The Hawke Memoirs*, p. 77; Pieters-Hawke, *Hazel*, p. 131; Hurst, *Hawke*, pp. 105–106; D'Alpuget, *Robert J. Hawke*, pp. 254–57; 'Report on Visit U.S.S.R., 21.7.71–24.7.71', by Hawke, MS 7348/3/14, D'Alpuget Papers, NLA.
4 Hawke, *The Hawke Memoirs*, p. 77; Pieters-Hawke, *Hazel*, p. 131; Hurst, *Hawke*, pp. 105–106; D'Alpuget, *Robert J. Hawke*, pp. 254–57.
5 Bob Hawke, 'Masada, Moscow and Melbourne', 6 October 1971, aild.org.au.
6 Hawke, *The Hawke Memoirs*, pp. 58–59; Harris, *Political Football*.
7 Philip Bentley, 'Australian Trade Unionism, 1970–71', *Journal of Industrial Relations*, December 1971, p. 413; *Australian*, 29 June 1971; D'Alpuget, *Robert J. Hawke*, p. 194.
8 D'Alpuget, *Robert J. Hawke*, p. 178; Hagan, *The History of the A.C.T.U.*, pp. 273–75; Hurst, *Hawke*, p. 107–109; *Tribune*, 8 September 1971; R.M. Martin, 'The A.C.T.U. Congress of 1971', *Journal of Industrial Relations*, December 1971; *Canberra Times*, 3 September 1971.
9 *Farrago*, 7 August 1970; Notes of an interview with 'Nugget' Coombs, 20 August 1976, MS 7348, Box 4, Folder 22, D'Alpuget Papers, NLA.
10 D'Alpuget, *Robert J. Hawke*, pp. 194–98; Pieters-Hawke, *Hazel*, pp. 133–35; *Australian*, 29 June 1971; *Woman's Day*, 19 April 1971. During the 1970s, Hawke was out of the office for up to 198 days each year, whether interstate, overseas, on holidays or away ill. For the details of his time away, see figures provided by Jean Sinclair to D'Alpuget, 23 June 1981, MS 7348/3/17, D'Alpuget Papers, NLA.
11 Pieters-Hawke (ed.), *Remembering Bob*, p. 41; Interview with Col Cunningham by D'Alpuget, 4 April 1981, MS 7348/2/12, D'Alpuget Papers, NLA; D'Alpuget, *Robert J. Hawke*, pp. 314–15.
12 David Hickie, *The Prince and the Premier*, Angus & Robertson, Sydney, 1985, pp. 113–14; For the details of Saffron's life and criminal enterprises, see Tony Reeves, *Mr Sin: The Abe Saffron Dossier*, Allen & Unwin, Sydney, 2007, and Alan Saffron, *Gentle Satan: My*

Father, Abe Saffron, Penguin, Melbourne, 2008, pp. 104–108, 110–11, 130; For a more sympathetic view of Saffron, see Duncan McNab, *The Usual Suspect: The Life of Abe Saffron*, Macmillan, Sydney, 2005; Louis Nowra, *Kings Cross: A Biography*, NewSouth Publishing, Sydney, 2013, p. 295; Biographical Details, Mr Eddie Kornhauser, compiled 14 February 1981, MS 7348/2/12, D'Alpuget Papers, NLA; *Australian Financial Review*, 15 December 1989, 10 February 2006; *Truth*, 30 September 1951; *Canberra Times*, 22 June 1991; *Sydney Morning Herald*, 14 March 2021.

13 D'Alpuget, *Robert J. Hawke*, pp. 179–87, 238–39; Interview with Peter Redlich by D'Alpuget, 30 March 1981, MS 7348/2/12, and Interview with Harold Souter by D'Alpuget, 27 June 1980, MS 7348/3/16, D'Alpuget Papers, NLA.

14 Interview with Peter Abeles by Daniel Connell, 1 January 1985, Oral History Collection, NLA; For Claire Dan's account of her life with Peter Abeles, see Claire Dan, *Ups and Downs*, Wild and Woolley, Sydney, 2008; D'Alpuget, *Robert J. Hawke*, pp. 23–40; Saffron, *Gentle Satan*, p. 99.

15 Richard Hall, *Disorganised Crime*, University of Queensland Press, Brisbane, 1986, pp. 92–93, 96–99, 102; Hickie, *The Prince and the Premier*, pp. 86–87; Tony Reeves, *The Real George Freeman*, Penguin, Melbourne, 2011, pp. 68, 89; Reeves, *Mr Sin*, pp. 216–17; for reminiscences from the former head of the National Crime Authority about the extent of corruption, see Don Stewart, *Recollections of an Unreasonable Man*, ABC Books, Sydney, 2007; Norm Lipson and Adam Walters, *The Accidental Gangster: The Life and Times of Bela Csidei*, Park Street Press, Sydney, 2006, p. 126; *Canberra Times*, 25 April 1967; Bob Bottom, *The Godfather in Australia*, Magistra Publishing, Melbourne, 1979, p. 194; *New York Times*, 28 June 1999; *Wall Street Journal*, 15 April 1983; *Bulletin*, 17 February 1973; 'Hawke and Sir Peter Abeles', Note by D'Alpuget, 2 September 1982, MS 7348/2/12, D'Alpuget Papers, NLA; *Tribune*, 10 September 1980; Caroline Butler-Bowden and Charles Pickett, 'Sir Paul Strasser', *Australian Dictionary of Biography*, Vol. 18.

16 Interview with Peter Abeles by Daniel Connell, 1 January 1985, Oral History Collection, NLA; D'Alpuget, *Robert J. Hawke*, pp. 234–40; Hall, *Disorganised Crime*, pp. 92–93, 96–99, 102; Hickie, *The Prince and the Premier*, pp. 86–87; Reeves, *The Real George Freeman*, pp. 68, 89; *Canberra Times*, 25 April 1967; Bottom, *The Godfather in Australia*, p. 194; *New York Times*, 28 June 1999; *Wall Street Journal*, 15 April 1983; *Bulletin*, 17 February 1973; 'Hawke and Sir Peter Abeles', Note by D'Alpuget, 2 September 1982, MS 7348/2/12, D'Alpuget Papers, NLA; *Tribune*, 10 September 1980; *Times*, 29 June 1999; 'Sir Paul Strasser', *Australian Dictionary of Biography*, Vol. 18.

17 Like Liberal premier Bob Askin, who was closely associated with Abeles and died wealthy, there were rumours about William McKell being paid off by brewers and sly grog traders. He was also a racehorse owner and keen punter who died wealthy. His biographer defended McKell against the charges of corruption, although his association with Abeles would suggest otherwise. It was left to his successor, James McGirr, to establish a royal commission that uncovered widespread corruption involving police and organised criminals, including Abe Saffron. See Christopher Cunneen, *William John McKell*, UNSW Press, Sydney, 2000, pp. 3, 84, 183–88, 213; Evan Whitton, *Can of Worms II*, Fairfax Library Sydney, 1987, p. 154; D'Alpuget, *Robert J. Hawke*, pp. 236–37; Reeves, *Mr Sin*, pp. 84–91, 143–44; John Pilger, *A Secret Country*, Jonathan Cape, London, 1989, pp. 190–95; Bradley Bowden, *Driving Force: The History of the Transport Workers' Union of Australia 1883–1992*, Allen & Unwin, Sydney, 1993, pp. 145–46; Bradley Bowden, 'The Origins and History of the Transport Workers' Union of Australia 1883–1975', PhD thesis, University of Wollongong, 1991, pp. 234–38, 261–310; *PM*, ABC Radio National, 25 June 1999; Transcript of 'Flying High: Sir Peter Abeles', *Four Corners*, ABC TV, 2 November 1987; Author interview with Marian Wilkinson; *National Times*, 18–24 October and 15–21 November 1985, 7–13 March 1986.

18 Lipson and Walters, *The Accidental Gangster*, pp. 124–27.

19 Jill Margo, *Frank Lowy*, HarperCollins, Sydney, 2000, pp. 284–85; Suzanne Rutland, 'Postwar Jewish Migration and Sydney's Cityscape', *Literature and Aesthetics*, December 2008; *Canberra Times*, 16 June 1972; *Australian Jewish Times*, 12 July 1973; *Bulletin*, 24 February, 3 March and 13 October 1973.

20 Bramston, *Bob Hawke*, p. 221; Graham Richardson, *Whatever It Takes*, Bantam, Sydney, 1994, p. 104; George Freeman, *George Freeman: An Autobiography*, George Freeman, Sydney, 1988, p. 184; Reeves, *The Real George Freeman*, p. 143; *Bulletin*, 13 October 1973.
21 D'Alpuget, *Robert J. Hawke*, pp. 234–32; Hagan, *The History of the A.C.T.U.*, pp. 381–83; see documents in MS 7348/1/1, D'Alpuget Papers, NLA; Press releases by R.J. Hawke, N68/542/79/664, and documents in N68/924, ACTU Papers, NBAC; Author interview with Neil Mitchell; *Australian*, 12 April and 30 July 1971; *Sun*, 28 August 1971.
22 Bramston, *Bob Hawke*, pp. 221–22; *Age*, 3 August 2010.
23 Pieters-Hawke, *Hazel*, p. 133.
24 D'Alpuget, *Robert J. Hawke*, pp. 194–98.
25 D'Alpuget, *Robert J. Hawke*, pp. 165, 352; Pieters-Hawke (ed.), *Remembering Bob*, p. 41; Zelda D'Aprano, *Zelda: The Becoming of a Woman*, Visa, Melbourne, 1977, pp. 115–21; Author interview with Ralph Willis; *Australian*, 29 June 1971; *Woman's Day*, 19 April 1971.
26 D'Alpuget, *Robert J. Hawke*, pp. 165, 352; Pieters-Hawke (ed.), *Remembering Bob*, p. 41; D'Aprano, *Zelda*, pp. 115–21; Author interview with Ralph Willis; *Australian*, 29 June 1971; *Woman's Day*, 19 April 1971.
27 Leunig's cartoon can be found reprinted in Gerster and Bassett, *Seizures of Youth*, p. 175; Hocking, *Gough Whitlam*, Vol. 1, pp. 371–80; Hagan, *The History of the A.C.T.U.*, p. 182.
28 Mullins, *Tiberius with a Telephone*, pp. 524–29; Hurst, *Hawke*, pp. 123–30; Hawke, *The Hawke Memoirs*, pp. 59–61; Hagan, *The History of the A.C.T.U.*, p. 281; *Australian*, 28 July 1972; *Age*, 31 July 1972; *Canberra Times*, 25 August 1972.
29 Author interview with John Stone. A year earlier, the rankings had been reversed, with McMahon on 55 per cent, Whitlam on 45 per cent and Hawke on 42 per cent. *Canberra Times*, 7 March and 14 August 1972.
30 *Canberra Times*, 31 August 1972; Hocking, *Gough Whitlam*, Vol. 1, pp. 382, 387.
31 *Canberra Times*, 31 August, 13 and 30 September, 5, 6 and 11 October 1972; *Sun*, 14 September 1972; *Age*, 14 September 1972; *Herald*, 14 September 1972.
32 *Canberra Times*, 20 June 1972; Graham Freudenberg, *A Certain Grandeur*, Penguin, Melbourne, 2009, pp. 280–82.
33 Hocking, *Gough Whitlam*, Vol. 1, pp. 384–96; Tom Uren, *Straight Left*, Random House Australia, Sydney, 1994, pp. 219–20; Mullins, *Tiberius with a Telephone*, pp. 560, 566–87; McMullin, *The Light on the Hill*, pp. 336–37.
34 Laurie Oakes and David Solomon, *The Making of an Australian Prime Minister*, Cheshire, Melbourne, 1973, pp. 164–65; Uren, *Straight Left*, p. 219; *Canberra Times*, 14 and 18 November 1972; Letter, Clyde Cameron to Joseph Cahill, 27 November 1972, Selected letters by Clyde Cameron, Vol. 1, MS 4614, NLA.
35 *Canberra Times*, 22 November 1972; Hurst, *Hawke*, pp. 130–32; Anne Longmire, *St. Kilda: The Show Goes On*, Hudson, Melbourne, 1989, p. 241; Hawke, *My Own Life*, pp. 115–17; Jenny Hocking, *Gough Whitlam*, Vol. II, Miegunyah Press, Melbourne, 2012, pp. 1–5; Hawke, *The Hawke Memoirs*, p. 61.
36 Hocking, *Gough Whitlam*, Vol. II, pp. 1–5; *Age*, 4 December 1972.

Chapter Fourteen: 1973–1974
1 Hocking, *Gough Whitlam*, Vol. II, pp. 3–26; Crowley, *Tough Times*, pp. 79–80; Malcolm Saunders, 'The ALP's Response to the Anti-Vietnam War Movement: 1965–73', *Labour History*, No. 44, May 1983, p. 89.
2 Hawke, *The Hawke Memoirs*, p. 61.
3 Guy, *A Life on the Left*, p. 254–57; Hagan, *The History of the A.C.T.U.*, pp. 402–403; Connell, *The Confessions of Clyde Cameron*, pp. 201–202.
4 Hawke, *The Hawke Memoirs*, pp. 60–61.
5 Connell, *The Confessions of Clyde Cameron*, pp. 202–203, 209–14; Guy, *A Life on the Left*, Chapters 22–25; Hagan, *The History of the A.C.T.U.*, p. 421.
6 Interview with Jean Sinclair by D'Alpuget, 23 November 1981, MS 7348/3/16, D'Alpuget Papers, NLA.
7 For a history of the green bans, see Meredith Burgmann and Verity Burgmann, *Green Bans, Red Union*, UNSW Press, Sydney, 1988; Philip Bentley, 'Australian Trade Unionism, 1972–73', *Journal of Industrial Relations*, December 1973.

8   Hagan, *The History of the A.C.T.U.*, pp. 414–16.
9   Hocking, *Gough Whitlam*, Vol. II, pp. 78–79; D'Alpuget, *Robert J. Hawke*, pp. 216–22; Richard Broinowski, *Fact or Fission?*, Scribe, Melbourne, 2003, pp. 107–10; Margaret Barrett, 'French Nuclear Testing in the Pacific, 1995–96, and its Fallout for French Australians', *French Australian Review*, No. 44, June 2008, pp. 25–31.
10 D'Alpuget, *Robert J. Hawke*, pp. 216–22; Hurst, *Hawke*, pp. 134–38; Hagan, *The History of the A.C.T.U.*, p. 418.
11 Hurst, *Hawke*, pp. 138–39; Hawke, *The Hawke Memoirs*, pp. 64–65; D'Alpuget, *Robert J. Hawke*, pp. 209, 225–26; *Canberra Times*, 10 July 1973.
12 Hawke, *The Hawke Memoirs*, pp. 64–65; Hurst, *Hawke*, pp. 138–40; D'Alpuget, *Robert J. Hawke*, p. 209.
13 D'Alpuget, *Robert J. Hawke*, p. 176; *Sydney Morning Herald*, 26 October 2015.
14 Interview by D'Alpuget, 31 July 1980, MS 7348/2/12, D'Alpuget Papers, NLA.
15 Interview by D'Alpuget, 31 July 1980, MS 7348/2/12, D'Alpuget Papers, NLA; Hawke, *My Own Life*, pp. 118–19.
16 Letter, D'Alpuget to Hawke, 20 March 1980, MS 7348/3/18, and Note by D'Alpuget on Helga Cammell, undated, MS 7348/3/15, D'Alpuget Papers, NLA; Lynn Milne, *The Clerks*, United Services Union, Sydney, 2008, pp. 210–11; Noel Tennison, *My Spin in PR*, Media Relations Publishing, Melbourne, 2008, pp. 74–76; Noel Tennison, *The Life of the Party*, Primrose Hall Publishing, Brisbane, 2014, pp. 251–53; *Age*, 11 March 1975.
17 Notes of an interview with George Polites by Jim Hagan, MS 7348/4/22, D'Alpuget Papers, NLA.
18 Tim Rowse, *Nugget Coombs: A Reforming Life*, Cambridge University Press, Melbourne, 2002, pp. 295–96; Strangio, *Keeper of the Faith*, pp. 261–65; Hocking, *Gough Whitlam*, Vol. II, pp. 102–05; Hurst, *Hawke*, p. 139; McMullin, *The Light on the Hill*, pp. 346–47; Hagan, *The History of the A.C.T.U.*, pp. 419–20.
19 Interview with Gough Whitlam by D'Alpuget, 26 June 1981, MS 7348/2/12, D'Alpuget, *Robert J. Hawke*, pp. 210–12; D'Alpuget Papers, NLA; *Australian Financial Review*, 4 September 1973.
20 Hocking, *Gough Whitlam*, Vol. II, pp. 100–101; Strangio, *Keeper of the Faith*, pp. 273–74.
21 *Age*, 18 October 1973; *Canberra Times*, 12 November 1973; Hocking, *Gough Whitlam*, Vol. II, pp. 110–11; Hurst, *Hawke*, pp. 146–50.
22 R.M. Martin, 'The A.C.T.U. Congress of 1973', *Journal of Industrial Relations*, December 1973.
23 *Age*, 18 October 1973; *Canberra Times*, 12 November 1973; Hocking, *Gough Whitlam*, Vol. II, pp. 105–106; 110–11; Hurst, *Hawke*, pp. 146–50; McMullin, *The Light on the Hill*, pp. 346–47.
24 Interview with Peter Abeles by D'Alpuget, 24 August 1981, MS 7348/2/12, D'Alpuget Papers, NLA; Hawke, *The Hawke Memoirs*, pp. 76–78.
25 D'Alpuget, *Robert J. Hawke*, pp. 258–62; Hawke, *The Hawke Memoirs*, pp. 76–77.
26 D'Alpuget, *Robert J. Hawke*, pp. 262–63; Hurst, *Hawke*, pp. 144–45; Chanan Reich, 'From "Endemically Pro-Israel" to Unsympathetic: Australia's Middle East Policy, 1967–1972', *Australian Journal of Politics and History*, Vol. 56, No. 4, 2010.
27 Diary entry, 25 November 1973, Hazel Hawke's diary for 1973, JCPML 1271/1-6/5, Hazel Hawke Papers, JCPML.
28 Interview with Peter Abeles by D'Alpuget, 24 August 1981, MS 7348/2/12, Interview with Jean Sinclair by D'Alpuget, 23 November 1981, MS 7348/3/16, D'Alpuget Papers, NLA; Hawke, *The Hawke Memoirs*, pp. 76–78; D'Alpuget, *Robert J. Hawke*, pp. 258–66.
29 Hurst, *Hawke*, pp. 152–53; D'Alpuget, *Robert J. Hawke*, pp. 266–67; Interview of Eddie Kornhauser by D'Alpuget, May 1981, MS 7348/2/12, D'Alpuget Papers, NLA.
30 Hurst, *Hawke*, pp. 145, 152–53; D'Alpuget, *Robert J. Hawke*, pp. 267–70; *Canberra Times*, 25 January 1974; *Bulletin*, 23 February 1974.
31 D'Alpuget, *Robert J. Hawke*, p. 271; Interview by D'Alpuget, 31 July 1980, MS 7348/2/12, D'Alpuget Papers, NLA.
32 Interview by D'Alpuget, 31 July 1980, MS 7348/2/12, D'Alpuget Papers, NLA.
33 Mike Willesee, *Memoirs*, Macmillan, Sydney, 2017, pp. 177–78.
34 *Canberra Times*, 1 April 1974; Willesee, *Memoirs*, pp. 194–95.

35 McMullin, *The Light on the Hill*, pp. 350–52; Guy, *A Life on the Left*, 289–91; Crowley, *Tough Times*, pp. 109–17; Hocking, *Gough Whitlam*, Vol. II, pp. 140–43.
36 *Canberra Times*, 18 April and 18 May 1974.
37 *Bulletin*, 11 May 1974; *Tharunka*, 8 May 1974.

Chapter Fifteen: 1974–1975

1 Malcolm Fraser and Margaret Simons, *Malcolm Fraser: The Political Memoirs*, Miegunyah Press, Melbourne, 2010, pp. 258–59; Souter, *Acts of Parliament*, pp. 493–94, 522; Hawke, *The Hawke Memoirs*, p. 65; Peter Blazey and Andrew Campbell, *The Political Dice Men*, Outback Press, Melbourne, 1974, pp. 186–89.
2 McMullin, *The Light on the Hill*, pp. 355–56; Crowley, *Tough Times*, pp. 19–20; Freudenberg, *A Certain Grandeur*, pp. 282–83; 'Australian Political Chronicle, January–April 1974', *Australian Journal of Politics and History*, August 1974, p. 227.
3 Hocking, *Gough Whitlam*, Vol. II, p. 207; Michelle Arrow, *The Seventies*, NewSouth Publishing, Sydney, 2019, pp. 98–102, 104–107; McMullin, *The Light on the Hill*, pp. 355–56; Crowley, *Tough Times*, pp. 85–87.
4 Hawke, *The Hawke Memoirs*, p. 65; *Sydney Morning Herald*, 4 March and 6 June 1974.
5 *Canberra Times*, 8, 10 and 11 July 1974; *Australian Women's Weekly*, 26 June 1974; *Sydney Morning Herald*, 22 April 2002; Author interview with Barry Donovan.
6 *Canberra Times*, 12, 15 and 17 July 1974; *New Daily*, 11 December 2015; *Sydney Morning Herald*, 22 April 2002; James Vyver, '"He was Almost Legless": How Bob Hawke and a Bottle of Brandy Saved Frank Sinatra from Tour Disaster', *The History Listen*, 20 November 2018, www.abc.net.au.
7 *Canberra Times*, 31 August 1972; *Bulletin*, 24 August and 5 October 1974.
8 Crowley, *Tough Times*, pp. 128–33; Freudenberg, *A Certain Grandeur*, pp. 308–12, 327; 'Australian Political Chronicle, May–August 1974', *Australian Journal of Politics and History*, December 1974; *Sun*, 21 August 1974.
9 Crowley, *Tough Times*, pp. 128–33; 'Australian Political Chronicle, September–December 1974', *Australian Journal of Politics and History*, March 1975.
10 *National Times*, 2 September 1974; *Herald*, 3 September 1974; 'Australian Political Chronicle, September–December 1974', *Australian Journal of Politics and History*, March 1975.
11 *Canberra Times*, 7 October 1974; excerpts from the 'Monday Conference' program can be found on www.AustralianPolitics.com.
12 *Sydney Morning Herald*, 28 September 1974.
13 Interview with Chris Crellin by D'Alpuget, 9 April 1981, MS 7348/2/12, D'Alpuget Papers, NLA; Pieters-Hawke, *Hazel*, pp. 113–14; 149–56; Hawke, *My Own Life*, pp. 128–29.
14 Interview with Col Cunningham by D'Alpuget, 4 April 1981; and Interview with Eddie Kornhauser by D'Alpuget, May 1981, MS 7348/2/12, D'Alpuget Papers, NLA.
15 Peter Butt, *Merchants of Menace*, Blackwattle Press, Sydney, 2015, pp. 16–19, 90; Jonathan Kwitny, *The Crimes of Patriots: A True Tale of Dope, Dirty Money, and the CIA*, Simon & Schuster, New York, 1987, pp. 82–73; Alfred W. McCoy, *The Politics of Heroin*, Lawrence Hill Books, New York, 1991, pp. 461–78; Brian Toohey and Marian Wilkinson, *The Book of Leaks*, Angus & Robertson, Sydney, 1987, pp. 196–220; *Sea Horse: The Voice of Ocean Shores*, June, September and November 1969, February and June 1971, May 1972; the author visited Ocean Shores in 2022, when the country club was celebrating its fiftieth anniversary.
16 Interview with Col Cunningham by D'Alpuget, 4 April 1981, MS 7348/2/12, D'Alpuget Papers, NLA.
17 Alan Ramsey, 'Labor "Stop Hawke" Plot', newspaper cutting c. September 1975, N21/2632, ACTU Papers, NBAC.
18 Interview with Gough Whitlam by D'Alpuget, 26 June 1981, MS 7348/2/12, D'Alpuget Papers, NLA.
19 Hocking, *Gough Whitlam*, Vol. II, pp. 192–95; Freudenberg, *A Certain Grandeur*, pp. 313–14; Strangio, *Keeper of the Faith*, pp. 317–18.
20 Strangio, *Keeper of the Faith*, pp. 319–20; Uren, *Straight Left*, pp. 243–45; Button, *As It Happened*, pp. 162–63; Freudenberg, *A Certain Grandeur*, pp. 323–28; *Sydney Morning Herald*, 13 December 2018; Bramston, *Bob Hawke*, p. 162.

21 Interview with Gay Davidson by D'Alpuget, 5 March 1980, MS 7348/2/12, D'Alpuget Papers, NLA.
22 Hocking, *Gough Whitlam*, Vol. II, pp. 196–99; Hurst, *Hawke*, pp. 184–85; D'Alpuget, *Robert J. Hawke*, pp. 275–76; 'Australian Political Chronicle, September–December 1974', *Australian Journal of Politics and History*, March 1975; Judith Walker, 'Labor in Government: The 1975 Federal Conference at Terrigal', *Politics*, Vol. 10, No. 2, 1975; a photo of the whipping appears in Pullan, *Bob Hawke*, p. 213.
23 *Sydney Morning Herald*, 21 August 1984 and 31 May 2007; *Guardian*, 14 and 15 September 2017; Kevin Perkins, *Bristow: Last of the Hard Men*, Bonmoat, Sydney, 2003, pp. 216, 221–22, 232; Reeves, *Mr Sin*, p. 166, the author is grateful to Paul Wray-McCann for bringing this episode to my attention.
24 Crowley, *Tough Times*, pp. 100–101.
25 Hawke, *My Own Life*, p. 123; Hawke, *The Hawke Memoirs*, pp. 66–67; Hocking, *Gough Whitlam*, Vol. II, pp. 222–23; D'Alpuget, *Robert J. Hawke*, pp. 279–80.
26 Hawke, *My Own Life*, pp. 124–27; Pieters-Hawke, *Hazel*, pp. 142–43; Tim Colebatch, *Dick Hamer: The Liberal Liberal*, Scribe, Melbourne, 2014, p. 286; Interview with Hazel Hawke by D'Alpuget, n.d., MS 7348/3/16, D'Alpuget Papers, NLA.
27 Hocking, *Gough Whitlam*, Vol. II, pp. 222–36; Wayne Reynolds, 'Tirath Hassaram Khemlani', *Australian Dictionary of Biography*, Vol. 19.
28 Hawke, *The Hawke Memoirs*, p. 68; D'Alpuget, *Robert J. Hawke*, p. 284; *Age*, 26 July 1975.
29 *Age*, 26 July 1975.
30 Hagan, *The History of the A.C.T.U.*, pp. 382–83; D'Alpuget, *Robert J. Hawke*, p. 286; Hurst, *Hawke*, pp. 196–97; *Sydney Morning Herald*, 23 July 1975; *Age*, 26 July 1975; *Australian Financial Review*, 23 October 1975; *Canberra Times*, 30 August, 3, 4 and 5 September, 1, 2 and 9 October 1975; 'Australian Political Chronicle, July–December 1975', *Australian Journal of Politics and History*, April 1976.
31 Hurst, *Hawke*, pp. 197–98; *Guardian*, 25 October 2020; Hocking, *Gough Whitlam*, Vol. II, Chapters 10–11; Freudenberg, *A Certain Grandeur*, Chapter 24; 'Australian Political Chronicle, July–December 1975', *Australian Journal of Politics and History*, April 1976.
32 Hocking, *Gough Whitlam*, Vol. II, pp. 324–49, 416–17; for Whitlam's account of his dismissal, see Gough Whitlam, *The Truth of the Matter* (third edition), Melbourne University Press, Melbourne, 2005; Freudenberg, *A Certain Grandeur*, pp. 381–416.
33 Hurst, *Hawke*, p. 198; D'Alpuget, *Robert J. Hawke*, pp. 288–90; Hocking, *Gough Whitlam*, Vol. II, pp. 338–62.
34 Pieters-Hawke (ed.), *Remembering Bob*, pp. 47–48; Joint letter by Hawke and Whitlam, 14 December 1975, N21/973, ACTU Papers, NBAC.
35 *Age*, 9, 10, 12 and 13 December 1975; D'Alpuget, *Robert J. Hawke*, pp. 290–93; Hocking, *Gough Whitlam*, Vol. II, pp. 368–70.

Chapter Sixteen: 1976–1977
1 *Age*, 10 and 15 December 1975; D'Alpuget, *Robert J. Hawke*, pp. 290–93; Hocking, *Gough Whitlam*, Vol. II, pp. 368–70; Hurst, *Hawke*, pp. 199–200; John Stubbs, *Hayden*, Mandarin, Melbourne, 1990, pp. 149–55; David Frost, *Whitlam and Frost*, Sundial Publications, London, 1974, p. 152.
2 *National Times*, 6 October 1979; Hawke, *The Hawke Memoirs*, p. 98; Hurst, *Hawke*, pp. 199–200; D'Alpuget, *Robert J. Hawke*, p. 292; Interview with Gough Whitlam by D'Alpuget, 26 June 1981, MS 7348/2/12, D'Alpuget Papers, NLA; *Bulletin*, 1 August 1978.
3 *Age*, 15 December 1975; Interview with Don Dunstan by D'Alpuget, March 1980, MS 7348/3/15, D'Alpuget Papers, NLA.
4 D'Alpuget, *Robert J. Hawke*, pp. 292–93, 302–303; Interview with Gough Whitlam by D'Alpuget, 26 June 1981, MS 7348/2/12, D'Alpuget Papers, NLA; *Age*, 16, 17, 18, 20 and 22 December 1975.
5 Pieters-Hawke (ed.), *Remembering Bob*, pp. 47–48; Paul Kelly, *The Hawke Ascendancy*, Angus & Robertson, Sydney, 1984, pp. 20–21; D'Alpuget, *Robert J. Hawke*, pp. 292–93; Hurst, *Hawke*, pp. 199–200; Hocking, *Gough Whitlam*, Vol. II, p. 370; Chanan Reich, 'From "Endemically Pro-Israel" to Unsympathetic: Australia's Middle East Policy, 1967–1972', *Australian Journal of Politics and History*, Vol. 56, No. 4, 2010, p. 588.

6   Kelly, *The Hawke Ascendancy*, pp. 20–21; D'Alpuget, *Robert J. Hawke*, pp. 293–301; Hurst, *Hawke*, pp. 200–202; Hawke, *The Hawke Memoirs*, pp. 78–80; Hocking, *Gough Whitlam*, Vol. II, pp. 370–75; *Canberra Times*, 26 February 1976; *Australian*, 25 February 1976; *Bulletin*, 19 January 1982.
7   Interview with Eddie Kornhauser by D'Alpuget, May 1981, MS 7348/2/12, D'Alpuget Papers, NLA; D'Alpuget, *Robert J. Hawke*, pp. 295–97.
8   Hurst, *Hawke*, pp. 201–203; Hocking, *Gough Whitlam*, Vol. II, pp. 371–75; Kelly, *The Hawke Ascendancy*, pp. 20–21; D'Alpuget, *Robert J. Hawke*, pp. 297–300; Transcript of press conference by Hawke, 7 March 1976, MS 7348/3/14, D'Alpuget Papers, NLA.
9   Kelly, *The Hawke Ascendancy*, pp. 21–22; Hurst, *Hawke*, pp. 202–203; Stubbs, *Hayden*, p. 168.
10 *Economist*, 27 March 1976; Fraser and Simons, *Malcolm Fraser*, p. 321; Bob Carr, 'Australian Trade Unionism in 1976', *Journal of Industrial Relations*, March 1977; T.O. Lloyd, *Empire to Welfare State: English History, 1906–1985* (third edition), Oxford University Press, Oxford, 1986, pp. 444, 450, 463.
11 Patrick Weller, *Malcolm Fraser PM*, Penguin, Melbourne, 1989, pp. 218–25; Hawke, *The Hawke Memoirs*, pp. 84–85; D'Alpuget, *Robert J. Hawke*, pp. 310–11; Fraser and Simons, *Malcolm Fraser*, pp. 365–66; Documents in MS 7348/1/1, D'Alpuget Papers, NLA.
12 Bob Carr, 'Australian Trade Unionism in 1976', *Journal of Industrial Relations*, March 1977; Hagan, *The History of the A.C.T.U.*, p. 430; Fraser and Simons, *Malcolm Fraser*, pp. 365–66.
13 Uren, *Straight Left*, pp. 288–89; D'Alpuget, *Robert J. Hawke*, pp. 310–11; Hocking, *Gough Whitlam*, Vol. II, pp. 178–80, 386; Crowley, *Tough Times*, pp. 151–53, 319–21.
14 Bob Carr, 'Australian Trade Unionism in 1976', *Journal of Industrial Relations*, March 1977; D'Alpuget, *Robert J. Hawke*, pp. 310–11; Hurst, *Hawke*, pp. 206–207; Tom Bramble, *Trade Unionism in Australia*, Cambridge University Press, Melbourne, 2008, pp. 96–97; Moss Cass, Vivien Encel and Anthony O'Donnell, *Moss Cass and the Greening of the Australian Labor Party*, Australian Scholarly Publishing, Melbourne, 2017, pp. 258–60.
15 Bob Hawke address at the National Press Club, 29 June 1976, ORAL TRC 436, NLA; *Australian Financial Review*, 5 July 1976; *Bulletin*, 10 July 1976.
16 *Nation Review*, 8 July 1976; *National Times*, 5 July 1976; *Bulletin*, 10 July 1976.
17 Interview with Eddie Kornhauser by D'Alpuget, May 1981; 'Hawke and Sir Peter Abeles', note by D'Alpuget, 2 September 1982; and Notes by D'Alpuget of talk with Gill Appleton, n.d., MS 7348/2/12, D'Alpuget Papers, NLA.
18 Transcript of 'Just Call Me Bob', *Australian Story*, ABC TV, 10 November 2014; D'Alpuget, *Robert J. Hawke*, pp. 305–307; Hawke, *My Own Life*, pp. 133–34; Interview with Chris Crellin by D'Alpuget, 9 April 1981, MS 7348/2/12, D'Alpuget Papers, NLA.
19 Pieters-Hawke, *Hazel*, pp. 158–59; Hawke, *My Own Life*, pp. 133–35; D'Alpuget, *Robert J. Hawke*, p. 316; Interview with Chris Crellin by D'Alpuget, 9 April 1981, MS 7348/2/12, D'Alpuget Papers, NLA.
20 Hagan, *The History of the A.C.T.U.*, pp. 385–86, 438; *Bulletin*, 8 May and 12 June 1976; *National Times*, 5 July 1976; *Australian Financial Review*, 28 June 1976; Kelly, *The Hawke Ascendancy*, p. 29.
21 *Nation Review*, 8 July 1976; *Sydney Morning Herald*, 30 July 1976; *Australian*, 27 August 1976; Interview with Peter Redlich by D'Alpuget, 30 March 1981, MS 7348/2/12, D'Alpuget Papers, NLA; Paul Ormonde, *A Foolish Passionate Man: A Biography of Jim Cairns*, Penguin, Melbourne, 1981, p. 237.
22 D'Alpuget, *Robert J. Hawke*, pp. 306–307; *Wheels*, December 1976.
23 Hawke's speech at the ceremony can be found in MS 7348/3/14, D'Alpuget Papers, NLA; a brief newsreel of the dedication ceremony can be found online at www.britishpathe.com; a detailed history of Ijzim can be found online at www.palestineremembered.com; see also Efrat Ben-Ze'ev, 'The Palestinian Village of Ijzim during the 1948 War', *History and Anthropology*, Vol. 13, No. 1, 2002; and Ilan Pappe, *A History of Modern Israel: One Land, Two Peoples*, Cambridge University Press, Cambridge, 2004, pp. 136–39; *Australian Jewish Times*, 6 January 1977.
24 'Sir Warwick Oswald Fairfax', *Australian Dictionary of Biography*, Vol. 17; Hawke, *My Own Life*, pp. 133–34; Kelly, *The Hawke Ascendancy*, p. 35; John Pilger, *A Secret Country*, Jonathan Cape, London, 1989, p. 183; Author interview with Tom Keneally; Author interview with Brian Toohey; Notes by D'Alpuget in MS 7348/1/5, D'Alpuget Papers, NLA.

25 Hocking, *Gough Whitlam*, Vol. II, pp. 391–92; McMullin, *The Light on the Hill*, pp. 383–84; Stubbs, *Hayden*, pp. 168–77.
26 For details of the dinner, see documents in N68/79/791, ACTU Papers, NBAC.
27 Braham Dabscheck and Jim Kitay, 'Malcolm Fraser's (Unsuccessful) 1977 Voluntary Wages and Prices Freeze', *Journal of Industrial Relations*, June 1991; Hagan, *The History of the A.C.T.U.*, p. 452; Hurst, *Hawke*, p. 209.
28 D'Alpuget, *Robert J. Hawke*, pp. 317–24; Author interview with Neil Mitchell.
29 Ormonde, *A Foolish Passionate Man*, p. 237; D'Alpuget, *Robert J. Hawke*, pp. 325–26; *Age*, 4 July 1977.
30 Interview with Gay Davidson by D'Alpuget, 5 March 1980, MS 7348/2/12, D'Alpuget Papers, NLA; D'Alpuget, *Robert J. Hawke*, pp. 317–25.
31 Uren, *Straight Left*, p. 300; *Canberra Times*, 2 and 8 July 1977; D'Alpuget, *Robert J. Hawke*, pp. 325–26; Crowley, *Tough Times*, p. 121; Weller, *Malcolm Fraser PM*, pp. 360–66; Hurst, *Hawke*, pp. 214–17.
32 D'Alpuget, *Robert J. Hawke*, pp. 327–31; Hurst, *Hawke*, pp. 218–20; Bob Carr, 'Australian Trade Unionism in 1977', *Journal of Industrial Relations*, March 1978; *Canberra Times*, 14 December 1977.
33 Hurst, *Hawke*, pp. 221–25; Weller, *Malcolm Fraser PM*, pp. 199–203; Kelly, *The Hawke Ascendancy*, pp. 40–42.
34 Kathryn Steel, 'Point of View: A Significant Regional Industrial Dispute from a Novel Perspective', *Provenance: The Journal of Public Record Office Victoria*, No. 12, 2013; Kathryn Steel, 'Injustice and Outcomes: A Comparative Analysis of Two Major Disputes', *Labor History*, Vol. 56, No. 5, 2015; Bob Carr, 'Australian Trade Unionism in 1977', *Journal of Industrial Relations*, March 1978; Hurst, *Hawke*, pp. 221–24.
35 Bramston, *Bob Hawke*, pp. 192–94; D'Alpuget, *Bob Hawke*, pp. 462–66; *Guardian*, 5 June 2015.

Chapter Seventeen: 1978–1979
1 Interview with Gill Appleton by D'Alpuget, 31 July 1980, MS 7348/2/12, D'Alpuget Papers, NLA; Hocking, *Gough Whitlam*, Vol. II, pp. 392–96; Souter, *Acts of Parliament*, pp. 564–65; D'Alpuget, *Robert J. Hawke*, pp. 333–34; Stubbs, *Hayden*, pp. 179–80.
2 The university course in question was taken by the author and taught by then senior lecturer, later professor David Kemp, who later became the Liberal minister for education in the Howard government; *Sun-Herald*, 5 August 1979.
3 Interview with Hawke by George Negus, *Weekend Australian*, 22–23 April 1978.
4 D'Alpuget, *Robert J. Hawke*, pp. 284–85; 'ALP Conference 1979 Adelaide', undated note by D'Alpuget, MS 7348/3/17, D'Alpuget Papers, NLA; Hawke, *My Own Story*, pp. 138–42; *Sun-Herald*, 5 August 1979; Transcript of 'Just Call Me Bob', Part One, *Australian Story*, ABC TV, 10 November 2014.
5 Interview with Col Cunningham by D'Alpuget, 4 April 1981, MS 7348/2/12, Notes of an interview with Sam Stoljar by D'Alpuget, and undated Note on 'RJH's Massage' by D'Alpuget, MS 7348/2/11, D'Alpuget Papers, NLA; Interview with Chris Crellin by D'Alpuget, 9 April 1981, MS 7348/2/12, D'Alpuget Papers, NLA; D'Alpuget, *Robert J. Hawke*, pp. 303–304, 335–37, 371; Hawke, *My Own Life*, pp. 141–43.
6 *Sydney Morning Herald*, 16 September 1979 and 17 November 1983; *Age*, 18 November 1983 and 9 September 1985; *Toledo Blade*, 27 September 1979; *San Francisco Chronicle*, 7 October 1988.
7 John Williams, *The Fortunate Life of a Vindicatrix Boy*, self-published, Adelaide, 2005, p. 137; *Hansard*, 17 November 1983; *Sydney Morning Herald*, 17 November 1983; *National Times*, 8–14 March 1981, 18–24 November 1983; Kwitny, *The Crimes of Patriots*, pp. 240–42; Bottom, *The Godfather in Australia*, pp. 73, 96–102; Perkins, *Bristow*, pp. 216, 221–22; Pilger, *A Secret Country*, pp. 189-93; *Daily News*, New York, 12 November 1978; *Sun-Herald*, 1 May 1983.
8 Letter (copy), Xavier Herbert to Hawke, 26 January 1979 and other docs in MS 7348/3/14, D'Alpuget Papers, NLA; D'Alpuget, *Robert J. Hawke*, pp. 353–54.
9 *Nation Review*, 12 April 1979; Hawke, *The Hawke Memoirs*, pp. 95–96; D'Alpuget, *Robert J. Hawke*, pp. 354–58; Hurst, *Hawke*, p. 237; Samuel Furphy, 'James Francis Roulston', *Australian Dictionary of Biography*, Vol. 18.

10 *Nation Review*, 12 April 1979.
11 *Bulletin*, 9 October 1979; Hawke, *The Hawke Memoirs*, p. 96; D'Alpuget, *Robert J. Hawke*, pp. 336–37; D'Alpuget, *On Longing*, pp. 30–37.
12 Hawke, *My Own Life*, pp. 145–50; Hawke, *The Hawke Memoirs*, pp. 89–92; D'Alpuget, *Robert J. Hawke*, pp. 358–71; Hurst, *Hawke*, pp. 237–39; Suzanne Rutland, *Lone Voice: The Wars of Isi Leibler*, Gefen Publishing, Jerusalem, 2021, pp. 270–82; see also Sam Lipski and Suzanne Rutland, *Let My People Go: The Untold Story of Australia and the Soviet Jews 1959–89*, Hybrid Publishers, Melbourne, 2015, Chapters 16 and 17; See Letter, Murray Bourchier to Hawke, 30 May 1980, and other docs in MS 7348/3/14, D'Alpuget Papers, NLA.
13 Hurst, *Hawke*, pp. 232–42; Kelly, *The Hawke Ascendancy*, pp. 109–12; Laurie Oakes, *Labor's 1979 Conference, Adelaide*, Objective Publications, Canberra, 1979, pp. 4–5; Rutland, *Lone Voice*, pp. 281–82.
14 Kelly, *The Hawke Ascendancy*, p. 82; D'Alpuget, *Robert J. Hawke*, pp. 372–74; Stubbs, *Hayden*, pp. 190–91; Hayden, *Hayden*, pp. 326–29; Oakes, *Labor's 1979 Conference*, pp. 15–19; 'Telecom Dispute of 12/13 July 1979', undated note by D'Alpuget, MS 7348/3/17, D'Alpuget Papers, NLA.
15 Kelly, *The Hawke Ascendancy*, pp. 82–83; Uren, *Straight Left*, pp. 313–14; D'Alpuget, *Robert J. Hawke*, pp. 372–74; Stubbs, *Hayden*, pp. 192–95; Oakes, *Labor's 1979 Conference*, pp. 20–25; *National Times*, 28 July 1979; *National Times*, 28 July 1979; Undated newspaper cutting, c. 28 July 1979, MS 7348/5, and 'ALP Conference 1979 Adelaide', undated note by D'Alpuget, MS 7348/3/17, D'Alpuget Papers, NLA.
16 Stubbs, *Hayden*, pp. 192–93; D'Alpuget, *Robert J. Hawke*, pp. 377–83; *Age*, 24 July 1979.
17 The meeting at the Boulevard Hotel took place on 5 September. 'Decision about not to seek preselection for Federal Parliament 1979', undated note by D'Alpuget, MS 7348/3/17, D'Alpuget Papers, NLA.
18 In his memoirs, Hawke has his mother's death occurring on 'Friday 8 September', when it was actually on Saturday, 8 September. Hawke, *The Hawke Memoirs*, pp. 3, 93; Death certificate of Edith Emily Hawke; Hawke, *My Own Life*, pp. 141–42; D'Alpuget, *Robert J. Hawke*, p. 383; Ross, 'Ellie Hawke, 1897–1979: The True Kingmaker', in Dunsford (ed.), *Remarkable Women of the South East*, South East Book Promotions Group, Mount Gambier, p. 17; Letter, D'Alpuget to Rogers, 14 October 1980, MS 7348/3/18, D'Alpuget Papers, NLA.
19 *Financial Review*, 11 September 1979; *Age*, 14 September 1979.
20 Hawke, *My Own Life*, pp. 151–53.
21 Ibid.
22 Ibid.; D'Alpuget, *Robert J. Hawke*, pp. 383–84; Hawke, *The Hawke Memoirs*, p. 93; *Canberra Times*, 12 September 197.
23 Hawke, *The Hawke Memoirs*, pp. 93–94; Bob Carr, 'Australian Trade Unionism in 1979', *Journal of Industrial Relations*, March 1980; *Sydney Morning Herald*, 15 September 1979; *Australian Financial Review*, 17 September 1979; *National Times*, 22 September 1979.
24 Bob Carr, 'Australian Trade Unionism in 1979', *Journal of Industrial Relations*, March 1980; *Australian Financial Review*, 13 and 17 September 1979; *Age*, 13 September 1979; *Sydney Morning Herald*, 15 September 1979; *National Times*, 22 September 1979.
25 *Australian Financial Review*, 17 September 1979; *Age*, 13 and 14 September 1979; *National Times*, 22 and 29 September 1979.
26 Mike Steketee and Milton Cockburn, *Wran: An Unauthorised Biography*, Allen & Unwin, Sydney, 1986, pp. 254–55, 289–91; Williams, *The Fortunate Life of a Vindicatrix Boy*, p. 137; 'ALP Conference 1979 Adelaide', undated note by D'Alpuget, MS 7348/3/17, and 'Hawke and Sir Peter Abeles', note by D'Alpuget, 2 September 1982, MS 7348/2/12, D'Alpuget Papers, NLA.
27 D'Alpuget, *Robert J. Hawke*, pp. 388–89; Kelly, *The Hawke Ascendancy*, p. 112.
28 Hawke, *The Hawke Memoirs*, p. 98; D'Alpuget, *Robert J. Hawke*, pp. 388–89; Kelly, *The Hawke Ascendancy*, p. 112; Pullan, *Bob Hawke*, pp. 210–18; Carr, 'Australian Trade Unionism in 1979', *Journal of Industrial Relations*, March 1980, p. 101.
29 Rutland, *Lone Voice*, p. 282.
30 Letter (copy), D'Alpuget to Hawke, 24 September 1979, MS7348/3/17, D'Alpuget Papers, NLA.

31 Kelly, *The Hawke Ascendancy*, pp. 113–14; *National Times*, 29 September 1979; *Wills Labor Call*, undated newssheet published in support of Hand's candidature, MS 7348/5, D'Alpuget Papers, NLA; *Australian Financial Review*, 1 December 1979.
32 D'Alpuget, *Robert J. Hawke*, p. 382; *Sydney Morning Herald*, 19 September 1979.
33 D'Alpuget, *Robert J. Hawke*, p. 390; *Australian Financial Review*, 1 December 1979.
34 Hawke, *The Hawke Memoirs*, pp. 97–98; *Australian Financial Review*, 1 December 1979.
35 *Bulletin*, 9 October 1979.
36 Kelly, *The Hawke Ascendancy*, pp. 114–15.
37 Notes by D'Alpuget, MS 7348/3/14, D'Alpuget Papers, NLA.
38 *National Times*, 6 October 1979; Interview with Harold Souter by D'Alpuget, 3 August 1976, MS 7348/4/22, D'Alpuget Papers, NLA; see also speech by Hawke to the National Press Club defending his time as ACTU president and listing his achievements. MS 7348/1/4, D'Alpuget Papers, NLA.

Bibliography

PRIMARY DOCUMENTS

Alexander Turnbull Library, Wellington, New Zealand
Cambridge Terrace Congregational Church, papers
Congregational Union of New Zealand, records
Terrace Congregational Church, papers
Trinity Congregational Church (Lower Hutt), papers

Australian Association of Social Workers Inc. (Victorian Branch)
Transcript of interview, Connie Benn

Australian National University Archives
Australian National University News, Canberra
Australian National University Report, 1956 and 1957
Interview with Robin Gollan by Stephen Foster, 1993
Interview with Geoffrey Sawyer by Daniel Connell, 1990
Student and staff files for Emily Sadka
Student and staff files for Robert Hawke

Battye Library, Perth
Albert Hawke, collection of biographical material
Interview with Albert Hawke by Phillip Pendal
Interview with Bob Hawke on behalf of Phillip Pendall
Western Australian Congregational Union, Papers

Bodleian Library, Oxford
R.J.L. Hawke, 'An appraisal of the role of the Australian Commonwealth Court of Conciliation and Arbitration with special reference to the development of the concept of a basic wage', B.Litt. Thesis, University of Oxford, 1956

Bordertown Council Chambers
Bob Hawke's School Report, 1937

Bordertown Library
Bordertown Congregational Church: A Centenary Report, 1874–1974
Congregational (Bordertown Pastorate), Papers
My Memories: Recollections and Images by Residents of the Tatiara,
    Bordertown High School, 1985
Tatiara Schools Commemoration, Tatiara Schools Commemoration
    Committee, Bordertown, 1988

Noel Butlin Archives Centre, Canberra
Australian Council of Trade Unions, Papers

Fryer Library, University of Queensland
Colin Clark, Papers

Genealogy Society of South Australia
Various birth, death and marriage certificates

Guild Council Archives, University of Western Australia
Annual reports, 1949–53
Minutes of Guild Council Meetings, 1949–53

Hawke Library, University of South Australia
Bob Hawke, Papers

John Curtin Prime Ministerial Library
Hazel Hawke, Papers

Mitchell Library, Sydney
Clyde Cameron, Papers

National Library of Australia
Blanche d'Alpuget, Papers
Russell Braddon, Papers
John Button, Papers
Clyde Cameron, Papers
Manning Clark, Papers
L.F. Crisp, Papers
Interview with Peter Abeles by Daniel Connell, 1985
Interview with Sir Robert Askin by Mel Pratt, 1976
Interview with Russell Braddon by Vivienne Rae-Ellis, 1984
Interview with Geoffrey Sawer by Mel Pratt, 1971

Interview with Gordon Scholes by Gary Sturgess, August 2010
Interview with Kenneth Wheare by Catherine Santamaria, 1975
Craig McGregor, Papers
National Union of Students, Papers
Emily Sadka, Papers
Geoffrey Sawer, Papers
Sir Billy Snedden, Papers

Parliamentary Library, Canberra
Official Report of the ALP Commonwealth Conference, Adelaide, 31 July 1967

Parliamentary Library, Perth
Phillip Pendal, *Son of Labor: A Biography of A.R.G. Hawke*, Phillip Pendal Publications, South Perth, 1995

Perth Modern School, Archives
Interview with Bob Hawke by Paula Hamilton, 13 March 2001
Perth Modern School, Papers and publications
The Sphinx, 1942–47

St Mark's College, Canberra
Footprints in Travancore: A Report of the Third World Conference of Christian Youth in Travancore, India, December 11–25, 1952, American Committee for the Third World Conference of Christian Youth, c. 1953

State Library of South Australia, Adelaide
Congregational Church Women's Society, papers
Congregational Union Executive Committee Minutes
Bordertown Congregational Church, papers
Houghton Congregational Church, papers
Maitland Congregational Church, papers
Maitland Watch, Maitland, 1934–39
Paracombe Congregational Church, papers
Parkin College, papers
Trustees of Rossawella Church, Minute Book

State Library of Victoria
Study Book for the World Christian Youth Conference, Travancore, India, December 1952, Australian Christian Youth Commission, Melbourne, 1952

State Records of South Australia
Education Department, employment records relating to Edith Emily Lee
Kapunda school records
The Education Gazette, 1915–39

State Records of Western Australia
Admission cards for Bob Hawke's entry into Perth Modern School
Education Department, Record of Service Cards, Edith Emily Hawke
West Leederville School Journal

Uniting Church of Australia Archives, Perth
Leederville and Subiaco Congregational Churches, Papers
Personnel records relating to Clem Hawke

Uniting Church History Centre, Adelaide
Congregational Youth Fellowship of Australia and New Zealand Conference Magazine, 1953

University College Archives, Oxford
Bob Hawke's student file
Dean's Cards relating to Bob Hawke
University College Record, 1952–1955

University of Western Australia Archives, Perth
Bob Hawke file, Rhodes Selection Committee Papers
Bob Hawke, student file
Emily Sadka, staff file

Woman's Christian Temperance Union, Perth
Minute Books of WCTU Executive Meetings and Conventions, 1939–56
Minute Books of Perth Branch of the WCTU

Author Interviews
Rev. Geoffrey Beck
Ruth Butterworth
Heather Copley
Barry Donovan
John Edwards
Gareth Evans
Niel Gunson
Bob Hawke
Tom Keneally
Don McIntosh
Chris Masters
Neil Mitchell
Nigel Powell
Robert Pullan
Susan Ryan

Margaret Steven
John Stone
Tom Uren
Brian Toohey
Marian Wilkinson
Ralph Willis

Email Correspondence
Niel Gunson, Canberra
Archbishop (ret.) Keith Rayner, Adelaide

Newspapers & Magazines
Advertiser, Adelaide
Argus, Melbourne
Australasian, Melbourne
Australasian Post, Melbourne
Australian Christian Commonwealth, Adelaide
Australian Jewish News, Melbourne
Australian Women's Weekly, Sydney
Barrier Miner, Broken Hill
Birmingham Daily Post, Birmingham
Border Chronicle, Bordertown
Border Mail, Albury
Border Watch, Mount Gambier
Call and Bailey's Weekly, Perth
Cambridge Post, Perth
Canberra Times, Canberra
Chronicle, Adelaide
Cobbers, Perth
Courier-Mail, Brisbane
Coventry Evening Telegraph, Coventry
Daily Herald, Adelaide
Daily Mercury, Mackay
Daily News, Perth
Education, Journal of the NSW Teachers' Federation
Evening Post, Wellington
Evening Star, Dunedin
Express and Telegraph, Adelaide
Financial Review, Sydney
Geelong Advertiser, Geelong
Geraldton Guardian, Geraldton
Glenelg Guardian, Adelaide
Guardian, London
Honi Soit, Sydney

Huon Times, Franklin
Kadina and Wallaroo Times, Kadina
Kapunda Herald, Kapunda
Laura Standard and Crystal Brook Courier, Laura
Mail, Adelaide
Maitland Watch, Maitland
Manchester Guardian, Manchester
Mirror, Perth
Mount Barker Courier, Mount Barker
Murray Pioneer and Australian River Record, Renmark
Narracoorte Herald, Narracoorte
Nelson Evening Mail, Nelson
New Idea, Sydney
News, Adelaide
New Weekly, Sydney
Northam Advertiser, Northam
Observer, Adelaide
Oxford Mail, Oxford
Papua New Guinea Post-Courier, Port Moresby
Pelican, UWA Student Guild
Pioneer, Yorketown
Press, Canterbury
Queensland Times, Ipswich
Record, Emerald Hill
Register, Adelaide
Sea Horse, Brunswick Heads
South Australian Congregationalist, Adelaide
South Pacific Post, Port Moresby
Sport, Adelaide
Standard-Post, Frankston
Sunday Times, Perth
Sydney Morning Herald, Sydney
Table Talk, Melbourne
Telegraph, Brisbane
Tharunka, Kensington, NSW
Times and Northern Advertiser, Peterborough
Tribune, Sydney
Troll, Melbourne
Uniken, University of New South Wales
Weekly Times, Melbourne
West Australian, Perth
Western Mail, Perth
Wheels, Sydney

Books

Gillon Aitken (ed.), *Between Father and Son: Family Letters: V.S. Naipaul*, Alfred A. Knopf, New York, 2000

Fred Alexander, *Campus at Crawley*, University of Western Australia Press, Crawley, 1963

Blanche d'Alpuget, *Bob Hawke: The Complete Biography*, Simon and Schuster, Sydney, 2019

Blanche d'Alpuget, *Mediator: A Biography of Richard Kirby*, Melbourne University Press, Carlton, 1977

Blanche d'Alpuget, *On Longing*, Melbourne University Press, Carlton, 2008

Blanche d'Alpuget, *Robert J. Hawke*, Penguin, Melbourne, 1984

Zelda D'Aprano, *Kath Williams: The Unions and the Fight for Equal Pay*, Spinifex, Melbourne, 2001

Zelda D'Aprano, *Zelda: The Becoming of a Woman*, Visa, Melbourne, 1977

Stan Anson, *Hawke: An Emotional Life* (updated ed.), McPhee Gribble, Melbourne, 1992

Gillian Appleton, *Diamond Cuts: An Affectionate Memoir of Jim McClelland*, Macmillan, Sydney, 2000

H.W. Arndt, *A Course Through Life: Memoirs of an Australian Economist*, Australian National University, Canberra, 1985

Michelle Arrow, *The Seventies: The Personal, the Political and the Making of Modern Australia*, NewSouth Publishing, Sydney, 2019

Australian Dictionary of Biography, Various vols., Melbourne University Press, Melbourne

Philip Ayres, *Malcolm Fraser: A Biography*, William Heinemann, Richmond, 1987

Robert Ayson, *Hedley Bull and the Accommodation of Power*, Palgrave Macmillan, Basingstoke, 2012

Brian Bamford, *The Substance: The Story of a Rhodes Scholar at Oxford*, R, Beerman Publishers, Cape Town, c. 1960

Margo Beasley, *Wharfies: A History of the Waterside Workers' Federation of Australia*, Halstead Press, Rushcutters Bay, 1996

Joan Beaumont (ed.), *Australia's War 1914-18*, Allen & Unwin, Sydney, 1995

Coral Bell and Meredith Thatcher (eds.), *Remembering Hedley*, ANU Press, Canberra, 2008

Elinor A. Bellman, *Bellman Family History: Cornwall to South Australia*, Saddleworth, 1984

John Blaxland, *The Official History of ASIO, 1963-1975: The Protest Years*, Allen & Unwin, Sydney, 2016

Peter Blazey and Andrew Campbell, *The Political Dice Men*, Outback Press, Fitzroy, 1974

Stephen Blundell and Michael Freeden (eds.), *Mansfield: Portrait of an Oxford College*, Third Millenium, London, 2012

Frank Bongiorno, *Dreamers and Schemers: A Political History of Australia*, La Trobe University Press, 2022

Frank Bongiorno, *The Sex Lives of Australians*, 2nd ed., Black Inc., Melbourne, 2015

Bob Bottom, *Bugged!*, Macmillan, South Melbourne, 1989

Bob Bottom, *Connections II: Crime Rackets and Networks of Influence in Australia*, Macmillan, South Melbourne, 1987

Bob Bottom, *Fighting Organised Crime: Triumph and Betrayal in a Lifelong Campaign*, BBP, Nelson Bay, 2009

Bob Bottom, *The Godfather in Australia*, Magistra Publishing, South Melbourne, 1979

Bob Bottom, *Shadow of Shame: How the Mafia Got Away With the Murder of Donald Mackay*, Sun Books, South Melbourne, 1988

Bob Bottom, *Without Fear or Favour*, Sun Books, Melbourne, 1984

Bradley Bowden, *Driving Force: The History of the Transport Workers' Union of Australia 1883–1992*, Allen & Unwin, Sydney 1993

Margaret Bowman and Michelle Grattan, *Reformers: Shaping Australian Society from the 60s to the 80s*, Collins Dove, Melbourne, 1989

Tom Bramble, *Trade Unionism in Australia: A History from Flood to Ebb Tide*, Cambridge University Press, Port Melbourne, 2008

Troy Bramston, *Bob Hawke: Demons and Destiny*, Viking, North Sydney, 2022

Joyce Branson, *Pioneer Pastor of the South: The Life and Work of Rev. Ridgway William Newland, 1790–1864*, Victor Harbour, 1989

Judith Brett (ed.), *Political Lives*, Allen & Unwin, Sydney, 1997

Clarrie Briese, *Corruption in High Places*, Noble Books, Sydney, 2021

Richard Broinowski, *Fact or Fission?: The Truth about Australia's Nuclear Ambitions*, Scribe, Melbourne, 2003

Judith Brown, *Town Life in Pioneer South Australia*, Rigby, Adelaide, 1980

Nicholas Brown, *A History of Canberra*, Cambridge University Press, Melbourne, 2014

Allen Buckley, *The Story of Mining in Cornwall*, Cornwall Editions, Fowey, 2005

H. T. Burgess (ed.), *Cyclopedia of South Australia*, Vol. II, Cyclopedia Company, Adelaide, 1899

Meredith Burgmann and Verity Burgmann, *Green Bans, Red Union: Environmental Activism and the New South Wales Builders Labourers' Federation*, UNSW Press, Sydney, 1998

Peter Butt, *Merchants of Menace*, Blackwattle Press, Sydney, 2015

Frank Cain, *Terrorism & Intelligence in Australia: A History of ASIO & National Surveillance*, Australian Scholarly Publishing, Melbourne, 2008

Clyde Cameron (ed.), *The Cameron Diaries*, Allen & Unwin, Sydney, 1990

Clyde Cameron, *Unions in Crisis*, Hill of Content, Melbourne, 1982

John Cameron, *In Stow's Footsteps: A Chronological History of the Congregational Churches in S.A. 1837–1977*, South Australian Congregational History Project Committee, Adelaide, 1987

Moss Cass, Vivien Encel and Anthony O'Donnell, *Moss Cass and the Greening of the Australian Labor Party*, Australian Scholarly Publishing, North Melbourne, 2017

A Celebration of Contribution: Tales of the Courage, Commitment and Creativity of Modernians 1911–1963, Department of Education, Perth, 2016

Bob Charlton, *The History of Kapunda*, Kapunda, 1971

Neil Chenoweth, *Rupert Murdoch: The Untold Story of the World's Greatest Media Wizard*, Random House, New York, 2001

Philip Chubb and Barry Donovan, *Chance is Worth a Thousand Plans: Peter Redlich & the Creation of a National Law Firm*, Holding, Redlich & Co., Melbourne, 2013

The Civic Record, 1836–1986, Wakefield Press, Adelaide, 1986

Colin Clark, *Australian Hopes and Fears*, Hollis and Carter, London, 1958

Colin Clark, *The Conditions of Economic Progress* (2nd ed.), Macmillan, London, 1951

David Clune (with John Upton), *Inside the Wran Era: The Ron Mulock Memoirs*, Connor Court Publishing, Ballarat, 2015

Tim Colebatch, *Dick Hamer: The liberal Liberal*, Scribe, Melbourne, 2014

Dudley Coleman, *Golden Heritage: A Story of Renmark*, Renmark Irrigation Trust, Renmark, 1954

Peter Coleman, Selwyn Cornish and Peter Drake, *Arndt's Story: The Life of an Australian Economist*, Asia Pacific Press, Canberra, 2007

Peter Coleman, *Memoirs of a Slow Learner* (2nd ed.), Connor Court, Ballarat, 2015

Peter Collins, *The Bear Pit: A Life in Politics*, Allen & Unwin, Sydney, 2000

Brian Costar, Peter Love and Paul Strangio (eds.), *The Great Labor Schism: A Retrospective*, Scribe, Melbourne, 2005

Colin Cowdrey, *M.C.C.: The Autobiography of a Cricketer*, Hodder and Stoughton, London, 1976

Joan Coxsedge, *Cold Tea for Brandy: A Tale of Protest, Painting and Politics*, Vulcan Press, Balwyn North, 2007

G.D. Crabb, *Baptists at Kapunda, 1865–1949*, self-published, Golden Grove, 2015

Frank Crowley, *Australia's Western Third: A History of Western Australia*, Heinemann, Melbourne, 1970

Frank Crowley (ed.), *Tough Times: Australia in the Seventies*, Heinemann, Melbourne, 1986

Christopher Cunneen, *William John McKell: Boilermaker, Premier, Governor-General*, UNSW Press, Sydney, 2000

F.M. Cutlack, *Renmark: The Early Years*, Nancy Basey, Melbourne, 1987

Claire Dan, *Ups and Downs*, Wild and Woolley, Sydney, 2008

Robin Darwell-Smith, *A History of University College Oxford*, Oxford University Press, Oxford, 2008

Jim Davidson, *A Three-Cornered Life: The Historian W.K. Hancock*, UNSW Press, Sydney, 2010

E.V. Davies, J.E. Hoffman and B.J. Price, *Canberra: A History of Australia's Capital*, ACT Ministry for Health, Education and the Arts, Canberra, 1990

J.R. Davis, *Principles and Pragmatism: A History of Girton, King's College and Pembroke School*, Hyde Park Press, Adelaide, 1991

David Day, *John Curtin: A Life*, HarperCollins, Sydney, 1999

Department of Local Government, *South Australia: The Civic Record, 1836–1986*, Wakefield Press, Adelaide, 1986

Phil Dickie, *The Road to Fitzgerald: Revelations of Corruption Spanning Four Decades*, University of Queensland Press, St Lucia, 1988

Phil Dickie, *The Road to Fitzgerald and Beyond*, University of Queensland Press, St Lucia, 1989

J.R. Digance, 'Congregationalism in South Australia', Unpublished thesis, n.d.

Graeme Disney and Valerie Tarrant, *Bayside Reflections: History and Heritage of Sandringham, Hampton, Black Rock & Beaumaris*, City of Sandringham, Sandringham, 1988

Marion Dixon, *Looking Back: A Short History of the UWA Law School, 1927–1992*, UWA Law School, Nedlands, 1992

Adair Dunsford (ed.), *Remarkable Women of the South East*, South East Book Promotions Group, Mount Gambier, 1994

Jim Faull, *The Cornish in Australia*, AL Press, Melbourne, 1983

Alan Fitzgerald, *Canberra in Two Centuries: A Pictorial History*, Clareville Press, Canberra, 1987

Bill Ford and David Plowman (eds.), *Australian Unions: An Industrial Relations Perspective* (2nd ed.), Macmillan, South Melbourne, 1989

S.G. Foster and Margaret Varghese, *The Making of the Australian National University: 1946–1996*, Allen & Unwin, Sydney, 1996

Malcolm Fraser and Margaret Simons, *Malcolm Fraser: The Political Memoirs*, Miegunyah Press, Carlton, 2010

George Freeman, *George Freeman: An Autobiography*, George Freeman, Sydney, 1988

Graham Freudenberg, *A Certain Grandeur: Gough Whitlam's Life in Politics*, Penguin, Melbourne, 2009

Graham Freudenberg, *A Figure of Speech: A Political Memoir*, Wiley, Brisbane, 2005

David Frost, *Whitlam and Frost*, Sundial Publications, London, 1974

Jim Gibbney, *Canberra, 1913–1953*, Australian Government Publishing Service, Canberra, 1988

Michael Gladwin, *Captains of the Soul: A History of Australian Army Chaplains*, Big Sky Publishing, Sydney, 2013

Malcolm Graham, *A Century of Oxford*, Sutton Publishing, Stroud, 1999

Jenny Gregory (ed.), *On the Homefront: Western Australia and World War II*, University of Western Australia Press, Nedlands, 1996

Jenny Gregory (ed.), *Seeking Wisdom: A Centenary History of the University of Western Australia*, University of Western Australia, Crawley, 2013

G. Arch Grosvenor, *Red Mud to Green Oasis*, Raphael Arts, Renmark, 1979

Bill Guy, *A Life on the Left: A Biography of Clyde Cameron*, Wakefield Press, Adelaide, 1999

Jim Hagan, *Australian Trade Unionism in Documents*, Longman Cheshire, Melbourne, 1986

Jim Hagan, *The History of the A.C.T.U.*, Longman Cheshire, Melbourne, 1981

Jim Hagan and Ken Turner, *A History of the Labor Party in New South Wales, 1891–1991*, Longman Cheshire, Melbourne, 1991

Richard Hall, *Disorganised Crime*, University of Queensland Press, St Lucia, 1986

Ian Hancock, *John Gorton: He Did It His Way*, Hodder, Sydney, 2002

G.C. Harcourt, *The Making of a Post-Keynsian Economist: Cambridge Harvest*, Palgrave Macmillan, Basingstoke, 2012

G.C. Harcourt, *Post-Keynsian Essays in Biography: Portraits of Twentieth-Century Political Economists*, Macmillan, Basingstoke, 1993

G.C. Harcourt, *Selected Essays on Economic Policy*, Palgrave, Basingstoke, 2001

Bryan Harding, *Always in Need of Reform: Reflections of a Policeman*, self-published, Kilmore, 2022

Stewart Harris, *Political Football: The Springbok Tour of Australia, 1971*, Gold Star Publications, Melbourne, 1972

Bob Hawke, *The Hawke Memoirs*, William Heinemann, Melbourne, 1994

Hazel Hawke, *My Own Life: An Autobiography*, Text Publishing, Melbourne, 1992

Hazel Hawke (ed.), *Reflections on Marriage*, Text, Melbourne, 1996

Mark Hearn and Harry Knowles, *One Big Union: A History of the Australian Workers Union, 1886–1994*, Cambridge University Press, Melbourne, 1996

Joyce Henderson, *The Strength of White Ribbon: For God, Home and Humanity 1892–1992*, Woman's Christian Temperance Union of Western Australia, Perth, 1992

David Hickie, *The Prince and the Premier*, Angus & Robertson, Sydney, 1985

Roy Higgins (with Terry Vine), *The Professor*, Caribou Publications, Melbourne, 1984

S. A. Hill, *An Illustrated Guide to Historic Kapunda*, Kapunda Historical Society, Kapunda, 1986

Jenny Hocking, *Gough Whitlam: A Moment in History: The Biography*, Vol. I, Miegunyah Press, Carlton, 2008

Jenny Hocking, *Gough Whitlam: His Time: The Biography*, Vol. II, Miegunyah Press, Carlton, 2014

Jenny Hocking, *Lionel Murphy: A Political Biography*, Cambridge University Press, Melbourne, 1997

Dino Hodge, *Don Dunstan: Intimacy & Liberty*, Wakefield Press, Adelaide, 2014

Ruth Hopkins, *Where Now Cousin Jack?*, Self-published, Bendigo, 1988

Arnold Hunt, *This Side of Heaven: A History of Methodism in South Australia*, Lutheran Publishing House, Adelaide, 1985

John Hurst, *Hawke: The Definitive Biography*, Angus & Robertson, Sydney, 1979

K.S. Inglis, *This Is The ABC: The Australian Broadcasting Commission 1932–1983*, Melbourne University Press, Carlton, 1983

Miles Jebb, *The Colleges of Oxford*, Constable, London, 1992

Y.M. Johnson, *The Renmark Hotel, 1897–1997: The First Community Hotel in the British Empire*, Y.M. Gurr, Renmark, 1997

Alan Jones, *Tatiara: The First 140 Years, 1845–1985*, District Council of Tatiara, Bordertown, 1986

Brian Lewis Jones, *Parkin's Passion: A History of the Parkin Congregational Mission of South Australia Incorporated, 1882–2007*, MediaCom Education, Unley, 2007

George Kaye, *Bygone Days in Lower Hutt*, Lower Hutt City Council, Lower Hutt, 1987

Paul Kelly, *The Hawke Ascendancy*, Angus & Robertson, Sydney, 1984

Julie Kennedy, *Summertown and Cutteslowe*, Robert Boyd Publications, Witney, 1995

Anthony Kenny (ed.), *The History of the Rhodes Trust, 1902–1999*, Oxford University Press, Oxford, 2001

Edward Kiek, *The First Hundred Years: The Centenary Record of the South Australian Congregational Union*, S.A. Congregational Union, Adelaide, 1950

Colm Kiernan, *Calwell: A Personal and Political Biography*, Nelson, Melbourne, 1978

Albert Maori Kiki, *Kiki: Ten Thousand Years in a Lifetime*, Cheshire, Melbourne, 1968

Perilla Kinchin, *Seven Roads in Summertown: Voices from an Oxford Suburb*, White Cockade Publishing, Oxford, 2006

Margaret Knauerhase, *Straight on Till Morning: A Brief Biography of Edward Sidney Kiek*, E.S. Wigg, Adelaide, 1963

Jonathan Kwitny, *The Crimes of Patriots: A True Tale of Dope, Dirty Money, and the CIA*, Simon and Schuster, New York, 1987

Brij Lal and Allison Ley (eds.), *The Coombs: A House of Memories* (2nd ed.), Australian National University Press, Canberra, 2014

Terry Lane, *As the Twig is Bent*, CollinsDove, North Blackburn, 1979

Constance Larmour, *Labor Judge: The Life and Times of Judge Alfred William Foster*, Hale & Iremonger, Sydney, 1985

Patricia Lay (ed.), *Cornish-Australian Heritage: A biographical register of Cornish-Australians, 1788–1988*, Heritage 2000 Plus, Queanbeyan, 1999

Simon Lee, *Vincent's: 1863–2013*, Third Millenium Publishing, London, 2014

Isi Leibler, *The Case for Israel*, Executive Council of Australian Jewry, Melbourne, 1972

Isi Leibler, *Soviet Jewry and Human Rights*, Human Rights Publications, Caulfield, 1965

Sam Lipski (ed.), *Soviet Jewry and the Australian Communist Party: Documents*, Human Rights Publications, Caulfield, 1966

Sam Lipski and Suzanne Rutland, *Let My People Go: The Untold Story of Australia and the Soviet Jews 1959–89*, Hybrid, Melbourne, 2015

Norm Lipson and Adam Walters, *The Accidental Gangster: The Life and Times of Bela Csidei*, Park Street Press, Sydney, 2006

Alfred W. McCoy, *Drug Traffic: Narcotics and Organized Crime in Australia*, Harper & Row, Sydney, 1980

Alfred W. McCoy, *The Politics of Heroin: CIA Complicity in the Global Drug Trade*, Lawrence Hill Books, New York, 1991

David McGill, *Lower Hutt: The First Garden City*, Lower Hutt City Council, Lower Hutt, 1991

Mark McKenna, *An Eye for Eternity: The Life of Manning Clark*, Melbourne University Press, Melbourne, 2011

David McKnight, *Rupert Murdoch: An Investigation of Political Power*, Allen & Unwin, Sydney, 2012

Ross McMullin, *The Light on the Hill: The Australian Labor Party 1891–1991*, Oxford University Press, Melbourne, 1991

Anne Macneill, *The Australian National University: People and Places in a Landscape*, ANU, Canberra, 1978

Desmond Manderson, *From Mr Sin to Mr Big: A History of Australian Drug Laws*, Oxford University Press, Melbourne, 1993

Vida Maney (compiler), *Great Women of the Good Country*, Border Chronicle, Bordertown, 1996

Bruce Mansfield, *Summer is Almost Over: A Memoir*, Barton Books, Canberra, 2012

Jill Margo, *Frank Lowy: Pushing the Limits*, HarperCollins, Sydney, 2000

David Marr, *Patrick White: A Life*, Random House, Sydney, 1991

David Marr (ed.), *Patrick White: Letters*, Jonathan Cape, London, 1994

Chris Masters, *Not for Publication*, ABC Books, Sydney, 2002

Brian Matthews, *Manning Clark: A Life*, Allen & Unwin, Sydney, 2008

John Menadue, *Things You Learn Along the Way*, David Lovell Publishing, Melbourne, 1999

Theodore Millon and Roger Davis (et. al.), *Personality Disorders in Modern Life*, John Wiley & Sons, New York

Lynn Milne, *The Clerks: A History of the Federated Clerks Union in New South Wales, 1907–2003*, United Services Union, Sydney, 2008

Patrick Mullins, *Tiberius with a Telephone: The Life and Stories of William McMahon*, Scribe, Melbourne, 2018
George Munster, *A Paper Prince*, Viking, Melbourne, 1985
John Murphy, *Imagining the Fifties: Private Sentiment and Political Culture in Menzies' Australia*, UNSW Press, Sydney, 2000
John Murphy and Judith Smart (eds.), *The Forgotten Fifties: Aspects of Australian Society and Culture in the 1950s*, Melbourne University Press, Carlton, 1997
Sarah Newton, *Maxwell Newton: A Biography*, Fremantle Arts Centre Press, South Fremantle, 1993
Louis Nowra, *Kings Cross: A Biography*, NewSouth Publishing, Sydney, 2013
Laurie Oakes, *On the Record: Politics, Politicians and Power*, Hachette, Sydney, 2010
Laurie Oakes, *Power Plays: The Real Stories of Australian Politics*, Hachette, Sydney, 2008
Laurie Oakes and David Solomon, *Grab for Power: Election '74*, Cheshire, Melbourne, 1974
Laurie Oakes and David Solomon, *The Making of an Australian Prime Minister*, Cheshire, Melbourne, 1973
Daniel Oakman, *Oppy: The Life of Sir Hubert Opperman*, Melbourne Books, Melbourne, 2018
The Official Civic Record of South Australia: Centenary Year, 1936, Universal Publicity Company, Adelaide, 1936
Bobbie Oliver, *Unity is Strength: A History of the Australian Labor Party and the Trades and Labor Council in Western Australia, 1899–1999*, API Network, Perth, 2003
H.H. Opperman, *Pedals, Politics and People*, Haldane Publishing, Sydney, 1977
Nicholas Orme (ed.), *Unity and Variety: A History of the Church in Devon and Cornwall*, University of Exeter Press, Exeter, 1991
Philip Payton, *The Cornish Farmer in Australia*, Dyllansow Truran, Trewirgie, 1987
Philip Payton, *The Cornish Miner in Australia*, Dyllansow Truran, Trewirgie, 1984
Philip Payton, *The Cornish Overseas*, Alexander Associates, Fowey, 1999
Philip Payton, *Making Moonta: The Invention of Australia's Little Cornwall*, University of Exeter Press, Exeter, 2007
Kevin Perkins, *Bristow: Last of the Hard Men*, Bonmoat, Ashfield, 2003
Kevin Perkins, *The Gambling Man*, Polynesian Press, Tonga, 1990
Sue Pieters-Hawke, *Hazel: My Mother's Story*, Macmillan, Sydney, 2011
Michael Piggott and Maggie Shapley, *Prime Ministers at the Australian National University: An Archival Guide*, ANU eView, Canberra, 2011
Robert Pullan, *Bob Hawke: A Portrait*, Methuen, Sydney, 1980
Julie Quinlivan (ed.), *Student Days: The University of Western Australia Student Guild, A Collection of Memoirs*, Guild of Undergraduates, Perth, 1988

Alan Ramsay, *A Matter of Opinion*, Allen & Unwin, Sydney, 2009
Alan Ramsay, *The Way they Were*, NewSouth, Sydney, 2011
Tony Reeves, *Mr Sin: The Abe Saffron Dossier*, Allen & Unwin, Sydney, 2007
Tony Reeves, *The Real George Freeman*, Penguin, Melbourne, 2011
G.S. Reid and M.R. Oliver, *The Premiers of Western Australia, 1890–1982*, University of Western Australia Press, Nedlands, 1982
Renmark Primary School, *Work Hard – Play Hard: One Hundred Years of Education at Renmark Primary School*, Renmark, 1988
Graham Richardson, *Whatever It Takes*, Bantam Books, Sydney, 1994
Matthew Ricketson (ed.), *The Best Australian Profiles*, Black Inc., Melbourne, 2004
Tim Rowse, *Nugget Coombs: A Reforming Life*, Cambridge University Press, Melbourne, 2002
Suzanne D. Rutland, *Lone Voice: The Wars of Isi Leibler*, Hybrid Publishers, Melbourne, 2021
Colleen Ryan, *Fairfax: The Rise and Fall*, Melbourne University Publishing, Carlton, 2013
Susan Ryan, *Catching the Waves: Life In and Out of Politics*, HarperCollins, Sydney, 1999
Alan Saffron, *Gentle Satan: My Father, Abe Saffron*, Penguin, Melbourne, 2008
Russell Schneider, *The Colt from Kooyong: Andrew Peacock, A Political Biography*, Angus & Robertson, Sydney, 1981
Barbara Scott (ed.), *Sun, Sand and Sweat: Recollections of a Seaside Village*, Petone Historical Society, Petone, 2015
Jocelynne Scutt (ed.), *Lionel Murphy: A Radical Judge*, McCulloch Publishing, Carlton, 1987
George Seddon and Gillian Lilleyman, *A Landscape for Learning: A History of the Grounds of the University of Western Australia*, University of Western Australia Press, Crawley, 2006
William Shawcross, *Rupert Murdoch*, Random House, Sydney, 1992
Christine Shervington, *University Voices: Traces from the Past*, University of Western Australia, Perth, 1987
Billy Mackie Snedden and M. Bernie Schedvin, *Billy Snedden: An Unlikely Liberal*, Macmillan, Melbourne, 1990
Michael Somare, *Sana: An Autobiography of Michael Somare*, Niugini Press, Port Moresby, 1975
Ian Soulsby, *A History of Cornwall*, Phillimore, Chichester, 1986
Gavin Souter, *Heralds and Angels: The House of Fairfax, 1841–1990*, Melbourne University Press, Carlton, 1991
The Sphinx Foundation, *Perth Modern School: The History and the Heritage*, B+G Resources Enterprises, Cottesloe, 2005
C.T. Stannage (ed.), *A New History of Western Australia*, University of Western Australia Press, Nedlands, 1981

Nigel Starck, *Proud Australian Boy: A Biography of Russell Braddon*, Australian Scholarly Publishing, North Melbourne, 2011

Alexander Stephan (ed.), *The Americanization of Europe: Culture, Diplomacy, and Anti-Americanism after 1945*, Berghahn Books, New York, 2008

Elizabeth Storry et al (eds.), *Pictorial History of Renmark: Celebrating 100 Years, 1887–1987*, Murray Pioneer, Renmark, 1987

Paul Strangio, *Keeper of the Faith: A Biography of Jim Cairns*, Melbourne University Press, Carlton South, 2002

John Stubbs, *Hayden*, Mandarin, Port Melbourne, 1990

Anne Summers, *Damned Whores and God's Police* (rev. ed.), Penguin, Ringwood, 1994

Roberta Sykes, *Snake Dancing*, Allen & Unwin, Sydney, 1998

Gwenda Tavan, *The Long, Slow Death of White Australia*, Scribe, Melbourne, 2005

Noel Tennison, *The Life of the Party*, Primrose Hall Publishing, Brisbane, 2014

Noel Tennison, *My Spin in PR*, Media Relations Publishing, Hampton, 2008

Brian Toohey and Marian Wilkinson, *The Book of Leaks*, Angus & Robertson, Sydney, 1987

Bruce Upham (ed.), *Congregationalism in Australia*, Uniting Church Press, Melbourne, 2001

Tom Uren, *Straight Left*, Random House, Sydney, 1995

Martyn F. Wakelin, *Language and History in Cornwall*, Leicester University Press, Leicester, 1975

Shane Warne (with Mark Nicholls), *No Spin*, Ebury Press, North Sydney, 2018

Vera Wasowski, *Vera: My Story*, Black Inc., Melbourne, 2015

Bill Waterhouse, *What Are the Odds: The Bill Waterhouse Story*, Vintage, North Sydney, 2010

Jill Waterhouse, *University House: As They Experienced It: A History 1954–2004*, University House, Canberra, 2004

Patrick Weller, *Malcolm Fraser PM: A Study in Prime Ministerial Power*, Penguin, Ringwood, 1989

Sydney Wells, *Paddle Steamers to Cornucopia: The Renmark–Mildura Experiment of 1887*, Murray Pioneer, Renmark, 1986

Derek Whitelock, *Adelaide: From Colony to Jubilee*, Savvas Publishing, Adelaide, 1985

Gough Whitlam, *The Truth of the Matter*, Melbourne University Press, Melbourne, 2005

Gough Whitlam, *The Whitlam Government*, Viking, Ringwood, 1985

Evan Whitton, *Can of Worms: A Citizen's Reference Book to Crime and the Administration of Justice*, Fairfax Library, Sydney, 1986

Evan Whitton, *Can of Worms II: A Citizen's Reference Book to Crime and the Administration of Justice*, Fairfax Library, Sydney, 1987

Mike Willesee, *Memoirs*, Macmillan, Sydney, 2017
John Williams, *The Fortunate Life of a Vindicatrix Boy*, self-published, 2005
David Wilson and Lindsay Murdoch, *Big Shots: A Who's Who in Australian Crime*, Sun Books, South Melbourne, 1985
David Wilson, *Big Shots II*, Macmillan, South Melbourne, 1987
Thomas Wilson, *Modern Capitalism and Economic Progress*, Macmillan, London, 1950
William T. Youngs, *The Congregationalists*, Greenwood Press, Westport, 1990

Journal Articles
'Australian Political Chronicle, January–April 1974', *Australian Journal of Politics and History*, August 1974
'Australian Political Chronicle, May–August 1974', *Australian Journal of Politics and History*, December 1974
'Australian Political Chronicle, July–December 1975', *Australian Journal of Politics and History*, April 1976
Joseph Warren Beach, 'The Salzburg Seminar', *CEA Critic*, Vol. 12, No. 7, October 1950
Melissa Bellanta, 'Transcending Class? Australia's Single Taxers in the Early 1890s', *Labour History*, No. 92, May 2007
Philip Bentley, 'Australian Trade Unionism, 1970–71', *Journal of Industrial Relations*, December 1971
Philip Bentley, 'Australian Trade Unionism, 1972–73', *Journal of Industrial Relations*, December 1973
Philip Bentley, 'Australian Trade Unionism, 1973–74', *Journal of Industrial Relations*, December 1974
Efrat Ben-Ze'ev, 'The Palestinian Village of Ijzim During the 1948 War', *History and Anthropology*, Vol. 13, No. 1, 2002
Bradley Bowden, 'The Rise and Decline of Australian Unionism: A History of Industrial Labour from the 1820s to 2010', *Labour History*, May 2011
Bob Carr, 'Australian Trade Unionism in 1975', *Journal of Industrial Relations*, December 1975
Bob Carr, 'Australian Trade Unionism in 1976', *Journal of Industrial Relations*, March 1977
Bob Carr, 'Australian Trade Unionism in 1977', *Journal of Industrial Relations*, March 1978
Bob Carr, 'Australian Trade Unionism in 1978', *Journal of Industrial Relations*, March 1979
Drew Cottle, 'The University of Western Australia Labour Club, 1925–1949: A Nursery of
Political Radicals?', *Critical Studies in Education*, Vol. 40, No. 1, 1999
C.J. Coventry, 'The "Eloquence" of Robert J. Hawke: United States Informer, 1973–79', *Australian Journal of Politics and History*, Vol. 67, No. 1, 2021

Braham Dabscheck and Jim Kitay, 'Malcolm Fraser's (Unsuccessful) 1977 Voluntary Wages and Prices Freeze', *Journal of Industrial Relations*, June 1991

G.C. Harcourt, 'The Systematic Downside of Flexible Labour Market Regimes: Salter Revisited', *Economic and Labour Relations Review*, Vol. 23, No. 2, 2012

K.W. Hince, 'Australian Trade Unionism, 1968–9', *Journal of Industrial Relations*, September 1969

Yacov Livne and Yossi Goldstein, '"Let My People Go": The Beginnings of Israel's Operation to Open Soviet Immigration Gates', *Soviet and Post-Soviet Review*, Vol. 47, No. 3, 2020

Donald Markwell, 'Keynes and Australia', *Research Discussion Paper*, Reserve Bank of Australia, September 1985

R.M. Martin, 'The ACTU Congress of 1967', *Journal of Industrial Relations*, September 1967

R.M. Martin, 'The A.C.T.U. Congress of 1969', *Journal of Industrial Relations*, September 1969

R.M. Martin, 'The A.C.T.U. Congress of 1971', *Journal of Industrial Relations*, December 1971

R.M. Martin, 'The A.C.T.U. Congress of 1973', *Journal of Industrial Relations*, December 1973

R.M. Martin, 'The A.C.T.U. Congress of 1977', *Journal of Industrial Relations*, December 1977

R.M. Martin, 'The A.C.T.U. Congress of 1979', *Journal of Industrial Relations*, December 1979

Robert Mead, 'The Salzburg Seminar in American Studies', *World Affairs*, Spring 1954

Philip Mendes, 'A Convergence of Political Interests: Isi Leibler, the Communist Party of Australia and Soviet Anti-Semitism, 1964–66', *Australian Journal of Politics and History*, Vol. 55, No. 2, 2009

John Merritt, 'The Trade Union Leader Who Went to Gaol', *Canberra Historical Journal*, Vol. 59, 2007

Alex Millmow, 'Colin Clark and Australia', *History of Economics Review*, Vol. 56, No. 1, 2012

Gail Reekie, 'War, Sexuality and Feminism: Perth Women's Organisations, 1938–1945', *Australian Historical Studies*, Vol. 21, No. 85, 1985

Chanan Reich, 'From "Endemically Pro-Israel" to Unsympathetic: Australia's Middle East Policy, 1967–1972', *Australian Journal of Politics and History*, Vol. 56, No. 4, 2010

T.H. Rigby, 'The Soviet Politburo: A Comparative Profile 1951–71', *Soviet Studies*, Vol. 24, No. 1, 1972

Grant Rodwell, '"There are Other Evils to be Put Down": Temperance, Eugenics and Education in Australia, 1900–1930', *Paedagogica Historica*, Vol. 34, Sup. 2, 1998

Seth Rosenthal et al, 'The Narcissistic Grandiosity Scale: A Measure to Distinguish Narcissistic Grandiosity from High Self-Esteem', *Assessment*, Vol. 27, No. 3, 2020

Malcolm Saunders, 'The ALP's Response to the Anti-Vietnam War Movement: 1965–73', *Labour History*, Vol. 44, 1983

Malcolm Saunders, 'Harry Samuel Taylor, the "William Lane" of the South Australian Riverland', *Labour History*, No. 72, May 1997

Malcolm Saunders, 'The Trade Unions in Australia and Opposition to Vietnam and Conscription: 1965–73', *Labour History*, Vol. 43, 1982

Tom Sheridan, 'Regulator *Par Excellence*: Sir Henry Bland and Industrial Relations 1950–1967', *Journal of Industrial Relations*, Vol. 41, No. 2, 1999

Henry Nash Smith, 'The Salzburg Seminar', *American Quarterly*, Vol. 1, No. 1, 1949

Kathryn Steel, 'Point of View: A Significant Regional Industrial Dispute from a Novel Perspective', *Provenance: The Journal of Public Record Office Victoria*, Vol. 12, 2013

Kathryn Steel, 'Injustice and Outcomes: A Comparative Analysis of Two Major Disputes', *Labor History*, Vol. 56, No. 5, 2015

Glenn Stevens, 'Inflation and Disinflation in Australia: 1950–91', *Reserve Bank of Australia Conference Paper*, 1992

Tony Thomas, 'Bob Hawke's Sugar Daddies', *Quadrant*, September 2022

Judith Walker, 'Labor in Government – The 1975 Federal Conference at Terrigal', *Politics*, Vol. 10, No. 2, 1975

Judith Walker, 'Restructuring the A.L.P. – N.S.W. and Victoria', *Australian Quarterly*, Vol. 43, No. 4, 1971

John Gillard Watson, 'The Salzburg Seminar', *Higher Education Quarterly*, Vol. 11, No. 4, 1957

Peter Yule, 'Hieser, Hawke and Harsanyi: Three "might-have-beens" in the history of CBE', *Margin*, ANU College of Business and Economics, Vol. 3, 2011

Reports, Booklets, Lectures etc

Geoffrey Beck, 'The Blackbird Leys Saga: Part of the story', Oxford, 2005

The Cyclopedia of New Zealand, Cyclopedia Company, Wellington, 1897

Bob Hawke, *In Memoriam, Albert Monk*, 1975

Lower Hutt: Past and Present, Lower Hutt Borough Council, 1941

Church History Committee, *Renmark Wilkinson Memorial Church, 60th Anniversary*, Renmark, 1949

Padraic McGuinness, '"The Economic Guerrillas": A lecture in honour of Maxwell Newton', Seminar Series, No. 2, Tasman Institute, 1991

Dennis Nutt, 'Thomas Hagger: A Burning Flame', Churches of Christ booklet, 2015

Perth Modern School Class of 1942–46, *Then – Now – And In Between: A Reunion Memento*, Perth, November 1996

Walter Phillips, *Edward Sidney Kiek: His Life and Thought*, Uniting Church Historical Society, South Australia, 1981

Joyce Riley and Douglas Riley, *The History of the Congregational National Memorial Church, Canberra*, City Uniting Church, Canberra, 1979

Harold Souter, *Commonwealth Industrial Regulation in Australia*, Victorian Fabian Society, Melbourne, 1957

Tatiara Heritage Survey: Report to the District Council of Tatiara, Historical Research Pty Ltd and Austral Archaeology Pty Ltd, 2004

Tatiara: The Good Country, Tatiara Pastoral, Agricultural and Industrial Society, Bordertown, 1976

Francis West, *University House: Portrait of an Institution*, Australian National University, Canberra, 1980

Peter Yule, 'History of the ANU College of Business and Economics', unpublished manuscript, 2012

Theses

Bradley Bowden, 'The Origins and History of the Transport Workers' Union of Australia 1883–1975', PhD Thesis, University of Wollongong, 1991

Brian Chalmers, 'Methodists and Revivalism in South Australia, 1838–1939: The Quest for "Vital Religion"', PhD Thesis, Flinders University, 2016

John Daniel Fitzgerald, 'Federal Intervention in the Victorian Branch of the Australian Labor Party, 1970', MA Thesis, La Trobe University, 1975

Michael Hopkins, 'Congregationalism in Oxford: The Growth and Development of Congregational Churches In and Around the City of Oxford since 1653', MA Thesis, University of Birmingham, 2010

Veronica O'Flaherty, 'A Very Dim Light, A Very Steep Hill: Women in the Victorian Branch of the Australian Labor Party', PhD Thesis, Victoria University, 2005

Ralph F. Pervan, 'The Western Australian Labor Movement, 1933–47', MA Thesis, University of Western Australia, 1966

Acknowledgments

During the course of researching my biography of Paul Keating, I had occasion to interview Bob Hawke and took the opportunity to ask for his cooperation in this planned biography of him. He readily agreed, noting that he felt an obligation to help academics who were researching his time as prime minister, given that he was still being paid the 'Queen's shilling'.

In the event, my subsequent requests for an interview went unanswered. Fortunately, that didn't prove to be an impediment to the completion of this book. For one thing, with Hawke having done so many interviews during the course of his life and being practised in deflecting questions that he didn't want to answer, it's doubtful whether another interview could have added much. More value lay in the archives that hadn't been explored, the people who hadn't been interviewed and the questions that hadn't previously been asked of the material.

As always, this biography is partly built on the work of earlier biographers and historians, Blanche d'Alpuget, John Hurst, Rob Pullen, Stan Anson and Troy Bramston, along with the contemporary journalists mentioned in the footnotes and the writers of the many other works listed in the bibliography. It's also built on the interviews with the many people who've been willing to share their memories of Hawke. And it wouldn't have been possible without the cooperation of the librarians and archivists who've provided access to the mountain of material dealing with the lives of Bob Hawke and his parents.

This has been a long journey over a decade or more, during which many debts have been incurred along the way. In New Zealand, thanks are due to the staff of the Alexander Turnbull Library in Auckland and the Lower Hutt Library for locating books and documents related to the time when Bob Hawke's parents were living and preaching in Alicetown, outside Auckland.

While visiting the various locations in South Australia where Bob Hawke's parents lived, and where Hawke was later born and raised, I was assisted by the librarians of the State Library of South Australia, the Bob Hawke Prime Ministerial Library at the University of South Australia, the staff of the State Records of South Australia and the Uniting Church History Centre, as well as the staff of museums and libraries in Bordertown, Maitland, Renmark and Kapunda. Particular thanks go to Renmark historian Heather Everingham for her hospitality and insights about the town's history.

In Perth, Lesley Annamalay and Maria Carvalho of the University of Western Australia Archives and the staff of the Student Guild helped to locate papers and photographs related to his time at the university and his winning of the Rhodes Scholarship; the archivist of the Perth Modern School was very helpful in making the school's records available; the president of the Western Australian branch of the WCTU, Christine White, kindly provided access to the voluminous records of that organisation, with which Hawke's mother was so deeply involved; Sally Laming and the staff of the John Curtin Prime Ministerial Library, where Hazel Hawke's papers are mostly located, provided great assistance over several days; as did the staff of the Battye Library, the State Records of Western Australia, the State Parliamentary Library in Perth and the Uniting Church of Australia Archives. Thanks are also due to David Hilliard for kindly making available a copy of the church magazine which published the speech made by Hawke after his return from India.

In Oxford, I am grateful to the staff of the Bodleian Library for providing access to Hawke's thesis, and to the archivist of University College, Dr Robin Darwell-Smith who made available various records relating to Hawke's time as a student at the college; the ninety-nine-year-old Rev. Geoffrey Beck told of his time hosting Hawke and Hazel at his Lonsdale Street home, while the present owner of that home, Julia Sleeper, described the set-up of the house at the time when Hawke and Hazel stayed there; Simon Offen and Simon Lee provided details of Vincent's Club, where Hawke was wont to socialise.

As with several of my other books, the research for this biography would have been much more complicated without the assistance of the

Trove website, run by the National Library of Australia. At a keystroke, it opened the pages of numerous Australian newspapers which would otherwise have been too difficult and time-consuming to access. The National Library was also the repository of numerous collections and interviews relating to Hawke. I am particularly grateful to Blanche d'Alpuget for depositing the many notes she made while interviewing subjects for her biography of Hawke and to Marian Sawer for allowing access to the papers of her father, Geoffrey Sawer, who was the supervisor of Hawke's failed attempt at a Ph.D. thesis. The ANU Archives complemented the collections at the NLA with papers from Hawke's time as a student and lecturer at the ANU. I am grateful to the ACTU for allowing access to its papers, which are located within the Noel Butlin Archives, now subsumed within the ANU Archives.

Apart from the many interviews provided online by the National Library, there were many people who gave up their time to be interviewed for this book, whether in person or by phone or email. Although he didn't agree to be interviewed for this book, Bob Hawke was interviewed for my biography of Paul Keating, which had benefits for this book and the subsequent volume dealing with Hawke's time as prime minister and beyond. The many other interviewees who were particularly helpful include Barry Jones, Gareth Evans, Ralph Willis, Kim Beazley, Neal Blewett and John Stone, who were most generous with their time, along with Rev. Geoffrey Beck, Moss Cass, Barry Donovan, Niel Gunson, Margaret Steven, Tom Keneally, Chris Masters, Neil Mitchell, Robert Pullan, Brian Toohey, Heather Copley and Marian Wilkinson.

At HarperCollins, I have been blessed with a patient and supportive publisher in Helen Littleton, while the text has been improved by the editing work of Scott Forbes, Neil Thomas, Julian Welch and Rachel Dennis.

La Trobe University has provided an academic home during the research and writing of this book, with the ever-helpful staff at the library answering my multitude of requests for sometimes hard-to-get books and articles.

My dear friend, the documentary producer John Moore, provided a sounding board during the course of writing this book, prior to his untimely death from a brain tumour. This book is dedicated to his memory.

As always, Silvia has been a boon companion on yet another long journey.

Index

ABC
  Monday Conference Hawke 1974
    appearance on 293–4
  Nation's Forum of the Air 92
  This Day Tonight 325
Abeles, Peter 252–4, 255, 256, 280, 282, 320, 336–7, 340, 345, 350
Aboriginal land rights 223
ACTU *see* Australian Council of Trade Unions (ACTU)
Adelaide 7, 11
Advertiser (Adelaide) 32
Allan, Jimmy 117, 119
Amarena, Sal 337
Anson, Stan 51, 352
anti-communism 130, 177
anti-conscriptionists 12, 159
Anzac Day 25, 28, 35
apartheid 240–3, 247–8
Arndt, Heinz 131–2
Asian invasion, 1960s fears of 187
Askin, Sir Robert 252, 253
Attlee, Clement 106
Austin, Mervyn 92–3, 94
Australia-Overseas Club, UWA 88, 94, 99
Australia Party 232
Australian Capital Territory cricket team 136
Australian Council of Employer Federations 170, 275
Australian Council of Trade Unions (ACTU)
  advocate for, acting as 157, 159–62, 164–5, 188
  affiliation with AWU 206
  campaigning for presidency 195, 196, 204, 205, 210, 214
  Carlton offices 150
  congress
    1969 213–14, 215–17
    1971 248–50, 259
    1973 278–9
    1979 345, 347, 348
    Hawke attendance at 137
  decline in importance 276
  Executive 196, 205, 210, 213, 216, 217, 224
  farewell dinner 354
  50th anniversary dinner 326
  gender-based wages 208
  Hawke reforms to 231
  'margins' cases 161–2, 170, 190, 199
  President, as 217, 224, 305, 330, 333–4, 354–5
  public attention from activities in 188
  public profile and appearances as President 228–9, 232, 239–40
  remuneration as President 232–3
  research officer 144, 145, 149, 150, 152
  spokesman for, acting as 183, 184
  staff 150
  style of leadership 225
  wage cases *see* wage cases
Australian Financial Review 130, 231, 349
Australian Institute of Political Science (AIPS)
  1962 Hawke speech 166, 167
Australian Labor Party (ALP) 11, 79, 111
  1961 Federal election 168, 169
  1975 conference 298–9
  1979 conference 342–4, 348
  ACT branch, joining 132
  Hawke's negative comments 315–16
  May 1977 leadership vote 325
  post-dismissal leadership jostling 311–13, 316
  President 272–3, 276, 301, 327
  retirement as President 336
  vice-president 264
  Victorian branch 229–30, 297
  Victorian branch split 130, 214
  Victorian state executive, 1970 election to 229, 230
Australian National University (ANU) 126, 149
  banning from University House 142
  disciplining of Hawke by vice-chancellor and deans 141–2

escalation of drinking 135, 136, 139–40, 146
ornamental pond incident 139–40
PhD scholarship 125
thesis 134, 137, 142
University Council 132, 142
University House 127–8, 134, 142
Australian Security Intelligence Organisation (ASIO) 242
Australian Student Christian Movement (ASCM) 72, 80, 81
Australian Workers' Union (AWU) 206
Ayres, Lily 60

'baby boomers' 232
Baillieu, Kate 333
Balogh, Thomas 106, 113
Baptist church 7, 9
Barblett, Alan 81, 83, 88
Barnard, Lance 267, 287, 302
Barnes, Allan 312
Bass electorate 302, 303
Batt, Neil 343–4
Bayliss, Professor Noel 90
Beasley, Frank 74, 85, 92
Beaufort Hotel, Melbourne 170–1
Beazley, Kim 110
Beck, Reverend Geoffrey 108–9, 112, 116, 123, 183
Beck, Joy 109
Beech, Tom 29
Beecham, Sir Thomas 106
Bemrose, Dawn 239
Benn, Connie 346
Bjelke-Petersen, Joh 247, 285
Blazey, Peter 338–9
Blewett, Neal 92
Bolte, Henry 230
Bordertown 27–9, 31, 33–7
Boulevarde Hotel, Sydney 254–5
Bourke's department store 236–7, 238, 239, 249, 251
Bowden, Glenda 299
Bowen, Lionel 312
Braddon, Russell 101–2
The Naked Island 101
Bristow, Tim 300, 301
Britain, social welfare measures 294
Broadbent, Maggie 53, 60
Brown, Horace 'Horrie' 137–8, 152, 157
Bruce, Stanley 31
Bryant, Gordon 312, 344
Builders Labourers Federation 269–70, 278, 348
Bull, Hedley 104, 105, 107, 109, 114, 116
The Bulletin 353
Button, John 167, 230

Cairns, Dr Jim 130, 204, 226, 276, 287, 292, 298, 299, 303, 304, 312, 322, 323, 328
Callaghan, James 316
Calwell, Arthur 168, 169, 177–8, 179, 188, 204, 262
Cameron, Clyde 175, 181, 230, 234, 264, 291, 293, 303
equal pay 268–9
Hawke's criticism of 269
Cammell, Helga 275, 302, 340
Canberra
1956, in 127, 128, 133, 142
The Canberra Times 293, 299
Hawke's correspondence to 132
Canberra University College 126, 129, 131, 144
Carr, Bob 353
Chamberlain, Joe 145
Channel 9 308
Charody, John 253
Chevron Hotel, South Yarra 296
Chifley, Ben 69, 71, 81, 126, 137, 265
Chipp, Don 350
Churchill, Winston 102, 203
Clark, Colin 110–12, 113–15, 130, 164, 166–7
Australian Hopes and Fears 149
The Conditions of Economic Progress 110
Clark, Manning 130, 131, 133–4, 135, 136, 263, 338
Clews, Bob 76–7
Cohen, Sam 242, 247
Memorial Lecture 247
Cold War 69, 129, 130, 131, 168, 187, 218, 259
Coleman, Peter 129, 134–5, 153, 235
Colombo Plan 151
Combe, David 195, 274, 311, 314, 315, 328, 333, 336
Commonwealth Labor Advisory Committee 224–5
Communist Party 71, 79, 95, 131, 179, 187, 215, 278–9
Conciliation and Arbitration Commission 152, 157–8
Congregational Church 17
socials and sporting events 62
Congregational Youth Fellowship Australia 84, 94, 97–8
Connor, Rex 303, 325
conscription
introduction for overseas service 189
plebiscites 12, 13–14
Vietnam War 203, 223
Coombs, Dr H.C. 'Nugget' 225, 249, 276–7, 338
Copland, Sir Douglas 164

Corio electorate 175, 204
  1963 Federal election 174–7, 179–81
Cornell, Bob 76
Cornish immigrants in South Australia 7, 8, 11
Cornish people 8–9
Cowdrey, Colin 112, 113, 120
Craig, Ailsa 239
Crawford, George 229, 230, 338
Crean, Frank 261, 277, 288, 292, 297, 312, 322
Crean, Simon 311, 322
Crellin, Chris 323
Crisp, Professor Finlay 'Fin' 129, 132
Cropper, Marjorie 239
Crossley, Ethel 50
Crowley, Bill 172
Csidei, Bela 254, 337
Cuban missile crisis 178
Cunningham, Col 250, 281–2, 295, 296, 297, 323, 336
Currie, George 87, 92
Curtin, John 55, 58, 71, 159
Cyclone Tracy 298

D'Alpuget, Blanche 41, 47, 50, 135, 227, 238, 258, 273, 352, 345, 351–2
  first meeting 227
  fling with Hawke 320
  talk of marriage with Bob 340, 347, 352
D'Aprano, Zelda 258–9
Dan, Claire 252
Darwin 298
Davidson, Gay 299
De Lisle, Frank 20
demarcation disputes 212, 289
Democratic Labor Party (DLP) 111, 130, 167, 177, 180, 181, 218–19, 232, 350
Diem, Ngo Dinh 179
dismissal of Whitlam 306–8
Docker, Ted 139
Dolan, Cliff 259
Donovan, Barry 228, 233, 290
Dougherty, Tom 206
Dowd, John 253
Ducker, John 226, 279, 328, 330, 343, 344
Dunlop 237–8, 239, 248
Dunshea, Eric 237, 238
Dunstan, Don 177, 291, 311–12, 329
Durack, Kim 72

early post-Federation years 8
Economic Planning Committee 184, 210–11
economic theory 137, 142, 160
The Economist 316

Edrich, Eddy 102–3, 108
Eggleston, Richard 'Dick' 138, 143, 157, 163
elections
  1961 Federal election 168, 169
  1963 Federal election 175–81
  1964 half-Senate election 188–9
  1969 Federal election 218–19, 265
  1972 Federal election 262, 263–6
  1974 Senate election and referendums 285–6, 287
  1975 Federal election 308–9, 310
  1977 Federal election 331–2, 333
Elliot, Doug 176
England 41, 112, 114, 124, 126
  1953, in 101, 103, 107
  Hazel on way to 109
equal pay 208, 216, 223, 258–9, 260, 268–9
Evatt, H.V. 'Doc' 126, 129, 130, 131, 132, 168, 204
Everingham, Doug 211

Fairfax, Sir Warwick 324
Farr, Reverend Alan 128
Farrell, James T. 129
feminism 187, 223
Festival of Christian Witness 84–5
Fieldhouse, David 128
Fischer, Henry 314, 315
Fitzgibbon, Charlie 216, 278, 347
Fitzpatrick, Brian
  The British Empire in Australia 122
  Short History of the Australian Labor Movement 122
Foote, Bob 76, 77
Forster 11, 14–15
Foster, Justice Alfred 159, 160, 161, 164
Fraser, Malcolm 130, 287, 302, 303, 304, 306, 313, 315, 316, 323, 348
  1975 election 310
  1976 budget 317
  1977 Federal election 331–2, 333
  attempts to compromise with 316–17
  caretaker Prime Minister 307, 308
  meetings with Hawke 317, 319
Fraser Government
  economic policies 325–6
  wage freeze, proposal for 326, 327
Fratianno, Jimmy 'the Weasel' 336–7
Freeman, George 256
French nuclear tests in the Pacific 271–2
Freudenberg, Graham 263, 310
Frost, David 261, 262, 310, 325

Gair, Vince 285
Gairdner, Sir Charles 86, 90, 94, 99
Gallagher, Justice Francis 161, 191, 197, 213

Index

Gallagher, Norm 278, 348, 354
Gaudron, Mary 268
Geater, Gwen 40–1, 42, 47, 48
Geelong Advertiser 176, 181
gender-based wages 208
George, Sir Arthur 253
Gietzelt, Ray 195, 210, 348
Gillett, John 91
Glasson, Reed 20, 22–3
Gleghorn, Geoff 231, 260, 265
Gollan, Robin 131
Goodhart, Arthur 104
Gordon, Adam Lindsay 64
Gorton, John 211, 216, 218, 219, 223, 225, 232, 265
Graduation Balls 83, 87
Grave, Selwyn 93
Great Depression 31–3
Great War 10, 12, 15
   Australian casualties 16
   chaplains serving in 13
   Western Front casualties, news of 13
Green Plains West 7, 9, 11, 37
Greenwood, Ivor 305
Greer, Germaine 235–6
Guild of Undergraduates 80–1, 83, 84, 98–9
   Hawke's presidency 84, 91, 94
Guinness Book of Records 116–17
Gunson, Niel 128–9, 133, 134, 135

Hackett Scholarship 82
Hagger, Thomas 36, 37, 38
Hall, John 86–7, 106
Hamer, Dick 302
Hancock, Keith 198
   Australia 122
Hand, Gerry 345, 351, 352, 353
Hand, Michael 296
Hansberry, Martin 42
Harding, Rosie 159, 162
Harris, Rolf 80
Hartley, Bill 229, 230, 282–3, 313, 315, 338, 339
Haselhurst, M.E. 85
Hawke, Albert 12, 49, 51, 70, 79, 110, 125, 149, 347
   Bob, influences on 54–5
   election losses 188
   Labor leader WA 94
   WA Cabinet Minister 47, 71
   WA State Premier 99, 115, 145
Hawke, Bob (Robert James Lee)
   1962 Canada and Britain study trip 183
   1966 New Guinea wage case 199–202
   1976 National Press Club address 319–20, 322

absences from home 165, 184, 235, 250, 257, 274, 295–6, 321
ACTU *see* Australian Council of Trade Unions (ACTU)
adulation from ACTU role 165, 166
Albert Hawke, influences of 54–5
alcohol consumption 78, 81, 92, 116, 131, 135, 136, 228, 283, 335
   ACTU job, in 153, 156, 162, 171–2, 174
   ANU, at 135, 136, 139–40, 146
alcohol poisoning 174, 335
ALP Club, UWA 80, 81
ANU *see* Australian National University (ANU)
approval ratings 261, 262, 291, 322
arts degree 84, 99, 116, 118
behaviour as a child 38, 51, 52, 54, 59, 61
behaviour when drunk 135, 139–40, 261, 283, 297, 320, 324–5, 329
betting on the horses 202, 250
birth 30
Blanche D'Alpuget *see* D'Alpuget, Blanche
charisma 73
Clem, bond with 31, 40, 41
Companion of the Order of Australia 337–8
Congregational Youth Fellowship Australia 84
conviction for dangerous driving and appeal, Oxford 118, 119
Corio electorate *see* Corio electorate
cricket 57–8, 73, 83–4, 91, 112, 136
death of Robbie 173–4
depression 335, 336
Ellie, relationship with 31, 40, 46–7, 50
expectations of Ellie on 30, 31, 40, 51, 53, 56
Father of the Year award 249–50, 258
Festival of Christian Witness 84–5
financial difficulties 192, 257
Greece family holiday 302
Guild of Undergraduates 80–1, 83, 84, 98–9
Guild presidency 84, 91, 94
Guinness Book of Records 116–17
Hackett Bursary 71
Hazel *see* Hawke, Hazel
ill health 209
Jewish community, friendships 251
Labour Club, UWA 72, 79, 80
law degree 74, 75
libel actions 193, 233
Maitland school 42–3
Maitland years 39–40, 43
'Male Chauvinist of the Month' award 258

marriage difficulties 165–6, 172, 173–4, 184–5, 209, 281–2, 335, 340
marriage to Hazel 124
motorbike crash 74–5, 94–5
narcissism 51, 73, 78, 141
organised religion, rejection of 95–6, 98, 171
Oxford University *see* Oxford University
Panther motorbike 74, 76
paranoia 283
parental absences, frequent 34, 41, 47, 54, 55, 59–61
Perth Modern School 56, 57
proposal to Hazel 81
public profile as ACTU President 228–9, 232, 239–40
Rhodes Scholarship *see* Rhodes Scholarship
Salzberg summer school scholarship 119–20
school results 65
sex education 62
sports played 57–8, 73
Sunday School teaching 64, 65, 73, 171
threats against himself and family 281, 283
University of Western Australia 65, 69–72
UWA *see* University of Western Australia (UWA)
Vacuum Oil Company 84, 85, 86
West Leederville 50, 51, 171
Whitlam, denigration of 262
womanising 78, 154–5, 156, 165–6, 184, 273–5, 284, 320, 329
World War Two 56–7
Hawke, Clem (Arthur Clemence) 7, 69, 71, 347
Bob, bond with 31, 40, 41
Bordertown 27–9, 31, 34–7
childhood 11
Congregational Church 17
Congregational Union, WA chairman 162
education 12–13, 19
enlistment 54, 61
Forster 11, 14, 15
Houghton 18
insurance salesman, as 64
Lower Hutt position 20, 21–2, 23
Maitland 38–9
marriage to Ellie 18
Methodist Home Mission 12–13, 15
Methodist Training Home 13
nervous breakdown 19
ordination 23
political activities 11
preacher positions 11, 12, 13, 14

Renmark 24–7
temperance 26, 33
Hawke, Cyril 12
Hawke, Ellie (Edith Emily) (née Lee) 7, 8, 71, 199
1978 strokes 334, 335
absences from home, frequent 34, 41, 47, 54, 55, 59–60
Bordertown 33–5
death 346
Forster 16
Girl Guides 25, 34, 40, 41
Maitland 39, 41, 43
marriage to Clem 18
religious upbringing 9–10
teacher training 10
teaching positions 10–11
temperance work 26, 33, 52, 53, 55
West Leederville 51, 52
WCTU work 26, 33, 47, 52–3, 55, 56, 59–61, 64
Hawke, Hazel (née Masterton) 51, 52, 265
abortion 89–90
background and upbringing 62–3
beginning relationship with Bob 77–8
births of children 138–9, 158–9, 165, 173
death of Robbie 173–4
early interactions with Bob 63–4, 76, 77
Ellie's funeral 347
Family Centre for Low Income People volunteering 295
financial difficulties, 1960s 192
home life, 1970s 233–6, 274, 281, 295, 302, 320–1
Indian High Commission job 134, 233
marriage 124
marriage difficulties 165–6, 172, 173–4, 184–5, 209, 281–2, 335, 340
Melbourne 154, 155, 156, 163
music 63
night classes 209–10, 212, 233
Oxford 108–9, 113
paid work, absence from 153
pregnancies 89, 134, 137, 151, 156, 172
proposal by Bob 81
Hawke, Neil (John Neil) 18, 26, 27, 30, 31, 43–6
death 45–6, 47
King's College, Adelaide 39, 44–5
Hawke, Robert James
birth and death 173, 184
Hawke, Rosslyn 184, 233, 302
birth 165
post-school life 321
secondary schooling 302–3

Hawke, Stephen 211, 233, 347
  birth 158–9
  post-school life 321, 347
  rebelliousness 302–3
  secondary schooling 302–3
Hawke, Susan Edith 155, 156, 202, 227, 302
  1971 Israel visit 244
  birth 138
  Firbank secondary education 212, 233
  Monash University 303, 321
Hawke Government 167
Hayden, Bill 169, 241, 304, 310, 315, 322, 323, 324, 325, 330
  1975 budget 305–6
  ALP leader, as 333, 342
Heller, Clemens 119
Herbert, Xavier 338
Hewett, Dorothy 71
Hieser, Ron 130, 131, 136, 163
Higgins, Roy 250
Hinze, Russ 251
Hogg, Bob 343, 353
Hogg, Don 201–2
Holding, Clyde 230, 297, 315, 329
Holt, Harold 203–4, 211, 218
Hughes, Billy 12, 13–14, 352
Hunt, Ralph 319, 320
Hussein, Saddam 313

immigration
  1960s, Australia 187
Indonesian-Malaysian 'confrontation', 1963 178–9, 187
industrial relations 84, 86, 123, 144, 166, 192, 234, 268, 317, 331, 349
  reforms 285
industrial unrest
  1960s 212–13
  1970s 225, 248, 259–60, 269–70, 289, 291, 322
  1972 oil industry strike 260
  fines and penalties imposed against unions 214–15
  strikes 214–15
influenza pandemic 16, 18, 27
Innes, Ted 262, 312
International Confederation of Free Trade Unions 271
International House, UWA
  Appeal, launch of 90, 91
  Bob, calls for 88–9
International Labour Organization (ILO) 228
  1970 226–7, 228
  1971 242
  1973 271–2
  1977 302

International Women's Year 1975 275
Iraqi loan affair 313–15, 322
Israel
  Hawke's support for 244, 247, 251, 281, 282–3
  Hawke's visits 244, 245, 323–4
  Yom Kippur War 279–80

Jenkins, Harry 312
John Curtin pub (Lygon pub) 150, 238, 239, 251, 311, 340
Johnson, Lyndon 203

Kapunda 7, 11, 39, 47
Keating, Paul 219, 329, 353–4
Keating Government 167
Kelly, Paul 320, 324
Kelty, Bill 241, 308, 311, 348
Keneally, Thomas 324
Kennedy, J.F., assassination 179–80
Kerr, John 190, 198, 215
  Whitlam dismissal 306, 307
Khemlani, Tirath 303, 304
Khrushchev, Nikita 129
Kiek, Dr Edward 17, 18, 19, 31, 43
Kiki, Albert Maori 225
King's College, Adelaide 39, 44–5, 48
Kirby, Sir Richard 143, 159–60, 161, 164, 182, 190, 191–2, 197, 213, 269, 320, 326
Knight, John 75, 131
Korean War 152, 288
Kornhauser, Eddie 250, 251, 296, 300, 314, 350

Landeryou, Bill 311, 352
Lee, William 8
Leibler, Isi 256, 341, 342, 351
Leschen, Bob 84
London, 1953 101–2
Lower Hutt, New Zealand 20–3
Lowy, Frank 255
Lynch, Phillip 260
Lyons, Joseph 32

MacCallum, Mungo 320, 323
McHarrie, Dawn 65
McHenry, Stephen 78
McIntosh, Don 193
McKell, Sir William 253
McKissack, Jill 192–3
McMahon, Billy 218, 219, 238, 241, 242, 259, 260, 261, 284
McWhirter, Norris 117
McWhirter, Ross 117
Maitland 37, 38–9, 43, 47–8
Maitland Watch 42
Malone, Frank 79, 81

Mandela, Nelson 240
Mansfield, Bill 163
Marsh, Jan 231, 319
Matthews, Peter 231
Mauldon, Frank 93
Medibank 304, 317, 318–19, 321
Medibank Private 318
Meir, Golda 245, 280
Melbourne 150–1
Melbourne Ports electorate 297, 322
Menzies, Robert 49, 69, 81, 126, 129, 130, 166, 168, 169, 187, 262–3
  1963 Federal election 177, 178, 179
  1964 half-Senate election 188–9
  conscription for overseas service 189
  retirement 203
Methodist church 7, 9
  South Australia, in 9
metric conversion 292
militancy experienced globally, 1968 212–13
Millane, Corinne 239
Miller, Rod 176, 178
minimum wage 268
Mitchell, Sir James 83, 86
Mitchell, Neil 257, 327
Monk, Albert 137, 144, 150, 159, 166, 171, 174, 183–4, 194, 196, 198, 205, 206, 213
  retirement 216
Moore, John 190, 197, 269
Morosi, Junie 300
Mundey, Jack 269–70
Munro, Paul 200–1, 231
Murdoch, Rupert 312–13, 314
Murdoch papers 263
  anti-Whitlam stance 313
  Iraqi loan 314–15
Murphy, Lionel 271, 300–1
Murray, Bob 229
Murray Pioneer 24
My Lai massacre 226

Naipaul, V.S. 104
Narungga people 8
National Union of Australian University Students (NUAUS) 88, 92, 98
  Hawke vice-presidency 91, 94
New South Wales Electoral Council 149
Newton, Jack 250
Newton, Max 57, 82, 130
Nixon, Richard 280
Nolan, Peter 349
North, Lindsay 276
Northborne Cricket Club 136
Nuclear Non-Proliferation Treaty 271
Nugan, Frank 296
Nugan Hand Bank 296

oil embargo, 1973 279–9, 288, 316
Oliphant, Mark 141
Olympic Games, 1956 151
Opperman, Hubert 175–7, 178, 180, 181, 204
O'Shea, Clarrie 214–15
Oxford 103
  Hazel's arrival in 108–9
Oxford University 78, 105–6, 107
  Bachelor of Letters 109–10, 111, 113–14, 116
  cricket, time spent on 112, 113, 114, 120, 121
  First XI cricket team 112–13
  Guinness Book of Records 116–17
  Oxford Authentics cricket team 112
  Philosophy, Politics and Economics (PPE) degree 105, 106, 109
  thesis submitted 121–3
  University College 103–5
  University College Record 112
Oxford University Air Squadron 106–7, 113, 117

Packer, Kerry 193, 252, 353
Papua and New Guinea
  1966 Indigenous public servants wage case 199–202
  independence movement 225
Parodi, Alexandre 272
Peacock, Andrew 350
Perth Modern School 56, 57, 61, 70
  1964 visit by Hawke family 186
  Bob, threat of expulsion 61
  segregation of boys and girls 62
  The Sphinx 57
Polites, George 170, 275–6
Port Neill 14
Poyser, George 176
Pratt, Tony 227
Prices Justification Tribunal 301, 317, 325
productivity 123, 138, 152, 157–8, 160–2, 165, 170, 197, 207
  improvements 182, 190–1, 194, 198–9, 316

Queen Elizabeth II 324

Ramsey, Alan 297
Rayner, Keith 95
Rea, Gavera 225
recessions 168, 288
  1961–62 169–70, 197
Redlich, Peter 233, 251–2, 323
Reeves, Tony 253
Renmark 24–7
resale price maintenance system 236, 237, 238, 239, 263

Reserve Bank board 277, 345, 346
Revelman, Lionel 236–7, 238, 251
Rhodes House 105, 111, 123
Rhodes Scholarship 82, 83, 85, 118
   application 86
   failure of first application 87
   Hawke awarded with 95
   referees 85, 92–3
   second application 91
Richards, Beverley 154–5, 165, 172, 177
Richardson, Graham 344
Riordan, Joe 210
Robinson, Jim 170, 171, 182, 190, 198
Rockey, George 252, 320, 323, 345
Roper, Tom 225
Rossiter, Dr James 90, 93
Roulston, Jim 330, 338, 343, 352
Russell, Enid 74
Russell, Eric 158, 160
Ryan, Morgan 301
Ryan, Susan 329

Sadka, Emily 135–6
Saffron, Abe 250–1, 252, 253, 254, 300, 301
Salter, Wilfred 158, 160
Sampson, Noel 61
San Francisco, 1978 visit 336–7
Sandringham branch of the Labor Party 229
Sandringham houses
   Keats Avenue 151–2, 155, 185, 193
   Royal Avenue 185–6, 187, 192, 193, 211, 233–4
Santamaria, B.A. 111, 129, 130, 164, 214
Saunders, John 255
Sawer, Geoffrey 126, 127, 134, 139, 141, 144, 145, 146, 149
Scholes, Gordon 176, 204
Scott, David 295
Scullin, James 32
Sears, James and Elizabeth 15, 17
Seligman, Ben 120
sexism
   1950s Australia 153
Shelepin, Alexander 246, 247, 280
Shrimpton, Jean 273
Sinatra, Frank 289–91
Sinclair, Jean 269, 282, 308, 345, 353, 354
Snedden, Bill 80, 81, 130, 226, 229, 285, 287, 302, 308
Solo petrol stations 305
Somare, Michael 200
Souter, Harold 137, 138, 143, 144, 150, 152, 153, 166, 171, 183, 198, 278, 305
   1969 ACTU congress 216–17
   rivalry with Hawke 184, 196, 205, 206, 207, 210, 213, 214

South African teams tour, boycott 240–3, 247–8
South Australia
   copper mines 7, 8
   Cornish immigrants 7, 8, 11
Southey, Bob 232
Soviet Union 218, 219, 245
   Hawke's visits 246, 280, 341
Springboks tour 240–3, 247, 259
Strachan, Peggy 34
Stalin, Joseph 129
Stanner, W.E.H. 140, 141
Steven, Margaret 135, 140
Stoljar, Sam 127, 135, 145
Stone, John 57, 58, 65, 70, 81, 82–3, 84, 106, 107, 123, 130, 261
Strasser, Sir Paul 253
strikes 1, 190–1, 197, 213, 224, 248, 259, 291, 293, 300, 331, 348
Sukarno, President 178, 179
Surtees, George 254
Sweeney, Justice Charles 191
Swinging Sixties 203, 211
   public demonstrations and marches 211
Sydney
   1970s corruption in 253, 256
   union 'green bans' 269–70
The Sydney Morning Herald 130, 324
   Hawke's correspondence 132

Tasman Bridge, Hobart 298
Taylor, Harry Samuel 24
television, arrival of 292
Tennison, Noel 275
Tham, Rudy 337
TNT 252, 253, 254, 336, 337
Toohey, Brian 337
Toohey, John 81
Torr, William 13
Transport Workers' Union (TWU) 253
Turner Cricket Club 136

unemployment 31–2, 43, 131, 163, 166, 168, 263, 288, 292, 299, 301, 307–8, 313, 317, 325, 331, 346
unions
   demarcation disputes 212, 289
   fines and penalties imposed against 214
   Hawke enlisting supporters among 194–5, 205
United Australia Party 32
United States
   nuclear testing 179
   Vietnam 179, 187–8
University of Western Australia (UWA) 65, 69–71
   ALP Club 79, 81, 84
   Australia-Overseas Club 88, 94, 99

Black Swan 71
drinking on campus 78
Guild of Undergraduates 80–1, 83, 84, 90–1, 94, 98–9
International House 88–9, 90
Labour Club 72, 79, 80
Liberal Club 84
The Pelican 84, 88
Student Christian Movement 84
uranium mining 327, 329, 348–9, 352
Uren, Tom 264, 327, 329, 343, 348

Vacuum Oil Company 84, 85, 86
Vernon, Sir James 196, 198, 199
Vernon report 197, 198
Victorian Trades Hall Council 215, 224, 338
Vietnam Moratorium 1970 225–7, 259
Vietnam War 169, 179, 187–8, 203, 211, 218, 223, 279
Vietnamese refugees 332
Vincent's Club 113, 117

wage cases
   1953 wage case 122, 152, 156, 159, 162, 164, 169, 182, 189
   1956–57 wage case 137, 138, 143
   1957–58 wage case 143–4, 157
   1959 wage case 152, 156, 159–62, 170, 191
   1960 wage case 163–4
   1961 wage case 164–5, 182, 191
   1962 wage case 170
   1963 wage case 170
   1964 wage case 182
   1965 wage case 189–92, 193–4, 197
   1966 wage case 196–9
   1967 wage case 207
   union anger at 1965 wage case decision 193–4
Wallace, Henry 80
Warne, Shane 234
Wasowski, Vera 235–6
Waterhouse, Bill 301
Watts, Reverend Ewen 85–6
Webb, Leicester 134
Wesley, John 9
West Leederville 49–50
West Leederville Primary School 50–1
Wheare, Kenneth 115, 118, 121, 126
Wheeldon, John 58
Wheeler, Sir Frederick 261
White, Jan *see* Marsh, Jan
White Australia policy 150, 203
Whitington, Don 242
Whitlam, Gough 168, 177, 178, 188, 204, 210, 230, 241, 251, 261, 277, 288, 291, 330
   1969 Federal election 218–19, 265
   1972 Federal election 263–6
   1974 Senate election and referendums 285–6, 287
   1975 Federal election 308–9, 310
   dismissal by Kerr 306–8
   Hawke as his heir, appointment 310–311
   Iraqi loan affair 313–15, 322
   Labor Party leader 211, 261
Whitlam, Margaret 264, 291
Whitlam, Tony 325
Whitlam Government 267–9, 277, 288–9, 292, 299–300
   1975 budget 305–6
   economic problems 294, 303–4
   loans affair 303–4, 307
   Prices Justification Tribunal 301, 317
   reforms 289
   tariff reduction 276, 292, 302
Wilkes, Frank 338
Willesee, Don 284
Willesee, Mike 284–5
Williams, Brigadier Bill 105, 113, 119, 121, 123
Willis, Ralph 162, 165, 170, 171, 177, 184, 189, 193, 195, 217, 224, 249, 319, 343
   research officer role 231
Wills electorate 344, 349
   indecision about nominating 349–51
   nomination for preselection 351
   preselection 345, 352, 353
Wilson, Harold 294, 316
Wilson, Tom 106, 107, 110
   Modern Capitalism and Economic Progress 106
Winter, Terry 199
Winthrop Hackett, Sir John 70
Women's Christian Temperance Union (WCTU) 26, 33, 47, 52–3, 59
   'racial hygiene', call for 52–3
World Conference of Christian Youth, India 94, 95–6
World War Two 151
   commencement 47
   fall of Singapore 56
   Pacific conflicts preceding 43
Wran, Neville 350
Wright, Justice Sid 197
Wyndham, Cyril 184

Yom Kippur War 279–80
Yorke Peninsula 7, 37, 39
Young, Mick 234–5, 265, 327

Zanetti, Terry 84, 91